The baroque wall fountain in the Villa Sciarra, Rome

Encounters

Readings for Advanced Composition

Revised Printing

William R. Epperson and Mark R. Hall
Oral Roberts University

Kendall Hunt
publishing company

Cover image © Shutterstock, Inc.

Kendall Hunt
publishing company

www.kendallhunt.com
Send all inquiries to:
4050 Westmark Drive
Dubuque, IA 52004-1840

Copyright © 2001 by William Epperson and Mark Hall
Revised Printing 2013.

ISBN 978-1-4652-2396-8

Printed in the United States of America
20 19 18 17 16 15 14 13 12

Contents

Introduction

"A well-chosen anthology is a complete dispensary of medicine for the more common mental disorders, and may be used as much for prevention as cure."

Robert Graves

*E*ncounters: Readings for Advanced Composition is intended as a series of readings to accompany a standard writing handbook for use in a second semester college composition course or an advanced writing course. Its selections and editorial viewpoint make it appropriate for adoption by a Christian college or university. Its companion volume, *Strategies For Reading and Writing,* may be used for an introductory freshman composition course or for senior English courses at the secondary school level. The editors have chosen the selections in both volumes as examples of thoughtful responses to crucial human concerns.

Part One of *Encounters* focuses on literature as a way of knowing, pointing students to the way that reading stories, poems, dramas, and essays can expand their horizons, allowing them vicarious participation in a variety of situations and settings. By careful, thoughtful reading that engages them in the lives of others, students are able to perceive the likenesses and differences of the human experience—and through this, it is hoped, to have their minds and hearts expanded. The sections of Part One focus on a few particular issues—such as the different attitudes of men and women, the different views of youth and age, and the different assumptions of various cultures—that make communication among humans so difficult.

Part Two introduces the students to the concepts of worldview, values, and assumptions that underlie their perceptions and establish their interpretations of what they read. Here students encounter particular problems posed by modern notions of work, ecology, and historical validity and meaning. They are challenged to engage these issues within the perspective of a Christian worldview. The writers represented here create a dialogue of voices—with differing views, differing methods of posing and answering questions, differing genres and styles. The "Christian" worldview revealed here is not narrowly sectarian, nor does it often conform to popular or stereotypical views labeled "evangelical," "liberal," or "conservative." The editors have tried to represent this view with respect to a common Christian heritage that includes voices from the past and present and from the major Christian communions—Orthodox, Roman Catholic, Anglican, and Protestant. We recognize that, historically, different Christian groups have viewed the relationship between Christ and culture in varying ways. As Richard Niebuhr has described in his study *Christ and Culture,* the relationship has been a dynamic spectrum ranging from "Christ against culture" to "Christ, the transformer of culture." No one "Christian perspective" can be considered comprehensive and definitive; rather, the whole Church, through history, has manifested its vision in a complex multiplicity of views and attitudes.

Part Three introduces students to the broad subjects of imagination and creativity, presenting selections that explore the aesthetic implications of Christian doctrine—particularly Creation and the Incarnation. The role of belief in artistic creation and evaluation; the relevance of story, myth, and fantasy; the relationship of the mundane and the transcendental; the importance of the particular, of the physical world, and of ordinary human life and activities—these are the subjects examined in this final section of the book.

The book is organized in such a way as to encourage students' interaction with the text. Active reading skills must be practiced—in many cases they must be learned. Students cannot respond well, in discussion or in writing, unless they have understood what they have been asked to respond to. The editors designed *Encounters* with a workbook format, unusual in an anthology, in order to teach and encourage active reading skills. Questions following each selection require students to mark or annotate the text, to analyze particulars of style or content, to explain relationships of textual units, and to question or apply the insights suggested by the readings. Synthesis questions require the students to compare, contrast, and evaluate the views of several authors within the unit or, sometimes, from different parts of the book. The editors have found manifold connections suggested by these various readings and are confident that meaningful writing assignments—representing analysis, synthesis, and evaluation—can come from considering several of these selections together.

The book is designed to foster critical inquiry and response. The writing selections challenge students to examine their own assumptions; to actively "hear" another voice and "see" another view; to analyze content, methods, and style; to exercise discernment; to evaluate and to synthesize ideas; and to apply insights to their own lives and cultures. By these activities, they make discoveries that generate strong, involved, and committed writing. The editors have found that these readings, when presented in a learning atmosphere that encourages free dialogue and honest response, can open up new horizons for students as they begin, consciously, to structure a personal vision that is founded upon the great heritage of Christian thought.

The purpose of a liberal arts education was originally, in Greek and Roman cultures, to educate *free* persons, making them responsible and wise citizens of the state. As the editors of this text view it, the task of modern liberal arts education is to lead students into their own freedom—freedom to live thoughtfully and critically in a society that surrounds them daily with the pervasive influences—good and bad—of popular culture and the plethora of voices carried by the many media our technology has provided. By acquainting students with examples of voices from the Christian tradition reasserting the "good, the true, and the beautiful," we hope to encourage them to develop a more mature and discerning taste for these qualities, a new respect for their cultural and religious heritage, a value system with balanced and incisive evaluative standards, and a fresh sense of wonder at the presence of divine holiness in the ordinary world.

Part One

Experiencing Through Literature

The academic disciplines that constitute a liberal arts curriculum represent the various ways humans have crafted their search for knowledge of reality. These methods of cognition vary according to the discipline, and each discipline asks its own appropriate questions, makes use of data in particular ways, and provides answers pertinent to, yet limited by, its specific methodology. Many of the disciplines represent a move toward abstract thinking. Mathematics is the best example of this, for the language of mathematics is a completely abstract language. Similarly, scientific classifications, for example, move from specific phenomena (concrete things, individual beings) to more abstract groupings (species, families). History, a discipline that yields knowledge and understanding of past events, is a method of cognition that also moves from concrete phenomena to abstract principles or explanations. Historians select details, then attempt to interpret them, giving more generalized explanations. Literary criticism and scholarship similarly proceed from specific texts to more general interpretations, for unlike the *art* of literature, which is decidedly concrete, the *study* of literature requires abstraction.

In contrast to these disciplines that move toward generalization, abstraction, interpretation, and categorization, the mimetic (representative) arts—drama, painting, sculpture, fiction, and poetry—favor the concrete, providing images drawn from sense experience and evoking similar experiences in the viewers' or readers' imaginations. Traditionally, a measure of success in these arts has been the fullness, accuracy, and power by which they have portrayed reality. Thus, critics in the eighteenth century considered whether a work mirrored reality well, speaking of its "justice to nature." While some contemporary literature has moved far from realism in its stylistic experimentation, it remains grounded in the fundamental experience of being human. A story in which the words do not mean anything can hardly be judged adequate as a work of art because it cannot communicate. The visual arts and music can and do depart from literal representation successfully, for the material of these arts—sounds, tones, rhythms, colors, lines, light and dark, masses, and shapes—communicate in their own non-verbal ways, but literature consists of the material of words, and words, by definition, denote meaning. Although the poet Archibald MacLeish said in his poem "Ars Poetica," "A poem should not mean / But be," a poem, as an artifice constructed of words, cannot "be" without "meaning."

Storytellers, poets, dramatists, essayists, and singers have given shape to our human community throughout history. The bards of the ancient world celebrated their heroes, telling adventures that would later be written down as *The Iliad, The Odyssey, Beowulf,* and other epic poems that have been preserved for modern readers. By celebrating qualities that characterized the hero in their societies, these epics shaped their listeners' imaginations and values, encouraging the love of virtues such as courage, friendship, loyalty, hospitality, strength, and skill. The world of the story perpetuated the moral values of the community. The storyteller delighted his listeners with his stories, even as he instructed, reminding them of the ways good and evil manifest themselves in the human world.

To delight and to instruct—these have been considered the ends of literature since antiquity. Literature, an art composed of words, is a mimetic art—that is, it presents readers with an image of reality. Whether the work be fantasy, science fiction, myth, or realistic fiction, the ideas and situations presented are grounded in what we know as human nature. We recognize the characters; we can identify with, or at least understand, their emotions—whether they inhabit a moor in England, a Greek battle camp outside the walls of Troy, an imaginary planet, or a modern urban ghetto.

Encountering such images of human reality in the art of literature interests us, delights us, and instructs us in a variety of ways. On the simplest level of a plot unfolding, we want to know "what happens next?" Suspense builds as an action is presented in a story. If the story is a mystery, we want to know "who did it?" The reader's anticipation of a plot answering these kinds of questions builds an effect of suspense in his or her mind—and the answer the plot gives fulfills this anticipation, resolving the suspense or solving the mystery in a way that satisfies the reader.

On a deeper level, the mimetic art of literature presents readers with a mirror by which they may see themselves reflected. Young readers often find in literature feelings expressed that they have had, but have never been able to put into words or to share with others. In finding their emotions mirrored in a story or a poem, these readers feel validated, their own identities clarified to themselves. This self-validation is one of the fundamental values of literature and one of its most powerful attractions. Books that trace a young person's coming of age, leaving childhood and entering the world of adult society, have been perennially popular—from Dickens' novels *David Copperfield, Great Expectations,* and *Oliver Twist* to J. D. Salinger's *Catcher in the Rye* and Alice Walker's *The Color Purple.*

Literature also provides readers with knowledge of others—characters and situations from other times and other places. Experience is a great teacher; we all learn from being in a real situation, but our personal experiencing is necessarily limited to the time and space that we inhabit at the present moment. Vicarious experience, however, also yields its knowledge to us. With the aid of mimetic art—especially the verbal arts of story and poetry—we exercise our ability to project ourselves imaginatively into situations far away in time or place. A good writer can present such a clear, realistic, and moving human situation that readers participate in the action of the story, gaining insight into different cultures, different values, different customs, and different ways of expressing their common humanity. Thus, stories from the perspective of a peasant goat-keeper in India or about a coastal village in Columbia, stories about two brothers growing up in Harlem or about an old woman who is losing her memory, or poems portraying the pride and materialism of a Renaissance duke or the erotic attractions of a beautiful woman—these broaden our horizons by providing vicarious experiences from times and places we have never been or may never personally experience. In the selections of *Encounters,* Part One, readers are able to see through the eyes of others as well as their own, encountering different people and places, thus experiencing the presence and power of literature.

Chapter 1

Ways of Knowing

If seventeenth-century adolescents could have traveled through time to the twenty-first century and visited a school where students their own age were studying, they might have concluded that these twenty-first century students possessed brain capacities immensely beyond their own. They might even imagine that some kind of super humans existed as they observe students sitting in front of a strange box performing unbelievable feats: composing music without instruments, making business transactions without currency, or carrying on conversations with people from all over the world within minutes.

Conversely, twenty-first century students traveling in time to the seventeenth century might initially assume their own superiority to their seventeenth century predecessors, basing their judgment on primitive surroundings and limited accessibility. On closer inspection, however, these pre-modern students would demonstrate knowledge and skills that contemporary students lack: an understanding of the classics of Western culture, a greater familiarity of language through competency in grammar and Latin, and a closer connection to the environment around them.

What we hope both groups would discover is that methods of knowing vary to meet prevailing cultural demands and that, in reality, modern advancements are not reflections of superior capacities but only indications of different experiences. Our technologically based culture requires methods foreign to an agriculturally based culture. The modern "knower" has benefited from the achievements of modern science by experiencing an improved quality of life—greater longevity, better nutrition and such—but some would say this advancement has not been without a price. With increased control over the environment has come a diminished capacity to enjoy it. As modern science reduces our understanding of the world to facts and statistics, the knower becomes more and more separated from his object of study, the known.

In his book *To Know As We Are Known*, Parker Palmer characterizes the modern way of knowing as one that is detached and disconnected, with its emphasis on objectivity and factual information, resulting in a society that no longer reaps the benefits of knowing through total engagement with one's whole being. He states, "The modern divorce of the knower from the known has led to the collapse of community and accountability between the knowing self and the known world." To Palmer, this separation can be repaired only when one's education includes an interdependence between the knower and the known, in which the knower becomes "coparticipant in a community of faithful relationships with other persons and creatures and things, with whatever our knowledge makes known."

The study of how we know, which is called *epistemology*, can enable us to understand ourselves as beings separate from other creatures, and for centuries philosophers have pondered how humans know, struggling with questions regarding the nature between the knower and the known and the relationship between the two. During antiquity, Plato claimed that knowledge involved a process of remembering the ideal world that existed beyond the material world, while Aristotle claimed that knowledge was not separated from the material world, but rather the material world revealed the true world to our senses. The Enlightenment thinkers of the eighteenth century believed that through reason alone humans could know complete reality, an emphasis that, through time, tended to exclude ways of knowing through one's experience, or as Christians believe, knowing through God's revelation.

These theories of how we know can help us differentiate among some of the ways through which we know—such as reason, experience, or revelation—yet other factors must contribute to our understanding of the world since we are able to experience only one lifetime. One of the ways in which we can know the world around us is through literature, which provides us with vicarious experiences through the lives of fictional characters or the figurative language of poets. The modern rhetorician Kenneth Burke, in his book *Philosophy of Literary Form,* describes literature's affective influence as "equipment for living" because of its unique ability to provide psychological health through strategies unavailable to our own experiences. In other words, the day-in-and-day-out stresses of life can be relieved through our imaginative engagement with literature.

In his book *Language in Thought and Action,* S. I. Hayakawa states that one can be nourished through literature that "introduces us to new sources of delight; literature that makes us feel that we are not alone in our misery; literature that shows us our problems in a new light; literature that opens new possibilities to us and opens new areas of possible experience; literature that offers us a variety of 'symbolic strategies' by means of which we can 'encompass' our situations."

Defending the place of literature against those who would criticize "fixing our inner eye earnestly on things that can never exist," C. S. Lewis asserts in his book *Experiment in Criticism* that the vicarious experiences available to us in literature help enlarge our perspectives. He states, "We want to be more than ourselves. Each of us by nature sees the whole world from one point of view with a perspective and a selectiveness peculiar to himself." He continues, "We want to see with other eyes, to imagine with other imaginations, to feel with other hearts, as well as with our own." "Reality," he reminds us, "even seen through the eyes of many is not enough. I will see what others have invented. Even the eyes of all humanity are not enough. I regret that the brutes cannot write books." Later, he states, "In reading great literature I become a thousand men and yet remain myself."

Although few would deny the value of literature as a way of knowing, Virginia Stem Owens claims that fiction is beginning to lose ground among moderns because it is associated with what is untrue. Like Palmer's indictment against the objectivist view of knowledge, Owens asserts that without the hope offered through the vicarious experiences contained in fiction, we are left as "cognitive shipwrecks, Robinson Crusoes who have to learn everything about their new surroundings from the beginning."

As you begin reading the following selections, you will discover how each author represents different ways of knowing, whether through differing men's and women's perceptions, the attitudes of youth and old age, a Christian's metaphysical view of the world, or the language of varying cultures or professions. For example, in the story "A Horse and Two Goats" the cultural disparity between the two characters makes it impossible for them to understand each other, forcing them to rely on each other's good will to attempt communication. Because cultures are separate, different ways of knowing can be isolating. Herein lies literature's ability to help readers understand what it is like to be in a world increasingly complicated by "exogenous variables," those niggling realities that need our attention and our best thinking. Owens tells us that books give us "clues as to how the world works." Hopefully, as you vicariously experience different ways of knowing, you will find some of the clues among these pages.

Helen Keller

SHE KNEW THE WORLD AROUND HER BY THE USE OF WORDS

The Day Language Came into My Life *AND BY HER SENSES*

Helen Keller (1880–1968), blind and deaf at eighteen months, lived a subhuman existence where she only knew the world around her through immediate, very limited, sensations (touch, smell, taste). When Helen was six, Anne Sullivan entered her life as her teacher and introduced her to language through signing words on Helen's hand; after this experience, her life was never the same. Leading her from total darkness to the world of words, this acquisition of language gave Helen access to ways of knowing reality and communicating that she had never possessed before. Helen Keller's writings have served as an inspiration for readers who are encouraged by her determination to learn. This selection taken from her autobiography, *The Story of My Life*, relates the experience that changed her life.

Vocabulary . . . .

confounding	quiver
languor	tussle
plummet	

The most important day I remember in all my life is the one on which my teacher, Anne Mansfield Sullivan, came to me. I am filled with wonder when I consider the immeasurable contrast between the two lives which it connects. It was the third of March 1887, three months before I was seven years old.

On the afternoon of that eventful day, I stood on the porch, dumb, expectant. I guessed vaguely from my mother's signs and from the hurrying to and fro in the house that something unusual was about to happen, so I went to the door and waited on the steps. The afternoon sun penetrated the mass of honeysuckle that covered the porch and fell on my upturned face. My fingers lingered almost unconsciously on the familiar leaves and blossoms which had just come forth to greet the sweet southern spring. I did not know what the future held of marvel or surprise for me. Anger and bitterness had preyed upon me continually for weeks and a deep languor had succeeded this passionate struggle.

Have you ever been at sea in a dense fog, when it seemed as if a tangible white darkness shut you in, and the great ship, tense and anxious, groped her way toward the shore with plummet and sounding-line, and you waited with beating heart for something to happen? I was like that ship before my education began, only I was without compass or sounding-line and had no way of knowing how near the harbor was. "Light! give me light!" was the wordless cry of my soul, and the light of love shone on me in that very hour.

I felt approaching footsteps. I stretched out my hand as I supposed to my mother. Someone took it, and I was caught up and held close in the arms of her who had come to reveal all things to me, and, more than all things else, to love me.

The morning after my teacher came she led me into her room and gave me a doll. The little blind children at the Perkins Institution had sent it and Laura Bridgman had dressed it; but I did not know this until afterward. When I had played with it a little while, Miss Sullivan slowly spelled into my hand the word "d-o-l-l." I was at once interested in this finger play and tried to imitate it. When I finally succeeded in making the letters correctly I was flushed with childish pleasure and pride. Running downstairs to my mother I held up my hand and made the letters for doll. I did not know that I was

From *The Story of My Life* by Helen Keller.

spelling a word or even that words existed; I was simply making my fingers go in monkeylike imitation. In the days that followed I learned to spell in this uncomprehending way a great many words, among them *pin, hat, cup* and a few verbs like *sit, stand* and *walk*. But my teacher had been with me several weeks before I understood that everything has a name.

One day, while I was playing with my new doll, Miss Sullivan put my big rag doll into my lap also, spelled "d-o-l-l" and tried to make me understand that "d-o-l-l" applied to both. Earlier in the day we had had a tussle over the words "m-u-g" and "w-a-t-e-r." Miss Sullivan had tried to impress it upon me that "m-u-g" is *mug* and that "w-a-t-e-r" is *water*, but I persisted in confounding the two. In despair she had dropped the subject for the time, only to renew it at the first opportunity. I became impatient at her repeated attempts and, seizing the new doll, I dashed it upon the floor. I was keenly delighted when I felt the fragments of the broken doll at my feet. Neither sorrow nor regret followed my passionate outburst. I had not loved the doll. In the still, dark world in which I lived there was no strong sentiment or tenderness. I felt my teacher sweep the fragments to one side of the hearth, and I had a sense of satisfaction that the cause of my discomfort was removed. She brought me my hat, and I knew I was going out into the warm sunshine. This thought, if a wordless sensation may be called a thought, made me hop and skip with pleasure.

We walked down the path to the well-house, attracted by the fragrance of the honeysuckle with which it was covered. Some one was drawing water and my teacher placed my hand under the spout. As the cool stream gushed over one hand she spelled into the other the word *water*, first slowly, then rapidly. I stood still, my whole attention fixed upon the motions of her fingers. Suddenly I felt a misty consciousness as of something forgotten a thrill of returning thought; and somehow the mystery of language was revealed to me. I knew then that "w-a-t-e-r" meant the wonderful cool something that was flowing over my hand. The living word awakened my soul, gave it light, hope, joy, set it free! There were barriers still, it is true, but barriers that could in time be swept away.

I left the well-house eager to learn. Everything had a name, and each name gave birth to a new thought. As we returned to the house every object which I touched seemed to quiver with life. That was because I saw everything with the strange, new sight that had come to me. On entering the door I remembered the doll I had broken. I felt my way to the hearth and picked up the pieces. I tried vainly to put them together. Then my eyes filled with tears; for I realized what I had done, and for the first time I felt repentance and sorrow.

I learned a great many new words that day. I do not remember what they all were; but I do know that *mother, father, sister, teacher* were among them— words that were to make the world blossom for me, "like Aaron's rod, with flowers." It would have been difficult to find a happier child than I was as I lay in my crib at the close of that eventful day and lived over the joys it had brought me, and for the first time longed for a new day to come. ■

[handwritten note] THE IDEA THAT WITHOUT WORDS TO THINK WITH HOW DO WE TRULY THINK.

Making Connections through Discussion and Writing

1. Keller did not experience emotions like regret or repentance until she learned to "name things."

    a. List the incidents that occurred after young Helen broke the doll that led to her later regret.

    _____
    _____
    _____
    _____
    _____
    _____
    _____
    _____
    _____

    b. Why was this experience so significant to her?

    _____
    _____
    _____
    _____
    _____
    _____
    _____
    _____

2. Keller uses the metaphor of a fog to illustrate how profoundly dark her world was.

    a. Circle additional metaphors she uses to help readers understand her experience.

    b. Explain how these metaphors make her experience more concrete to her readers.

    _____
    _____
    _____
    _____
    _____
    _____
    _____
    _____
    _____
    _____
    _____
    _____
    _____
    _____

3. Helen Keller's first attempts at sign language were what she called "monkey-like imitations." Explain how her change from mimicking words to understanding them affected her relationship to the world around her.

    _____
    _____
    _____
    _____
    _____
    _____
    _____
    _____

4. Keller describes her childhood world as all sensation until she understood the concept of language, implying that thought is impossible without language. From your study and experience, do you believe thought precedes language or language precedes thought? Write a paragraph assuming one of these positions.

    _____
    _____
    _____
    _____
    _____
    _____
    _____
    _____
    _____
    _____
    _____
    _____
    _____
    _____
    _____
    _____

Virginia Stem Owens
Telling the Truth in Lies

Virginia Stem Owens (b. 1941), novelist and essayist, directed the Milton Center at Kansas Newman College. Her non-fiction books include *Assault on Eden: A Memoir of Communal Life in the Early 70s; And the Trees Clap Their Hands: Faith, Perception, and the New Physics; Wind River Winter; If You Do Love Old Men;* and *Daughters of Eve: Women of the Bible Speak to Women of Today.* She has also written several novels, including *Generations of Women.* In the essay below, Owens discusses the art of fiction as a cognitive device, a "way of knowing."

Vocabulary ....

actuarial chart	peruse
amorphous	philology
bewails	purdah
castigated	rhapsodizing
chiaroscuro (chiaroscura)	semblance
chimeric (chimerical)	speculative
cognitive	tacit
collate	virtuoso
disclaimer	voyeurism
genocide	

A few years ago, the nonfiction writer Annie Dillard published a book titled *Living by Fiction.* I have loved, and indeed "lived by" fiction ever since I was old enough to listen to my mother read me stories at bedtime. When I say I lived by fiction as a child, I mean that all those stories of endangered children—"Hansel and Gretel", "Snow White", the "Reed Girl"—gave me a certain understanding of the world, one that included hope.

I do not think adults often consider how much children, even young children, need hope. We have forgotten what it is like to arrive in this world with very little information about how it works; we are thrown up on its shores as cognitive shipwrecks, Robinson Crusoes who have to learn everything about their new surroundings from the beginning. If even that fact were not mercifully concealed from us, we would no doubt give up at the start.

After only a few years, however, children do begin to catch on to the fact the world demands a good deal of knowledge and expertise in order to operate in it successfully. They begin to sense their own vulnerability, their own peripheral position in the events that shape their lives. It is at this point that they begin to rely on fiction as a kind of basic survival training. For one thing, the characters in children's stories are most often hidden heroes who, not until the end, are revealed as the bravest and most resourceful people in the story. Informed by these stories, children begin to feel they have some reason for building the same expectations into themselves. If Jack, though small and insignificant, could outwit the giant in the end, perhaps they too will one day be as clever.

I remember as a child the feeling growing in me that someday I too would be vindicated. This was the way life worked. Story after story told me so. This was the secret key to understanding that every child searches for. And it is to verify this hope that they inevitably and anxiously enquire when the story is finished, "Is it true?" There is no place else they can turn at this age to have this hope confirmed except in fiction. Only in fairy tales and stories where the weakest and most abused ("Black

From *Theology News and Notes,* December 1991 by Virginia Stem Owens. Reprinted by permission of Fuller Theological Seminary

Beauty"), the orphan ("Anne of Green Gables"), and the poor ("Jack and the Beanstalk") were at last revealed as the noblest or at least the cleverest, did I find that understanding and hope nourished.

Fiction Transcends Time and Place

Fiction first enters our lives as a cognitive instrument, a device for learning something significant about the world. This remains one of fiction's primary functions, even after we grow up and discovered other ways of learning about the world. We still turn to narratives of imaginary lives in order to find out what it is like to be somebody else.

Fiction brings us a certain kind of news about the world we can get in no other way, because all other ways are abstract and detached, while fiction's way is particular. Thus it can tell us what it is like to be a soldier on the beaches of ancient Troy or a modern oilfield worker in Tripoli. It brings us news of life in prison and life under purdah. In short, it tells us about all those worlds which would otherwise be closed to us, because of the simple fact that an individual consciousness can only experience a limited number of situations first-hand in one lifetime.

Fiction works out of those paradoxes that seem to fuel the world: by limiting itself to the particular, it transcends time and space. The standard opening line of a fairy tale underscores this limitation: "*Once upon a time.*" Every life is only once, the audience is reminded; what follows is a singular event, just as your own life is unrepeatable and isolate. Yet here is your chance to transcend that limitation, to be transported to another time, another place; transformed into another being, through imagination.

This kind of knowledge is of a different sort than that supplied by, say, statistics. An actuarial chart may tell us the statistical probability of our living to a ripe old age, but it cannot tell us what being old is like. Fiction focuses the spectrum of possibilities that abstractions provide into clearcut, hard-edged actualities.

The narrative hunger we all have for the "news" of the world that fiction supplies is not mere voyeurism nor idle curiosity about how the rest of the world lives. It is an urgent necessity. The time for discovering the tacit rules by which our lives operate is short; not even an actuarial chart can guarantee enough years. On the very threshold of adulthood, one must already begin to make decisions, to act, to shape one's life into sometimes unalterable patterns. How are we possibly to peruse all the evidence before we have to commit ourselves in a career, marriage, politics? But though

life is short, art is long. It is, in fact, an accumulated hoard of information.

Annie Dillard tells us in her book, *Living by Fiction*, that the novelist "is interested in knowing the world in order to make honest sense of it. He worries the world and probes it; collects the world and collates it. No part of it is outside his field. . . That is, the novel's potential field is the whole world; any given novel's actual field is only a small wedge of it. But that wedge may include anything: philology, genocide, childbirth, naval architecture, microphysics, love, the dressing of game."

As an example of the novelist's voracious appetite for knowledge of the world, consider Balzac who reported in a letter written during the period when he was working on *Madame Bovary* that he had "spent all last evening frantically poring over surgical texts. I am studying the theory of clubfeet. In three hours I devoured an entire volume on this interesting topic and took notes. . . . One ought to know everything, to write."

Yet despite the novelist's devotion to learning about the world, fiction has been castigated throughout history for not being real. Its detractors claim it *cannot* tell us anything. Beginning with Plato, who banished poets from his utopian Republic, to St. Augustine, who censured the fourth-century theater, to a political science professor who recently told me he had not had time to "waste" on a novel in ten years, fiction has the reputation of being chimeric, false, an unreliable source of information.

Plato's popularizers often condense his arguments against that "poetic tribe" who "wander about rhapsodizing" into the single charge that poets are liars. His arguments against fiction are slightly more complex than that, however. First, he advises abolishing poetry because it "feeds and waters the passions instead of drying them up." But even worse, he finds the creations of poets, even those of Homer whose skill he obviously admired, at a third remove from reality, no more than copies of copies. Stories of heroic exploits he values at a lower rate than the sandals made by a simple cobbler, who is at least copying an eternal ideal. Fictional imitations, he claims, are "easy to produce without knowledge of the truth. For it is phantoms, not realities, that they produce. . . . Do you suppose, then, that if a man were able to produce both the exemplar and the semblance, he would be eager to abandon himself to the fashioning of phantoms and set this in the forefront of his life as the best thing he had?"

He continues in this vein, claiming that the poet, "if he had genuine knowledge of the things he imitates . . . would far rather devote himself to real things than to the imitation of them, and would endeavor to leave after him many noble deeds and works as memorials of himself, and would be more eager to be the theme of praise than the praiser." For example, he argues, if Homer had really known anything about medicine, he would have preferred to be a doctor instead of merely describing one. The same argument supposedly would apply to Balzac; he should have become a podiatrist instead of merely dabbling in clubfeet.

Augustine's objections to fiction come from another quarter. He found it an abomination that people should waste their tears on the imaginary afflictions of Dido when there were plenty of actual occasions for grief. He found it immoral to squander one's sympathy on characters who had never really existed.

In more recent times, Sir Peter Medawar, one of the greatest interpreters of science in our age, has described scientists as those who "are building explanatory structures, *telling stories*, which are scrupulously tested to see if they are stories about real life." Although he brings science and fiction very close here, he still maintains the superiority of science on the grounds that the stories science tells are "real," whereas fiction's are purely imaginary.

Disillusion and Discovery

Such have been the bases for arguments against fiction over the centuries. Fiction is not "real"; it is therefore lies. It deceives even our very sympathies. These are not, let me emphasize, just the objections of the ancients or the puritanical.

I checked a book out of the library last week by Saul Bellow, a Nobel Prize-winning novelist. The book was not a novel, however, but an autobiographical account of the author's trip to the Middle East, entitled *To Jerusalem and Back*. My husband, who teaches English at a university, happened to pick it up. He looked at the cover and quickly put it down again with a gesture of dismissal, obviously surprised that I should be devoting my time to what he assumed was a work of modern fiction.

"It's not what you think," I hurried to reassure him. "It's a *non*-fiction. It really is about his trip to Jerusalem. It's not just a story." Suddenly the tone of my own apologetic disclaimer revealed to me that people who live in the late twentieth century, at least in the West, are just as disillusioned with, and even contemptuous of fiction as Plato or St. Augustine ever were.

If discovering the world, a bigger world than any single consciousness has access to experientially, has always been a large part of the appeal of fiction, then the steady decline in the publication of fiction over the past few decades should tell us something. In the United States last year, new fiction titles accounted for less than 5% of books published in this country, though when reprints of older fiction are added, the figure rises to something like 12%. Non-fiction has taken over publishing almost entirely, not just in books, but in periodicals as well. The miniscule amount of serially published fiction is proportionally far smaller than the already tiny sliver it maintains in book publishing. Most periodicals today publish no fiction at all.

On the other hand, the fastest selling hardcover book in the history of publishing, *Iacocca*, sold over a million copies during its first two months in print. It is the autobiography of an Italian immigrant who rose to fame, fortune, and power as the president of the Chrysler Corporation. The book has the same plot, one hardly need point out, as many fairy tales. And adults read such a book for the same reason that children listen to Snow White or Jack and the Beanstalk—for clues as to how the world works. Their unspoken question remains "Is it true?" *Iacocca* is information about the desire for wealth and how to get it. Adults test this story against their own experience to assess their chances of becoming rich and powerful too. They want to know how smart one has to be, or how lucky, what it costs in terms of effort, attention, and relationships, and if it was worth it.

The literary community generally bewails this preference of the public for non-fiction. To them, the shift toward non-fiction only indicates aesthetic callousness and moral insensitivity on the public's part. People who read autobiographies of corporation executives instead of novels by Nobel Prize winners are dismissed by the literary establishment as crass, materialistic clods. Clods who, like Plato, claim it is better to *be* a doctor than to create a fictional phantom of one.

Now Plato was certainly no populist, nor would he have approved of the public's taste for *Iacocca*'s autobiography. Yet I believe that, in a backhanded way, the modern popular preference for non-fiction ultimately bears out Plato's objection. People have always depended on fiction to tell them about the world. And it is this cognitive task of fiction that many modern writers have either failed to carry out or else have repudiated altogether.

Annie Dillard, in describing contemporary modernist fiction says, "In many works, the world is an arena of possibilities. Anything may happen. This 'anything' is fiction's new subject. Traditional writers labour to make their 'what-ifs' seems plausible. But contemporary modernists flaunt the speculative nature of their fiction."

Modern readers, however, turn away from this kind of contemporary literary fiction because they do not find it credible. It tells them nothing true about life; it does not even pretend to know anything true about life. It no longer operates as a cognitive device. It is primarily interested in virtuoso performances with language. Though other writers may be interested in virtuosity, the man on the street already has hobbies of his own. He wants to know about the world. Time is passing. How is he to make sense of amorphous information, of the chiaroscura of experience? How is he to shape life into meaning? Where is the handle by which to grasp it?

Reynolds Price, an American novelist who, like several of his colleagues, has almost given up the fictional project,[1] says in his essay, "The Origins and Life of Narrative," which serves as an introduction to his book *A Palpable God*, that "the first—and final—aim of fiction is to compel belief in an ordered world." Cognition is not often linked with compulsion these days, but that is the bit of leverage fiction has that sets it apart from other non-fiction forms of writing.

Whatever cognition comes to us through any mediation of language, the route it must necessarily travel, as far as I can tell, is that of transference. This is true whether we are talking about metaphor (see Aristotle's Rhetoric 1401 b 14.25) or fiction. The only difference between the cognitive transference of metaphor and that of fiction is one of magnitude. With metaphors, one transfers certain qualities recognized as belonging to one object or action to a seemingly unrelated object or situation. If the metaphor is apt, miraculously the qualities thus transferred not only stick, but tell us something fresh about their new host. Except for direct sensory experience, the apprehension of likeness is our primary way of learning about the world. In fact, the question we most often ask when we enquire about anything novel in our experience is "What is it like?"

Fiction attempts to answer this question on a much larger scale than a single metaphor. For fiction, the referent is that amorphous and transient subject, human life. Fiction claims to tell us what life itself is like. And as with metaphor, it achieves this end by the means of transference.

The psychological dynamics of fiction are such that the audience inevitably identifies with the central character in a narrative. The identification happens whether the protagonist is admirable or otherwise, whether the audience seeks this psychic intimacy or not. In fact, a good deal of the dissatisfaction expressed today with contemporary fiction arises from the fact that the central character is not admirable, and the audience feels uneasy inhabiting that particular consciousness. Yet, for as long as they continue with the story, it is impossible for them to escape that position.

In any case, the reader learns something of what life is like as seen through the eyes of, say, a rogue, or a child, or a gullible saint. The story is a cognitive device that shows us at least a glimpse of the world through other eyes, a glimpse that would not otherwise have been possible. And once the imagination is committed, once the process of transference begins and we are inside another skin, we are compelled to believe in that life, at least for as long as the story goes on. Stories, then, have the unique power—more than Plato's reason, more than Medawar's science—to compel belief. Reynolds Price even raises the fascinating question, "does canonical (approved, acceptable) in the matter of Hebrew and Christian sacred texts finally mean credible?"

All literary genres involving fiction are certainly in a state of flux today. Except for the documented staying-power of some form of story-telling from the very beginning of our history, one might almost fear for the loss of narrative altogether. There is, however, a whole new genre arising from the dissolution of fictional categories. It is becoming increasingly difficult, for instance, to tell the difference between a personal essay and a short story. Shusako Endo has brought the Japanese tradition of autobiographical fiction to the West. Collections of story-essays, for example Richard Seltzer's *Mortal Lessons* and Garrison Kiellor's *Lake Wobegone Days*, are enjoying enormous popularity.

I think their broad appeal is because these writers are saying quite straight-forwardly, "If you want to know what being a surgeon, or a young boy growing up in small town America, or a student in Japan during the Second World War is like, let me tell you." They are more interested in their subject than in their skill.

Altogether they still seek to delight with the way they use language; they do not try to dazzle. Their focus is on the world itself, a world they believe in so strongly that they want the reader to believe in it too. They are still trying to answer the question all of us have been asking since we got here: "Is it true?" ∎

Making Connections through Discussion and Writing

1. According to the author, what lies behind a contemporary dismissal of the value of fiction?

   _____
   _____
   _____
   _____

2. Owens claims that fiction operates as a "cognitive instrument" helping readers learn something about unknown worlds that would otherwise be closed to them. Explain how she believes fiction is able to do this.

   _____
   _____
   _____
   _____
   _____

3. Circle the names of two historical critics of fiction who dismiss its importance as an art form, and summarize each critic's explanation by describing his or her attitudes.

   _____
   _____
   _____
   _____
   _____
   _____
   _____

4. Owens states that Reynolds Price "has almost given up the fictional project." Complete an internet search and determine how many fiction works Reynolds has published since 1991 when Owens made this comment. List titles that you find. Then analyse Owen's comment in light of your research.

   _____
   _____
   _____
   _____
   _____
   _____
   _____
   _____
   _____
   _____

5. Defending fiction's ability to provide the "particulars" in life, Owens cites the axiom "though life is short, art is long." In a brief paragraph, explain what she means by this statement.

_____
_____
_____
_____
_____
_____
_____

6. To help us make sense of "that amorphous and transient subject, human life," Owens says that fiction tells us what life is like through transference.

a. What does "transference" mean in this context?

_____
_____
_____
_____
_____
_____

b. How does transference facilitate "belief in an ordered world"?

_____
_____
_____
_____
_____

7. Write a paragraph describing your own experience with fiction and how it has influenced your own ways of knowing.

_____
_____
_____
_____
_____
_____
_____
_____
_____
_____
_____

Adam Smith

You Keep Bringing up Exogenous Variables

Adam Smith (b. 1930) is the pseudonym chosen by George J. W. Goodman, who began writing columns on economics for the *New York* magazine in 1966 under the name "Adam Smith," the name of a famous 18th century economist and philosopher. He has since published four books under this pseudonym: *Powers of the Mind, Super Money, The Money Game,* and *Paper Money.* He has served on the editorial board of *The New York Times* and frequently publishes in *The Atlantic Monthly.* The following article illustrates the problems inherent in perceiving life strictly through an abstract, theoretical view.

Vocabulary ....

elasticities	myopia
exogenous	pejorative
lemmas	stochastic equilibria

I have a friend called Arthur, who has a pleasant smile, a wife, two children, two sets of skis, and who has, in economics, what is called an ideal quantitative background. Practically from second grade, Arthur loved math. It was a mystery to him why some people had to chew their pencils in math exams; to him, math was as easy as watching television was to some of his contemporaries. And although excellent marks came showering upon him all through school, he was never a serious, innovative mathematician. Great mathematicians, like competitive swimmers, mature early. At sixteen they have solved Fermat's Last Theorem, and at twenty-six they had better be teaching somewhere, because they are burned out. Arthur knew, at eighteen, that he was not that kind of scholar-mathematician, so he looked around at college and found a congenial home in economics. Arthur's hardest course came in his freshman year; it was English, and he had to write a paper on two Joseph Conrad stories, *Heart of Darkness* and *The Secret Agent.* He had a ghastly time with it. When he finished the Conrad paper, he says, he was very glad that he would never again have to do anything like that.

The graduate students who taught sections of the economics courses were very strong in econometrics, which is a mathematical and statistical form of economics, and Arthur was marvelously adept at that. After he got his Ph.D., Arthur thought about teaching. But one of his professors was a consultant to a commercial firm I will call Economics, Inc., which had built a computer model of the whole economy and which sold this service to various businesses. Economics, Inc., offered Arthur such a high starting salary that he went right to work there and has been very happy ever since.

At various times I visited Arthur, and we would sit at his computer console. His cuffs would shoot out of his sport jacket, and his fingers would be poised over the computer keyboard like those of E. Power Biggs at the organ. The computer keyboard was like a typewriter keyboard, *q-w-e-r-t-y-u-i-o-p,* except that it had a lot of extra keys you had to press before you could ask it questions. Once, I had just come back from the Middle East and I was worried that the price of oil might go to $15 a barrel, or even $20 a barrel.

"Ask it what the inflation rate will be if oil goes to fifteen dollars a barrel," I would say, and Arthur would go tapety-tapety-tap on the keyboard. The answer—when the computer did not ask us for more information, or tell us to start over—would appear on the CRT screen. "Wow," said Arthur. "Inflation of nine percent, all other things being equal."

"Ask it what the mortgage rate will be with oil at fifteen dollars a barrel," I said. Tapety-tapety-tap.

"Ten percent?" Arthur said. "That's awfully high. It can't be right. Maybe we have to have an assumption about housing starts, too." Tapety-tapety-tapety-tapety-*tap*.

I have called Arthur, periodically, over the years, but I have never had to act specifically on his information. In 1973, for example, Economics, Inc., missed the inflation rate by a wide margin. "Well, we did better than the Council of Economic Advisers," Arthur said, referring to the group appointed by the President, which sits in Washington. "They predicted inflation would be down to two and a half percent." Indeed they had, and Economics, Inc., had done better.

In order to have something as neat and symmetrical as an equation, you have to have assumptions, even if the assumption is very basic—let x equal the unknown, let $\sum$ mean "the sum of." There is an old joke, used by economists at departmental dinners, in which three men are stranded on a desert island and all they have is one huge can of tuna, but the tuna is inside the can and they are starving. The first man, a physicist, suggests a way to make a fire hot enough to melt the can. The second is an engineer, who is thinking up a complicated slingshot that will hurl the can against a rock with enough force to puncture it. The third is an economist. He has the answer. He says, "Assume a can opener." Then he proceeds with a theory.

Economics, Inc., had all kinds of assumptions and all kinds of assessments.

None of this, by the way, hurt Economics, Inc. Businessmen and institutions quested for certainty, and the computer at Economics, Inc., was very certain, even if it was not always right. The CRT screen would say ERROR if the processing was inconsistent, but not if the conclusions didn't match the brawling world outside.

As I said, I was worried about the Middle East. If the price of oil went high enough fast enough, we would have a depression because all that money for imports would get taken out of our economy, unless the oil countries reinvested the money productively, unless the Federal Reserve loosened the money to make up for the oil, unless the new price of oil brought up more oil . . . you see the process. So I was talking to Arthur about Saudi Arabia, and the health of King Khalid, and the Shiites of the eastern province who worked in the oil fields, and I could tell it all sounded to Arthur like Conrad's Congo in *Heart of Darkness*—unfathomable. Revolutionary Iran had thrown out the Shah, the price of oil was doubling, gold was going to new highs, and I had been saying how far off the great Economics, Inc.,

model was; it wasn't telling me what I so urgently needed to know. Arthur lost his temper.

"You keep bringing up exogenous variables!" he shouted.

Like *economist, exogenous* is another Greek-rooted word, from *exo*, "outside, coming from outside."

"Who the hell knew there was an ayatollah?" Arthur said. "Who knew the Russian wheat crop was going to bomb? Who cares about whoever it is in the eastern province?"

"But *life* is exogenous variables," I said. All I wanted was the answers. I was worried that if *one* ayatollah could, in a short time, cause oil to go up, the truckers then to go on strike, the airlines to flirt with bankruptcy, the defense budget to gather momentum, the Japanese to replace us as the buyers of Iranian oil—what if there was *another* fanatic Islamic cleric somewhere dictating into cassettes? What if there was a sorehead colonel in an oil country deciding that Allah wished the prime minister to meet with a nine-millimeter bullet?

But Arthur had hung up. And suddenly I knew one of the problems with economics. Arthur was brilliant. He had never sold a can of shoe polish, or bought a carload of lumber, or hired anybody, or fired anybody, or even worried about his checking account; in fact, he had never done anything but economics. In his own shop he could make lemmas dance around stochastic equilibria, he could rip off multiple regressions, he could make equations whistle "Dixie." The trouble came from that joke, "Assume a can opener." For deep, deep in the Economics, Inc., computer was a very tiny person upon whom the assumptions were based. Would the tiny person spend? Would the tiny person save? If you tapped the tiny person on the knee, his leg would jerk; if you tickled him, he would laugh. But the tiny, tiny person, upon whom all the vast panoply of computer modeling had been done, *was an economist*. If you asked him something, he would take a tiny sheet of yellow paper and ask, "What are the costs, and what are the benefits?" With a column for each, very coolly and rationally. He never threw an ashtray at his tiny wife, breaking a window and raising the gross national product by the price of the new window. Fear and greed and panic and emotion and nationalism and religious fervor, ayatollahs and Shiites and sinister Middle Eastern colonels were not part of his world.

This is *not* meant to be a trivial complaint about the limits of models. That is of interest to the people who use them, who naturally want to do the best possible job, and the subject has been well debated by such respected figures as Harvard's

Hendrik Houthakker, an expert on econometric models and the varying relationships known as elasticities. I have another friend, Princeton's Geoffrey Watson, who, many years ago, with James Durbin, derived an equation that made them both famous in the field. The Durbin-Watson equation is one test for the mathematical work upon which the complex computer models are based. "Mathematics has so much prestige," Geoffrey says, "that people sometimes back away from their own intuitive judgments. What used to be called 'political economy' at Oxford and Cambridge has been overshadowed. I had a distinguished economics professor at Cambridge, Richard Stern, whose background was in classics."

There were once two kinds of economists, one might argue: the Smiths and the Ricardos. The Smith is the 1723 Adam Smith, and the Ricardo is David Ricardo, his immediate successor. Both the Smiths and the Ricardos were concerned with human activity and with the institutions that produce, preserve, and distribute wealth. The Smiths observed; the Ricardos sought the universal and logical principles, using algebra and its succeeding languages. The Smiths looked for what is to be explained, the Ricardos for the principles that did the explaining. Until comparatively recently, economists could write in both languages; that is, they could describe human activity in some detail, using the detail in written analysis, and they could reason mathematically and abstractly about the governing principles.

Today the Ricardos are fashionable and the Smiths are not. Economists who write well in English—there may be eight of them—run the risk of being labeled with the pejorative term "literary." The Ricardos admire the elegance of perfect equations; the highest terms of their praise are "rigorous" and "scientific."

When the problem was contained enough, when the numbers were discrete enough, the mathematical descriptions of the Ricardos worked. Government economists who favored deregulation of the airline industry found that scenario unfolding much as they had planned. But too often the real world did not match the movements of that tiny economist inside the computer. All through the 1970s, the economists missed the impact of OPEC because, when they described it mathematically, they treated it as if it were a rational, profit-maximizing convention of economists. They did not know about *asibaya*, the Arab sense of community,

nor could they quantify Third World indignation at past histories, or Middle East rivalries, or Western myopia, all of which became more important than the more easily quantified data. Some years ago the sociologist and pollster Daniel Yankelovich described a process he called the McNamara fallacy, after the Secretary of Defense who had so carefully quantified the Vietnam War.

"The first step," he said, "is to measure what can easily be measured. The second is to disregard what can't be measured, or give it an arbitrary quantitative value. This is artificial and misleading. The third step is to presume that what can't be measured easily isn't very important. This is blindness. The fourth step is to say that what can't be easily measured really doesn't exist." The philosopher A. N. Whitehead called this tendency, in another form, "the fallacy of misplaced concreteness."

The Hopi language, an American Indian language, contains no words, grammatical forms, constructions, or expressions that refer to what we call "time," or to past, present, or future. The whole structure we base on "time"—wages, rent, credit, interest, depreciation, insurance—cannot be expressed in Hopi and is not part of that world view. The main Eskimo language has twenty-seven different words for snow, each connoting another nuance of texture, utility, and consistency, so the Eskimo's ability to communicate about snow is far greater than ours. The picture of the universe, of "reality," shifts from language to language. The economists whose counsel we seek—as do presidents and prime ministers—speak from a world within the world, just as the Hopi spoke from a world without time, credit, wages, and rent. That cold, neat, elegant world of mathematics views a different reality than blunt, ambiguous English.

Poets know they must use the slippery sibilances and jagged edges of language, as well as the meanings of the words, to communicate. Poets know that life throws up exogenous variables. I made a note that at the next meeting of the Advisory Council of the university Department of Economics on which I serve I would propose that we recruit some poets. I am sure the council will treat the suggestion as merely amusing, and I'm not totally sure it's a great idea; but I know it's aimed in the right direction. I sent Arthur the classic *Language, Thought, and Reality* by Benjamin Whorf, from which I took the example of the Hopi, but I haven't heard back. Maybe it reminds him of *Heart of Darkness*, and maybe he's just too busy. ■

Making Connections through Discussion and Writing

1. This humorous narrative describes two views regarding the interpretation of economics articulated by the "Smiths" and the "Ricardos."

   a. Briefly summarize each view.

   Smiths _____
   _____
   _____
   _____
   _____

   Ricardos _____
   _____
   _____
   _____
   _____

   b. Compare and contrast them, explaining why over the years one theory eventually gained precedence over the other.

   _____
   _____
   _____
   _____
   _____
   _____
   _____
   _____
   _____

2. Refusing to acknowledge "exogenous variables," people like Arthur believe life is completely rational and predictable. Compare and contrast the two worlds described by the writer: the world of exogenous variables and Arthur's neat, tidy world.

   _____
   _____
   _____
   _____
   _____
   _____
   _____
   _____
   _____
   _____
   _____
   _____
   _____
   _____

3. This piece uses humor to discuss why some have a need for certainty in an uncertain world. Explain why the writer believes literature can act as an antidote to a modernist's need for certainty.

_____

_____

_____

_____

4. The writer identifies four steps that lead to the "fallacy of misplaced concreteness." List these steps and discuss how this way of viewing reality works against a Christian view that affirms the supernatural. (For further understanding, see "The Poison of Subjectivism" by C. S. Lewis in *Encounters*, Part Three.)

Step 1

_____

_____

_____

_____

_____

_____

_____

Step 2

_____

_____

_____

_____

_____

_____

_____

Step 3

_____

_____

_____

_____

_____

_____

_____

Step 4

_____
_____
_____
_____
_____
_____
_____
_____
_____

Step 4

Chapter 2

Perspectives on Men and Women

Although in the last few decades women have enjoyed greater equality in the work place, assumptions surrounding women's personalities have been fraught with misunderstanding. However, breaking new ground in gender studies, Carol Gilligan, in her book *In a Different Voice*, has attempted to demystify psychologists' avoidance of what has been called "the dark continent" for psychology, a woman's psyche. Tracing Freud's inability to fit women into his theories of personality development, Gilligan concludes that the experiences of relationships germane to women have been difficult to pin down to a theory, especially when being compared to men's relationships.

Gilligan uses Lawrence Kohlberg's publicized theory of moral development (a Harvard University study that initially focused on young boys' moral decision-making) to illustrate how differences between genders in moral decision-making reflect the different worlds that exist inside the heads of girls and boys instead of what was previously assumed—that girls' thinking is inferior. Designed to explore how the genders define conceptions of morality and the self, Kohlberg had presented two eleven-year-old children with a moral dilemma; while the boy answered from a position of logic (he even commented that considering a moral dilemma is sort of like solving a math problem with humans), the girl's answers were more ambivalent. Seeing the problem more from a relational perspective than from an analytical one, the girl was unable to resolve the dilemma to the satisfaction of those administering the test. She wondered if others involved could communicate about the problem, which, according to Kohlberg's standard of measurement, revealed that the girl's moral development was further behind the boy's because it was "naïve and cognitively immature."

Gilligan challenges Kohlberg's theory and the standard he used to create it, based on a construction, which, she claims, studied males only and provided a narrow scope of possibilities that excluded women. She states that a woman's world "is a world of relationships and psychological truths where an awareness of the connection between people gives rise to a responsibility for one another, a perception of the need for response." Gilligan concludes that women filter decisions from a communitarian construct, which, although it certainly reflects a different way of knowing, it does not indicate an inferior or immature epistemology. Gilligan's studies have created a venue for women to be recognized on their own merit as moral agents and have opened the door for additional studies of women's ethical behavior in decision-making.

As far back as Greek classical theatre, playwrights have created conflicts that revolved around the clashing views of men and women. These tensions have continued to inspire drama, from Sophocles' play *Antigone* to Shakespeare's *King Lear* and Ibsen's *A Doll's House*. The modern play *Trifles* by Susan Glaspell presents a compelling social issue between the genders that contrasts the moral decision-making process of males and females. Using irony to demonstrate how the truth is lost to males whose sense of self- importance propels them to look at more obvious possibilities for clues, the play reveals the women's intuitive sense of relationship that enables them to uncover "trifles" that solve the mystery.

As you begin reading *Trifles*, notice how the men in the play attempt a more logical approach but miss the subtle signs of a dysfunctional marriage—the house, the unattended food, the erratic sewing—all of which reveal Minnie Wright's emotional state. These clues are not lost on the women who, as Gilligan would point out, possess an awareness of the connection between people and a responsibility for one another.

The poetry in this section presents various masculine views of women, from the witty appreciations of Ben Jonson and Robert Herrick, two late seventeenth-century poets, to the callous comments of Browning's aristocratic narrator in "My Last Duchess." Modern attitudes, influenced by feminist thinking, should provide a stimulus for critical discussions of these poems and the views taken by the narrators they employ. They may also challenge the student readers to distinguish between the views of the authors and narrators.

The two modern stories, Kate Chopin's "Story of an Hour" and Andre Dubus' "A Father's Story," sensitively trace the thoughts and reactions of male and female protagonists faced with crises. While neither character should be presented as revealing rigid or defining "feminine" or "masculine" tendencies in their reactions, their concerns and values may still reveal cultural patterns of gender identity current in late nineteenth-century and mid-twentieth-century America.

Susan Glaspell

Trifles

Susan Glaspell (1882-1948) founded the Provincetown Players on Cape Cod, Massachusetts, along with her husband George Cook. This talented group of artists included Eugene O'Neill and Edna St. Vincent Millay. Glaspell wrote six novels, but she is best remembered for her plays, which include *Inheritors* (1921), *The Verge* (1922), *Alison's House* (1930), *Ambrose Holt and Family* (1931) and *Judd Rankin's Daughter* (1945). Many of Glaspell's works deal with women's issues and the relationship between men and women. The play *Trifles* was originally a story titled "A Jury of Her Peers," based on a murder that Glaspell covered while working as a reporter for the *Des Moines Daily News*.

Scene: The kitchen in the now abandoned farmhouse of John Wright, a gloomy kitchen, and left without having been put in order—the walls covered with a faded wall paper. Down right is a door leading to the parlor. On the right wall above this door is a built-in kitchen cupboard with shelves in the upper portion and drawers below. In the rear wall at right, up two steps is a door opening onto stairs leading to the second floor. In the rear wall at left is a door to the shed and from there to the outside. Between these two doors is an old-fashioned black iron stove. Running along the left wall from the shed door is an old iron sink and sink shelf, in which is set a hand pump. Downstage of the sink is an uncurtained window. Near the window is an old wooden rocker. Center stage is an unpainted wooden kitchen table with straight chairs on either side. There is a small chair down right. Unwashed pans under the sink, a loaf of bread outside the breadbox, a dish towel on the table—other signs of incompleted work. At the rear the shed door opens and the SHERIFF *comes in followed by the* COUNTY ATTORNEY *and* HALE. *The* SHERIFF *and* HALE *are men in middle life, the* COUNTY ATTORNEY *is a young man; all are much bundled up and go at once to the stove. They are followed by the two women—the Sheriffs wife,* MRS. PETERS, *first; she is a slight wiry woman, a thin nervous face.* MRS. HALE *is larger and would ordinarily be called more comfortable looking, but she is disturbed now and looks fearfully about as she enters. The women have come in slowly, and stand close together near the door.*

COUNTY ATTORNEY *(at stove rubbing his hands)*. This feels good. Come up to the fire, ladies.

MRS. PETERS *(after taking a step forward)*. I'm not—cold.

SHERIFF *(unbuttoning his overcoat and stepping away from the stove to right of table as if to mark the beginning of official business)*. Now, Mr. Hale, before we move things about, you explain to Mr. Henderson just what you saw when you came here yesterday morning.

COUNTY ATTORNEY *(crossing down to left of the table)*. By the way, has anything been moved? Are things just as you left them yesterday?

SHERIFF *(looking about)*. It's just about the same. When it dropped below zero last night I thought I'd better send Frank out this morning to make a fire for us—*(sits right of center table)* no use getting pneumonia with a big case on, but I told him not to touch anything except the stove—and you know Frank.

COUNTY ATTORNEY. Somebody should have been left here yesterday.

SHERIFF. Oh—yesterday. When I had to send Frank to Morris Center for that man who went crazy—I want you to know I had my hands full yesterday. I knew you could get back from Omaha by today and as long as I went over everything here myself—

From *Plays* by Susan Glaspell, Dodd, Mead & Company, Inc., 1920.

COUNTY ATTORNEY. Well, Mr. Hale, tell just what happened when you came here yesterday morning.

HALE (*crossing down to above table*). Harry and I had started to town with a load of potatoes. We came along the road from my place and as I got here I said, "I'm going to see if I can't get John Wright to go in with me on a party telephone." I spoke to Wright about it once before and he put me off, saying folks talked too much anyway, and all he asked was peace and quiet—I guess you know about how much he talked himself, but I thought maybe if I went to the house and talked about it before his wife, though I said to Harry that I didn't know as what his wife wanted made much difference to John—

COUNTY ATTORNEY. Let's talk about that later, Mr. Hale. I do want to talk about that, but tell now just what happened when you got to the house.

HALE. I didn't hear or see anything; I knocked at the door, and still it was all quiet inside. I knew they must be up, it was past eight o'clock. So I knocked again, and I thought I heard somebody say, "Come in." I wasn't sure, I'm not sure yet, but I opened the door—this door (*indicating the door by which the two women are still standing*) and there in that rocker—(*pointing to it*) sat Mrs. Wright. (*They all look at the rocker down left.*)

COUNTY ATTORNEY. What—was she doing?

HALE. She was rockin' back and forth. She had her apron in her hand and was kind of—pleating it.

COUNTY ATTORNEY. And how did she—look?

HALE. Well, she looked queer.

COUNTY ATTORNEY. How do you mean—queer?

HALE. Well, as if she didn't know what she was going to do next. And kind of done up.

COUNTY ATTORNEY (*takes out notebook and pencil and sits left of center table*). How did she seem to feel about your coming?

HALE. Why, I don't think she minded—one way or other. She didn't pay much attention. I said, "How do, Mrs. Wright, it's cold, ain't it?' And she said, "Is it"—and went on kind of pleating at her apron. Well, I was surprised; she didn't ask me to come up to the stove, or to set down, but just sat there, not even looking at me, so I said, "I want to

see John." And then she—laughed. I guess you would call it a laugh. I thought of Harry and the team outside, so I said a little sharp: "Can't I see John?" "No," she says, kind o' dull like. "Ain't he home?" says I. "Yes," says she, "he's home." "Then why can't I see him?" I asked her, out of patience. "'Cause he's dead," says she. *"Dead?"* says I. She just nodded her head, not getting a bit excited, but rockin' back and forth. "Why—where is he?" says I, not knowing what to say. She just pointed upstairs—like that. (*Himself pointing to the room above.*) I started for the stairs, with the idea of going up there. I walked from there to here—then I says, "Why, what did he die of?" "He died of a rope round his neck," says she, and just went on pleatin' at her apron. Well, I went out and called Harry. I thought I might—need help. We went upstairs and there he was lyin'—

COUNTY ATTORNEY. I think I'd rather have you go into that upstairs, where you can point it all out. Just go on now with the rest of the story.

HALE. Well, my first thought was to get that rope off. It looked . . . (*stops, his face twitches*) . . . but Harry, he went up to him, and he said, "No, he's dead all right, and we'd better not touch anything." So we went back downstairs. She was still sitting that same way. "Has anybody been notified?" I asked. "No," says she, unconcerned. "Who did this, Mrs. Wright?" said Harry. He said it business-like—and she stopped pleatin' of her apron. "I don't know," she says. "You don't *know?*" says Harry. "No," says she. "Weren't you sleepin' in the bed with him?" says Harry. "Yes," says she, "but I was on the inside." "Somebody slipped a rope round his neck and strangled him and you didn't wake up?" says Harry. "I didn't wake up," she said after him. We must 'a' looked as if we didn't see how that could be, for after a minute she said, "I sleep sound." Harry was going to ask her more questions but I said maybe we ought to let her tell her story first to the coroner, or the sheriff. So Harry went fast as he could to Rivers' place, where there's a telephone.

COUNTY ATTORNEY. And what did Mrs. Wright do when she knew that you had gone for the coroner?

HALE. She moved from the rocker to that chair over there (*pointing to a small chair in the down right corner*) and just sat there with her hands held together and looking down. I got a feeling that I ought to make some conversation, so I said I had come in to see if John wanted to put in a telephone, and at that she started to laugh, and then she stopped and looked at me—scared. *(The* COUNTY ATTORNEY, *who has had his notebook out, makes a note.)* I dunno, maybe it wasn't scared. I wouldn't like to say it was. Soon Harry got back, and then Dr. Lloyd came and you, Mr. Peters, and so I guess that's all I know that you don't.

COUNTY ATTORNEY *(rising and looking around).* I guess we'll go upstairs first—and then out to the barn and around there. *(To the* SHERIFF.*)* You're convinced that there was nothing important here—nothing that would point to any motive?

SHERIFF Nothing here but kitchen things. *(The* COUNTY ATTORNEY, *after again looking around the kitchen, opens the door of a cupboard closet in right wall. He brings a small chair from right—gets on it and looks on a shelf. Pulls his hand away, sticky.)*

COUNTY ATTORNEY. Here's a nice mess. *(The women draw nearer up center.)*

MRS. PETERS *(to the other woman).* Oh, her fruit; it did freeze. *(To the lawyer.)* She worried about that when it turned so cold. She said the fire'd go out and her jars would break.

SHERIFF *(rises).* Well, can you beat the woman! Held for murder and worryin' about her preserves.

COUNTY ATTORNEY *(getting down from chair).* I guess before we're through she may have something more serious than preserves to worry about. *(Crosses down right center.)*

HALE. Well, women are used to worrying over trifles. *(The two women move a little closer together.)*

COUNTY ATTORNEY *(with the gallantry of a young politician).* And yet, for all their worries, what would we do without the ladies? *(The women do not unbend. He goes below the center table to the sink, takes a dipperful of water from the pail and pouring it into a basin, washes his hands. While he is doing this the* SHERIFF *and* HALE *cross to cupboard, which they inspect. The* COUNTY ATTORNEY *starts to wipe his hands on the roller towel, turns it for a cleaner place.)* Dirty towels! *(Kicks his foot against the pans under the sink.)* Not much of a housekeeper, would you say, ladies?

MRS. HALE *(stiffly).* There's a great deal of work to be done on a farm.

COUNTY ATTORNEY. To be sure. And yet *(with a little bow to her)* I know there are some Dickson County farmhouses which do not have such roller towels. *(He gives it a pull to expose its full length again.)*

MRS. HALE. Those towels get dirty awful quick. Men's hands aren't always as clean as they might be.

COUNTY ATTORNEY. Ah, loyal to your sex, I see. But you and Mrs. Wright were neighbors. I suppose you were friends, too.

MRS. HALE *(shaking her head).* I've not seen much of her of late years. I've not been in this house—it's more than a year.

COUNTY ATTORNEY *(crossing to women up center).* And why was that? You didn't like her?

MRS. HALE. I liked her all well enough. Farmers' wives have their hands full, Mr. Henderson. And then—

COUNTY ATTORNEY. Yes—?

MRS. HALE *(looking about).* It never seemed a very cheerful place.

COUNTY ATTORNEY. No—it's not cheerful. I shouldn't say she had the homemaking instinct.

MRS. HALE. Well, I don't know as Wright had, either.

COUNTY ATTORNEY. You mean that they didn't get on very well?

MRS. HALE. No, I don't mean anything. But I don't think a place'd be any cheerfuller for John Wright's being in it.

COUNTY ATTORNEY. I'd like to talk more of that a little later. I want to get the lay of things upstairs now. *(He goes past the women to up right where steps lead to a stair door.)*

SHERIFF. I suppose anything Mrs. Peters does'll be all right. She was to take in some clothes for her, you know, and a few little things. We left in such a hurry yesterday.

COUNTY ATTORNEY. Yes, but I would like to see what you take, Mrs. Peters, and keep an eye out for anything that might be of use to us.

MRS. PETERS. Yes, Mr. Henderson. *(The men leave by up right door to stairs. The women listen to the men's steps on the stairs, then look about the kitchen.)*

MRS. HALE *(crossing left to sink).* I'd hate to have men coming into my kitchen, snooping around and criticizing. *(She arranges the pans under sink which the lawyer had shoved out of place.)*

MRS. PETERS. Of course it's no more than their duty. *(Crosses to cupboard up right.)*

MRS. HALE. Duty's all right, but I guess that deputy sheriff that came out to make the fire might have got a little of this on. (*Gives the roller towel a pull.*) Wish I'd thought of that sooner. Seems mean to talk about her for not having things slicked up when she had to come away in such a hurry. (*Crosses right to* MRS. PETERS *at cupboard.*)

MRS. PETERS (*who has been looking through cupboard, lifts one end of towel that covers a pan*). She had bread set. (*Stands still.*)

MRS. HALE (*eyes fixed on a loaf of bread beside the breadbox, which is on a low shelf the cupboard.*) She was going to put this in there. (*Picks up loaf, then abruptly drops it. In a manner of returning to familiar things.*) It's a shame about her fruit. I wonder if it's all gone. (*Gets up on the chair and looks.*) I think there's some here that's all right, Mrs. Peters. Yes—here; (*holding it toward the window*) this is cherries, too. (*Looking again.*) I declare I believe that's the only one. (*Gets down, jar in her hand. Goes to the sink and wipes it off on the outside.*) She'll feel awful bad after all her hard work in the hot weather. I remember the afternoon I put up my cherries last summer.

She puts the jar on the big kitchen table, center of the room. With a sigh, is about to sit down in the rocking chair. Before she is seated realizes what chair it is; with a slow look at it, steps back. The chair which she has touched rocks back and forth. Mrs. Peters moves to center table and they both watch the chair rock for a moment or two.

MRS. PETERS (*shaking off the mood which the empty rocking chair has evoked. Now in a business-like manner she speaks*). Well I must get those things from the front room closet. (*She goes to the door at the right but, after looking into the other room, steps back*). You coming with me, Mrs. Hale? You could help me carry them. (*They go in the other room; reappear,* MRS. PETERS *carrying a dress, petticoat and skirt,* MRS. HALE *following with a pair of shoes.*) My, it's cold in there. (*She puts the clothes on the big table, and hurries to the stove.*)

MRS. HALE (*right of center table examining the skirt*). Wright was close. I think maybe that's why she kept so much to herself. She didn't even belong to the Ladies' Aid. I suppose she felt she couldn't do her part, and then you don't enjoy things when you feel shabby. I heard she used to wear pretty clothes and be lively, when she was Minnie Foster, one of the town girls singing in the choir. But that— oh, that was thirty years ago. This all you want to take in?

MRS. PETERS. She said she wanted an apron. Funny thing to want, for there isn't much to get you dirty in jail, goodness knows. But I suppose just to make her feel more natural. (*Crosses to cupboard.*) She said they was in the top drawer in this cupboard. Yes, here. And then her little shawl that always hung behind the door. (*Opens stair door and looks.*) Yes, here it is. (*Quickly shuts door leading upstairs.*)

MRS. HALE (*abruptly moving toward her*). Mrs. Peters?

MRS. PETERS. Yes, Mrs. Hale? (*At up right door.*)

MRS. HALE. Do you think she did it?

MRS. PETERS (*in a frightened voice*). Oh, I don't know.

MRS. HALE. Well, I don't think she did. Asking for an apron and her little shawl. Worrying about her fruit.

MRS. PETERS (*starts to speak, glances up, where footsteps are heard in the room above. In a low voice*). Mr. Peters says it looks bad for her. Mr. Henderson is awful sarcastic in a speech and he'll make fun of her sayin' she didn't wake up.

MRS. HALE. Well, I guess John Wright didn't wake when they was slipping that rope under his neck.

MRS. PETERS (*crossing slowly to table and placing shawl and apron on table with other clothing*). No, it's strange. It must have been done awful crafty and still. They say it was such a—funny way to kill a man, rigging it all up like that.

MRS. HALE (*crossing to left of* MRS. PETERS *at table*). That's just what Mr. Hale said. There was a gun in the house. He says that's what he can't understand.

MRS. PETERS. Mr. Henderson said coming out that what was needed for the case was a motive; something to show anger, or—sudden feeling.

MRS. HALE (*who is standing by the table*). Well, I don't see any signs of anger around here. (*She puts her hand on the dish towel which lies on the table, stands looking down at table, one-half of which is clean, the other half messy.*) It's wiped to here. (*Makes a move as if to finish work, then turns and looks at loaf of bread outside the breadbox. Drops towel. In that voice of coming back to familiar things.*) Wonder how they are finding things upstairs. (*Crossing below table to down right.*) I hope she had it a little more red-up up there. You know, it seems kind of *sneaking*. Locking her up in town and then coming out here and trying to get her own house to turn against her!

MRS. PETERS. But, Mrs. Hale, the law is the law.

MRS. HALE. I s'pose 'tis. (*Unbuttoning her coat.*) Better loosen up your things, Mrs. Peters. You won't feel them when you go out.

Mrs. Peters takes off her fur tippet, goes to hang it on chair back left of table, stands looking at the work basket on floor near down left window.

MRS. PETERS. She was piecing a quilt.

She brings the large sewing basket to the center table and they look at the bright pieces, MRS. HALE above the table and MRS. PETERS left of it.

MRS. HALE. It's a log cabin pattern. Pretty, isn't it? I wonder if she was goin' to quilt it or just knot it? (*Footsteps have been heard coming down the stairs. The SHERIFF enters followed by HALE and the COUNTY ATTORNEY.*)

SHERIFF. They wonder if she was going to quilt it or just knot it! (*The men laugh, the women look abashed.*)

COUNTY ATTORNEY (*rubbing his hands over the stove*). Frank's fire didn't do much up there, did it? Well, let's go out to the barn and get that cleared up. (*The men go outside by up left door.*)

MRS. HALE (*resentfully*). I don't know as there's anything so strange, our takin' up our time with little things while we're waiting for them to get the evidence. (*She sits in chair right of table smoothing out a block with decision.*) I don't see as it's anything to laugh about.

MRS. PETERS (*apologetically*). Of course they've got awful important things on their minds. (*Pulls up a chair and joins MRS. HALE at the left of the table.*)

MRS. HALE (*examining another block*). Mrs. Peters, look at this one. Here, this is the one she was working on, and look at the sewing! All the rest of it has been so nice and even. And look at this! It's all over the place! Why, it looks as if she didn't know what she was about! (*After she has said this they look at each other, then start to glance back at the door. After an instant MRS. HALE has pulled at a knot and ripped the sewing.*)

MRS. PETERS. Oh, what are you doing, Mrs. Hale?

MRS. HALE (*mildly*). Just pulling out a stitch or two that's not sewed very good. (*Threading a needle.*) Bad sewing always made me fidgety.

MRS. PETERS (*with a glance at door, nervously*). I don't think we ought to touch things.

MRS. HALE. I'll just finish up this end. (*Suddenly stopping and leaning forward.*) Mrs. Peters?

MRS. PETERS. Yes, Mrs. Hale?

MRS. HALE. What do you suppose she was so nervous about?

MRS. PETERS. Oh—I don't know. I don't know as she was nervous. I sometimes sew awful queer when I'm just tired. (MRS. HALE *starts to say something, looks at* MRS. PETERS, *then goes on sewing.*) Well, I must get these things wrapped up. They may be through sooner than we think. (*Putting apron and other things together.*) I wonder where I can find a piece of paper, and string. (*Rises.*)

MRS. HALE. In that cupboard, maybe.

MRS. PETERS (*crosses right looking in cupboard*). Why, here's a bird-cage. (*Holds it up.*) Did she have a bird, Mrs. Hale?

MRS. HALE. Why, I don't know whether she did or not—I've not been here for so long. There was a man around last year selling canaries cheap, but I don't know as she took one; maybe she did. She used to sing real pretty herself.

MRS. PETERS (*glancing around*). Seems funny to think of a bird here. But she must have had one, or why would she have a cage? I wonder what happened to it?

MRS. HALE. I s'pose maybe the cat got it.

MRS. PETERS. No, she didn't have a cat. She's got that feeling some people have about cats—being afraid of them. My cat got in her room and she was real upset and asked me to take it out.

MRS. HALE. My sister Bessie was like that. Queer, ain't it?

MRS. PETERS (*examining the cage*). Why, look at this door. It's broke. One hinge is pulled apart. (*Takes a step down to MRS. HALE's right.*)

MRS. HALE (*looking too*). Looks as if someone must have been rough with it.

MRS. PETERS. Why, yes. (*She brings the cage forward and puts it on the table.*)

MRS. HALE (*glancing toward up left door*). I wish if they're going to find any evidence they'd be about it. I don't like this place.

MRS. PETERS. But I'm awful glad you came with me, Mrs. Hale. It would be lonesome for me sitting here alone.

MRS. HALE. It would, wouldn't it? (*Dropping her sewing.*) But I tell you what I do wish, Mrs. Peters. I wish I had come over sometimes when *she* was here. I—(*looking around the room*)—wish I had.

MRS. PETERS. But of course you were awful busy, Mrs. Hale—your house and your children.

MRS. HALE (*rises and crosses left*). I could've come. I stayed away because it weren't cheerful—and that's why I ought to have come. I—(*looking out left window*)—I've never liked this place. Maybe because it's down in a hollow and you don't see the road. I dunno what it is, but it's a lonesome place and always was. I wish I had come over to see Minnie Foster sometimes. I can see now—(*Shakes her head.*)

MRS. PETERS (*left of table and above it*). Well, you mustn't reproach yourself, Mrs. Hale. Somehow we just don't see how it is with other folks until—something turns up.

MRS. HALE. Not having children makes less work—but it makes a quiet house, and Wright out to work all day, and no company when he did come in. (*Turning from window.*) Did you know John Wright, Mrs. Peters?

MRS. PETERS. Not to know him; I've seen him in town. They say he was a good man.

MRS. HALE. Yes—good; he didn't drink, and kept his word as well as most, I guess, and paid his debts. But he was a hard man, Mrs. Peters. Just to pass the time of day with him—(*Shivers.*) Like a raw wind that gets to the bone. (*Pauses, her eye falling on the cage.*) I should think she would 'a' wanted a bird. But what do you suppose went with it?

MRS. PETERS. I don't know, unless it got sick and died. (*She reaches over and swings the broken door, swings it again, both women watch it.*)

MRS. HALE. You weren't raised round here, were you? (*MRS. PETERS shakes her head.*) You didn't know—her?

MRS. PETERS. Not till they brought her yesterday.

MRS. HALE. She—come to think of it, she was kind of like a bird herself—real sweet and pretty, but kind of timid and— fluttery. How—she—did—change. (*Silence: then as if struck by a happy thought and relieved to get back to everyday things. Crosses right above* MRS. PETERS *to cupboard, replaces small chair used to stand on to its original place down right.*) Tell you what, Mrs. Peters, why don't you take the quilt in with you? It might take up her mind.

MRS. PETERS. Why, I think that's a real nice idea, Mrs. Hale. There couldn't possibly be any objection to it could there? Now, just what would I take? I wonder if her patches are in here—and her things. (*They look in the sewing basket.*)

MRS. HALE (*crosses to right of table*). Here's some red. I expect this has got sewing things in it. (*Brings out a fancy box.*) What a pretty box. Looks like something somebody would give you. Maybe her scissors are in here. (*Opens box. Suddenly puts her hand to her nose.*) Why—(MRS. PETERS *bends nearer, then turns her face away.*) There's something wrapped up in this piece of silk.

MRS. PETERS. Why, this isn't her scissors.

MRS. HALE (*lifting the silk*). Oh, Mrs. Peters—it's—(MRS. PETERS *bends closer.*)

MRS. PETERS. It's the bird.

MRS. HALE. But, Mrs. Peters—look at it! Its neck! Look at its neck! It's all—other side *to*.

MRS. PETERS. Somebody—wrung—its neck.

Their eyes meet. A look of growing comprehension, of horror. Steps are heard outside. MRS. HALE *slips box under quilt pieces, and sinks into her chair. Enter* SHERIFF *and* COUNTY ATTORNEY. MRS. PETERS *steps down left and stands looking out of window.*

COUNTY ATTORNEY (*as one turning from serious things to little pleasantries*). Well, ladies, have you decided whether she was going to quilt it or knot it? (*Crosses to center above table.*)

MRS. PETERS. We think she was going to—knot it. (SHERIFF *crosses to right of stove, lifts stove lid and glances at fire, then stands warming hands at stove.*)

COUNTY ATTORNEY. Well, that's interesting, I'm sure. (*Seeing the bird-cage.*) Has the bird flown?

MRS. HALE (*putting more quilt pieces over the box*). We think the—cat got it.

COUNTY ATTORNEY (*preoccupied*). Is there a cat? (MRS. HALE *glances in a quick covert way at MRS. PETERS.*)

MRS. PETERS (*turning from window, takes a step in*). Well, not *now*. They're superstitious, you know. They leave.

COUNTY ATTORNEY (*to SHERIFF PETERS, continuing an interrupted conversation*). No sign at all of anyone having come from the outside. Their own rope. Now let's go up again and go over it piece by piece. (*They start upstairs.*) It would have to have been someone who knew just the—

MRS. PETERS *sits down left of table. The two women sit there not looking at one another, but as if peering into something and at the same time holding back. When they talk now it is in the manner of feeling their way over strange ground, as if afraid of what they are saying, but as if they cannot help saying it.*

MRS. HALE (*hesitatively and in hushed voice*). She liked the bird. She was going to bury it in that pretty box.

MRS. PETERS (*in a whisper*). When I was a girl—my kitten—there was a boy took a hatchet, and before my eyes—and before I could get there —(*Covers her face an instant.*) If they hadn't held me back I would have—(*catches herself, looks upstairs where steps are heard, falters weakly*)—hurt him.

MRS. HALE (*with a slow look around her*). I wonder how it would seem never to have had any children around. (*Pause.*) No, Wright wouldn't like the bird—a thing that sang. She used to sing. He killed that, too.

MRS. PETERS (*moving uneasily*). We don't know who killed the bird.

MRS. HALE. I knew John Wright.

MRS. PETERS. It was an awful thing was done in this house that night, Mrs. Hale. Killing a man while he slept, slipping a rope around his neck that choked the life out of him.

MRS. HALE. His neck. Choked the life out of him. (*Her hand goes out and rests on the bird-cage.*)

MRS. PETERS (*with rising voice*). We don't know who killed him. We don't *know*.

MRS. HALE (*her own feeling not interrupted*). If there'd been years and years of nothing, then a bird to sing to you, it would be awful—still, after the bird was still.

MRS. PETERS (*something within her speaking*). I know what stillness is. When we homesteaded in Dakota, and my first baby died—after he was two years old, and me with no other then—

MRS. HALE (*moving*). How soon do you suppose they'll be through looking for the evidence?

MRS. PETERS. I know what stillness is. (*Pulling herself back.*) The law has got to punish crime, Mrs. Hale.

MRS. HALE (*not as if answering that*). I wish you'd seen Minnie Foster when she wore a white dress with blue ribbons and stood up there in the choir and sang. (*A look around the room.*) Oh I *wish* I'd come over here once in a while! That was a crime! That was a crime! Who's going to punish that?

MRS. PETERS (*looking upstairs*). We mustn't—take on.

MRS. HALE. I might have known she needed help! I know how things can be—for women. I tell you, it's queer, Mrs. Peters. We live close together and we live far apart. We all go through the same things—it's all just a different kind of the same thing. (*Brushes her eyes, noticing the jar of fruit, reaches out for it.*) If I was you I wouldn't tell her her fruit was gone. Tell her it *ain't*. Tell her it's all right. Take this in to prove it to her. She—she may never know whether it was broke or not.

MRS. PETERS (*takes the jar, looks about for something to wrap it in; takes petticoat from the clothes brought from the other room, very nervously begins winding this around the jar. In a false voice*). My, it's a good thing the men couldn't hear us. Wouldn't they just laugh! Getting all stirred up over a little thing like a—dead canary. As if that could have anything to do with—with—wouldn't they *laugh*! (*The men are heard coming downstairs.*)

MRS. HALE (*under her breath*). Maybe they would—maybe they wouldn't.

COUNTY ATTORNEY. No, Peters, it's all perfectly clear except a reason for doing it. But you know juries when it comes to women. If there was some definite thing. (*Crosses slowly to above table. SHERIFF crosses down right. MRS. HALE and MRS. PETERS remain seated at either side of table.*) Something to show— something to make a story about—a thing that would connect up with this strange way of doing it—(*The women's eyes meet for an instant. Enter HALE from outer door.*)

HALE (*remaining by door*). Well, I've got the team around. Pretty cold out there.

COUNTY ATTORNEY. I'm going to stay awhile by myself. (*To the* SHERIFF.) You can send Frank out for me, can't you? I want to go over everything. I'm not satisfied that we can't do better.

SHERIFF Do you want to see what Mrs. Peters is going to take in? (*The lawyer picks up the apron, laughs.*)

COUNTY ATTORNEY. Oh, I guess they're not very dangerous things the ladies have picked out. (*Moves a few things about, disturbing the quilt pieces which cover the box. Steps back.*) No, Mrs. Peters doesn't need supervising. For that matter a sheriffs wife is married to the law. Ever think of it that way, Mrs. Peters?

MRS. PETERS. Not—just that way.

SHERIFF (*chuckling*). Married to the law. (*Moves to down right door to the other room.*) I just want you to come in here a minute, George. We ought to take a look at these windows.

COUNTY ATTORNEY (*scoffingly*). Oh, windows!

SHERIFF. We'll be right out, Mr. Hale.

HALE *goes outside. The* SHERIFF *follows the* COUNTY ATTORNEY *into the room. Then* MRS. HALE *rises, hands tight together, looking intensely at* MRS. PETERS, *whose eyes make a slow turn, finally meeting* MRS. HALE's. *A moment* MRS. HALE *holds her, then her own eyes point the way to where the box is concealed. Suddenly* MRS. PETERS *throws back quilt pieces and tries to put the box in the bag she is carrying. It is too big. She opens box, starts to take bird out, cannot touch it, goes to pieces, stands there helpless. Sound of a knob turning in the other room.* MRS. HALE *snatches the box and puts it in the pocket of her big coat. Enter* COUNTY ATTORNEY *and* SHERIFF, *who remains down right.*

COUNTY ATTORNEY (*crosses to up left door facetiously*). Well, Henry, at least we found out that she was not going to quilt it. She was going to—what is it you call it, ladies?

MRS. HALE (*standing center below table facing front, her hand against her pocket*). We call it—knot it, Mr. Henderson.

Curtain ■

Making Connections through Discussion and Writing

1. How does the setting of this play provide insight into the lives of John and Minnie Wright?

_____

_____

_____

_____

2. As the men search for clues, they make patronizing comments about the women, yet the reader is aware of the irony in the men's "expertise." List the missed clues that the women find.

_____

_____

_____

_____

_____

_____

_____

_____

3. Trace Mrs. Wright's moral decision-making path from the beginning of the play to the end.

_____

_____

_____

_____

_____

_____

_____

_____

4. a. Compare and contrast the men's and women's ways of knowing.

_____

_____

_____

_____

_____

_____

_____

_____

b.   How does this play demonstrate Gilligan's conclusions about men and women?

_____

_____

_____

_____

_____

_____

_____

Robert Herrick
Delight in Disorder

Robert Herrick (1591–1674) is classified with the witty seventeenth-century poets Richard Lovelace, Thomas Carew, and others as a "Cavalier" poet, poets who were "Royalists" (loyal to the monarchy) in their political sympathies during the civil conflicts of late seventeenth-century England. Their works were characterized by grace, polish, arrogance, and an air of worldliness and sensuality. Herrick was one of the young poets who made up the group called "sons of Ben," that is, poetic disciples of Ben Jonson. In the poem below, Herrick's elegant style has similar characteristics to Jonson's poem "Still To Be Neat."

Vocabulary . . . .

bewitch
civility
enthralls
erring

kindles
tempestuous
wantonness

A sweet disorder in the dress
Kindles in clothes a wantonness.
A lawn[1] about the shoulders thrown
Into a fine distractiön,
An erring lace, which here and there
Enthralls the crimson stomacher,[2]
A cuff neglectful, and thereby
Ribbands[3] to flow confusedly;
A winning wave, deserving note,
In the tempestuous petticoat;
A careless shoestring, in whose tie
I see a wild civility;
Do more bewitch me than when art
Is too precise in every part. ■

Notes

[1] lawn—a scarf of fine linen

[2] stomacher—ornamental covering for the breasts

[3] Ribbands—ribbons

Making Connections through Discussion and Writing

1. a. The images used in this poem reveal the speaker's taste for a certain style in a woman. List five images he uses to describe her.

   _____
   _____
   _____
   _____
   _____

   b. Do these images suggest the woman's moral qualities or the speaker's interpretation? Explain your answer.

   _____
   _____
   _____
   _____
   _____
   _____
   _____

2. In the poem, the author juxtaposes disparate terms to create antithesis.

   a. Underline his use of such opposing terms.

   b. Describe their effects on the theme of the poem.

   _____
   _____
   _____
   _____
   _____
   _____

3. Herrick's use of images demands that readers use their imaginations to create this woman as a mental picture. Write a paragraph describing your impression of this young woman.

   _____
   _____
   _____
   _____
   _____
   _____
   _____
   _____
   _____

Ben Jonson

Still to Be Neat

Ben Jonson (1572–1637) was a dramatist and poet whose reputation for versatility and wit influenced a group of admirers who called themselves "sons of Ben." He is best known for his plays, such as *Volpone* (1606), *The Alchemist* (1610), and *Bartholomew Fair* (1614). Although his explosive personality caused him a great deal of trouble, including time in jail and a loss of possessions, he was appointed poet laureate in England in 1616 and later was appointed City Chronologer of London in 1628. Jonson is buried in Westminster Abbey under a plain slab on which his friends later carved the words "O rare Ben Jonson!"

Still[1] to be neat, still to be dressed,
As you were going to a feast;
Still to be powdered, still perfumed;
Lady, it is to be presumed,
Though art's hid causes are not found,
All is not sweet, all is not sound.

Give me a look, give me a face
That makes simplicity a grace;
Robes loosely flowing, hair as free;
Such sweet neglect more taketh me
Than all th' adulteries of art.
They strike mine eyes, but not my heart. ■

Note

[1] Still—continually

Making Connections through Discussion and Writing

1. What does the woman's "powdered and perfumed" perfection reveal to the speaker?

    _____
    _____
    _____
    _____

2. a. What is the effect of the repetition of words in the poem?

    _____
    _____
    _____
    _____

    b. How do they help create the image of stylized beauty that the speaker finds unsatisfactory?

    _____
    _____
    _____
    _____

3. Compare or contrast the view of women taken by Jonson and by Herrick in these two representative poems.

    _____
    _____
    _____
    _____
    _____
    _____
    _____
    _____
    _____
    _____

Robert Browning
My Last Duchess

Robert Browning (1812–1899) grew up on the outskirts of London. He became a poet, but his work was not widely accepted, and he depended on his family for income well into his adult life. Browning married the poet Elizabeth Barrett in 1846, and they lived in Florence, Italy, until her death in 1861. His publication of dramatic monologues titled *Men and Women* (1855) represents his best work. Browning is known for his perfection of the dramatic monologue, his insight into the psychological motivations of characters, and his depictions of characters who reveal more about themselves than they realize. All of these characteristics of Browning can be seen in "My Last Duchess," published in *Dramatic Lyrics* (1842).

Vocabulary . . . .

countenance	munificence
dowry	officious
durst	pretense
mantle	trifling

Ferrara[1]

That's my last Duchess painted on the wall,
Looking as if she were alive. I call
That piece a wonder, now; Frà Pandolf's[2] hands
Worked busily a day, and there she stands.
Will 't please you sit and look at her? I said
"Frà Pandolf" by design, for never read
Strangers like you that pictured countenance,
The depth and passion of its earnest glance,
But to myself they turned (since none puts by
The curtain I have drawn for you, but I)
And seemed as they would ask me, if they durst,
How such a glance came there; so, not the first
Are you to turn and ask thus. Sir, 'twas not
Her husband's presence only, called that spot
Of joy into the Duchess' cheek; perhaps
Frà Pandolf chanced to say, "Her mantle laps
Over my lady's wrist too much," or "Paint
Must never hope to reproduce the faint
Half-flush that dies along her throat." Such stuff
Was courtesy, she thought, and cause enough
For calling up that spot of joy. She had
A heart—how shall I say?—too soon made glad,
Too easily impressed; she liked whate'er
She looked on, and her looks went everywhere.

Sir, 'twas all one! My favor at her breast,
The dropping of the daylight in the West,
The bough of cherries some officious fool
Broke in the orchard for her, the white mule
She rode with round the terrace—all and each
Would draw from her alike the approving speech,
Or blush, at least. She thanked men,—good! but thanked
Somehow—I know not how—as if she ranked
My gift of a nine-hundred-years-old name
With anybody's gift. Who'd stoop to blame
This sort of trifling? Even had you skill
In speech—which I have not—to make your will
Quite clear to such an one, and say "Just this
Or that in you disgusts me; here you miss,
Or there exceed the mark"—and if she let
Herself be lessoned so, nor plainly set
Her wits to yours, forsooth, and made excuse—
E'en then would be some stooping; and I choose
Never to stoop. Oh sir, she smiled, no doubt,
Whene'er I passed her; but who passed without
Much the same smile? This grew; I gave commands;
Then all smiles stopped together. There she stands
As if alive. Will 't please you rise? We'll meet
The company below, then. I repeat,
The Count your master's known munificence
Is ample warrant that no just pretense
Of mine for dowry will be disallowed;
Though his fair daughter's self, as I avowed
At starting, is my object. Nay, we'll go
Together down, sir. Notice Neptune[3] though,
Taming a sea-horse, thought a rarity,
Which Claus of Innsbruck[4] cast in bronze for me! ◼

Notes

[1] Ferrara—a city in Northern Italy

[2] Frà Pandolf—a fictitious artist

[3] Neptune—Roman god of the sea

[4] Claus of Innsbruck—a fictitious sculptor

Making Connections through Discussion and Writing

1. a. As you reread this poem, underline words the speaker uses to describe himself and his station in life.

   b. Write a brief description of the speaker.

   _____
   _____
   _____
   _____

2. a. Describe the woman in the painting, the speaker's "last duchess."

   _____
   _____
   _____
   _____

   b. What does the duke seem to think about her?

   _____
   _____
   _____

   c. Explain how you, as the reader, interpret his comments to view her differently.

   _____
   _____
   _____
   _____

3. a. Why is the speaker being visited?

   _____
   _____
   _____
   _____

   b. To whom is he speaking?

   _____
   _____

   c. Note passages in the Duke's monologue where he seems to be responding to his visitor's reactions. Underline these lines and suggest how the visitor's actions, words or attitudes may have elicited the Duke's words.

   _____
   _____
   _____

4.   a.   What is significant about the painting of the duchess and the bronze statue of Neptune?

_____

_____

_____

_____

   b.   What do these objects reveal about the speaker and his attitude toward the duchess?

_____

_____

_____

_____

_____

5.   What is implied by the line, "I gave commands; / Then all smiles stopped together"?

_____

_____

_____

Nathaniel Hawthorne
Young Goodman Brown

Nathaniel Hawthorne (1804–1864) was born in Salem, Massachusetts, the son of a sea captain and great-grandson of a judge who officiated at the Salem witch trials. After completing college in 1825, he lived in his mother's house for twelve years, writing stories for newspapers. He published his first collection of short stories *Twice Told Tales* in 1837, making enough money to marry Sophia Peabody. He then published four novels: *The Scarlet Letter* (1848), *The House of Seven Gables* (1851), *The Blithedale Romance* (1852), and *The Marble Faun* (1860). Hawthorne was instrumental in shaping the American short story into a legitimate form. From his nineteenth-century perspective, which is often critical, his fiction revolves around Puritan New England, emphasizing its sin and guilt. Hawthorne generally focuses on the condition of the human heart, as seen in the following story.

Vocabulary ....

anathema	lurid
athwart	ocular
bane	pendent
benignantly	proselytes
catechism	sable
cinquefoil	scruples
cognizance	similitude
festoon	

Young Goodman Brown came forth at sunset into the street at Salem village; put his head back, after crossing the threshold, to exchange a parting kiss with his young wife. And Faith, as the wife was aptly named, thrust her own pretty head into the street, letting the wind play with the pink ribbons of her cap while she called to Goodman Brown.

"Dearest heart," whispered she, softly and rather sadly, when her lips were close to his ear, "prithee put off your journey until sunrise and sleep in your own bed tonight. A lone woman is troubled with such dreams and such thoughts that she's afeard of herself sometimes. Pray tarry with me this night, dear husband, of all nights in the year."

"My love and my Faith," replied Goodman Brown, "of all nights in the year, this one night must I tarry away from thee. My journey, as thou callest it, forth and back again, must needs be done 'twixt now and sunrise. What, my sweet, pretty wife, dost thou doubt me already, and we but three months married?"

"Then God bless you!" said Faith, with the pink ribbons; "and may you find all well when you come back."

"Amen!" cried Goodman Brown. "Say thy prayers, dear Faith, and go to bed at dusk, and no harm will come to thee."

So they parted; and the young man pursued his way until, being about to turn the corner by the meeting-house, he looked back and saw the head of Faith still peeping after him with a melancholy air, in spite of her pink ribbons.

"Poor little Faith!" thought he, for his heart smote him. "What a wretch am I to leave her on such an errand! She talks of dreams, too. Methought as she spoke there was trouble in her face, as if a dream had warned her what work is to be done tonight. But no, no; 'twould kill her to think it. Well, she's a blessed angel on earth; and after this one night I'll cling to her skirts and follow her to heaven."

With this excellent resolve for the future, Goodman Brown felt himself justified in making more haste on his present evil purpose. He had taken a dreary road, darkened by all the gloomiest trees of the forest, which barely stood aside to let the narrow path creep through, and closed immediately behind. It was all as lonely as could be; and there is this peculiarity in such a solitude, that the traveller knows not who may be concealed by the innumerable trunks and the thick boughs overhead; so that with lonely footsteps he may yet be passing through an unseen multitude.

"There may be a devilish Indian behind every tree," said Goodman Brown to himself; and he glanced fearfully behind him as he added, "What if the devil himself should be at my very elbow!"

His head being turned back, he passed a crook of the road, and, looking forward again, beheld the figure of a man, in grave and decent attire, seated at the foot of an old tree. He arose at Goodman Brown's approach and walked onward side by side with him.

"You are late, Goodman Brown," said he. "The clock of the Old South[1] was striking as I came through Boston, and that is full fifteen minutes agone.

"Faith kept me back a while," replied the young man, with a tremor in his voice, caused by the sudden appearance of his companion, though not wholly unexpected.

It was now deep dusk in the forest, and deepest in that part of it where these two were journeying. As nearly as could be discerned, the second traveller was about fifty years old, apparently in the same rank of life as Goodman Brown, and bearing a considerable resemblance to him, though perhaps more in expression than features. Still they might have been taken for father and son. And yet, though the elder person was as simply clad as the younger, and as simple in manner too, he had an indescribable air of one who knew the world, and who would not have felt abashed at the governor's dinner table or in King William's court, were it possible that his affairs should call him thither. But the only thing about him that could be fixed upon as remarkable was his staff, which bore the likeness of a great black snake, so curiously wrought that it might almost be seen to twist and wriggle itself like a living serpent. This, of course, must have been an

ocular deception, assisted by the uncertain light.

"Come, Goodman Brown," cried his fellow traveller, "this is a dull place for the beginning of a journey. Take my staff, if you are so soon weary."

"Friend," said the other, exchanging his slow pace for a full stop, "having kept covenant by meeting thee here, it is my purpose now to return whence I came. I have scruples touching the matter thou wot'st of."

"Sayest thou so?" replied he of the serpent, smiling apart. "Let us walk on, nevertheless, reasoning as we go; and if I convince thee not thou shalt turn back. We are but a little way in the forest yet."

"Too far! too far!" exclaimed the goodman, unconsciously resuming his walk. "My father never went into the woods on such an errand, nor his father before him. We have been a race of honest men and good Christians since the days of the martyrs; and shall I be the first of the name of Brown that ever took this path and kept—"

"Such company, thou wouldst say," observed the elder person, interpreting his pause. "Well said, Goodman Brown! I have been as well acquainted with your family as with ever a one among the Puritans; and that's no trifle to say. I helped your grandfather, the constable, when he lashed the Quaker woman so smartly through the streets of Salem; and it was I that brought your father a pitch-pine knot, kindled at my own hearth, to set fire to an Indian village, in King Philip's war. They were my good friends, both; and many a pleasant walk have we had along this path, and returned merrily after midnight. I would fain be friends with you for their sake."

"If it be as thou sayest," replied Goodman Brown, "I marvel they never spoke of these matters; or, verily, I marvel not, seeing that the least rumor of the sort would have driven them from New England. We are a people of prayer, and good works to boot, and abide no such wickedness."

"Wickedness or not," said the traveller with the twisted staff, "I have a very general acquaintance here in New England. The deacons of many a church have drunk the communion wine with me; the selectmen of divers towns make me their chairman; and a majority of the Great and General Court are firm supporters of my interest. The governor and I, too—But these are state secrets."

"Can this be so?" cried Goodman Brown, with a stare of amazement at his undisturbed companion. "Howbeit, I have nothing to do with the governor and council; they have their own ways, and are no rule for a simple husbandman like me. But, were I to go on with thee, how should I meet the eye of that good old man, our minister, at Salem village? Oh, his voice would make me tremble both Sabbath day and lecture day."

Thus far the elder traveller had listened with due gravity; but now burst into a fit of irrepressible mirth, shaking himself so violently that his snake-like staff actually seemed to wriggle in sympathy.

"Ha! ha! ha!" shouted he again and again; then composing himself, "Well, go on, Goodman Brown, go on; but, prithee, don't kill me with laughing."

"Well, then, to end the matter at once," said Goodman Brown, considerably nettled, "there is my wife, Faith. It would break her dear little heart; and I'd rather break my own."

"Nay, if that be the case," answered the other, "e'en go thy ways, Goodman Brown. I would not for twenty old women like the one hobbling before us that Faith should come to any harm."

As he spoke he pointed his staff at a female figure on the path, in whom Goodman Brown recognized a very pious and exemplary dame, who had taught him his catechism in youth, and was still his moral and spiritual adviser, jointly with the minister and Deacon Gookin.

"A marvel, truly, that Goody Cloyse should be so far in the wilderness at nightfall," said he. "But with your leave, friend, I shall take a cut through the woods until we have left this Christian woman behind. Being a stranger to you, she might ask whom I was consorting with and whither I was going."

"Be it so," said his fellow-traveller. "Betake you to the woods, and let me keep the path."

Accordingly the young man turned aside, but took care to watch his companion, who advanced softly along the road until he had come within a staff's length of the old dame. She, meanwhile, was making the best of her way, with singular speed for so aged a woman and mumbling some indistinct words—a prayer, doubtless—as she went. The traveller put forth his staff and touched her withered neck with what seemed the serpent's tail.

"The devil!" screamed the pious old lady.

"Then Goody Cloyse knows her old friend?" observed the traveller, confronting her and leaning on his writhing stick.

"Ah, forsooth, and is it your worship indeed?" cried the good dame. "Yea, truly it is, and in the very image of my old gossip, Goodman Brown, the grandfather of the silly fellow, that now is. But— would your worship believe it?—my broomstick hath strangely disappeared, stolen, as I suspect, by that unhanged witch, Goody Cory, and that, too,

when I was all anointed with the juice of smallage, and cinquefoil, and wolf's bane—"

"Mingled with fine wheat and the fat of a new-born babe," said the shape of old Goodman Brown.

"Ah, your worship knows the recipe," cried the old lady, cackling aloud. "So, as I was saying, being all ready for the meeting, and no horse to ride on, I made up my mind to foot it; for they tell me there is a nice young man to be taken into communion tonight. But now your good worship will lend me your arm, and we shall be there in a twinkling."

"That can hardly be," answered her friend. "I may not spare you my arm, Goody Cloyse; but here is my staff, if you will."

So saying, he threw it down at her feet, where, perhaps, it assumed life, being one of the rods which its owner had formerly lent to the Egyptian magi[2]. Of this fact, however, Goodman Brown could not take cognizance. He had cast up his eyes in astonishment, and, looking down again, beheld neither Goody Cloyse nor the serpentine staff, but his fellow-traveller alone, who waited for him as calmly as if nothing had happened.

"That old woman taught me my catechism," said the young man; and there was a world of meaning in this simple comment.

They continued to walk onward, while the elder traveller exhorted his companion to make good speed and persevere in the path, discoursing so aptly that his arguments seemed rather to spring up in the bosom of his auditor than to be suggested by himself. As they went, he plucked a branch of maple to serve for a walking stick, and began to strip it of the twigs and little boughs, which were wet with evening dew. The moment his fingers touched them they became strangely withered and dried up as with a week's sunshine. Thus the pair proceeded, at a good free pace, until suddenly, in a gloomy hollow of the road, Goodman Brown sat himself down on the stump of a tree and refused to go any farther.

"Friend," said he, stubbornly, "my mind is made up. Not another step will I budge on this errand. What if a wretched old woman do choose to go to the devil when I thought she was going to heaven: is that any reason I should quit my dear Faith and go after her?"

"You will think better of this by and by," said his acquaintance, composedly. "Sit here and rest yourself a while; and when you feel like moving again, there is my staff to help you along."

Without more words, he threw his companion the maple stick, and was as speedily out of sight as if he had vanished into the deepening gloom. The young man sat a few moments by the roadside, applauding himself greatly, and thinking with how clear a conscience he should meet the minister in his morning walk, nor shrink from the eye of good old Deacon Gookin. And what calm sleep would be his that very night, which was to have been spent so wickedly, but so purely and sweetly now, in the arms of Faith! Amidst these pleasant and praiseworthy meditations, Goodman Brown heard the tramp of horses along the road, and deemed it advisable to conceal himself within the verge of the forest, conscious of the guilty purpose that had brought him thither, though now so happily turned from it.

On came the hoof tramps and the voices of the riders, two grave old voices, conversing soberly as they drew near. These mingled sounds appeared to pass along the road, within a few yards of the young man's hiding-place; but, owing doubtless to the depth of the gloom at that particular spot, neither the travellers nor their steeds were visible. Though their figures brushed the small boughs by the wayside, it could not be seen that they intercepted, even for a moment, the faint gleam from the strip of bright sky athwart which they must have passed. Goodman Brown alternately crouched and stood on tiptoe, pulling aside the branches and thrusting forth his head as far as he durst without discerning so much as a shadow. It vexed him the more, because he could have sworn, were such a thing possible, that he recognized the voices of the minister and Deacon Gookin, jogging along quietly, as they were wont to do, when bound to some ordination or ecclesiastical council. While yet within hearing, one of the riders stopped to pluck a switch.

"Of the two, reverend sir," said the voice like the deacon's, "I had rather miss an ordination dinner than tonight's meeting. They tell me that some of our community are to be here from Falmouth and beyond, and others from Connecticut and Rhode Island, besides several of the Indian pow-wows, who, after their fashion, know almost as much deviltry as the best of us. Moreover, there is a goodly young woman to be taken into communion."

"Mighty well, Deacon Gookin!" replied the solemn old tones of the minister. "Spur up, or we shall be late. Nothing can be done, you know, until I get on the ground."

The hoofs clattered again; and the voices, talking so strangely in the empty air, passed on through the forest, where no church had ever been gathered or solitary Christian prayed. Whither, then, could these holy men be journeying so deep into the heathen wilderness? Young Goodman Brown caught hold of a tree for support, being ready to sink down on the ground, faint and overburdened with the heavy sickness of his heart. He looked up to the sky, doubting whether there really was a heaven above him. Yet there was the blue arch, and the stars brightening in it.

"With heaven above and Faith below, I will yet stand firm against the devil!" cried Goodman Brown.

While he still gazed upward into the deep arch of the firmament and had lifted his hands to pray, a cloud, though no wind was stirring, hurried across the zenith and hid the brightening stars. The blue sky was still visible, except directly overhead, where this black mass of cloud was sweeping swiftly northward. Aloft in the air, as if from the depths of the cloud, came a confused and doubtful sound of voices. Once the listener fancied that he could distinguish the accents of townspeople of his own, men, and women, both pious and ungodly, many of whom he had met at the communion table, and had seen others rioting at the tavern. The next moment, so indistinct were the sounds, he doubted whether he had heard aught but the murmur of the old forest, whispering without a wind. Then came a stronger swell of those familiar tones, heard daily in the sunshine at Salem village, but never until now from a cloud of night. There was one voice, of a young woman, uttering lamentations, yet with an uncertain sorrow, and entreating for some favor, which, perhaps, it would grieve her to obtain; and all the unseen multitude, both saints and sinners, seemed to encourage her onward.

"Faith!" shouted Goodman Brown, in a voice of agony and desperation, and the echoes of the forest mocked him, crying, "Faith! Faith!" as if bewildered wretches were seeking her all through the wilderness.

The cry of grief, rage, and terror was yet piercing the night, when the unhappy husband held his breath for a response. There was a scream, drowned immediately in a louder murmur of voices, fading into far-off laughter, as the dark cloud swept away, leaving the clear and silent sky above Goodman Brown. But something fluttered lightly down through the air and caught on the branch of a tree. The young man seized it, and beheld a pink ribbon.

"My Faith is gone!" cried he, after one stupefied moment. "There is no good on earth; and sin is but a name. Come, devil; for to thee is this world given."

And, maddened with despair, so that he laughed loud and long, did Goodman Brown grasp his staff and set forth again, at such a rate that he seemed to fly along the forest path rather than to walk or run. The road grew wilder and drearier and more faintly traced, and vanished at length, leaving him in the heart of the dark wilderness, still rushing onward with the instinct that guides mortal man to evil. The whole forest was peopled with frightful sounds—the creaking of the trees, the howling of wild beasts, and the yell of Indians; while sometimes the wind tolled like a distant church bell, and sometimes gave a broad roar around the traveller, as if all Nature were laughing him to scorn. But he was himself the chief horror of the scene, and shrank not from its other horrors.

"Ha! ha! ha!" roared Goodman Brown when the wind laughed at him. "Let us hear which will laugh loudest. Think not to frighten me with your deviltry. Come witch, come wizard, come Indian powwow, come devil himself, and here comes Goodman Brown. You may as well fear him as he fear you."

In truth, all through the haunted forest there could be nothing more frightful than the figure of Goodman Brown. On he flew among the black pines, brandishing his staff with frenzied gestures, now giving vent to an inspiration of horrid blasphemy, and now shouting forth such laughter as set all the echoes of the forest laughing like demons around him. The fiend in his own shape is less hideous than when he rages in the breast of man. Thus sped the demoniac on his course, until, quivering among the trees, he saw a red light before him, as when the felled trunks and branches of a clearing have been set on fire, and throw up their lurid blaze against the sky, at the hour of midnight. He paused, in a lull of the tempest that had driven him onward, and heard the swell of what seemed a hymn, rolling solemnly from a distance with the weight of many voices. He knew the tune; it was a familiar one in the choir of the village meeting-house. The verse died heavily away, and was lengthened by a chorus, not of human voices, but of all the sounds of the benighted wilderness pealing in awful harmony together. Goodman Brown cried out, and his cry was lost to his own ear by its unison with the cry of the desert.

In the interval of silence he stole forward until the light glared full upon his eyes. At one extremity of an open space, hemmed in by the dark wall of the forest, arose a rock, bearing some rude, natural resemblance either to an altar or a pulpit, and surrounded by four blazing pines, their tops aflame, their stems untouched, like candles at an evening meeting. The mass of foliage that had overgrown the summit of the rock was all on fire, blazing high into the night and fitfully illuminating the whole field. Each pendent twig and leafy festoon was in a blaze. As the red light arose and fell, a numerous congregation alternately shone forth, then disappeared in shadow, and again grew, as it were, out of the darkness, peopling the heart of the solitary woods at once.

"A grave and dark-clad company," quoth Goodman Brown.

In truth they were such. Among them, quivering to and fro between gloom and splendor, appeared faces that would be seen next day at the council board of the province, and others which, Sabbath after Sabbath, looked devoutly heavenward, and benignantly over the crowded pews, from the holiest pulpits in the land. Some affirm that the lady of the governor was there. At least there were high dames well known to her, and wives of honored husbands, and widows, a great multitude, and ancient maidens, all of excellent repute, and fair young girls, who trembled lest their mothers should espy them. Either the sudden gleams of light flashing over the obscure field bedazzled Goodman Brown, or he recognized a score of the church members of Salem village famous for their especial sanctity. Good old Deacon Gookin had arrived, and waited at the skirts of that venerable saint, his revered pastor. But, irreverently consorting with these grave, reputable, and pious people, these elders of the church, these chaste dames and dewy virgins, there were men of dissolute lives and women of spotted fame, wretches given over to all mean and filthy vice, and suspected even of horrid crimes. It was strange to see that the good shrank not from the wicked, nor were the sinners abashed by the saints. Scattered also among their pale-faced enemies were the Indian priests, or powwows, who had often scared their native forest with more hideous incantations than any known to English witchcraft.

"But where is Faith?" thought Goodman Brown; and, as hope came into his heart, he trembled.

Another verse of the hymn arose, a slow and mournful strain, such as the pious love, but joined to words which expressed all that our nature can conceive of sin, and darkly hinted at far more.

Unfathomable to mere mortals is the lore of fiends. Verse after verse was sung; and still the chorus of the desert swelled between like the deepest tone of a mighty organ; and with the final peal of that dreadful anthem there came a sound, as if the roaring wind, the rushing streams, the howling beasts, and every other voice of the unconverted wilderness were mingling and according with the voice of guilty man in homage to the prince of all. The four blazing pines threw up a loftier flame, and obscurely discovered shapes and visages of horror on the smoke wreaths above the impious assembly. At the same moment the fire on the rock shot redly forth and formed a glowing arch above its base, where now appeared a figure. With reverence be it spoken, the figure bore no slight similitude, both in garb and manner, to some grave divine of the New England churches.

"Bring forth the converts!" cried a voice that echoed through the field and rolled into the forest.

At the word, Goodman Brown stepped forth from the shadow of the trees and approached the congregation, with whom he felt a loathful brotherhood by the sympathy of all that was wicked in his heart. He could have well-nigh sworn that the shape of his own dead father beckoned him to advance, looking downward from a smoke wreath, while a woman, with dim features of despair, threw out her hand to warn him back. Was it his mother? But he had no power to retreat one step, nor to resist, even in thought, when the minister and good old Deacon Gookin seized his arms and led him to the blazing rock. Thither came also the slender form of a veiled female, led between Goody Cloyse, that pious teacher of the catechism, and Martha Carrier, who had received the devil's promise to be queen of hell. A rampant hag was she. And there stood the proselytes beneath the canopy of fire.

"Welcome my children," said the dark figure, "to the communion of your race. Ye have found thus young your nature and your destiny. My children, look behind you!"

They turned; and flashing forth, as it were, in a sheet of flame, the fiend worshippers were seen; the smile of welcome gleamed darkly on every visage.

"There," resumed the sable form, "are all whom ye have reverenced from youth. Ye deemed them holier than yourselves, and shrank from your own sin, contrasting it with their lives of righteousness and prayerful aspirations heavenward. Yet here are they all in my worshipping assembly. This night it shall be granted you to know their secret deeds: how hoary-bearded elders of the church have whispered wanton words to the young maids of their households; how many a woman, eager for widows' weeds, has given her husband a drink at bedtime and let him sleep his last sleep in her bosom; how beardless youths have made haste to inherit their fathers' wealth; and how fair damsels—blush not, sweet ones—have dug little graves in the garden, and bidden me, the sole guest, to an infant's funeral. By the sympathy of your human hearts for sin ye shall scent out all the places—whether in church, bed-chamber, street, field, or forest where crime has been committed, and shall exult to behold the whole earth one stain of guilt, one mighty blood spot. Far more than this. It shall be yours to penetrate, in every bosom, the deep mystery of sin, the fountain of all wicked arts, and which inexhaustibly supplies more evil impulses than human power—than my power at its utmost—can make manifest in deeds. And now, my children, look upon each other."

They did so; and, by the blaze of the hell-kindled torches, the wretched man beheld his Faith, and the wife her husband, trembling before that unhallowed altar.

"Lo, there ye stand, my children," said the figure, in a deep and solemn tone, almost sad with its despairing awfulness, as if his once angelic nature could yet mourn for our miserable race. "Depending upon one another's hearts, ye had still hoped that virtue were not all a dream. Now are ye undeceived. Evil is the nature of mankind. Evil must be your only happiness. Welcome again, my children, to the communion of your race."

"Welcome," repeated the fiend worshippers, in one cry of despair and triumph.

And there they stood, the only pair, as it seemed, who were yet hesitating on the verge of wickedness in this dark world. A basin was hollowed, naturally, in the rock. Did it contain water, reddened by the lurid light? or was it blood? or, perchance, a liquid flame? Herein did the shape of evil dip his hand and prepare to lay the mark of baptism upon their foreheads, that they might be partakers of the mystery of sin, more conscious of the secret guilt of others, both in deed and thought, than they could now be of their own. The husband cast one look at his pale wife, and Faith at him. What polluted wretches would the next glance show them to each other, shuddering alike at what they disclosed and what they saw!

"Faith! Faith!" cried the husband, "look up to heaven, and resist the wicked one."

Whether Faith obeyed he knew not. Hardly had he spoken when he found himself amid calm night and solitude, listening to a roar of the wind which died heavily away through the forest. He staggered against the rock, and felt it chill and damp; while a hanging twig, that had been all on fire, besprinkled his cheek with the coldest dew.

The next morning young Goodman Brown came slowly into the street of Salem village, staring around him like a bewildered man. The good old minister was taking a walk along the graveyard to get an appetite for breakfast and meditate his sermon, and bestowed a blessing, as he passed, on Goodman Brown. He shrank from the venerable saint as if to avoid an anathema. Old Deacon Gookin was at domestic worship, and the holy words of his prayer were heard through the open window. "What God doth the wizard pray to?" quoth Goodman Brown. Goody Cloyse, that excellent old Christian, stood in the early sunshine at her own lattice, catechizing a little girl who had brought her a pint of morning's milk. Goodman Brown snatched away the child as from the grasp of the fiend himself. Turning the corner by the meetinghouse, he spied the head of Faith, with the pink ribbons, gazing anxiously forth, and bursting into such joy at the sight of him that she skipped along the street and almost kissed her husband before the whole village. But Goodman Brown looked sternly and sadly into her face, and passed on without a greeting.

Had Goodman Brown fallen asleep in the forest and only dreamed a wild dream of a witch-meeting?

Be it so if you will; but, alas! it was a dream of evil omen for young Goodman Brown. A stern, a sad, a darkly meditative, a distrustful, if not a desperate man did he become from the night of that fearful dream. On the Sabbath day, when the congregation were singing a holy psalm, he could not listen because an anthem of sin rushed loudly upon his ear and drowned all the blessed strain. When the minister spoke from the pulpit with power and fervid eloquence, and, with his hand on the open Bible, of the sacred truths of our religion, and of saint-like lives and triumphant deaths, and of future bliss or misery unutterable, then did Goodman Brown turn pale, dreading lest the roof should thunder down upon the gray blasphemer and his hearers. Often, waking suddenly at midnight, he shrank from the bosom of Faith; and at morning or eventide, when the family knelt down at prayer, he scowled and muttered to himself, and gazed sternly at his wife, and turned away. And when he had lived long, and was borne to his grave a hoary corpse, followed by Faith, an aged woman, and children and grandchildren, a goodly procession, besides neighbors not a few, they carved no hopeful verse upon his tombstone, for his dying hour was gloom. ■

Notes

1 Old South—the Old South Church in Boston

2 Egyptian magi—Egyptian magicians who imitated some of the miracles of Moses before Pharoah, e.g., turning staffs into snakes.

Making Connections through Discussion and Writing

1. Hawthorne's use of impending darkness in the setting foreshadows what is going to happen. For example, in the first paragraph he crosses the threshold at sunset.

    a. Underline other references to darkness.

    b. Explain their significance to the story.

    _____
    _____
    _____
    _____
    _____
    _____
    _____
    _____
    _____

    c. What light images are used to contrast the dark images?

    _____
    _____
    _____
    _____
    _____
    _____

2. Goodman Brown's formidable companion is described as one who bore a considerable resemblance to him but also as one who seemed to know the world. Why would the young man's tempter look like himself?

    _____
    _____
    _____

3. In another reference to the formidable companion, Hawthorne describes him as one whose deep and solemn tone was "almost sad with its despairing awfulness, as if his once angelic nature could yet mourn for our miserable race." Explain the significance of this passage in terms of Young Goodman Brown's own choices.

    _____
    _____
    _____
    _____
    _____
    _____

4. An author wanting to convey a message or belief may use the technique of allegory, turning the message or belief into a story in which the people represent or personify abstract qualities or ideas, such as love or death. What allegorical figures are in this story, and what do they personify?

_____   _____

_____   _____

_____   _____

_____   _____

_____   _____

5. Young Goodman Brown's young wife, Faith, seems to function as his lifeline throughout the story, yet their relationship changes. What could Hawthorne be saying here about Brown's spiritual condition?

_____

_____

_____

_____

_____

_____

6. a. What is the theme of the story?

_____

_____

_____

   b. Explain how the symbols and allegorical figures support the theme.

_____

_____

_____

_____

_____

_____

_____

7. a. What does this story suggest about human depravity.

_____

_____

_____

_____

_____

_____

   b. What does the story suggest about grace?

_____

_____

_____

_____

_____

_____

8. a. Hawthorne's ambiguous conclusion leaves the interpretive decision to the reader. List the ambiguities in the story.

_____

_____

_____

_____

_____

_____

_____

_____

    b. What do you think really happened?

_____

_____

_____

_____

_____

_____

Kate Chopin

The Story of an Hour

Kate Chopin (show-pan) (1851–1904) was born in St. Louis into an affluent family. She married Oscar Chopin in 1870 and moved to New Orleans. Two years after Oscar died of malaria in 1882, Chopin, with their six children, moved back to St. Louis to live with her mother. She began writing and published two collections of her stories, *Bayoued Folk* (1894) and *A Night in Acadia* (1897), resulting in a decade of popularity. However, with the publication of *The Awakening* (1899), which depicts a woman attempting to become free from years of marital repression, her popularity declined for about sixty years. In the "Story of an Hour" Chopin's character, having discovered her newfound freedom, is unable to survive when her freedom is removed.

Vocabulary ....

bespoke	imploring
elixir	importunities
illumination	tumultuously

Knowing that Mrs. Mallard was afflicted with a heart trouble, great care was taken to break to her as gently as possible the news of her husband's death.

It was her sister Josephine who told her, in broken sentences; veiled hints that revealed in half concealing. Her husband's friend Richards was there, too, near her. It was he who had been in the newspaper office when intelligence of the railroad disaster was received, with Brently Mallard's name leading the list of "killed." He had only taken the time to assure himself of its truth by a second telegram, and had hastened to forestall any less careful, less tender friend in bearing the sad message.

She did not hear the story as many women have heard the same, with a paralyzed inability to accept its significance. She wept at once, with sudden, wild abandonment, in her sister's arms. When the storm of grief had spent itself she went away to her room alone. She would have no one follow her.

There stood, facing the open window, a comfortable, roomy armchair. Into this she sank, pressed down by a physical exhaustion that haunted her body and seemed to reach into her soul.

She could see in the open square before her house the tops of trees that were all aquiver with the new spring life. The delicious breath of rain was in the air. In the street below a peddler was crying his wares. The notes of a distant song which some one was singing reached her faintly, and countless sparrows were twittering in the eaves.

There were patches of blue sky showing here and there through the clouds that had met and piled one above the other in the west facing her window.

She sat with her head thrown back upon the cushion of the chair, quite motionless, except when a sob came up into her throat and shook her, as a child who has cried itself to sleep continues to sob in its dreams.

She was young, with a fair, calm face, whose lines bespoke repression and even a certain strength. But now there was a dull stare in her eyes, whose gaze was fixed away off yonder on one of those patches of blue sky. It was not a glance of reflection, but rather indicated a suspension of intelligent thought.

There was something coming to her and she was waiting for it, fearfully. What was it? She did not know; it was too subtle and elusive to name. But she felt it, creeping out of the sky, reaching toward her through the sounds, the scents, the color that filled the air.

Now her bosom rose and fell tumultuously. She was beginning to recognize this thing that was approaching to possess her, and she was striving to beat it back with her will—as powerless as her two white slender hands would have been.

When she abandoned herself a little whispered word escaped her slightly parted lips. She said it over and over under her breath: "free, free, free!" The vacant stare and the look of terror that had followed it went from her eyes. They stayed keen and bright. Her pulses beat fast, and the coursing blood warmed and relaxed every inch of her body.

She did not stop to ask if it were or were not a monstrous joy that held her. A clear and exalted perception enabled her to dismiss the suggestion as trivial.

She knew that she would weep again when she saw the kind, tender hands folded in death; the face that had never looked save with love upon her, fixed and gray and dead. But she saw beyond that bitter moment a long procession of years to come that would belong to her absolutely. And she opened and spread her arms out to them in welcome.

There would be no one to live for her during those coming years; she would live for herself. There would be no powerful will bending hers in that blind persistence with which men and women believe they have a right to impose a private will upon a fellow-creature. A kind intention or a cruel intention made the act seem no less a crime as she looked upon it in that brief moment of illumination.

And yet she had loved him—sometimes. Often she had not. What did it matter! What could love,

the unsolved mystery, count for in face of this possession of self-assertion which she suddenly recognized as the strongest impulse of her being!

"Free! Body and soul free!" she kept whispering.

Josephine was kneeling before the closed door with her lips to the keyhole, imploring for admission. "Louise, open the door! I beg; open the door—you will make yourself ill. What are you doing, Louise? For heaven's sake open the door."

"Go away. I am not making myself ill." No; she was drinking in a very elixir of life through that open window.

Her fancy was running riot along those days ahead of her. Spring days, and summer days, and all sorts of days that would be her own. She breathed a quick prayer that life might be long. It was only yesterday she had thought with a shudder that life might be long.

She arose at length and opened the door to her sister's importunities. There was a feverish triumph in her eyes, and she carried herself unwittingly like a goddess of Victory. She clasped her sister's waist, and together they descended the stairs. Richards stood waiting for them at the bottom.

Some one was opening the front door with a latchkey. It was Brently Mallard who entered, a little travel-stained, composedly carrying his gripsack and umbrella. He had been far from the scene of accident, and did not even know there had been one. He stood amazed at Josephine's piercing cry; at Richards' quick motion to screen him from the view of his wife.

But Richards was too late.

When the doctors came they said she had died of heart disease—of joy that kills. ◼

Andre Dubus

A Father's Story

Andre   bus (1936–1999), a consummate writer of novellas and short stories in the real-
ist trac   n, won many awards for his fiction, including the Rea Award for the Short
Story, tl   EN/Malamud Award, and the American Academy of Arts and Letters Award.
His ficti   orks include *Separate Flights* (1975), *Finding a Girl in America* (1980), *The Times
Are Neve   Bad* (1983), *Voices from the Moon* (1984), *The Last Worthless Evening* (1986), and
Dancing   · Hours (1996). Two late books of non-fiction, *Broken Vessels* (1991) and
Meditation   m a Movable Chair (1998), movingly tell of the accident that left him crip-
pled and c   s sustaining Christian faith. The following story depicts a character who
must strugg   ) live out his faith, his ethics, and his love for his daughter when a tragedy
brings these   lties into conflict.

Vocabulary . . . .

baw	lee
cante	pantheism
celebi	rye
celibac	sacristy
decidu	silo
exorcise	slacking
gauge	sorrel
Host	unabashed

My name is Luke Ripley, ¿   ere is what I call
my life: I own a stable o   ty horses, and I
have young people who tea   ding, and we
board some horses too. This   northeastern
Massachusetts. I have a barn wi   indoor ring,
and outside I've got two fenced-i   ¿s and a pasture that ends at a woods with trai   all it my life
because it looks like it is, and peop   :now call it
that, but it's a life I can get away fro   hen I hunt
and fish, and some nights after dinn   ien I sit in
the dark in the front room and listen   ɔera. The
room faces the lawn and the road, a tv   ιe country road. When cars come around the   ᵓ northwest of the house, they light up the .   for an
instant, the leaves of the maple out by tl   ιd and
the hemlock closer to the window. Ther   alone
again, or I'd appear to be if someone crep   ɔ the
house and looked through a window: a b   tted
grey-haired guy, drinking tea and smoki   ga-
rettes, staring out at the dark woods acı   he
road, listening to a grieving soprano.

My real life is the only one nobody talks about
anymore, except Father Paul LeBoeuf, another old
buck. He has a decade on me: he's sixty-four, a big
man, bald on top with grey at the sides; when he
had hair, it was black. His face is ruddy, and he
jokes about being a whiskey priest,[1] though he's
not. He gets outdoors as much as he can, goes for a
long walk every morning, and hunts and fishes
with me. But I can't get him on a horse anymore.
Ten years ago I could badger him into a trail ride! I
had to give him a western saddle, and he'd hold the
pommel and bounce through the woods with me,
and be sore for days. He's looking at seventy with
eyes that are younger than many I've seen in people in their twenties. I do not remember ever feeling the way they seem to; but I was lucky, because
even as a child I knew that life would try me, and I
must be strong to endure, though in those early
days I expected to be tortured and killed for my
faith, like the saints I learned about in school.

Father Paul's family came down from Canada,

From *The Times Are Never So Bad* by Andre Dubus. Reprii   · permission of David R. Godine, Publisher, Inc. Copyright © 1983 by
Andre Dubus.

and he grew up speaking more French than English, so he is different from the Irish priests who abound up here. I do not like to make general statements, or even to hold general beliefs, about people's blood, but the Irish do seem happiest when they're dealing with misfortune or guilt, either their own or somebody's else's, and if you think you're not a victim of either one, you can count on certain Irish priests to try to change your mind. On Wednesday nights Father Paul comes to dinner. Often he comes on other nights too, and once, in the old days when we couldn't eat meat on Fridays, we bagged our first ducks of the season on a Friday, and as we drove home from the marsh, he said: For the purposes of Holy Mother Church, I believe a duck is more a creature of water than land, and is not rightly meat. Sometimes he teases me about never putting anything in his Sunday collection, which he would not know about if I hadn't told him years ago. I would like to believe I told him so we could have a philosophical talk at dinner, but probably the truth is I suspected he knew, and I did not want him to think I so loved money that I would not even give his church a coin on Sunday. Certainly the ushers who pass the baskets know me as a miser.

I don't feel right about giving money for buildings, places. This starts with the Pope, and I cannot respect one of them till he sells his house and everything in it, and that church too, and uses the money to feed the poor. I have rarely, and maybe never, come across saintliness, but I feel certain it cannot exist in such a place. But I admit, also, that I know very little, and maybe the popes live on a different plane and are tried in ways I don't know about. Father Paul says his own church, St. John's, is hardly the Vatican. I like his church: it is made of wood, and has a simple altar and crucifix, and no padding on the kneelers. He does not have to lock its doors at night. Still it is a place. He could say Mass in my barn. I know this is stubborn, but I can find no mention by Christ of maintaining buildings, much less erecting them of stone or brick, and decorating them with pieces of metal and mineral and elements that people still fight over like barbarians. We had a Maltese woman taking riding lessons, she came over on the boat when she was ten, and once she told me how the nuns in Malta used to tell the little girls that if they wore jewelry, rings and bracelets and necklaces, in purgatory snakes would coil around their fingers and wrists and throats. I do not believe in frightening children or telling them lies, but if those nuns saved a few girls from devotion to things, maybe they were right. That Maltese woman laughed about it, but I noticed she wore only a watch, and that with a leather strap.

The money I give to the church goes in people's stomachs, and on their backs, down in New York City. I have no delusions about the worth of what I do, but I feel it's better to feed somebody than not. There's a priest in Times Square giving shelter to runaway kids, and some Franciscans who run a bread line; actually it's a morning line for coffee and a roll, and Father Paul calls it the continental breakfast for winos and bag ladies. He is curious about how much I am sending, and I know why: he guesses I send a lot, he has said probably more than tithing, and he is right; he wants to know how much because he believes I'm generous and good, and he is wrong about that; he has never had much money and does not know how easy it is to write a check when you have everything you will ever need, and the figures are mere numbers, and represent no sacrifice at all. Being a real Catholic is too hard; if I were one, I would do with my house and barn what I want the Pope to do with his. So I do not want to impress Father Paul, and when he asks me how much, I say I can't let my left hand know what my right is doing.

He came on Wednesday nights when Gloria and I were married, and the kids were young; Gloria was a very good cook (I assume she still is, but it is difficult to think of her in the present), and I liked sitting at the table with a friend who was also a priest. I was proud of my handsome and healthy children. This was long ago, and they were all very young and cheerful and often funny, and the three boys took care of their baby sister, and did not bully or tease her. Of course they did sometimes, with that excited cruelty children are prone to, but not enough so that it was part of her days. On the Wednesday after Gloria left with the kids and a U-Haul trailer, I was sitting on the front steps, it was summer, and I was watching cars go by on the road, when Father Paul drove around the curve and into the driveway. I was ashamed to see him because he is a priest and my family was gone, but I was relieved too. I went to the car to greet him. He got out smiling, with a bottle of wine, and shook my hand, then pulled me to him, gave me a quick hug, and said: 'It's Wednesday, isn't it? Let's open some cans.'

With arms about each other we walked to the house, and it was good to know he was doing his work but coming as a friend too, and I thought what good work he had. I have no calling. It is for me to keep horses.

In that other life, anyway. In my real one I go to bed early and sleep well and wake at four forty-five, for an hour of silence. I never want to get out of bed then, and every morning I know I can sleep for another four hours, and still not fail at any of my duties. But I get up, so have come to believe my life can be seen in miniature in that struggle in the dark of morning. While making the bed and boiling water for coffee, I talk to God: I offer Him my day, every act of my body and spirit, my thoughts and moods, as a prayer of thanksgiving, and for Gloria and my children and my friends and two women I made love with after Gloria left. This morning offertory is a habit from my boyhood in a Catholic school; or then it was a habit, but as I kept it and grew older it became a ritual. Then I say the Lord's Prayer, trying not to recite it, and one morning it occurred to me that a prayer, whether recited or said with concentration, is always an act of faith.

I sit in the kitchen at the rear of the house and drink coffee and smoke and watch the sky growing light before sunrise, the trees of the woods near the barn taking shape, becoming single pines and elms and oaks and maples. Sometimes a rabbit comes out of the treeline, or is already sitting there, invisible till the light finds him. The birds are awake in the trees and feeding on the ground, and the little ones, the purple finches and titmice and chickadees, are at the feeder I rigged outside the kitchen window; it is too small for pigeons to get a purchase. I sit and give myself to coffee and tobacco that get me brisk again, and I watch and listen. In the first year or so after I lost my family, I played the radio in the mornings. But I overcame that, and now I rarely play it at all. Once in the mail I received a questionnaire asking me to write down everything I watched on television during the week they had chosen. At the end of those seven days I wrote in *The Wizard of Oz* and returned it. That was in winter and was actually a busy week for my television, which normally sits out the cold months without once warming up. Had they sent the questionnaire during baseball season, they would have found me at my set. People at the stables talk about shows and performers I have never heard of, but I cannot get interested; when I am in the mood to watch television, I go to a movie or read a detective novel. There are always good detective novels to be found, and I like remembering them next morning with my coffee.

I also think of baseball and hunting and fishing, and of my children. It is not painful to think about them anymore, because even if we had lived together, they would be gone now, grown into their own lives, except Jennifer. I think of death too, not sadly, or with fear, though something like excitement does run through me, something more quickening than the coffee and tobacco. I suppose it is an intense interest, and an outright distrust: I never feel certain that I'll be here watching birds eating at tomorrow's daylight. Sometimes I try to think of other things, like the rabbit that is warm and breathing but not there till twilight. I feel on the brink of something about the life of the senses, but either am not equipped to go further or am not interested enough to concentrate. I have called all of this thinking, but it is not, because it is unintentional; what I'm really doing is feeling the day, in silence, and that is what Father Paul is doing too on his five-to-ten-mile walks.

When the hour ends I take an apple or carrot and I go to the stable and tack up a horse. We take good care of these horses, and no one rides them but students, instructors, and me, and nobody rides the horses we board unless an owner asks me to. The barn is dark and I turn on lights and take some deep breaths, smelling the hay and horses and their manure, both fresh and dried, a combined odor that you either like or you don't. I walk down the wide space of dirt between stalls, greeting the horses, joking with them about their quirks, and choose one for no reason at all other than the way it looks at me that morning. I get my old English saddle that has smoothed and darkened through the years, and go into the stall, talking to this beautiful creature who'll swerve out of a canter if a piece of paper blows in front of him, and if the barn catches fire and you manage to get him out he will, if he can get away from you, run back into the fire, to his stall. Like the smells that surround them, you either like them or you don't. I love them, so am spared having to try to explain why. I feed one the carrot or apple and tack up and lead him outside, where I mount, and we go down the driveway to the road and cross it and turn northwest and walk, then trot then canter to St. John's.

A few cars are on the road, their drivers looking serious about going to work. It is always strange for me to see a woman dressed for work so early in the morning. You know how long it takes them, with the makeup and hair and clothes, and I think of them waking in the dark of winter or early light of other seasons, and dressing as they might for an evening's entertainment. Probably this strikes me because I grew up seeing my father put on those suits he never wore on weekends or his two weeks off, and so am accustomed to the men, but when I see these women I think something went wrong, to send all those dressed-up people out on the road when the dew hasn't dried yet. Maybe it's because I so dislike getting up early, but am also doing what I choose to do, while they have no choice. At heart I am lazy, yet I find such peace and delight in it that I believe it is a natural state, and in what looks like my laziest periods I am closest to my center. The ride to St. John's is fifteen minutes. The horses and I do it in all weather; the road is well plowed in winter, and there are only a few days a year when ice makes me drive the pickup. People always look at someone on horseback, and for a moment their faces change and many drivers and I wave to each other. Then at St. John's, Father Paul and five or six regulars and I celebrate the Mass.

Do not think of me as a spiritual man whose every thought during those twenty-five minutes is at one with the words of the Mass. Each morning I try, each morning I fail, and know that always I will be a creature who, looking at Father Paul and the altar, and uttering prayers, will be distracted by scrambled eggs, horses, the weather, and memories and daydreams that have nothing to do with the sacrament I am about to receive. I can receive, though: the Eucharist, and also, at Mass and at other times, moments and even minutes of contemplation. But I cannot achieve contemplation, as some can; and so, having to face and forgive my own failures, I have learned from them both the necessity and wonder of ritual. For ritual allows those who cannot will themselves out of the secular to perform the spiritual, as dancing allows the tongue-tied man a ceremony of love. And, while my mind dwells on breakfast, or Major or Duchess tethered under the church eave, there is, as I take the Host from Father Paul and place it on my tongue and return to the pew, a feeling that I am thankful I have not lost in the forty-eight years since my first Communion. At its center is excitement; spreading out from it is the peace of certainty. Or the certainty of peace. One night Father Paul and I talked about faith. It was long ago, and all I remember is him saying: Belief is believing in God; faith is believing that God believes in you. That is the excitement, and the peace; then the Mass is over, and I go into the sacristy and we have a cigarette and chat, the mystery ends, we are two men talking like any two men on a morning in America, about baseball, plane crashes, presidents, governors, murders, the sun, the clouds. Then I go to the horse and ride back to the life people see, the one in which I move and talk, and most days I enjoy it.

It is late summer now, the time between fishing and hunting, but a good time for baseball. It has been two weeks since Jennifer left, to drive home to Gloria's after her summer visit. She is the only one who still visits; the boys are married and have children, and sometimes fly up for a holiday, or I fly down or west to visit one of them. Jennifer is twenty, and I worry about her the way fathers worry about daughters but not sons. I want to know what she's up to, and at the same time I don't. She looks athletic, and she is: she swims and runs and of course rides. All my children do. When she comes for six weeks in summer, the house is loud with girls, friends of hers since childhood, and new ones. I am glad she kept the girl friends. They have been young company for me and, being with them, I have been able to gauge her growth between summers. On their riding days, I'd take them back to the house when their lessons were over and they had walked the horses and put them back in the stalls, and we'd have lemonade or Coke, and cookies if I had some, and talk until their parents came to drive them home. One year their breasts grew, so I wasn't startled when I saw Jennifer in July. Then they were driving cars to the stable, and beginning to look like young women, and I was passing out beer and ashtrays and they were talking about college.

When Jennifer was here in summer, they were at the house most days. I would say generally that as they got older they became quieter, and though I enjoyed both, I sometimes missed the giggles and shouts. The quiet voices, just low enough for me not to hear from wherever I was, rising and falling in proportion to my distance from them, frightened me. Not that I believed they were planning or recounting anything really wicked, but there was a female seriousness about them, and it was secretive, and of course I thought: love, sex. But it was more than that: it was womanhood they were entering, the deep forest of it, and no matter how many women and men too are saying these days that there is little difference between us, the truth is that men find their way into that forest only on clearly marked trails, while women move about in it like birds. So hearing Jennifer and her friends talking so quietly, yet intensely, I wanted very much to have a wife.

But not as much as in the old days, when Gloria had left but her presence was still in the house as strongly as if she had only gone to visit her folks for a week. There were no clothes or cosmetics, but potted plants endured my neglectful care as long as they could, and slowly died; I did not kill them on purpose, to exorcise the house of her, but I could not remember to water them. For weeks, because I did not use it much, the house was as neat as she had kept it, though dust layered the order she had made. The kitchen went first: I got the dishes in and out of the dishwasher and wiped the top of the stove, but did not return cooking spoons and pot holders to their hooks on the wall, and soon the burners and oven were caked with spillings, the refrigerator had more space and was spotted with juices. The living room and my bedroom went next; I did not go into the children's rooms except on bad nights when I went from room to room and looked and touched and smelled, so they did not lose their order until a year later when the kids came for six weeks. It was three months before I ate the last of the food Gloria had cooked and frozen: I remember it was a beef stew, and very good. By then I had four cookbooks, and was boasting a bit, and talking about recipes with the women at the stables, and looking forward to cooking for Father Paul. But I never looked forward to cooking at night only for myself, though I made myself do it; on some nights I gave in to my daily temptation, and took a newspaper or detective novel to a restaurant. By the end of the second year, though, I had stopped turning on the radio as soon as I woke in the morning, and was able to be silent and alone in the evening too, and then I enjoyed my dinners.

It is not hard to live through a day, if you can live through a moment. What creates despair is the imagination, which pretends there is a future, and insists on predicting millions of moments, thousands of days, and so drains you that you cannot live the moment at hand. That is what Father Paul told me in those first two years, on some of the bad nights when I believed I could not bear what I had to: the most painful loss was my children, then the loss of Gloria, whom I still loved despite or maybe because of our long periods of sadness that rendered us helpless, so neither of us could break out of it to give a hand to the other. Twelve years later I believe ritual would have healed us more quickly than the repetitious talks we had, perhaps even kept us healed. Marriages have lost that, and I wish I had known then what I know now, and we had performed certain acts together every day, no matter how we felt, and perhaps then we could have subordinated feeling to action, for surely that is the essence of love. I know this from my distractions during Mass, and during everything else I do, so that my actions and feelings are seldom one. It does happen every day, but in proportion to everything else in a day, it is rare, like joy. The third most painful loss, which became second and sometimes first as months passed, was the knowledge that I could never marry again, and so dared not even keep company with a woman.

On some of the bad nights I was bitter about this with Father Paul, and I so pitied myself that I cried, or nearly did, speaking with damp eyes and breaking voice. I believe that celibacy is for him the same trial it is for me, not of the flesh, but the spirit: the heart longing to love. But the difference is he chose it, and did not wake one day to a life with thirty horses. In my anger I said I had done my service to love and chastity, and I told him of the actual physical and spiritual pain of practicing rhythm: nights of striking the mattress with a fist, two young animals lying side by side in heat, leaving the bed to pace, to smoke, to curse, and too passionate to question, for we were so angered and oppressed by our passion that we could see no further than our loins. So now I understand how people can be enslaved for generations before they throw down their tools or use them as weapons, the form of their slavery—the cotton fields, the shacks and puny cupboards and untended illnesses—absorbing their emotions and thoughts until finally they have little or none at all to direct with clarity and energy at the owners and legislators. And I told him of the trick of passion and its slaking: how during what we had to believe were safe periods, though all four children were conceived at those times, we were able with some coherence to question the tradition and reason and justice of the law against birth control, but not with enough conviction to soberly act against it, as though regular satisfaction in bed tempered our revolutionary as well as our erotic desires. Only when abstinence drove us hotly away from each other did we receive an urge so strong it lasted all the way to the drugstore and back; but always, after release, we threw away the remaining condoms; and after going through this a few times, we knew what would happen, and from then on we submitted to the calendar she so precisely marked on the bedroom wall. I told him that living two lives each month, one as celibates, one as lovers, made us tense and short-tempered, so we snapped at each other like dogs.

To have endured that, to have reached a time when we burned slowly and could gain from bed the comfort of lying down at night with one who loves you and whom you love, could for weeks on end go to bed tired and peacefully sleep after a kiss, a touch of the hands, and then to be thrown out of the marriage like a bundle from a moving freight car, was unjust, was intolerable, and I could not or would not muster the strength to endure it. But I did, a moment at a time, a day, a night, except twice, each time with a different woman and more than a year apart, and this was so long ago that I clearly see their faces in my memory, can hear the pitch of their voices, and the way they pronounced words, one with a Massachusetts accent, one midwestern, but I feel as though I only heard about them from someone else. Each rode at the stables and was with me for part of an evening; one was badly married, one divorced, so none of us was free. They did not understand this Catholic view, but they were understanding about my having it, and I remained friends with both of them until the married one left her husband and went to Boston, and the divorced one moved to Maine. After both those evenings, those good women, I went to Mass early while Father Paul was still in the confessional, and received his absolution. I did not tell him who I was, but of course he knew, though I never saw it in his eyes. Now my longing for a wife comes only once in a while, like a cold: on some late afternoons when I am alone in the barn, then I lock up and walk to the house, daydreaming, then suddenly look at it and see it empty, as though for the first time, and all at once I'm weary and feel I do not have the energy to broil meat, and I think of driving to a restaurant, then shake my head and go on to the house, the refrigerator, the oven; and some mornings when I wake in the dark and listen to the silence and run my hand over the cold sheet beside me; and some days in summer when Jennifer is here.

Gloria left first me, then the Church, and that was the end of religion for the children, though on visits they went to Sunday Mass with me, and still do, out of a respect for my life that they manage to keep free of patronage. Jennifer is an agnostic, though I doubt she would call herself that, any more than she would call herself any other name that implied she had made a decision, a choice, about existence, death, and God. In truth she tends to pantheism, a good sign, I think; but not wanting to be a father who tells his children what they ought to believe, I do not say to her that Catholicism includes pantheism, like onions in a stew. Besides, I have no missionary instincts and do not believe everyone should or even could live with the Catholic faith. It is Jennifer's womanhood that renders me awkward. And womanhood now is frank, not like when Gloria was twenty and there were symbols: high heels and cosmetics and dresses, a cigarette, a cocktail. I am glad that women are free now of false modesty and all its attention paid the flesh; but, still, it is difficult to see so much of your daughter, to hear her talk as only men and bawdy women used to, and most of all to see in her face the deep and unabashed sensuality of women, with no tricks of the eyes and mouth to hide the pleasure she feels at having a strong young body. I am certain, with the way things are now, that she has very happily not been a virgin for years. That does not bother me. What bothers me is my cer-

tainty about it, just from watching her walk across a room or light a cigarette or pour milk on cereal.

She told me all of it, waking me that night when I had gone to sleep listening to the wind in the trees and against the house, a wind so strong that I had to shut all but the lee windows, and still the house cooled; told it to me in such detail and so clearly that now, when she has driven the car to Florida, I remember it all as though I had been a passenger in the front seat, or even at the wheel. It started with a movie, then beer and driving to the sea to look at the waves in the night and the wind, Jennifer and Betsy and Liz. They drank a beer on the beach and wanted to go in naked but were afraid they would drown in the high surf. They bought another six-pack at a grocery store in New Hampshire, and drove home. I can see it now, feel it: the three girls and the beer and the ride on country roads where pines curved in the wind and the big deciduous trees swayed and shook as if they might leap from the earth. They would have some windows partly open so they could feel the wind; Jennifer would be playing a cassette, the music stirring them, as it does the young, to memories of another time, other people and places in what is for them the past.

She took Betsy home, then Liz, and sang with her cassette as she left the town west of us and started home, a twenty-minute drive on the road that passes my house. They had each had four beers, but now there were twelve empty bottles in the bag on the floor at the passenger seat, and I kept focusing on their sound against each other when the car shifted speeds or changed directions. For I want to understand that one moment out of all her heart's time on earth, and whether her history had any bearing on it, or whether her heart was then isolated from all it had known, and the sound of those bottles urged it. She was just leaving the town, accelerating past a night club on the right, gaining speed to climb a long, gradual hill, then she went up it, singing, patting the beat on the steering wheel, the wind loud through her few inches of open window, blowing her hair as it did the high branches alongside the road, and she looked up at them and watched the top of the hill for someone drunk or heedless coming over it in part of her lane. She crested to an open black road, and there he was: a bulk, a blur, a thing running across her headlights, and she swerved left and her foot went for the brake and was stomping air above its pedal when she hit him, saw his legs and body in the air, flying out of her light, into the dark. Her brakes were screaming into the wind, bottles clinking in the fallen bag, and with the music and wind inside the car was his sound, already a memory but as real as an echo, that car-shuddering thump as though she had struck a tree. Her foot was back on the accelerator. Then she shifted gears and pushed it. She ejected the cassette and closed the window. She did not start to cry until she knocked on my bedroom door, then called: "Dad?"

Her voice, her tears, broke through my dream and the wind I heard in my sleep, and I stepped into jeans and hurried to the door, thinking harm, rape, death. All were in her face, and I hugged her and pressed her cheek to my chest and smoothed her blown hair, then led her, weeping, to the kitchen and sat her at the table where still she could not speak, nor look at me; when she raised her face it fell forward again, as of its own weight, into her palms. I offered tea and she shook her head, so I offered beer twice, then she shook her head, so I offered whiskey and she nodded. I had some rye that Father Paul and I had not finished last hunting season, and I poured some over ice and set it in front of her and was putting away the ice but stopped and got another glass and poured one for myself too, and brought the ice and bottle to the table where she was trying to get one of her long menthols out of the pack, but her fingers jerked like severed snakes, and I took the pack and lit one for her and took one for myself. I watched her shudder with her first swallow of rye, and push hair back from her face, it is auburn and gleamed in the overhead light, and I remember how beautiful she looked riding a sorrel; she was smoking fast, then the sobs in her throat stopped, and she looked at me and said it, the words coming out with smoke: 'I hit somebody. With the *car*.'

Then she was crying and I was on my feet, moving back and forth, looking down at her, asking *Who? Where? Where?* She was pointing at the wall over the stove, jabbing her fingers and cigarette at it, her other hand at her eyes, and twice in horror I actually looked at the wall. She finished the whiskey in a swallow and I stopped pacing and asking and poured another, and either the drink or the exhaustion of tears quieted her, even the dry sobs, and she told me; not as I tell it now, for that was later as again and again we relived it in the kitchen or living room, and, if in daylight, fled it on horseback out on the trails through the woods and, if at night, walked quietly around in the moonlit pasture, walked around and around it, sweating through our clothes. She told it in bursts, like she was a child again, running to me, injured from play. I put on boots and a shirt and left her with the bottle and her streaked face and a cigarette twitching

between her fingers, pushed the door open against the wind, and eased it shut. The wind squinted and watered my eyes as I leaned into it and went to the pickup.

When I passed St. John's I looked at it, and Father Paul's little white rectory in the rear, and wanted to stop, wished I could as I could if he were simply a friend who sold hardware or something. I had forgotten my watch but I always know the time within minutes, even when a sound or dream or my bladder wakes me in the night. It was nearly two; we had been in the kitchen about twenty minutes; she had hit him around one-fifteen. Or her. The road was empty and I drove between blowing trees; caught for an instant in my lights, they seemed to be in panic. I smoked and let hope play its tricks on me: it was neither man nor woman but an animal, a goat or calf or deer on the road; it was a man who had jumped away in time, the collision of metal and body glancing not direct, and he had limped home to nurse bruises and cuts. Then I threw the cigarette and hope both out the window and prayed that he was alive, while beneath that prayer, a reserve deeper in my heart, another one stirred: that if he were dead, they would not get Jennifer.

From our direction, east and a bit south, the road to that hill and the night club beyond it and finally the town is, for its last four or five miles, straight through farming country. When I reached that stretch I slowed the truck and opened my window for the fierce air; on both sides were scattered farmhouses and barns and sometimes a silo, looking not like shelters but like unsheltered things the wind would flatten. Corn bent toward the road from a field on my right, and always something blew in front of me: paper, leaves, dried weeds, branches. I slowed approaching the hill, and went up it in second, staring through my open window at the ditch on the left side of the road, its weeds alive, whipping, a mad dance with the trees above them. I went over the hill and down and, opposite the club, turned right onto a side street of houses, and parked there, in the leaping shadows of trees. I walked back across the road to the club's parking lot, the wind behind me, lifting me as I strode, and I could not hear my boots on pavement. I walked up the hill, on the shoulder, watching the branches above me, hearing their leaves and the creaking trunks and the wind. Then I was at the top, looking down the road and at the farms and fields; the night was clear, and I could see a long way; clouds scudded past the half-moon and stars, blown out to sea.

I started down, watching the tall grass under

the trees to my right, glancing into the dark of the ditch, listening for cars behind me; but as soon as I cleared one tree, its sound was gone, its flapping leaves and rattling branches far behind me, as though the greatest distance I had at my back was a matter of feet, while ahead of me I could see a barn two miles off. Then I saw her skid marks: short, and going left and downhill, into the other lane. I stood at the ditch, its weeds blowing; across it were trees and their moving shadows, like the clouds. I stepped onto its slope, and it took me sliding on my feet, then rump, to the bottom, where I sat still, my body gathered to itself, lest a part of me should touch him. But there was only tall grass, and I stood, my shoulders reaching the sides of the ditch, and I walked uphill, wishing for the flashlight in the pickup, walking slowly, and down in the ditch I could hear my feet in the grass and on the earth, and kicking cans and bottles. At the top of the hill I turned and went down, watching the ground above the ditch on my right, praying my prayer from the truck again, the first one, the one I would admit, that he was not dead, was in fact home, and began to hope again, memory telling me of lost pheasants and grouse I had shot, but they were small and the colors of their home, while a man was either there or not; and from that memory I left where I was and while walking in the ditch under the wind was in the deceit of imagination with Jennifer in the kitchen, telling her she had hit no one, or at least had not badly hurt anyone, when I realized he could be in the hospital now and I would have to think of a way to check there, something to say on the phone. I see now that, once hope returned, I should have been certain what it prepared me for: ahead of me, in high grass and the shadows of trees, I saw his shirt. Or that is all my mind would allow itself: a shirt, and I stood looking at it for the moments it took my mind to admit the arm and head and the dark length covered by pants. He lay face down, the arm I could see near his side, his head turned from me, on its cheek.

"Fella?" I said. I had meant to call, but it came out quiet and high, lost inches from my face in the wind. Then I said, 'Oh God,' and felt Him in the wind and the sky moving past the stars and moon and the field around me, but only watching me as He might have watched Cain or Job, I did not know which, and I said it again, and wanted to sink to the earth and weep till I slept there in the weeds. I climbed, scrambling up the side of the ditch, pulling at clutched grass, gained the top on hands and knees, and went to him like that, panting, moving through the grass as high and higher than my face, crawling under that sky, making sounds too, like some animal, there being no words to let him know I was here with him now. He was long; that is the word that came to me, not tall. I kneeled beside him, my hands on my legs. His right arm was by his side, his left arm straight out from the shoulder, but turned, so his palm was open to the tree above us. His left cheek was cleanshaven, his eye closed, and there was no blood. I leaned forward to look at his open mouth and saw the blood on it, going down into the grass. I straightened and looked ahead at the wind blowing past me through grass and trees to a distant light, and I stared at the light, imagining someone awake out there, wanting someone to be, a gathering of old friends, or someone alone listening to music or painting a picture, then I figured it was a night light at a farmyard whose house I couldn't see. *Going,* I thought. *Still going.* I leaned over again and looked at dripping blood.

So I had to touch his wrist, a thick one with a watch and expansion band that I pushed up his arm, thinking *he's left-handed,* my three fingers pressing his wrist, and all I felt was my tough fingertips on that smooth underside flesh and small bones, then relief, then certainty. But against my will, or only because of it, I still don't know, I touched his neck, ran my fingers down it as if petting, then pressed, and my hand sprang back as from fire. I lowered it again, held it there until it felt that faint beating that I could not believe. There was too much wind. Nothing could make a sound in it. A pulse could not be felt in it, nor could mere fingers in that wind feel the absolute silence of a dead man's artery. I was making sounds again; I grabbed his left arm and his waist, and pulled him toward me, and that side of him rose, turned, and I lowered him to his back, his face tilted up toward the tree that was groaning, the tree and I the only sounds in the wind. Turning my face from his, looking down the length of him at his sneakers, I placed my ear on his heart, and heard not that but something else, and I clamped a hand over my exposed ear, heard something liquid and alive, like when you pump a well and after a few strokes you hear air and water moving in the pipe, and I knew I must raise his legs and cover him and run to a phone, while still I listened to his chest, thinking *raise with what? cover with what?* and amid the liquid sound I heard the heart, then lost it, and pressed my ear against bone, but his chest was quiet, and I did not know when the liquid had stopped, and do not know now when I heard air, a faint rush of it, and whether under my ear or at his mouth or whether I heard it at all. I straightened and looked at the light, dim and yellow. Then I touched his throat, looking him full in the face. He was blond and young. He could have been sleeping in the shade of a tree, but for the smear of blood from his mouth to his hair, and the night sky, and the weeds blowing against his head, and the leaves shaking in the dark above us.

I stood. Then I kneeled again and prayed for his soul to join in peace and joy all the dead and living; and, doing so, confronted my first sin against him, not stopping for Father Paul, who could have given him the last rites, and immediately then my second one, or, I saw then, my first, not calling an ambulance to meet me there, and I stood and turned into the wind, slid down the ditch and crawled out of it, and went up the hill and down it, across the road to the street of houses whose people I had left behind forever, so that I moved with stealth in the shadows to my truck.

When I came around the bend near my house, I saw the kitchen light at the rear. She sat as I had left her, the ashtray filled, and I looked at the bottle, felt her eyes on me, felt what she was seeing too: the dirt from my crawling. She had not drunk much of the rye. I poured some in my glass, with the water from melted ice, and sat down and swallowed some and looked at her and swallowed some more, and said: 'He's dead.'

She rubbed her eyes with the heels of her hands, rubbed the cheeks under them, but she was dry now.

'He was probably dead when he hit the ground. I mean, that's probably what killed—'

'Where was he?'

'Across the ditch, under a tree.'

'Was he—did you see his face?'

'No, Not really. I just felt. For life, pulse. I'm going out to the car.'

'What for? Oh.'

I finished the rye, and pushed back the chair, then she was standing too.

'I'll go with you.'

'There's no need.'

'I'll go.'

I took a flashlight from a drawer and pushed open the door and held it while she went out. We turned our faces from the wind. It was like on the hill, when I was walking, and the wind closed the distance behind me: after three or four steps I felt there was no house back there. She took my hand, as I was reaching for hers. In the garage we let go, and squeezed between the pickup and her little car, to the front of it, where we had more room, and we stepped back from the grill and I shone the light on the fender, the smashed headlight turned into it, the concave chrome staring to the right, at the garage wall.

'We ought to get the bottles,' I said.

She moved between the garage and the car, on the passenger side, and had room to open the door and lift the bag. I reached out, and she gave me the bag and backed up and shut the door and came around the car. We sidled to the doorway, and she put her arm around my waist and I hugged her shoulders.

'I thought you'd call the police,' she said.

We crossed the yard, faces bowed from the wind, her hair blowing away from her neck, and in the kitchen I put the bag of bottles in the garbage basket. She was working at the table: capping the rye and putting it away, filling the ice tray, washing the glasses, emptying the ashtray, sponging the table.

'Try to sleep now,' I said.

She nodded at the sponge circling under her hand, gathering ashes. Then she dropped it in the sink and, looking me full in the face, as I had never seen her look, as perhaps she never had, being for so long a daughter on visits (or so it seemed to me and still does: that until then our eyes had never seriously met), she crossed to me from the sink and kissed my lips, then held me so tightly I lost balance, and would have stumbled forward had she not held me so hard.

I sat in the living room, the house darkened, and watched the maple and the hemlock. When I believed she was asleep I put on *La Boheme*,[2] and kept it at the same volume as the wind so it would not wake her. Then I listened to *Madame Butterfly*, and in the third act had to rise quickly to lower the sound: the wind was gone. I looked at the still maple near the window, and thought of the wind leaving farms and towns and the coast, going out over the sea to die on the waves. I smoked and gazed out the window. The sky was darker, and at daybreak the rain came. I listened to *Tosca*, and at six-fifteen went to the kitchen where Jennifer's purse lay on the table, a leather shoulder-purse crammed with the things of an adult woman, things she had begun accumulating only a few years back, and I nearly wept, thinking of what sandy foundations they were: driver's license, credit card, disposable lighter, cigarettes, checkbook, ballpoint pen, cash, cosmetics, comb, brush, Kleenex, these the rite of passage from childhood, and I took one of them—her keys—and went out, remembering a jacket and hat when the rain struck me, but I kept going to the car, and squeezed and lowered myself into it, pulled the seat belt over my shoulder and fastened it and backed out, turning in the drive, going forward into the road, toward St. John's and Father Paul.

Cars were on the road, the workers, and I did not worry about any of them noticing the fender and light. Only a horse distracted them from what they drove to. In front of St. John's is a parking lot; at its far side, past the church and at the edge of the lawn, is an old pine, taller than the steeple now. I shifted to third, left the road, and, aiming the right headlight at the tree, accelerated past the white blur of church, into the black trunk growing bigger till it was all I could see, then I rocked in that resonant thump she had heard, had felt, and when I turned off the ignition it was still in my ears, my blood, and I saw the boy flying in the wind. I lowered my forehead to the wheel. Father Paul opened the door, his face white in the rain.

'I'm all right.'

'What happened?'

'I don't know. I fainted.'

I got out and went around to the front of the car, looked at the smashed light, the crumpled and torn fender.

'Come to the house and lie down.'

'I'm all right.'

'When was your last physical?'

'I'm due for one. Let's get out of this rain.'

'You'd better lie down.'

'No. I want to receive.'

That was the time to say I want to confess, but I have not and will not. Though I could now, for Jennifer is in Florida, and weeks have passed, and perhaps now Father Paul would not feel that he must tell me to go to the police. And, for that very reason, to confess now would be unfair. It is a world of secrets, and now I have one from my best, in truth my only, friend. I have one from Jennifer too, but that is the nature of fatherhood.

Most of that day it rained, so it was only in early evening, when the sky cleared, with a setting sun, that two little boys, leaving their confinement for some play before dinner, found him. Jennifer and I got that on the local news, which we listened to every hour, meeting at the radio, standing with cigarettes, until the one at eight o'clock; when she stopped crying, we went out and walked on the wet grass, around the pasture, the last of sunlight still in the air and trees. His name was Patrick Mitchell, he was nineteen years old, was employed by CETA,[3] lived at home with his parents and brother and sister. The paper next day said he had been at a friend's house and was walking home, and I thought of that light I had seen, then knew it was not for him; he lived on one of the streets behind the club. The paper did not say then, or in the next few days, anything to make Jennifer think

he was alive while she was with me in the kitchen. Nor do I know if we—I—could have saved him.

In keeping her secret from her friends, Jennifer had to perform so often, as I did with Father Paul and at the stables, that I believe the acting, which took more of her than our daylight trail rides and our night walks in the pasture, was her healing. Her friends teased me about wrecking her car. When I carried her luggage out to the car on that last morning, we spoke only of the weather for her trip—the day was clear, with a dry cool breeze—and hugged and kissed, and I stood watching as she started the car and turned it around. But then she shifted to neutral and put on the parking brake and unclasped the belt, looking at me all the while, then she was coming to me, as she had that night in the kitchen, and I opened my ams.

I have said I talk with God in the mornings, as I start my day, and sometimes I sit with coffee, looking at the birds, and the woods. Of course He has never spoken to me, but that is not something I require. Nor does He need to. I know Him, as I know the part of myself that knows Him, that felt Him watching from the wind and the night as I knelt over the dying boy. Lately I have taken to arguing with Him, as I can't with Father Paul, who, when he hears my monthly confession, has not heard and will not hear anything of failure to do all that one can to save an anonymous life, of injustice to a family in their grief, of deepening their pain at the chance and mystery of death by giving them nothing—no one—to hate. With Father Paul I feel lonely about this, but not with God. When I received the Eucharist while Jennifer's car sat twice-damaged, so redeemed, in the rain, I felt neither loneliness nor shame, but as though He were watching me, even from my tongue, intestines, blood, as I have watched my sons at times in their young lives when I was able to judge but without anger, and so keep silent while they, in the agony of their youth, decided how they must act; or found reasons, after their actions, for what they had done. Their reasons were never as good or as bad as their actions, but they needed to find them, to believe they were living by them, instead of the awful solitude of the heart.

I do not feel the peace I once did: not with God, nor the earth, or anyone on it. I have begun to prefer this state, to remember with fondness the other one as a period of peace I neither earned nor deserved. Now in the mornings while I watch purple finches driving larger titmice from the feeder, I say to Him: I would do it again. For when she knocked on my door, then called me, she woke what had flowed dormant in my blood since her birth, so that what rose from the bed was not a stable owner or a Catholic or any other Luke Ripley I had lived with for a long time, but the father of a girl.

And He says: I am a Father too.

Yes, I say, as You are a Son Whom this morning I will receive; unless You kill me on the way to church, then I trust You will receive me. And as a Son You made Your plea.

Yes, He says, but I would not lift the cup.

True, and I don't want You to lift it from me either. And if one of my sons had come to me that night, I would have phoned the police and told them to meet us with an ambulance at the top of the hill.

Why? Do you love them less?

I tell Him no, it is not that I love them less, but that I could bear the pain of watching and knowing my sons' pain, could bear it with pride as they took the whip and nails. But You never had a daughter and, if You had, You could not have borne her passion.

So, He says, you love her more than you love Me.

I love her more than I love truth.

Then you love in weakness, He says.

As You love me, I say, and I go with an apple or carrot out to the barn. ■

Notes

[1] Vernacular term for a priest addicted to alcohol.

[2] This and the two titles just below are operas by Giacomo Puccini (1858–1924).

[3] Comprehensive Employment and Training Act— a government program to assist people into the job market.

Making Connections through Discussion and Writing

1. a. Dubus' story is told in first-person narrative voice. What is the effect of this technique?

_____

_____

_____

_____

_____

    b. What would be different about the story if it had been told by an omniscient narrator?

_____

_____

_____

_____

_____

2. Luke distinguishes between "what I call my life" and his "real life." What is the difference between these two?

_____

_____

_____

_____

_____

_____

_____

_____

3. Give an example of Luke's comments that indicate spiritual humility.

_____

_____

_____

_____

_____

4. List actions or thoughts that suggest Luke's spiritual faithfulness.

_____

_____

_____

_____

_____

_____

5. a. Why doesn't Luke call the police about the accident?

_____

_____

_____

_____

    b. Why does he consider his negligence a sin?

_____

_____

_____

_____

    c. Why doesn't he confess this sin?

_____

_____

_____

_____

6. In the last dialogue, God says Luke loves in "weakness"; Luke responds that God loves him in "weakness." What does this mean?

_____

_____

_____

_____

_____

_____

_____

Chapter 3
Perspectives on Youth and Age

In the Biblical book of Proverbs, the first seven verses begin with advice from a father to his son, promising him long life and peace if he obeys his father's words. These verses demonstrate the wisdom of an older man whose experiences provide his offspring with insight that can be obtained only through living. Maturity's perspective offers the hindsight that youth lacks, and although children often become weary of parental advice, they may find themselves giving the same advice when they become parents.

Literature, too, expresses the concerns of youth and old age. William Blake devoted two volumes of poetry, *Songs of Innocence* and *Songs of Experience,* to pondering the chasm dividing the world of the immature from the world of the mature. As Blake's titles indicate, both innocence and experience are capable of teaching us about the frailties of human existence.

The perspective of youth is forward looking—impatient with waiting, repetition, practice, and routine—ready to meet life's challenges, yet also eager to enjoy the present moment. In Hemingway's "A Clean, Well-Lighted Place," the young waiter's impatience reflects his inexperience with the loneliness and despair experienced by the old man as he remarks about him, "He's lonely. I'm not lonely. I have a wife waiting in bed for me."

This impatience is not a character flaw but rather indicative of the impetuous energy germane to the younger generation. In the poem, "Birches," Frost compares the two perspectives of youth and age, depicting a boy who is assertive, conquering the stiffness in the trees "by riding them down over and over again," and who is confident, like the young waiter in Hemingway's story. For example, he is described as learning "all there was about launching out too soon," and yet even so, he keeps his poise.

In contrast to the perspective of youth, maturity looks at the past and often interprets the present and the future in light of it. Although no one would deny its more melancholy position, maturity has much to teach us as we learn how age can soften the heart but harden one's hopes, or how it can enlarge one's vision but diminish the possibilities for realizing that vision.

Hemingway's older waiter is both compassionate and despondent, filled with empathy for the old man but in despair for his own life, while Frost's speaker has learned through life's challenges that while he can still dream of being a swinger of birches, the possibility no longer exists.

In poetry, the seasons often personify youth and age, where metaphors of spring and new growth, as in "Fern Hill," create images of childhood and all its promise. In Shakespeare's "Sonnet 73," the speaker recognizes the approaching winter of his life, yet also realizes how age has also given him an awareness of his love's lingering devotion.

In this section you will discover literature that allows you to experience the vitality of youth and the reflection and wisdom of old age.

William Shakespeare

Sonnet 73

William Shakespeare (1564–1616) was an English poet and dramatist of the Elizabethan and early Jacobean period. His early plays include *A Midsummer Night's Dream* (1594), *The Merchant of Venice* (1596), *Much Ado About Nothing* (1598-1600), and *Twelfth Night* (1599–1600). His tragedies include *Hamlet* (1600–1601), *Othello* (1604), *King Lear* (1605–1606), and *Macbeth* (1606). His sonnets are among the most quoted and loved in the English language. The following sonnet is about mature love and the losses that occur with the passing of life's seasons.

That time of year thou mayst in me behold
When yellow leaves, or none, or few, do hang
Upon those boughs which shake against the cold,
Bare ruined choirs[1] where late[2] the sweet birds sang.
In me thou seest the twilight of such day
As after sunset fadeth in the west,
Which by and by black night doth take away,
Death's second self, that seals[3] up all in rest.
In me thou seest the glowing of such fire
That[4] the ashes of his[5] youth doth lie
As the deathbed whereon it must expire,
Consumed with[6] that[7] which it was nourished by.
    This thou perceiv'st, which makes thy love more strong,
    To love that well which thou must leave[8] ere long. ∎

Notes

[1] choirs—in a traditional church, the area where the choir sits

[2] late—of late, or lately

[3] seals—closes

[4] That—as

[5] his—its

[6] with—along with or by

[7] that—may refer to the speaker or to youth and life

[8] leave—that is, lose when the speaker dies

Making Connections through Discussion and Writing

1. a. Whom is the speaker addressing in this poem?

   _____

   b. What do lines 5, 10, and 14 tell the reader about the relationship of the speaker and his beloved?

   _____
   _____
   _____
   _____

2. a. Underline three fundamental metaphors describing loss and diminishment that are developed separately in the three opening quatrains.

   b. Explain how these metaphors build to strengthen the theme in the concluding couplets.

   _____
   _____
   _____
   _____

3. a. Describe the tone of this poem.

   _____
   _____
   _____

   b. What does the poem tell us about mature love?

   _____
   _____
   _____
   _____

4. Write an emulation (in verse or prose) in which you use three metaphors to illustrate an abstraction such as friendship or alienation.

   _____
   _____
   _____
   _____
   _____
   _____
   _____
   _____

Robert Frost

Birches

Robert Frost (1874–1963) was born in San Francisco, but his mother moved to New England after the death of his father in 1885. He briefly attended Dartmouth and Harvard, then was employed as a shoemaker, schoolteacher, editor, and farmer. He moved to England and published his first book of poetry, *A Boy's Will* (1913), followed shortly by his second one, *North of Boston* (1914), which contains some of his more famous poems including "Mending Wall" and "Death of a Hired Man." Frost moved back to America in 1915, settling on a farm in New Hampshire. He then published *Mountain Interval* (1916), which contains "The Road Not Taken." He won the Pulitzer Prize for poetry in 1924, 1931, 1937, and 1943. He was one of America's best known poets and read "The Gift Outright" at John F. Kennedy's inauguration in 1960. Frost's poetry speaks of rural settings and nature by using traditional verse form, yet his poetry examines the struggles and the darkness that lurk within the souls of individuals.

Vocabulary ....

        bracken
        crazes

When I see birches bend to left and right
Across the lines of straighter darker trees,
I like to think some boy's been swinging them.
But swinging doesn't bend them down to stay
As ice-storms do. Often you must have seen them
Loaded with ice a sunny winter morning
After a rain. They click upon themselves
As the breeze rises, and turn many-colored
As the stir cracks and crazes their enamel.
Soon the sun's warmth makes them shed crystal shells
Shattering and avalanching on the snow-crust—
Such heaps of broken glass to sweep away
You'd think the inner dome of heaven had fallen.
They are dragged to the withered bracken by the load,
And they seem not to break; though once they are bowed
So low for long, they never right themselves:
You may see their trunks arching in the woods
Years afterwards, trailing their leaves on the ground
Like girls on hands and knees that throw their hair
Before them over their heads to dry in the sun.
But I was going to say when Truth broke in
With all her matter-of-fact about the ice-storm
I should prefer to have some boy bend them
As he went out and in to fetch the cows—

From *The Poetry of Robert Frost*, Henry Holt and Company, 1916.

Some boy too far from town to learn baseball,
Whose only play was what he found himself,
Summer or winter, and could play alone.
One by one he subdued his father's trees
By riding them down over and over again
Until he took the stiffness out of them,
And not one but hung limp, not one was left
For him to conquer. He learned all there was
To learn about not launching out too soon
And so not carrying the tree away
Clear to the ground. He always kept his poise
To the top branches, climbing carefully
With the same pains you use to fill a cup
Up to the brim, and even above the brim.
Then he flung outward, feet first, with a swish,
Kicking his way down through the air to the ground.
So was I once myself a swinger of birches.
And so I dream of going back to be.
It's when I'm weary of considerations,
And life is too much like a pathless wood
Where your face burns and tickles with the cobwebs
Broken across it, and one eye is weeping
From a twig's having lashed across it open.
I'd like to get away from earth awhile
And then come back to it and begin over.
May no fate willfully misunderstand me
And half grant what I wish and snatch me away
Not to return. Earth's the right place for love:
I don't know where it's likely to go better.
I'd like to go by climbing a birch tree,
And climb black branches up a snow-white trunk
Toward Heaven, till the tree could bear no more,
But dipped its top and set me down again.
That would be good both going and coming back.
One could do worse than be a swinger of birches. ■

Making Connections through Discussion and Writing

1. A literal reading tells us that birches can be bent by swinging but are more likely bent by ice-storms; however, closer reading reveals that the damage Frost is talking about may have to do with life experiences rather than merely literal ice storms.

   a. Circle the details Frost gives in the poem as he describes the effects of an ice storm.

   b. What is he suggesting about life?

   _____
   _____
   _____
   _____

2. Robert Frost frequently used images of nature in his poetry; however, these images often reflect a darker side of life. For example, the first twenty lines reveal his more melancholy use of nature.

   a. Underline the places that show nature's darkness.

   b. How does the poem make the connection between nature and a person's aging?

   _____
   _____
   _____

3. a. List images of nature that are used by the persona to compare the confidence of childhood to the more complex attitudes of adulthood.

   _____   _____
   _____   _____
   _____   _____
   _____   _____

   b. How do these images reflect two ways of knowing?

   _____
   _____
   _____
   _____

   c. Highlight places in the poem that suggest the difficult experiences of aging.

4.   a.   Why is it important that the boy have time alone, where his "only play was what he found himself"?

_____

_____

_____

_____

_____

   b.   How does climbing birches prepare him for adulthood?

_____

_____

_____

_____

5.   a.   List phrases characterizing heaven and earth.

_____   _____

_____   _____

_____   _____

_____   _____

   b.   Discuss what he means when he says, "Earth's the right place for love."

_____

_____

_____

_____

_____

_____

Dylan Thomas

Fern Hill

Dylan Thomas (1914–1953) was born in Wales and attended only grammar school for his education. He published his first collection of poetry in 1934 titled *Eighteen Poems.* Later poetic works include *The Collected Poems of Dylan Thomas* (1953) and *Under Milkwood (1955).* Thomas' *Quite Early One Morning* (1954) is composed of autobiographical sketches and essays. Because of his radio work in England and his many poetry readings throughout American universities, Thomas became a celebrated figure. Plagued by alcoholism and lung problems, Thomas died an early death. His poetry is most noted for its emotion, transcendence, vision, and imagination. William York Tindall, an expositor of Thomas' poems, notes that the main theme of "Fern Hill" is "not how it feels to be young, . . . [but] how it feels to have been young."

Now as I was young and easy under the apple boughs
About the lilting house and happy as the grass was green,
    The night above the dingle[1] starry,
      Time let me hail and climb
    Golden in the heydays of his eyes,
And honoured among wagons I was prince of the apple towns
And once below a time I lordly had the trees and leaves
      Trail with daisies and barley
    Down the rivers of the windfall light.

And as I was green and carefree, famous among the barns
About the happy yard and singing as the farm was home,
    In the sun that is young once only,
      Time let me play and be
    Golden in the mercy of his means,
And green and golden I was huntsman and herdsman, the calves
Sang to my horn, the foxes on the hills barked clear and cold,
      And the sabbath rang slowly
    In the pebbles of the holy streams.

All the sun long it was running, it was lovely, the hay
Fields high as the house, the tunes from the chimneys, it was air
    And playing, lovely and watery
      And fire green as grass.
    And nightly under the simple stars
As I rode to sleep the owls were bearing the farm away,
All the moon long I heard, blessed among stables, the nightjars[2]
    Flying with the ricks,[3] and horses
      Flashing into the dark.

And then to awake, and the farm, like a wanderer white
With the dew, come back, the cock on his shoulder: it was all
      Shining, it was Adam and maiden,
         The sky gathered again
      And the sun grew round that very day.
So it must have been after the birth of the simple light
In the first, spinning place, the spellbound horses walking warm
      Out of the whinnying green stable
        On to the fields of praise.

And honoured among foxes and pheasants by the gay house
Under the new made clouds and happy as the heart was long
      In the sun born over and over,
        I ran my heedless ways,
      My wishes raced through the house high hay
And nothing I cared, at my sky blue trades, that time allows
In all his tuneful turning so few and such morning songs
      Before the children green and golden
        Follow him out of grace.

Nothing I cared, in the lamb white days, that time would take me
Up to the swallow thronged loft by the shadow of my hand,
      In the moon that is always rising,
        Nor that riding to sleep
      I should hear him fly with the high fields
And wake to the farm forever fled from the childless land.
Oh as I was young and easy in the mercy of his means,
      Time held me green and dying
      Though I sang in my chains like the sea. ■

Notes

[1] dingle—wooded valley

[2] nightjars—night-birds

[3] ricks—haystacks

Making Connections through Discussion and Writing

1. a. Underline the occurrences of the words "golden" and green."

    b. What do you think these words symbolize?

    _____
    _____
    _____
    _____

    c. What is he emphasizing through his repetition of these words?

    _____
    _____
    _____
    _____

2. a. Thomas loves to use unusual conceits and word combination, e.g., "the lilting house" and "happy as the grass was green." Circle all of these in the poem.

    b. Explain what each means in your own words.

    _____
    _____
    _____
    _____
    _____
    _____
    _____
    _____

3. a. Time is an ever-present character in the poem. Put brackets around all references to Time.

    b. How does Time function in this poem?

    _____
    _____
    _____
    _____

    c. What might the chains signify in the last line?

    _____
    _____
    _____
    _____

4. Identifiy and discuss a major theme of the poem.

    _____
    _____
    _____
    _____

Ernest Hemingway
A Clean, Well-Lighted Place

Ernest Hemingway (1899–1961) is one of the most famous American writers of the twentieth century. His well-known fictional works include *The Sun Also Rises (1926), A Farewell to Arms (1929), For Whom the Bell Tolls (1940),* and *The Old Man and the Sea (1952).* In 1952 he was awarded the Pulitzer Prize and, in 1954, the Nobel Prize for literature. Hemingway described his unadorned writing style as a boiled-down picture of the world. Exemplifying his simple style and narrative detachment, "A clean well-lighted place" uses dialogue to suggest conflicting attitudes and strong emotion.

It was late and every one had left the café except an old man who sat in the shadow the leaves of the tree made against the electric light. In the day time the street was dusty, but at night the dew settled the dust and the old man liked to sit late because he was deaf and now at night it was quiet and he felt the difference. The two waiters inside the café knew that the old man was a little drunk, and while he was a good client they knew that if he became too drunk he would leave without paying, so they kept watch on him.

"Last week he tried to commit suicide," one waiter said.

"Why?"

"He was in despair."

"What about?"

"Nothing."

"How do you know it was nothing?"

"He has plenty of money."

They sat together at a table that was close against the wall near the door of the café and looked at the terrace where the tables were all empty except where the old man sat in the shadow of the leaves of the tree that moved slightly in the wind. A girl and a soldier went by in the street. The street light shone on the brass number on his collar. The girl wore no head covering and hurried beside him.

"The guard will pick him up," one waiter said.

"What does it matter if he gets what he's after?"

"He had better get off the street now. The guard will get him. They went by five minutes ago."

The old man sitting in the shadow rapped on his saucer with his glass. The younger waiter went over to him.

"What do you want?"

The old man looked at him. "Another brandy," he said.

"You'll be drunk," the waiter said. The old man looked at him. The waiter went away.

"He'll stay all night," he said to his colleague. "I'm sleepy now. I never get into bed before three o'clock. He should have killed himself last week."

The waiter took the brandy bottle and another saucer from the counter inside the café and marched out to the old man's table. He put down the saucer and poured the glass full of brandy.

"You should have killed yourself last week," he said to the deaf man. The old man motioned with his finger. "A little more," he said. The waiter poured on into the glass so that the brandy slopped over and ran down the stem into the top saucer of the pile. "Thank you," the old man said. The waiter took the bottle back inside the café. He sat down at the table with his colleague again.

"He's drunk now," he said.

"He's drunk every night."

"What did he want to kill himself for?"

"How should I know."

"How did he do it?"

"He hung himself with a rope."

"Who cut him down?"

"His niece."

"Why did they do it?"

"Fear for his soul."

"How much money has he got?"

"He's got plenty."

"He must be eighty years old."

"Anyway I should say he was eighty."

"I wish he would go home. I never get to bed before three o'clock. What kind of hour is that to go to bed?"

"He stays up because he likes it."

"He's lonely. I'm not lonely. I have a wife waiting in bed for me."

"He had a wife once too."

"A wife would be no good to him now."

"You can't tell. He might be better with a wife."

"His niece looks after him. You said she cut him down."

"I know."

"I wouldn't want to be that old. An old man is a nasty thing."

"Not always. This old man is clean. He drinks without spilling. Even now, drunk. Look at him."

"I don't want to look at him. I wish he would go home. He has no regard for those who must work."

The old man looked from his glass across the square, then over at the waiters.

"Another brandy," he said, pointing to his glass. The waiter who was in a hurry came over.

"Finished," he said, speaking with that omission of syntax stupid people employ when talking to drunken people or foreigners. "No more tonight. Close now."

"Another," said the old man.

"No. Finished." The waiter wiped the edge of the table with a towel and shook his head.

The old man stood up, slowly counted the saucers, took a leather coin purse from his pocket and paid for the drinks, leaving half a peseta[1] tip.

The waiter watched him go down the street, a very old man walking unsteadily but with dignity.

"Why didn't you let him stay and drink?" the unhurried waiter asked. They were putting up the shutters. "It is not half-past two."

"I want to go home to bed."

"What is an hour?"

"More to me than to him."

"An hour is the same."

"You talk like an old man yourself. He can buy a bottle and drink at home."

"It's not the same."

"No, it is not," agreed the waiter with a wife. He did not wish to be unjust. He was only in a hurry.

"And you? You have no fear of going home before your usual hour?"

"Are you trying to insult me?"

"No, hombre,[2] only to make a joke."

"No," the waiter who was in a hurry said, rising from pulling down the metal shutters. "I have confidence. I am all confidence."

"You have youth, confidence, and a job," the older waiter said. "You have everything."

"And what do you lack?"

"Everything but work."

"You have everything I have."

"No. I have never had confidence and I am not young."

"Come on. Stop talking nonsense and lock up."

"I am of those who like to stay late at the café," the older waiter said. "With all those who do not want to go to bed. With all those who need a light for the night."

"I want to go home and into bed."

"We are of two different kinds," the older waiter said. He was now dressed to go home. "It is not only a question of youth and confidence although those things are very beautiful. Each night I am reluctant to close up because there may be some one who needs the café."

"Hombre, there are bodegas[3] open all night long."

"You do not understand. This is a clean and pleasant café. It is well lighted. The light is very good and also, now, there are shadows of the leaves."

"Good night," said the younger waiter.

"Good night," the other said. Turning off the electric light he continued the conversation with himself. It is the light of course but it is necessary that the place be clean and pleasant. You do not want music. Certainly you do not want music. Nor can you stand before a bar with dignity although that is all that is provided for these hours. What did he fear? It was not fear or dread. It was a nothing that he knew too well. It was all a nothing and a man was nothing too. It was only that and light was all it needed and a certain cleanness and order. Some lived in it and never felt it but he knew it all was nada y pues[4] nada y nada y pues nada. Our nada who art in nada, nada be thy name thy kingdom nada thy will be nada in nada as it is in nada. Give us this nada our daily nada and nada us our nada as we nada our nadas and nada us not into nada but deliver us from nada; pues nada. Hail nothing full of nothing, nothing is with thee. He smiled and stood before a bar with a shining steam pressure coffee machine.

"What's yours?" asked the barman.

"Nada."

"Otro loco mas,"[5] said the barman and turned away.

"A little cup," said the waiter.

The barman poured it for him.

"The light is very bright and pleasant but the bar is unpolished," the waiter said.

The barman looked at him but did not answer. It was too late at night for conversation.

"You want another copita?"[6] the barman asked.

"No, thank you," said the waiter and went out. He disliked bars and bodegas. A clean, well-lighted café was a very different thing. Now, without thinking further, he would go home to his room. He would lie in the bed and finally, with daylight, he would go to sleep. After all, he said to himself, it is probably only insomnia. Many must have it. ∎

Notes

[1] peseta—a coin from Spain

[2] hombre—man, fellow

[3] bodega—bar or tavern (usually dark, like a wine cellar)

[4] nada y pues—nothing and then (nothing more)

[5] otro loco mas—another crazy one

[6] copita—a little cup (used for alcoholic beverages)

Making Connections through Discussion and Writing

1. The two waiters are not named, but rather, different ways of referring to them reveal their natures. (For example, one waiter is referred to as the waiter "who was in a hurry" and the other waiter is referred to as "the unhurried waiter," yet even these characteristics are not provided until much of the conversation between the waiters takes place.) Write a description of the two waiters based on their conversation.

    _____
    _____
    _____
    _____

    _____
    _____
    _____
    _____

2. The story relates the perspective of two waiters, one who is young and the other who is old.

    a. How does youth affect the younger waiter's behavior toward the old man?

    _____
    _____
    _____

    b. How does the older waiter perceive the old man?

    _____
    _____
    _____
    _____

3. In addition to using dialogue to establish character, Hemingway employs dark and light imagery in his settings to create the tone in his fiction.

    a. Contrast the light in the café to the darker bodega.

    _____
    _____
    _____

    b. How do these images intensify his theme?

    _____
    _____
    _____

4. As the old waiter walks home, his disturbing thoughts repeat a sad, but familiar litany: "Our nada who art in nada, nada be thy name. . . . Hail nothing full of nothing. . . ." What do these lines reveal about the attitude of the old waiter and Hemingway's theme?

_____

_____

_____

_____

_____

5. James Joyce said about this story, "He [Hemingway] has reduced the distance between literature and life, which is what every writer strives to do. Have you read 'A Clean, Well-Lighted Place'? . . . It is masterly. Indeed, it is one of the best stories ever written."

In a paragraph, write your own response to this story. Comment on Hemingway's technique of using dialogue as the major way of conveying the story.

_____

_____

_____

_____

_____

_____

_____

_____

_____

_____

_____

_____

_____

_____

_____

_____

Helen Norris

Mrs. Moonlight

Helen Norris (b. 1916) is an American Southern writer of short stories. She graduated from the University of Alabama with bachelors and masters degrees. She published *The Christmas Wife* in 1985, on which an HBO film starring Julie Harris and Jason Robards was based. In 1999 PBS produced another of her stories entitled "The Cracker Man." Author of two books of poetry, *Whatever is Round* (1994) and *Rain Pulse* (1997), Norris was selected as Poet Laureate of Alabama from 1999-2003. Her work is particularly noted for the characters who must reconcile the real world with the kind of world they would like to possess. This can be seen especially in the following story, "Mrs. Moonlight," which is from the short story collection *Water into Wine*, published in 1988.

During the night she would forget about the tree-house. In the morning when she heard the hammering, like a woodpecker gone just a little wild, she would go outside and look at Mr. Snider halfway up the tree and say to him, "What are you building?" And he would stop and tell her gravely, "Ma'am, I'm making you this treehouse like you ast me to do." And then she would remember. To forget and then remember made a wonderful surprise at the start of each day. Sometimes she remembered without having to be told. But whichever way it was, she was happy about the treehouse.

She didn't tell him that she planned to live in it. She knew better than that. She told him that she wanted it for her granddaughter Mitzi. He didn't guess she would live there to be out of her daughter's hair once and for all so the question of the nursing home would disappear.

Her daughter was to be away from home for two weeks; she sold cosmetics on the road. And Mrs. Gideon figured she could get the treehouse ready in that length of time and be all moved in when her daughter got back. So she asked Mr. Snider what his charge would be. He added up numbers in his little gray notebook with the stub of a pencil he kept hanging from it on a piece of string. He told her he could do it for four hundred if she wanted the best. If she wanted less than that, he could make it three fifty. "I want the best," she said.

"What about plumbing?" she inquired.

"Plumbing? Oh, ma'am, they got restrictions."

"It's all right," she said. "I can come down for that."

"You planning on being up here some yourself?"

"I might," she said. "You can't tell."

He looked at her slantwise. "I wouldn't recommend it."

"What about a stove?"

"A stove?"

"For cooking."

"That ain't exactly possible. Unless . . ." He consulted the sky, the tree, and the ground. He turned and spat with care on the far side of her. "Unless a 'lectrician could run a line up the trunk. You might could have a little hot plate, something of that nature. I said might. They got restrictions."

"That's what I'll do," she said.

"I said he might could do it, ma'am."

"It's all right either way. I can fix sandwiches. And I'm very fond of junk food."

Sometimes the way he looked at her she thought he might have guessed her plans, but she didn't care. He was being paid and that was that. She was sick to death of everybody dabbling in her business. Mattie the maid was always snooping. She had been told to do it. "Miss Fanny, you ain't et a bite a lunch." "Miss Fanny, I wouldn't walk that far if I was you." Her daughter was gone all day and Mitzi was in school till three o'clock. So Mattie trailed her. "Mattie, don't you have some cleaning you can do?"

Mrs. Gideon had a special treehouse in mind. She drew the plan for Mr. Snider on a paper napkin. "It has to look this way. I had a treehouse once and it was just like this. I want a window here, and just a little platform where I can sit and watch the moon."

He looked slantwise again. "I wouldn't recommend a person being up here after dark. A ladder ain't that safe."

"Make it safe," she said.

When the house was well along, she looked up one morning and was amazed to see that it was like the treehouse she had had when she was young. "Mr. Snider, this is wonderful! This is just the way my treehouse looked when I was young, the little porch and all."

"Ma'am, I'm building it the way you ast me to do."

"Did I?" she said in wonder. "Well, I'm glad." She had forgotten all about it.

But the treehouse of the past was very clear in her mind. It had been built when she was ten, and there the best years of her life had been spent. Sometimes she had slipped up to watch the sunrise. She had watched the moonrise too, heard the wind in the leaves and the treefrogs after rain and the chatter of the squirrels and birds going to sleep, all as if she had belonged to the world of the tree. Especially she remembered how clear her mind had been. Everything that happened seemed to fall into a crystal pool and she could look down and see it lying on the bottom whenever she chose. Not like it was today. Not like that at all.

Again she asked Mr. Snider what his charge would be. Then she wrote him out a check and pinned it to the leaf of the tree he was in. "I might forget it later on. Things slip my mind." She thought of telling him that she was seventy-eight. Or was she older than that? Or maybe she was younger. She would have to look it up, but it didn't matter.

She waited till one day when the house was almost finished. All it needed was the ladder and a second coat of fern green paint. Then she made a phone call. Just dialing made her happy.

He answered her at once, as if he had been waiting. He sounded just the same, but older of course.

"Robert, this is Fanny Gideon."

"Fanny Gideon!" he said, as if they shared something precious, which of course they did.

"I know it's a long way, but I got something to show you."

"Have you, now?"

"I know it's a long way."

"Not for me. Ten miles is not far. I got wheels." And he laughed. "That's what my grandson says."

"They let you drive?" she said. "That's wonderful, Robert. They took my wheels away."

"They wouldn't try it with me. I can outdrive 'em all."

"Can you come right away?"

"You bet I can." He sounded happy about it.

She made a little note for herself and put it on the door, just in case she forgot, which she didn't think she would. It said: "Robert is coming over to see the treehouse."

But she didn't need the note. She was waiting in the swing on the porch. And when he drove up and got out of his car, she knew again that they had made the big mistake of their lives when they hadn't gotten married when they were fifteen, hadn't run away again when they were caught and brought back, hadn't told the family just to go to hell.

She had seen him the last time, oh, she couldn't remember when. She would have to ask him. He came toward her, not as tall as then, not as steady on his feet, but just as straight. All his hair. All his teeth, as far as she could tell. A beautiful man.

She stood up to greet him. "I see you got both eyes and both hands and both feet."

He looked down at his feet and then he held up his hands. "So I have," he said, surprised. And with his hands he took hers.

"But we have to wear glasses," she said, gay and happy.

"No, we don't. But they tell us to do it, and we humor 'em."

She led him out to the treehouse. Mr. Snider was standing on his painting ladder. The ladder for the house he was going to build last. Only his paint-speckled shoes could be seen.

"What do you think?" she said.

His eyes misted over. He circled the tree. Leaves were winking in the sunlight.

"What do you think?"

"It's perfect," he said, moved. "It's just the way it was."

"I thought you would like it."

"Like it! It's the best thing been built in the last sixty years. Maybe sixty-five. How old are we, Fanny?"

"I can't remember. But I know how old we were. We were fifteen then. It was the best year of my life."

He gazed up at the treehouse, narrowing his eyes. He took off his glasses and sighted through one lens. "Mine too. The best."

"You see the little porch where we used to watch the moon?"

"I do," he said.

"You used to call me Mrs. Moonlight. You said it was because my hair was like moonlight."

"It still is," he said.

"Of course it's not. It never was . . . I wanted you to see what I was up to here."

"Why you doin' it, Fanny?"

"Well, because I have a little trouble remembering things. But I remember that, up there, things were clear as ice. I could look down on things and see the way they were. And I was closer to the sun and it warmed up my brain and made it work fine, and the moon cooled it off so it didn't overheat."

He laughed out loud. "You gonna climb up and heat up and cool off and recall things?"

She laughed along with him. "I aim to do just that."

"I might come and join you."

"Do you think your wife would mind?"

"She died," he said.

"Did I know that?" she said.

"You came to the funeral."

She was silent for a bit. "You see what I mean?" It must have been at the funeral that she had seen him last. She added, "I'm sorry . . . I'm sorry again."

He put his arm around her. "It was five years ago."

"Did you grieve a lot?"

He thought about it for a while. "She didn't like me very much."

She touched his hand lightly. "How could she not?"

Her daughter came back before the ladder was made. She stood and looked up at the treehouse in the early sun. She was smartly dressed. Her face was made up with some of the cosmetics she'd been selling on the road. A purplish shade of lipstick that was catching on. Eye shadow to match. Nail polish to match. She wore white sandals, a white pleated skirt, a silk and linen sweater in a fuchsia shade, and a little white scarf to hide the lines in her throat. She left to talk with Mattie. She came out again and lay in wait for Mr. Snider. She told him she was sorry but it had to come down. He shook his head from side to side.

"Don't worry, you'll be paid."

"I done been paid," he said. "It's a shame to knock it down. I done my best work."

"Mr. Snider. I'm surprised at you. You should have known better."

"Better 'n what?" he said, indignant. "I work for hire."

Mrs. Gideon kept to her room. Through her door she heard the murmur of Mattie telling on her. When her daughter knocked, she stiffened every muscle in her body. "Come in," she said, although she didn't want to say it. She hardly knew her daughter with the purple lipstick on and her purple lids.

"Mama, I hope you know we can't leave it there."

"Why? Why?" said Mrs. Gideon. "I had it built to live in."

"To live in!" said her daughter. "When you have a nice room in a comfortable house?" She tore off her scarf as if she couldn't breathe.

"But I get in your way. You talk of putting me somewhere." She would not say the word. "I should think you'd be happy to have me out of the house."

Her daughter dropped to Mrs. Gideon's bed and thrust her face into her purple-tipped fingers. "Mama, I want to keep you here, but you make it very hard when you do things like this. I have to work. I have to travel. I have to leave you alone. And Mattie can't keep up with you every minute of the day. How could you imagine you could live in a treehouse?"

"Well, I didn't," said Mrs. Gideon, seeing how the wind was blowing. "I thought it would be nice for Mitzi to play in."

"Mitzi is seventeen. She doesn't want a treehouse. She wants clothes and a car."

"I had a treehouse when I was fifteen, but maybe times have changed."

"It has to come down."

Mrs. Gideon was holding back the tears. "Why does it? Why does it? It looks lovely in the tree."

"Because, Mama, if I leave it you'll be climbing up some day."

"How could I when it doesn't have a ladder made?"

"You will find one somehow and you will fall and I will be to blame."

"No one would blame you if I fell."

"I would blame myself."

Mrs. Gideon thought tearfully that many of the wretched things that happen in the world grow out of people's saying that they don't want the blame for something that in the first place is totally not their business. She said with dignity, "I've never even seen what it is like inside, but if you like I'll promise you I won't go up."

"Mama, you'll forget. You always forget. You light the stove and forget. You plug in the iron and then you forget. You almost burn the house down once a week. You took the bus to town and forgot to come home."

"I didn't forget. I wasn't ready."

"Mama, you forgot. You've even forgotten now that you forgot."

"I can't win," said Mrs. Gideon. She blew her nose and looked through the window. "About the treehouse, I paid for it," she said at last, "entirely with my money. I remember that quite clearly. I wrote a check."

"Your money. Well, Mama, it's your money and it isn't. Because when you spend it up it's mine that keeps you going."

"I have enough to last me."

"Not at this rate you don't."

Afterward Mrs. Gideon lay on the bed and thought that she was tired of being treated as if she were too young to have sense and at the same time too old to have sense. She wouldn't let herself believe that they would tear the treehouse down . . .

But late in the morning she heard the sound of hammering and splintering wood. And she cried into her pillow as if her heart would break.

She would not come out for lunch, so Mattie left a tray on the floor outside her room. When her daughter had gone to work in the afternoon she ventured from the room, stepping over the tray of food, and looked out the back door. In the tree there was nothing. It was as if the treehouse had never been. It was just the way the other one had gone when she was young. Gone in an hour. Nothing left.

She turned away, tears blinding her eyes. Mattie was working in the bedroom upstairs. She passed the telephone and thought of calling Robert, for he would grieve too. But what could he do? The phone book was opened to the yellow pages, and there she saw marked the name of a nursing home, the number outlined.

She was cold all over. Her fingers were numb, but she found Robert's number. "I need you," she said.

He heard the cry in her voice. "I'm coming," he said.

When he came she was sitting in the swing on the porch. "Go look at the treehouse." She did not want to see its ruination again.

He returned in a moment. "What happened?" he asked.

"She had it torn down. That's what happened."

He saw her eyes red from weeping. After a while he said, "But we can remember it. She can't tear that down."

She swung for a little, while he stood below her in the grass. "I didn't tell you, Robert, but I was planning to live there. Be out of her way. Get all moved in by the time she got back . . . It's not crazy," she said. "I was going to have a little hot plate put in. Be out of her way . . ." The chain creaked as she swung. "But now you know what? I made the thing happen I didn't want to happen. The reason I did it was to keep it away. She called a nursing home. I saw the number by the phone. I'm so afraid, Robert. I'm so afraid."

He climbed the steps then and sat down beside her. They swung together. He held her hand.

"I'm so tired of being treated like I don't have sense enough to live here."

"I know," he said. "I get it too. But when he gets too out of line I tell my son off."

"You do? I wish I could."

"You gotta have guts, the older you get." He thought of it, swinging. "It takes more guts than it does when you're young."

"If we had got married when we tried to then . . . If we had been faster so they couldn't have caught us . . ."

He squeezed her hand.

"I don't ever think about my husband," she said. "Isn't that strange? I never think about him. It was like when he died I had got that over with. I must have been sad, though. I can't recall."

They swung in silence.

"I wish I could start my life over again. I'd fix it so I wouldn't have to be afraid."

"I'm thinking," he said. "I'm thinking now. You wanta live in a treehouse? My kid brother has a little house in the woods. You remember Alfie. It's in the next county. Trees around it. You can't hardly see it for all the trees. Nothing fancy inside. He goes there to hunt in the wintertime."

She was suddenly so happy she began to cry. "You mean we could go?"

"Why not?" he said. "I slipped around and saw where he hides the key."

Her eyes were shining as she thought of it.

"You go in and leave a note for your daughter. Say you're with me and we've gone to the woods. I'll be in the car."

"I'll do it," she said. She went inside but didn't write the note. She grabbed her purse from the dresser and a sweater from the bed and slipped out when Mattie was running water in the sink. She climbed in beside him in the Pontiac.

Down the road a ways he said, "Did you leave her the note?"

"I think I forgot it."

"You didn't forget. You just didn't want to do it. I know you, Fanny Gideon, from way, way back."

"I was afraid she'd come and get me. Are you mad with me, Robert?"

"Hell, no, I'm not mad. She deserves what she gets."

"You didn't tell your son."

"I never tell him a thing. Once you start leaving notes it's like asking permission."

She couldn't remember when she had been so happy. "This is like when we were young and ran away to get married." She was smiling at him.

He was smiling too but looking hard at the road. Drivers everywhere were getting crazier all the time. Just stay out of their way. If he lost his license now he wouldn't get it back.

"Robert," she said, "can you remember things?"

"Not as well as I did, but well enough I guess."

"Good,"she said. "You take care of the past and I'll handle the present."

"Who's in charge of the future?"

"Oh, it's in charge of itself."

It seemed to him a very funny thing for her to say. "So should we finish what we started back then and get married?" He hadn't planned to say it, but it was said and he was glad.

"What about your wife?"

He tensed to make a turn. "She died."

". . . I'm truly very sorry."

"It's all right," he said. "It's over and done. So do you want to get married?"

"I sort of like the idea of living in sin. Don't you?"

"I do," he said.

At length he put it to her gravely, "If you married me I think they'd leave us alone. We could live somewhere."

"It's too late for that."

"Too late? Like you said, the future is in charge of itself."

A shade passed over her. "I'm too late."

They left the pavement. They drove into the country and now he relaxed. Beside them were fields of greening oats crosshatched with shadows from the passing clouds. Swarms of keening birds swept out of the sky. A whirl of wind whipped out of a tunnel beneath the road. It raked the pasture grasses and combed them all backward and followed the road. The willows in the ditches bridled and dipped.

She tied her sweater loosely in a knot about her throat. "It was raining before. We were driving through rain."

"The windshield misted up. I had to go slow."

"I remember everything about that day." They passed cattle standing knee deep in a lake. "We're running from them now like we did before."

"We're not running from them. Don't think about running. Don't think about them. Think about they're young, with the memories they're proud of crammed with junk, plain junk. There's not much about them we could recommend."

"They're faster," she said. "The people who come after you are always faster. Or they wouldn't win."

He turned into the trees and shifted gears. With a howl from the engine they drove up, up on a pine-needled road. And soon, very soon he pointed to the house tucked away in trees. She exclaimed with delight. There was a series of steps they must climb to reach it. Like a ladder, she laughed. He wanted to help her, but she waved him away. "I've still got my legs." "So you have," he observed her. "You're like a mountain goat. I've gotten slower."

Inside was a small and airless room with a hearth at one end and a bed at the other. There was a smell of ash. Against one wall was a rusting stove. "I told you not fancy."

"I didn't come for fancy." It made her think of an acorn, brown and secret, the way a room should be that lives in trees. She could feel the swaying of her childhood treehouse when the wind blew at dusk and she pulled her long hair over her head to match the birds snug in their rippling feathers.

"It's got a bathroom off that door by the bed."

"And a porch," she whispered, knowing it was there on the other side of another door. She pulled it open and walked out slowly. The sun was nesting in a giant maple full of summer. The lowest branches swept the weathered boards. The massive trunk fell out of sight below. She dropped her purse and settled like a wren among the leaves.

He watched her from the doorway. Then he joined her, stepping through the branches to inspect what lay beneath. The floor of the forest dropped sharply away. The porch had the look of being blown into the hillside and the house that followed it propped on piles. Fanny's own treehouse had been better made.

He returned to her and stood among the mammoth branches, their leaf clusters hanging like fruit in the motionless air. He smiled at her but he could not speak. He had lost the power and the spell of a tree, lost how it was to feel himself all gone into the green . . . to desire it so much . . . to climb anything, to swing from anything, a rope, a vine, daring death to get it . . . a craving so strong it was strange it wasn't called immoral or illegal. But then the moralists were all grown up. He had been young and full of the craving and Fanny Gideon had given him her tree. If she hadn't had a treehouse, would they have loved?

She looked up at him with happiness. "We have always been married."

He held out his hand. She pulled it down and kissed it and kept it in hers. "Your hand is just the way I need a hand to be. Not young and not old. Take care of it," she said.

"I will," he said, moved, and knowing he would have loved her without her tree. "Are you hungry?" he asked. "There might be something in there."

She shook her head. "I'm too happy to eat. This is the happiest I've ever been. I've forgotten the rest."

Her happiness began to make him afraid. Like the tree before them, it was larger than life. There was nothing to tell him if it was real, or if she had made it to hide her fear. Her fear was real, for he felt it stir in the deep of his throat, in the palm of his hand, the way he would know whatever was wrong when she was a girl. When they climbed the ladder it was always there for the tree to know. For him to know if he knew the tree. He had learned the tree. On the calmest day he could feel it wanting to circle and toss, have some fun, give them something to think about. On a windy day he would spin with it, going green inside, getting into its marrow, feeling within it the way she was, knowing he would marry the way she was, the way he felt the way she was . . . And now he was troubled with the empty years. They turned in his bones where they must have lain but he hadn't known. What he dreaded most at this time of his life was to live through anything over again. The flight they'd begun being ended again, the door they had opened being shut once more. Life had come to seem like a series of things that repeated themselves, until one day he had closed his heart. It was better perhaps to forget . . . like Fanny. He could feel something break like a bough in the woods.

Her eyes had never left the tree. The air was stirring. A shudder swept through the leaves and into her. "How long will we be here?"

"Till we want to leave."

"Till they find us, you mean?"

He did not reply. He was aware that the tree was growing dark within. Only the tips of branches were still green-gold. Somewhere deep within it was a whir of wings. He went inside and found some coffee to brew in a pan. There were crackers in a tin, but they seemed too stale. He came out with her coffee. "It's the best we have."

She took the cup absently and drank a little. "It's very good, Robert." She laid the cup on the floor. Her voice, it seemed to him, was just as it had been. In the failing light he saw her face again young and kindling the treehouse they had never let go. Her hair was the color it had been in the moonlight . . .

He found a weathered chair that had been tipped against the wall. He drew it across the floor and sat beside her in the dusk. It was dark in the tree. They could hear the birds within settling into the night, and somewhere an owl. And a wind came from nowhere to sleep in the woods, bedding down in the leaves but restless, turning, sighing, troubled with dreams, sleepwalking in leaf mold, crouching in the chimney, falling into the ravine . . . It was turning cooler. "Where is the moon?" she asked with longing in her voice.

"It isn't time, Mrs. Moonlight. Give it time." He stroked her hair while they sat between the tree dark and the dark of their room, between two darks with an equal claim, and neither would release them into the other. But fireflies wove the darks into night . . . He took her hand and led her, it seemed to her, into the tree, but it must have been the room. For she lay on the bed and he took off her glasses and then her shoes. He covered her with a blanket that smelled of smoke.

"I want you near me," she said.

So he lay down beside her. "There isn't a light," he whispered. "Do you mind the dark?"

"Not when you are with me."

He found her hands and kissed them. They were trembling and cold. He drew the blanket closely about her throat.

She said, "I won't think about anything but now. Or remember . . . I won't remember anything but then. I fight all the time to keep from losing myself. They try to make me remember the things they want me to remember. Why do I have to remember *their* things? Never mine. My things. Go to a nursing home because I left my coat in the park? Such a fuss she made. I didn't care about the coat. I never liked it. I didn't try to remember it. I don't have room in my mind for all the things they want me to remember. I just have room for when you kissed me in the treehouse . . . and I was Mrs. Moonlight. It fills up my brain. There's no room for the rest."

"Don't think about the rest." He kissed her hair.

"I have to think of it. I have to," she said.

He could feel that she was losing all the joy of the tree, as if the wind they heard were blowing it away and blowing her with it away from him. "Don't think," he begged her.

"I have to think of it," she said. He could feel her pain. "When she tore down the treehouse it was like she tore me down. Like she tore down the things of mine I need to remember. I can't forgive her for that. And now I want to forget her . . . along with the rest. She will put me in that home so I might as well forget her . . . Help me do it," she said.

She was weeping now. "Help me forget her and just remember you."

He held her face in his hands. "I would if I could but I don't know how. I have never known how." He took his hands away. His mind was heavy with the chirring of the crickets round their bed. Birds had flown in and were muttering in the gloom above the open door. After a time he said through her weeping, as if to himself, "Whiskey is a good thing but it doesn't last. I tried it for a while when my wife stopped loving me . . . It doesn't last."

"I need something to last."

"I know," he said. "I know. But it always comes back. I closed myself up for most of my life. Till today when you called . . ."

She turned to embrace him. "You will be always in my mind. All the rest will go but you. Do you believe it?" she said.

"I believe it, Mrs. Moonlight. I truly do."

She lay quietly beside him, sleeping a little, waking to find him sleeping, then waking again to find him waking too. A full moon had risen behind the tree. The churning leaves were frothing the light that struck the bed. "I'm trying to forget her. It's hard, so hard. It's like your own children get stuck in your mind. Maybe when they're born to you they aren't all born. Maybe a part of them is left inside . . . Hold me," she said.

He folded his arms about her.

"When you hold me I can almost . . . There's so much . . . so much. She would run and always open her little hands to fall. They were full of stone bruises and splinters and cuts . . . I would look at her hands and I'd kiss them and cry . . ."

"Try to sleep," he said.

"Red flowers made her smile . . ." It was a while before she asked, "Do you think they'll come?"

"My son is smart enough to figure this out."

"But not before morning?"

He felt the brush of a moth upon his lips. "Not before then."

"So we have tonight. We mustn't fall asleep."

But they did. When he woke she was gone. He sat up in panic. His fear was so strong his heart was beating in his throat. He could not hear a sound but the wind in the tree. Suppose she had forgotten where she was and fallen down the steps or walked into the woods and fallen into the ravine . . .

He stumbled to the porch, where he found her in the moonlight among the moving leaves. He did not trust his voice to speak. He drew her up to him and held her. She was as soft as a girl. As small as she had been. As yielding as then.

"Robert?" she said. "Robert?" Her voice was breaking with bewilderment. "Why are we here?" She pulled away from his arms. "This isn't our tree-house. Who does it belong to? My daughter tore it down . . . the one I had made. Why are we here?" she said again. "Are we running away?"

"There's no reason," he said. "Come inside," he begged.

"Don't let them take us back."

"No," he whispered. "No."

She caught her breath. "I forget . . . But the old things are there." She reached a hand to the tree. "New things that happen are so hard to keep. They fall through the leaves . . . Unless they break your heart. Unless they're what she did." She turned to search his face. "How did we get here? There's a room . . . and a bed."

"Yes, inside. Come inside."

"There's one way," she said.

"Tell me," he said, hardly hearing her words. She was trembling in his arms.

"Then I have to tell you this one thing you never knew. After they brought us back, they tore down our treehouse."

"I knew that," he said. "I went to see it one night and it was gone."

"But you didn't know that after that I tried to kill myself. I was crazy with grief. I didn't want to live. I cut my wrist. I wanted that much to die. When you're fifteen you're crazy like a fox, they said. I was ashamed of it later."

After a moment she pulled back her sleeve and showed him the scar. He found it in the moonlight and kissed it slowly.

"What if they hadn't found me and made me live?"

"What are you saying?"

"I want to go back and die to the rest of my life. I want to go back and die before my daughter came."

"But you went on living."

"What if I hadn't?"

"Then what are we now tonight?" he asked in despair.

"This is another life. Don't you feel it?" she said.

"You're saying it isn't real?"

"Oh, no, it's the realest thing that's ever been."

He was stroking her hair. "Your hair is like moonlight . . . Come back to bed."

He led her inside and they lay down together, side by side, hands touching, eyes closed against the dark. "I love you, Mrs. Moonlight." He heard her breath growing faint. "Please don't die," he pled. Her hair was like smoke. He drew the smoke of their blanket to cover them both.

"No, I'm only going backward. A part of me will die." She was weeping. They wept together. He held her in his arms.

"Don't go to sleep," she said. "I need you to help me."

"I don't know how," he wept. "I don't know what you're doing."

"I'm making it that she never happened to me."

"Are you sure it's what you want?"

"Yes, I am. I'm sure. You're the only one ever that belonged in my life . . . Think about the way we were. Think about the moon."

He could hear the owl. Beyond her hair, through the door he could see how the wind was slicing the moonlight, tossing it with leaves, thrusting it deep . . . and deeper into the tree. "You never let me kiss you but once a day, even though we said that we were going to be married. You were that shy."

"I'm not now," she said. "Kiss me now."

He kissed her long and gently, like an echo of the way it used to be. And the way it used to be reechoed till at last she was hearing nothing else, not the wind in the leaves, not the owl, not her daughter's voice . . . After a time she whispered, "It all slips away unless I hold on. It's like I am singing and the words blow away."

"Marry me," he said, "and I'll remember for you." Beneath his hand her head was tracing a refusal. "Everything you need to keep I'll keep for you."

"There's just a little bit and I can keep it myself and let go the rest."

He was losing his breath in the smoke of her hair. "If you do she'll put you in the home all the sooner."

"I know it," she said. "But this way it will be like a stranger has done it. Nothing a stranger does to you can make any difference."

It was morning when they woke to a thrasher's song. Beyond the door the tree was like another country in another season. It glistened. It unfolded. Light and shadow flew about in it like restless birds.

They heard the car outside. He rose and went to the window. "Well, they're here," he said. "It's my son's gray car."

Then her daughter entered, hair disheveled, eyes wild with reproach.

"Mama, why have you done this? Why are you here?"

Fanny Gideon looked up at her serenely. "Do I know you?" she said.

The birdsong throbbed in the maple tree and circled the bed where Fanny Gideon lay with her hair on the pillow like a bridal veil. Her daughter turned upon him her shocked, accusing face. "How dare you take her?"

Long ago, when he was still a boy who swung from trees, before she was born, someone who was like her had asked him the same. It seemed to him that now he had grown into the answer. He summoned all his force to make a stand against her and against all the ones who ride you down to take you back and stash you in some corner, flush you down some snakehole, throw you away.

"Not this time," he said to her, calling up the memory of that ancient flight and capture. "This time we're married."

He saw her face give way . . . He found Fanny's glasses and put them on her.

She sat up in bed and looked past the strange woman standing beside her. The tree itself seemed to sing with the bird. She had only to rise to belong to the tree world, belong to its mystery, the mystery of greenness, her own sweet youth. She smiled at him, seeing him deep in the green, seeing him already shadowed with leaves. On this first morning of the rest of their life she remembered him. As she always would. ■

Making Connections through Discussion and Writing

1. a. Who tells the story in "Mrs. Moonlight"?
    _____

    b. How does this point of view make the story particularly effective?
    _____
    _____
    _____
    _____

2. How does the title, "Mrs. Moonlight," reveal something about the main character as a young woman and now as an older woman?
    _____
    _____
    _____
    _____

3. a. Describe the relationship between the mother and daughter.
    _____
    _____
    _____
    _____

    b. How do their different perceptions reflect their ages?
    _____
    _____
    _____
    _____

4. a. Discuss how the symbols of the moon and the treehouse relate particularly to Mrs. Moonlight.
    _____
    _____
    _____
    _____
    _____
    _____

    b. How do they provide insight into the character and theme?
    _____
    _____
    _____
    _____

c.   How does the treehouse represent both the past and the future in the story?

_____

_____

_____

_____

_____

_____

_____

_____

5.   As they discuss marrying, Mrs. Gideon tells Robert, "You take care of the past and I'll handle the present." Then she says that the future is "in charge of itself." Why is this distribution of time important to her?

_____

_____

_____

_____

6.   We do not often have descriptions of old people in love. Describe the relationship between Mrs. Gideon and Robert and the quality of understanding that exists between them.

_____

_____

_____

_____

7.   a.   What happens at the conclusion of the story?

_____

_____

_____

_____

b.   Do you think Mrs. Moonlight has dementia, or does she selectively forget?

_____

_____

_____

c.   What kind of resolution does Norris provide for the reader?

_____

_____

_____

_____

Chapter 4

Perspectives on the Self and the Other

S cripture tells us that to gain life, we must lose our lives, and even though this directive seems paradoxical, experience and maturity validate its truthfulness. We often find that giving ourselves to others brings
far greater rewards than holding ourselves back, even though this giving may involve great personal risk. In
his best-selling book *The Road Less Traveled*, Scott Peck claims that the courage to love involves the two-fold
principle of both extending ourselves through unbiased acceptance and expending ourselves through self-
sacrificing actions; thus, through these behaviors, we become more truly ourselves.

Identifying the human progression leading from self-centeredness to an authentic awareness of another,
Richard E. Palmer, in his book *Hermeneutics* cites the ideas of the contemporary German philosopher Hans-
Georg Gadamer (found in *Wahrheit und Methode*) describing three normative positions of interpersonal relationships. Palmer describes Gadamer's first position, "thou as object," as one in which the "other person is
seen as something specific within one's field of experience, most often something which can serve as a means
of achieving one's goals." We recognize this kind of perspective, the "thou as object," in the story "A Very
Old Man with Enormous Wings" in which the townspeople treat the winged stranger as a carnival act or an
antiquated angel who can help them achieve selfish ends. They are incapable of seeing him beyond their own
needs or even extending hospitality to someone so unfamiliar to their own experiences.

The second position involving the forming of interpersonal relationships attempts to understand the
"thou" by seeing him or her from the perspective of one's own reflection and so thereby objectifying the person and destroying any real possibility of understanding another person. This perspective can be understood
more fully by examining the behavior of the two characters in "A Horse and Two Goats," in which both Muni
and the American are unable to understand each other, so they rely on their own assumptions about the other
that virtually tell them nothing and get them nowhere. Although this particular story has humorous consequences, Gadamer recognizes more insidious possibilities with this second position that sees one merely as
a projection of oneself, and where, as Palmer states, "in claiming to recognize the other in all his condi-
tionedness, in claiming to be objective, the knower is really claiming to be master."

In the third kind of "I-Thou" relationship, meaning is not projected from the "I" but occurs from an
authentic openness to the "thou." As Palmer says, "It is the kind of openness that wills to hear rather than to
master, is willing to be modified by the other." In other words, an authentic awareness of the other removes
all expectation from the other, even what is perceived as the highest and best, allowing the other to exist as
an entity apart from oneself, not as a projection, but as an authentic and separate being. In the story "Mrs.
Moonlight" the main character perceives that she is being treated inauthentically by her daughter. The
daughter tends to see her mother in the "thou as object" type of perspective; however, Robert validates her
as a person, a "thou," even when she continually forgets something she had just said.

Similarly, in "Sonny's Blues" we become aware of the progression of the narrator's acceptance of his
brother's way of being, not as one who interprets this way of being from his own objectifications, but as one
who is finally able to remove all of his own expectations from Sonny and see him as the "other," an authentic and separate being. In this story, the narrator extends himself into Sonny's world and discovers through
Sonny's music a reality he had not imagined before.

Clearly, "Sonny's Blues" and "Mrs. Moonlight" demonstrate how extending oneself through unbiased
acceptance characterizes authentic love, just as "A Worn Path" demonstrates how expending oneself through

self-sacrificing actions can help complete the courageous act of loving. Through Phoenix's persistence, the reader becomes aware of the "habit of love" that pervades her being, even though she forgets the objective of her task. Welty describes old Phoenix's journey as "an errand of love carried out," one in which she is so habitually moving in the direction of self-sacrifice that she needs no external incentive to keep her going.

As you begin reading the works contained in "Perspectives on the Self and the Other," you may be challenged to be more open to the voice of the other, the stranger, the alien. You may find your horizons broadened as you learn the customs and values of those whom you may never get a chance to know personally, but yet are responsible for understanding and reverencing as fellow humans, willing to love, to expend and extend your very self in a life of sacrificial giving.

Eudora Welty

A Worn Path

Eudora Welty (1909-2001) was born in Jackson, Mississippi, graduated from the University of Wisconsin, and extended her studies at Columbia University in New York City. Other than those few years away, she spent her entire life in Jackson living in her family home. Her Southern heritage is reflected through her settings and her characters' reactions to their environment. She has written novels, such as *The Robber Bridegroom* (1942), *Losing Battles* (1970), and *The Optimist's Daughter* (1972), which won the Pulitzer Prize; memoirs, such as *One Writer's Beginnings* (1984); nonfiction, such as *The Eye of the Story* (1977); and short stories such as "Livvie," and "A Worn Path," the latter of which appears here.

Vocabulary . . . .

cur	pullets
furrow	ravine
lolling	rouse
lye	

It was December—a bright frozen day in the early morning. Far out in the country there was an old Negro woman with her head tied in a red rag, coming along a path through the pinewoods. Her name was Phoenix Jackson.[1] She was very old and small and she walked slowly in the dark pine shadows, moving a little from side to side in her steps, with the balanced heaviness and lightness of a pendulum in a grandfather clock. She carried a thin, small cane made from an umbrella, and with this she kept tapping the frozen earth in front of her. This made a grave and persistent noise in the still air, that seemed meditative like the chirping of a solitary little bird.

She wore a dark striped dress reaching down to her shoe tops, and an equally long apron of bleached sugar sacks, with a full pocket: all neat and tidy, but every time she took a step she might have fallen over her shoelaces, which dragged from her unlaced shoes. She looked straight ahead. Her eyes were blue with age. Her skin had a pattern all its own of numberless branching wrinkles and as though a whole little tree stood in the middle of her forehead, but a golden color ran underneath, and the two knobs of her cheeks were illuminated by a yellow burning under the dark. Under the red rag her hair came down on her neck in the frailest of ringlets, still black, and with an odor like copper.

Now and then there was a quivering in the thicket. Old Phoenix said, "Out of my way, all you foxes, owls, beetles, jack rabbits, coons and wild animals! . . . Keep out from under these feet, little bob-whites. . . . Keep the big wild hogs out of my path. Don't let none of those come running my direction. I got a long way." Under her small black-freckled hand her cane, limber as a buggy whip, would switch at the brush as if to rouse up any hiding things.

On she went. The woods were deep and still. The sun made the pine needles almost too bright to look at, up where the wind rocked. The cones dropped as light as feathers. Down in the hollow was the mourning dove—it was not too late for him.

The path ran up a hill. "Seem like there is chains about my feet, time I get this far," she said, in the voice of argument old people keep to use with themselves. "Something always take a hold of me on this hill—pleads I should stay."

After she got to the top she turned and gave a full, severe look behind her where she had come. "Up through pines," she said at length. "Now down through oaks."

Her eyes opened their widest, and she started down gently. But before she got to the bottom of the hill a bush caught her dress.

Her fingers were busy and intent, but her skirts were full and long, so that before she could pull them free in one place they were caught in another. It was not possible to allow the dress to tear. "I in the thorny bush," she said. "Thorns, you do your appointed work. Never want to let folks pass, no sir. Old eyes thought you was a pretty little *green* bush."

Finally, trembling all over, she stood free, and after a moment dared to stoop for her cane.

"Sun so high!" she cried, leaning back and looking, while the thick tears went over her eyes. "The time getting all gone here."

At the foot of this hill was a place where a log was laid across the creek.

"Now comes the trial," said Phoenix.

Putting her right foot out, she mounted the log and shut her eyes. Lifting her skirt, leveling her cane fiercely before her, like a festival figure in some parade, she began to march across. Then she opened her eyes and she was safe on the other side.

"I wasn't as old as I thought," she said.

But she sat down to rest. She spread her skirts on the bank around her and folded her hands over her knees. Up above her was a tree in a pearly cloud of mistletoe. She did not dare to close her eyes, and when a little boy brought her a plate with a slice of marble-cake on it she spoke to him. "That would be acceptable," she said. But when she went to take it there was just her own hand in the air.

So she left that tree, and had to go through a barbed-wire fence. There she had to creep and crawl, spreading her knees and stretching her fingers like a baby trying to climb the steps. But she talked loudly to herself: she could not let her dress be torn now, so late in the day, and she could not pay for having her arm or leg sawed off if she got caught fast where she was.

At last she was safe through the fence and risen up out in the clearing. Big dead trees, like black men with one arm, were standing in the purple stalks of the withered cotton field. There sat a buzzard.

"Who you watching?"

In the furrow she made her way along.

"Glad this is not the season for bulls," she said, looking sideways, "and the good Lord made his snakes to curl up and sleep in the winter. A pleasure I don't see no two-headed snake coming around that tree, where it come once. It took a while to get by him, back in the summer."

She passed through the old cotton and went into a field of dead corn. It whispered and shook and was taller than her head. "Through the maze now," she said, for there was no path.

Then there was something tall, black, and skinny there, moving before her.

At first she took it for a man. It could have been a man dancing in the field. But she stood still and listened, and it did not make a sound. It was as silent as a ghost.

"Ghost," she said sharply, "who be you the ghost of? For I have heard of nary death close by."

But there was no answer—only the ragged dancing in the wind.

She shut her eyes, reached out her hand, and touched a sleeve. She found a coat and inside that an emptiness, cold as ice.

"You scarecrow," she said. Her face lighted. "I ought to be shut up for good," she said with laughter. "My senses is gone. I too old. I the oldest people I ever know. Dance, old scarecrow," she said, "while I dancing with you."

She kicked her foot over the furrow, and with mouth drawn down, shook her head once or twice in a little strutting way. Some husks blew down and whirled in steamers about her skirts.

Then she went on, parting her way from side to side with the cane, through the whispering field. At last she came to the end, to a wagon track where the silver grass blew between the red ruts. The quail were walking around like pullets, seeming all dainty and unseen.

"Walk pretty," she said. "This is the easy place. This the easy going."

She followed the track, swaying through the quiet bare fields, through the little strings of trees silver in their dead leaves, past cabins silver from weather, with the doors and windows boarded shut, all like old women under a spell sitting there. "I walking in their sleep," she said, nodding her head vigorously.

In a ravine she went where a spring was silently flowing through a hollow log. Old Phoenix bent and drank. "Sweet-gum makes the water sweet," she said, and drank more. "Nobody know who made this well, for it was here when I was born."

The track crossed a swampy part where the moss hung as white as lace from every limb. "Sleep on, alligators, and blow your bubbles." Then the track went into the road.

Deep, deep the road went down between the high green-colored banks. Overhead the live-oaks met, and it was as dark as a cave.

A black dog with a lolling tongue came up out of the weeds by the ditch. She was meditating, and not ready, and when he came at her she only hit him a little with her cane. Over she went in the ditch, like a little puff of milkweed.

Down there, her sense drifted away. A dream visited her, and she reached her hand up, but nothing reached down and gave her a pull. So she lay there and presently went to talking. "Old woman," she said to herself, "that black dog come up out of the weeds to stall you off, and now, there he sitting on his fine tail smiling at you."

A white man finally came along and found her—a hunter, a young man, with his dog on a chain.

"Well, Granny!" he laughed. "What are you doing there?"

"Lying on my back like a June-bug waiting to be turned over, mister," she said, reaching up her hand.

He lifted her up, gave her a swing in the air, and set her down. "Anything broken, Granny?"

"No sir, them old dead weeds is springy enough," said Phoenix, when she had got her breath. "I thank you for your trouble."

"Where do you live, Granny?" he asked, while the two dogs were growling at each other.

"Away back yonder, sir, behind the ridge. You can't even see it from here."

"On your way home?"

"No sir, I going to town."

"Why, that's too far! That's as far as I walk when I come out myself, and I get something for my trouble." He patted the stuffed bag he carried, and there hung down a little closed claw. It was one of the bob-whites, with its beak hooked bitterly to show it was dead. "Now you go on home, Granny!"

"I bound to go to town, mister," said Phoenix. "The time come around."

He gave another laugh, filling the whole landscape. "I know you old colored people! Wouldn't miss going to town to see Santa Claus!"

But something held old Phoenix very still. The deep lines in her face went into a fierce and different radiation. Without warning, she had seen with her own eyes a flashing nickel fall out of the man's pocket onto the ground.

"How old are you, Granny?" he was saying.

"There is no telling, mister," she said, "no telling."

Then she gave a little cry and clapped her hands and said, "Git on away from here, dog! Look! Look at that dog!" She laughed as if in admiration. "He ain't scared of nobody. He a big black dog." She whispered, "Sic him!"

"Watch me get rid of that cur," said the man. "Sic him, Pete! Sic him!"

Phoenix heard the dogs fighting, and heard the man running and throwing sticks. She even heard a gunshot. But she was slowly bending forward by that time, further and further forward, the lids stretched down over her eyes, as if she were doing this in her sleep. Her chin was lowered almost to her knees. The yellow palm of her hand came out from the fold of her apron. Her fingers slid down and along the ground under the piece of money with the grace and care they would have in lifting an egg from under a setting hen. Then she slowly straightened up, she stood erect, and the nickel was in her apron pocket. A bird flew by. Her lips moved. "God watching me the whole time. I come to stealing."

The man came back, and his own dog panted about them. "Well, I scared him off that time," he said, and then he laughed and lifted his gun and pointed it at Phoenix.

She stood straight and faced him.

"Doesn't the gun scare you?" he said, still pointing it.

"No, sir. I seen plenty go off closer by, in my day, and for less than what I done," she said, holding utterly still.

He smiled, and shouldered the gun. "Well, Granny," he said, "you must be a hundred years old, and scared of nothing. I'd give you a dime if I had any money with me. But you take my advice and stay home, and nothing will happen to you."

"I bound to go on my way, mister," said Phoenix. She inclined her head in the red rag. Then they went in different directions, but she could hear the gun shooting again and again over the hill.

She walked on. The shadows hung from the oak trees to the road like curtains. Then she smelled wood-smoke, and smelled the river, and she saw a steeple and the cabins on their steep steps. Dozens of little black children whirled around her. There ahead was Natchez[2] shining. Bells were ringing. She walked on.

In the paved city it was Christmas time. There were red and green electric lights strung and criss-crossed everywhere, and all turned on in the daytime. Old Phoenix would have been lost if she had not distrusted her eyesight and depended on her feet to know where to take her.

She paused quietly on the sidewalk where people were passing by. A lady came along in the crowd, carrying an armful of red-, green-, and silver-wrapped presents; she gave off perfume like the red roses in hot summer, and Phoenix stopped her.

"Please, missy, will you lace up my shoe?" She held up her foot.

"What do you want, Grandma?"

"See my shoe," said Phoenix. "Do all right for out in the country, but wouldn't look right to go in a big building."

"Stand still then, Grandma," said the lady. She put her packages down on the sidewalk beside her and laced and tied both shoes tightly.

"Can't lace 'em with a cane," said Phoenix. "Thank you, missy. I doesn't mind asking a nice lady to tie up my shoe, when I gets out on the street."

Moving slowly and from side to side, she went into the big building, and into a tower of steps, where she walked up and around and around until her feet knew to stop.

She entered a door, and there she saw nailed up on the wall the document that had been stamped with the gold seal and framed in the gold frame, which matched the dream that was hung up in her head.

"Here I be," she said. There was a fixed and ceremonial stiffness over her body.

"A charity case, I suppose," said an attendant who sat at the desk before her.

But Phoenix only looked above her head. There was sweat on her face, the wrinkles in her skin shone like a bright net.

"Speak up, Grandma," the woman said. "What's your name? We must have your history, you know. Have you been here before? What seems to be the trouble with you?"

Old Phoenix only gave a twitch to her face as if a fly were bothering her.

"Are you deaf?" cried the attendant.

But then the nurse came in.

"Oh, that's just old Aunt Phoenix," she said. "She doesn't come for herself—she has a little grandson. She makes these trips just as regular as clockwork. She lives away back off the Old Natchez Trace."[3] She bent down. "Well, Aunt Phoenix, why don't you just take a seat? We won't keep you standing after your long trip." She pointed.

The old woman sat down, bolt upright in the chair.

"Now, how is the boy?" asked the nurse.

Old Phoenix did not speak.

"I said, how is the boy?"

But Phoenix only waited and stared straight ahead, her face very solemn and withdrawn into rigidity.

"Is his throat any better?" asked the nurse. "Aunt Phoenix, don't you hear me? Is your grandson's throat any better since the last time you came for the medicine?"

With her hands on her knees, the old woman waited, silent, erect, and motionless, just as if she were in armor.

"You mustn't take up our time this way, Aunt Phoenix," the nurse said. "Tell us quickly about your grandson, and get it over. He isn't dead, is he?"

At last there came a flicker and then a flame of comprehension across her face, and she spoke.

"My grandson. It was my memory had left me. There I sat and forgot why I made my long trip."

"Forgot?" the nurse frowned. "After you came so far?"

Then Phoenix was like an old woman begging a dignified forgiveness for waking up frightened in the night. "I never did go to school, I was too old at the Surrender,"[4] she said in a soft voice. "I'm an old woman without an education. It was my memory fail me. My little grandson, he is just the same, and I forgot it in the coming."

"Throat never heals, does it?" said the nurse, speaking in a loud, sure voice to old Phoenix. By now she had a card with something written on it, a little list. "Yes. Swallowed lye. When was it?— January—two, three years ago—"

Phoenix spoke unasked now. "No missy, he not dead, he just the same. Every little while his throat begin to close up again, and he not able to swallow. He not get his breath. He not able to help himself. So the time come around, and I go on another trip for the soothing medicine."

"All right. The doctor said as long as you came to get it, you could have it," said the nurse. "But it's an obstinate case."

"My little grandson, he sit up there in the house all wrapped up, waiting by himself," Phoenix went on. "We is the only two left in the world. He suffer and it don't seem to put him back at all. He got a sweet look. He going to last. He wear a little patch quilt and peep out holding his mouth open like a little bird. I remembers so plain now. I not going to forget him again, no, the whole enduring time. I could tell him from all the others in creation."

"All right." The nurse was trying to hush her now. She brought her a bottle of medicine. "Charity," she said, making a check mark in a book.

Old Phoenix held the bottle close to her eyes, and then carefully put it into her pocket.

"I thank you," she said.

"It's Christmas time, Grandma," said the attendant. "Could I give you a few pennies out of my purse?"

"Five pennies is a nickel," said Phoenix stiffly.

"Here's a nickel," said the attendant.

Phoenix rose carefully and held out her hand. She received the nickel and then fished the other nickel out of her pocket and laid it beside the new one. She stared at her palm closely, with her head on one side.

Then she gave a tap with her cane on the floor.

"This is what come to me to do," she said, "I going to the store and buy my child a little windmill they sells, made out of paper. He going to find it hard to believe there such a thing in the world. I'll march myself back where he waiting, holding it straight up in this hand."

She lifted her free hand, gave a little nod, turned around, and walked out of the doctor's office. Then her slow step began on the stairs, going down. ■

Notes

[1] Phoenix—the mythical bird that rose out of flames

[2] Natchez—a city in Mississippi

[3] Old Natchez Trace—an old Indian trail, later a commercial and military route from Natchez, Mississippi, to Nashville, Tennessee. Many settlers moving into the South took this route.

[4] the Surrender—the surrender at the end of the Civil War

Making Connections through Discussion and Writing

1. Most of the story is a narration of Phoenix's journey. List the various obstacles she faces, and describe how she deals with each one.

_____   _____
_____   _____
_____   _____
_____   _____
_____   _____
_____   _____
_____   _____
_____   _____

2. Throughout the story Phoenix carries on conversations with herself, with the wildlife in the woods, the bushes and trees, the scarecrow, and the Lord. What do these conversations reveal about her character?

_____
_____
_____
_____
_____

3. When Phoenix encounters the hunter who surprises her by pointing a gun at her and then asking her if the gun scares her, she replies, "No sir. I seen plenty go off closer by, in my day, and for less than what I done."

   a. What had she done?

   _____
   _____
   _____
   _____

   b. What does this action reveal about Phoenix and the hunter?

   _____
   _____
   _____
   _____

4. a. What attitudes do the various characters reveal by their actions and words to Phoenix?

   _____
   _____
   _____

   b. How do these attitudes reveal the social milieu of the story?

   _____
   _____
   _____
   _____

5. Regarding this story, Welty says, "A worn path is not its circumstances but its subject: the deep-grained habit of love." She also says, "The path is the thing that matters." Explain what these quotations mean in terms of the title and Phoenix, the main character.

_____

_____

_____

_____

_____

_____

_____

6. a. Underline images that become symbols in the text.

   b. What are their possible meanings?

   _____

   _____

   _____

   _____

   _____

   _____

   _____

James Baldwin

Sonny's Blues

James Baldwin (1924–1987) was born in New York City and grew up in poverty in Harlem, the son of a revivalist preacher. At the age of 14 he pastored the Fireside Pentecostal Church. He moved to Paris when he was twenty-four and there wrote *Go Tell It on the Mountain* (1953), a novel depicting the religious awakening of a fourteen-year-old black youth, based closely on his own earlier experiences. His other novels, which focus on black men in a racist white society, include *Another Country* (1962), *If Beale Street Could Talk* (1974), and *Harlem Quartet* (1987). He was very active in the Civil Rights Movement in the 1960s, supporting it through essays included in *The Fire Next Time* (1963). His style and subject matter in the story presented here reflect his Christian heritage and his growing up in America.

Vocabulary . . . .

chasm	insular
corroborated	parody
evocations	quicksilver
furlough	sardonic
indigo	

I read about it in the paper, in the subway, on my way to work. I read it, and I couldn't believe it, and I read it again. Then perhaps I just stared at it, at the newsprint spelling out his name, spelling out the story. I stared at it in the swinging lights of the subway car, and in the faces and bodies of the people, and in my own face, trapped in the darkness which roared outside.

It was not to be believed and I kept telling myself that, as I walked from the subway station to the high school. And at the same time I couldn't doubt it. I was scared, scared for Sonny. He became real to me again. A great block of ice got settled in my belly and kept melting there slowly all day long, while I taught my classes algebra. It was a special kind of ice. It kept melting, sending trickles of ice water all up and down my veins, but it never got less. Sometimes it hardened and seemed to expand until I felt my guts were going to come spilling out or that I was going to choke or scream. This would always be at a moment when I was remembering some specific thing Sonny had once said or done.

When he was about as old as the boys in my classes his face had been bright and open, there was a lot of copper in it; and he'd had wonderfully direct brown eyes, and great gentleness and privacy. I wondered what he looked like now. He had been picked up, the evening before, in a raid on an apartment downtown, for peddling and using heroin.

I couldn't believe it: but what I mean by that is that I couldn't find any room for it anywhere inside me. I had kept it outside me for a long time. I hadn't wanted to know. I had had suspicions, but I didn't name them, I kept putting them away. I told myself that Sonny was wild, but he wasn't crazy. And he'd always been a good boy, he hadn't ever turned hard or evil or disrespectful, the way kids can, so quick, so quick, especially in Harlem. I didn't want to believe that I'd ever see my brother going down, coming to nothing, all that light in his face gone out, in the condition I'd already seen so many others. Yet it had happened and here I was, talking about algebra to a lot of boys who might, every one of them for all I knew, be popping off needles every time they went to the head.[1] Maybe it did more for them than algebra could.

I was sure that the first time Sonny had ever had horse,[2] he couldn't have been much older than these boys were now. These boys, now, were living as we'd been living then, they were growing up with a rush and their heads bumped abruptly against the low ceiling of their actual possibilities. They were filled with rage. All they really knew were two darknesses, the darkness of their lives, which was now closing in on them, and the darkness of the movies, which had blinded them to that other darkness, and in which they now, vindictively, dreamed, at once more together than they were at any other time, and more alone.

When the last bell rang, the last class ended, I let out my breath. It seemed I'd been holding it for all that time. My clothes were wet—I may have looked as though I'd been sitting in a steam bath, all dressed up, all afternoon. I sat alone in the classroom a long time. I listened to the boys outside, downstairs, shouting and cursing and laughing. Their laughter struck me for perhaps the first time. It was not the joyous laughter which—God knows why—one associates with children. It was mocking and insular, its intent was to denigrate. It was disenchanted, and in this, also, lay the authority of their curses. Perhaps I was listening to them because I was thinking about my brother and in them I heard my brother. And myself.

One boy was whistling a tune, at once very complicated and very simple, it seemed to be pouring out of him as though he were a bird, and it sounded very cool and moving through all that harsh, bright air, only just holding its own through all those other sounds.

I stood up and walked over to the window and looked down into the courtyard. It was the beginning of the spring and the sap was rising in the boys. A teacher passed through them every now and again, quickly, as though he or she couldn't wait to get out of that courtyard, to get those boys out of their sight and off their minds. I started collecting my stuff. I thought I'd better get home and talk to Isabel.

The courtyard was almost deserted by the time I got downstairs. I saw this boy standing in the shadow of a doorway, looking just like Sonny. I almost called his name. Then I saw that it wasn't Sonny, but somebody we used to know, a boy from around our block. He'd been Sonny's friend. He'd never been mine, having been too young for me, and, anyway, I'd never liked him. And now, even though he was a grown-up man, he still hung around that block, still spent hours on the street corners, was always high and raggy. I used to run into him from time to time and he'd often work around to asking me for a quarter or fifty cents. He always had some real good excuse, too, and I always gave it to him, I don't know why.

But now, abruptly, I hated him. I couldn't stand the way he looked at me, partly like a dog, partly like a cunning child. I wanted to ask him what the hell he was doing in the school courtyard.

He sort of shuffled over to me, and he said, "I see you got the papers. So you already know about it."

"You mean about Sonny? Yes, I already know about it. How come they didn't get you?"

He grinned. It made him repulsive and it also brought to mind what he'd looked like as a kid. "I wasn't there. I stay away from them people."

"Good for you." I offered him a cigarette and I watched him through the smoke. "You come all the way down here just to tell me about Sonny?"

"That's right." He was sort of shaking his head and his eyes looked strange, as though they were about to cross. The bright sun deadened his damp dark brown skin and it made his eyes look yellow and showed up the dirt in his kinked hair. He smelled funky.[3] I moved a little away from him and I said, "Well, thanks. But I already know about it and I got to get home."

"I'll walk you a little ways," he said. We started walking. There were a couple of kids still loitering in the courtyard and one of them said goodnight to me and looked strangely at the boy beside me.

"What're you going to do?" he asked me. "I mean, about Sonny?"

"Look. I haven't seen Sonny for over a year, I'm not sure I'm going to do anything. Anyway, what the hell *can* I do?"

"That's right," he said quickly, "ain't nothing you can do. Can't much help old Sonny no more, I guess."

It was what I was thinking and so it seemed to me he had no right to say it.

"I'm surprised at Sonny, though," he went on—he had a funny way of talking, he looked straight ahead as though he were talking to himself— "I thought Sonny was a smart boy, I thought he was too smart to get hung."

"I guess he thought so too," I said sharply, "and that's how he got hung. And how about you? You're pretty goddamn smart, I bet."

Then he looked directly at me, just for a minute. "I ain't smart," he said. "If I was smart, I'd have reached for a pistol a long time ago."

"Look. Don't tell *me* your sad story, if it was up to me, I'd give you one." Then I felt guilty—guilty, probably, for never having supposed that the poor bastard *had* a story of his own, much less a sad one, and I asked, quickly, "What's going to happen to him now?"

He didn't answer this. He was off by himself some place.

"Funny thing," he said, and from his tone we might have been discussing the quickest way to get to Brooklyn, "when I saw the papers this morning, the first thing I asked myself was if I had anything to do with it. I felt sort of responsible."

I began to listen more carefully. The subway station was on the corner, just before us, and I stopped. He stopped, too. We were in front of a bar and he ducked slightly, peering in, but whoever he was looking for didn't seem to be there. The juke box was blasting away with something black and bouncy and I half watched the barmaid as she danced her way from the juke box to her place behind the bar. And I watched her face as she laughingly responded to something someone said to her, still keeping time to the music. When she smiled one saw the little girl, one sensed the doomed, still-struggling woman beneath the battered face of the semi-whore.

"I never *give* Sonny nothing," the boy said finally, "but a long time ago I come to school high and Sonny asked me how it felt." He paused, I couldn't bear to watch him, I watched the barmaid, and I listened to the music which seemed to be causing the pavement to shake. "I told him it felt great." The music stopped, the barmaid paused and watched the juke box until the music began again. "It did."

All this was carrying me some place I didn't want to go. I certainly didn't want to know how it felt. It filled everything, the people, the houses, the music, the dark, quicksilver barmaid, with menace; and this menace was their reality.

"What's going to happen to him now?" I asked again.

"They'll send him away some place and they'll try to cure him." He shook his head. "Maybe he'll even think he's kicked the habit. Then they'll let him loose"—he gestured, throwing his cigarette into the gutter. "That's *all*."

"What do you mean, that's *all*?"

But I knew what he meant.

"I *mean*, that's *all*." He turned his head and looked at me, pulling down the corners of his mouth. "Don't you know what I mean?" he asked, softly.

"How the hell *would* I know what you mean?" I almost whispered it, I don't know why.

"That's right," he said to the air, "how would *he* know what I mean?" He turned toward me again, patient and calm, and yet I somehow felt him shaking, shaking as though he were going to fall apart. I felt that ice in my guts again, the dread I'd felt all afternoon; and again I watched the barmaid, moving about the bar, washing glasses, and singing. "Listen. They'll let him out and then it'll just start all over again. That's what I mean."

"You mean—they'll let him out. And then he'll just start working his way back in again. You mean he'll never kick the habit. Is that what you mean?"

"That's right," he said, cheerfully. "*You* see what I mean."

"Tell me," I said at last, "why does he want to die? He must want to die, he's killing himself, why does he want to die?"

He looked at me in surprise. He licked his lips. "He don't want to die. He wants to live. Don't nobody want to die, ever."

Then I wanted to ask him—too many things. He could not have answered, or if he had, I could not have borne the answers. I started walking. "Well, I guess it's none of my business."

"It's going to be rough on old Sonny," he said. We reached the subway station. "This is your station?" he asked. I nodded. I took one step down. "Damn!" he said, suddenly. I looked up at him. He grinned again. "Damn it if I didn't leave all my money home. You ain't got a dollar on you, have you? Just for a couple of days, is all."

All at once something inside gave and threatened to come pouring out of me. I didn't hate him any more. I felt that in another moment I'd start crying like a child.

"Sure," I said. "Don't sweat." I looked in my wallet and didn't have a dollar, I only had a five. "Here," I said. "That hold you?"

He didn't look at it—he didn't want to look at it. A terrible, closed look came over his face, as though he were keeping the number on the bill a secret from him and me. "Thanks," he said, and now he was dying to see me go. "Don't worry about Sonny. Maybe I'll write him or something."

"Sure," I said. "You do that. So long."

"Be seeing you," he said. I went on down the steps.

And I didn't write Sonny or send him anything for a long time. When I finally did, it was just after my little girl died, he wrote me back a letter which made me feel like a bastard.

Here's what he said:

Dear brother,

You don't know how much I needed to hear from you. I wanted to write you many a time but I dug how much I must have hurt you and so I didn't write. But now I feel like a man who's been trying to climb up out of some deep, real deep and funky hole and just saw the sun up there, outside. I got to get outside.

I can't tell you much about how I got here. I mean I don't know how to tell you. I guess I was afraid of something or I was trying to escape from something and you know I have never been very strong in the head (smile). I'm glad Mama and Daddy are dead and can't see what's happened to their son and I swear if I'd known what I was doing I would never have hurt you so, you and a lot of other fine people who were nice to me and who believed in me.

I don't want you to think it had anything to do with me being a musician. It's more than that. Or maybe less than that. I can't get anything straight in my head down here and I try not to think about what's going to happen to me when I get outside again. Sometime I think I'm going to flip and *never* get outside and sometime I think I'll come straight back. I tell you one thing, though, I'd rather blow my brains out than go through this again. But that's what they all say, so they tell me. If I tell you when I'm coming to New York and if you could meet me, I sure would appreciate it. Give my love to Isabel and the kids and I was sure sorry to hear about little Gracie. I wish I could be like Mama and say the Lord's will be done, but I don't know it seems to me that trouble is the one thing that never does get stopped and I don't know what good it does to blame it on the Lord. But maybe it does some good if you believe it.

Your brother,
Sonny

Then I kept in constant touch with him and I sent him whatever I could and I went to meet him when he came back to New York. When I saw him many things I thought I had forgotten came flooding back to me. This was because I had begun, finally, to wonder about Sonny, about the life that Sonny lived inside. This life, whatever it was, had made him older and thinner and it had deepened the distant stillness in which he had always moved. He looked very unlike my baby brother. Yet, when he smiled, when we shook hands, the baby brother I'd never known looked out from the depths of his private life, like an animal waiting to be coaxed into the light.

"How you been keeping?" he asked me.

"All right. And you?"

"Just fine." He was smiling all over his face. "It's good to see you again."

"It's good to see you."

The seven years' difference in our ages lay between us like a chasm: I wondered if these years would ever operate between us as a bridge. I was remembering, and it made it hard to catch my breath, that I had been there when he was born; and I had heard the first words he had ever spoken. When he started to walk, he walked from our mother straight to me. I caught him just before he fell when he took the first steps he ever took in this world.

"How's Isabel?"

"Just fine. She's dying to see you."

"And the boys?"

"They're fine, too. They're anxious to see their uncle."

"Oh, come on. You know they don't remember me."

"Are you kidding? Of course they remember you."

He grinned again. We got into a taxi. We had a lot to say to each other, far too much to know how to begin.

As the taxi began to move, I asked, "You still want to go to India?"

He laughed. "You still remember that. Hell, no. This place is Indian enough for me."

"It used to belong to them," I said. And he laughed again. "They damn sure knew what they were doing when they got rid of it."

Years ago, when he was around fourteen, he'd been all hipped on the idea of going to India. He read books about people sitting on rocks, naked, in all kinds of weather, but mostly bad, naturally, and walking barefoot through hot coals and arriving at wisdom. I used to say that it sounded to me as though they were getting away from wisdom as fast as they could. I think he sort of looked down on me for that.

Do you mind," he asked, "if we have the driver drive alongside the park? On the west side—I haven't seen the city in so long."

"Of course not," I said. I was afraid that I might sound as though I were humoring him, but I hoped he wouldn't take it that way.

So we drove along, between the green of the park and the stony, lifeless elegance of hotels and apartment buildings, toward the vivid, killing streets of our childhood. These streets hadn't changed, though housing projects jutted up out of them now like rocks in the middle of a boiling sea. Most of the houses in which we had grown up had vanished, as had the stores from which we had stolen, the basements in which we had first tried sex, the rooftops from which we had hurled tin cans and bricks. But houses exactly like the houses of our past yet dominated the landscape, boys exactly like the boys we once had been found themselves smothering in these houses, came down into the streets for light and air and found themselves encircled by disaster. Some escaped the trap, most didn't. Those who got out always left something of themselves behind, as some animals amputate a leg and leave it in the trap. It might be said, perhaps, that I had escaped, after all, I was a school teacher; or that Sonny had, he hadn't lived in Harlem for years. Yet, as the cab moved uptown through streets which seemed, with a rush, to darken with dark people, and as I covertly studied Sonny's face, it came to me that what we both were seeking through our separate cab windows was that part of ourselves which had been left behind. It's always at the hour of trouble and confrontation that the missing member aches.

We hit 110th Street and started rolling up Lenox Avenue. And I'd known this avenue all my life, but it seemed to me again, as it had seemed on the day I'd first heard about Sonny's trouble, filled with a hidden menace which was its very breath of life.

"We almost there," said Sonny.

"Almost." We were both too nervous to say anything more.

We live in a housing project. It hasn't been up long. A few days after it was up it seemed uninhabitably new, now, of course, it's already run-down. It looks like a parody of the good, clean, faceless life—God knows the people who live in it do their best to make it a parody. The beat-looking grass lying around isn't enough to make their lives green, the hedges will never hold out the streets, and they know it. The big windows fool no one, they aren't big enough to make space out of no space. They don't bother with the windows, they watch the TV screen instead. The playground is most popular with the children who don't play at jacks, or skip rope, or roller skate, or swing, and they can be found in it after dark. We moved in partly because it's not too far from where I teach, and partly for the kids; but it's really just like the houses in which Sonny and I grew up. The same things happen, they'll have the same things to remember. The moment Sonny and I started into the house I had the feeling that I was simply bringing him back into the danger he had almost died trying to escape.

Sonny has never been talkative. So I don't know why I was sure he'd be dying to talk to me when supper was over the first night. Everything went fine, the oldest boy remembered him, and the youngest boy liked him, and Sonny had remembered to bring something for each of them; and Isabel, who is really much nicer than I am, more open and giving, had gone to a lot of trouble about dinner and was genuinely glad to see him. And she's always been able to tease Sonny in a way that I haven't. It was nice to see her face so vivid again and to hear her laugh and watch her make Sonny laugh. She wasn't, or, anyway, she didn't seem to be, at all uneasy or embarrassed. She chatted as though there were no subject which had to be avoided and she got Sonny past his first, faint stiffness. And thank God she was there, for I was filled with that icy dread again. Everything I did seemed awkward to me, and everything I said sounded freighted with hidden meaning. I was trying to remember everything I'd heard about dope addiction and I couldn't help watching Sonny for signs. I wasn't doing it out of malice. I was trying to find out something about my brother. I was dying to hear him tell me he was safe.

"Safe!" my father grunted, whenever Mama suggested trying to move to a neighborhood which might be safer for children. "Safe, hell! Ain't no place safe for kids, nor nobody."

He always went on like this, but he wasn't, ever, really as bad as he sounded, not even on weekends, when he got drunk. As a matter of fact, he was always on the lookout for "something a little better," but he died before he found it. He died suddenly, during a drunken weekend in the middle of the war, when Sonny was fifteen. He and Sonny hadn't ever got on too well. And this was partly because Sonny was the apple of his father's eye. It was because he loved Sonny so much and was frightened for him, that he was always fighting with him. It doesn't do any good to fight with Sonny. Sonny just moves back, inside himself, where he can't be reached. But the principal reason that they never hit it off is that they were so much alike. Daddy was big and rough and loud-talking, just the opposite of Sonny, but they both had—that same privacy.

Mama tried to tell me something about this, just after Daddy died. I was home on leave from the army.

This was the last time I ever saw my mother alive. Just the same, this picture gets all mixed up in my mind with pictures I had of her when she was younger. The way I always see her is the way she used to be on a Sunday afternoon, say, when the old folks were talking after the big Sunday dinner. I always see her wearing pale blue. She'd be sitting on the sofa. And my father would be sitting in the easy chair, not far from her. And the living room would be full of church folks and relatives. There they sit, in chairs all around the living room, and the night is creeping up outside, but nobody knows it yet. You can see the darkness growing against the window panes and you hear the street noises every now and again, or maybe the jangling beat of a tambourine from one of the churches close by, but it's real quiet in the room. For a moment nobody's talking, but every face looks darkening, like the sky outside. And my mother rocks a little from the waist, and my father's eyes are closed. Everyone is looking at something a child can't see. For a minute they've forgotten the children. Maybe a kid is lying on the rug, half asleep. Maybe somebody's got a kid in his lap and is absent-mindedly stroking the kid's head. Maybe there's a kid, quiet and big-eyed, curled up in a big chair in the corner. The silence, the darkness coming, and the darkness in the faces frighten the child obscurely. He hopes that the hand which strokes his forehead will never stop—will never die. He hopes that there will never come a time when the old folks won't be sitting around the living room, talking about where they've come from, and what they've seen, and what's happened to them and their kinfolk.

But something deep and watchful in the child knows that this is bound to end, is already ending. In a moment someone will get up and turn on the light. Then the old folks will remember the children and they won't talk any more that day. And when light fills the room, the child is filled with darkness. He knows that every time this happens he's moved just a little closer to that darkness outside. The darkness outside is what the old folks have been talking about. It's what they've come from. It's what they endure. The child knows that they won't talk any more because if he knows too much about what's happened to *them*, he'll know too much too soon, about what's going to happen to *him*.

The last time I talked to my mother, I remember I was restless. I wanted to get out and see Isabel. We weren't married then and we had a lot to straighten out between us.

There Mama sat, in black, by the window. She was humming an old church song, *Lord, you brought me from a long ways off.* Sonny was out somewhere. Mama kept watching the streets.

"I don't know," she said, "if I'll ever see you again, after you go off from here. But I hope you'll remember the things I tried to teach you."

"Don't talk like that," I said, and smiled. "You'll be here a long time yet."

She smiled, too, but she said nothing. She was quiet for a long time. And I said, "Mama, don't you worry about nothing. I'll be writing all the time, and you be getting the checks. . . ."

"I want to talk to you about your brother," she said, suddenly. "If anything happens to me he ain't going to have nobody to look out for him."

"Mama," I said, "ain't nothing going to happen to you *or* Sonny. Sonny's all right. He's a good boy and he's got good sense."

"It ain't a question of his being a good boy," Mama said, "nor of his having good sense. It ain't only the bad ones, nor yet the dumb ones that gets sucked under." She stopped, looking at me. "Your Daddy once had a brother," she said, and she smiled in a way that made me feel she was in pain. "You didn't never know that, did you?"

"No," I said, "I never knew that," and I watched her face.

"Oh, yes," she said, "your Daddy had a brother." She looked out of the window again. "I know you never saw your Daddy cry. But *I* did—many a time, through all these years.

I asked her, "What happened to his brother? How come nobody's ever talked about him?"

This was the first time I ever saw my mother look old.

"His brother got killed," she said, "when he was just a little younger than you are now. I knew him. He was a fine boy. He was maybe a little full of the devil, but he didn't mean nobody no harm."

Then she stopped and the room was silent, exactly as it had sometimes been on those Sunday afternoons. Mama kept looking out into the streets.

"He used to have a job in the mill," she said, "and, like all young folks, he just liked to perform on Saturday nights. Saturday nights, him and your father would drift around to different place, go to dances and things like that, or just sit around with people they knew, and your father's brother would sing, he had a fine voice, and play along with himself on his guitar. Well, this particular Saturday night, him and your father was coming home from some place, and they were both a little drunk and there was a moon that night, it was bright like day. Your father's brother was feeling kind of good, and he was whistling to himself, and he had his guitar slung over his shoulder. They was coming down a hill and beneath them was a road that turned off from the highway. Well, your father's brother, being always kind of frisky, decided to run down this hill, and he did, with that guitar banging and clanging behind him, and he ran across the road, and he was making water behind a tree. And your father was sort of amused at him and he was still coming down the hill, kind of slow. Then he heard a car motor and that same minute his brother stepped from behind the tree, into the road, in the moonlight. And he started to cross the road. And your father started to run down the hill, he says he don't know why. This car was full of white men. They was all drunk, and when they seen your father's brother they let out a great whoop and holler and they aimed the car straight at him. They was having fun, they just wanted to scare him, the way they do sometimes, you know. But they was drunk. And I guess the boy, being drunk, too, and scared, kind of lost his head. By the time he jumped it was too late. Your father says he heard his brother scream when the car rolled over him, and he heard the wood of that guitar when it give, and he heard them strings go flying, and he heard them white men shouting, and the car kept on a-going and it ain't stopped till this day. And, time your father got down the hill, his brother weren't nothing but blood and pulp."

Tears were gleaming on my mother's face. There wasn't anything I could say.

"He never mentioned it," she said, "because I never let him mention it before you children. Your Daddy was like a crazy man that night and for many a night thereafter. He says he never in his life seen anything as dark as that road after the lights of that car had gone away. Weren't no thing, weren't nobody on that road, just your Daddy and his brother and that busted guitar. Oh, yes. Your Daddy never did really get right again. Till the day he died he weren't sure but that every white man he saw was the man that killed his brother."

She stopped and took out her handkerchief and dried her eyes and looked at me.

"I ain't telling you all this," she said, "to make you scared or bitter or to make you hate nobody. I'm telling you this because you got a brother. And the world ain't changed."

I guess I didn't want to believe this. I guess she saw this in my face. She turned away from me, toward the window again, searching those streets.

"But I praise my Redeemer," she said at last, "that He called your Daddy home before me. I ain't saying it to throw no flowers at myself, but, I declare, it keeps me from feeling too cast down to know I helped your father get safely through this world. Your father always acted like he was the roughest, strongest man on earth. And everybody took him to be like that. But if he hadn't had *me* there—to see his tears!"

She was crying again. Still, I couldn't move. I said, "Lord, Lord, Mama, I didn't know it was like that."

"Oh, honey," she said, "there's a lot that you don't know. But you are going to find out." She stood up from the window and came over to me. "You got to hold on to your brother," she said, "and don't let him fall, no matter what it looks like is happening to him and no matter how evil you gets with him. You going to be evil with him many a time. But don't you forget what I told you, you hear?"

"I won't forget," I said. "Don't you worry, I won't forget. I won't let nothing happen to Sonny."

My mother smiled as though she were amused at something she saw in my face. Then, "You may not be able to stop nothing from happening. But you got to let him know you's *there*."

———————

Two days later I was married, and then I was gone. And I had a lot of things on my mind and I pretty well forgot my promise to Mama until I got shipped home on a special furlough for her funeral.

And, after the funeral, with just Sonny and me alone in the empty kitchen, I tried to find out something about him.

"What do you want to do?" I asked him.

"I'm going to be a musician," he said.

For he had graduated, in the time I had been away, from dancing to the juke box to finding out who was playing what, and what they were doing with it, and he had bought himself a set of drums.

"You mean, you want to be a drummer?" I somehow had the feeling that being a drummer might be all right for other people but not for my brother Sonny.

"I don't think," he said, looking at me very gravely, "that I'll ever be a good drummer. But I think I can play a piano."

I frowned. I'd never played the role of the older brother quite so seriously before, had scarcely ever, in fact, *asked* Sonny a damn thing. I sensed myself in the presence of something I didn't really know how to handle, didn't understand. So I made my frown a little deeper as I asked: "What kind of musician do you want to be?"

He grinned. "How many kinds do you think there are?"

"Be *serious*," I said.

He laughed, throwing his head back, and then looked at me. "I *am* serious."

"Well, then, for Christ's sake, stop kidding around and answer a serious question. I mean, do you want to be a concert pianist, you want to play classical music and all that, or—or what?" Long before I finished he was laughing again. "For Christ's *sake*, Sonny!"

He sobered, but with difficulty. "I'm sorry. But you sound so—*scared*!" and he was off again.

"Well, you may think it's funny now, baby, but it's not going to be so funny when you have to make your living at it, let me tell you *that*." I was furious because I knew he was laughing at me and I didn't know why.

"No," he said, very sober now, and afraid, perhaps, that he'd hurt me, "I don't want to be a classical pianist. That isn't what interests me. I mean"—he paused, looking hard at me, as though his eyes would help me to understand, and then gestured helplessly, as though perhaps his hand would help—"I mean, I'll have a lot of studying to do, and I'll have to study *everything*, but, I mean, I want to play *with*—jazz musicians." He stopped. "I want to play jazz," he said.

Well, the word had never before sounded as heavy, as real, as it sounded that afternoon in Sonny's mouth. I just looked at him and I was probably frowning a real frown by this time. I simply couldn't see why on earth he'd want to spend his time hanging around nightclubs, clowning around on bandstands, while people pushed each other around a dance floor. It seemed—beneath him, somehow. I had never thought about it before, had never been forced to, but I suppose I had always put jazz musicians in a class with what Daddy called "good-time people."

"Are you *serious*?"

"Hell, *yes*, I'm serious."

He looked more helpless than ever, and annoyed, and deeply hurt.

I suggested, helpfully: "You mean—like Louis Armstrong?"[4]

His face closed as though I'd struck him. "No. I'm not talking about none of that old-time, down home crap."

"Well, look, Sonny, I'm sorry, don't get mad. I just don't altogether get it, that's all. Name somebody—you know, a jazz musician you admire."

"Bird."

"Who?"

"Bird! Charlie Parker![5] Don't they teach you nothing in the goddamn army?"

I lit a cigarette. I was surprised and then a little amused to discover that I was trembling. "I've been out of touch," I said. "You'll have to be patient with me. Now. Who's this Parker character?"

"He's just one of the greatest jazz musicians alive," said Sonny, sullenly, his hands in his pockets, his back to me. "Maybe *the* greatest," he added, bitterly, "that's probably why *you* never heard of him."

"All right," I said, "I'm ignorant. I'm sorry. I'll go out and buy all the cat's records right away, all right?"

"It don't," said Sonny, with dignity, "make any difference to me. I don't care what you listen to. Don't do me no favors."

I was beginning to realize that I'd never seen him so upset before. With another part of my mind I was thinking that this would probably turn out to be one of those things kids go through and that I shouldn't make it seem important by pushing it too hard. Still, I didn't think it would do any harm to ask: "Doesn't all this take a lot of time? Can you make a living at it?"

He turned back to me and half leaned, half sat, on the kitchen table. "Everything takes time," he said, "and—well, yes, sure, I can make a living at it. But what I don't seem to be able to make you understand is that it's the only thing I want to do."

"Well, Sonny," I said, gently, "you know people can't always do exactly what they *want* to do—"

"*No*, I don't know that," said Sonny, surprising me. "I think people *ought* to do what they want to do, what else are they alive for?"

"You getting to be a big boy," I said desperately, "it's time you started thinking about your future."

"I'm thinking about my future," said Sonny, grimly. "I think about it all the time."

I gave up. I decided, if he didn't change his mind, that we could always talk about it later. "In the meantime," I said, "you got to finish school." We had already decided that he'd have to move in with Isabel and her folks. I knew this wasn't the ideal arrangement because Isabel's folks are inclined to be dicty and they hadn't especially wanted Isabel to marry me. But I didn't know what else to do. "And we have to get you fixed up at Isabel's."

There was a long silence. He moved from the kitchen table to the window. "That's a terrible idea. You know it yourself."

"Do you have a *better* idea?"

He just walked up and down the kitchen for a minute. He was as tall as I was. He had started to shave. I suddenly had the feeling that I didn't know him at all.

He stopped at the kitchen table and picked up my cigarettes. Looking at me with a kind of mocking, amused defiance, he put one between his lips. "You mind?"

"You smoking already?"

He lit the cigarette and nodded, watching me through the smoke. "I just wanted to see if I'd have the courage to smoke in front of you." He grinned and blew a great cloud of smoke to the ceiling. "It was easy." He looked at my face. "Come on, now, I bet you was smoking at my age, tell the truth."

I didn't say anything but the truth was on my face, and he laughed. But now there was something very strained in his laugh. "Sure. And I bet that ain't all you was doing."

He was frightening me a little. "Cut the crap," I said. "We already decided that you was going to go and live at Isabel's. Now, what's got into you all of a sudden?"

"*You* decided it," he pointed out. "*I* didn't decide nothing." He stopped in front of me, leaning against the stove, arms loosely folded. "Look, brother. I don't want to stay in Harlem no more, I really don't." He was very earnest. He looked at me, then over toward the kitchen window. There was something in his eyes I'd never seen before, some thoughtfulness, some worry all his own. He rubbed the muscle of one arm. "It's time I was getting out of here."

"Where do you want to *go*, Sonny?"

"I want to join the army. Or the navy, I don't care. If I say I'm old enough, they'll believe me."

Then I got mad. It was because I was so scared. "You must be crazy. You . . . fool, what the hell do you want to go and join the *army* for?"

"I just told you. To get out of Harlem."

"Sonny, you haven't even finished *school*. And if you really want to be a musician, how do you expect to study if you're in the *army*?"

He looked at me, trapped, and in anguish. "There's ways. I might be able to work out some kind of deal. Anyway, I'll have the G.I. Bill[6] when I come out."

"*If* you come out." We stared at each other. "Sonny, please. Be reasonable. I know the setup is far from perfect. But we got to do the best we can."

"I ain't learning nothing in school," he said. "Even when I go." He turned away from me and opened the window and threw his cigarette out into the narrow alley. I watched his back. "At least, I ain't learning nothing you'd want me to learn." He slammed the window so hard I thought the glass would fly out, and turned back to me, "And I'm sick of the stink of these garbage cans!"

"Sonny," I said, "I know how you feel. But if you don't finish school now, you're going to be sorry later that you didn't." I grabbed him by the shoulders. "And you only got another year. It ain't so bad. And I'll come back and I swear I'll help you do *whatever* you want to do. Just try to put up with it till I come back. Will you please do that? For me?"

He didn't answer and he wouldn't look at me.

"Sonny. You hear me?"

He pulled away. "I hear you. But you never hear anything *I* say."

I didn't know what to say to that. He looked out of the window and then back at me. "OK," he said, and sighed. "I'll try."

Then I said, trying to cheer him up a little, "They got a piano at Isabel's. You can practice on it."

And as a matter of fact, it did cheer him up for a minute. "That's right," he said to himself. "I forgot that." His face relaxed a little. But the worry, the thoughtfulness, played on it still, the way shadows play on a face which is staring into the fire.

But I thought I'd never hear the end of that piano. At first, Isabel would write me, saying how nice it was that Sonny was so serious about his music and how, as soon as he came in from school, or wherever he had been when he was supposed to be at school, he went straight to that piano and stayed there until suppertime. And, after supper, he went back to that piano and stayed there until everybody went to bed. He was at the piano all day Saturday and all day Sunday. Then he bought a record player and started playing records. He'd play one record over and over again, all day long sometimes, and he'd improvise along with it on the piano. Or he'd play one section of the record, one chord, one change, one progression, then he'd do it on the piano. Then back to the record. Then back to the piano.

Well, I really don't know how they stood it. Isabel finally confessed that it wasn't like living with a person at all, it was like living with sound. And the sound didn't make any sense to her, didn't make any sense to any of them—naturally. They began, in a way, to be afflicted by this presence that was living in their home. It was as though Sonny were some sort of god, or monster. He moved in an atmosphere which wasn't like theirs at all. They fed him and he ate, he washed himself, he walked in and out of their door; he certainly wasn't nasty or unpleasant or rude, Sonny isn't any of those things;

but it was as though he were all wrapped up in some cloud, some fire, some vision all his own; and there wasn't any way to reach him.

At the same time, he wasn't really a man yet, he was still a child, and they had to watch out for him in all kinds of ways. They certainly couldn't throw him out. Neither did they dare to make a great scene about that piano because even they dimly sensed, as I sensed, from so many thousands of miles away, that Sonny was at that piano playing for his life.

But he hadn't been going to school. One day a letter came from the school board and Isabel's mother got it—there had, apparently, been other letters but Sonny had torn them up. This day, when Sonny came in, Isabel's mother showed him the letter and asked where he'd been spending his time. And she finally got it out of him that he'd been down in Greenwich Village,[7] with musicians and other characters, in a white girl's apartment. And this scared her and she started to scream at him and what came up, once she began—though she denies it to this day—was what sacrifices they were making to give Sonny a decent home and how little he appreciated it.

Sonny didn't play the piano that day. By evening, Isabel's mother had calmed down but then there was the old man to deal with, and Isabel herself. Isabel says she did her best to be calm but she broke down and started crying. She says she just watched Sonny's face. She could tell, by watching him, what was happening with him. And what was happening was that they penetrated his cloud, they had reached him. Even if their fingers had been a thousand times more gentle than human fingers ever are, he could hardly help feeling that they had stripped him naked and were spitting on that nakedness. For he also had to see that his presence, that music, which was life or death to him, had been torture for them and that they had endured it, not at all for his sake, but only for mine. And Sonny couldn't take that. He can take it a little better today than he could then but he's still not very good at it and, frankly, I don't know anybody who is.

The silence of the next few days must have been louder than the sound of all the music ever played since time began. One morning, before she went to work, Isabel was in his room for something and she suddenly realized that all of his records were gone. And she knew for certain that he was gone. And he was. He went as far as the navy would carry him. He finally sent me a postcard from some place in Greece and that was the first I knew that Sonny was still alive. I didn't see him

any more until we were both back in New York and the war had long been over.

He was a man by then, of course, but I wasn't willing to see it. He came by the house from time to time, but we fought almost every time we met. I didn't like the way he carried himself, loose and dreamlike all the time, and I didn't like his friends, and his music seemed to be merely an excuse for the life he led. It sounded just that weird and disordered.

Then we had a fight, a pretty awful fight, and I didn't see him for months. By and by I looked him up, where he was living, in a furnished room in the Village, and I tried to make it up. But there were lots of other people in the room and Sonny just lay on his bed, and he wouldn't come downstairs with me, and he treated these other people as though they were his family and I weren't. So I got mad and then he got mad, and then I told him that he might just as well be dead as live the way he was living. Then he stood up and he told me not to worry about him any more in life, that he *was* dead as far as I was concerned. Then he pushed me to the door and the other people looked on as though nothing were happening, and he slammed the door behind me. I stood in the hallway, staring at the door. I heard somebody laugh in the room and then the tears came to my eyes. I started down the steps, whistling to keep from crying, I kept whistling to myself, *You going to need me, baby, one of these cold, rainy days.*

I read about Sonny's trouble in the spring. Little Grace died in the fall. She was a beautiful little girl. But she only lived a little over two years. She died of polio and she suffered. She had a slight fever for a couple of days, but it didn't seem like anything and we just kept her in bed. And we would certainly have called the doctor, but the fever dropped, she seemed to be all right. So we thought it had just been a cold. Then, one day, she was up, playing, Isabel was in the kitchen fixing lunch for the two boys when they'd come in from school, and she heard Grace fall down in the living room. When you have a lot of children you don't always start running when one of them falls, unless they start screaming or something. And, this time, Gracie was quiet. Yet, Isabel says that when she heard that *thump* and then that silence, something happened in her to make her afraid. And she ran to the living room and there was little Grace on the floor, all twisted up, and the reason she hadn't screamed was that she couldn't get her breath. And when she did scream, it was the worst sound, Isabel says, that she'd ever heard in all her life, and she still hears it sometimes in her dreams. Isabel will sometimes wake me up with a low, moaning, strangled sound and I have to be quick to awaken her and hold her to me and where Isabel is weeping against me seems a mortal wound.

I think I may have written Sonny the very day that little Grace was buried. I was sitting in the living room in the dark, by myself, and I suddenly thought of Sonny. My trouble made his real.

One Saturday afternoon, when Sonny had been living with us, or anyway, been in our house, for nearly two weeks, I found myself wandering aimlessly about the living room, drinking from a can of beer, and trying to work up courage to search Sonny's room. He was out, he was usually out whenever I was home, and Isabel had taken the children to see their grandparents. Suddenly I was standing still in front of the living room window, watching Seventh Avenue. The idea of searching Sonny's room made me still. I scarcely dared to admit to myself what I'd be searching for. I didn't know what I'd do if I found it. Or if I didn't.

On the sidewalk across from me, near the entrance to a barbecue joint, some people were holding an old-fashioned revival meeting. The barbecue cook, wearing a dirty white apron, his conked[8] hair reddish and metallic in the pale sun, and a cigarette between his lips, stood in the doorway, watching them. Kids and older people paused in their errands and stood there, along with some older men and a couple of very tough-looking women who watched everything that happened on the avenue, as though they owned it, or were maybe owned by it. Well, they were watching this, too. The revival was being carried on by three sisters in black, and a brother. All they had were their voices and their Bibles and tambourine. The brother was testifying and while he testified two of the sisters stood together, seeming to say, amen, and the third sister walked around with the tambourine outstretched and a couple of people dropped coins into it. Then the brother's testimony ended and the sister who had been taking up the collection dumped the coins into her palm and transferred them to the pocket of her long robe. Then she raised both hands, striking the tambourine against the air, and then against one hand, and she started to sing. And the two other sisters and the brother joined in.

It was strange, suddenly, to watch, though I had been seeing these meetings all my life. So, of course, had everybody else down there. Yet, they paused and watched and listened and I stood still at the window. *"'Tis the old ship of Zion,"* they sang, and the sister with the tambourine kept a steady,

jangling beat, *"it has rescued many a thousand!"* Not a soul under the sound of their voices was hearing this song for the first time, not one of them had been rescued. Nor had they seen much in the way of rescue work being done around them. Neither did they especially believe in the holiness of the three sisters and the brother, they knew too much about them, knew where they lived, and how. The woman with the tambourine, whose voice dominated the air, whose face was bright with joy, was divided by very little from the woman who stood watching her, a cigarette between her heavy, chapped lips, her hair a cuckoo's nest, her face scarred and swollen from many beatings, and her black eyes glittering like coal. Perhaps they both knew this, which was why, when, as rarely, they addressed each other, they addressed each other as Sister. As the singing filled the air the watching, listening faces underwent a change, the eyes focusing on something within; the music seemed to soothe a poison out of them; and time seemed, nearly, to fall away from the sullen, belligerent, battered faces, as though they were fleeing back to their first condition, while dreaming of their last. The barbecue cook half shook his head and smiled, and dropped his cigarette and disappeared into his joint. A man fumbled in his pockets for change and stood holding it in his hand impatiently, as though he had just remembered a pressing appointment further up the avenue. He looked furious. Then I saw Sonny, standing on the edge of the crowd. He was carrying a wide, flat notebook with a green cover, and it made him look, from where I was standing, almost like a schoolboy. The coppery sun brought out the copper in his skin, he was very faintly smiling, standing very still. Then the singing stopped, the tambourine turned into a collection plate again. The furious man dropped in his coins and vanished, so did a couple of the women, and Sonny dropped some change in the plate, looking directly at the woman with a little smile. He started across the avenue, toward the house. He has a slow, loping walk, something like the way Harlem hipsters[9] walk, only he's imposed on this his own half-beat. I had never really noticed it before.

I stayed at the window, both relieved and apprehensive. As Sonny disappeared from my sight, they began singing again. And they were still singing when his key turned in the lock.

"Hey," he said.

"Hey, yourself. You want some beer?"

"No. Well, maybe." But he came up to the window and stood beside me, looking out. "What a warm voice," he said.

They were singing *If I could only hear my mother pray again!*

"Yes," I said, "and she can sure beat that tambourine."

"But what a terrible song," he said, and laughed. He dropped his notebook on the sofa and disappeared into the kitchen. "Where's Isabel and the kids?"

"I think they went to see their grandparents. You hungry?"

"No." He came back into the living room with his can of beer. "You want to come some place with me tonight?"

I sensed, I don't know how, that I couldn't possibly say no. "Sure. Where?"

He sat down on the sofa and picked up his notebook and started leafing through it. "I'm going to sit in with some fellows in a joint in the Village."

"You mean, you're going to play, tonight?"

"That's right." He took a swallow of his beer and moved back to the window. He gave me a sidelong look. "If you can stand it."

"I'll try," I said.

He smiled to himself and we both watched as the meeting across the way broke up. The three sisters and the brother, heads bowed, were singing *God be with you till we meet again*. The faces around them were very quiet. Then the song ended. The small crowd dispersed. We watched the three women and the lone man walk slowly up the avenue.

"When she was singing before," said Sonny, abruptly, "her voice reminded me for a minute of what heroin feels like sometimes—when it's in your veins. It makes you feel sort of warm and cool at the same time. And distant. And—and sure." He sipped his beer, very deliberately not looking at me. I watched his face. "It makes you feel—in control. Sometimes you've got to have that feeling."

"Do you?" I sat down slowly in the easy chair.

"Sometimes." He went to the sofa and picked up his notebook again. "Some people do."

"In order," I asked, "to play?" And my voice was very ugly, full of contempt and anger.

"Well"—he looked at me with great, troubled eyes, as though, in fact, he hoped his eyes would tell me things he could never otherwise say—"they *think* so. And *if* they think so—!"

"And what do *you* think?" I asked.

He sat on the sofa and put his can of beer on the floor. "I don't know," he said, and I couldn't be sure if he were answering my question or pursuing his thoughts. His face didn't tell me. "It's not so much to *play*. It's to *stand* it, to be able to make it at all. On

any level." He frowned and smiled: "In order to keep from shaking to pieces."

"But these friends of yours," I said, "they seem to shake themselves to pieces pretty goddamn fast."

"Maybe." He played with the notebook. And something told me that I should curb my tongue, that Sonny was doing his best to talk, that I should listen. "But of course you only know the ones that've gone to pieces. Some don't—or at least they haven't *yet* and that's just about all *any* of us can say." He paused. "And then there are some who just live, really, in hell, and they know it and they see what's happening and they go right on. I don't know." He sighed, dropped the notebook, folded his arms. "Some guys, you can tell from the way they play, they on something *all* the time. And you can see that, well, it makes something real for them. But of course," he picked up his beer from the floor and sipped it and put the can down again, "they *want* to, too, you've got to see that. Even some of them that say they don't—*some*, not all."

"And what about you?" I asked—I couldn't help it, "What about you? Do *you* want to?"

He stood up and walked to the window and I remained silent for a long time. Then he sighed. "Me," he said. Then: "While I was downstairs before, on my way here, listening to that woman sing, it struck me all of a sudden how much suffering she must have had to go through—to sing like that. It's *repulsive* to think you have to suffer that much."

I said: "But there's no way not to suffer—is there, Sonny?"

"I believe not," he said and smiled, "but that's never stopped anyone from trying." He looked at me. "Has it?" I realized, with this mocking look, that there stood between us, forever, beyond the power of time or forgiveness, the fact that I had held silence—so long!—when he had needed human speech to help him. He turned back to the window. "No, there's no way not to suffer. But you try all kinds of ways to keep from drowning in it, to keep on top of it, and to make it seem—well, like *you*. Like you did something, all right, and now you're suffering for it. You know?" I said nothing. "Well you know," he said, impatiently, "why *do* people suffer? Maybe it's better to do something to give it a reason, *any* reason."

"But we just agreed," I said, "that there's no way not to suffer. Isn't it better, then, just to—take it?"

"But nobody just takes it," Sonny cried, "that's what I'm telling you! *Everybody* tries not to. You're just hung up on the *way* some people try—it's not *your* way!"

The hair on my face began to itch, my face felt wet. "That's not true," I said, "that's not true. I don't give a damn what other people do, I don't even care how they suffer. I just care how *you* suffer." And he looked at me. "Please believe me," I said, "I don't want to see you—die—trying not to suffer."

"I won't," he said flatly, "die trying not to suffer. At least, not any faster than anybody else."

"But there's no need," I said, trying to laugh, "is there? in killing yourself."

I wanted to say more, but I couldn't. I wanted to talk about will power and how life could be—well, beautiful. I wanted to say that it was all within; but was it? or, rather, wasn't that exactly the trouble? And I wanted to promise that I would never fail him again. But it would all have sounded—empty words and lies.

So I made the promise to myself and prayed that I would keep it.

"It's terrible sometimes, inside," he said, "that's what's the trouble. You walk these streets, black and funky and cold, and there's not really a living ass to talk to, and there's nothing shaking, and there's no way of getting it out—that storm inside. You can't talk it and you can't make love with it, and when you finally try to get with it and play it, you realize *nobody's* listening. So *you've* got to listen. You got to find a way to listen."

And then he walked away from the window and sat on the sofa again, as though all the wind had suddenly been knocked out of him. "Sometimes you'll do *anything* to play, even cut your mother's throat." He laughed and looked at me. "Or your brother's." Then he sobered. "Or your own." Then: "Don't worry. I'm all right now and I think I'll *be* all right. But I can't forget—where I've been. I don't mean just the physical place I've been, I mean where I've *been*. And *what* I've been."

"What have you been, Sonny?" I asked.

He smiled—but sat sideways on the sofa, his elbow resting on the back, his fingers playing with his mouth and chin, not looking at me. "I've been something I didn't recognize, didn't know I could be. Didn't know anybody could be." He stopped, looking inward, looking helplessly young, looking old. "I'm not talking about it now because I feel *guilty* or anything like that—maybe it would be better if I did, I don't know. Anyway, I can't really talk about it. Not to you, not to anybody," and now he turned and faced me. "Sometimes, you know, and it was actually when I was most *out* of the world, I felt that I was in it, that I was *with* it, really, and I could play or I didn't really have to *play*, it just came out of me, it was there. And I don't know how I played, thinking about it now, but I know I did awful things, those times, sometimes, to people. Or it wasn't that I *did* anything to them—it was that they weren't real." He picked up the beer can; it was empty; he rolled it between his palms: "And other times—well, I needed a fix, I needed to find a place to lean, I needed to clear a space to *listen*— and I couldn't find it, and I—went crazy, I did terrible things to *me*, I was terrible *for* me." He began pressing the beer can between his hands, I watched the metal begin to give. It glittered, as he played with it like a knife, and I was afraid he would cut himself, but I said nothing. "Oh well. I can never tell you. I was all by myself at the bottom of something, stinking and sweating and crying and shaking, and I smelled it, you know? *My* stink, and I thought I'd die if I couldn't get away from it and yet, all the same, I knew that everything I was doing was just locking me in with it. And I didn't know," he paused, still flattening the beer can, "I didn't know, I still *don't* know, something kept telling me that maybe it was good to smell your own stink, but I didn't think that *that* was what I'd been trying to do—and—who can stand it?" and he abruptly dropped the ruined beer can, looking at me with a small, still smile, and then rose, walking to the window as though it were the lodestone rock. I watched his face, he watched the avenue. "I couldn't tell you when Mama died—but the reason I wanted to leave Harlem so bad was to get away from drugs. And then, when I ran away, that's what I was running from—really. When I came back, nothing had changed, *I* hadn't changed, I was just—older." And he stopped, drumming with his fingers on the windowpane. The sun had vanished, soon darkness would fall. I watched his face. "It can come again," he said, almost as though speaking to himself. Then he turned to me. "It can come again," he repeated. "I just want you to know that."

"All right," I said, at last. "So it can come again. All right."

He smiled, but the smile was sorrowful. "I had to try to tell you," he said.

"Yes," I said. "I understand that."

"You're my brother," he said, looking straight at me, and not smiling at all.

"Yes," I repeated, "yes. I understand that."

He turned back to the window, looking out. "All that hatred down there," he said, "all that hatred and misery and love. It's a wonder it doesn't blow the avenue apart."

We went to the only nightclub on a short, dark street, downtown. We squeezed through the narrow, chattering, jampacked bar to the entrance of the big room, where the bandstand was. And we stood there for a moment, for the lights were very dim in this room and we couldn't see. Then, "Hello, boy," said a voice and an enormous black man, much older than Sonny or myself, erupted out of all that atmospheric lighting and put an arm around Sonny's shoulder. "I been sitting right here," he said, "waiting for you."

He had a big voice, too, and heads in the darkness turned toward us.

Sonny grinned and pulled a little away, and said, "Creole, this is my brother. I told you about him."

Creole shook my hand. "I'm glad to meet you, son," he said, and it was clear that he was glad to meet me *there*, for Sonny's sake. And he smiled, "You got a real musician in *your* family," and he took his arm from Sonny's shoulder and slapped him, lightly, affectionately, with the back of his hand.

"Well. Now I've heard it all," said a voice behind us. This was another musician, and a friend of Sonny's, a coal-black, cheerful-looking man, built close to the ground. He immediately began confiding to me, at the top of his lungs, the most terrible things about Sonny, his teeth gleaming like a lighthouse and his laugh coming up out of him like the beginning of an earthquake. And it turned out that everyone at the bar knew Sonny, or almost everyone; some were musicians, working there, or nearby, or not working, some were simply hangers-on, and some were there to hear Sonny play. I was introduced to all of them and they were all very polite to me. Yet, it was clear that, for them, I was only Sonny's brother. Here, I was in Sonny's world. Or, rather: his kingdom. Here, it was not even a question that his veins bore royal blood.

They were going to play soon and Creole installed me, by myself, at a table in a dark corner. Then I watched them, Creole, and the little black man, and Sonny, and the others, while they horsed around, standing just below the bandstand. The light from the bandstand spilled just a little short of them and, watching them laughing and gesturing and moving about, I had the feeling that they, nevertheless, were being most careful not to step into that circle of light too suddenly: that if they moved into the light too suddenly, without thinking, they would perish in flame. Then, while I watched, one of them, the small black man, moved into the light and crossed the bandstand and started fooling around with his drums. Then—being funny and being, also, extremely ceremonious—Creole took Sonny by the arm and led him to the piano. A woman's voice called Sonny's name and a few hands started clapping. And Sonny, also being funny and being ceremonious, and so touched, I think, that he could have cried, but neither hiding it nor showing it, riding it like a man, grinned, and put both hands to his heart and bowed from the waist.

Creole then went to the bass fiddle and a lean, very bright-skinned brown man jumped up on the bandstand and picked up his horn. So there they were, and the atmosphere on the bandstand and in the room began to change and tighten. Someone stepped up to the microphone and announced them. Then there were all kinds of murmurs. Some people at the bar shushed others. The waitress ran around, frantically getting in the last orders, guys and chicks got closer to each other, and the lights on the bandstand, on the quartet, turned to a kind of indigo. Then they all looked different there. Creole looked about him for the last time, as though he were making certain that all his chickens were in the coop, and then he jumped and struck the fiddle. And there they were.

All I know about music is that not many people ever really hear it. And even then, on the rare occasions when something opens within, and the music enters, what we mainly hear, or hear corroborated, are personal, private, vanishing evocations. But the man who creates the music is hearing something else, is dealing with the roar rising from the void and imposing order on it as it hits the air. What is evoked in him, then, is of another order, more terrible because it has no words, and triumphant, too, for that same reason. And his triumph, when he triumphs, is ours. I just watched Sonny's face. His face was troubled, he was working hard, but he wasn't with it. And I had the feeling that, in a way, everyone on the bandstand was waiting for him, both waiting for him and pushing him along. But as I began to watch Creole, I realized that it was Creole who held them all back. He had them on a short rein. Up there, keeping the beat with his whole body, wailing on the fiddle, with his eyes half closed, he was listening to everything, but he was listening to Sonny. He was having a dialogue with Sonny. He wanted Sonny to leave the shoreline and strike out for the deep water. He was Sonny's witness that deep water and drowning were not the same thing—he had been there, and he knew. And he wanted Sonny to know. He was waiting for Sonny to do the things on the keys which would let Creole know that Sonny was in the water.

And, while Creole listened, Sonny moved, deep within, exactly like someone in torment. I had never before thought of how awful the relationship must be between the musician and his instrument. He has to fill it, this instrument, with the breath of life, his own. He has to make it do what he wants it to do. And a piano is just a piano. It's made out of so much wood and wires and little hammers and big ones, and ivory. While there's only so much you can do with it, the only way to find this out is to try; to try and make it do everything.

And Sonny hadn't been near a piano for over a year. And he wasn't on much better terms with his life, not the life that stretched before him now. He and the piano stammered, started one way, got scared, stopped; started another way, panicked, marked time, started again; then seemed to have found a direction, panicked again, got stuck. And the face I saw on Sonny I'd never seen before. Everything had been burned out of it, and, at the same time, things usually hidden were being burned in, by the fire and fury of the battle which was occurring in him up there.

Yet, watching Creole's face as they neared the end of the first set, I had the feeling that something had happened, something I hadn't heard. Then they finished, there was scattered applause, and then, without an instant's warning, Creole started into something else, it was almost sardonic, it was *Am I Blue*. And, as though he commanded, Sonny began to play. Something began to happen. And Creole let out the reins. The dry, low, black man said something awful on the drums, Creole answered, and the drums talked back. Then the horn insisted, sweet and high, slightly detached perhaps, and Creole listened, commenting now and then, dry, and driving, beautiful and calm and old. Then they all came together again, and Sonny was part of the family again. I could tell this from his face. He seemed to have found, right there beneath his fingers, a damn brand new piano. It seemed that he couldn't get over it. Then, for a while, just being happy with Sonny, they seemed to be agreeing with him that brand-new pianos certainly were a gas.

Then Creole stepped forward to remind them that what they were playing was the blues. He hit something in all of them, he hit something in me, myself, and the music tightened and deepened, apprehension began to beat the air. Creole began to tell us what the blues were all about. They were not about anything very new. He and his boys up there were keeping it new, at the risk of ruin, destruction, madness, and death, in order to find new ways to make us listen. For, while the tale of how we suffer, and how we are delighted, and how we may triumph is never new, it always must be heard. There isn't any other tale to tell, it's the only light we've got in all this darkness.

And this tale, according to that face, that body, those strong hands on those strings, has another aspect in every country, and a new depth in every generation. Listen, Creole seemed to be saying, listen. Now these are Sonny's blues. He made the little black man on the drums know it, and the bright, brown man on the horn. Creole wasn't trying any longer to get Sonny in the water. He was wishing him Godspeed. Then he stepped back, very slowly, filling the air with the immense suggestion that Sonny speak for himself.

Then they all gathered around Sonny and Sonny played. Every now and again one of them seemed to say, amen. Sonny's fingers filled the air with life, his life. But that life contained so many others. And Sonny went all the way back, he really began with the spare, flat statement of the opening phrase of the song. Then he began to make it his. It was very beautiful because it wasn't hurried and it was no longer a lament. I seemed to hear with what burning he had made it his, with what burning we had yet to make it ours, how we could cease lamenting. Freedom lurked around us and I understood, at last, that he could help us to be free if we would listen, that he would never be free until we did. Yet, there was no battle in his face now, I heard what he had gone through, and would continue to go through until he came to rest in earth. He had made it his: that long line, of which we knew only Mama and Daddy. And he was giving it back, as everything must be given back, so that, passing through death, it can live forever. I saw my mother's face again, and felt, for the first time, how the stones of the road she had walked on must have bruised her feet. I saw the moonlit road where my father's brother died. And it brought something else back to me, and carried me past it, I saw my little girl again and felt Isabel's tears again, and I felt my own tears begin to rise. And I was yet aware that this was only a moment, that the world waited outside, as hungry as a tiger, and that trouble stretched above us, longer than the sky.

Then it was over. Creole and Sonny let out their breath, both soaking wet, and grinning. There was a lot of applause and some of it was real. In the dark, the girl came by and I asked her to take drinks to the bandstand. There was a long pause, while they talked up there in the indigo light and after awhile I saw the girl put a Scotch and milk on top of the piano for Sonny. He didn't seem to notice it, but just before they started playing again, he sipped from it and looked toward me, and nodded. Then he put it back on top of the piano. For me, then, as they began to play again, it glowed and shook above my brother's head like the very cup of trembling.[10] ■

Notes

[1] head—restroom

[2] horse—heroin

[3] funky—musty

[4] Louis Armstrong—(1900–1971), a famous trumpet player

[5] Charlie Parker—(1920–1955) nicknamed "Bird," a saxophone player and jazz musician

[6] G.I. Bill—federal government benefits earned from serving in the military

[7] Greenwich Village—a part of New York City known for being avant garde

[8] conked—a hair treatment that straightens hair with chemicals

[9] Harlem hipsters—a term used during the 1930s and 40s for the "in" crowd of Harlem

[10] See Isaiah 51:17, 22-23.

Making Connections through Discussion and Writing

1. Baldwin's narrative technique in this story may present some difficulty in reading. Sonny's brother, in telling the story, moves around in time freely, so the chronology of events may be confusing. Label the different sections according to the time period they present (i.e., their childhood, their father's childhood), marking the beginning and ending of each one.

2. a. Underline the images of darkness and light and of music.

   b. Explain the possible symbolic meanings contained in these images.

   _____
   _____
   _____
   _____
   _____
   _____
   _____

   c. Examine the first paragraph carefully in view of the images you have underlined. How does the setting, an artificially lit subway that makes its way through the darkness, foreshadow the narrator's own fears?

   _____
   _____
   _____
   _____
   _____
   _____

3. a. Circle the parts in the text where we find each brother expressing his fears.

   b. What are the two brothers' strategies for freeing themselves from the limitations and threats of their situation and environment?

   _____
   _____
   _____
   _____
   _____

4. When the narrator tells about the old folks reciting "what they've seen, and what's happened to them and their kinfolk," he says that when they remember that the children are there, they stop telling the stories and turn on the lights. Then the narrator comments, "When light fills the room, the child is filled with darkness." How do you explain this paradox?

   _____
   _____
   _____
   _____
   _____

5. a. What is the significance of the mother's story of what happened in the past to her husband and his brother?

_____

_____

_____

_____

    b. How does that story relate to the narrator and Sonny?

_____

_____

_____

_____

_____

6. a. The narrator's mother asks that he be "there" for Sonny. Explain what this means in the story.

_____

_____

_____

_____

    b. When is he "there," and when is he not?

_____

_____

_____

_____

    c. How does the narrator change the way he expresses his love for his brother?

_____

_____

_____

_____

7. a. The narrator says of Sonny's music, "He was giving it all back, as everything must be given back, so that passing through death, it can live forever." Review this statement in context and comment on how it reflects Baldwin's Christian background.

_____

_____

_____

_____

_____

b. What does the statement reveal about the narrator's changing attitude toward Sonny and his music?

_____

_____

_____

_____

_____

c. What is Baldwin suggesting about the tranforming and redeeming power of art?

_____

_____

_____

_____

_____

8. Explain how Baldwin uses his Christian background, by explicit and implicit allusions and images, to enrich the meaning and effect of his story.

_____

_____

_____

_____

_____

_____

_____

_____

_____

_____

_____

_____

9. a. What is the theme of the story?

_____

_____

_____

b. What does the story suggest about our responsibilities to family members and our acceptance of their unique individuality?

_____

_____

_____

_____

_____

R. K. Narayan

A Horse and Two Goats ✫

R. K. Narayan (1906-2001) was born in Madras, India, into a Hindu Brahmin family. Narayan has been awarded the National Prize of the Indian Literary Academy, the Sahitya Award, the Padma Bhushan, the National Association of Independent Schools Award, and an honorary doctorate in literature from the University of Leeds in England. His novels and stories center around Malgudi, a fictional city in South India, where he describes the lives of characters ranging from the highest level of Indian culture to the lowest level, all with a sense of humor and compassion as reflected in "A Horse and Two Goats." A prodigious writer, Narayan continues to publish into his eighties. He published five collections of stories, including Malgudi Days (1982), and thirty four novels, including The Grandmothers Tale (1994).

Vocabulary ....

accosted	ingratiatingly
aquiline	itinerant
avatars	lorries
balustrade	meandered
bog	millet
brooding	pinioned
camphor	pundit
coriander	tethered
extricate	unobtrusively
gargoyles	urchin

Of the seven hundred thousand villages dotting the map of India, in which the majority of India's five hundred million live, flourish, and die, Kritam was probably the tiniest, indicated on the district survey map by a microscopic dot, the map being meant more for the revenue offical out to collect tax than for the guidance of the motorist, who in any case could not hope to reach it since it sprawled far from the highway at the end of a rough track furrowed up by the iron-hooped wheels of bullock carts. But its size did not prevent its giving itself the grandiose name Kritam, which meant in Tamil "coronet" or "crown" on the brow of this subcontinent. The village consisted of fewer than thirty houses, only one of them built with brick and cement. Painted a brilliant yellow and blue all over with gorgeous carvings of gods and gargoyles on its balustrade, it was known as the Big House. The other houses, distributed in four streets, were generally of bamboo thatch, straw, mud, and other unspecified material. Muni's was the last house in the fourth street, beyond which stretched the fields. In his prosperous days, Muni had owned a flock of forty sheep and goats and sallied forth every morning driving the flock to the highway a couple of miles away. There he would sit on the pedestal of a clay statue of a horse while his cattle grazed around. He carried a crook at the end of a bamboo pole and snapped foliage from the avenue trees to feed his flock; he also gathered faggots and dry sticks, bundled them, and carried them home for fuel at sunset.

His wife lit the domestic fire at dawn, boiled water in a mud pot, threw into it a handful of millet flour, added salt, and gave him his first nourishment for the day. When he started out, she would put in his hand a packed lunch, once again the same millet cooked into a little ball, which he could swallow with a raw onion at midday. She was old, but he was older and needed all the attention she could give him in order to be kept alive.

His fortunes had declined gradually, unnoticed. From a flock of forty which he drove into a pen at night, his stock had now come down to two goats, which were not worth the rent of a half rupee[1] a month the Big House charged for the use of the pen in their backyard. And so the two goats were tethered to the trunk of a drumstick tree[2] which grew in front of his hut and from which occasionally Muni could shake down drumsticks. This morning he got six. He carried them in with a sense of triumph. Although no one could say precisely who owned the tree, it was his because he lived in its shadow.

She said, "If you were content with the drumstick leaves alone, I could boil and salt some for you."

"Oh, I am tired of eating those leaves. I have a craving to chew the drumstick out of sauce, I tell you."

"You have only four teeth in your jaw, but your craving is for big things. All right, get the stuff for the sauce, and I will prepare it for you. After all, next year you may not be alive to ask for anything. But first get me all the stuff, including a measure of rice or millet, and I will satisfy your unholy craving. Our store is empty today. Dhall,[3] chili, curry leaves, mustard, coriander, gingelley oil,[4] and one large potato. Go out and get all this." He repeated the list after her in order not to miss any item and walked off to the shop in the third street.

He sat on an upturned packing case below the platform of the shop. The shopman paid no attention to him. Muni kept clearing his throat, coughing, and sneezing until the shopman could not stand it any more and demanded, "What ails you? You will fly off that seat into the gutter if you sneeze so hard, young man." Muni laughed inordiriately, in order to please the shopman, at being called "young man." The shopman softened and said, "You have enough of the imp inside to keep a second wife busy, but for the fact the old lady is still alive." Muni laughed appropriately again at this joke. It completely won the shopman over; he liked his sense of humor to be appreciated. Muni engaged his attention in local gossip for a few minutes, which always ended with a reference to the postman's wife, who had eloped to the city some months before.

The shopman felt most pleased to hear the worst of the postman, who had cheated him. Being an itinerant postman, he returned home to Kntam only once in ten days and every time managed to slip away again without passing the shop in the third street. By thus humoring the shopman, Muni could always ask for one or two items of food, promising repayment later. Some days the shopman was in a good mood and gave in, and sometimes he would lose his temper suddenly and bark at Muni for daring to ask for credit. This was such a day, and Muni could not progress beyond two items listed as essential components. The shopman was also displaying a remarkable memory for old facts and figures and took out an oblong ledger to support his observations. Muni felt impelled to rise and flee. But his self-respect kept him in his seat and made him listen to the worst things about himself. The shopman concluded, "If you could find five rupees and a quarter, you will have paid off an ancient debt and then could apply for admission to swarga.[5] How much have you got now?"

"I will pay you everything on the first of the next month."

"As always, and whom do you expect to rob by then?"

Muni felt caught and mumbled, "My daughter has sent word that she will be sending me money."

"Have you a daughter?" sneered the shopman. "And she is sending you money! For what purpose, may I know?"

"Birthday, fiftieth birthday," said Muni quietly.

"Birthday! How old are you?"

Muni repeated weakly, not being sure of it himself. "Fifty." He always calculated his age from the time of the great famine when he stood as high as the parapet around the village well, but who could calculate such things accurately nowadays with so many famines occurring? The shopman felt encouraged when other customers stood around to watch and comment. Muni thought helplessly, My poverty is exposed to everybody. But what can I do?

"More likely you are seventy," said the shopman. "You also forget that you mentioned a birthday five weeks ago when you wanted castor oil for your holy bath."

"Bath! Who can dream of a bath when you have to scratch the tank-bed for a bowl of water? We would all be parched and dead but for the Big House, where they let us take a pot of water from their well." After saying this Muni unobtrusively rose and moved off.

He told his wife, "That scoundrel would not give me anything. So go out and sell the drumsticks for what they are worth."

He flung himself down in a corner to recoup from the fatigue of his visit to the shop. His wife said, "You are getting no sauce today, nor anything else. I can't find anything to give you to eat. Fast till the evening, it'll do you good. Take the goats and be gone now," she cried and added, "Don't come back before the sun is down." He knew that if he obeyed her she would somehow conjure up some food for him in the evening. Only he must be careful not to argue and irritate her. Her temper was undependable in the morning but improved by evening time. She was sure to go out and work—grind corn in the Big House, sweep or scrub somewhere, and earn enough to buy foodstuff and keep a dinner ready for him in the evening.

Unleashing the goats from the drumstick tree, Muni started out, driving them ahead and uttering weird cries from time to time in order to urge them on. He passed through the village with his head bowed in thought. He did not want to look at anyone or be accosted. A couple of cronies lounging in the temple corridor hailed him, but he ignored their call. They had known him in the days of affluence when he lorded over a flock of fleecy sheep, not the miserable gawky goats that he had today. Of course he also used to have a few goats for those who fancied them, but real wealth lay in sheep; they bred fast and people came and bought the fleece in the shearing season; and then that famous butcher from the town came over on the weekly market days bringing him betel leaves, tobacco, and often enough some bhang[6] which they smoked in a hut in the coconut grove, undisturbed by wives and well-wishers. After a smoke one felt light and elated and inclined to forgive everyone including that brother-in-law of his who had once tried to set fire to his home. But all this seemed like the memories of a previous birth. Some pestilence afflicted his cattle (he could of course guess who had laid his animals under a curse), and even the friendly butcher would not touch one at half the price...and now here he was left with the two scraggy creatures. He wished someone would rid him of their company, too. The shopman had said that he was seventy. At seventy, one only waited to be summoned by God. When he was dead what would his wife do? They had lived in each other's company since they were children. He was told on their day of wedding that he was ten years old and she was eight. During the wedding ceremony they had had to recite their respective ages and names. He had thrashed her only a few times in their career, and later she had the upper hand. Progeny, none. Perhaps a large progeny would have brought him the blessing of the gods. Fertility brought merit. People with fourteen sons were always so prosperous and at peace

with the world and themselves. He recollected the thrill he had felt when he mentioned a daughter to that shopman; although it was not believed, what if he did not have a daughter?—his cousin in the next village had many daughters, and any one of them was as good as his; he was fond of them all and would buy them sweets if he could afford it. Still, everyone in the village whispered behind their backs that Muni and his wife were a barren couple. He avoided looking at anyone; they all professed to be so high up, and everyone else in the village had more money than he. "I am the poorest fellow in our caste and no wonder that they spurn me, but I won't look at them either," and so he passed on with his eyes downcast along the edge of the street, and people left him also very much alone, commenting only to the extent, "Ah, there he goes with his two goats; if he slits their throats, he may have more peace of mind." "What has he to worry about anyway? They live on nothing and have none to worry about." Thus people commented when he passed through the village. Only on the outskirts did he lift his head and look up. He urged and bullied the goats until they meandered along to the foot of the horse statue on the edge of the village. He sat on its pedestal for the rest of the day. The advantage of this was that he could watch the highway and see the lorries and buses pass through to the hills, and it gave him a sense of belonging to a larger world. The pedestal of the statue was broad enough for him to move around as the sun travelled up and westward; or he could also crouch under the belly of the horse, for shade.

The horse was nearly life-size, molded out of clay, baked, burnt, and brightly colored, and reared its head proudly, prancing its forelegs in the air and flourishing its tail in a loop; beside the horse stood a warrior with scythe-like mustachios, bulging eyes, and aquiline nose. The old image-makers believed in indicating a man of strength by bulging out his eyes and sharpening his moustache tips, and also decorated the man's chest with beads which looked today like blobs of mud through the ravages of sun and wind and rain (when it came), but Muni would insist that he had known the beads to sparkle like the nine gems at one time in his life. The horse itself was said to have been as white as a dhobi-washed sheet, and had had on its back a cover of pure brocade of red and black lace, matching the multicolored sash around the waist of the warrior. But none in the village remembered the splendor as no one noticed its existence. Even Muni, who spent all his waking hours at its foot, never bothered to look up. It was untouched even by the young vandals of the village who gashed tree trunks with knives and tried to topple off milestones and inscribed lewd designs on all walls. This statue had been closer to the population of the village at one time, when this spot bordered the village; but when the highway was laid through (or perhaps when the tank and wells dried up completely here) the village moved a couple of miles inland.

Muni sat at the foot of the statue, watching his two goats graze in the arid soil among the cactus and lantana bushes. He looked at the sun; it was tilted westward no doubt, but it was not the time yet to go back home; if he went too early his wife would have no food for him. Also he must give her time to cool off her temper and feel sympathetic, and then she would scrounge and manage to get some food. He watched the mountain road for a time signal. When the green bus appeared around the bend he could leave, and his wife would feel pleased that he had let the goats feed long enough.

He noticed now a new sort of vehicle coming down at full speed. It looked like both a motor car and a bus. He used to be intrigued by the novelty of such spectacles, but of late work was going on at the source of the river on the mountain and an assortment of people and traffic went past him, and he took it all casually and described to his wife, later in the day, everything he saw. Today, while he observed the yellow vehicle coming down, he was wondering how to describe it later to his wife, when it sputtered and stopped in front of him. A red-faced foreigner, who had been driving it, got down and went round it, stooping, looking, and poking under the vehicle; then he straightened himself up, looked at the dash-board, stared in Muni's direction, and approached him. "Excuse me, is there a gas station nearby, or do I have to wait until another car comes—" He suddenly looked up at the clay horse and cried, "Marvellous," without completing his sentence. Muni felt he should get up and run away, and cursed his age. He could not readily put his limbs into action; some years ago he could outrun a cheetah, as happened once when he went to the forest to cut fuel and it was then that two of his sheep were mauled—a sign that bad times were coming. Though he tried, he could not easily extricate himself from his seat, and then there was also the problem of the goats. He could not leave them behind.

The red-faced man wore khaki clothes—evidently a policeman or a soldier. Muni said to himself, He will chase or shoot if I start running. Some dogs chase only those who run—O Siva,[7] protect

me. I don't know why this man should be after me. Meanwhile the foreigner cried, "Marvellous!" again, nodding his head. He paced around the statue with his eyes fixed on it. Muni sat frozen for a while, and then fidgeted and tried to edge away. Now the other man suddenly pressed his palms together in a salute, smiled, and said, "Namaste![8] How do you do?"

At which Muni spoke the only English expressions he had learnt, "Yes, no." Having exhausted his English vocabulary, he started in Tamil: "My name is Muni. These two goats are mine, and no one can gainsay it—though our village is full of slanderers these days who will not hesitate to say that what belongs to a man doesn't belong to him." He rolled his eyes and shuddered at the thought of evil-minded men and women peopling his village.

The foreigner faithfully looked in the direction indicated by Muni's fingers, gazed for a while at the two goats and the rocks, and with a puzzled expression took out his silver cigarette case and lit a cigarette. Suddenly remembering the courtesies of the season, he asked "Do you smoke?" Muni answered "Yes, no." Whereupon the red-faced man took a cigarette and gave it to Muni, who received it with surprise, having had no offer of a smoke from anyone for years now. Those days when he smoked bhang were gone with his sheep and the large-hearted butcher. Nowadays he was not able to find even matches, let alone bhang. (His wife went across and borrowed a fire at dawn from a neighbor.) He had always wanted to smoke a cigarette; only once did the shopman give him one on credit, and he remembered how good it had tasted. The other flicked the lighter open and offered a light to Muni. Muni felt so confused about how to act that he blew on it and put it out. The other, puzzled but undaunted, flourished his lighter, presented it again, and lit Muni's cigarette. Muni drew a deep puff and started coughing; it was racking, no doubt, but extremely pleasant. When his cough subsided he wiped his eyes and took stock of the situation, understanding that the other man was not an Inquisitor of any kind. Yet, in order to make sure, he remained wary. No need to run away from a man who gave him such a potent smoke. His head was reeling from the effect of one of those strong American cigarettes made with roasted tobacco. The man said "I come from New York," took out a wallet from his hip pocket, and presented his card.

Muni shrank away from the card. Perhaps he was trying to present a warrant and arrest him. Beware of khaki, one part of his mind warned. Take all the cigarettes or bhang or whatever is offered, but don't get caught. Beware of khaki. He wished he weren't seventy as the shopman had said. At seventy one didn't run, but surrendered to whatever came. He could only ward off trouble by talk. So he went on, all in the chaste Tamil for which Kritam was famous. (Even the worst detractors could not deny that the famous poetess Avaiyar was born in this area, although no one could say whether it was in Kritam or Kuppam, the adjoining village.) Out of this heritage the Tamil language gushed through Muni in an unimpeded flow. He said, "Before God, sir, Bhagwan, who sees everything, I tell you, sir, that we know nothing of the case. If the murder was committed, whoever did it will not escape. Bhagwan[9] is all-seeing. Don't ask me about it. I know nothing." A body had been found mutilated and thrown under a tamarind tree at the border between Kritam and Kuppam a few weeks before, giving rise to much gossip and speculation. Muni added an explanation. "Anything is possible there. People over there will stop at nothing." The foreigner nodded his head and listened courteously though he understood nothing.

"I am sure you know when this horse was made," said the red man and smiled ingratiatingly.

Muni reacted to the relaxed atmosphere by smiling himself, and pleaded, "Please go away, sir, I know nothing. I promise we will hold him for you if we see any bad character around, and we will bury him up to his neck in a coconut pit if he tries to escape; but our village has always had a clean record. Must definitely be the other village."

Now the red man implored, "Please, please, I will speak slowly, please try to understand me. Can't you understand even a simple word of English? Everyone in this country seems to know English. I have gotten along with English everywhere in this country, but you don't speak it. Have you any religious or spiritual scruples against English speech?"

Muni made some indistinct sounds in his throat and shook his head. Encouraged, the other went on to explain at length, uttering each syllable with care and deliberation. Presently he sidled over and took a seat beside the old man, explaining, "You see, last August, we probably had the hottest summer in history, and I was working in shirtsleeves in my office on the fortieth floor of the Empire State Building. We had a power failure one day, you know, and there I was stuck for four hours, no elevator, no air conditioning. All the way in the train I kept thinking, and the minute I reached home in Connecticut, I told my wife, Ruth,

'We will visit India this winter, it's time to look at other civilizations.' Next day she called the travel agent first thing and told him to fix it, and so here I am. Ruth came with me but is staying back at Srinagar,[10] and I am the one doing the rounds and joining her later."

Muni looked reflective at the end of this long oration and said, rather feebly, "Yes, no," as a concession to the other's language, and went on in Tamil, "When I was this high"—he indicated a foot high—"I had heard my uncle say. . ."

No one can tell what he was planning to say, as the other interrupted him at this stage to ask, "Boy, what is the secret of your teeth? How old are you?"

The old man forgot what he had started to say and remarked, "Sometimes we too lose our cattle. Jackals or cheetahs may sometimes carry them off, but sometimes it is just theft from over in the next village, and then we will know who has done it. Our priest at the temple can see in the camphor flame the face of the thief, and when he is caught. . . ." He gestured with his hands a perfect mincing of meat.

The American watched his hands intently and said, "I know what you mean. Chop something? Maybe I am holding you up and you want to chop wood? Where is your axe? Hand it to me and show me what to chop. I do enjoy it, you know, just a hobby. We get a lot of driftwood along the backwater near my houses, and on Sundays I do nothing but chop wood for the fireplace. I really feel different when I watch the fire in the fireplace, although it may take all the sections of the Sunday *New York Times* to get a fire started." And he smiled at this reference.

Muni felt totally confused but decided the best thing would be to make an attempt to get away from this place. He tried to edge out, saying, "Must go home," and turned to go. The other seized his shoulder and said desperately, "Is there no one, absolutely no one here, to translate for me?" He looked up and down the road, which was deserted in this hot afternoon; a sudden gust of wind churned up the dust and dead leaves on the roadside into a ghostly column and propelled it toward the mountain road. The stranger almost pinioned Muni's back to the statue and asked, "Isn't this statue yours? Why don't you sell it to me?"

The old man now understood the reference to the horse, thought for a second, and said in his own language, "I was an urchin this high when I heard my grandfather explain this horse and warrior, and my grandfather himself was this high when he heard his grandfather, whose grandfather. . ."

The other man interrupted him. "I don't want to seem to have stopped here for nothing. I will offer you a good price for this," he said, indicating the horse. He had concluded without the least doubt that Muni owned this mud horse. Perhaps he guessed by the way he sat on its pedestal, like other souvenir sellers in this country presiding over their wares.

Muni followed the man's eyes and pointing fingers and dimly understood the subject matter and, feeling relieved that the theme of the mutilated body had been abandoned at least for the time being, said again, enthusiastically, "I was this high when my grandfather told me about this horse and the warrior, and my grandfather was this high when he himself . . ." and he was getting into a deeper bog of reminiscence each time he tried to indicate the antiquity of the statue.

The Tamil that Muni spoke was stimulating even as pure sound, and the foreigner listened with fascination. "I wish I had my tape-recorder here," he said, assuming the pleasantest expression. "Your language sounds wonderful. I get a kick out of every word you utter, here—he indicated his ears—"but you don't have to waste your breath in sales talk. I appreciate the article. You don't have to explain its points."

"I never went to a school, in those days only Brahmin[11] went to schools, but we had to go out and work in the fields morning till night, from sowing to harvest time . . . and when Pongal[12] came and we had cut the harvest, my father allowed me to go out and play with others at the tank, and so I don't know the Parangi language you speak, even little fellows in your country probably speak the Parangi language, but here only learned men and officers know it. We had a postman in our village who could speak to you boldly in your language, but his wife ran away with someone and he does not speak to anyone at all nowadays. Who would if a wife did what she did? Women must be watched; otherwise they will sell themselves and the home." And he laughed at his own quip.

The foreigner laughed heartily, took out another cigarette, and offered it to Muni, who now smoked with ease, deciding to stay on if the fellow was going to be so good as to keep up his cigarette supply. The American now stood up on the pedestal in the attitude of a demonstrative lecturer and said, running his finger along some of the carved decorations around the horse's neck, speaking slowly and uttering his words syllable by syllable, "I could give a sales talk for this better than anyone else. . . . This is a marvelous combination of

yellow and indigo, though faded now. . . . How do you people of this country achieve these flaming colors?"

Muni, now assured that the subject was still the horse and not the dead body, said, "This is our guardian, it means death to our adversaries. At the end of Kali Yuga,[13] this world and all other worlds will be destroyed, and the Redeemer will come in the shape of a horse called Kalki; this horse will come to life and gallop and trample down all bad men." As he spoke of bad men the figures of his shopman and his brother-in-law assumed concrete forms in his mind, and he revelled for a moment in the predicament of the fellow under the horse's hoof: served him right for trying to set fire to his home. . . .

While he was brooding on this pleasant vision, the foreigner utilized the pause to say, "I assure you that this will have the best home in the U.S.A. I'll push away the bookcase, you know I love books and am a member of five book clubs, and the choice and bonus volumes mount up to a pile really in our living room, as high as this horse itself. But they'll have to go. Ruth may disapprove, but I will convince her. The TV may have to be shifted, too. We can't have everything in the living room. Ruth will probably say what about when we have a party? I'm going to keep him right in the middle of the room. I don't see how that can interfere with the party—we'll stand around him and have our drinks."

Muni continued his description of the end of the world. "Our pundit discoursed at the temple once how the oceans are going to close over the earth in a huge wave and swallow us—this horse will grow bigger than the biggest wave and carry on its back only the good people and kick into the floods the evil ones—plenty of them about"—he said reflectively. "Do you know when it is going to happen?" he asked.

The foreigner now understood by the tone of the other that a question was being asked and said, "How am I transporting it? I can push the seat back and make room in the rear. That van can take in an elephant"—waving precisely at the back of the seat.

Muni was still hovering on visions of avatars and said again, "I never missed our pundit's discourses at the temple in those days during every bright half of the month, although he'd go on all night, and he told us that Vishnu[14] is the highest god. Whenever evil men trouble us, he comes down to save us. He has come many times. The first time he incarnated as a great fish, and lifted the scriptures on his back when the flood and sea waves . . ."

"I am not a millionaire, but a modest business-man. My trade is coffee."

Amidst all this wilderness of obscure sound Muni caught the word "coffee" and said, "If you want to drink 'kapi,' drive further up, in the next town, they have Friday market and there they open 'kapi-otels'—so I learn from passersby. Don't think I wander about. I go nowhere and look for nothing." His thoughts went back to the avatars. "The first avatar was in the shape of a little fish in a bowl of water, but every hour it grew bigger and bigger and became in the end a huge whale which the seas could not contain, and on the back of the whale the holy books were supported, saved, and carried." Once he had launched on the first avatar, it was inevitable that he should go on to the next, a wild boar on whose tusk the earth was lifted when a vicious conqueror of the earth carried it off and hid it at the bottom of the sea. After describing this avatar Muni concluded, "God will always save us whenever we are troubled by evil beings. When we were young we staged at full moon the story of the avatars. That's how I know the stories; we played them all night until the sun rose, and sometimes the European collector would come to watch, bringing his own chair. I had a good voice and so they always taught me songs and gave me the women's roles. I was always Goddess Lakshmi,[15] and they dressed me in a brocade sari,[16] loaned from the Big House . . ."

The foreigner said, "I repeat I am not a millionaire. Ours is a modest business; after all, we can't afford to buy more than sixty minutes of TV time in a month, which works out to two minutes a day, that's all, although in the course of time we'll maybe sponsor a one-hour show regularly if our sales graph continues to go up . . ."

Muni was intoxicated by the memory of his theatrical days and was about to explain how he had painted his face and worn a wig and diamond earrings when the visitor, feeling that he had spent too much time already, said, "Tell me, will you accept a hundred rupees or not for the horse? I'd love to take the whiskered soldier also but no space for him this year. I'll have to cancel my air ticket and take a boat home, I suppose. Ruth can go by air if she likes, but I will go with the horse and keep him in my cabin all the way if necessary." And he smiled at the picture of himself voyaging across the seas hugging this horse. He added, "I will have to pad it with straw so that it doesn't break . . ."

"When we played *Ramayana*,[17] they dressed me as Sita," added Muni. "A teacher came and taught us the songs for the drama and we gave him fifty rupees. He incarnated himself as Rama, and he alone could destroy Ravana, the demon with ten heads who shook all the worlds; do you know the story of *Ramayana*?"

"I have my station wagon as you see. I can push the seat back and take the horse in if you will just lend me a hand with it."

"Do you know *Mahabharata*?[18] Krishna was the eighth avatar of Vishnu, incarnated to help the Five Brothers regain their kingdom. When Krishna was a baby he danced on the thousand-hooded giant serpent and trampled it to death; and then he suckled the breasts of the demoness and left them flat as a disc, though when she came to him her bosoms were large, like mounds of earth on the banks of a dug-up canal." He indicated two mounds with his hands.

The stranger was completely mystified by the gesture. For the first time he said, "I really wonder what you are saying because your answer is crucial. We have come to the point when we should be ready to talk business."

"When the tenth avatar comes, do you know where you and I will be?" asked the old man.

"Lend me a hand and I can lift off the horse from its pedestal after picking out the cement at the joints. We can do anything if we have a basis of understanding."

At this stage the mutual mystification was complete, and there was no need even to carry on a guessing game at the meaning of words. The old man chattered away in a spirit of balancing off the credits and debits of conversational exchange, and said in order to be on the credit sale, "Oh, honorable one, I hope God has blessed you with numerous progeny. I say this because you seem to be a good man, willing to stay beside an old man and talk to him, while all day I have none to talk to except when somebody stops by to ask for a piece of tobacco. But I seldom have it, tobacco is not what it used to be at one time, and I have given up chewing. I cannot afford it nowadays." Noting the other's interest in his speech, Muni felt encouraged to ask, "How many children have you?" with appropriate gestures with his hands.

Realizing that a question was being asked, the red man replied, "I said a hundred," which encouraged Muni to go into details. "How many of your children are boys and how many girls? Where are they? Is your daughter married? Is it difficult to find a son-in-law in your country also?"

In answer to these questions the red man dashed his hand into his pocket and brought forth his wallet in order to take immediate advantage of the bearish trend in the market. He flourished a hundred-rupee currency note and said, "Well, this is what I meant."

The old man now realized that some financial element was entering their talk. He peered closely at the currency note, the like of which he had never seen in his life; he knew the five and ten by their colors although always in other people's hands, while his own earning at any time was in coppers and nickels. What was this man flourishing the note for? Perhaps asking for change. He laughed to himself at the notion of anyone coming to him for changing a thousand- or ten-thousand-rupee note. He said with a grin, "Ask our village headman who is also a moneylender; he can change even a lakh[19] of rupees in gold sovereigns if you prefer it that way; he thinks nobody knows, but dig the floor of his puja room[20] and your head will reel at the sight of the hoard. The man disguises himself in rags just to mislead the public. Talk to the headman yourself because he goes mad at the sight of me. Someone took away his pumpkins with the creeper and he, for some reason, thinks it was me and my goats . . . that's why I never let my goats be seen anywhere near the farms." His eyes travelled to his goats nosing about, attempting to wrest nutrition from minute greenery peeping out of rock and dry earth.

The foreigner followed his look and decided that it would be a sound policy to show an interest in the old man s pets. He went up casually to them and stroked their backs with every show of courteous attention. Now the truth dawned on the old man. His dream of a lifetime was about to be realized. He understood that the red man was actually making an offer for the goats. He had reared them up in the hope of selling them some day and, with the capital, opening a small shop on this very spot. Sitting here, watching toward the hills, he had often dreamt how he would put up a thatched roof here, spread a gunny sack out on the ground, and display on it fried nuts, colored sweets, and green coconut for the thirsty and famished wayfarers on the highway, which was sometimes very busy. The animals were not prize ones for a cattle show, but he had spent his occasional savings to provide them some fancy diet now and then, and they did not look too bad. While he was reflecting thus, the red man shook his hand and left on his palm one hundred rupees in tens now, suddenly realizing that this was what the old man was asking. "It is all for you or you may share it if you have a partner."

The old man pointed at the station wagon and asked, "Are you carrying them off in that?"

"Yes, of course," said the other, understanding the transportation part of it.

The old man said, "This will be their first ride in a motor car. Carry them off after I get out of sight, otherwise they will never follow you, but only me even if I am travelling on the path to Yama Loka.[21] He laughed at his own joke, brought his palms together in a salute, turned around and went off, and was soon out of sight beyond a clump of thicket.

The red man looked at the goats grazing peacefully. Perched on the pedestal of the horse, as the westerly sun touched off the ancient faded colors of the statue with a fresh splendor, he ruminated, "He must be gone to fetch some help. I suppose!" and settled down to wait. When a truck came downhill, he stopped it and got the help of a couple of men to detach the horse from its pedestal and place it in his station wagon. He gave them five rupees each, and for a further payment they siphoned off gas from the truck, and helped him to start his engine.

Muni hurried homeward with the cash securely tucked away at his waist in his dhoti.[22] He shut the street door and stole up softly to his wife as she squatted before the lit oven wondering if by a miracle food would drop from the sky. Muni displayed his fortune for the day. She snatched the notes from him, counted them by the glow of the fire, and cried, "One hundred rupees! How did you come by it? Have you been stealing?"

"I have sold our goats to a red-faced man. He was absolutely crazy to have them, gave me all this money and carried them off in his motor car!"

Hardly had these words left his lips when they heard bleating outside. She opened the door and saw the two goats at her door. "Here they are!" she said. "What's the meaning of all this?"

He muttered a great curse and seized one of the goats by its ears and shouted, "Where is that man? Don't you know you are his? Why did you come back?" The goat only wriggled in his grip. He asked the same question of the other, too. The goat shook itself off. His wife glared at him and declared, "If you have thieved, the police will come tonight and break your bones. Don't involve me. I will go away to my parents. . . ." ∎

Notes

1 rupee—a monetary unit of India, Nepal, and Pakistan

2 Drumstick tree—a tree that produces a vegetable that looks like elongated okra

3 dhall—a sauce made from lentils and spices

4 gengelly oil—sesame oil

5 swarga—heaven

6 bhang—a mild form of marijuana prepared from Indian hemp

7 Siva—the Hindu god known as "the Destroyer"

8 Namaste—a customary greeting

9 Bhagwan—another word for god

10 Srinager—a city in northern India; capital of the state of Kashmir

11 Brahmin—a Hindu priest; also the name of the highest caste in India

12 Pongal—a Harvest festival

13 Kali Yuga—the fourth and final age of the world, full of conflict and sin

14 Vishnu—the Hindu god known as "the Preserver"

15 Goddess Lakshmi—the Hindu goddess of fortune

16 sari—a long, single piece garment worn by Hindu women

17 *Ramayana*—an epic of India relating the adventures of Ramachandra and his wife, Sita

18 *Mahabharata*—an epic poem of India dealing mainly with the conflict between the Pandavas and the Kauravas, with many digressions; includes the *Bhagavad-Gita*

19 lakh—the sum of 100,000 (especially of rupees)

21 puja room—a worship room

22 Yama Loka—the place where Yama, a Vedic god who rules the underworld, resides

21 dhoti—a long loincloth worn by many Hindu men in India

Making Connections through Discussion and Writing

1. The story is told from a limited omniscient point of view in which only the thoughts of the main character, Muni, are revealed to the reader. How does he imagine himself to be perceived through the eyes of his wife and the people of Kritam?

   _____
   _____
   _____
   _____
   _____

2. Although Muni cannnot understand a word the red-faced American says, he begins to change during their attempted conversations, which are at cross-purposes.

   a. What happens to cause Muni to feel different about himself?

   _____
   _____
   _____
   _____

   b. What are the signs of Muni's changing during their conversation?

   _____
   _____
   _____
   _____

3. Muni and the American man are unable to understand each other and must rely on object and nonverbal language to attempt communication. For example, the American is unaware that the khaki clothes are threatening to Muni. Make a list of objects and nonverbal cues that each character uses to try to understand one another.

   _____   _____
   _____   _____
   _____   _____
   _____   _____
   _____   _____

4. a. Describe the American.

   _____
   _____
   _____
   _____

   b. How do this description and the American's actions depict him as a stereotypical American?

   _____
   _____
   _____
   _____

   c. Why is he continually referred to as red-faced?

_____

_____

5. a. What does the statue signify to Muni?

_____

_____

_____

   b. How does the American's view of the statue differ from Muni's?

_____

_____

_____

   c. Given their differing cultural values and assumptions, would Muni and the American have been able to communicate well even if they both spoke the same language? Explain.

_____

_____

_____

6. This story is told with a humorous tone. At what point in the story is the reader made aware of its lighter tone?

_____

_____

_____

_____

7. This story demonstrates how much can happen when such disparity exists between individuals who are trying to communicate. Write a well-developed paragraph about an experience in which you were unable to understand, or to be understood, by a person from another culture.

_____

_____

_____

_____

_____

_____

_____

_____

_____

_____

_____

_____

_____

Gabriel Garcia Marquez
A Very Old Man with Enormous Wings

Gabriel Garcia Marquez (b. 1928) is a famous Latin American writer who won the Nobel Prize for literature in 1982. Combining a style that incorporates the fantastic and the realistic, Marquez adapted his grandmother's Caribbean Colombian folklore to his novels and short stories in the form of "magic realism." His most famous novel is *One Hundred Years of Solitude* (1967). Other novels by Marquez, include *An Evil Hour* (1962), *The Autumn of the Patriarch* (1975), and *Love in the Time of Cholera* (1975). His *Collected Stories* was published in 1999.

Although reading magic realism may seem a bit strange at first, almost like reading fantasy for the first time, the effects of this style offer imaginative possibilities for the reader. As you begin reading this story, notice how Marquez calls the reader's attention to the story through a mixture of earthy realism and surprising surrealism. His use of magic realism engages images, opening possibilities of meaning.

Vocabulary . . . .

antiquarian	iridescent
bailiff	magnanimous
celestial	penitents
decrepit/decrepitude	primate
hermetic	proliferated
impeded	sidereal
impertinences	terrestrial
infamies	warren
ingenuous	

On the third day of rain they had killed so many crabs inside the house that Pelayo had to cross his drenched courtyard and throw them into the sea, because the newborn child had a temperature all night and they thought it was due to the stench. The world had been sad since Tuesday. Sea and sky were a single ash-gray thing and the sands of the beach, which on March nights glimmered like powdered light, had become a stew of mud and rotten shellfish. The light was so weak at noon that when Pelayo was coming back to the house after throwing away the crabs, it was hard for him to see what it was that was moving and groaning in the rear of the courtyard. He had to go very close to see that it was an old man, a very old man, lying face down in the mud, who, in spite of his tremendous efforts, couldn't get up, impeded by his enormous wings.

Frightened by that nightmare, Pelayo ran to get Elisenda, his wife, who was putting compresses on the sick child, and he took her to the rear of the courtyard. They both looked at the fallen body with mute stupor. He was dressed like a ragpicker. There were only a few faded hairs left on his bald skull and very few teeth in his mouth, and his pitiful condition of a drenched great-grandfather had taken away any sense of grandeur he might have had. His huge buzzard wings, dirty and half-plucked, were forever entangled in the mud. They looked at him so long and so closely that Pelayo and Elisenda very soon overcame their surprise and in the end found him familiar. Then they dared speak to him, and he answered in an incomprehensible dialect with a strong sailor's voice. That was how they skipped over the inconvenience of the wings and quite intelligently concluded that he was a lonely castaway from some foreign ship wrecked by the storm. And yet, they called in a neighbor woman who knew everything about life and death to see him, and all she needed was one look to show them their mistake.

"He's an angel," she told them. "He must have been coming for the child, but the poor fellow is so old that the rain knocked him down."

On the following day everyone knew that a flesh-and-blood angel was held captive in Pelayo's house. Against the judgment of the wise neighbor woman, for whom angels in those times were the fugitive survivors of a celestial conspiracy, they did not have the heart to club him to death. Pelayo watched over him all afternoon from the kitchen, armed with his bailiff's club, and before going to bed he dragged him out of the mud and locked him up with the hens in the wire chicken coop. In the middle of the night, when the rain stopped, Pelayo and Elisenda were still killing crabs. A short time afterward the child woke up without a fever and with a desire to eat. Then they felt magnanimous and decided to put the angel on a raft with fresh water and provisions for three days and leave him to his fate on the high seas. But when they went out into the courtyard with the first light of dawn, they found the whole neighborhood in front of the chicken coop having fun with the angel, without the slightest reverence, tossing him things to eat through the openings in the wires as if he weren't a supernatural creature but a circus animal.

Father Gonzaga arrived before seven o'clock, alarmed at the strange news. By that time onlookers less frivolous than those at dawn had already arrived and they were making all kinds of conjectures concerning the captive's future. The simplest among them thought that he should be named mayor of the world. Others of sterner mind felt that he should be promoted to the rank of five-star general in order to win all wars. Some visionaries hoped that he could be put to stud in order to implant on earth a race of winged wise men who could take charge of the universe. But Father Gonzaga, before becoming a priest, had been a robust woodcutter. Standing by the wire, he reviewed his catechism[1] in an instant and asked them to open the door so that he could take a close look at that pitiful man who looked more like a huge decrepit hen among the fascinated chickens. He was lying in a corner drying his open wings in the sunlight among the fruit peels and breakfast leftovers that the early risers had thrown him. Alien to the impertinences of the world, he only lifted his antiquarian eyes and murmured something in his dialect when Father Gonzaga went into the chicken coop and said good morning to him in Latin.[2] The parish priest had his first suspicion of an impostor when he saw that he did not understand the language of God or know how to greet His ministers. Then he noticed that seen close up he was much too human: he had an unbearable smell of the outdoors, the back side of his wings was strewn with parasites and his main feathers had been mistreated by terrestrial winds, and nothing about him measured up to the proud dignity of angels. Then he came out of the chicken coop and in a brief sermon warned the curious against the risks of being ingenuous. He reminded them that the devil had the bad habit of making use of carnival tricks in order to confuse the unwary. He argued that if wings were not the essential element in determining the difference between a hawk and an airplane, they were even less so in the recognition of angels. Nevertheless, he promised to write a letter to his bishop so that the latter would write to his primate so that the latter would write to the Supreme Pontiff[3] in order to get the final verdict from the highest courts.

His prudence fell on sterile hearts. The news of the captive angel spread with such rapidity that after a few hours the courtyard had the bustle of a marketplace and they had to call in troops with fixed bayonets to disperse the mob that was about to knock the house down. Elisenda, her spine all twisted from sweeping up so much marketplace trash, then got the idea of fencing in the yard and charging five cents admission to see the angel.

The curious came from far away. A travelling carnival arrived with a flying acrobat who buzzed over the crowd several times, but no one paid any attention to him because his wings were not of those of an angel but, rather, those of a sidereal bat. The most unfortunate invalids on earth came in search of health: a poor woman who since childhood had been counting her heartbeats and had run out of numbers; a Portuguese man who couldn't sleep because the noise of the stars disturbed him; a sleepwalker who got up at night to undo the things he had done while awake; and many others with less serious ailments. In the midst of that shipwreck disorder that made the earth tremble, Pelayo and Elisenda were happy with fatigue, for in less than a week they had crammed their rooms with money and the line of pilgrims waiting their turn to enter still reached beyond the horizon.

The angel was the only one who took no part in his own act. He spent his time trying to get comfortable in his borrowed nest, befuddled by the hellish heat of the oil lamps and sacramental candles that had been placed along the wire. At first they tried to make him eat some mothballs, which, according to the wisdom of the wise neighbor woman, were the food prescribed for angels. But he turned them down, just as he turned down the papal lunches[4] that the penitents brought him, and they never found out whether it was because he was an angel or because he was an old man that in the end he ate nothing but eggplant mush. His only supernatural virtue seemed to be patience. Especially during the first days, when the hens pecked at him, searching for the stellar parasites that proliferated in his wings, and the cripples pulled out feathers to touch their defective parts with, and even the most merciful threw stones at him, trying to get him to rise so they could see him standing. The only time they succeeded in arousing him was when they burned his side with an iron for branding steers, for he had been motionless for so many hours that they thought he was dead. He awoke with a start, ranting in his hermetic language and with tears in his eyes, and he flapped his wings a couple of times, which brought on a whirlwind of chicken dung and lunar dust and a gale of panic that did not seem to be of this world. Although many thought that his reaction had been one not of rage but of pain, from then on they were careful not to annoy him, because the majority understood that his passivity was not that of a hero taking his ease but that of a cataclysm in repose.

Father Gonzaga held back the crowd's frivolity with formulas of maidservant inspiration while awaiting the arrival of a final judgment on the nature of the captive. But the mail from Rome[5] showed no sense of urgency. They spent their time finding out if the prisoner had a navel, if his dialect had any connection with Aramaic, how many times he could fit on the head of a pin,[6] or whether he wasn't just a Norwegian with wings. Those meager letters might have come and gone until the end of time if a providential event had not put an end to the priest's tribulations.

It so happened that during those days, among so many other carnival attractions, there arrived in town the traveling show of the woman who had been changed into a spider for having disobeyed her parents. The admission to see her was not only less than the admission to see the angel, but people were permitted to ask her all manner of questions about her absurd state and to examine her up and down so that no one would ever doubt the truth of her horror. She was a frightful tarantula the size of a ram and with the head of a sad maiden. What was most heartrending, however, was not her outlandish shape but the sincere affliction with which she recounted the details of her misfortune. While still practically a child she had sneaked out of her parents' house to go to a dance, and while she was coming back through the woods after having danced all night without permission, a fearful thunderclap rent the sky in two and through the crack came the lightning bolt of brimstone that changed her into a spider. Her only nourishment came from the meatballs that charitable souls chose to toss into her mouth. A spectacle like that, full of so much human truth and with such a fearful lesson, was bound to defeat without even trying that of a haughty angel who scarcely deigned to look at mortals. Besides, the few miracles attributed to the angel showed a certain mental disorder, like the blind man who didn't recover his sight but grew three new teeth, or the paralytic who didn't get to walk but almost won the lottery, and the leper whose sores sprouted sunflowers. Those consolation miracles, which were more like mocking fun, had already ruined the angel's reputation when the woman who had been changed into a spider finally crushed him completely. That was how Father Gonzaga was cured forever of his insomnia and Pelayo's courtyard went back to being as empty as during the time it had rained for three days and crabs walked through the bedrooms.

The owners of the house had no reason to lament. With the money they saved they built a two-story mansion with balconies and gardens and high netting so that crabs wouldn't get in during the winter, and with iron bars on the windows so that angels wouldn't get in. Pelayo also set up a rabbit warren close to town and gave up his job as bailiff for good, and Elisenda bought some satin pumps with high heels and many dresses of iridescent silk, the kind worn on Sunday by the most desirable women in those times. The chicken coop was the only thing that didn't receive any attention. If they washed it down with creolin and burned tears of myrrh[7] inside it every so often, it was not in homage to the angel but to drive away the dungheap stench that still hung everywhere like a ghost and was turning the new house into an old one. At first, when the child learned to walk, they were careful that he not get too close to the chicken coop. But then they began to lose their fears and got used to the smell, and before the child got his second teeth he'd gone inside the chicken coop to play, where the wires were falling apart. The angel was no less standoffish with him than with other mortals, but he tolerated the most ingenious infamies with the patience of a dog who had no illusions. They both came down with the chicken pox at the same time. The doctor who took care of the child couldn't resist the temptation to listen to the angel's heart, and he found so much whistling in the heart and so many sounds in his kidneys that it seemed impossible for him to be alive. What surprised him most, however, was the logic of his wings. They seemed so natural on that completely human organism that he couldn't understand why other men didn't have them too.

When the child began school it had been some time since the sun and rain had caused the collapse of the chicken coop. The angel went dragging himself about here and there like a stray dying man. They would drive him out of the bedroom with a broom and a moment later find him in the kitchen. He seemed to be in so many places at the same time that they grew to think that he'd been duplicated, that he was reproducing himself all through the house, and the exasperated and unhinged Elisenda shouted that it was awful living in that hell full of angels. He could scarcely eat and his antiquarian eyes had also become so foggy that he went about bumping into posts. All he had left were the bare cannulae[8] of his last feathers. Pelayo threw a blanket over him and extended him the charity of letting him sleep in the shed, and only then did they notice that he had a temperature at night, and was delirious with the tongue twisters of an old Norwegian. That was one of the few times they became alarmed, for they thought he was going to die and not even the wise neighbor woman had been able to tell them what to do with dead angels.

And yet he not only survived his worst winter, but seemed improved with the first sunny days. He remained motionless for several days in the farthest corner of the courtyard, where no one would see him, and at the beginning of December some large, stiff feathers began to grow on his wings, the feathers of a scarecrow, which looked more like another misfortune of decrepitude. But he must have known the reason for those changes, for he was quite careful that no one should notice them, that no one should hear the sea chanteys that he sometimes sang under the stars. One morning Elisenda was cutting some bunches of onions for lunch when a wind that seemed to come from the high sea blew into the kitchen. Then she went to the window and caught the angel in his first attempts at flight. They were so clumsy that his fingernails opened a furrow in the vegetable patch and he was on the point of knocking the shed down with the ungainly flapping that slipped on the light and couldn't get a grip on the air. But he did manage to gain altitude. Elisenda let out a sigh of relief, for herself and for him, when she saw him pass over the last houses, holding himself up in some way with the risky flapping of a senile vulture. She kept watching him even when she was through cutting the onions and she kept on watching until it was no longer possible for her to see him, because then he was no longer an annoyance in her life but an imaginary dot on the horizon of the sea. ■

Notes

1 catechism—set form of religious instruction

2 Latin—the language of the Roman Catholic mass

3 Bishop . . . Supreme Pontiff—Bishops are officials in the Roman Catholic Church hierarchy; the Supreme Pontiff is the Pope, the spiritual leader of Roman Catholicism.

4 papal lunches—lunches blessed by the Pope

5 Rome—the city where the Vatican, headquarters of the Roman Catholic Church, is located

6 navel . . . head of a pin—tests to prove the authenticity of an angel. A navel would indicate a human birth. Aramaic was the dialect spoken by Jesus. Medieval Christians speculated on whether angels took up physical space—hence the question of how many of them could "fit on the head of a pin."

7 creolin . . . myrrh—Creolin is used as a disinfectant and myrrh is used as incense.

8 cannulae—the quills of feathers

Making Connections through Discussion and Writing

1. a. What surprising thing is introduced into the realistic setting established by the first paragraph?

    _____
    _____
    _____
    _____
    _____

    b. How would you explain this event or label this thing?

    _____
    _____
    _____
    _____
    _____

2. a. We often perceive new phenomena through the lenses of our unconscious assumptions. Explain how the townspeople view the old man/angel.

    _____
    _____
    _____
    _____

    b. How do their assumptions lead to their interpretations about him?

    _____
    _____
    _____
    _____
    _____

3. Although strange and miraculous phenomena do occur as the people seek the old man/angel's powers, the narrator says these occurrences "showed a certain mental disorder." Describe some of the things that happen to the people.

    _____
    _____
    _____
    _____
    _____
    _____
    _____
    _____

4. As the carnival-like setting grows more and more surreal, the town's treatment of the old man begins to change. Describe this change.

    _____

    _____

    _____

    _____

    _____

    _____

    _____

    _____

5. Several times the old man is referred to as being indifferent or standoffish. The narrator also relates, "The majority understood that his passivity was not that of a hero taking his ease but that of a cataclysm in repose." Explain what this suggests about the old man.

    _____

    _____

    _____

    _____

6. Compare and contrast the behavior of Pelayo and Elisenda, Father Gonzaga, and the townspeople to the behavior of the old man.

    _____

    _____

    _____

    _____

    _____

    _____

    _____

    _____

    _____

    _____

    _____

    _____

7. The priest suspects that the old man is an imposter because "he did not know the language of God" and "he was much too human." What could Marquez be saying about religious institutions and their need for "predictable holiness"?

    _____

    _____

    _____

    _____

    _____

8. The old man's wings were described from various perspectives throughout the story, sometimes with disgust, sometimes with fascination. Describe the different reactions to his wings, beginning with Pelayo and Elisenda to the doctor who treated the old man for chicken pox.

_____

_____

_____

_____

_____

_____

_____

_____

_____

9. Throughout the story the old man is seen as an annoyance; he is kept in a shed; he is an object of derision; he is ignored; he flies away—much to Elisenda's relief. Suggest different ways they could have treated the old man.

_____

_____

_____

_____

_____

_____

_____

_____

_____

Part Two

Identifying Assumptions and Worldview

The lively art of debate begins with at least two differing opinions: "I love spinach"; "Spinach tastes awful"; "That is a beautiful dress you're wearing"; "I really don't like that color on you." "Mr. Smith should be president of the United States"; "There is no way I would ever vote for Mr. Smith." In order to surmise how and why we hold differing opinions, we must ask some basic questions: Why do we hold the opinions that we do? What is the basis for truth? How do we distinguish between fact and opinion? From what presuppositions do we form our opinions and shape our views? What basic questions about God, the universe, humanity, and our world do we ask that form the foundation for our worldview?

A key element in this search for understanding "how we know" is distinguishing between fact and opinion. Some "laws" exist with little or no debate. If an apple falls from a tree, it falls down, not up, demonstrating the "law" of gravity. Rain can fall only from a sky that contains clouds, never from a clear, blue one. Without water, all living things will eventually die. These "laws" can be demonstrated by observation and experience. They are statements of fact, not opinion.

Dorothy Sayers in her book *The Mind of the Maker* asserts that there also exists "a universal moral law . . . which consists of certain statements of fact about the nature of man; and by behaving in conformity with which, man enjoys his true freedom." She believes that this law is "discoverable" and "it cannot be promulgated; it can only be ascertained because it is a question not of opinion but of fact." According to Sayers, the pronouncements found in Christianity about morality are "statements of fact about man and the moral universe, and upon which the whole moral code depends for its authority and its validity in practice. These statements do not rest on human consent; they are either true or false." Sayers accuses many people of mixing categories of fact and opinion regarding the creeds and the fundamental statements of Scripture that require obedience to moral law. Sayers illustrates the difference between fact and opinion by saying that a law requiring a chef to wear a top hat while cooking omelets is a law that would be "arbitrary and irrational"; on the other hand, a law stating the omelets cannot be prepared until the shell is broken is irrefutable. She concludes, "The Christian creeds are too frequently assumed to be in the top-hat category; this is an error; they belong to the category of egg-breaking." An assertion like the one Sayers makes becomes fundamental to the shaping of worldview and our perception of the reality that surrounds us.

Whether an individual perceives moral law as irrefutable and immutable or arbitrary and changeable colors how he or she perceives right and wrong, truth and falsehood; it influences the study of ethics and determines the pattern of one's life. This discussion brings us to the maxim that is central to the theme of this text: What we believe affects who we are and what we do. Belief shapes our essence and our conduct. Our belief system affects the way we view God, the way we treat others, and even the way we see ourselves. Just as the direction and destination of a train are determined by the switches on a track, so are an individual's presuppositions, one's epistemological framework, the guiding force behind belief and action. From this foundation arises the formation of worldview.

Every individual has a worldview, whether or not he or she acknowledges it. James Sire in his classic work *Discipleship of the Mind* defines worldview and lists seven fundamental questions that must be answered in order to *clearly* establish a worldview. How these questions are answered determines the course of individual thought and action. According to Sire, worldview is "a set of presuppositions (assumptions that may be true or entirely false) which we hold (consciously or subconsciously, consistently or inconsistently) about the makeup of the world." He continues, "A worldview is a set of *presuppositions,* that's a combination of fundamental commitments to the way we think things are." In other words, worldview is the way we *see* the world. It answers the following questions: (1) "What is prime reality—the really real?"; (2) "What is the nature of external reality, that is, the world around us?" (metaphysics); (3) "What is a human being?"; (4) "What happens to a person at death?"; (5) "Why is it possible to know anything at all?" In other words, How do we know? (epistemology); (6) "How do we know what is right and wrong?" (ethics); and (7) "What is the meaning of human history?"

The answers to these questions arise from basically three positions: naturalism, which postulates that everything arose from nothing and that the universe is all that exists; pantheism, which asserts that there is no distinction between God, the human being, and the universe; and theism, which maintains that the universe originated from God, that everything is held together by God, and that all things are working providentially for His purpose. Are these views equally valid, or does one answer the worldview questions more adequately? As James Sire observes, "What one does in the laboratory or library affects the worldview undergirding one's efforts." For this reason, it is essential that a valid way of examining the world be established. Having a valid worldview is like wearing properly fitting lenses. It puts everything in focus. According to Ronald Nash, author of *Worldviews in Conflict,* the validity of a worldview is determined by applying three tests: the test of reason, the test of experience, and the test of practice. Fundamentally, for the Christian, reason is not an enemy of faith; it is an ally.

The Christian responses to the questions noted above provide a legitimate foundation on which to discover and delineate all knowledge and truth. Because Christians view truth in relationship to the revelation of God and knowledge itself is a conduit of truth, a fruitful quest for epistemology must begin and end with God. (This statement in itself contains assumptions; what we must determine is whether or not these assumptions are the most legitimate way to view reality.) This search should become the cardinal principle for university education and the traditional academic disciplines as well as the shaping principle by which we choose to pattern our lives. These theological presuppositions thus provide the basis that should undergird all proper scholarship. Perhaps John Henry Cardinal Newman said it best in his book *The Idea of a University*: "All branches of knowledge are connected together because the subject matter of knowledge is intimately united in itself, as being the acts and the works of the Creator." Newman, and most Christians, would agree that if scientists and scholars truly understand the world, then they have discovered knowledge that emanates from God, whether or not they recognize this truth. Because this knowledge does indeed come from God and His creation, scientists and scholars can, as a result of their methodologies, know some things with certainty.

If knowledge cannot be known with certainty, then the act of knowing itself becomes suspect. A highly influential post-modern view questions whether reality can in fact be known or whether it is simply a cultural construct. C. S. Lewis logically demonstrates that a view that abrogates the ability of an individual to know something is in itself untenable. In his book *Miracles*, Lewis writes:

> It follows that no account of the universe can be true unless that account leaves it possible for our thinking to be a real insight. A theory which explained everything else in the whole universe but which made it impossible to believe that our thinking was valid, would be utterly out of court. For the theory would itself have been reached by thinkers, and if thinking is not valid that theory would, of course, be itself demolished. It would have destroyed its own credentials. It would be an argument which proved that no argument was sound—a proof that there are no such things as proofs—which is nonsense.

This section of *Encounters* is especially concerned with shaping our Christian perspectives. Exactly how does an individual think as a Christian? Many in the Church do not realize that much of what passes as authentic Christian thinking is actually secular reasoning sugarcoated with Christian jargon and moralism. Many of the authors in this chapter of *Encounters* claim that the Church by and large no longer knows how to think Christianly. This section seeks to recapture in some way that lost art and to establish a true Christian way of knowing, one that emerges from reason inexplicably intertwined with faith. If we truly think Christianly, then our minds will be transformed, enlightenment will come, and we will discover the joy and richness of Christian understanding and living.

We have chosen to accomplish this purpose largely by looking through the lenses of Christian thinkers although occasionally interspersed throughout the readings are works that view the world differently. These have been provided to contrast and complement the Christian way of seeing. By looking through the lenses of others, we often see our own world more clearly. Even so, before we look too long and too hard into other realms, we must make sure we understand our own. Thus, we embark on an expedition of discovery, seeking out our God-ordained vocation; seeing God in the art of men and women; traveling to worlds of wonder, places where the Unseen dwells; realizing that moments in the past become the map of the present and the blueprint of the future; and finding in nature the fingerprint of God, noting especially the responsibility of human beings toward creation.

Chapter 5

Values and Beliefs

*I*n what many call a "post-modern, post-Christian" world, all ideas vie for equal weight. At times it seems that the only ideas not acceptable are those that say that someone else is wrong. Tolerance is the buzz-word of the day, and anyone who has the audacity to assert that a certain action or conduct is wrong may be held in suspicion and contempt. This attitude is antithetical to Christianity which unequivocally states that there are clear demarcations between right and wrong and between truth and falsehood.

In "The Poison of Subjectivism," C. S. Lewis concurs with Dorothy L. Sayers that there exists "a universal moral law": "Until modern times no thinker of the first rank ever doubted that our judgments of value were rational judgments or that what they discovered was objective." The "whole attempt to jettison traditional values as something subjective and to substitute a new scheme of values for them," Lewis maintains, "is like trying to lift yourself by your own collar." He shows the folly of the human endeavor to create new values: "The human mind has no more power of inventing a new value than of planting a new sun in the sky or a new primary colour in the spectrum." Here Lewis shapes his argument to logically demonstrate the validity of his assumptions. He concludes, "If we returned to the objective view we should demand qualities much rarer, and much more beneficial—virtue, knowledge, diligence and skill. 'Vision' is for sale, or claims to be for sale, everywhere. But give me a man who will do a day's work for a day's pay, who will refuse bribes, who will not make up his facts, and who has learned his job."

Glenn Tinder in his clear, thorough, and insightful essay "Can We Be Good Without God" has also asserted truth claims regarding the morality of our present culture. While he acknowledges the influence of the Enlightenment thinkers such as Thomas Jefferson and John Locke as important to the foundation of democracy, he maintains that their ideas arose out of a Christian response toward society. Refusing to exalt capitalism and societal institutions, he demonstrates the dignity of all human beings as well as their fallenness. Inherent in this assertion is the acknowledgment that change is necessary in society as long as it is based on the assumption that destiny beckons to each human being confirming his soul and providing him or her with the utmost value. The Christian assertion about God and his relationship to humans and to goverment provide the basis for the formation of a just rule in the midst of a broken world.

A value-laden society advances according to the guidance of the immutable and omniscient God. In the face of finite evil, human beings confront the possibility of infinite good.

C. S. Lewis
The Poison of Subjectivism

C. S. Lewis (1898–1963) was born in Belfast, Northern Ireland. Raised Anglican, he became a professed atheist during his teenage years. Returning to Christianity in 1929, he chronicled this journey in his autobiography, *Surprised by Joy* (1955). At the time of his death, he was a professor of Medieval and Renaissance literature at Cambridge University. He is known for both his literary scholarship, as in *Preface to* Paradise Lost (1942), and his ability to explain (often with wit) Christian beliefs, such as in *The Great Divorce* (1945) and *The Problem of Pain* (1940). His writings also include the *Screwtape Letters* (1942), *The Chronicles of Narnia* series (1950–1956), and a space trilogy—*Out of the Silent Planet* (1938), *Perelandra* (1944), and *That Hideous Strength* (1946)—as well as a number of poems, essays, and other nonfiction books. In the essay below, first published in 1943, Lewis demonstrates how the subjective values promoted by modernists result in a nonsensical and meaningless way of viewing reality. He fleshes out this argument in more detail in his book *The Abolition of Man* (1947).

Vocabulary ....

contingency	peccadillo
disapprobation	platitudes
dyarchy	retrogressively
epiphenomenon	status quo
monomaniac	terminus
omnipotent	unanimity

One cause of misery and vice is always present with us in the greed and pride of men, but at certain periods in history this is greatly increased by the temporary prevalence of some false philosophy. Correct thinking will not make good men of bad ones; but a purely theoretical error may remove ordinary checks to evil and deprive good intentions of their natural support. An error of this sort is abroad at present. I am not referring to the Power philosophies of the Totalitarian states, but to something that goes deeper and spreads wider and which, indeed, has given these Power philosophies their golden opportunity. I am referring to Subjectivism.

After studying his environment man has begun to study himself. Up to that point, he had assumed his own reason and through it seen all other things. Now, his own reason has become the object: it is as if we took out our eyes to look at them. Thus studied, his own reason appears to him as the epiphenomenon which accompanies chemical or electrical events in a cortex which is itself the by-product of a blind evolutionary process. His own logic, hitherto the king whom events in all possible worlds must obey, becomes merely subjective. There is no reason for supposing that it yields truth.

As long as this dethronement refers only to the theoretical reason, it cannot be wholehearted. The scientist has to assume the validity of his own logic (in the stout old fashion of Plato or Spinoza) even in order to prove that it is merely subjective, and therefore he can only flirt with subjectivism. It is true that this flirtation sometimes goes pretty far. There are modern scientists, I am told, who have dropped the words *truth* and *reality* out of their vocabulary and who hold that the end of their work is not to know what is there but simply to get practical results. This is, no doubt, a bad symptom. But, in the main, subjectivism is such an uncomfortable yokefellow for research that the danger, in this quarter, is continually counteracted.

But when we turn to practical reason the ruinous effects are found operating in full force. By practical reason I mean our judgement of good and evil. If you are surprised that I include this under the heading of reason at all, let me remind you that your surprise is itself one result of the subjectivism I am discussing. Until modern times no thinker of the first rank ever doubted that our judgements of value were rational judgements or that what they discovered was objective. It was taken for granted that in temptation passion was opposed, not to some sentiment, but to reason. Thus Plato thought, thus Aristotle, thus Hooker, Butler and Doctor Johnson. The modern view is very different. It does not believe that value judgements are really judgements at all. They are sentiments, or complexes, or attitudes, produced in a community by the pressure of its environment and its traditions, and differing from one community to another. To say that a thing is good is merely to express our feeling about it; and our feeling about it is the feeling we have been socially conditioned to have.

But if this is so, then we might have been conditioned to feel otherwise. 'Perhaps', thinks the reformer or the educational expert, 'it would be better if we were. Let us improve our morality.' Out of this apparently innocent idea comes the disease that will certainly end our species (and, in my view, damn our souls) if it is not crushed; the fatal superstition that men can create values, that a community can choose its 'ideology' as men choose their clothes. Everyone is indignant when he hears the Germans define justice as that which is to the interest of the Third Reich. But it is not always remembered that this indignation is perfectly groundless if we ourselves regard morality as a subjective sentiment to be altered at will. Unless there is some objective standard of good, over-arching Germans, Japanese and ourselves alike whether any of us obey it or no, then of course the Germans are as competent to create their ideology as we are to create ours. If 'good' and 'better' are terms deriving their sole meaning from the ideology of each people, then of course ideologies themselves cannot be better or worse than one another. Unless the measuring rod is independent of the things measured, we can do no measuring. For the same reason it is useless to compare the moral ideas of one age with those of another: progress and decadence are alike meaningless words.

All this is so obvious that it amounts to an iden-

tical proposition. But how little it is now understood can be gauged from the procedure of the moral reformer who, after saying that 'good' means 'what we are conditioned to like' goes on cheerfully to consider whether it might be 'better' that we should be conditioned to like something else. What in Heaven's names does he mean by 'better'?

He usually has at the back of his mind the notion that if he throws over traditional judgement of value, he will find something else, something more 'real' or 'solid' on which to base a new scheme of values. He will say, for example, 'We must abandon irrational taboos and base our values on the good of the community'—as if the maxim 'Thou shalt promote the good of the community' were anything more than a polysyllabic variant of 'Do as you would be done by' which has itself no other basis than the old universal value judgement he claims to be rejecting. Or he will endeavour to base his values on biology and tell us that we must act thus and thus for the preservation of our species. Apparently he does not anticipate the question, 'Why should the species be preserved?' He takes it for granted that it should, because he is really relying on traditional judgements of value. If he were starting, as he pretends, with a clean slate, he could never reach this principle. Sometimes he tries to do so by falling back on 'instinct'. 'We have an instinct to preserve our species', he may say. But have we? And if we have, who told us that we must obey our instincts? And why should we obey this instinct in the teeth of many others which conflict with the preservation of the species? The reformer knows that some instincts are to be obeyed more than others only because he is judging instincts by a standard, and the standard is, once more, the traditional morality which he claims to be superseding. The instincts themselves obviously cannot furnish us with grounds for grading the instincts in a hierarchy. If you do not bring a knowledge of their comparative respectability *to* your study of them, you can never derive it *from* them.

This whole attempt to jettison traditional values as something subjective and to substitute a new scheme of values for them is wrong. It is like trying to lift yourself by your own coat collar. Let us get two propositions written into our minds with indelible ink.

1. The human mind has no more power of inventing a new value than of planting a new sun in the sky or a new primary colour in the spectrum.

2. Every attempt to do so consists in arbitrarily selecting some one maxim of traditional morality, isolating it from the rest, and erecting it into an *unum necessarium*.[1]

The second proposition will bear a little illustration. Ordinary morality tells us to honour our parents and cherish our children. By taking the second precept alone you construct a Futurist Ethic in which the claims of 'posterity' are the sole criterion. Ordinary morality tells us to keep promises and also to feed the hungry. By taking the second precept alone you get a Communist Ethic in which 'production', and distribution of the products to the people, are the sole criteria. Ordinary morality tells us, *ceteris paribus*,[2] to love our kindred and fellow-citizens more than strangers. By isolating this precept you can get either an Aristocratic Ethic with the claims of our class as sole criterion, or a Racialist Ethic where no claims but those of blood are acknowledged. These monomaniac systems are then used as a ground from which to attack traditional morality; but absurdly, since it is from traditional morality alone that they derive such semblance of validity as they possess. Starting from scratch, with no assumptions about value, we could reach none of them. If reverence for parents or promises is a mere subjective by-product of physical nature, so is reverence for race or posterity. The trunk to whose root the reformer would lay the axe is the only support of the particular branch he wishes to retain.

All idea of 'new' or 'scientific' or 'modern' moralities must therefore be dismissed as mere confusion of thought. We have only two alternatives. Either the maxims of traditional morality must be accepted as axioms of practical reason which neither admit nor require argument to support them and not to 'see' which is to have lost human status; or else there are no values at all, what we mistook for values being 'projections' of irrational emotions. It is perfectly futile, after having dismissed traditional morality with the question, 'Why should we obey it?' then to attempt the reintroduction of value at some later stage in our philosophy. Any value we reintroduce can be countered in just the same way. Every argument used to support it will be an attempt to derive from premises in the indicative mood a conclusion in the imperative. And this is impossible.

Against this view the modern mind has two lines of defence. The first claims that traditional morality is different in different times and places—in fact, that there is not one morality but a thousand. The second exclaims that to tie ourselves to an immutable moral code is to cut off all progress and acquiesce in 'stagnation'. Both are unsound.

Let us take the second one first. And let us strip it of the illegitimate emotional power it derives from the word 'stagnation' with its suggestion of puddles and mantled pools. If water stands too long it stinks. To infer thence that whatever stands long must be unwholesome is to be the victim of metaphor. Space does not stink because it has preserved its three dimensions from the beginning. The square on the hypotenuse has not gone mouldy by continuing to equal the sum of the squares on the other two sides. Love is not dishonoured by constancy, and when we wash our hands we are seeking stagnation and 'putting the clock back', artificially restoring our hands to the *status quo* in which they began the day and resisting the natural trend of events which would increase their dirtiness steadily from our birth to our death. For the emotive term 'stagnant' let us substitute the descriptive term 'permanent'. Does a permanent moral standard preclude progress? On the contrary, except on the supposition of a changeless standard, progress is impossible. If good is a fixed point, it is at least possible that we should get nearer and nearer to it; but if the terminus is as mobile as the train, how can the train progress towards it? Our ideas of the good may change, but they cannot change either for the better or the worse if there is no absolute and immutable good to which they can approximate or from which they can recede. We can go on getting a sum more and more nearly right only if the one perfectly right answer is 'stagnant'.

And yet it will be said, I have just admitted that our ideas of good may improve. How is this to be reconciled with the view that 'traditional morality' is a *depositum fidei*[3] which cannot be deserted? The answer can be understood if we compare a real moral advance with a mere innovation. From the Stoic and Confucian, 'Do not do to others what you would not like them to do to you'; to the Christian, 'Do as you would be done by' is a real advance. The morality of Nietzsche is a mere innovation. The first is an advance because no one who did not admit the validity of the old maxim could see reason for accepting the new one, and anyone who accepted the old would at once recognize the new as an extension of the same principle. If he rejected it, he would have to reject it as a superfluity, something that went too far, not as something simply heterogeneous from his own ideas of value. But the Nietzschean ethic can be accepted only if we are ready to scrap traditional morals as a mere error and then to put ourselves in a position where we can find no ground for any value judgements at all. It is the difference between a man who says to us: 'You like your vegetables moderately fresh; why not grow your own and have them perfectly fresh?' and a man who says, 'Throw away that loaf and try eating bricks and centipedes instead.' Real moral advances, in fine, are made *from within* the existing moral tradition and in the spirit of that tradition and can be understood only in the light of that tradition. The outsider who has rejected the tradition cannot judge them. He has, as Aristotle said, no *arche*,[4] no premises.

And what of the second modern objection—that the ethical standards of different cultures differ so widely that there is no common tradition at all? The answer is that this is a lie—a good, solid, resounding lie. If a man will go into a library and spend a few days with the *Encyclopedia of Religion and Ethics* he will soon discover the massive unanimity of the practical reason in man. From the Babylonian *Hymn to Samos*, from the Laws of Manu, the *Book of the Dead*, the Analects, the Stoics, the Platonists, from Australian aborigines and Redskins, he will collect the same triumphantly monotonous denunciations of oppression, murder, treachery and falsehood, the same injunctions of kindness to the aged, the young, and the weak, of almsgiving and impartiality and honesty. He may be a little surprised (I certainly was) to find that precepts of mercy are more frequent than precepts of justice; but he will no longer doubt that there is such a thing as the Law of Nature. There are, of course, differences. There are even blindnesses in particular cultures—just as there are savages who cannot count up to twenty. But the pretence that we are presented with a mere chaos—though no outline of universally accepted value shows through—is simply false and should be contradicted in season and out of season wherever it is met. Far from finding a chaos, we find exactly what we should expect if good is indeed something objective and reason the organ whereby it is apprehended—that is, a substantial agreement with considerable local differences of emphasis and, perhaps, no one code that includes everything.

The two grand methods of obscuring this agreement are these: First, you can concentrate on those divergences about sexual morality which most serious moralists regard as belonging to positive rather than to Natural Law, but which rouse strong emotions. Differences about the definition of incest or between polygamy and monogamy come under this head. (It is untrue to say that the Greeks thought sexual perversion innocent. The continual tittering of Plato is really more evidential than the stern prohibition of Aristotle. Men titter thus only about what they regard as, at least, a *peccadillo*: the jokes about drunkenness in *Pickwick*, far from proving that the nineteenth-century English thought it innocent, prove the reverse.

There is an enormous difference of *degree* between the Greek view of perversion and the Christian, but there is not opposition.) The second method is to treat as differences in the judgement of value what are really differences in belief about fact. Thus human sacrifice, or persecution of witches, are cited as evidence of a radically different morality. But the real difference lies elsewhere. We do not hunt witches because we disbelieve in their existence. We do not kill men to avert pestilence because we do not think pestilence can thus be averted. We do 'sacrifice' men in war, and we do hunt spies and traitors.

So far I have been considering the objections which unbelievers bring against the doctrine of objective value, or the Law of Nature. But in our days we must be prepared to meet objections from Christians too. 'Humanism' and 'liberalism' are coming to be used simply as terms of disapprobation, and both are likely to be so used of the position I am taking up. Behind them lurks a real theological problem. If we accept the primary platitudes of practical reason as the unquestioned premises of all action, are we thereby trusting our own reason so far that we ignore the Fall, and are we retrogressively turning our absolute allegiance away from a person to an abstraction?

As regards the Fall, I submit that the general tenor of scripture does not encourage us to believe that our knowledge of the Law has been depraved in the same degree as our power to fulfil it. He would be a brave man who claimed to realize the fallen condition of man more clearly than St. Paul. In that very chapter (Romans 7) where he asserts most strongly our inability to keep the moral law he also asserts most confidently that we perceive the Law's goodness and rejoice in it according to the inward man. Our righteousness may be filthy and ragged; but Christianity gives us no ground for holding that our perceptions of right are in the same condition. They may, no doubt, be impaired; but there is a difference between imperfect sight and blindness. A theology which goes about to represent our practical reason as radically unsound is heading for disaster. If we once admit that what God means by 'goodness' is sheerly different from what we judge to be good, there is no difference left between pure religion and devil worship.

The other objection is much more formidable. If we once grant that our practical reason is really reason and that its fundamental imperatives are as absolute and categorical as they claim to be, then unconditional allegiance to them is the duty of man. So is absolute allegiance to God. And these two allegiances must, somehow, be the same. But how is the relation between God and the moral law to be represented? To say that the moral law is God's law is no final solution. Are these things right because God commands them or does God command them because they are right? If the first, if good is to be *defined* as what God commands, then the goodness of God Himself is emptied of meaning and the commands of an omnipotent fiend would have the same claim on us as those of the 'righteous Lord'. If the second, then we seem to be admitting a cosmic dyarchy, or even making God Himself the mere executor of a law somehow external and antecedent to His own being. Both views are intolerable.

At this point we must remind ourselves that Christian theology does not believe God to be a person. It believes Him to be such that in Him a trinity of persons is consistent with a unity of Deity. In that sense it believes Him to be something very different from a person, just as a cube, in which six squares are consistent with unity of the body, is different from a square. (Flatlanders, attempting to imagine a cube, would either imagine the six squares coinciding, and thus destroy their distinctness, or else imagine them set out side by side, and thus destroy the unity. Our difficulties about the Trinity are of much the same kind.) It is therefore possible that the duality which seems to force itself upon us when we think, first, of our Father in Heaven, and, secondly, of the self-evident imperatives of the moral law, is not a mere error but a real (though inadequate and creaturely) perception of things that would necessarily be two in any mode of being which enters our experience, but which are not so divided in the absolute being of the superpersonal God. When we attempt to think of a person and a law, we are compelled to think of this person either as obeying the law or as making it. And when we think of Him as making it we are compelled to think of Him either as making it in conformity to some yet more ultimate pattern of goodness (in which case that pattern, and not He, would be supreme) or else as making it arbitrarily by a *sic volo, sic jubeo*[5] (in which case He would be neither good nor wise). But it is probably just here that our categories betray us. It would be idle, with our merely mortal resources, to attempt a positive correction of our categories—*ambulavi in mirabilibus supra me.*[6] But it might be permissible to lay down two negations: that God neither *obeys* nor *creates* the moral law. The good is uncreated; it never could have been otherwise; it has in it no shadow of contingency; it lies, as Plato said, on the other side of existence. It is the *Rita* of the Hindus by which the gods themselves are divine, the *Tao* of the Chinese from which all realities proceed. But we, favoured beyond the wisest pagans, know what lies beyond existence, what admits no contingency, what lends divinity to all else, what is the ground of all existence, is not simply a law but also a begetting love, a love begotten, and the love which, being between these two, is also imminent in all those who are caught up to share the unity of their self-caused life. God is not merely good, but goodness; goodness is not merely divine, but God.

These may seem fine-spun speculations: yet I believe that nothing short of this can save us. A Christianity which does not see moral and religious experience converging to meet at infinity, not at a negative infinity, but in the positive infinity of the living yet superpersonal God, has nothing, in the long run, to divide it from devil worship; and a philosophy which does not accept value as eternal and objective can lead us only to ruin. Nor is the matter of merely speculative importance. Many a popular 'planner' on a democratic platform, many a mild-eyed scientist in a democratic laboratory means, in the last resort, just what the Fascist means. He believes that 'good' means whatever men are conditioned to approve. He believes that it is the function of him and his kind to condition men; to create consciences by eugenics, psychological manipulation of infants, state education and mass propaganda. Because he is confused, he does not yet fully realize that those who create conscience cannot be subject to conscience themselves. But he must awake to the logic of his position sooner or later; and when he does, what barrier remains between us and the final division of the race into a few conditioners who stand themselves outside morality and the many conditioned in whom such morality as the experts choose is produced at the experts' pleasure? If 'good' means only the local ideology, how can those who invent the local ideology be guided by any idea of good themselves? The very idea of freedom presupposes some objective moral law which overarches rulers and ruled alike. Subjectivism about values is eternally incompatible with democracy. We and our rulers are of one kind only so long as we are subject to one law. But if there is no Law of Nature, the *ethos* of any society is the creation of its rulers, educators and conditioners; and every creator stands above and outside his own creation.

Unless we return to the crude and nursery-like belief in objective values, we perish. If we do, we may live, and such a return might have one minor advantage. If we believed in the absolute reality of elementary moral platitudes, we should value those who solicit our votes by other standards than have recently been in fashion. While we believe that good is something to be invented, we demand of our rulers such qualities as 'vision', 'dynamism', 'creativity', and the like. If we returned to the objective view we should demand qualities much rarer, and much more beneficial—virtue, knowledge, diligence and skill. 'Vision' is for sale, or claims to be for sale, everywhere. But give me a man who will do a day's work for a day's pay, who will refuse bribes, who will not make up his facts, and who has learned his job. ■

[handwritten: If only these qualities, Hitler, Trump]

Notes

[1] *unum necessarium*—(Latin) one necessary thing

[2] *ceteris paribus*—(Latin) other things being equal

[3] *depositum fidei*—(Latin) deposit of faith

[4] *arche*—(Greek) beginning point

[5] *sic volo, sic jubeo*—(Latin) so will, so order

[6] *ambulavi in mirabilibus supra me*—(Latin) I have walked in marvels beyond me.

Making Connections through Discussion and Writing

1. a. What, according to Lewis, is the modern view toward values?

   _____
   _____
   _____
   _____
   _____

   b. List the problems Lewis sees with this view.

   _____
   _____
   _____
   _____
   _____
   _____
   _____

2. a. Underline the two propositions Lewis presents as irrefutable—"written into our minds with indelible ink."

   b. What evidence does he give to support his arguments?

   _____
   _____
   _____
   _____
   _____
   _____

3. a. What does Lewis mean by objective values?

   _____
   _____
   _____
   _____

   b. Why does he consider objectivity rather than subjectivity the necessary foundation for values?

   _____
   _____
   _____
   _____

4. a.   What is Lewis' definition of "good"?

   _____

   _____

   b.   According to Lewis, how does one attain the good?

   _____

   _____

   _____

   _____

   c.   Why is the good necessary?

   _____

   _____

   _____

   _____

   d.   How does goodness relate to God?

   _____

   _____

   _____

   _____

5. Lewis writes, "Real moral advances, in fine, are made *from within* the existing moral tradition and in the spirit of that tradition and can be understood only in the light of that tradition."
   a.   Explain what he means by this statement.

   _____

   _____

   _____

   _____

   b.   Give at least one example that demonstrates its validity.

   _____

   _____

   _____

   _____

6. How does Lewis answer the charge that values must be subjective because they differ in various cultures?

   _____

   _____

   _____

   _____

   _____

7. Lewis writes, "Subjectivism about values is eternally incompatible with democracy." What is his defense of this statement?

_____

_____

_____

_____

Glenn Tinder

Can We Be Good without God?

Glenn Tinder (b. 1923) was a professor of political science at the University of Massachusetts in Boston. He is the author of several books, including *Community: Reflections on a Tragic Ideal* (1980) and *The Political Meaning of Christianity* (1989). In this book, Tinder states, "Christianity requires not a program but a posture called the prophetic stance." This prophetic stance necessitates Christian community's participating in contemporary political and social processes.

Vocabulary ....

acquiescing	indefeasible
alluring	iniquitous
banal	intimations
contravention	intrinsically
demoralization	matrix
dichotomy	maxim
efficacy	predisposition
egalitarianism	presumptuous
emphatically	profundity
enunciated	proletariat
epitomized	protagonists
equivocations	purveyors
expediency	Stoics
fallible	subversive
fascism	sybaritic
flagrant	transcendental
Hellenic	truncated
impetus	virulent
implausible	

We are so used to thinking of spirituality as withdrawal from the world and human affairs that it is hard to think of it as political. Spirituality is personal and private, we assume, while politics is public. But such a dichotomy drastically diminishes spirituality, construing it as a relationship to God without implications for one's relationship to the surrounding world. The God of Christian faith (I shall focus on Christianity, although the God of the New Testament is also the God of the Old Testament) created the world and is deeply engaged in the affairs of the world. The notion that we can be related to God and not to the world—that we can practice a spirituality that is not political—is in conflict with the Christian understanding of God.

And if spirituality is properly political, the converse also is true, however distant it may be from prevailing assumptions: politics is properly spiritual. The spirituality of politics was affirmed by Plato at the very beginnings of Western political philosophy and was a commonplace of medieval political thought. Only in modern times has it come to be taken for granted that politics is entirely secular. The inevitable result is the demoralization of politics. Politics loses its moral structure and purpose, and turns into an affair of group interest and personal ambition. Government comes to the aid of only the well organized and influential, and it is limited only where it is checked by countervailing forces. Politics ceases to be understood as a preeminently human activity and is left to those who find it profitable, pleasurable, or in some other way useful to themselves. Political action thus comes to be carried out purely for the sake of power and privilege.

It will be my purpose in this essay to try to connect the severed realms of the spiritual and the political. In view of the fervent secularism of many Americans today, some will assume this to be the opening salvo of a fundamentalist attack on "pluralism." Ironically, as I will argue, many of the undoubted virtues of pluralism—respect for the individual and a belief in the essential equality of all human beings, to cite just two—have strong roots in the union of the spiritual and the political achieved in the vision of Christianity. The question that secularists have to answer is whether these values can survive without these particular roots. In short, can we be good without God? Can we affirm the dignity and equality of individual persons—values we ordinarily regard as secular—without giving them transcendental backing? Today these values are honored more in the breach than in the observance; Manhattan Island alone, with its extremes of sybaritic wealth on the one hand and Calcuttan poverty[1] on the other, is testimony to how little equality really counts for in contemporary America. To renew these indispensable values, I shall argue, we must rediscover their primal spiritual grounds.

Many will disagree with my argument, and I cannot pretend there are no respectable reasons for doing so. Some may disagree, however, because of misunderstandings. A few words at the outset may help to prevent this. First, although I dwell on Christianity, I do not mean thus to slight Judaism or its contribution to Western values. It is arguable that every major value affirmed in Christianity originated with the ancient Hebrews. Jewish sensitivities on this matter are understandable. Christians sometimes speak as though unaware of the elemental facts that Jesus was a Jew, that he died before even the earliest parts of the New Testament were written, and that his scriptural matrix was not Paul's Letter to the Romans or the Gospel of John but the Old Testament. Christianity

diverged from Judaism in answering one question: Who was Jesus? For Christians, he was the anticipated Messiah, whereas for traditional Jews (Paul and the first Christians were of course also Jews), he was not. This divergence has given Christianity its own distinctive character, even though it remains in a sense a Jewish faith.

The most adamant opposition to my argument is likely to come from protagonists of secular reason—a cause represented pre-eminently by the Enlightenment[2]. Locke and Jefferson[3], it will be asserted, not Jesus and Paul, created our moral universe. Here I cannot be as disarming as I hope I was in the paragraph above, for underlying my argument is the conviction that Enlightenment rationalism is not nearly so constructive as is often supposed. Granted, it has sometimes played a constructive role. It has translated certain Christian values into secular terms and, in an age becoming increasingly secular, has given them political force. It is doubtful, however, that it could have created those values or that it can provide them with adequate metaphysical foundations. Hence if Christianity declines and dies in coming decades, our moral universe and also the relatively humane political universe that it supports will be in peril. But I recognize that if secular rationalism is far more dependent on Christianity than its protagonists realize, the converse also is in some sense true. The Enlightenment carried into action political ideals that Christians, in contravention of their own basic faith, often shamefully neglected or denied. Further, when I acknowledged that there are respectable grounds for disagreeing with my argument, I had secular rationalism particularly in mind. The foundations of political decency are an issue I wish to raise, not settle.

Christian Love

Love seems as distant as spirituality from politics, yet any discussion of the political meaning of Christianity must begin by considering (or at least making assumptions about) love. Love is for Christians the highest standard of human relationships, and therefore governs those relationships that make up politics. Not that political relationships are expected to exhibit pure love. But their place in the whole structure of human relationships can be understood only by using the measure that love provides.

The Christian concept of love requires attention not only because it underlies Christian political ideas but also because it is unique. Love as Christians understand it is distinctly different from

[handwritten top margin: You cannot judge salvation, but you can judge fruit.]

[handwritten left margin: Without God there'd be no agape]

[handwritten annotation: Agape — philia, eros, storgics]

what most people think of as love. In order to dramatize the Christian faith in an incarnate and crucified God, Paul spoke ironically of "the folly of what we preach," and it may be said that Christian love is as foolish as Christian faith. Marking its uniqueness, Christian love has a distinctive name, *agape*, which sets it apart from other kinds of love, such as *philia*, or friendship, and *eros*, or erotic passion. *[handwritten: All other loves need to be controlled by agape]*

When John wrote that "God so loved the world, that he gave his only Son," he illuminated the sacrificial character of divine love. This is the mark of *agape*. It is entirely selfless. If one could love others without judging them, asking anything of them, or thinking of one's own needs, one would meet the Christian standard. Obviously, no one can. Many of us can meet the requirements of friendship or erotic love, but *agape* is beyond us all. It is not a love toward which we are naturally inclined or for which we have natural capacities. Yet it is not something exclusively divine, like omnipotence, which human beings would be presumptuous to emulate. In fact, it is demanded of us. *Agape* is the core of Christian morality. Moreover, as we shall see, it is a source of political standards that are widely accepted and even widely, if imperfectly, realized.

The nature of *agape* stands out sharply against the background of ordinary social existence. The life of every society is a harsh process of mutual appraisal. People are ceaselessly judged and ranked, and they in turn ceaselessly judge and rank others. This is partly a necessity of social and political order; no groups whatever—clubs, corporations, universities, or nations—can survive without allocating responsibilities and powers with a degree of realism. It is partly also a struggle for self-esteem; we judge ourselves for the most part as others judge us. Hence outer and inner pressures alike impel us to enter the struggle.

The process is harsh because all of us are vulnerable. All of us manifest deficiencies of natural endowment—of intelligence, temperament, appearance, and so forth. And all personal lives reveal moral deficiencies as well—blamable failures in the past, and vanity, greed, and other such qualities in the present. The process is harsh also because it is unjust. Not only are those who are judged always imperfect and vulnerable, but the judges are imperfect too. They are always fallible and often cruel. Thus few are rated exactly, or even approximately, as they deserve.

There is no judgment so final nor rank so high that one can finally attain security. Many are ranked high; they are regarded as able, or wise, or courageous. But such appraisals are never unanimous or stable. A few reach summits of power and honor where it seems for a moment that their victory is definitive. It transpires, however, that they are more fully exposed to judgment than anyone else, and often they have to endure torrents of derision.

[handwritten right margin: Discernment is distinct from Judgement]

Agape means refusing to take part in this process. It lifts the one who is loved above the level of reality on which a human being can be equated with a set of observable characteristics. The *agape* of God, according to Christian faith, does this with redemptive power; God "crucifies" the observable, and always deficient, individual, and "raises up" that individual to new life. The *agape* of human beings bestows new life in turn by accepting the work of God.

The power of *agape* extends in two directions. Not only is the one who is loved exalted but so is the one who loves. To lift someone else above the process of mutual scrutiny is to stand above that process oneself. To act on the faith that every human being is a beneficiary of the honor that only God can bestow is to place oneself in a position to receive that honor. (That is not the aim, of course; if it were, *agape* would be a way of serving oneself and would thus be nullified.) *Agape* raises all those touched by it into the community brought by Christ, the Kingdom of God. Everyone is glorified. No one is judged and no one judges.

[handwritten right margin: Woman in Adultery: God only can judge, yet Jesus made it clear to sin no more.]

Here we come to the major premise (in the logic of faith, if not invariably in the history of Western political philosophy) of all Christian social and political thinking—the concept of the exalted individual. Arising from *agape*, this concept more authoritatively than any other shapes not only Christian perceptions of social reality but also Christian delineations of political goals.

The Exalted Individual

To grasp fully the idea of the exalted individual is not easy, but this is not because it rests on a technical or complex theory. The difficulty of grasping the concept is due to its being beyond the whole realm of theory. It refers to something intrinsically mysterious, a reality that one cannot see by having someone else point to it or describe it. It is often spoken of, but the words we use—"the dignity of the individual," "the infinite value of a human being," and so forth—have become banal and no longer evoke the mystery that called them forth. Hence we must try to understand what such phrases mean. In what way, from a Christian standpoint, are individuals exalted? In trying to answer this question, the concept of destiny may provide some help.

In the act of creation God grants a human being glory, or participation in the goodness of all that has been created. The glory of a human being, however, is not like that of a star or a mountain. It is not objectively established but must be freely affirmed by the one to whom it belongs. In this sense the glory of a human being is placed in the future. It is not a mere possibility, however, nor does it seem quite sufficient to say that it is a moral norm. It is a fundamental imperative, even though all of us, in our sinfulness, to some degree refuse it. This fusion of human freedom and divine necessity may be summarily characterized by saying that the glory of an individual, rather than being immediately given, is destined.

Destiny is not the same as fate. The word refers not to anything terrible or even to anything inevitable, in the usual sense of the word, but to the temporal and free unfoldment of a person's essential being. A destiny is a spiritual drama.

A destiny is never completely fulfilled in time, in the Christian vision, but leads onto the plane of eternity. It must be worked out in time, however, and everything that happens to a person in time enters into eternal self-hood and is there given meaning and justification. My destiny is what has often been referred to as my soul.

Realizing a destiny is not a matter of acquiescing in some form of relentless causality. If it were, there would be no sin. A destiny can be failed or refused. That is why it is not a fate. True, the very word "destiny" is indicative of necessity, but the necessity of a destiny is not like the necessity that makes an object fall when it is dropped. Rather, it is the kind I recognize when I face a duty I am tempted to evade and say to myself, "This I *must* do." Yet my destiny has a weight unlike that of any particular duty, since it is the life given to me by God. As is recognized in words like "salvation" and "damnation," the call of destiny has a peculiar finality.

The *agape* of God consists in the bestowal of a destiny, and that of human beings in its recognition through faith. Since a destiny is not a matter of empirical observation, a person with a destiny is, so to speak, invisible. But every person has a destiny. Hence the process of mutual scrutiny is in vain, and even the most objective judgments of other people are fundamentally false. *Agape* arises from a realization of this and is therefore expressed in a refusal to judge.

The Lord of all time and existence has taken a personal interest in every human being, an interest that is compassionate and unwearying. The Christian universe is peopled exclusively with royalty. What does this mean for society?

To speak cautiously, the concept of the exalted individual implies that governments—indeed, all persons who wield power—must treat individuals with care. This can mean various things—for example, that individuals are to be fed and sheltered when they are destitute, listened to when they speak, or merely left alone so long as they do not break the law and fairly tried if they do. But however variously care may be defined, it always means that human beings are not to be treated like the things we use and discard or just leave lying about. They deserve attention. This spare standard has of course been frequently and grossly violated by people who call themselves Christians. It has not been without force, however. Even in our own secularized times people who are useless or burdensome, hopelessly ill or guilty of terrible crimes, are sometimes treated with extraordinary consideration and patience.

The modest standard of care implies other, more demanding standards. Equality is one of these; *no one* is to be casually sacrificed. No natural, social, or even moral differences justify exceptions to this rule. Of course destinies make people not equal but, rather, incomparable; equality is a measurement and dignity is immeasurable. But according to Christian claims, every person has been immeasurably dignified. Faith discerns no grounds for making distinctions, and the distinctions made by custom and ambition are precarious before God. "Many that are first will be last, and the last first." Not only love but humility as well—the humility of not anticipating the judgments of God—impels us toward the standard of equality.

No one, then, belongs at the bottom, enslaved, irremediably poor, consigned to silence; this is equality. This points to another standard: that no one should be left outside, an alien and a barbarian. *Agape* implies universality. Greeks and Hebrews in ancient times were often candidly contemptuous of most of the human race. Even Jesus, although not contemptuous of Gentiles, conceived of his mission as primarily to Israel. However, Jesus no doubt saw the saving of Israel as the saving of all humankind, and his implicit universalism became explicit, and decisive for the history of the world, in the writings and missionary activity of Paul. Christian universalism (as well as Christian egalitarianism) was powerfully expressed by Paul when he wrote that "there is neither Jew nor Greek, there is neither slave nor free, there is neither male nor female; for you are all one in Christ Jesus."

Christian universalism was reinforced by the universalism of the later Stoics, who created the ideal of an all-embracing city of reason—*cosmopolis*. Medieval Christians couched their universalist outlook in Hellenic terms. Thus two streams of thought, from Israel and Greece, flowed together. As a result the world today, although divided among nations often ferociously self-righteous and jealous, is haunted by the vision of a global community. War and national rivalry seem unavoidable, but they burden the human conscience. Searing poverty prevails in much of the world, as it always has, but no longer is it unthinkingly accepted in either the rich nations or the poor. There is a shadowy but widespread awareness, which Christianity has had much to do with creating, that one person cannot be indifferent to the destiny of another person anywhere on earth. It is hardly too much to say that the idea of the exalted individual is the spiritual center of Western politics. Although this idea is often forgotten and betrayed, were it erased from our minds our politics would probably become altogether what it is at present only in part—an affair of expediency and self-interest.

The exalted individual is not an exclusively Christian principle. There are two ways in which, without making any religious assumptions, we may sense the infinite worth of an individual. One way is love. Through personal love, or through the sympathy by which personal love is extended (although at the same time weakened), we sense the measureless worth of a few, and are able to surmise that what we sense in a few may be present in all. In short, to love some (it is, as Dostoevsky[4] suggested, humanly impossible to love everyone) may give rise to the idea that all are worthy of love. Further, the idea of the exalted individual may become a secular value through reason, as it did for the Stoics. Reason tells me that each person is one and not more than one. Hence my claims upon others are rightfully matched by their claims upon me. Simple fairness, which even a child can understand, is implicitly egalitarian and universal; and it is reasonable.

Can love and reason, though, undergird our politics if faith suffers a further decline? That is doubtful. Love and reason are suggestive, but they lack definite political implications. Greeks of the Periclean Age[5], living at the summit of the most brilliant period of Western civilization, showed little consciousness of the notion that every individual bears an indefeasible and incomparable dignity. Today why should those who assume that God is dead entertain such a notion? This question is particularly compelling in view of a human characteristic very unlike exaltation.

The Fallen Individual

The fallen individual is not someone other than the exalted individual. Every human being is fallen and exalted both. This paradox is familiar to all informed Christians. Yet it is continually forgotten—partly, perhaps, because it so greatly complicates the task of dealing with evil in the world, and no doubt partly because we hate to apply it to ourselves; although glad to recall our exaltation, we are reluctant to remember our fallenness. It is vital to political understanding, however, to do both. If the concept of the exalted individual defines the highest value under God, the concept of the fallen individual defines the situation in which that value must be sought and defended.

The principle that a human being is sacred yet morally degraded is hard for common sense to grasp. It is apparent to most of us that some people are morally degraded. It is ordinarily assumed, however, that other people are morally upright and that these alone possess dignity. From this point of view all is simple and logical. The human race is divided roughly between good people, who possess the infinite worth we attribute to individuals, and bad people, who do not. The basic problem of life is for the good people to gain supremacy over, and perhaps eradicate, the bad people. This view appears in varied forms: in Marxism[6], where the human race is divided between a world-redeeming class and a class that is exploitative and condemned; in some expressions of American nationalism, where the division—at least, until recently—has been between "the free world" and demonic communism; in Western films, where virtuous heroes kill bandits and lawless Indians.

This common model of life's meaning is drastically irreligious, because it places reliance on good human beings and not on God. It has no room for the double insight that the evil are not beyond the reach of divine mercy nor the good beyond the need for it. It is thus antithetical to Christianity, which maintains that human beings are justified by God alone, and that all are sacred and none are good.

The proposition that none are good does not mean merely that none are perfect. It means that all are persistently and deeply inclined toward evil. All are sinful. In a few sin is so effectively suppressed that it seems to have been destroyed. But this is owing to God's grace, Christian principles imply, not to human goodness, and those in whom it has happened testify emphatically that this is so. Saints claim little credit for themselves.

Nothing in Christian doctrine so offends people today as the stress on sin. It is morbid and self-destructive, supposedly, to depreciate ourselves in this way. Yet the Christian view is not implausible. The twentieth century, not to speak of earlier ages (often assumed to be more barbaric), has displayed human evil in extravagant forms. Wars and massacres, systematic torture and internment in concentration camps, have become everyday occurrences in the decades since 1914. Even in the most civilized societies subtle forms of callousness and cruelty prevail through capitalist and bureaucratic institutions. Thus our own experience indicates that we should not casually dismiss the Christian concept of sin.

According to that concept, the inclination toward evil is primarily an inclination to exalt ourselves rather than allowing ourselves to be exalted by God. We exalt ourselves in a variety of ways: for example, by power, trying to control all the things and people around us; by greed, accumulating an inequitable portion of the material goods of the world; by self righteousness, claiming to be wholly virtuous; and so forth. Self-exaltation is carried out sometimes by individuals, sometimes by groups. It is often referred to, in all of its various forms, as "pride."

The Christian concept of sin is not adequately described, however, merely by saying that people frequently engage in evil actions. Our predisposition toward such actions is so powerful and so unyielding that it holds us captive. As Paul said, "I do not do what I want, but I do the very thing I hate." This does not imply, of course, that I am entirely depraved. If I disapprove of my evil acts, then I am partly good. However, if I persist in evil in the face of my own disapproval, then I am not only partly evil but also incapable of destroying the evil in my nature and enthroning the good. I am, that is to say, a prisoner of evil, even if I am not wholly evil.

This imprisonment is sometimes called "original sin," and the phrase is useful, not because one must take the story of Adam's disobedience literally but because it points to the mysterious truth that our captivity by evil originates in a primal and iniquitous choice on the part of every person. I persistently fail to attain goodness because I have turned away from goodness and set my face toward evil.

The political value of the doctrine of original sin lies in its recognition that our evil tendencies are not in the nature of a problem that we can rationally comprehend and deliberately solve. To say that the source of sin is sin is to say that sin is underivable and inexplicable. A sinful society is not like a malfunctioning machine, something to be checked and quickly repaired.

Sin is ironic. Its intention is self-exaltation, its result is self-debasement. In trying to ascend, we fall. The reason for this is not hard to understand. We are exalted by God; in declaring our independence from God, we cast ourselves down. In other words, sin concerns not just our actions and our nature but also the setting of our lives. By sin we cast ourselves into a degraded sphere of existence, a sphere Christians often call "the world." Human beings belong to the world through sin. They look at one another as objects; they manipulate, mutilate, and kill one another. In diverse ways, some subtle and some shocking, some relatively innocuous and some devastating, they continually depersonalize themselves and others. They behave as inhabitants of the world they have sinfully formed rather than of the earth created by God. Original sin is the quiet determination, deep in everyone, to stay inside the world. Every sinful act is a violation of the personal being that continually, in freedom, vision, and love, threatens the world. The archetype of sin is the reduction of a person to the thing we call a corpse.

The Man-god Versus the God-man

When the paradox of simultaneous exaltation and fallenness collapses, it is either cynicism or (to use a term that is accurate but masks the destructive character of the attitude it refers to) idealism.

Cynicism measures the value of human beings by their manifest qualities and thus esteems them very slightly. It concludes, in effect, that individuals are not exalted, because they are fallen. Idealism refuses this conclusion. It insists that the value of human beings, or of some of them, is very great. It is not so simplistic, however, as to deny the incongruity of their essential value and their manifest qualities. Rather, it asserts that this incongruity can be resolved by human beings on their own, perhaps through political revolution or psychotherapy. Human beings can exalt themselves.

We shall dwell in this discussion on idealism, partly because idealism is much more tempting and therefore much more common than cynicism. Idealism is exhilarating, whereas cynicism, as anything more than a youthful experiment, is grim and discouraging. We shall dwell on idealism also because it is so much more dangerous than it looks. The dangers of cynicism are evident; that a general contempt for human beings is apt to be socially and politically destructive scarcely needs to be argued. But idealism looks benign. It is important to understand why its appearance is misleading.

Idealism in our time is commonly a form of collective pride. Human beings exalt themselves by exalting a group. Each one of course exalts the singular and separate self in some manner. In most people, however, personal pride needs reinforcement through a common ideal or emotion, such as nationalism. Hence the rise of collective pride. To exalt ourselves, we exalt a nation, a class, or even the whole of humanity in some particular manifestation like science. Such pride is alluring. It assumes grandiose and enthralling proportions yet it seems selfless, because not one person alone but a class or nation or some other collectivity is exalted. It can be at once more extreme and less offensive than personal pride.

To represent the uncompromising and worldly character of modern idealism we may appropriately use the image of the man-god. This image is a reversal of the Christian concept of the God-man, Christ. The order of the terms obviously is crucial. In the case of the God-man, it indicates the source of Christ's divinity as understood in Christian faith. God took the initiative. To reverse the order of the terms and affirm the man-god is to say that human beings become divine on their own initiative. Here pride reaches its most extreme development. The dignity bestowed on human beings by God, in Christian faith, is now claimed as a quality that human beings can acquire through their own self-creating acts.

In using the concept of the man-god, I do not mean to suggest that divinity is explicitly attributed to certain human beings. Even propagandists, to say nothing of philosophers, are more subtle than that. What happens is simply that qualities traditionally attributed to God are shifted to a human group or type. The qualities thus assigned are various—perfect understanding, perhaps, or unfailing fairness. Illustrative are the views of three great intellectual figures, familiar to everyone, yet so diversely interpreted that the fundamental character of their thought—and their deep similarity—is sometimes forgotten.

Friedrich Nietzsche[7] set forth the ideal of the man-god more literally and dramatically than any other writer. Nietzsche's thinking was grounded in a bitter repudiation of Christianity, and he devoted much of his life to scouring human consciousness in order to cleanse it of every Christian idea and emotion. In this way his philosophy became a comprehensive critique of Western civilization, as well as a foreshadowing of an alternative civilization. It is, as practically everyone now recognizes, remarkable in its range, subtlety, and complexity; Nietzsche is not easily classified or epitomized. It can nevertheless be argued that the dramatic center of his lifework lay in the effort to overthrow the standard of Christian love and to wipe out the idea that every human being deserves respect— leading Nietzsche to attack such norms in the field of politics as equality and democracy. If Christian faith is spurned, Nietzsche held, with the courage that was one of the sources of his philosophical greatness, then Christian morality must also be spurned. *Agape* has no rightful claim on our allegiance. And not only does *agape* lack all moral authority but it has a destructive effect on society and culture. It inhibits the rise of superior human beings to the heights of glory, which, we realize at last, are not inhabited by God. By exalting the common person, who is entirely lacking in visible distinction and glory, *agape* subverts the true order of civilization. The divine quality that Nietzsche claimed for humanity was power—the power not only of great political leaders like Julius Caesar and Napoleon but also of philosophers, writers, and artists, who impose intricate and original forms of order on chaotic material. Such power, in the nature of things, can belong only to a few. These few are human gods. Their intrinsic splendor overcomes the absurdity that erupted with the death of the Christian God, and justifies human existence.

Karl Marx is perhaps not only as well known among Christian intellectuals as even the most celebrated theologians but also as influential. The familiar saying "We are all Marxists now" dramatizes the fact that Marx's views on such matters as class and capitalism are part of the furniture of the modern mind. Christian writers are not exceptions; spontaneously they think in some measure in Marxist terms. A considerable number of them can even be called Marxist Christians—an appellation fully justified in the case of most liberation theologians. Marx has in that sense become a familiar member of the Christian household. When he is thus domesticated, however, we tend to forget what he really thought. We may forget that he was as apocalyptically secular and humanistic as Nietzsche, even though he disdained the kind of elevated and poetic rhetoric that abounds in Nietzsche's writings. He called for the entire transformation of human life by human beings, and this, in Marx's mind, included the transformation of nature. The universe was to become radically—in its roots, in its sources and standards—human. True, like the Christians he scorned, and unlike

Nietzsche, Marx was egalitarian. The transformation of humanity and being was envisioned as the work of multitudes, the proletariat, and not of exceptional individuals, and ahead lay justice and community rather than glorious solitude, as in Nietzsche. Nevertheless, Marx tacitly claimed for the proletariat qualities much like those attributed in the Old Testament to God—omniscience, righteousness, and historical sovereignty, all devoted to avenging past wrongs and transfiguring human existence.

Sigmund Freud,[8] of course, avoided both the rhetoric of redemption and the thought; he regarded any great change in the character of human beings or the conditions of human life as unlikely, and by intention was a scientist, not a prophet or a revolutionary. He belongs among the heralds of the man-god, however, because of the conviction that underlay all his psychological investigations. Disorders of the soul, which for Christians derive in one way or another from sin, and hence in their ultimate origins are mysterious, Freud believed to be scientifically explicable. From this conviction it followed that the healing work Christians believe to be dependent on divine grace Freud could assign altogether to human therapy. The soul was thus severed from God (for Freud, a childish illusion) and placed in the province of human understanding and action. Not that psychoanalysis and Christianity are in all ways mutually exclusive; the many Christians who have learned from Freud testify to the contrary. But for Freud and his major followers, psychoanalysis is a comprehensive faith, not merely a set of useful hypotheses and techniques. As a faith, it attributes to humanity alone powers and responsibilities that Christians regard as divine. Human beings are exalted by virtue of purely human faculties. Freud's attitude of resignation was a matter mainly of temperament; his methods, theories, and basic assumptions have reinforced the efforts of human beings to seize the universal sovereignty that Christians assign exclusively to God.

Nietzsche, Marx, and Freud represent a movement by no means restricted to those who consciously follow any one of them or even to those familiar with their writings. Not only are we "all Marxists now"; it could be said with nearly equal justification that we are all Nietzscheans and Freudians. Most of us have come to assume that we ourselves are the authors of human destiny. The term "man-god" may seem extreme, but I believe that our situation is extreme. Christianity poses sweeping alternatives—destiny and fate, redemption and eternal loss, the Kingdom of God and the void of Hell. From centuries of Christian culture and education we have come habitually to think of life as structured by such extremes. Hence Christian faith may fade, but we still want to live a destiny rather than a mere life, to transform the conditions of human existence and not merely to effect improvements, to establish a perfect community and not simply a better society. Losing faith in the God-man, we inevitably begin to dream of the man-god, even though we often think of the object of our new faith as something impersonal and innocuous, like science, thus concealing from ourselves the radical nature of our dreams.

Political Idolatry

The political repercussions are profound. Most important is that all logical grounds for attributing an ultimate and immeasurable dignity to every person, regardless of outward character, disappear. Some people may gain dignity from their achievements in art, literature, or politics, but the notion that all people without exception—the most base, the most destructive, the most repellent—have equal claims on our respect becomes as absurd as would be the claim that all automobiles or all horses are of equal excellence. The standard of *agape* collapses. It becomes explicable only on Nietzsche's terms: as a device by which the weak and failing exact from the strong and distinguished a deference they do not deserve. Thus the spiritual center of Western politics fades and vanishes. If the principle of personal dignity disappears, the kind of political order we are used to—one structured by standards such as liberty for all human beings and equality under the law—becomes indefensible.

Nietzsche's stature is owing to the courage and profundity that enabled him to make this all unmistakably clear. He delineated with overpowering eloquence the consequences of giving up Christianity, and every like view of the universe and humanity. His approval of those consequences and his hatred of Christianity give force to his argument. Many would like to think that there are no consequences—that we can continue treasuring the life and welfare, the civil rights and political authority, of every person without believing in a God who renders such attitudes and conduct compelling. Nietzsche shows that we cannot. We cannot give up the Christian God—and the transcendence given other names in other faiths—and go on as before. We must give up Christian morality too. If the God-man is nothing more than an illusion, the same thing is true of the idea that every individual possesses incalculable worth.

It is true, as we have seen, that love and reason provide intimations of such worth—but intimations alone; they provide little basis for overruling the conclusions of our senses. The denial of the God-man and of God's merciful love of sinful humanity is a denial of destiny, and without destiny there is simply life. But life calls forth respect only in proportion to its intensity and quality. Except in the case of infants and children, we ordinarily look on those lacking in purposeful vitality with pity or disgust. Respect we spontaneously reserve for the strong and creative. If it is life we prize, then institutions that protect and care for people whose lives are faltering are worse than senseless. It is hard to think of anyone else, with the single exception of Dostoevsky, who has understood all of this as profoundly as did Nietzsche.

Marx certainly did not. His mind was on matters of a different kind, matters less philosophical. The result was an illogical humanitarianism. Marx was incensed by the squalor in which the common people of his time were forced to live and by the harsh conditions and endless hours of their work. Marx sympathized deeply with the downtrodden and disinherited. But this expressed his personal qualities, not his philosophy or faith. His philosophy was a materialism that can be interpreted in differing ways but that implied, at the very least, that reality was not created by and is not governed by God; his faith was in science and human will. He provided no philosophical or religious grounds whatever for the idea that every person must be treated with care. In spite of Marx's humanitarianism, therefore, there is a link between Marxist thought and the despotic regimes that have ruled in his name. It is perfectly true, as his defenders aver, that Marx adhered to political principles quite unlike those manifest in the purges and prison camps of the Soviet Union. That such practices should claim the authority of his name is thus outrageous in a sense. Nonetheless, the connection between Marx himself and modern Marxist despots is not entirely accidental. They share the principle that a single individual does not necessarily matter.

If the denial of the God-man has destructive logical implications, it also has dangerous emotional consequences. Dostoevsky wrote that a person "cannot live without worshipping something." Anyone who denies God must worship an idol—which is not necessarily a wooden or metal figure. In our time we have seen ideologies, groups, and leaders receive divine honors. People proud of their critical and discerning spirit have rejected Christ and bowed down before Hitler, Stalin, Mao, or some other secular savior.

When disrespect for individuals is combined with political idolatry, the results can be atrocious. Both the logical and the emotional foundations of political decency are destroyed. Equality becomes nonsensical and breaks down under attack from one or another human god. Consider Lenin: as a Marxist, and like Marx an exponent of equality, under the pressures of revolution he denied equality in principle—except as an ultimate goal—and so systematically nullified it in practice as to become the founder of modern totalitarianism. When equality falls, universality is likely also to fall. Nationalism or some other form of collective pride becomes virulent, and war unrestrained. Liberty, too, is likely to vanish; it becomes a heavy personal and social burden when no God justifies and sanctifies the individual in spite of all personal deficiencies and failures.

The idealism of the man-god does not, of course, bring as an immediate and obvious consequence a collapse into unrestrained nihilism. We all know many people who do not believe in God and yet are decent and admirable. Western societies, as highly secularized as they are, retain many humane features. Not even tacitly has our sole governing maxim become the one Dostoevsky thought was bound to follow the denial of the God-man: "Everything is permitted." *If you do away with God*

This may be, however, because customs and habits formed during Christian ages keep people from professing and acting on such a maxim even though it would be logical for them to do so. If that is the case, our position is precarious, for good customs and habits need spiritual grounds, and if those are lacking, they will gradually, or perhaps suddenly in some crisis, crumble.

To what extent are we now living on moral savings accumulated over many centuries but no longer being replenished? To what extent are those savings already severely depleted? Again and again we are told by advertisers, counselors, and other purveyors of popular wisdom that we have a right to buy the things we want and to live as we please. We should be prudent and farsighted, perhaps (although even those modest virtues are not greatly emphasized), but we are subject ultimately to no standard but self-interest. If nihilism[9] is most obvious in the lives of wanton destroyers like Hitler, it is nevertheless present also in the lives of people who live purely as pleasure and convenience dictate.

And aside from intentions, there is a question concerning consequences. Even idealists whose good intentions for the human race are pure and strong are still vulnerable to fate because of the pride that causes them to act ambitiously and recklessly in history. Initiating chains of unforeseen and destructive consequences, they are often overwhelmed by results drastically at variance with their humane intentions. Modern revolutionaries have willed liberty and equality for everyone, not the terror and despotism they have actually created. Social reformers in the United States were never aiming at the great federal bureaucracy or at the pervasive dedication to entertainment and pleasure that characterizes the welfare state they brought into existence. There must always be a gap between intentions and results, but for those who forget that they are finite and morally flawed the gap may become a chasm. Not only Christians but almost everyone today feels the fear that we live under the sway of forces that we have set in motion—perhaps in the very process of industrialization, perhaps only at certain stages of that process, as in the creation of nuclear power—and that threaten our lives and are beyond our control.

There is much room for argument about these matters. But there is no greater error in the modern mind than the assumption that the God-man can be repudiated with impunity. The man-god may take his place and become the author of deeds wholly unintended and the victim of terrors starkly in contrast with the benign intentions lying at their source. The irony of sin is in this way reproduced in the irony of idealism: exalting human beings in their supposed virtues and powers, idealism undermines them. Exciting fervent expectations, it leads toward despair.

Ideology and Ambiguity

Practically everyone today agrees that "being good," in a political sense, depends on recognizing the measureless worth of the human being. When this recognition is translated into ideological terms, such as liberalism and conservatism, however, agreement vanishes. The main moral assumption underlying the discussion above becomes controversial. Nevertheless, we have to ask what the ideological implications of Christianity are, for this is simply to inquire about the practical meaning of the ideas that we have been discussing and thus to carry the argument to its logical conclusion.

In asking about ideology, however, we immediately encounter something that seemingly undermines any ideological commitment. This is an implicit political ambiguity. This ambiguity is deeply rooted in Christian principles, and must at the outset be taken into account.

In the Christian view, while every individual is exalted, society is not. On the contrary, every society is placed in question, for a society is a mere worldly order and a mere human creation and can never do justice to the glory of the human beings within it. The exaltation of the individual reveals the baseness of society. It follows that our political obligations are indeterminate and equivocal. If we recognize what God has done—so Christian principles imply—we shall be limitlessly respectful of human beings but wary of society. Yet human beings live in society, and we meet them there or not at all. Hence we cannot stand wholly apart from society without failing in our responsibilities to the human beings whom God has exalted. So far as we are responsive to God, we must live within human kingdoms as creatures destined to be fellow citizens in God's Kingdom. This obligation gives rise to a political stance that is ambiguous and, in a world of devastatingly unambiguous ideologies, unique: humane and engaged, but also hesitant and critical.

Christianity implies skepticism concerning political ideals and plans. For Christianity to be wedded indissolubly to any of them (as it often has been, "Christian socialism" and Christian celebrations of "the spirit of democratic capitalism" being examples) is idolatrous and thus subversive of Christian faith.

Trying to take into account both the profound evil in human nature and the immense hope in the human situation, as Christians must, leads inevitably to what reformers and radicals—particularly those of the Third World, surrounded as they are by impoverished multitudes—are apt to regard as fatal equivocations. It leads, as I have already indicated, to a critical spirit and to qualified commitments. It would be easy to charge that such a posture reflects the self-interest and complacency of those who do not suffer from the injustice characterizing existing structures. Equivocation, it may be said, is one of the luxuries of bourgeois life in the industrial world.

Still, a Christian in the United States, without being particularly discerning or morally sensitive, can see at least two things not so clearly visible to Third World Christian writers, particularly those liberation theologians who long for immediate social transformation. One of these is the universal disaster of revolution. There is perhaps not a single example in our time of a determined effort to produce swift and sweeping change which has not ended in tyranny; such efforts have often also ended in abominations, such as those witnessed in recent times in Cambodia, incalculably worse than those perpetrated by the old social order.

(2) The second thing a Christian in a prosperous industrial nation can see is visible because it is near at hand: that life can be culturally vulgar, morally degraded, and spiritually vacuous even under conditions of substantial justice. Not that justice has been fully achieved in the United States. But it has been approximated closely enough for us to begin to gauge its significance. We can begin to see that justice does not necessarily mean an entirely good society. The great masses of people in the United States enjoy historically unprecedented prosperity, in stark contrast with conditions in the Third World. Accompanying this prosperity, however, are signs—too numerous and flagrant to need mentioning—of moral cynicism, spiritual frivolity, and despair. If revolutions make plain the power of sin—its ability to captivate idealistic reformers—mass society displays the ingenuity of sin. Human beings in their passion for justice have not devised institutions that they cannot in their pride and selfishness outwit.

It may seem that the ideological meaning of Christianity is becoming clear: Christianity is solidly, if covertly, on the side of the status quo. It is conservative. There are good reasons for arguing, however, that Christianity cannot logically be conservative but is rather—in its own distinctive fashion—radical.

A Hesitant Radicalism

The Christian record in the annals of reform, it must be granted, is not impressive. Christians have accepted, and sometimes actively supported, slavery, poverty, and almost every other common social evil. They have often condemned such evils in principle but failed to oppose them in practice. Faith does not necessarily conquer selfishness and is particularly unlikely to do so when connected with an established religion and thus with privileged groups. That Christianity has in various times and places, and in various ways, been an established religion is perhaps the major reason why it has been implicated in injustices such as slavery, serfdom, and the oppressive wage labor of early capitalism.

Nevertheless, Christianity in essence is not conservative. The notion that it is (the historical record aside) probably stems mainly from the fact that Christians share with conservatives a consciousness of the fallibility of human beings. The two camps occupy common anthropological ground. But the consciousness of human fallibility is far keener among Christians than among conservatives, for Christians are skeptical of human

arrangements that typically command deep respect in conservatives. Thus, Christians cannot logically assume that the antiquity of institutions provides any assurance of their justice or efficacy. They realize, if they consult Christian principles, that long-standing customs and traditions embody not only the wisdom of generations but also the wickedness—in particular, the determination of dominant groups to preserve their powers and privileges.

Christians are also mistrustful of aristocracies and elites. Conservatives typically commend the rule of long-ascendant minorities, those certified by the established order as wise and noble. But Paul, addressing early Christians in Corinth, noted that "not many of you were wise according to worldly standards, not many were powerful, not many were of noble birth." New Testament passages indicate that Christ had a special concern for the despised and disinherited, the ignorant and unsophisticated. "God chose what is foolish in the world to shame the wise." The attitude expressed in such a passage is remote from the typical conservative reverence for minorities of inherited rank and traditional learning.

Conservatives (like non-Christian radicals) commonly assume that sin can be circumvented by human skill. In the conservative view, allowing only those institutional changes that are gradual and protracted, and according authority to traditional elites, will accomplish this. For Christians, sin is circumvented only by grace. It is certainly not circumvented by society, the form that sinful men and women give to the fallen world.

In America conservatives believe that sin is effectively redirected to the common good through the market. The alchemy of capitalist competition transmutes sin into virtue. But it is difficult to see how any Christian who fully grasps Christian principles can be an unqualified supporter of capitalism. Insofar as the market governs social relations, people are forced into acquisitive rivalry; to count in any way on a gift of "daily bread" rather than on money in the bank would be the mark of a fool. Acquisitive success is candidly equated with virtue and personal worth naively measured in material terms. Charity is often bestowed on the needy, but it is a matter of personal generosity, not of justice or community; and it is unsanctioned in capitalist theory. No principles could be more thoroughly anticommunal than those of capitalism. Indeed, capitalism is probably more anticommunal in theory than in practice, for human beings cannot be as consistently selfish and calculating as capitalist doctrine calls on them to be. Capitalism has one bond with Christianity—the premise that human beings are ordinarily selfish. A system that enables an industrial society to achieve a degree of order and efficiency without depending on either human goodness or governmental coercion cannot be entirely despised. Nevertheless, even if capitalism worked as well as its supporters claim, it would by Christian standards fail morally and spiritually.

But if Christians are more pessimistic about human beings and about social devices like the market than are conservatives, how can they act on the side of serious social change? How can they do anything but cling to all institutions, however unjust, that counteract the chaotic potentialities of human beings and achieve some sort of order? There are three answers to these questions.

First of all, Christian ideas place one in a radical—that is, critical and adverse—relationship to established institutions. The Kingdom of God is a judgment on existing society, and a symbol of its impermanence. Jesus was crucified because his presence and preaching were profoundly unsettling to reigning religious and political groups. Jesus did not seek the violent overthrow of these groups, but neither did he show much concern for their stability.

Further, these attitudes have to be acted on. This is a matter of spiritual integrity. To anticipate the coming of the Kingdom of God is merely sentimental, a private frivolity, unless one tries to reshape society according to the form of the imminent community, a form defined by equality and universality and requiring particular attention to the disinherited and oppressed.

Finally, however, to take it for granted that all attempted reforms will fail would be as presumptuous as to assume that they will succeed. It is not only sinful human beings who are at work in history, Christians believe, but God as well. *Agape* is not merely a standard of personal conduct, powerless over events. In exalting individuals, it discloses the inner meaning of history. To practice love is to be allied with the deepest currents of life. From a Christian standpoint, a frightened refusal of all social change would be highly inappropriate.

Clearly the immediate political aims of Christians are not necessarily different from those of secular radicals and reformers. Their underlying attitudes are different, however. The Christian sense of the depth and stubbornness of evil in human beings, along with the faith that the universe under the impetus of grace is moving toward radical re-creation, gives a distinctive cast to the Christian conception of political action and social progress.

Secular conceptions of reform are apt to be characterized by optimistic oversimplifications and distortions. American reformers, for example, typically assume that human beings are both reasonable and just and that beneficent social change is therefore easy. The main thing necessary, after identifying a problem, is to devise and propagate a rational solution. Poverty, crime, class conflict, war, and all other great social evils can gradually but surely be eliminated. Good will and intelligence, well organized and fully informed (through the studies of social scientists), will suffice. Such illusions stem from a dilemma noted above. It is difficult for secular reformers to reconcile their sense of the dignity of individuals with a recognition of the selfishness and perversity of individuals. They are thus led persistently to exaggerate human goodness. Trying to match their view of human nature with their belief in human dignity, they fail to see how human beings actually behave or to understand the difficulties and complexities of reform.

Tocqueville suggested approvingly that Christianity tends to make a people "circumspect and undecided," with "its impulses…checked and its works unfinished." This expresses well the spirit of reform inherent in Christian faith. Christianity is radical, but it is also hesitant. This is partly, of course, because Christianity restrains our self-assurance. Efforts at social transformation must always encounter unforeseen complexities, difficulties, limits, and tragedies. Caution is in order. But Christian hesitancy has deeper grounds than prudence and more compelling motives than wariness of practical blunders. Hesitation expresses a consciousness of the mystery of being and the dignity of every person. It provides a moment for consulting destiny. Recent decades have seen heroic political commitments in behalf of social reform, but hesitation has been evident mainly in the service of self-interest. Christian faith, however, suggests that hesitation should have a part in our most conscientious deeds. It is a formality that is fitting when we cross the frontier between meditation and action. And like all significant formalities, it is a mark of respect—for God and for the creatures with whom we share the earth.

Some will dislike the implication that "being good" consists in being radical; others will think it strange to link radicalism with hesitation or religious faith. I suggest, however, that the main task facing political goodness in our time is that of maintaining responsible hope. Responsible hope is hesitant because it is cognizant of the discouraging actualities of collective life; it is radical because it measures those actualities against the highest standards of imagination and faith. Whether so para-doxical a stance can be sustained without transcen-dental connections—without God—is doubtful.

We live in a disheartening century—"the worst so far," as someone has said. There have never before been wars so destructive as the series of con-flicts that erupted in 1914; never have tyrannies been so frenzied and all-consuming as those estab-lished by Nazism and communism. All great polit-ical causes have failed. Socialism has eventuated in the rule either of privileged ideological bureaucrats or of comfortable, listless masses; liberal reform in America has at least for a time passed away, leav-ing stubborn injustices and widespread cynicism; conservatism has come to stand for an illogical combination of market economics and truculent nationalism. Most of the human race lives in crush-ing poverty, and the privileged minority in soci-eties where industrial abundance undergirds a preoccupation with material comfort and an atmos-phere of spiritual inanity.

It is not just that hope itself is difficult to main-tain in our situation. One is forced, so to speak, to hope alone. After all that has happened, in what party or cause or movement can one find a hope that can be unreservedly shared? Inherent in the disheartenment of our century is the impossibility of believing any longer in political commitment. And to draw back from commitment is to face political solitude. The individual must find a way of standing for authentic values with little or no human support. A radicalism that is hesitant must also be solitary.

If the great causes and movements all have failed, and unqualified political commitments have become impossible, why not, as Paul asked, eat and drink, since tomorrow we die? This is a question that secular reason should take far more seriously than it ever has.

It is a question to which all of us need an answer. The need is partly political. There can be no decent politics unless many people can resist the historical discouragement so natural in our times. The consumer society and fascism exemplify the possible outcome when nations are populated pre-dominantly by people incapable of the hesitation in which reality needs to be faced or the hope in which it must be judged and reshaped.

The need is also personal. In its depths the life of an individual is historical and political because it is one with the lives of all human beings. To despair of history is to despair of one's own humanity. Today we are strongly tempted to split the individ-ual and history, the personal and the political. When this occurs, personal being is truncated and impoverished. People in earlier times of bewilder-ment and disillusionment, such as the era of the downfall of the ancient city-state system, were sim-ilarly tempted, and a standard of life first clearly enunciated by Epicurus[10] in the aftermath of the Macedonian[11] conquest of the city-states is still, in the twentieth century, attractive. Epicurus called for withdrawal from public life and political activi-ty; he argued that everything essential to one's humanity, such as friendship, can be found in the private sphere. Personal life thus is salvaged from the raging torrent of history. But it is also mutilated, for it is severed from the human situation in its global scope and its political contours.

The absorption of Americans in the pleasures of buying and consuming, of mass entertainment and sports, suggests an Epicurean response to our historical trials. The dangers—erosion of the grounds of political health and impairment of per-sonal being—are evident.

Being good politically means not only valuing the things that are truly valuable but also having the strength to defend those things when they are everywhere being attacked and abandoned. Such strength is exemplified by Dietrich Bonhoeffer, the great German pastor and theologian, who uncom-promisingly opposed the Nazi regime from the beginning, even to the extent of returning to Germany from a guaranteed haven in America to join the anti-Hitler resistance. Arrested by the Gestapo, he was killed at the end of the war. One of Bonhoeffer's prayers, composed in prison, was, "Give me the hope that will deliver me from fear and faintheartedness." Much that I have tried to say in the preceding pages might be summarized simply in this question: If we turn away from tran-scendence, from God, what will deliver us from a politically fatal fear and faintheartedness? ∎

Notes

1 Manhattan Island . . . Calcutta poverty—Manhattan Island, part of New York City, boasts some very wealthy people and business-es, whereas Calcutta, India, has a great deal of poverty.

2 Enlightenment—the eighteenth century, the "Age of Reason"

3 Locke and Jefferson—John Locke (1632–1704) an English philosopher who maintained that the mind is a blank slate until it acquires knowledge through the five senses; Thomas Jefferson (1743–1826), third president of the United States and author of the Declaration of

Independence. He believed in religious freedom and the separation of church and state.

4 Dostoevsky—Fyodor Dostoevsky (1821–1881) a Russian novelist known for his psychologically complex novels that exemplify his Christian view of life.

5 Periclean Age—in ancient Greece, the time of Athenian leadership under the statesman Pericles (500?–429 B.C.), who believed in the democratic ideal

6 Marx—Karl Marx (1818–1883) a German socialist who established the modern political philosophy of communism in his book *Das Kapital*

7 Friedrich Nietzsche—(1844–1900) a German philosopher known for his book *Man and Superman*

8 Sigmund Freud—(1856–1939) an Austrian physician and neurologist known for his founding of the theories of psychoanalysis

9 nihilism—a belief that nothing has meaning or can be communicated

10 Epicurus—(340–270? B.C.) a Greek philosopher who advocated freedom from pain and emotional disturbances; his followers are known for their pursuit of pleasure.

11 Macedonia—an ancient country located in the area around the Adriatic Sea in what is now Greece; home of Alexander the Great

●

Making Connections through Discussion and Writing

1. a. Underline Tinder's thesis statement that occurs in his first paragraph.

   b. Outline the main points and subpoints by putting roman numerals and letters in the margins.

2. a. At beginning of his essay, Tinder identifies two objections to his argument. What are they?

   _____

   _____

   _____

   b. How does he refute these objections?

   _____

   _____

   _____

3. a. Tinder claims that the Christian concept of love, *agape*, is what makes our faith unique and separate from a society that ceaselessly judges and ranks others. According to Tinder, how does a society based on *agape* treat its citizens?

   _____

   _____

   _____

   _____

   _____

   _____

●

   b. How should *agape* affect how we view others?

   _____

   _____

   _____

   _____

4. a. Tinder asserts that idealism will always fail to provide the necessary philosophy for modern humankind. How does he define idealism?

   _____

   _____

   _____

   _____

   b. Why, according to Tinder, is idealism inadequate?

   _____

   _____

   _____

   _____

●

5. Identify the three thinkers who, according to Tinder, have contributed to the idea of the man-god. In a sentence in your own words, explain how they attributed to humans the ability to create their own destiny as man-gods.

_____

_____

_____

_____

_____

_____

_____

_____

_____

_____

_____

_____

_____

6. a. Examine the context of Tinder's statements, "Christianity is not conservative," and "Christianity is radical." Paraphrase his definitions of "conservative" and "radical."

conservative _____

_____

_____

_____

radical _____

_____

_____

_____

b. Do his definitions reflect a departure from what you have believed to be true about Christianity? Explain why you agree or disagree.

_____

_____

_____

_____

_____

7. Why does Tinder feel capitalism fails, both morally and spiritually, by Christian standards?

_____

_____

_____

_____

_____

8. To resolve the dilemma posed by severing the political from the spiritual, what does Tinder propose?

_____

_____

_____

_____

_____

Chapter 6

Vocation

To many people today, "vocation" simply means the work one does in order to make a living, a necessary job that allows one to enjoy a comfortable material existence and have some leisure time in which to "enjoy life." Some are fortunate enough to enjoy their work, and some take real pleasure in the craftsmanship or skills they can employ in their work activities, but to many others work is a necessary evil, a drudgery of routine and boring tasks, whether on an assembly line or at an office desk. In this environment, education has increasingly become a matter of technical training. Students are prepared to take jobs in the "real world" by learning to master computer skills, teaching skills, accounting skills, or skills with the equipment used by contemporary media. The traditional ends of a "liberal education" are increasingly obscured in the process of making students fit into the technological and professional structures of modern society. Traditional liberal education, however, was more concerned with the shaping of the person as a physical, social, and spiritual being than with the training of a worker. The inculcation of ideas of truth, beauty, and goodness were educational goals fit for human beings who were respected as ends in themselves, worthy of nurturing, worthy of caring love.

The traditional meaning of "vocation" has also been obscured in the modern social environment. Only in religious circles does one often hear the term used in its original sense—a calling from God—and then it is used in the narrow sense of being called to religious ministry (e.g., as a "vocation" to enter the priesthood or to become a missionary or a monk). But in traditional Christian thought, every person has a "calling," a vocation to a particular work. It may be to religious ministry, but it may also be to any other kind of legitimate work. If one hears and follows this vocation, the work itself becomes fulfilling and joy-giving. It serves God, man, and oneself.

In his book *Preface to* Paradise Lost, C. S. Lewis defines "vocation" as a "desired duty." Using the hero of the classic Roman epic *The Aenead* as his example, Lewis illustrates how Aeneas sacrifices merely personal goals, such as fulfilling his love for Dido, the queen of Carthage, in order to follow his vocation, the founding of Rome, a goal set for him by his "gods." In obeying his vocation, he achieves his destiny and finds his true joy. Christians who are able to recover this sense of vocation can find in their work true satisfaction, taking pleasure in the integrity of their crafting and in the quality of their products. Even activities that may seem like distractions from their callings—such as relatively mundane summer jobs or even some courses required for a college degree—can be viewed as parts of the overall process leading into their vocations. If an individual is following his or her calling, the work done well not only yields its own satisfaction, but it also becomes a part of service to God, a part of worship. As Richard Wilbur states in his poem "A Plain Song for Comadre," even the scrubwater thrown out by the faithful cleaning woman shines with "grimy rainbows," and its "suds flash like angel feathers."

As seen in this section of *Encounters*, G. K. Chesterton, Dorothy L. Sayers, and the contemporary poet Richard Wilbur affirm the value, significance, and joy of work from a Christian viewpoint. The apocryphal Jewish book "Ecclesiasticus" portrays the ancient Hebrew validation of the work of artists, scholars, craftsmen, and others who maintain the economic and social life of a community. In the poem "The Man Had No Useful Work," the Indian poet Tagore writes a parable that reveals the value of aesthetic as well as practical work. Finally, the contemporary American novelist and essayist Alice Walker, in "In Search of Our Mothers'

Gardens," turns to her own African-American heritage to affirm the aesthetic work of women who did not have access to the "fine arts," but who made beauty from their own environments in the forms of their gardens and quilts. These essays and poems attest to the human desire for work that is both useful and beautiful, yielding to the worker a sense of joy, worth, and worship.

Dorothy L. Sayers
Why Work?

Dorothy L. Sayers (1893–1957) was an English writer who was one of the first women to receive a degree at Oxford. Considered one of the masters of the detective story, Sayers was one of the most popular mystery writers in England. A friend and frequent correspondent with C. S. Lewis, Sayers is also known for her religious essays and plays and for her translation of Dante's *Divine Comedy*. Her talents as a lay apologist and as a contributor to Christian aesthetics are seen in her work *The Mind of the Maker*. This selection is taken from her collection of essays *Creed or Chaos*.

Vocabulary ....

acquiescing
cumbered
fob
inexorable

sanction
superfluous
trumpery

I have already, on a previous occasion,[1] spoken at some length on the subject of Work and Vocation. What I urged then was a thorough-going revolution in our whole attitude to work. I asked that it should be looked upon—not as a necessary drudgery to be undergone for the purpose of making money, but as a way of life in which the nature of man should find its proper exercise and delight and so fulfil itself to the glory of God. That it should, in fact, be thought of as a creative activity undertaken for the love of the work itself; and that man, made in God's image, should make things, as God makes them, for the sake of doing well a thing that is well worth doing.

It may well seem to you—as it does to some of my acquaintances—that I have a sort of obsession about this business of the right attitude to work. But I do insist upon it, because it seems to me that what becomes of civilization after this war is going to depend enormously on our being able to effect this revolution in our ideas about work. Unless we do change our whole way of thought about work, I do not think we shall ever escape from the appalling squirrel-cage of economic confusion in which we have been madly turning for the last three centuries or so, the cage in which we landed ourselves by acquiescing in a social system based upon Envy and Avarice. A society in which con-sumption has to be artificially stimulated in order to keep production going is a society founded on trash and waste, and such a society is a house built upon sand.

It is interesting to consider for a moment how our outlook has been forcibly changed for us in the last twelve months by the brutal presence of war. War is a judgment that overtakes societies when they have been living upon ideas that conflict too violently with the laws governing the universe. People who would not revise their ideas voluntarily find themselves compelled to do so by the sheer pressure of the events which these very ideas have served to bring about. Never think that wars are irrational catastrophes: they happen when wrong ways of thinking and living bring about intolerable situations; and whichever side may be the more outrageous in its aims and the more brutal in its methods, the root causes of conflict are usually to be found in some wrong way of life in which all parties have acquiesced, and for which everybody must, to some extent, bear the blame. It is quite true that false Economics are one of the root causes of the present war; and one of the false ideas we had about Economics was a false attitude both to Work and to the goods produced by Work. This attitude we are now being obliged to alter, under the compulsion of war—and a very strange and painful

From *Creed or Chaos* © 1949 by Dorothy L. Sayers. Reprinted by permission of the Estate of Dorothy Sayers and the Waktins/Loomis Agency.

process it is in some ways. It is always strange and painful to have to change a habit of mind; though, when we have made the effort, we may find a great relief, even a sense of adventure and delight, in getting rid of the false and returning to the true.

Can you remember—it is already getting difficult to remember—what things were like before the war? The stockings we bought cheap and threw away to save the trouble of mending? The cars we scrapped every year to keep up with the latest fashion in engine-design and streamlining? The bread and bones and scraps of fat that littered the dustbins—not only of the rich, but of the poor? The empty bottles that even the dustman scorned to collect, because the manufacturers found it cheaper to make new ones than to clean the old? The mountains of empty tins that nobody found it worth while to salvage, rusting and stinking on the refuse-dumps? The food that was burnt or buried because it did not pay to distribute it? The land choked and impoverished with thistle and ragwort, because it did not pay to farm it? The handkerchiefs used for paint-rags and kettle-holders? The electric lights left blazing because it was too much trouble to switch them off? The fresh peas we could not be bothered to shell, and threw aside for something out of a tin? The paper that cumbered the shelves, and lay knee-deep in the parks, and littered the seats of railway-trains? The scattered hairpins and smashed crockery, the trumpery knick-knacks of steel and wood and rubber and glass and tin that we bought to fill in an odd half-hour at Woolworth's and forgot as soon as we had bought them? The advertisements imploring and exhorting and cajoling and menacing and bullying us to glut ourselves with things we did not want, in the name of snobbery and idleness and sex-appeal? And the fierce international scramble to find in helpless and backward nations a market on which to fob off all the superfluous rubbish which the inexorable machines ground out hour by hour, to create money and to create employment? Do you realize how we have had to alter our whole scale of values, now that we are no longer being urged to consume but to conserve? We have been forced back to the social morals of our great-grandparents. When a piece of lingerie costs three precious coupons, we have to consider, not merely its glamour-value, but how long it will wear. When fats are rationed, we must not throw away scraps, but jealously use to advantage what it cost so much time and trouble to breed and rear. When paper is scarce we must—or we should—think whether what we have to say is worth saying before writing or printing it. When our life depends on the land, we have

to pay in short commons for destroying its fertility by neglect or overcropping. When a haul of herrings takes valuable manpower from the forces, and is gathered in at the peril of men's lives by bomb and mine and machine-gun, we read a new significance into those gloomy words which appear so often in the fishmonger's shop: NO FISH TODAY. . . . We have had to learn the bitter lesson that in all the world there are only two sources of real wealth: the fruit of the earth and the labour of men; and to estimate work—not by the money it brings to the producer, but by the worth of the thing that is made.

The question that I will ask you to consider today is this: When the war is over, are we likely, and *do we want* to keep this attitude to work and the results of work? Or are we preparing and *do we want*, to go back to our old habits of thought? Because I believe that on our answer to this question the whole economic future of society will depend. Sooner or later the moment will come when we have to make a decision about this. At the moment, we are not making it—don't let us flatter ourselves that we are. It is being made for us. And don't let us imagine that a war-time economy has stopped waste. It has not. It has only transferred it elsewhere. The glut and waste that used to clutter our own dustbins have been removed to the field of battle. That is where all the surplus consumption is going to. The factories are roaring more loudly than ever, turning out night and day goods that are of no conceivable value for the maintenance of life; on the contrary, their sole object is to destroy life, and instead of being thrown away they are being blown away—in Russia, in North Africa, over Occupied France, in Burma and China, and the Spice Islands, and on the Seven Seas. What is going to happen when the factories stop turning out armaments? No nation has yet found a way to keep the machines running and whole nations employed under modern industrial conditions without wasteful consumption. For a time, a few nations could contrive to keep going by securing a monopoly of production and forcing their waste products on to new and untapped markets. When there are no new markets and all nations are industrial producers, the only choice we have been able to envisage so far has been that between armaments and unemployment. This is the problem that some time or other will stare us in the face again, and this time we must have our minds ready to tackle it. It may not come at once—for it is quite likely that after the war we shall have to go through a further period of managed consumption while the shortages caused by the war are being made good. But sooner or later we shall have to grapple with this difficulty, and everything will depend on our attitude of mind about it. Shall we be prepared to take the same attitude to the arts of peace as to the arts of war? I see no reason why we should not sacrifice our convenience and our individual standard of living just as readily for the building of great public works as for the building of ships and tanks—but when the stimulus of fear and anger is removed, shall we be prepared to do any such thing? Or shall we *want* to go back to that civilization of greed and waste which we dignify by the name of a 'high standard of living'? I am getting very much afraid of that phrase about the standard of living. And I am also frightened by the phrase 'after the war'—it is so often pronounced in a tone that suggests: 'after the war, we want to relax, and go back, and live as we did before'. And that means going back to the time when labour was valued in terms of its cash returns, and not in terms of the work.

Now the answer to this question, if we are resolute to know what we are about, will not be left to rich men—to manufacturers and financiers. If these people have governed the world of late years it is only because we ourselves put the power into their hands. The question can and should be answered by the worker and the consumer. It is extremely important that the worker should really understand where the problem lies. It is a matter of brutal fact that in these days labour, more than any other section of the community, has a vested interest in war. Some rich employers make profit out of war—that is true; but what is infinitely more important is that for all working people war means full employment and high wages. When war ceases, then the problem of employing labour at the machines begins again. The relentless pressure of hungry labour is behind the drive towards wasteful consumption, whether in the destruction of war or in the trumpery of peace. The problem is far too much simplified when it is presented as a mere conflict between labour and capital, between employed and employer. The basic difficulty remains, even when you make the State the sole employer, even when you make Labour into the employer. It is not simply a question of profits and wages or living conditions—but of what is to be done with the work of the machines, and what work the machines are to do. If we do not deal with this question now, while we have time to think about it, then the whirligig of wasteful production and wasteful consumption will start again and will again end in war. And the driving-power of labour will be thrusting to turn the wheels, because it is to the financial interest of labour to keep the whirligig going faster and faster till the inevitable catastrophe comes.

And, so that the wheels may turn, the consumer—that is, you and I, including the workers, who are consumers also—will again be urged to consume and waste; and unless we change our attitude—or rather unless we keep hold of the new attitude forced upon us by the logic of war—we shall again be bamboozled by our vanity, indolence, and greed into keeping the squirrel-cage of wasteful economy turning. We could—you and I—bring the whole fantastic economy of profitable waste down to the ground overnight, without legislation and without revolution, merely by refusing to co-operate with it. I say, we could—as a matter of fact, we have; or rather, it has been done for us. If we do not want it to rise up again after the war, we can prevent it—simply by preserving the war-time habit of valuing work instead of money. The point is: do we *want* to? . . . Whatever we do, we shall be faced with grave difficulties. That cannot be disguised. But it will make a great difference to the result if we are genuinely aiming at a real change in economic thinking. And by that I mean a radical change from top to bottom—a new system; not a mere adjustment of the old system to favour a different set of people. The habit of thinking about work as something one does to make money is so ingrained in us that we can scarcely imagine what a revolutionary change it would be to think about it instead in terms of the work done. It would mean taking the attitude of mind we reserve for our unpaid work—our hobbies, our leisure interests, the things we make and do for pleasure—and making *that* the standard of all our judgments about things and people. We should ask of an enterprise, not 'will it pay?' but, 'is it good?' of a man, not 'what does he make?' but 'what is his work worth?' of goods, not 'can we induce people to buy them?' but 'are they useful things well made?' of employment, not 'how much a week?' but 'will it exercise my faculties to the utmost?' And shareholders in—let us say—brewing companies, would astonish the directorate by arising at shareholders' meetings and demanding to know, not merely where the profits go or what dividends are to be paid, not even merely whether the workers' wages are sufficient and the conditions of labour satisfactory, but loudly, and with a proper sense of personal responsibility: What goes into the beer?

You will probably ask at once: How is this altered attitude going to make any difference to the question of employment? Because it sounds as though it would result in not more employment, but less. I am not an economist, and I can only point to a peculiarity of war economy that usually goes without notice in economic text-books. In war, production for wasteful consumption still goes on: but there is one great difference in the goods produced. None of them is valued for what it will fetch, but only for what it is worth in itself. The gun and the tank, the aeroplane and the warship have to be the best of their kind. A war consumer does not buy shoddy. He does not buy to sell again. He buys the thing that is good for its purpose, asking nothing of it but that it shall do the job it has to do. Once again, war forces the consumer into a right attitude to the work. And, whether by strange coincidence, or whether because of some universal law, so soon as nothing is demanded of the thing made but its own integral perfection, its own absolute value, the skill and labour of the worker are fully employed and likewise acquire an absolute value.

This is probably not the kind of answer that you will find in any theory of economics. But the professional economist is not really trained to answer, or even to ask himself questions about absolute values. The economist is inside the squirrel-cage and turning with it. Any question about absolute values belongs to the sphere, not of economics, but of religion. And it is very possible that we cannot deal with economics at all, unless we can see economy from outside the cage; that we cannot begin to settle the relative values without considering absolute values. And if so, this may give a very precise and practical meaning to the words: 'Seek first the kingdom of God and righteousness, and all these things shall be added to you.'. . . I am persuaded that the reason why the Churches are in so much difficulty about giving a lead in the economic sphere is because they are trying to fit a Christian standard of economics to a wholly false and pagan understanding of work.

What is the Christian understanding of work? . . . I should like to put before you two or three propositions arising out of the doctrinal position which I stated at the beginning: namely, that work is the natural exercise and function of man—the creature who is made in the image of his Creator. You will find that any one of them, if given in effect everyday practice, is so revolutionary (as compared with the habits of thinking into which we have fallen), as to make all political revolutions look like conformity.

The first, stated quite briefly, is that work is not, primarily, a thing one does to live, but the thing one lives to do. It is, or it should be, the full expression of the worker's faculties, the thing in which he finds spiritual, mental, and bodily satisfaction, and the medium in which he offers himself to God.

Now the consequences of this are not merely that the work should be performed under decent living and working conditions. That is a point we have begun to grasp, and it is a perfectly sound point. But we have tended to concentrate on it to the exclusion of other considerations far more revolutionary.

1. There is, for instance, the question of profits and remuneration. We have all got it fixed in our heads that the proper end of work is to be paid for—to produce a return in profits or payment to the worker which fully or more than compensates the effort he puts into it. But if our proposition is true, this does not follow at all. So long as Society provides the worker with a sufficient return in real wealth to enable him to carry on the work properly, then he has his reward. For his work is the measure of his life, and his satisfaction is found in the fulfilment of his own nature, and in contemplation of the perfection of his work. That, in practice, there is this satisfaction, is shown by the mere fact that a man will put loving labour into some hobby which can never bring him in any economically adequate return. His satisfaction comes, in the god-like manner, from looking upon what he has made and finding it very good. He is no longer bargaining with his work, but serving it. It is only when work has to be looked on as a means to gain that it becomes hateful; for then, instead of a friend, it becomes an enemy from whom tolls and contributions have to be extracted. What most of us demand from society is that we should always get out of it a little *more* than the value of the labour we give to it. By this process, we persuade ourselves that society is always in our debt—a conviction that not only piles up actual financial burdens, but leaves us with a grudge against society.

2. Here is the second consequence. At present we have no clear grasp of the principle that every man should do the work for which he is fitted by nature. The employer is obsessed by the notion that he must find cheap labour, and the worker by the notion that the best-paid job is the job for him. Only feebly, inadequately, and spasmodically do we ever attempt to tackle the problem from the other end, and inquire: What type of worker is suited to this type of work? People engaged in education see clearly that this *is* the right end to start from; but they are frustrated by economic pressure, and by the failure of parents on the one hand and employers on the other to grasp the fundamental importance of this

approach. And that the trouble results far more from a failure of intelligence than from economic necessity is seen clearly under war conditions, when, though competitive economics are no longer a governing factor, the right men and women are still persistently thrust into the wrong jobs, through sheer inability on everybody's part to imagine a purely vocational approach to the business of fitting together the worker and his work.

3. A third consequence is that, if we really believed this proposition and arranged our work and our standard of values accordingly, we should no longer think of work as something that we hastened to get through in order to enjoy our leisure; we should look on our leisure as the period of changed rhythm that refreshed us for the delightful purpose of getting on with our work. And, this being so, we should tolerate no regulations of any sort that prevented us from working as long and as well as our enjoyment of work demanded. We should resent any such restrictions as a monstrous interference with the liberty of the subject. How great an upheaval of our ideas that would mean I leave you to imagine. It would turn topsy-turvy all our notions about hours of work, rates of work, unfair competition, and all the rest of it. We should all find ourselves fighting, as now only artists and the members of certain professions fight, for precious time in which to get on with the job—instead of fighting for precious hours saved from the job.

4. A fourth consequence is that we should fight tooth and nail, not for mere employment, but for the quality of the work that we had to do. We should clamour to be engaged on work that was worth doing, and in which we could take a pride. The worker would demand that the stuff he helped to turn out should be good stuff—he would no longer be content to take the cash and let the credit go. Like the shareholders in the brewery, he would feel a sense of personal responsibility, and clamour to know, and to control, what went into the beer he brewed. There would be protests and strikes—not only about pay and conditions, but about the quality of the work demanded and the honesty, beauty, and usefulness of the goods produced. The greatest insult which a commercial age has offered to the worker has been to rob him of all interest in the end-product of the work and to force him to dedicate his life to making badly things which were not worth making.

This first proposition chiefly concerns the worker as such. My second proposition directly concerns Christians as such, and it is this: It is the business of the Church to recognize that the secular vocation, as such, is sacred. Christian people, and particularly perhaps the Christian clergy, must get it firmly into their heads that when a man or woman is called to a particular job of secular work, that is as true a vocation as though he or she were called to specifically religious work. The Church must concern herself not only with such questions as the just price and proper working conditions: she must concern herself with seeing that the work itself is such as a human being can perform without degradation—that no one is required by economic or any other considerations to devote himself to work that is contemptible, soul-destroying, or harmful. It is not right for her to acquiesce in the notion that a man's life is divided into the time he spends on his work and the time he spends in serving God. He must be able to serve God *in* his work, and the work itself must be accepted and respected as the medium of divine creation.

In nothing has the Church so lost her hold on reality as in her failure to understand and respect the secular vocation. She has allowed work and religion to become separate departments, and is astonished to find that, as a result, the secular work of the world is turned to purely selfish and destructive ends, and that the greater part of the world's intelligent workers have become irreligious, or at least, uninterested in religion. But is it astonishing? How can any one remain interested in a religion which seems to have no concern with nine-tenths of his life? The Church's approach to an intelligent carpenter is usually confined to exhorting him not to be drunk and disorderly in his leisure hours, and to come to church on Sundays. What the Church *should* be telling him is this: that the very first demand that his religion makes upon him is that he should make good tables. Church by all means, and decent forms of amusement, certainly—but what use is all that if in the very centre of his life and occupation he is insulting God with bad carpentry? No crooked table-legs or ill-fitting drawers ever, I dare swear, came out of the carpenter's shop at Nazareth. Nor, if they did, could any one believe that they were made by the same hand that made heaven and earth. No piety in the worker will compensate for work that is not true to itself; for any work that is untrue to its own technique is a living lie. Yet in her own buildings, in her own ecclesiastical art and music, in her hymns and prayers, in her sermons and in her little books of devotion, the Church will tolerate, or permit a pious intention to excuse, work so ugly, so pretentious, so tawdry and twaddling, so insincere and insipid, so *bad* as to shock and horrify any decent draftsman. And why? Simply because she has lost all sense of the fact that the living and eternal truth is expressed in work only so far as that work is true in itself, to itself, to the standards of its own technique. She has forgotten that the secular vocation is sacred. Forgotten that a building must be good architecture before it can be a good church; that a painting must be well painted before it can be a good sacred picture; that work must be good work before it can call itself God's work.

Let the Church remember this: that every maker and worker is called to serve God *in* his profession or trade—not outside it. The Apostles complained rightly when they said it was not meet they should leave the word of God and serve tables; their vocation was to preach the word. But the person whose vocation it is to prepare the meals beautifully might with equal justice protest: It is not meet for us to leave the service of our tables to preach the word. The official Church wastes time and energy, and, moreover, commits sacrilege, in demanding that secular workers should neglect their proper vocation in order to do Christian work—by which she means ecclesiastical work. The only Christian work is good work well done. Let the Church see to it that the workers are Christian people and do their work well, as to God: then all the work will be Christian work, whether it is Church embroidery, or sewage-farming. As Jacques Maritain says: 'If you want to produce Christian work, be a Christian, and try to make a work of beauty into which you have put your heart; do not adopt a Christian pose.' He is right. And let the Church remember that the beauty of the work will be judged by its own, and not by ecclesiastical standards. Let me give you an illustration of what I mean. When my play *The Zeal of Thy House* was produced in London, a dear old pious lady was much struck by the beauty of the four great archangels who stood throughout the play in their heavy, gold robes, eleven feet high from wing-tip to sandal-tip. She asked with great innocence 'whether I selected the actors who played the angels for the excellence of their moral character?' I replied that the angels were selected, to begin with, not by me but by the producer, who had the technical qualifications for selecting suitable actors—for that was part of his vocation. And that he selected, in the first place, young men who were six feet tall, so that they would match properly together. Secondly, angels had to be of good physique, so as

to be able to stand stiff on the stage for two and a half hours, carrying the weight of their wings and costumes, without wobbling, or fidgeting, or fainting. Thirdly, they must be able to speak verse well, in an agreeable voice and audibly. Fourthly, they must be reasonably good actors. When all these technical conditions were fulfilled, we might come to the moral qualities, of which the first would be the ability to arrive on the stage punctually and in a sober condition, since the curtain must go up on time, and a drunken angel would be indecorous. After that, and only after that, one might take character into consideration, but that—provided his behaviour was not so scandalous as to cause dissension among the company—the right kind of actor with no morals would give a far more reverent and seemly performance than a saintly actor with the wrong technical qualifications. The worst religious films I ever saw were produced by a company which chose its staff exclusively for their piety. Bad photography, bad acting, and bad dialogue produced a result so grotesquely irreverent that the pictures could not have been shown in churches without bringing Christianity into contempt. God is not served by technical incompetence; and incompetence and untruth always result when the secular vocation is treated as a thing alien to religion. . . . And conversely: when you find a man who is a Christian praising God by the excellence of his work—do not distract him and take him away from his proper vocation to address religious meetings and open church bazaars. Let him serve God in the way to which God has called him. If you take him away from that, he will exhaust himself in an alien technique and lose his capacity to do his dedicated work. It is your business, you churchmen, to get what good you can from observing his work—not to take him away from it, so that he may do ecclesiastical work for you. But, if you have any power, see that he is set free to do his own work as well as it may be done. He is not there to serve you; he is there to serve God by serving his work.

This brings me to my third proposition, and this may sound to you the most revolutionary of all. It is this: the worker's first duty is to *serve the work*. The popular 'catch' phrase of to-day is that it is everybody's duty to serve the community. It is a well-sounding phrase, but there *is* a catch in it. It is the old catch about the two great commandments. 'Love God—and your neighbour; on those two commandments hang all the Law and the Prophets.' The catch in it, which nowadays the world has largely forgotten, is that the second commandment depends upon the first, and that without the first, it is a delusion and a snare. Much of our present trouble and disillusionment have come from putting the second commandment before the first. If we put our neighbour first, we are putting man above God, and that is what we have been doing ever since we began to worship humanity and make man the measure of all things. Whenever man is made the centre of things, he becomes the storm-centre of trouble—and that is precisely the catch about serving the community. It ought perhaps to make us suspicious of that phrase when we consider that it is the slogan of every commercial scoundrel and swindler who wants to make sharp business practice pass muster as social improvement. 'Service' is the motto of the advertiser, of big business, and of fraudulent finance. And of others, too. Listen to this: 'I expect the judicature to understand that the nation does not exist for their convenience, but that justice exists to serve the nation.' That was Hitler yesterday—and that is what becomes of 'service', when the community, and not the work, becomes its idol. There is, in fact, a paradox about working to serve the community, and it is this: that to aim directly at serving the community is to falsify the work; the only way to serve the community is to forget the community and serve the work. There are three very good reasons for this:

The first is, that you cannot do good work if you take your mind off the work to see how the community is taking it—any more than you can make a good drive from the tee if you take your eye off the ball. 'Blessed are the single-hearted' (for that is the real meaning of the word we translate *'the pure in heart'*). If your heart is not wholly in the work, the work will not be good—and work that is not good serves neither God nor the community; it only serves Mammon.

The second reason is that the moment you think of serving other people, you begin to have a notion that other people owe you something for your pains; you begin to think that you have a claim on the community. You will begin to bargain for reward, to angle for applause, and to harbour a grievance if you are not appreciated. But if your mind is set upon serving the work, then you know you have nothing to look for; the only reward the *work* can give you is the satisfaction of beholding its perfection. The work takes all and gives nothing but itself; and to serve the work is a labour of pure love.

And thirdly, if you set out to serve the community, you will probably end by merely fulfilling a public demand—and you may not even do that. A public demand is a changeable thing. Nine-tenths of the bad plays put on in theatres owe their badness to the fact that the playwright has aimed at pleasing the audience, instead of at producing a good and satisfactory play. Instead of doing the work as its own integrity demands that it should be done, he has falsified the play by putting in this or that which he thinks will appeal to the groundlings (who by that time have probably come to want something else), and the play fails by its insincerity. The work has been falsified to please the public—and in the end even the public is not pleased. As it is with works of art, so it is with all work. We are coming to the end of an era of civilization which began by pandering to public demand, and ended by frantically trying to create public demand for an output so false and meaningless that even a doped public revolted from the trash offered to it and plunged into war rather than swallow any more of it. The danger of 'serving the community' is that one is part of the community, and that in serving it one may only be serving a kind of communal egotism. The only true way of serving the community is to be truly in sympathy with the community—to be one's self part of the community—and then to serve the work, without giving the community another thought. Then the work will endure, because it will be true to itself. It is the work that serves the community; the business of the worker is to serve the work.

Where we have become confused is in mixing up the *ends* to which our work is put with the *way* in which the work is done. The end of the work will be decided by our religious outlook: as we *are* so we *make*. It is the business of religion to make us Christian people, and then our work will naturally be turned to Christian ends, because our work is the expression of ourselves. But the *way* in which the work is done is governed by no sanction except the good of the work itself; and religion has no direct connexion with that, except to insist that the workman should be free to do his work well according to its own integrity. Jacques Maritain—one of the very few religious writers of our time who really understands the nature of creative work—has summed the matter up in a sentence:

'What is required is the perfect practical discrimination between the end pursued by the workman *(finis operantis)* and the end to be served by the work *(finis operis)*, so that the workman may work for his wages but the work be controlled and set in being only in relation to its proper good and nowise in relation to the wages earned; so that the artist may work for any and every human intention he likes, but the work taken by itself be performed and constructed for its proper beauty alone.'

Or perhaps we may put it more shortly still: If work is to find its right place in the world, it is the duty of the Church to see to it that the work serves God, and that the worker serves the work. ∎

Notes

[1] At Brighton, March 1941. The major part of the address was printed in *A Christian Basis for the Post-War World* (S.C.M. Press).

Making Connections through Discussion and Writing

1. Dorothy L. Sayers wrote this selection during World War II. Explain how Sayers uses wartime conditions in Great Britain as an opportunity to encourage a reevaluation of society's attitude toward work.

   _____

   _____

   _____

   _____

   _____

   _____

2. Underline Sayers' favored definition of "work" in the first paragraph of this selection.

3. Sayers characteristically bases her thought on particular Christian doctrines. Circle the statement in which Sayers clarifies that her ideas about work stem from a specific doctrine.

4. Sayers' essay is clearly structured. Outline below the three propositions that follow from the doctrine she cites and the consequences or points that follow the propositions.

   _____

   _____

   _____

   _____

   _____

   _____

   _____

   _____

   _____

   _____

   _____

   _____

   _____

   _____

   _____

   _____

   _____

   _____

5. In a brief paragraph, evaluate current American attitudes toward work and consumption against the standard Sayers sets in this essay.

    _____
    _____
    _____
    _____
    _____
    _____
    _____
    _____
    _____
    _____
    _____
    _____
    _____
    _____
    _____
    _____

from Ecclesiasticus 38–39

Ecclesiasticus is an ancient Hebrew book in the tradition of the Wisdom literature, like Proverbs and Ecclesiastes. Unlike these books, it was never included in the Jewish Canon; however, it was a part of the Greek Bible, and the Roman Catholic Church accepts it as part of the Apocrypha. In the excerpt here, the writer honors the work of tradesmen, craftsmen, and scholars.

Vocabulary . . . .

furrows   pummels
goad   wield
puddles

Trades and Crafts

Leisure is what gives the scribe the opportunity to acquire wisdom;
    the man with few business affairs grows wise.
How can the ploughman[1] become wise,
    whose sole ambition is to wield the goad
driving his oxen, engrossed in their work,
    his conversation is of nothing but cattle?
His mind is fixed on the furrows he traces,
    and his evenings pass in fattening his heifers.
So it is with every workman and craftsman,
    toiling day and night;
those who engrave seals,
    always trying to think of new designs:
they set their heart on producing a good likeness,
    and stay up perfecting the work.
So it is with the blacksmith sitting by his anvil;
    he considers what to do with the pig-iron,[2]
the breath of the fire scorches his skin,
    as he contends with the heat of the furnace;
he batters his ear with the din of the hammer,
    his eyes are fixed on the pattern;
he sets his heart on completing his work,
    and stays up putting the finishing touches.
So it is with the potter, sitting at his work,
    turning the wheel with his feet;
constantly on the alert over his work,
    each flick of the finger premeditated;
he pummels the clay with his arm,
    and puddles it with his feet;
he sets his heart on perfecting the glaze,
    and stays up cleaning the kiln.
All these put their trust in their hands,
    and each is skilled at his own craft.

A town could not be built without them,
> there would be no settling, no travelling.
But they are not required at the council,
> they do not hold high rank in the assembly.
They do not sit on the judicial bench,
> and have no grasp of the law.
They are not remarkable for culture or sound judgement,
> and are not found among the inventors of maxims.
But they give solidity to the created world,
> while their prayer is concerned with what pertains to their trade.

The scholar

It is otherwise with the man who devotes his soul
> to reflecting on the Law of the Most High.
He researches into the wisdom of all the Ancients,
> he occupies his time with the prophecies.
He preserves the discourses of famous men,
> he is at home with the niceties of parables.
He researches into the hidden sense of proverbs,
> he ponders the obscurities of parables.
He enters the service of princes,
> he is seen in the presence of rulers.
He travels in foreign countries,
> he has experienced human good and human evil.
At dawn and with all his heart
> he resorts to the Lord who made him;
he pleads in the presence of the Most High,
> he opens his mouth in prayer
> and makes entreaty for his sins.
If it is the will of the great Lord,
> he will be filled with the spirit of understanding,
he will shower forth words of wisdom,
> and in prayer give thanks to the Lord.
He will grow upright in purpose and learning,
> he will ponder the Lord's hidden mysteries.
He will display the instruction he has received,
> taking his pride in the Law of the Lord's covenant.
Many will praise his understanding,
> and it will never be forgotten.
His memory will not disappear,
> generation after generation his name will live. ■

Notes

[1] ploughman—plowman

[2] pig-iron—crude iron that has been cast in blocks

Making Connections through Discussion and Writing

1. In this selection, the writer observes that our work requires our hearts. Why is it important to set our hearts on the quality of our work?

    _____
    _____
    _____
    _____
    _____

2   a. How does the author give honor to craftsmen and manual laborers?

    _____
    _____
    _____
    _____

    b. Does our society bestow such honor or give generous reward to tradesmen, craftsmen, or artists? If so, how? If not, should this attitude be changed? How?

    _____
    _____
    _____
    _____
    _____
    _____

3. a. What do you think is meant by the phrase "they give solidity to the created world"?

    _____
    _____
    _____
    _____

    b. Give some examples to support your answer.

    _____
    _____
    _____
    _____
    _____
    _____

4. Compare or contrast the portrait of the scholar given here to the activities of a contemporary scholar. You may wish to interview a college professor to identify how he or she spends time pursuing modern scholarly activities.

    _____

    _____

    _____

    _____

    _____

    _____

    _____

    _____

    _____

    _____

    _____

    _____

    _____

    _____

    _____

    _____

    _____

    _____

5. In a well-developed paragraph, describe a vocation you feel you might have, one on which you could "set your heart." Give details of the work you would do and the satisfaction you anticipate from that work.

    _____

    _____

    _____

    _____

    _____

    _____

    _____

    _____

    _____

    _____

G. K. Chesterton
The Little Birds Who Won't Sing

G. K. Chesterton (1874–1936) was the author of many poems, essays, articles, and novels including the famous "Father Brown" stories. As a child, Chesterton was a liberal Unitarian, but because of his wife's influence, he later became a convert to Roman Catholicism. After this conversion, he believed that true freedom came from following God's commandments through the Church. The following excerpt is from his book *Tremendous Trifles*. Here Chesterton laments modern humanity's failure to incorporate joy expressed in song in their daily existence.

Vocabulary ....

collectivist	reaping
Gothic	Socialists
indecipherable	steeds
nascent	

On my last morning on the Flemish coast,[1] when I knew that in a few hours I should be in England, my eye fell upon one of the details of Gothic carving of which Flanders[2] is full. I do not know whether the thing was old, though it was certainly knocked about and indecipherable, but at least it was certainly in the style and tradition of the early Middle Ages. It seemed to represent men bending themselves (not to say twisting themselves) to certain primary employments. Some seemed to be sailors tugging at ropes; others, I think, were reaping; others were energetically pouring something into something else. This is entirely characteristic of the pictures and carvings of the early thirteenth century, perhaps the most purely vigorous time in all history. The great Greeks preferred to carve their gods and heroes doing nothing. Splendid and philosophic as their composure is there is always about it something that marks the master of many slaves. But if there was one thing the early medievals liked it was representing people doing something—hunting or hawking, or rowing boats, or treading grapes, or making shoes, or cooking something in a pot. "Quicquid agunt homines votum timor ira voluptas."[3] (I quote from memory.) The Middle Ages is full of that spirit in all its monuments and manuscripts. Chaucer[4] retains it in his jolly insistence on

everybody's type of trade and toll. It was the earliest and youngest resurrection of Europe, the time when social order was strengthening, but had not yet become oppressive; the time when religious faiths were strong, but had not yet been exasperated. For this reason the whole effect of Greek and Gothic carving is different. The figures in the Elgin marbles,[5] though often rearing their steeds for an instant in the air, seem frozen for ever at that perfect instant. But a mass of medieval carving seems actually a sort of bustle or hubbub in stone. Sometimes one cannot help feeling that the groups actually move and mix, and the whole front of a great cathedral has the hum of a huge hive.

But about these particular figures there was a peculiarity of which I could not be sure. Those of them that had any heads had very curious heads, and it seemed to me that they had their mouths open. Whether or not this really meant anything or was an accident of nascent art I do not know; but in the course of wondering I recalled to my mind the fact that singing was connected with many of the tasks there suggested, that there were songs for reapers reaping and songs for sailors hauling ropes. I was still thinking about this small problem when I walked along the pier at Ostend,[6] and I heard some sailors uttering a measured shout as they laboured, and I remembered that sailors still sing in

From *Everlasting Man* by G. K. Chesterton, published 1925.

chorus while they work, and even sing different songs according to what part of their work they are doing. And a little afterwards, when my sea journey was over, the sight of men working in the English fields reminded me again that there are still songs for harvest and for many agricultural routines. And I suddenly wondered why if this were so it should be quite unknown for any modern trade to have a ritual poetry. How did people come to chant rude poems while pulling certain ropes or gathering certain fruit, and why did nobody do anything of the kind while producing any of the modern things? Why is a modern newspaper never printed by people singing in chorus? Why do shopmen seldom, if ever, sing?

If reapers sing while reaping, why should not auditors sing while auditing and bankers while banking? If there are songs for all the separate things that have to be done in a boat, why are there not songs for all the separate things that have to be done in a bank? As the train from Dover flew through the Kentish[7] gardens, I tried to write a few songs suitable for commercial gentlemen. Thus, the work of bank clerks when casting up columns might begin with a thundering chorus in praise of Simple Addition.

> "Up my lads, and lift the ledgers,
>   sleep and ease are o'er.
> Hear the Stars of Morning shout-
>   ing: 'Two and Two are Four.'
> Though the creeds and realms are
>   reeling, though the sophists roar,
> Though we weep and pawn our
>   watches, Two and Two are Four."

And then, of course, we should need another song for times of financial crisis and courage, a song with a more fierce and panic-stricken metre, like the rushing of horses in the night:

> "There's a run upon the Bank—
>   Stand away!
> For the Manager's a crank and the
>   Secretary drank, and the Upper
>   Tooting Bank
>   Turns to bay!
> Stand close: there is a run
>   On the Bank.
> Of our ship, our royal one, let the
>   ringing legend run,
> that she fired every gun
>   Ere she sank."

And as I came into the cloud of London I met a friend of mine who actually is in a bank, and submitted these suggestions in rhyme to him for use among his colleagues. But he was not very hopeful about the matter. It was not (he assured me) that he underrated the verses, or in any sense lamented their lack of polish. No; it was rather, he felt, an indefinable something in the very atmosphere of the society in which we live that makes it spiritually difficult to sing in banks. And I think he must be right; though the matter is very mysterious. I may observe here that I think there must be some mistake in the calculations of the Socialists. They put down all our distress not to a moral tone, but to the chaos of private enterprise. Now, banks are private; but post offices are Socialistic: therefore I naturally expected that the post office would fall into the collectivist idea of a chorus. Judge of my surprise when the lady in my local post office (whom I urged to sing) dismissed the idea with far more coldness than the bank clerk had done. She seemed, indeed, to be in a considerably greater state of depression than he. Should anyone suppose that this was the effect of the verses themselves, it is only fair to say that the specimen verse of the Post Office Hymn ran thus:

> "O'er London our letters are shaken
>   like snow,
> Our wires o'er the world like the
>   thunderbolts go.
> The news that may marry a maiden
>   in Sark,
> Or kill an old lady in Finsbury
>   Park."
> Chorus (with a swing of joy and energy):
> "Or kill an old lady in Finsbury
>   Park."

And the more I thought about the matter the more painfully certain it seemed that the most important and typical modern things could not be done with a chorus. One could not, for instance, be a great financier and sing; because the essence of being a great financier is that you keep quiet. You could not even in many modern circles be a public man and sing; because in those circles the essence of being a public man is that you do nearly everything in private. Nobody would imagine a chorus of moneylenders. Everyone knows the story of the solicitors' corps of volunteers who, when the Colonel on the battlefield cried "Charge!" all said simultaneously, "Six-and eightpence."[8] Men can sing while charging in a military, but hardly in a legal sense. And at the end of my reflections I had really got no further than the subconscious feeling of my friend the bank clerk—that there is something spiritually suffocating about our life; not about our laws merely, but about our life. Bank clerks are without songs not because they are poor, but because they are sad. Sailors are much poorer. As I passed homewards I passed a little tin building of some religious sort, which was shaken with shouting as a trumpet is torn with its own tongue. *They* were singing anyhow; and I had for an instant a fancy I had often had before: that with us the superhuman is the only place where you can find the human. Human nature is hunted, and has fled into sanctuary. ■

Notes

[1] Flemish coast—the coast of Belgium

[2] Flanders—a section of Belgium

[3] *Quicquid agunt homines votum timor ira voluptas*— (Latin) Whatever humans do concerning a vow, [it is to them] fear, anger, pleasure.

[4] Chaucer—Geoffrey Chaucer (1343–1400) English writer

[5] Elgin marbles—Greek sculptures collected by Lord Elgin and taken to England in 1803

[6] Ostend—A town in Belgium. Ships traveling from the Continent to England often travel between Ostend, Belgium, and Dover, England.

[7] Kentish—Kent is a section of southern England.

[8] "Six-and eightpence"—Six shillings (an English unit of money, no longer used) and eight pence (pennies)

Making Connections through Discussion and Writing

1. Chesterton introduces the theme of this piece through commenting on statues. How does his observation prepare the reader for the discussion that follows?

    _____
    _____
    _____
    _____
    _____

2. Why does Chesterton feel that songs and work should go together?

    _____
    _____
    _____
    _____
    _____

3. According to Chesterton, why is modern humanity devoid of song in the workplace, particularly in the world of business?

    _____
    _____
    _____
    _____
    _____

4. Do you agree with Chesterton's assessment of modern society: "There is something spiritually suffocating about our life; not about our laws merely, but about our life"? In a persuasive paragraph, defend your answer, supporting it with specific examples and with citations from Chesterton's text.

    _____
    _____
    _____
    _____
    _____
    _____
    _____
    _____
    _____
    _____
    _____
    _____
    _____
    _____

5. What does Chesterton mean when he writes "that with us the superhuman is the only place where you can find the human"?

_____

_____

_____

_____

_____

_____

_____

6. In earlier times vocation was connected to God's calling on individual lives. Today vocation is thought of as work that is done to support what is considered "important" in people's lives. Explain how the division between real life and one's work affects the activities and relationships of family members, co-workers, and friends.

_____

_____

_____

_____

_____

_____

_____

_____

_____

_____

_____

_____

_____

_____

_____

Rabindranath Tagore
The Man Had No Useful Work

Rabindranath Tagore (1861–1941), winner of the Nobel Prize for literature in 1913, is one of modern India's most famous poets. He founded an influential educational institution, Visva-Bharati, in 1901, a school dedicated to "the ideal of the spiritual unity of all races." He published more than sixty volumes of poetry, eight novels, eight short-story collections, and twenty-four plays. The following poem affirms the value of aesthetic creativity in the face of a wholly pragmatic society.

Vocabulary ....

con (verb)
rents (noun)
vagaries

The man had no useful work, only vagaries of various kinds.

Therefore it surprised him to find himself in Paradise after a life spent perfecting trifles.

Now the guide had taken him by mistake to the wrong Paradise—one meant only for good, busy souls.

In this Paradise, our man saunters along the road only to obstruct the rush of business.

He stands aside from the path and is warned that he tramples on sown seed. Pushed, he starts up: hustled, he moves on.

A very busy girl comes to fetch water from the well. Her feet run on the pavement like rapid fingers over harp-strings. Hastily she ties a negligent knot with her hair, and loose locks on her forehead pry into the dark of her eyes.

The man says to her, "Would you lend me your pitcher?"

"My pitcher?" she asks, "to draw water?"

"No, to paint patterns on."

"I have no time to waste," the girl retorts in contempt.

Now a busy soul has no chance against one who is supremely idle.

Every day she meets him at the well, and every day he repeats the same request, till at last she yields.

Our man paints the pitcher with curious colors in a mysterious maze of lines.

The girl takes it up, turns it round and asks, "What does it mean?"

"It has no meaning," he answers.

The girl carries the pitcher home. She holds it up in different lights and tries to con its mystery.

At night she leaves her bed, lights a lamp, and gazes at it from all points of view.

This is the first time she has met with something without meaning.

On the next day the man is again near the well.

The girl asks, "What do you want?"

"To do more work for you!"

"What work?" she enquires.

"Allow me to weave colored strands into a ribbon to bind your hair."

"Is there any need?" she asks.

"None whatever," he allows.

The ribbon is made, and thenceforward she spends a great deal of time over her hair.

The even stretch of well-employed time in that Paradise begins to show irregular rents.

The elders are troubled; they meet in council.

The guide confesses his blunder, saying that he has brought the wrong man to the wrong place.

The wrong man is called. His turban, flaming

From *The Fugitive and Other Poems* by Rabindranath Tagore.

with color, shows plainly how great that blunder has been.

The chief of the elders says, "You must go back to the earth."

The man heaves a sigh of relief: "I am ready."

The girl with the ribbon round her hair chimes in: "I also!"

For the first time the chief of the elders is faced with a situation which has no sense in it. ■

Name: _____   Section: _____   Date: _____

Making Connections through Discussion and Writing

1. What irony is expressed in the opening three lines of the poem?

_____
_____
_____
_____
_____

2. Underline the images and phrases that indicate the appropriateness of the girl's being in this "practical" paradise.

3. Why is the girl so fascinated by the man's answer about his design having "no meaning"?

_____
_____
_____
_____
_____

4. a. Why is the man so willing to return to earth?

_____
_____
_____
_____

   b. Why does the girl decide to return there also?

_____
_____
_____
_____

5. What theme or themes do you find in this short poem?

_____
_____
_____
_____
_____
_____
_____

Thomas Merton
What Is a Monk?

Thomas Merton (1915–1968), an ordained Roman Catholic priest and a Trappist monk, was a highly influential voice on religious and social issues during the last half of the twentieth century. He published more than fifty books and is known for his ability to critically evaluate contemporary culture. *The Seven Storey Mountain* (1948) is considered a modern classic of spiritual autobiography. Other works include *The New Man* (1961), *Seeds of Destruction* (1964), and *Mystics and Zen Masters* (1967). He was accidentally electrocuted on a visit to Thailand, where he was engaged in dialogue with Buddhist monks and scholars. The selection below is taken from his book describing the monastic life, *The Silent Life* (1957).

A monk is a man who has been called by the Holy Spirit to relinquish the cares, desires and ambitions of other men, and devote his entire life to seeking God. The concept is familiar. The reality which the concept signifies is a mystery. For in actual fact, no one on earth knows precisely what it means to "seek God" until he himself has set out to find Him. No man can tell another what his search means unless that other is enlightened, at the same time, by the Spirit speaking within his own heart. In the end, no one can seek God unless he has already begun to find Him. No one can find God without having first been found by Him. A monk is a man who seeks God because he has been found by God.

In short, a monk is a "man of God."

Since all men were created by God that they might find Him, all men are called in some sense to be "men of God." But not all are called to be monks. A monk is therefore one who is called to give himself exclusively and perfectly to the one thing necessary for all men—the search for God. It is permissible for others to seek God by a road less direct, to lead a good life in the world, to raise a Christian family. The monk puts these things aside, though they may be good. He travels to God by the direct path, *recto tramite*.[1] He withdraws from "the world." He gives himself entirely to prayer, meditation, study, labor, penance, under the eyes of God. The monk is distinguished even from other religious vocations by the fact that he is essentially and exclusively dedicated to seeking God, rather than seeking souls for God.

Let us face the fact that the monastic vocation tends to present itself to the modern world as a problem and as a scandal.

In a basically religious culture, like that of India, or of Japan, the monk is more or less taken for granted. When all society is oriented beyond the mere transient quest of business and pleasure, no one is surprised that men should devote their lives to an invisible God. In a materialistic culture which is fundamentally irreligious the monk is incomprehensible because he "produces nothing." His life appears to be completely useless. Not even Christians have been exempt from anxiety over this apparent "uselessness" of the monk, and we are familiar with the argument that the monastery is a kind of dynamo which, though it does not "produce" grace, procures this infinitely precious spiritual commodity for the world.

The first Fathers of monasticism were concerned with no such arguments, valid though they may be in their proper context. The Fathers did not feel that the search for God was something that needed to be defended. Or rather, they saw that if men did not realize in the first place that God was to be sought, no other defence of monasticism would avail with them.

Is God, then, to be sought?

The deepest law in man's being is his need for God, for life God is Life. "In Him was life, and the life was the light of men, and the light shineth in the darkness and the darkness comprehended it not" (John 1:5). The deepest need of our darkness is to comprehend the light which shines in the midst of it. Therefore God has given us as His first commandment: "Thou shalt love the Lord thy God with thy whole heart, and with thy whole soul and with all thy strength." The monastic life is nothing but the life of those who have taken the first commandment in deadly earnest, and have, in the words of St. Benedict, "preferred nothing to the love of Christ."

But Who is God? Where is He? Is Christian monasticism a search for some pure intuition of the Absolute? A cult of the supreme Good? A worship of perfect and changeless Beauty? The very emptiness of such abstractions strikes the heart cold. The Holy One, the Invisible, the Almighty is infinitely greater and more real than any abstraction of man's devising. But He has said: "No one shall see me and live" (Exodus 33:20). Yet the monk persists in crying out with Moses: "Show me Thy face" (Exodus 33:13).

The monk, then, is one who is so intent upon the search for God that he is ready to die in order to see Him. That is why the monastic life is a "martyrdom" as well as a "paradise," a life that is at once "angelic" and "crucified."

St. Paul resolves the problem: "God who commanded the light to shine out of darkness, hath shined in our hearts to give the light of the knowledge of the glory of God, in the face of Christ Jesus" (2 Corinthians 4:6).

The monastic life is the rejection of all that obstructs the spiritual rays of this mysterious light. The monk is one who leaves behind the fictions and illusions of a merely human spirituality in order to plunge himself in the faith of Christ. Faith is the light which illumines him in mystery. Faith is the power which seizes upon the inner depths of his soul and delivers him up to the action of the divine Spirit, the Spirit of liberty, the Spirit of love. Faith takes him, as the power of God took the ancient prophets, and "stands him upon his feet" (Ezekiel 2:2) before the Lord. The monastic life is life in the Spirit of Christ, life in which the Christian gives himself entirely to the love of God which transforms him in the light of Christ.

"The Lord is a Spirit, and where the Spirit of the Lord is, there is liberty. But we all, beholding the glory of the Lord with open face, are transformed into the same image from glory to glory, as by the Spirit of the Lord" (2 Corinthians 3:17–18). What St. Paul has said of the inner life of every Christian becomes in all truth the main objective of the monk, living in his solitary cloister. In seeking Christian perfection the monk seeks the fullness of the Christian life, the complete maturity of Christian faith. For him, "to live is Christ."

In order to be free with the freedom of the children of God, the monk gives up his own will, his power to own property, his love of ease and comfort, his pride, his right to raise a family, his freedom to dispose of his time as he pleases, to go where he likes and to live according to his own judgment. He lives alone, poor, in silence. Why? Because of what he believes. He believes the word of Christ, Who has promised: "There is no man who has left house or parents or brethren or wife or children for the Kingdom of God's sake, who shall not receive much more in this present time, and in the world to come life everlasting" (Luke 18:29–30).

∎

Note

[1] *recto tramite*—(Latin) the right or direct pathway

Making Connections through Discussion and Writing

1. In this essay Merton seeks to explain the vocation, or calling, of a monk as a special way of dedicating oneself to God.

   a. Underline the sentence in which Merton says that this calling is different from other religious callings.

   b. Explain how and why you agree or disagree with Merton's ideas on this subject.

   _____
   _____
   _____
   _____
   _____
   _____
   _____
   _____
   _____
   _____

2. According to Merton, why does the modern world consider the monastic life "completely useless"?

   _____
   _____
   _____
   _____
   _____

3. How does Merton defend the monastic life's producing an "infinitely precious spiritual commodity for the world"?

   _____
   _____
   _____
   _____
   _____

4. a. Compare or contrast the way Merton defends the vocation of the monk and the way Tagore, in his poem "The Man Had No Useful Work," defends that of the artist.

   _____
   _____
   _____
   _____
   _____
   _____

b.   How do they attempt to convince readers?

_____

_____

_____

_____

_____

_____

5.   Sayers, in "Why Work?" asserts the value of work as a way of fulfilling our natures as human beings. How might the "work" of a monk satisfy Sayers' propositions?

_____

_____

_____

_____

_____

_____

_____

_____

_____

_____

_____

_____

_____

_____

_____

_____

Richard Wilbur
A Plain Song for Comadre

Richard Wilbur (b. 1921) is an American poet whose carefully crafted poetry usually contains rhyme and regular meter. He is known for his use of reason as a framework to discuss the meaning of life experiences. He has been influenced by the metaphysical poets, especially Andrew Marvell, and the contemporary poet, Wallace Stevens. His books of poetry include *The Beautiful Changes* (1947); *Things of This World* (1956), a book that won a Pulitzer Prize; *The Poems of Richard Wilbur* (1963); *Walking to Sleep: New Poems and Translations* (1969); and *The Mind-Reader* (1976). He is also known for his elegant translations of French drama. In the poem below Wilbur affirms the value of work that is well done. Such work, he suggests, becomes a form of worship.

Vocabulary . . . .

> furrow
> upbraids

[handwritten: Holy Things:]

Though the unseen may vanish, though insight fails
And doubter and downcast saint
Join in the same complaint,
What holy things were ever frightened off
By a fly's buzz, or itches, or a cough?
Harder than nails   6

They are, more warmly constant than the sun,
At whose continual sign
The dimly prompted vine   *[handwritten: holy things are always there whether you see them or not.]*
Upbraids itself to a green excellence.
What evening, when the slow and forced expense
Of sweat is done,   12

[handwritten: high quality] Does not the dark come flooding the straight furrow
Or filling the well-made bowl?
What night will not the whole
Sky with its clear studs and steady spheres
Turn on a sound chimney? It is seventeen years
Come tomorrow   18

That Bruna Sandoval has kept the church
Of San Ysidro, sweeping
And scrubbing the aisles, keeping
The candlesticks and the plaster faces bright,
And seen no visions but the thing done right
From the clay porch   24

To the white altar. For love and in all weathers
This is what she has done.
Sometimes the early sun
Shines as she flings the scrubwater out, with a crash
Of grimy rainbows, and the stained suds flash
Like angel-feathers.   30 ∎

Note

[1] comadre—(Spanish) godmother

Making Connections through Discussion and Writing

1. In this poem, the first five lines voice a complaint that is shared at times by both sinner and saint. What is that complaint?

   _____

   _____

   _____

   _____

   _____

2. a. Underline the words and phrases that assert the strength of holy things.

   b. How do these images suggest the abiding nature and positive influence of these things?

   _____

   _____

   _____

   _____

   _____

3. The natural darkness that "floods" and "fills" the things man makes, and the night sky that "turns," may appear to be negative forces, rendering human creations futile. A reading more consistent with the theme of the poem, however, suggests that the good work of humans *shapes* nature, refocuses natural forces around the artifacts of human making. How do the adjectives from lines 13–17—"straight," "well-made," and "sound,"—suggest the importance of *quality* in these made things and in their power to shape nature?

   _____

   _____

   _____

   _____

   _____

4. The passage from line 11 through line 17 is probably the most difficult part of the poem.

   a. Suggest how Wilbur may be using this section to link the holy things of the opening lines to the work of Bruna Sandoval described in the last half of the poem.

   _____

   _____

   _____

   _____

   _____

   _____

b. What does this link suggest about the ordinary, menial work of this woman?

_____

_____

_____

_____

5. a. Describe Bruna Sandoval and her work.

_____

_____

_____

_____

_____

b. How does her daily work become a form of worship?

_____

_____

_____

_____

_____

6. a. Underline the images in the last stanza of the poem.

b. How do the images that come at the end of the poem create a sense of transcendence and resolution?

_____

_____

_____

_____

_____

7. a. There is textual evidence that Bruna Sandoval does not herself perceive the "rainbows" or notice that the suds are like "angel-feathers." How may this lack of awareness relate her to the "doubter and down-cast saint" of the poem's opening lines?

_____

_____

_____

_____

b. What does this suggest about the "holiness" of her work?

_____

_____

_____

_____

8. a. Indicate the meter of the poem by marking the stressed syllables with "✓" and unstressed syllables with "◡".

    b. What's the rhyme scheme?

    _____

    c. Do you think this poem is itself an example of the kind of crafting that gives order and shape to human experience? Explain your answer, especially noting the structure and imagery of the poem.

    _____
    _____
    _____
    _____
    _____
    _____
    _____
    _____
    _____
    _____
    _____
    _____
    _____
    _____

Ann Patchett

The Language of Faith

Ann Patchett (b. 1964) is a prize-winning novelist who grew up in Nashville, Tennessee. Her first novel, *The Patron Saint of Liars,* was listed as one of the *New York Times* "Notable Books of the Year" in 1992. She has since published several other novels, including *The Magician's Assistant* (1998) and *Taft* (1999). The following informal essay, reprinted from an issue of *Image: A Journal of Arts and Religion*, traces how Patchett developed habits of discipline she believes to be essential to an artist's success.

Once I loved a man who loved tennis. This was years ago. He had given up the game long before we met, but I took great pleasure in watching him follow matches on television. Wimbledon was a sacred time in his house. He knew the game better than he knew himself. He could spot a foot fault before the toe of the shoe crossed the line. He understood tennis because he had played it when he was a boy, an hour before school in the morning, three hours after school in the afternoon, all day on Saturday and Sunday. His parents drove him to matches in the distant corners of the state. He played in wind, scorching heat, bitter cold. He was good, he told me so. Maybe there was a flicker of hope that he would be a professional player, but then one year some other boy was better and he lost his ranking. It doesn't matter. He didn't become a tennis star. He became a novelist.

I know many young people who want to be novelists. There are flocks of them everywhere I go, and yet the young person I know now who I think would make the best novelist doesn't write at all. I met her last year when I was speaking at her high school. She was sixteen then and she sat in the front of the class. When I asked if there were any questions, her hand shot up with such urgency I thought she was going to tell me there was a man at the door with a gun. "What do you do when you know you're faking the emotion in your art?" she asked me. "What if you're really good and so nobody else can see it, but you know that instead of creating something genuine, you're creating the illusion of something genuine? Does it bother you? What happens when you don't know how to stop it?"

I stared at her. She was looking at me as if this was information she desperately needed. I should say here that I've been asked many questions about my work: Do you write in the morning? Do you use a computer? Are these characters based on people you really know? No one had ever asked me about the nature of faking emotion, and it is a question that deserves to be asked. On the other side of the room, her teacher looked uncomfortable. "Eun-Mee is a violinist," the woman said by way of explanation.

Eun-Mee followed me from class to class, asking how I could write about things I had never experienced. How could I write about having children when I didn't even want children? And what should she do when she was instructed to play with passion when passion was a subject with which she had little experience? When my day at the school was over, she hugged me and asked for my address. I keep all of her letters. I have yet to hear her play, but if she puts half of the intensity into her music that she does into her sentences, I imagine she could make the concert hall draperies burst into flame. Even if she never becomes famous, these letters are a remarkable accountant of a rare and brilliant youth.

Eun-Mee plays the violin not unlike the way the man I loved played tennis. She plays in the morning and after school and in any other hour she can find. On the weekends her mother drives her the eight hours each way to and from Cincinnati so that she can study at a proper conservatory. She does her schoolwork for the week in the car. What other time is there for homework when a girl has everything to learn about the violin?

Of course, I have many friends who are writers who didn't start out with the grinding hours of tennis or violins or figure skating. Most of us wasted our childhoods in the normal ways—tormenting our sisters, walking our dogs, dreaming of being in love. But the ones who learned discipline by whatever vehicle they were given are the ones, I think, who are best groomed for writing. There is an art to repetition, to staying perfectly still and keeping your eye on the ball, to doing anything so long that some part of your body aches and begs you to stop. The same line of music played over and over again until you can't really hear it anymore begins to shape a person as slowly and completely as any rock was ever shaped by water. You can't see it, but it's happening. I had my own discipline in my youth, though it wasn't nearly so interesting—no contests, no trophies. The rewards for my sort of practice were much more abstract. If I was a rock, then my water was Catholicism. What I did through my childhood was pray.

I think all the girls with whom I spent twelve years in Catholic school were reconfigured by the experience of religion. If they weren't praying as hard, they were certainly going through the motions, and this is a case where I think it's safe to say form and content will lead you to similar places. When I was very young, before the school made a few attempts to be modern and attract some Protestant girls who paid higher tuition rates, we marched up the narrow back stairs of the convent to the chapel every morning and said the rosary. This is where it begins, lined up in that hallway, the nuns keeping us silent and still simply by glancing in our general direction. We filed past the glass-topped relic table which contained sacred chips of bone and tiny scraps of sheeting that had touched a saint's dead body or had touched a piece of sheeting that had once touched a saint's dead body. The relics were labeled with names pinned to the felt that lined the case. Every morning, I looked in and every morning the sight of those minuscule bits of bone seemed spectacularly holy, as if Christ himself had been waiting beneath the glass. It was an honor; that's the only word that seems fitting. To file past the presence of real saints, the physical remnants of sacred lives, was something I never grew tired of. I loved it with pure passion. I loved the blue walls of the convent, the painted statue of Mary outside the sisters' living room on the second floor with her gold star crown, the plain sandstone Mary in the chapel that stood on the left-hand side of the altar near the communion rail. Her feet were bare and she crushed a snake beneath her toes. I memorized her feet, the sleeping lines of the snake, every fold and drape of her gown, her open palms, the kindness of her face. I was careful to divide my time evenly between her statue and the statue of Saint Joseph that stood to the right of the altar, but it was Mary I loved.

We said the rosary together, grades one through twelve, with the older girls saying the first half of the Hail Mary[1] and the younger girls repeating the second half like a chorus. The young girls were each given a chunky plastic rosary every morning on our way up the stairs and we returned it before we went down to class. The thinking was that an average child was not to be trusted with a rosary of her own until First Communion. For me that was still two years away.

The problem with writing about one's self is that people are too in love with the details of their own lives. They go on and on about things that fascinate them when in fact those things are utterly boring to everyone else. I know this is true and yet still I want to go on, to recount the shape of every bead beneath my fingertips, the wording of every prayer. You will think at first it is all a matter of simple repetition, but it's not. No two Hail Marys, no matter how many of them there are prayed, can mean exactly the same thing. Ask the young violinist who plays a Bach violin concerto for five hours at a stretch. Every time, it is a surprise. I could tell you about every pew, every red leather kneeler, because there was not one that hadn't bent to the shape of my knees. I could tell you about the designs on the floors and the stained glass windows, the thrilling, narrow walkway behind the altar, the sacristy where the priest, on those rare and lucky occasions a priest came to say a mass, hung his vestments. And if you were chosen to be the one who lit the candles, or better yet, the one to snuff them out after the mass had ended, then your heart soared for the rest of the day. There was no better prize for all the hours logged there on your knees.

The answer to Eun-Mee's question about faking the emotion is that some days you do. Some days you mouth your Hail Mary's while your mind skims over the plots of sitcoms seen ten years before. Some days the mass is a meditation on what light does to dust in the air. But you keep showing up. You play the Bach again, you write another paragraph, you repeat the prayer. You hold on to the form through the stretches when the content has vanished. You observe the mass in all its glorious dullness. You practice. And then, in a storm in the middle of the night, all of the love comes rushing back to you. There is no reason why it left or why it should return, but it does. You play like a girl reaching into her chest to show her own heart. I write with so much assurance I feel like I am simply copying it down from some other source. And the prayers that you say—suddenly they are the rope that binds you to God.

After the school did away with the compulsory rosary[2] in the morning, I went to school early to go to chapel and said my prayers alone. Alone, I could forsake the pews and go to the front, near the statues, where I thought my prayers had a better chance of being heard. What was I praying for? I cannot even begin to remember. It wasn't about a thing, something to have, a larger allowance or peace in the world; it was about prayer itself. It was about how straight I could hold my back. It was about repetition, the pleasure of the words I could not help but whisper.

Look at the girl who kneels at the front of the church on the cold marble floor, saying her rosary alone for Mary the Mother of God. That is me. I am learning to write.

I knew even then that I wanted to be a writer. I practiced. I wrote poems and stories. I read books. I prayed. How do we separate the things we learn? When they told us at the end of second grade that when we came back in the fall everything we wrote would be in cursive, they might as well have told me that everything I wrote would be in French. Those loops, those tails that grew down from letters, formed a language unto itself. But I learned to reconfigure my letters at the same time that I learned how to make the letters mean something by their combinations, and so those two acts stay locked together in my mind: the pencil moving back and forth between the lines becomes a creative act. I practice my letters. I practice writing poems. I pray.

I'm disappointed with myself for never having learned to speak a foreign language. I wish with all the hindsight of age that someone would have forced it on me in my youth. I wish that while they were teaching me to speak Spanish and Italian they had also taught me to downhill ski, another thing I feel I should have mastered before I understood how difficult it was. But I did learn the language of faith. I learned it the easiest way: by immersing myself in a world of native speakers. I spent my childhood in the specific and peculiar culture of nuns. There are two stories I could tell here and both would be equally true: one in which I suffer all kinds of injustice and lunacy at the hands of nuns, another in which I am shown enormous kindness

and tenderness by these women. With a few startling exceptions, I loved the sisters and admired them. Nuns, at least the ones I knew, operated off of faith the way the rest of us operate off of air. Faith was the currency, the law, and the philosophy of their society. More than anything it was the language, the spoken or unspoken answer to any question. I have known nuns who left the church, but I have never known one who had forgotten her faith. In its first stages, faith is the ability to believe in something, to trust absolutely. When you are more fluent in the language, faith is the ability to believe and trust in something you will never see, to love absolutely something that is not there. In the final phase, when faith becomes second nature, the language in which you dream, faith is the ability to see all around you that which cannot be seen. To take this from the very comfortable abstract to the less comfortable concrete, advanced faith is the ability to see God in all things. Advanced skills in the language of faith mean that when you don't see God in something, you roll up your sleeves and seek Him out, because you know, absolutely, that He is there.

Because my family lived in the country, far away from where my sister and I went to school, my mother would drop us off at the convent early in the morning, an hour or more before school started, so that she could get to work on time, and we would stay at the convent for hours after the other children had gone home, doing homework or being helpful. I remember sorting silverware in the big kitchen of the sisters' dining room where I didn't study faith but overheard it spoken casually.

Literature has a great tradition of brilliant, soulful atheists, but I think it has an even greater tradition of faith: Tolstoy and Dostoevsky, Eliot and Yeats, Graham Greene and Flannery O'Connor.[3] What is writing, after all, but the ability to believe in that which you cannot see, to in the end believe in it so completely that you see it everywhere? Every day that I write it is in this secret language of faith. I cannot imagine how I will get to the end of any novel I begin. I do not know who the characters will become. I do not know how they will travel through their stories, how they will manage the fates I dole out to them. I have no idea if I will have the strength or courage to complete what I have started, but I am sure of my faith. It's a little like closing your eyes and stepping forward, one step and then another and another. It is trusting that I will be able to do this thing even when I don't understand exactly what it is I am doing.

Here's another way that faith prepared me to

be a novelist: it introduced me to the ways of God. When I was a child, my greatest career goal was to be a saint, a human manifestation of God's love. I didn't mention it to anyone, but the nuns, possibly sensing my natural impertinence, said that it was a sin to think we could be like God. The delicate balance was to try to live by God's example while knowing with full humility that you would fail. But why did I have to fail? I liked the challenge of tireless goodness, I liked the expectations of perfection. I thought about the Amish and their quilts, the way they would tilt the last block that was sewn on to create a mistake so that their creation did not achieve perfection and presume to stand with God. But isn't that the greatest admission of the perfection of their work? It was so flawless that a error had to be wittingly inserted into the pattern. Tilt the block back to its proper position and there is God in the art. Why not try?

As I got older and gave up my childhood dreams of matching God in terms of perfection, I became a novelist and decided to match Him in more ambitious ways. Like Him, my intention was to set out to create the world, maybe even in my own likeness. I would scoop people out of the air and shape them with my hands. The cities they lived in, the houses, the countries—those were my creation. The texture of their hair, the cereal they chose for breakfast and the way they chewed it, who they loved, the lies they told—every word of it was mine. I decided when they would have children and how those children would grow. I decided when their story would come to an end. People ask me, do your characters surprise you? Do you know everything that happens to them before you start to write, or do they take turns you had never imagined? It is not unlike predestination, one of the many religious questions I spent my youth trying to puzzle out. What I decided then was that God knew the future. We were not simple marionettes. He did not lift our hand and set it down again, but being the One who set us into motion, being the One who knows everything, He knows what we're going to do without having to control it. Yes, that was how I would write my books, as much as I believed God had written me. It is through my mimicking of the order of the universe that I offer God praise.

Children dream of complete access to candy stores, or they did when I was a child. Maybe now they dream they have keys to the entire mall. Adults often dream of the writer's life. Sometimes it's because they want to write and to this I say, yes, you are exactly right. It is something worth wanting. Most people have a story to tell. They've been putting sentences together all their lives and so would like the chance to do it on a professional basis. They would like to see a book with their name on it sitting in a store and again I say, yes, pursue that. It is indeed as fine a feeling as you imagine it to be. But that's not about writing. That's about having written. The other part of my life that people claim they want, I have to wonder about. Very few people are suited to live in a total absence of structure. What compels you to get out of bed when no one cares at all whether you do or you don't? I live alone with my dog, and walking her is as much of a routine as I manage. I don't sell my novels until I finish them, so if one takes me six months or six years to complete, there aren't going to be any badgering phone calls reminding me of looming deadlines. I can play computer solitaire by the hour. I have spent days at a time on the sofa, reading novel after novel, and no one complains. I tell myself it is related to my work, that I am thinking, and even I'm not sure whether or not I'm telling the truth. But I never stray too far. I have something inside me that gets me up again, gets me back to my work. I have an almost unnatural ability to hold still, and this is the thing I think most people lack, the thing that separates the writers from the non-writers: the simple act of focusing. That came from faith as well.

Or not exactly from faith. That focus came from church, and church and faith are not the same thing. When I was very small, still capable of being formed, my parents were still married, and I still lived in Los Angeles. My mother did not participate in the ritual of Sunday Mass, but for my father it was extremely important. I don't know if mass was important to him personally at that point in his life, but it was important to him that his daughters went to mass. Because my sister was three and a half years older, I never remember her being anything but the poster girl for good church behavior. I, on the other hand, wanted to flip through the hymnals. There was no greater pleasure than locking your toe beneath the kneeler,[4] lifting it up a half an inch, dropping it. Stretching out on the pew was a great temptation, but I knew I would get caught long before I made myself comfortable. The trick was to recline right up to the limit of good taste and then recline a half an inch more, which usually involved touching a stranger with your shoe. At this point my father would yank me up and take me outside.

This was thirty years ago and more, a time when people spanked their children, hit their children, in order to correct misbehavior, and no one called it abuse. I do not call it abuse. I call it taking my place in a long family history. I certainly know my father had been yanked out of plenty of masses to get smacked by his father for crimes that far exceeded my own (I will only say they had to do with the contents of the collection plate.) My grandfather, who lived to be a very lucid ninety-three years of age, told stories of getting knocked around with the best of them by his father. Several years ago my father took a parenting class as part of his work as a police officer. He was supposed to counsel parents who were having problems with their children. He called me one evening when he got home from school.

"I wasn't supposed to hit you," he said. "I feel terrible about this."

"Don't be ridiculous," I said.

"No, really," he said. "It turns out you aren't supposed to hit children at all."

But as every police officer knows, there is a connection between fear and respect, and nowhere is that connection clearer than in the Catholic Church. Heaven and hell, God's love, God's wrath, Revelations and Micah all in one Bible. If love is the backbone, then fear is the muscle that wraps around it. Fear makes us work. Fear makes us eager to please. God grants us unconditional love and acceptance but only if we ask for it, only if we know enough to say how terribly sorry we are. Forget that part of the deal and you are out of the garden for good.

By instilling in me an element of fear to temper his love, my father taught me a wonderful trick that the children I see today don't know how to perform: he taught me to sit still and to listen. This is an important point. Sitting still was only half of what my father was after. He wanted me to pay attention. He seemed to have the ability to watch my mind wander off as clearly as he saw my leg kick the pew in front of me, and time and again he stilled the leg and called back my wandering thoughts. "Listen to the priest," he whispered, his voice making it very clear that this was a warning and the next time there would be action without words. I was a smart kid and I put it all together. I held still. I paid attention. I listened.

Try to become a prodigy on the violin without those qualities. Try to write a novel. I suppose there are a few very lucky people who are born into stillness and concentration. The rest of us need to be reminded.

It was my parents' divorce that sent me to Catholic school on the other side of the country. My father wanted my sister and me to have a religious education, the kind that he could have provided but now had to entrust to the Sisters of Mercy. They pursued my father's objectives of stillness and concentration without ever having met him, something I found an eerie coincidence until I realized that Catholic schools were all more or less cut from the same cloth—from the one my father attended in Los Angeles in the 1940s to the one I attended in Tennessee in the late 1960s and 1970s. The Sisters[5] swatted and spanked in the early years of my education but then were moved away from corporal punishment. Someone told them not to hit us and all at once they stopped. But there was still a lesson to be taught, and they were never deterred from their lessons. What I remember most about those early years was that crimes were punished collectively. When some girl had done something wrong, we were all made to leave our work and stand until the perpetrator confessed, and when she did confess she was sent to the chapel alone to pray while the rest of us were to pray for her, if we chose to do so, at our desks. In short, she was not sent to the principal for hiding the gym shoes of another girl in a foolish prank, she was sent to God. The nuns shook their heads grimly, unable to imagine how God would forgive such a thing.

When I was in seventh grade I entered the dreaded science class of Sister Lawrence Mary, the most feared nun in the convent. The rumors of how she had beaten her students in the days before that privilege was revoked were the stuff of legends. By the time I came to her she was old and terrifying, and I had no idea why she ever needed to hit anyone, as the respect she commanded was absolute. Still, it is her punishment that stays with me most clearly: nothing annoyed her more than a student who said "is when," as in, "Photosynthesis is when a plant. . . ." We were to say, "Photosynthesis is the process by which a plant. . . ." "The process by which"—a phrase I still use no matter how stilted it sounds. If one of us slipped up, forgot, Sister Lawrence Mary told us all to stand, stretch our arms straight out to the sides, and contemplate Christ's suffering on the cross. Christ had died for us, in all our stupidity, in all our unworthiness. He could remember every detail of our lives and we couldn't even remember to say, "The process by which." Somehow these two things were connected, and it was hinted that if we could only have remembered to speak properly, then perhaps Christ would not have been nailed to the cross. Even though it had happened two thousand years before our birth, He knew how we would fail Him and so He was forced to die.

It is a simple exercise. Try it sometime. Stand with your arms out to the side and contemplate anything, Christ's death, the poor quality of tomatoes in winter, anything. You won't last long unless Sister Lawrence Mary is there to scare you into compliance. You won't last until you learn how to last, to figure out exactly in what you are being instructed and take the lesson.

The girl in Introduction to Biology, standing with all the other girls who are dressed exactly alike, standing with her arms out to her sides, she is learning to be a writer.

When people tell stories of Catholic school they are either hysterically funny in some off-Broadway play or they are the bitter and furious explanation of why they will never darken the door of the Church of Rome again. My story is something in between. I believe there are many different ways to learn, and I was taught in a complex combination of styles. But learn I did. I know how to sit and think for hours alone in silence, to keep looking at something long after I'm ready to turn my face away. Maybe I would have come to that without the beautiful and painful lessons of my faith. I suppose I will never know.

I am a Catholic. That doesn't mean I follow all the teachings of the church or that many of those teachings don't make me want to hide my face in my hands. That doesn't mean I make it to mass every week. That doesn't mean that I believe anyone else needs to sign up for Catholicism or any religion at all as a way to have a relationship with God. I am simply stating a fact about myself. "I used to be a Catholic," people will say to me. Or, for those who prefer to express themselves through bumper stickers, there is the one that simply says, "Recovering Catholic." For years I said the same thing. I shopped for a religion the way other people looked for houses. Then a man named Robert Tannenbaum, a college professor and former rabbi, set me straight. "Stick with your tribe," he told me. "The religion isn't the point. They're all pretty much the same. Stay with the one that you know and use it to help you look for God." It was simple, logical, and completely accurate advice. I stopped being angry, I reconsidered the past, and I took up with my church again.

I have a theory that in life we are given a set of categories by which to define ourselves: our family, our country, our race, our religion, along with a whole host of other, smaller subsets of identification. Even when they are terrible, our families are very difficult to leave completely. Our race we are stuck with, even when we are persecuted because of it or feel shamed by it. Our country, well, most expatriates come home eventually. I haven't always felt good about being an American—certain wars, certain administrations, certain decisions about spending, have made my stomach turn, but I didn't pack up for France. How can you leave your country? How can you leave who you are? That leaves religion as the thing we can most comfortably step out of. We can carry around a story of a philandering priest as the answer for our hasty departure. We can disconnect ourselves from our faith when we can't deny some poisonous uncle at a family reunion. I will only say it is a loss because it is important to have groups with whom to stand as a member. I have been to Catholic churches in cities where I didn't know a soul, and countries where I did not speak the language, but I could always follow along, and, by doing so, I could feel that there were some edges in my world. The church does not define my relationship with God, but it taught me how to believe. It taught me to be faithful to God, to be loyal. And I am. I only expanded the lesson, so that I am faithful to myself as well, to the people I love, and to my work. Without faith, I would never be able to find the end of the story. ■

Notes

1 Hail Mary—a prayer addressing the mother of Jesus

2 rosary—a set number of prayers said with the use of prayer beads (a "rosary")

3 Tolstoy . . . O'Connor—these are renowned writers: Leo Tolstoy and Fyodor Dostoevsky, nineteenth-century Russian novelists; T. S. Eliot, a twentieth-century English poet; William Butler Yeats, a twentieth-century Irish poet; Graham Greene, a twentieth-century English novelist; and Flannery O'Connor, a twentieth-century American novelist and short story writer.

4 kneeler—a cushion upon which one kneels to pray

5 Sisters—the nuns who served as teachers

Making Connections through Discussion and Writing

1. Ann Patchett introduces her idea that discipline is necessary for the vocation of a writer by telling about what two people she knew. Who were they, and how did they achieve the discipline she values?

   _____
   _____
   _____
   _____
   _____
   _____
   _____
   _____
   _____

2. Why does Patchett go into such detail about her early life in a Catholic school?

   _____
   _____
   _____
   _____

3. Patchett finds that the ability to "hold still," to "sit still and listen," and to "focus" is an essential part of her creativity. What, according to her, were the experiences that built this ability in her?

   _____
   _____
   _____
   _____
   _____
   _____
   _____
   _____
   _____
   _____
   _____
   _____
   _____

4. Explain Patchett's statement: "Every day that I write it is in this secret language of faith."

   _____
   _____
   _____
   _____

5. Like Sayers in "Toward a Christian Aesthetic," Patchett clarifies her thoughts about her artistry by an analogy with God's creativity.

    a. Circle the paragraph in which she explains this.

    b. How does she use this analogy to give insight into God's foreknowledge and man's free will?

    _____

    _____
    _____
    _____
    _____
    _____
    _____

Alice Walker

In Search of Our Mothers' Gardens

Alice Walker (b. 1944), African-American novelist, short story writer, and essayist, is best known for her novel *The Color Purple* (1982), which was made into a major motion picture. This novel won the American Book award and the Pulitzer Prize for fiction. Her early stories were contained in the two volumes *In Love and Trouble* and *You Can't Keep a Good Woman Down*. In the essay below, Walker values the heritage of artistic work done by African-American women with the humble materials available to them.

I described her own nature and temperament. Told how they needed a larger life for their expression. . . . I pointed out that in lieu of proper channels, her emotions had overflowed into paths that dissipated them. I talked beautifully I thought, about an art that would be born, an art that would open the way for women the likes of her. I asked her to hope, and build up an inner life against the coming of that day. . . . I sang, with a strange quiver in my voice, a promise song.

— "Avey," Jean Toomer, *Cane*

The poet speaking to a prostitute who falls asleep while he's talking —

When the poet Jean Toomer walked through the South in the early twenties, he discovered a curious thing: Black women whose spirituality was so intense, so deep, so *unconscious*, they were themselves unaware of the richness they held. They stumbled blindly through their lives: creatures so abused and mutilated in body, so dimmed and confused by pain, that they considered themselves unworthy even of hope. In the selfless abstractions their bodies became to the men who used them, they became more than "sexual objects," more even than mere women: they became Saints. Instead of being perceived as whole persons, their bodies became shrines: what was thought to be their minds became temples suitable for worship. These crazy "Saints" stared out at the world, wildly, like lunatics—or quietly, like suicides; and the "God" that was in their gaze was as mute as a great stone.

Who were these "Saints"? These crazy, loony, pitiful women?

Some of them, without a doubt, were our mothers and grandmothers.

In the still heat of the post-Reconstruction South, this is how they seemed to Jean Toomer: exquisite butterflies trapped in an evil honey, toiling away their lives in an era, a century, that did not acknowledge them, except as "the *mule* of the world." They dreamed dreams that no one knew— not even themselves, in any coherent fashion—and saw visions no one could understand. They wandered or sat about the countryside crooning lullabies to ghosts, and drawing the mother of Christ in charcoal on courthouse walls.

They forced their minds to desert their bodies and their striving spirits sought to rise, like frail whirlwinds from the hard red clay. And when those frail whirlwinds fell, in scattered particles, upon the ground, no one mourned. Instead, men lit candles to celebrate the emptiness that remained, as people do who enter a beautiful but vacant space to resurrect a God.

Our mothers and grandmothers, some of them: moving to music not yet written. And they waited.

They waited for a day when the unknown thing that was in them would be made known; but guessed, somehow in their darkness, that on the day of their revelation they would be long dead. Therefore to Toomer they walked, and even ran, in slow motion. For they were going nowhere immediate, and the future was not yet within their grasp. And men took our mothers and grandmothers, "but got no pleasure from it." So complex was their passion and their calm.

To Toomer, they lay vacant and fallow as autumn fields, with harvest time never in sight: and he saw them enter loveless marriages, without joy; and become prostitutes, without resistance; and become mothers of children without fulfillment.

For these grandmothers and mothers of ours were not "Saints," but Artists; driven to a numb and bleeding madness by the springs of creativity in them for which there was no release. They were Creators, who lived lives of spiritual waste, because they were so rich in spirituality—which is the basis of Art—that the strain of enduring their unused and unwanted talent drove them insane. Throwing away this spirituality was their pathetic attempt to lighten the soul to a weight their work-worn, sexually abused bodies could bear.

What did it mean for a Black woman to be an artist in our grandmothers' time? In our great-grandmothers' day? It is a question with an answer cruel enough to stop the blood.

Did you have a genius of a great-great-grand-mother who died under some ignorant and depraved white overseer's lash? Or was she required to bake biscuits for a lazy backwater tramp, when she cried out in her soul to paint watercolors of sunsets, or the rain falling on the green and peaceful pasturelands? Or was her body broken and forced to bear children (who were more often than not sold away from her)—eight, ten, fif-teen, twenty children—when her one joy was the thought of modeling heroic figures of Rebellion, in stone or clay?

How was the creativity of the Black woman kept alive, year after year and century after century, when for most of the years Black people have been in America, it was a punishable crime for a Black person to read or write? And the freedom to paint, to sculpt, to expand the mind with action, did not exist. Consider, if you can bear to imagine it, what might have been the result if singing, too, had been forbidden by law. Listen to the voices of Bessie Smith, Billie Holiday, Nina Simone, Roberta Flack, and Aretha Franklin,[1] among others, and imagine those voices muzzled for life. Then you may begin to comprehend the lives of our "crazy," "Sainted" mothers and grandmothers. The agony of the lives of women who might have been Poets, Novelists, Essayists, and Short Story Writers (over a period of centuries), who died with their real gifts stifled within them.

And, if this were the end of the story, we would have cause to cry out in my paraphrase of Okot p'Bitek's[2] great poem:

O, my clanswomen
Let us all cry together!
Come,

Let us mourn the death of our mother,
The death of a Queen
The ash that was produced
By a great fire!
O this homestead is utterly dead
Close the gates
With *lacari* thorns,
For our mother
The creator of the Stool is lost!
And all the young women
Have perished in the wilderness!

But this is not the end of the story, for all the young women—our mothers and grandmothers, *ourselves*—have not perished in the wilderness. And if we ask ourselves why, and search for and find the answer, we will know beyond all efforts to erase it from our minds, just exactly who, and of what, we Black American women are.

One example, perhaps the most pathetic, most misunderstood one, can provide a backdrop for our mothers' work: Phillis Wheatley, a slave in the 1700s.

Virginia Woolf, in her book, *A Room of One's Own*, wrote that in order for a woman to write fiction she must have two things, certainly: a room of her own (with key and lock) and enough money to support herself.

What then are we to make of Phillis Wheatley, a slave, who owned not even herself? This sickly, frail, Black girl who required a servant of her own at times—her health was so precarious—and who, had she been white would have been easily considered the intellectual superior of all the women and most of the men in the society of her day.

Virginia Woolf wrote further, speaking of course not of our Phillis, that any woman born with a great gift in the sixteenth century [insert *eighteenth century*, insert *Black woman*, insert *born or made a slave*] would certainly have gone crazed, shot herself, or ended her days in some lonely cottage outside the village, half witch, half wizard [insert *Saint*], feared and mocked at. For it needs little skill and psychology to be sure that a highly gifted girl who had tried to use her gift for poetry would have been so thwarted and hindered by contrary instincts [add *chains, guns, the lash, the ownership of one's body by someone else, submission to an alien religion*], that she must have lost her health and sanity to a certainty."

The key words, as they relate to Phillis, are "contrary instincts." For when we read the poetry of Phillis Wheatley—as when we read the novels of Nella Larsen or the oddly false-sounding autobiography of that freest of all Black women writers,

Zora Hurston[3]—evidence of "contrary instincts" is everywhere. Her loyalties were completely divided, as was, without question, her mind.

But how could this be otherwise? Captured at seven, a slave of wealthy, doting whites who instilled in her the "savagery" of the Africa they "rescued" her from . . . one wonders if she was even able to remember her homeland as she had known it, or as it really was.

Yet, because she did try to use her gift for poetry in a world that made her a slave, she was "so thwarted and hindered by . . . contrary instincts that she . . . lost her health. . . ." In the last years of her brief life, burdened not only with the need to express her gift but also with a penniless, friendless "freedom" and several small children for whom she was forced to do strenuous work to feed, she lost her health, certainly. Suffering from malnutrition and neglect and who knows what mental agonies, Phillis Wheatley died.

So torn by "contrary instincts" was Black, kidnapped, enslaved Phillis that her description of "the Goddess"—as she poetically called the Liberty she did not have—is ironically, cruelly humorous. And, in fact, has held Phillis up to ridicule for more than a century. It is usually read prior to hanging Phillis's memory as that of a fool. She wrote:

The Goddess comes, she moves divinely fair,
Olive and laurel binds her *golden* hair:
Wherever shines this native of the skies,
Unnumber'd charms and recent graces rise.
[Emphasis mine]

It is obvious that Phillis, the slave, combed the "Goddess's" hair every morning; prior, perhaps, to bringing in the milk, or fixing her mistress's lunch. She took her imagery from the one thing she saw elevated above all others.

With the benefit of hindsight we ask, "How could she?"

But at last, Phillis, we understand. No more snickering when your stiff, struggling, ambivalent lines are forced on us. We know now that you were not an idiot nor a traitor; only a sickly little Black girl, snatched from your home and country and made a slave; a woman who still struggled to sing the song that was your gift, although in a land of barbarians who praised you for your bewildered tongue. It is not so much what you sang, as that you kept alive, in so many of our ancestors, *the notion of song.*

Black women are called, in the folklore that so aptly identifies one's status in society, "the *mule* of the world," because we have been handed the burdens that everyone else—*everyone* else—refused to carry. We have also been called "Matriarchs," "Superwomen," and "Mean and Evil Bitches." Not to mention "Castraters" and "Sapphire's Mama." When we have pleaded for understanding, our character has been distorted; when we have asked for simple caring, we have been handed empty inspirational appellations, then stuck in the farthest corner. When we have asked for love, we have been given children. In short, even our plainer gifts, our labors of fidelity and love, have been knocked down our throats. To be an Artist and a Black woman, even today, lowers our status in many respects, rather than raises it: and yet, Artists we will be.

Therefore we must fearlessly pull out of ourselves and look at and identify with our lives the living creativity some of our great-grandmothers were not allowed to know. I stress *some* of them because it is well known that the majority of our great-grandmothers knew, even without "knowing" it, the reality of their spirituality, even if they didn't recognize it beyond what happened in the singing at church—and they never had any intention of giving it up.

How they did it: those millions of Black women who were not Phillis Wheatley, or Lucy Terry or Frances Harper or Zora Hurston or Nella Larsen or Bessie Smith—nor Elizabeth Catlett, nor Katherine Dunham, either—brings me to the title of this essay, "In Search of Our Mothers' Gardens," which is a personal account that is yet shared, in its theme and its meaning, by all of us. I found, while thinking about the far-reaching world of the creative Black woman, that often the truest answer to a question that really matters can be found very close.

In the late 1920s my mother ran away from home to marry my father. Marriage, if not running away, was expected of seventeen-year-old girls. By the time she was twenty, she had two children and was pregnant with a third. Five children later, I was born. And this is how I came to know my mother: she seemed a large, soft, loving-eyed woman who was rarely impatient in our home. Her quick, violent temper was on view only a few times a year, when she battled with the white landlord who had the misfortune to suggest to her that her children did not need to go to school.

She made all the clothes we wore, even my brothers' overalls. She made all the towels and sheets we used. She spent the summers canning vegetables and fruits. She spent the winter evenings making quilts enough to cover all our beds.

During the "working" day, she labored beside—not behind—my father in the fields. Her day began before sunup, and did not end until late at night. There was never a moment for her to sit down, undisturbed, to unravel her own private thoughts; never a time free from interruption—by work or the noisy inquiries of her many children. And yet, it is to my mother—and all our mothers who were not famous—that I went in search of the secret of what has fed that muzzled and often mutilated, but vibrant, creative spirit that the Black woman has inherited, and that pops out in wild and unlikely places to this day.

But when, you will ask, did my overworked mother have time to know or care about feeding the creative spirit?

The answer is so simple that many of us have spent years discovering it. We have constantly looked high, when we should have looked high—and low.

For example: in the Smithsonian Institution in Washington, D.C., there hangs a quilt unlike any other in the world. In fanciful, inspired, and yet simple and identifiable figures, it portrays the story of the Crucifixion. It is considered rare, beyond price. Though it follows no known pattern of quilt-making, and though it is made of bits and pieces of worthless rags, it is obviously the work of a person of powerful imagination and deep spiritual feeling. Below this quilt I saw a note that says it was made by "an anonymous Black woman in Alabama, a hundred years ago."

If we could locate this "anonymous" Black woman from Alabama, she would turn out to be one of our grandmothers—an artist who left her mark in the only materials she could afford, and in the only medium her position in society allowed her to use.

As Virginia Woolf wrote further, in *A Room of One's Own*:

"Yet genius of a sort must have existed among women as it must have existed among the working class. [Change this to *slaves* and *the wives and daughters of sharecroppers*.] Now and again an Emily Brontë or a Robert Burns [change this to *a Zora Hurston or a Richard Wright*] blazes out and proves its presence. But certainly it never got itself on to paper. When, however, one reads of a witch being ducked, of a woman possessed by devils [or *Sainthood*], of a wise woman selling herbs [our root-workers], or even a very remarkable man who had a mother, then I think we are on the track of a lost novelist, a suppressed poet, of some mute and inglorious Jane Austen. . . . Indeed, I would venture to guess that Anon, who wrote so many poems without singing them, was often a woman. . . ."

And so our mothers and grandmothers have, more often than not anonymously, handed on the creative spark, the seed of the flower they themselves never hoped to see: or like a sealed letter they could not plainly read.

And so it is, certainly, with my own mother. Unlike Ma Rainey's songs, which retained their creator's name even while blasting forth from Bessie Smith's mouth, no song or poem will bear my mother's name. Yet so many of the stories that I write, that we all write, are my mother's stories. Only recently did I fully realize this: that through years of listening to my mother's stories of her life, I have absorbed not only the stories themselves, but something of the manner in which she spoke, something of the urgency that involves the knowledge that her stories—like her life—must be recorded. It is probably for this reason that so much of what I have written is about characters whose counterparts in real life are so much older than I am.

But the telling of these stories, which came from my mother's lips as naturally as breathing, was not the only way my mother showed herself as an artist For stories, too, were subject to being distracted, to dying without conclusion. Dinners must be started, and cotton must be gathered before the big rains. The artist that was and is my mother showed itself to me only after many years. This is what I finally noticed:

Like Mem, a character in *The Third Life of Grange Copeland*, my mother adorned with flowers whatever shabby house we were forced to live in. And not just your typical straggly country stand of zinnias, either. She planted ambitious gardens—and still does—with over fifty different varieties of plants that bloom profusely from early March until late November. Before she left home for the fields, she watered her flowers, chopped up the grass, and laid out new beds. When she returned from the fields she might divide clumps of bulbs, dig a cold pit, uproot and replant roses, or prune branches from her taller bushes or trees—until night came and it was too dark to see.

Whatever she planted grew as if by magic, and her fame as a grower of flowers spread over three counties. Because of her creativity with her flowers, even my memories of poverty are seen through a screen of blooms—sunflowers, petunias, roses, dahlias, forsythia, spirea, delphiniums, verbena . . . and on and on.

And I remember people coming to my mother's yard to be given cuttings from her flowers; I hear again the praise showered on her because whatever rocky soil she landed on, she turned into a garden. A garden so brilliant with colors, so original in its design, so magnificent with life and creativity, that to this day people drive by our house in Georgia—perfect strangers and imperfect strangers—and ask to stand or walk among my mother's art.

I notice that it is only when my mother is working in her flowers that she is radiant, almost to the point of being invisible—except as Creator: hand and eye. She is involved in work her soul must have. Ordering the universe in the image of her personal conception of Beauty.

Her face, as she prepares the Art that is her gift, is a legacy of respect she leaves to me, for all that illuminates and cherishes life. She has handed down respect for the possibilities—and the will to grasp them.

For her, so hindered and intruded upon in so many ways, being an artist has still been a daily part of her life. This ability to hold on, even in very simple ways, is work Black women have done for a very long time.

This poem is not enough, but it is something, for the woman who literally covered the holes in our walls with sunflowers:

> They were women then
> My mama's generation
> Husky of voice—Stout of
> Step
> With fists as well as
> Hands
> How they battered down
> Doors
> And ironed
> Starched white
> Shirts
> How they led
> Armies
> Headragged Generals
> Across mined
> Fields
> Booby-trapped
> Ditches
> To discover books
> Desks
> A place for us
> How they knew what we
> *Must* know
> Without knowing a page
> Of it
> Themselves.

Guided by my heritage of a love of beauty and a respect for strength—in search of my mother's garden, I found my own.

And perhaps in Africa over two hundred years ago, there was just such a mother; perhaps she painted vivid and daring decorations in oranges and yellows and greens on the walls of her hut; perhaps she sang—in a voice like Roberta Flack's—*sweetly* over the compounds of her village; perhaps she wove the most stunning mats or told the most ingenious stories of all the village story-tellers. Perhaps she was herself a poet—though only her daughter's name is signed to the poems that we know.

Perhaps Phillis Wheatley's mother was also an artist.

Perhaps in more than Phillis Wheatley's biological life is her mother's signature made clear. ■

Notes

1 Bessie Smith . . . Aretha Franklin—famous American blues and jazz singers

2 Okot p'Bitek—African author; the poem is from *Song of Lawino: An Africa Lament.*

3 Phillis Wheatley . . . Nella Larsen . . . Zora Hurston—African-American authors

Making Connections through Discussion and Writing

1. a. Why were black women called "saints" by many?

    b. What leads Walker to call them "artists"?

    _____
    _____
    _____
    _____
    _____
    _____
    _____

2. a. Walker proceeds through part one of this essay by asking key questions. Underline the questions that lead the author to examine different aspects of the "artistry" of Black women.

    b. Explain how each question functions to reveal insights into American social history.

    _____
    _____
    _____
    _____
    _____
    _____
    _____
    _____
    _____
    _____
    _____
    _____

3. a. What is Walker's attitude toward the early American poet, Phyllis Wheatley?

    _____
    _____
    _____
    _____
    _____

    b. What does she mean by the phrase "contrary instincts"?

    _____
    _____
    _____
    _____

4. How does Walker use her own mother's story to make it yield historical significance?

_____
_____
_____
_____
_____
_____
_____

5. a. What artistic forms does Walker identify as revealing the unrecognized artistry of Black women?

_____
_____
_____
_____
_____

b. What is significant in the fact that this artistry was anonymous?

_____
_____
_____
_____
_____

c. Why does Walker believe it is important to speak about this artistry?

_____
_____
_____
_____
_____

6. Alice Walker, in "In Search of Our Mothers' Gardens," searches her own heritage for evidence of artistic sensitivity and creativity. What can you discover in your family background (such as arts, crafts, or customs) that reveals character traits, the values associated with work or with aesthetics?

_____
_____
_____
_____
_____
_____
_____
_____
_____

Synthesis/Essay Suggestions: Vocation

1. Write an essay in which you employ Sayers' ideas about consumption and the meaning of work to urge a renewed emphasis on Christian stewardship of the environment, drawing on the materials from the "Ecology" section, such as Lynn White, Jr.'s essay, as you make your point.

2. Use Sayers' analysis of attitudes toward work to examine Chesterton's observation that most modern workers do not sing at their workplaces.

3. Some critics of the monastic life suggest that it is "sub-Christian" because it fails to be of service to human society. Do you agree? Examine the ethical dimension of the monastic calling, using Sayers' analysis to evaluate Merton's defense of the cloistered life.

4. Authors in this section affirm the meaningfulness of work. Dorothy L. Sayers finds work a way of fulfilling our vocations, a way of obeying God, finding our true selves, and moving toward our destinies. The poet Richard Wilbur in "A Plain Song for Comadre" suggests that the faithful daily work of a person can become an act of praise. G. K. Chesterton asserts that daily work should result in fulfillment and joy. Building on these ideas, suggest how Merton's description of the life of a monk, combining a daily regimen of work and prayer, reveals this life to be a true vocation.

5. A charge of ethical inadequacy could be made against a life devoted to aesthetics. Use Sayers' essay to evaluate the positions taken by characters in the Tagore poem, "The Man Had No Useful Work."

6. Alice Walker praises her ancestors' artistry expressed through their gardens and quilts. Evaluate this work according to the ideas of Sayers and Tagore.

7. Tagore and Patchett emphasize different stages of artistic creativity in their works in this section. Examine J. R. R. Tolkien's story "Leaf by Niggle," and distinguish the various stages of creativity described there.

Chapter 7

Historical Knowledge

Historical knowing—the telling of human events, what has happened, and why it has happened—is a way of knowing reality as old as humans themselves. Stories of hunting for food, battling with enemies, seeking new places for the clan to live, facing the dangers of the forest or the plains—these are stories that underlie the oldest tales that came to be cast into written language. These were the stories that gathered up the memories of the tribal elders and passed on a communal identity to younger generations.

Later documents—such as trading accounts, government documents, laws, religious writings, and private letters—all witnessed to the rise of various cultures in the ancient world. Early historians recorded the military and civil achievements of their nations or the mighty acts of their kings. Always the events were represented as being true and accurate, but the accounts were likely to be questioned by historians from different cultures or by later historians.

This brings us to a major problem of historiography: how can it claim to be "objective" if every observer of any event is himself or herself inextricably engaged in the "subject" being observed. That is to say, if someone decides to write on the causes of World War I, for example, the very selection of what that historian selects as significant facts will be conditioned by his or her attitudes toward the conflict, attitudes and assumptions that the historian may not even be aware of. It is said that the victors write the history of wars, and that has generally been true in the past, but with modern communications media creating instant awareness of many dimensions of any event, the voice of the victims finds expression also. No clearly defined history of the Viet Nam War was possible, for "revisionist" histories in the form of newscasts, photojournalism, and commentary were being produced simultaneously with news releases announced by the American and United Nations armed forces.

A review of histories written over the course of civilization reveals that underlying assumptions have shaped the way data have been selected as being historically significant, the way the events have been interpreted, and the way lessons of the resulting histories have been applied. Religious cultures have produced "providential" history, such as the Old Testament account of the Jewish exodus from Egypt or Governor Bradford's journal recording the small band of English pilgrims coming from Holland and settling the Plymouth colony in the wilderness of the New World. (Even the term "New World" indicates a particular cultural bias; it was certainly not new to the native inhabitants. And to call these inhabitants "Indians" or "Native Americans" indicates other biases.)

"Intellectual histories" or "histories of ideas" have been written attempting to describe the worldviews of past cultures, focusing on the dominant attitudes of a particular period (works such as E. M. W. Tillyard's *Elizabethan World Picture* or Frank Lovejoy's *The Great Chain of Being*). Often the sources of such histories are accounts by thinkers, artists, religious, or social leaders of the culture being focused on.

More recently, the influence of Marxism has led historians to focus on economic forces determining social strata and the quality of life among the common people. Popular and scholarly studies have described "everyday" life, the domestic life of ordinary people from various eras. Such things as the work of the lower classes, the training of apprentices, folk beliefs and superstitions, initiation rituals, marriage customs, family structures are valid areas for historians to explore, and they equip themselves with knowledge from modern economic theory, anthropological and psychological insights, and many other areas to help them probe the meaning of past events.

As cultural attitudes change, new questions are asked about past events, yielding new historical insights. The changes in the American literary canon are an example of new cultural attitudes leading to questions that revise notions of literary value. As recently as the 1960s, few women or minority writers were represented in American literature anthologies. Today, because of a new sense of the value of America's multicultural heritage and the new attention of feminist scholars, American literature anthologies have greatly increased in scope, with early Spanish colonial accounts, slave narratives, Native American legends, and a wide variety of nineteenth- and twentieth-century poems, essays, and stories from women and minority writers being added to the canon. This kind of revision is simply one example of the ongoing process of historical revaluation of past events or past achievements.

Students may still wonder why histories must continue to be written about events that have already been dealt with extensively. Do we really need another study of Thomas Jefferson? And why must yet another American history text be produced for high school students? Why not just issue a set of supplements to update the older texts with more current events?

Other, even more basic, questions one might ask about history as a way of knowing reality are "What is a historical fact?" and "Who decides what is a historical fact?" If such a fact is simply something that happened, is a male student's shaving himself in the morning a historical fact? Could any approach or methodology of history make this act have historical significance? The act of shaving no doubt would be irrelevant to a study of the military history of the twentieth century, but a social historian could find it to be significant to a study of the American middle class customs or manners and the various reactions to middle class values, such as the Beat or Hippie movements of the 1950s and 1960s.

The following readings encourage students to explore these and other questions about the nature and methods of historical inquiry. Luke Timothy Johnson briefly sketches out the guidelines for what he considers valid historiography. Robert Darnton, in "Workers Revolt . . . ," illustrates a modern historian at work. Finding himself intrigued by a "joke" he does not "get" in a journal entry of an early eighteenth-century printer's apprentice in France, Darnton keeps asking questions, the answers to which inform him of the life and general attitudes of a whole class of people ignored by previous historians. In "The Discovery of the Past and the Idea of Progress," Richard Morris, taking a far more general approach, surveys the history of a cultural attitude toward time itself—past and future—and the belief in progress. Kay Boyle, using the vehicle of a fictional story, communicates to readers the effect of a historical catastrophe on an individual, thus bringing alive the human experience of historical events that might otherwise be known only in abstract terms.

Luke Timothy Johnson
The Character of Historical Knowing

Luke Timothy Johnson (b. 1943) is the Robert W. Woodruff Professor of New Testament and Christian Origins at the Chandler School of Theology at Emory University. Johnson, a Benedictine monk and a priest, received his Ph.D. from Yale University in 1976 and has become a leading Biblical scholar. He has published many books on the New Testament, the latest of which is *Living Jesus: Learning the Heart of the Gospel* (1999). This selection is taken from his book *The Real Jesus: The Misguided Quest for the Historical Jesus and the Truth of the Traditional Gospels* (1996).

Vocabulary ....

a priori
cognition
constitutive
demarcation

epistemology
historiography
proclivities

Popular equations are enabled by imprecise concepts and unexamined terms. The term *history* manifestly cannot be used simply for "the past" or "what happened in the past," any more than *historical* can be used simply as a synonym for "what was real about the past." History is, rather, the product of human intelligence and imagination. It is one of the ways in which human beings negotiate their present experience and understanding with reference to group and individual memory.

In its essence, history is a mode of human knowing. It is an interpretive activity. The stuff with which history works is human events in time and space, various kinds of records of such experiences (often but not necessarily written, and functioning basically as aide-mémoire),[1] and the effort to make sense of, or interpret, such experiences.

The intrinsic limitations to this form of knowing are, upon reflection, quickly evident. It is clear, first of all, that a great deal of what human beings consider "real" escapes historical knowledge. If history deals with human events in time and space (granting that time and space are meaningful and not simply themselves a priori categories of cognition), it misses a great deal. At the lower level, it misses things like fingernails and facial tics that partake of the human but never really surface as

parts of "events." At the upper end, it misses a great deal of what is most properly human, things like alienation and forgiveness, compassion and despair, meaning and value, love and hope.

Only with considerable stretching can these "realities" be called "historical." Yet, we insist, they are real. They are not necessarily "events"; they do not necessarily surface for our inspection; they may not enter collective memory. Nevertheless, they are often the most defining elements of our humanity. But they are not the stuff of history. Historical knowing is like a sieve that catches big chunks but lets much fine stuff slip through.

Even when we look more closely at the material history deals with best, "human events in time and space," we begin to recognize how slippery such cognition is. What constitutes a "human event"? We may speak of the "birth of the United Nations" 1945 as something that is inarguably a "historical event." And we are right. But what constituted it as an event? Who participated? When did it start? When did it end? If we press such issues, we become aware that to "do history," we must artificially edit out "stop frames" in the cinematic flow of human experience, must draw lines of demarcation that enable us to focus, describe, define, and interpret. Yet, if we are honest, we also

---

recognize that even in this simple editorial act, we are already engaging in interpretation. Our *selection* and *naming* of something as "event" is itself constitutive of the "event."

If so obvious and epochal an event as the founding of the United Nations turns out to be more elusive the closer we examine it, how much more is historical knowing limited when it comes to less public and prolonged events. As a teacher, for example, I may refer to one of my favorite lectures as a historical event: "The Historical Jesus Lecture of 1995." But what constituted such a lecture, after all? Was I the only significant character in the event, or were its hearers also constitutive of it? If they were, then did it matter whether they understood the lecture? We could ask further, when did that lecture begin? Was it when I started speaking, or had it begun when I first thought of the topic and outlined the talk? When did the lecture end? Or has it ended? Will the lecture be over before the last memory of the last hearer fades? For this "event," after all, was not about moving boundaries and rearranging national territory, but about moving minds in a certain direction and transforming internal terrain.

The same sort of ambiguity attends the second component of historical knowing, namely, the records of human events. Such records are inevitably selective. Not everything that happens is recorded, nor is everything that is recorded preserved. Not everything preserved is edited, translated, read, or understood. The documentary basis of our historical knowledge of some "great events" is astonishingly slender. Some events from antiquity are known only by a single sentence in a single work, preserved in a single manuscript. Records of human events are also selective because they represent only certain perspectives and interpretations. Even the most material historical data, such as inscriptions, inevitably result from *interpretations* by participants or observers of events. Historical knowing is limited to what this fragile skein of evidence allows.

The third component of history is most explicitly interpretive. It seeks to take the often sparse and accidental evidence of past human events and connect them in some meaningful pattern. The point or purpose of such a construal, however, has been a matter of debate from the birth of historiography. One position has held that the point of history is constructive: the memory of the past should serve as the source of positive and negative examples for the guidance of human behavior in the present. The other position has held that the proper

function of history is critical: the analysis of specific evidence acts as a corrective to distorted memory and current claims made on the basis of such memory. Both positions give implicit recognition to the fact that historical knowing is not disinterested knowledge. The search of "the past" is very much generated by questions posed by the present, and by debates concerning the shape of the future. Both constructive and critical historians are concerned with claims made in the present on the basis of an understanding of the past. Even the most positivist of historians, who insists that his or her only concern is to "get the record straight," must sooner or later respond to the question, Why should the record be straight?, just as the person who spends the whole day "just keeping my room straight" should be confronted with the question of why a room should be kept straight at such expenditure of time and effort.

The ideal of self-conscious critical historians is that "criticism" should be applied not only to the records of the past (testing their perspective, bias, interest), but equally to the ideological commitments of the present, including those of the historian. Part of the complexity and difficulty of the best historical research lies in sorting through the maze of subjectivity and self-interest operative not only in the past but also in the present. The difficulty of carrying out such self-criticism in a consistent fashion, together with the difficulty of even locating, much less allocating, the pieces of evidence of past memory, makes the doing of authentic historiography a daunting business and the examples of its accomplishment all the more worthy of appreciation.

Epistemology—the critical analysis of cognition—can become an irritant when it demands attention. This is because human knowing seems to work best when the subject is something other than itself. Aesthetic knowledge is better at discerning the beautiful in great art than it is at defining the nature of beauty and how the mind grasps it. Moral knowledge is better at distinguishing good behavior from nasty than it is at defining the nature of the virtuous and how the mind recognizes it. In the same way, historical knowing works best when it is puttering around with evidence from the past, but becomes progressively fuzzier when asked about the nature of historical knowledge. Fair enough. Excessive epistemology becomes cognitive cannibalism. But a little bit of it is important as a hedge against easy assumptions and arrogant certainties in any branch of knowledge.

The best practitioners of critical historiography,

therefore, are careful to make clear the character of their craft as a limited mode of knowledge, dependent on the frailties of the records of memory and the proclivities of self-interest. No serious historian, for example, would claim to render the "real" event or person, whether the event was Pearl Harbor or the person was Douglas MacArthur. The "real" event in all its complex particularity happened only once and cannot be recovered by any means. The serious historian recognizes that a "History of the Attack on Pearl Harbor" is a construction by the historian out of the available pieces.

If the historian is fortunate, there are many pieces, many forms of evidence and memory, so that the process of criticism can better sort out bias and the influences of subjective experience. If the historian is fortunate, there is rich information as well with which to contextualize a specific event, so that guesses concerning cause and effect might take on a higher level of probability. What is most important, however, is that the serious historian knows and acknowledges that historical knowl-edge deals only in degrees of probability, and never with certainty. The best historians candidly acknowledge their inability to penetrate the "reality" of the past, and confess that their craft involves in equal measure the attempt to verify the remaining evidence and the willingness to exercise creative guesswork to supply the most plausible or probable version that the evidence allows.

Because of the necessarily fragmentary character of all historical evidence, and because of the inevitable role of interpretive creativity on the part of the historian, serious practitioners of the craft are characterized by deep humility. They above all know how fragile their reconstructions are, how subject to revision, how susceptible to distortion when raised from the level of the probable to the certain. ∎

Note

[1] aide-mémoire—(French) a memory aid

Making Connections through Discussion and Writing

1. Identify the three components of "historical knowing" as given by Johnson.

_____
_____
_____

_____
_____
_____

_____
_____
_____

2. Explain why each component presents difficulties or ambiguities.

_____
_____
_____

_____
_____
_____

_____
_____
_____

3. Explain what Johnson means by his opening statement: "History is . . . the product of human intelligence and imagination."

_____
_____
_____
_____
_____

4. Remember some event that you experienced earlier in your life or some more recent event covered by new reports. Present it as a "historical event" by taking it through the process suggested by Johnson; then write a paragraph on your topic as a "historical account."
   a. Select and name the event.

_____

b. Describe any documentation or records about the event.

_____

_____

_____

_____

c. Interpret the event; tell what larger pattern of meaning it is a part of.

_____

_____

_____

_____

d. Compose a paragraph in which you treat the event as a historian might.

_____

_____

_____

_____

_____

_____

_____

_____

_____

_____

_____

_____

_____

_____

_____

_____

Robert Darnton

Workers Revolt:
The Great Cat Massacre of the Rue Saint-Séverin

Robert Darnton (b. 1939) is professor of history at Princeton University. He was named a Chevalier of the Legion d'Honneur (1999), the most prestigious award given by the French government. In 1995, Darnton was awarded the National Book Critics Circle Award in criticism for *The Forbidden Best Sellers of Pre-Revolutionary France.* The following selection is taken from his 1984 study of eighteenth-century French social history, *The Great Cat Massacre and Other Episodes from French Cultural History.*

Vocabulary . . . .

artisanal	ethnological
bludgeoning	ethos
bourgeois	Gargantuan
cassowaries	journeymen
caterwauling	oblique
charivari	opaque
compunction	pharisaical
confessor	repertory
cuckolding	

The funniest thing that ever happened in the printing shop of Jacques Vincent, according to a worker who witnessed it, was a riotous massacre of cats. The worker, Nicolas Contat, told the story in an account of his apprenticeship in the shop, rue Saint-Séverin, Paris, during the late 1730s.[1] Life as an apprentice was hard, he explained. There were two of them: Jerome, the somewhat fictionalized version of Contat himself, and Léveillé. They slept in a filthy, freezing room, rose before dawn, ran errands all day while dodging insults from the journeymen and abuse from the master, and received nothing but slops to eat. They found the food especially galling. Instead of dining at the master's table, they had to eat scraps from his plate in the kitchen. Worse still, the cook secretly sold the leftovers and gave the boys cat food—old rotten bits of meat that they could not stomach and so passed on to the cats, who refused it.

This last injustice brought Contat to the theme of cats. They occupied a special place in his narrative and in the household of the rue Saint-Séverin. The master's wife adored them, especially *la grise* (the gray), her favorite. A passion for cats seemed to have swept through the printing trade, at least at the level of the masters, or *bourgeois* as the workers called them. One bourgeois kept twenty-five cats. He had their portraits painted and fed them on roast fowl. Meanwhile, the apprentices were trying to cope with a profusion of alley cats who also thrived in the printing district and made the boys' lives miserable. The cats howled all night on the roof over the apprentices' dingy bedroom, making it impossible to get a full night's sleep. As Jerome and Léveillé had to stagger out of bed at four or five in the morning to open the gate for the earliest arrivals among the journeymen, they began the day in a state of exhaustion while the bourgeois slept late. The master did not even work with the men, just as he did not eat with them. He let the foreman run the shop and rarely appeared in it, except to vent his violent temper, usually at the expense of the apprentices.

One night the boys resolved to right this inequitable state of affairs. Léveillé, who had an extraordinary talent for mimickry, crawled along the roof until he reached a section near the master's bedroom, and then he took to howling and meowing so horribly that the bourgeois and his wife did not sleep a wink. After several nights of this treatment, they decided they were being bewitched. But instead of calling the curé—the master was exceptionally devout and the mistress exceptionally attached to her confessor—they commanded the apprentices to get rid of the cats. The mistress gave the order, enjoining the boys above all to avoid frightening her *grise*.

Gleefully Jerome and Léveillé set to work, aided by the journeymen. Armed with broom handles, bars of the press, and other tools of their trade, they went after every cat they could find, beginning with *la grise*. Léveillé smashed its spine with an iron bar and Jerome finished it off. Then they stashed it in a gutter while the journeymen drove the other cats across the rooftops, bludgeoning every one within reach and trapping those who tried to escape in strategically placed sacks. They dumped sackloads of half-dead cats in the courtyard. Then the entire workshop gathered round and staged a mock trial, complete with guards, a confessor, and a public executioner. After pronouncing the animals guilty and administering last rites, they strung them up on an improvised gallows. Roused by gales of laughter, the mistress arrived. She let out a shriek as soon as she saw a bloody cat dangling from a noose. Then she realized it might be *la grise*. Certainly not, the men assured her: they had too much respect for the house to do such a thing. At this point the master appeared. He flew into a rage at the general stoppage of work, though his wife tried to explain that they were threatened by a more serious kind of insubordination. Then master and mistress withdrew, leaving the men delirious with "joy," "disorder," and "laughter."[2]

The laughter did not end there. Léveillé reenacted the entire scene in mime at least twenty times during subsequent days when the printers wanted to knock off for some hilarity. Burlesque reenactments of incidents in the life of the shop, known as *copies* in printers' slang, provided a major form of entertainment for the men. The idea was to humiliate someone in the shop by satirizing his peculiarities. A successful *copie* would make the butt of the joke fume with rage—*prendre la chèvre* (take the

goat) in the shop slang—while his mates razzed him with "rough music." They would run their composing sticks across the tops of the type cases, beat their mallets against the chases, pound on cupboards, and bleat like goats. The bleating (*bais* in the slang) stood for the humiliation heaped on the victims, as in English when someone "gets your goat." Contat emphasized that Léveillé produced the funniest *copies* anyone had ever known and elicited the greatest choruses of rough music. The whole episode, cat massacre compounded by *copies*, stood out as the most hilarious experience in Jerome's entire career.

Yet it strikes the modern reader as unfunny, if not downright repulsive. Where is the humor in a group of grown men bleating like goats and banging with their tools while an adolescent reenacts the ritual slaughter of a defenseless animal? Our own inability to get the joke is an indication of the distance that separates us from the workers of preindustrial Europe. The perception of that distance may serve as the starting point of an investigation, for anthropologists have found that the best points of entry in an attempt to penetrate an alien culture can be those where it seems to be most opaque. When you realize that you are not getting something—a joke, a proverb, a ceremony—that is particularly meaningful to the natives, you can see where to grasp a foreign system of meaning in order to unravel it. By getting the joke of the great cat massacre, it may be possible to "get" a basic ingredient of artisanal culture under the Old Regime [pre-revolutionary France].

It should be explained at the outset that we cannot observe the killing of the cats at firsthand. We can study it only through Contat's narrative, written about twenty years after the event. There can be no doubt about the authenticity of Contat's quasi-fictional autobiography, as Giles Barber has demonstrated in his masterful edition of the text. It belongs to the line of autobiographical writing by printers that stretches from Thomas Platter to Thomas Gent, Benjamin Franklin, Nicholas Restif de la Bretonne, and Charles Manby Smith. Because printers, or at least compositors, had to be reasonably literate in order to do their work, they were among the few artisans who could give their own accounts of life in the working classes two, three, and four centuries ago. With all its misspellings and grammatical flaws, Contat's is perhaps the richest of these accounts. But it cannot be regarded as a mirror-image of what actually happened. It should be read as Contat's version of a happening, as his attempt to tell a story. Like all story telling, it sets the action in a frame of reference; it assumes a certain repertory of associations and responses on the part if its audience; and it provides meaningful shape to the raw stuff of experience. But since we are attempting to get at its meaning in the first place, we should not be put off by its fabricated character. On the contrary, by treating the narrative as fiction or meaningful fabrication we can use it to develop an ethnological *explication de texte* [interpretation of text].

The first explanation that probably would occur to most readers of Contat's story is that the cat massacre served as an oblique attack on the master and his wife. Contat set the event in the context of remarks about the disparity between the lot of workers and the bourgeois—a matter of the basic elements in life: work, food, and sleep. The injustice seemed especially flagrant in the case of the apprentices, who were treated like animals while the animals were promoted over their heads to the position the boys should have occupied, the place at the master's table. Although the apprentices seem most abused, the text makes it clear that the killing of the cats expressed a hatred for the bourgeois that had spread among all the workers: "The masters love cats; consequently [the workers] hate them." After masterminding the massacre, Léveillé became the hero of the shop, because "all the workers are in league against the masters. It is enough to speak badly of them [the masters] to be esteemed by the whole assembly of typographers."[3]

Historians have tended to treat the era of artisanal manufacturing as an idyllic period before the onset of industrialization. Some even portray the workshop as a kind of extended family in which master and journeymen labored at the same tasks, ate at the same table, and sometimes slept under the same roof.[4] Had anything happened to poison the atmosphere of the printing shops in Paris by 1740?

During the second half of the seventeenth century, the large printing houses, backed by the government, eliminated most of the smaller shops, and an oligarchy of masters seized control of the industry.[5] At the same time, the situation of the journeymen deteriorated. Although estimates vary and statistics cannot be trusted, it seems that their number remained stable: approximately 335 in 1666, 339 in 1701, and 340 in 1721. Meanwhile the number of masters declined by more than half, from eighty-three to thirty-six, the limit fixed by an edict in 1686. That meant fewer shops with larger work forces, as one can see from statistics on the density of presses: in 1644 Paris had seventy-five printing shops with a total of 180 presses; in 1701 it had fifty-one shops with 195 presses. This trend made it virtually impossible for journeymen to rise into the ranks of the masters. About the only way for a worker to get ahead in the craft was to marry a master's widow, for masterships had become hereditary privileges, passed on from husband to wife and from father to son.

The journeymen also felt threatened from below because the masters tended increasingly to hire *alloués*, or underqualified printers, who had not undergone the apprenticeship that made a journeyman eligible, in principle, to advance to a mastership. The *alloués* were merely a source of cheap labor, excluded from the upper ranks of the trade and fixed, in their inferior status, by an edict of 1723. Their degradation stood out in their name: they were *à louer* (for hire), not *compagnons* (journeymen) of the master. They personified the tendency of labor to become a commodity instead of a partnership. Thus Contat served his apprenticeship and wrote his memoirs when times were hard for journeymen printers, when the men in the shop in the rue Saint-Séverin stood in danger of being cut off from the top of the trade and swamped from the bottom.

How this general tendency became manifest in an actual workshop may be seen from the papers of the Société typographique de Neuchâtel (STN). To be sure, the STN was Swiss, and it did not begin business until seven years after Contat wrote his memoirs (1762). But printing practices were essentially the same way everywhere in the eighteenth century. The STN's archives conform in dozens of details to Contat's account of his experience. (They even mention the same shop foreman, Colas, who supervised Jerome for a while at the Imprimerie Royale and took charge of the STN's shop for a brief stint in 1779.) And they provide the only surviving record of the way masters hired, managed, and fired printers in the early modern era.

The STN's wage book shows that workers usually stayed in the shop for only a few months.[6] They left because they quarreled with the master, they got in fights, they wanted to pursue their fortune in shops further down the road, or they ran out of work. Compositors were hired by the job, *labeur* or *ouvrage* in printer's slang. When they finished a job, they frequently were fired, and a few pressmen had to be fired as well in order to maintain the balance between the two halves of the shop, the *casse* or composing sector and the *presse* or pressroom (two compositors usually set enough type to occupy a team of two pressmen.) When the foreman took on new jobs, he hired new hands. The hiring and firing went on at such a fierce pace that the work force was rarely the same from one week to the next. Jerome's fellow workers in the rue Saint-Séverin seem to have been equally volatile. They, too, were hired for specific *labeurs,* and they sometimes walked off the job after quarrels with the bourgeois—a practice common enough to have its own entry in the glossary of their slang which Contat appended to his narrative: *emporter son Saint Jean* (to carry off your set of tools or quit). A man was known as an *ancien* if he remained in the shop for only a year. Other slang terms suggest the atmosphere in which the work took place: *une chévre capitale* (a fit of rage), *se donner la gratte* (to get in a fight), *prendre la barbe* (to get drunk), *faire la déroute* (to go pub crawling), *promener sa chape* (to knock off work), *faire des loups* (to pile up debts).[7]

The violence, drunkenness, and absenteeism show up in the statistics of income and output one can compile from the STN's wage book. Printers worked in erratic spurts—twice as much in one week as in another, the weeks varying from four to six days and the days beginning anywhere from four in the morning until nearly noon. In order to keep the irregularity within bounds, the masters sought out men with two supreme traits: assiduousness and sobriety. If they also happened to be skilled, so much the better. A recruiting agent in Geneva recommended a compositor who was willing to set out for Neuchâtel in typical terms: "He is a good worker, capable of doing any job he gets, not at all a drunkard and assiduous at his labor."[8]

The STN relied on recruiters because it did not have an adequate labor pool in Neuchâtel and the streams of printers on the typographical *tours de France* sometimes ran dry. The recruiters and employers exchanged letters that reveal a common set of assumptions about eighteenth-century artisans: they were lazy, flighty, dissolute, and unreliable. They could not be trusted, so the recruiter should not loan them money for travel expenses and the employer could keep their belongings as a kind of security deposit in case they skipped off after collecting their pay. It followed that they could be discarded without compunction, whether or not they had worked diligently, had families to support, or fell sick. The STN ordered them in "assortments" just as it ordered paper and type. It complained that a recruiter in Lyon "sent us a couple in such a bad state that we were obliged to ship them off"[9] and lectured him about failing to inspect the goods: "Two of those whom you have sent to us have arrived all right, but so sick that they could infect all the rest; so we haven't been able to hire them. No one in town wanted to give them lodg-

ing. They have therefore left again and took the route for Besançon, in order to turn themselves in at the *hôpital.*"[10] A bookseller in Lyon advised them to fire most of their men during a slack period in their printing in order to flood the labor supply in eastern France and "give us more power over a wild and undisciplinable race, which we cannot control."[11] Journeymen and masters may have lived together as members of a happy family at some time somewhere in Europe, but not in the printing houses of eighteenth-century France and Switzerland.

Contat himself believed that such a state had once existed. He began his description of Jerome's apprenticeship by invoking a golden age when printing was first invented and printers lived as free and equal members of a "republic," governed by its own laws and traditions in a spirit of fraternal "union and friendship."[12] He claimed that the republic still survived in the form of the *chapelle* or workers' association in each shop. But the government had broken up general associations; the ranks had been thinned by *alloués*; the journeymen had been excluded from masterships; and the masters had withdrawn into a separate world of *baute cuisine* and *grasses matinées*. The master in the rue Saint-Séverin ate different food, kept different hours, and talked a different language. His wife and daughters dallied with worldly abbés. They kept pets. Clearly, the bourgeois belonged to a different subculture—one which meant above all that he did not work. In introducing his account of the cat massacre, Contat made explicit the contrast between the worlds of worker and master that ran throughout the narrative: "Workers, apprentices, everyone works. Only the masters and mistresses enjoy the sweetness of sleep. That makes Jerome and Léveillé resentful. They resolve not to be the only wretched ones. They want their master and mistress as associates (*associés*)."[13] That is, the boys wanted to restore a mythical past when masters and men worked in friendly association. They also may have had in mind the more recent extinction of the smaller printing shops. So they killed the cats.

But why cats? And why was the killing so funny? Those questions take us beyond the consideration of early modern labor relations and into the obscure subject of popular ceremonies and symbolism.

Folklorists have made historians familiar with the ceremonial cycles that marked off the calendar year for early modern man.[14] The most important of these was the cycle of carnival and Lent, a period of revelry followed by a period of abstinence. During carnival the common people suspended the normal rules of behavior and ceremoniously reversed the social order or turned it upside down in riotous procession. Carnival was a time for cutting up by youth groups, particularly apprentices, who organized themselves in "abbeys" ruled by a mock abbot or king and who staged charivaris or burlesque processions with rough music in order to humiliate cuckolds, husbands who had been beaten by their wives, brides who had married below their age group, or someone else who personified the infringement of traditional norms. Carnival was high season for hilarity, sexuality, and youth run riot—a time when young people tested social boundaries by limited outbursts of deviance, before being reassimilated in the world of order, submission, and Lentine seriousness. It came to an end on Shrove Tuesday or Mardi Gras, when a straw mannequin, King Carnival or Caramantran, was given a ritual trial and execution. Cats played an important part in some charivaris. In Burgundy, the crowd incorporated cat torture into its rough music. While mocking a cuckold or some other victim, the youths passed around a cat, tearing its fur to make it howl. *Faire le chat*, they called it. The Germans called charivaris *Katzenmusik*, a term that may have been derived from the howls of tortured cats.[15]

Cats also figured in the cycle of Saint John the Baptist, which took place on June 24, at the time of the summer solstice. Crowds made bonfires, jumped over them, danced around them, and threw into them objects with magical power, hoping to avoid disaster and obtain good fortune during the rest of the year. A favorite object was cats—cats tied up in bags, cats suspended from ropes, or cats burned at the stake. Parisians liked to incinerate cats by the sackful, while the Courimauds (*cour á miaud* or cat chasers) of Saint Chamond preferred to chase a flaming cat through streets. In parts of Burgundy and Lorraine they danced around a kind of burning May pole with a cat tied to it. In the Metz region they burned a dozen cats at a time in a basket on top of a bonfire. The ceremony took place with great pomp in Metz itself, until it was abolished in 1765. The town dignitaries arrived in procession at the Place du Grand-Sauley, lit the pyre, and a ring of riflemen from the garrison fired off volleys while the cats disappeared screaming in the flames. Although the practice varied from place to place, the ingredients were everywhere the same: a *feu de joie* (bonfire), cats, and an aura of hilarious witch-hunting.[16]

In addition to these general ceremonies, which involved entire communities, artisans celebrated ceremonies peculiar to their craft. Printers processed and feasted in honor of their patron, Saint John the Evangelist, both on his saint's day, December 27, and on the anniversary of his martyrdom, May 6, the festival of Saint Jean Porte Latine. By the eighteenth century, the masters had excluded the journeymen from the confraternity devoted to the saint, but the journeymen continued to hold ceremonies in their chapels.[17] On Saint Martin's day, November 11, they held a mock trial followed by a feast. Contat explained that the chapel was a tiny "republic," which governed itself according to its own code of conduct. When a worker violated the code, the foreman, who was the head of the chapel and not part of the management, entered a fine in a register: leaving a candle lit, five sous; brawling, three livres; insulting the good name of the chapel, three livres; and so on. On Saint Martin's the foreman read out the fines and collected them. The workers sometimes appealed their cases before a burlesque tribunal composed of the chapel's "ancients," but in the end they had to pay up amidst more bleating, banging of tools, and riotous laughter. The fines went for food amd drink in the chapel's favorite tavern, where the hell-raising continued until late in the night.[18]

Taxation and commensality characterized all the other ceremonies of the chapel. Special dues and feasts marked a man's entry into the shop (*bienvenue*), his exit (*conduite*), and even his marriage (*droit de chevet*). Above all, they punctuated a youth's progress from apprentice to journeyman. Contat described four of these rites, the most important being the first, called the taking of the apron, and the last, Jerome's initation as a full-fledged *compagnon*.

The taking of the apron (*la prise de tablier*) occurred soon after Jerome joined the shop. He had to pay six livres (about three days' wages for an ordinary journeyman) into a kitty, which the journeymen supplemented by small payments of their own (*faire la reconnaissance*). Then the chapel repaired to its favorite tavern, Le Panier Fleury in the rue de la Huchette. Emissaries were dispatched to procure provisions and returned loaded down with bread and meat, having lectured the shopkeepers of the neighborhood on which cuts were worthy of typographers and which could be left for cobblers. Silent and glass in hand, the journeymen gathered around Jerome in a special room on the second floor of the tavern. The subforeman approached, carrying the apron and followed by two "ancients," one from each of the "estates" of the shop, the *casse* and the *presse*. He handed the apron, newly made from close-woven linen, to the foreman, who took Jerome by the hand and led him to the center of the room, the subforeman and "ancients" falling in behind. The foreman made a short speech, placed the apron over Jerome's head and tied the strings behind him, as everyone drank to the health of the initiate. Jerome was then given a seat with the chapel dignitaries at the head of the table. The rest rushed for the best places they could find and fell on the food. They gobbled and guzzled and called out for more. After several Gargantuan rounds, they settled down to shop talk—and Contat lets us listen in:

> "Isn't it true," says one of them, "that printers know how to shovel it in? I am sure that if someone presented us with a roast mutton, as big as you like, we would leave nothing but the bones behind . . . ." They don't talk about theology nor philosophy and still less of politics. Each speaks of his job: one will talk to you about the *casse*, another the *presse*, this one of the tympan, another of the ink ball leathers. They all speak at the same time, whether they can be heard or not.

At last, early in the morning after hours of swilling and shouting, the workers separated—sotted but ceremonial to the end: "Bonsoir, Monsieur notre prote [foreman]"; Bonsoir, Messieurs les compositeurs"; "Bonsoir, Messieurs les imprimeurs"; "Bonsoir Jerome." The text explains that Jerome will be called by his first name until he is received as a journeyman.[19]

That moment came four years later, after two intermediary ceremonies (the *admission á l'ouvrage* and the *admission á la banque*) and a vast amount of hazing. Not only did the men torment Jerome, mocking his ignorance, sending him on wild goose chases, making him the butt of practical jokes, and overwhelming him with nasty chores; they also refused to teach him anything. They did not want another journeyman in their over-flooded labor pool, so Jerome had to pick up the tricks of the trade by himself. The work, the food, the lodging, the lack of sleep, it was enough to drive a boy mad, or at least out of the shop. In fact, however, it was standard treatment and should not be taken too seriously. Contat recounted the catalogue of Jerome's troubles in a light-hearted manner, which suggested a stock comic genre, the *misére des apprentis*.[20] The *miséres* provided farcical accounts, in doggerel verse or broadsides, of a stage in life that was familiar and funny to everyone in the artisanate. It was a transitional stage, which marked the passage from childhood to adulthood. A young

man had to sweat his way through it so that he would have paid his dues—the printers demanded actual payments, called *bienvenues* or *quatre beures*, in addition to razzing the apprentices—when he reached full membership in a vocational group. Until he arrived at that point, he lived in a fluid or liminal state, trying out adult conventions by subjecting them to some hell-raising of his own. His elders tolerated his pranks, called *copies* and *joberies* in the printing trade, because they saw them as wild oats, which needed to be sewn before he could settle down. Once settled, he would have internalized the conventions of his craft and acquired a new identity, which was often symbolized by a change in his name.[21]

Jerome became a journeyman by passing through the final rite, *compagnonnage*. It took the same form as the other ceremonies, a celebration over food and drink after the candidate paid an initiation fee and the journeymen chipped in with *reconnaissance*. But this time Contat gave a summary of the foreman's speech:[22]

> The newcomer is indoctrinated. He is told never to betray his colleagues and to maintain the wage rate. If a worker doesn't accept a price [for a job] and leaves the shop, no one in the house should do the job for a smaller price. Those are the laws among the workers. Faithfulness and probity are recommended to him. Any worker who betrays the others, when something forbidden, called *marron* [chestnut], is being printed, must be expelled ignominiously from the shop. The workers blacklist him by circular letters sent around all the shops of Paris and the provinces . . . . Aside from that, anything is permitted: excessive drinking is considered a good quality, gallantry and debauchery as youthful feats, indebtedness as a sign of wit, irreligion as sincerity. It's a free and republican territory in which everything is permitted. Live as you like but be an *honnéte homme*, no hypocrisy.

Hypocrisy turned out in the rest of the narrative to be the main characteristic of the bourgeois, a superstitious religious bigot. He occupied a separate world of pharasaical bourgeois morality. The workers defined their "republic" against that world and against other journeymen's groups as well—he cobblers, who ate inferior cuts of meat, and the masons or carpenters who were always good for a brawl when the printers, divided into "estates" (the *casse* and the *presse*) toured country taverns on

Sundays. In entering an "estate," Jerome assimilated an ethos. He identified himself with a craft; and as a full-fledged journeyman compositor, he received a new name. Having gone through a rite of passage in the full, anthropological sense of the term, he became a *Monsieur*.[23]

So much for ceremonies. What about cats? It should be said at the outset that there is an indefinable *je ne sais quoi* about cats, a mysterious something that has fascinated mankind since the time of the ancient Egyptians. One can sense a quasi-human intelligence behind a cat's eyes. One can mistake a cat's howl at night for a human scream, torn from some deep, visceral part of a man's animal nature. Cats appealed to poets like Baudelaire and painters like Manet, who wanted to express the humanity in animals along with the animality of men—and especially of women.[24]

This ambiguous ontological position, a straddling of conceptual categories, gives certain animals—pigs, dogs, and cassowaries as well as cats—in certain cultures an occult power associated with the taboo. That is why Jews do not eat pigs, according to Mary Douglas, and why Englishmen can insult one another by saying "son-of-a-bitch" rather than "son-of-a-cow," according to Edmund Leach.[25] Certain animals are good for swearing, just as they are "good for thinking" in Lévi-Strauss's famous formula. I would add that others—cats in particular—are good for staging ceremonies. They have ritual value. You cannot make a charivari with a cow. You do it with cats: you decide to *faire le chat*, to make *Katzenmusik*.

The torture of animals, especially cats, was a popular amusement throughout early modern Europe. You have only to look at Hogarth's *Stages of Cruelty* to see its importance, and once you start looking you see people torturing animals everywhere. Cat killings provided a common theme in literature, from *Don Quixote* in early seventeenth-century Spain to *Germinal* in late nineteenth-century France.[26] Far from being a sadistic fantasy on the part of a few half-crazed authors, the literary versions of cruelty to animals expressed a deep current of popular culture, as Mikhail Bakhtin has shown in his study of Rabelais.[27] All sorts of ethnographic reports confirm that view. On the *dimanche des brandous* in Semur, for example, children used to attach cats to poles and roast them over bonfires. In the *jeu du chat* at the Fete-Dieu in Aix-en-Provence, they threw cats high in the air and smashed them on the ground. They used expressions like "patient as a cat whose claws are being pulled out" or "patient as a cat whose paws are being grilled." The English

were just as cruel. During the Reformation in London, a Protestant crowd shaved a cat to look like a priest, dressed it in mock vestments, and hanged it on the gallows at Cheapside.[28] It would be possible to string out many other examples, but the point should be clear: there was nothing unusual about the ritual killing of cats. On the contrary, when Jerome and his fellow workers tried and hanged all the cats they could find in the rue Saint-Séverin, they drew on a common element in their culture. But what significance did that culture attribute to cats?

To get a grip on that question, one must rummage through collections of folktales, superstitions, proverbs, and popular medicine. The material is rich, varied, and vast but extremely hard to handle. Although much of it goes back to the Middle Ages, little can be dated. It was gathered for the most part by folklorists in the late nineteenth and early twentieth centuries, when sturdy strains of folklore still resisted the influence of the printed word. But the collections do not make it possible to claim that this or that practice existed in the printing houses of mid-eighteenth-century Paris. One can only assert that printers lived and breathed in an atmosphere of traditional customs and beliefs which permeated everything. It was not everywhere the same— France remained a patchwork of *pays* rather than a unified nation until late in the nineteenth century— but everywhere some common motifs could be found. The commonest were attached to cats. Early modern Frenchmen probably made more symbolic use of cats than of any other animal, and they used them in distinct ways, which can be grouped together for the purposes of discussion, despite the regional peculiarities.

First and foremost, cats suggested witchcraft. To cross one at night in virtually any corner of France was to risk running into the devil or one of his agents or a witch abroad on an evil errand. White cats could be as satanic as the black, in the daytime as well as at night. In a typical encounter, a peasant woman of Bigorre met a pretty white house cat who had strayed in the fields. She carried it back to the village in her apron, and just as they came to the house of a woman suspected of witchcraft, the cat jumped out, saying "Merci, Jeanne."[29] Witches transformed themselves into cats in order to cast spells on their victims. Sometimes, especially on Mardi Gras, they gathered for hideous sabbaths at night. They howled, fought, and copulated horribly under the direction of the devil himself in the form of a huge tomcat. To protect yourself from sorcery by cats there was one, classic remedy: maim it. Cut its tail, clip its ears, smash one of its legs, tear or burn its fur, and you would break its malevolent power. A maimed cat could not attend a sabbath or wander abroad to cast spells. Peasants frequently cudgeled cats who crossed their paths at night and discovered the next day that bruises had appeared on women believed to be witches—or so it was said in the lore of their village. Villagers also told stories of farmers who found strange cats in barns and broke their limbs to save the cattle. Invariably a broken limb would appear on a suspicious woman the following morning.

Cats possessed occult power independently of their association with witchcraft and deviltry. They could prevent the bread from rising if they entered bakeries in Anjou. They could spoil the catch if they crossed the path of fishermen in Brittany. If buried alive in Béarn, they could clear a field of weeds. They figured as staple ingredients in all kinds of folk medicine aside from witches' brews. To recover from a bad fall, you sucked the blood out of a freshly amputated tail of a tomcat. To cure yourself from pneumonia, you drank blood from a cat's ear in red wine. To get over colic, you mixed your wine with cat excrement. You could even make yourself invisible, at least in Brittany, by eating the brain of a newly killed cat, provided it was still hot.

There was a specific field for the exercise of cat power: the household and particularly the person of the master or mistress of the house. Folktales like "Puss 'n Boots" emphasized the identification of master and cat, and so did superstitions such as the practice of tying a black ribbon around the neck of a cat whose mistress had died. To kill a cat was to bring misfortune upon its owner or its house. If a cat left a house or stopped jumping on the sickbed of its master or mistress, the person was likely to die. But a cat lying on the bed of a dying man might be the devil, waiting to carry his soul off to hell. According to a sixteenth-century tale, a girl from Quintin sold her soul to the devil in exchange for some pretty clothes. When she died, the pallbearers could not lift her coffin: they opened the lid, and a black cat jumped out. Cats could harm a house. They often smothered babies. They understood gossip and would repeat it out of doors. But their power could be contained or turned to your advantage if you followed the right procedures, such as greasing their paws with butter or maiming them when they first arrived. To protect a new house, Frenchmen enclosed live cats within its walls—a very old rite, judging from cat skeletons that have been exhumed from the walls of medieval buildings.

Finally, the power of cats was concentrated on the most intimate aspect of domestic life: sex. *Le cbat, la chatte, le minet* mean the same thing in French slang as "pussy" does in English, and they have served as obscenities for centuries.[30] French folklore attaches special importance to the cat as a sexual metaphor or metonym. As far back as the fifteenth century, the petting of cats was recommended for success in courting women. Proverbial wisdom identified women with cats: "He who takes good care of cats will have a pretty wife." If a man loved cats, he would love women; and vice versa: "As he loves his cat, he loves his wife," went another proverb. If he did not care for his wife, you could say of him, "He has other cats to whip." A woman who wanted to get a man should avoid treading on a cat's tail. She might postpone marriage for a year—or for seven years in Quimper and for as many years as the cat meowed in parts of the Loire Valley. Cats connoted fertility and female sexuality everywhere. Girls were commonly said to be "in love like a cat"; and if they became pregnant, they had "let the cat go to the cheese." Eating cats could bring on pregnancy in itself. Girls who consumed them in stews gave birth to kittens in several folktales. Cats could even make diseased apple trees bear fruit, if buried in the correct manner in upper Brittany.

It was an easy jump from the sexuality of women to the cuckolding of men. Caterwauling could come from a satanic orgy, but it might just as well be toms howling defiance at each other when their mates were in heat. They did not call as cats, however. They issued challenges in their masters' names, along with sexual taunts about their mistresses: "Reno! Francois!" "Où allez-vous?—Voir la femme a vous.—Voir la femme á moi! Rouah!" (Where are you going?—To see your wife,—To see my wife! Ha!) Then the toms would fly at each other like the cats of Kilkenny, and their sabboth would end in a massacre. The dialogue differed according to the imaginations of the listeners and the onomatopoetic of their dialect, but it usually emphasized predatory sexuality.[31] "At night all cats are gray," went the proverb, and the gloss in an eighteenth-century proverb collection made the sexual hint explicit: "That is to say that all women are beautiful enough at night."[32] Enough for what? Seduction, rape, and murder echoed in the air when the cats howled at night in early modern France. Cat calls summoned up *Katzenmusik*, for charivaris often took the form of howling under a cuckold's window on the eve of Mardi Gras, the favorite time for cat sabbaths.

Witchcraft, orgy, cuckoldry, charivari, and massacre, the men of the Old Regime could hear a great deal in the wail of a cat. What the men of the rue

Saint-Séverin actually heard is impossible to say. One can only assert that cats bore enormous symbolic weight in the folklore of France and that the lore was rich, ancient, and widespread enough to have penetrated the printing shop. In order to determine whether the printers actually drew on the ceremonial and symbolic themes available to them, it is necessary to take another look at Contat's text. ∎

Author's Notes

1. Nicolas Contat, *Anecdotes typographiques oú l'on voit la description des coutumes, moeurs et usages singluliers des compagnons imprimeurs*, ed. Giles Barber (Oxford, 1980). The original manuscript is dated 1762. Barber provides a thorough description of its background and of Contat's career in his introduction. The account of the cat massacre occurs on pp. 48-56.

2. Contat, *Anecdotes typographiques*, p. 53.

3. *Ibid.*, pp. 52 and 53.

4. See, for example, Albert Soboul, *La France á la veille de la Révolution* (Paris, 1966), p. 140; and Edward Shorter, "The History of Work in the West: An Overview" in *Work and Community in the West*, ed. Edward Shorter (New York, 1973).

5. The following discussion is derived from Henri-Jean Martin, *Livre, pouvoirs at société a Paris au XVI siécle (1598-1701)* (Geneva, 1969); and Paul Chauvet, *Les Ouvriers du livre en France, des origines á la Révolution de 1789* (Paris, 1959). The statistics come from investigations by the authorities of the Old Regime as reported by Martin (II. 699-700) and Chauvet (pp. 126 and 154).

6. For a more detailed discussion of this material, see Robert Darnton, "Work and Culture in an Eighteenth-Century Printing Shop," an Englehard lecture at the Library of Congress to be published by the Library of Congress.

7. Contat, *Anecdotes typographiques*, pp. 68-73.

8. Christ to STN, Jan. 8, 1773, papers of the Société typographique de Neuchâtel, Bibliotheque de la Ville de Neuchâtel, Switzerland, hereafter cited as STN.

9. STN to Joseph Duplain, July 2, 1777.

10. STN to Louis Vernange, June 26, 1777.

11. Joseph Duplain to STN, Dec. 10, 1778.

12. Contat, *Anecdotes typographiques*, pp. 30-31.

13. *Ibid.*, p. 52.

14. For a recent overview of the vast literature on folklore and French history and bibliographic references, see Nicole Belmont, *Mythes et croyances dans l'ancienne France* (Paris, 1973). The following discussion is based primarily on the material collected in Eugène Rolland, *Faune populaire de la France* (Paris, 1881), IV; Paul Sébillot, *Le Folk-lore de France* (Paris, 1904-7), 4 vols., especially III, 72-155 and IV, 90-98; and to a lesser extent Arnold Van Gennep, *Manuel de folklore français contemporain* (Paris, 1937-38), 9 vols.

15. In Germany and Switzerland, *Katzenmusik* sometimes included mock trials and executions. The etymology of the term is not clear. See E. Hoffmann-Krayer and Hans Bächtold-Stäubli, *Handwörterbuch des deutschen Aberglaubens* (Berlin and Leipzig, 1931-32), IV, 1125-32 and Paul grebe et al., *Duden Etymologie: Herkunftswörterbuch der deutschen Sprache* (Mannheim, 1963), p. 317.

16. Information on the cat burning in Saint Chamond comes from a letter kindly sent to me by Elinor Accampo of Colorado College. The Metz ceremony is described in A. Benoist, "Traditions et anciennes coutumes du pays messin," *Revue des traditions populaires*, XV (1900), 14.

17. Contat, *Anecdotes typographiques*, pp. 30 and 66-67; and Chauvet, *Les Ouvriers du livre*, pp. 7-12.

18. Contat, *Anecdotes typographiques*, pp. 65-67.

19. *Ibid.*, pp. 37-41, quotation from pp. 39-40.

20. A good example of the genre, *La Misére des apprentis imprimeurs* (1710) is printed as an appendix to Contat, *Anecdotes typographiques*, pp. 101-10. For other examples, see A.C. Cailleau, *Les Miséres de ce monde, ou complaintes facétieuses sur les apprentissages des différents arts et métiers de la villa et faubourg de Paris* (Paris, 1783).

21. The classic study of this process is Arnold Van Gennep, *Les Rites de passage* (Paris, 1908). It has been extended by subsequent ethnographic research, notably that of Victor Turner: *The Forest of Symbols: Aspects of Ndembu Ritual* (Ithaca, N.Y., 1967) and *The Ritual Process* (Chicago, 1969). Jerome's experience fits the Van Gennep-Turner model very well, except in a few respects. He

was not considered sacred and dangerous, although the chapel could fine journeymen for drinking with him. He did not live outside adult society, although he left his home for a makeshift room at the edge of the master's household. And he was not exposed to secret *sacra*, although he had to acquire an esoteric lingo and to assimilate a craft ethos after a great deal of tribulation climaxed by a communal meal. Joseph Moxon, Thomas Gent, and Benjamin Franklin mention similar practices in England. In Germany the initiation rite was much more elaborate and had structural similarities to the rites of tribes in Africa, New Guinea, and North America. The apprentice wore a filthy headdress adorned with goat's horns and a fox's tail, indicating that he had reverted to an animal state. As a *Cornut* or *Mittelding*, part man, part beast, he underwent ritual tortures, including the filing of his fingertips. At the final ceremony, the head of the shop knocked off the hat and slapped him in the face. He then emerged newborn—sometimes newly named and even baptized—as a full-fledged journeyman. Such at least was the practice described in German typographical manuals, notably Christian Gottlob Täubel, *Praktisches Handbuch der Buchdruckerkunst für Anfanger* (Leipzig, 1791); Wilhelm Gottlieb Kircher, *Anweisung in der Buchdruckerkunst so veil davon das Drunken betrifft* (Brunswick, 1793); and Johann Christoph Hildebrand, *Handbuch für Buckdrucker-Lebrlinge* (Eisenach, 1835). The rite was related to an ancient popular play, the *Depositio Cornuti typographici*, which was printed by Jacob Redinger in his *Neu aufgesetztes Format Büchlein* (Frankfurt-am-Main, 1679).

22 Contat, *Anecdotes typographiques*, pp. 65-66.

23 The text does not give Jerome's last name, but it stresses the name change and the acquisition of the "Monsieur": "It is only after the end of the apprenticeship that one is called Monsieur; this quality belongs only to journeymen and not to apprentices" (p. 41). In the wage book of the STN, the journeymen always appear with their "Monsieur," even when they were called by nicknames, such as "Monsieur Bonnemain."

24 The black cat in Manet's *Olympia* represents a common motif, the animal "familiar" of a nude. On Baudelaire's cats, see Roman Jakobson and Claude Lévi-Strauss, "Les Chats de Charles Baudelaire,"*L'Homme*, II (1962), 5-21; and Michael Riffaterre, "Describing Poetic Structures: Two Approaches to Baudelaire's *Les Chats*," in *Structuralism*, ed. Jacques Ehrmann (New Haven, 1966).

25 Mary Douglas, *Purity and Danger: An Analysis of Concepts of Pollution and Taboo* (London, 1966); and E.R. Leach, "Anthropological Aspects of Language: Animal Categories and Verbal Abuse," in *New Directions in the Study of Language*, ed. E.H. Lenneberg, (Cambridge, Mass., 1964).

26 Cervantes and Zola adapted traditional cat lore to the themes of their novels. In *Don Quixote* (part II, chap. 46), a sack full of hollowing cats interrupts the hero's serenade to Altisidora. Taking them for devils, he tries to mow them down with his sword, only to be bested by one of them in single combat. In *Germinal* (part V, chap. 6), the symbolism works in the opposite way. A mob of workers pursues Maigrat, their class enemy, as if he were a cat trying to escape across the rooftops. Screaming "Get the cat! Get the cat!" they castrate his body "like a tomcat" after he falls from the roof. For an example of cat killing as a satire on French legalism, see Friar John's plan to massacre the Furry Lawcats in Rabelais' *Gargantua and Pantagruel*, book V, chap. 15.

27 Mikhail Baktin, *Rabelais and His World*, trans. Helene Iswolsky (Cambridge, Mass., 1968). The most important literary version of cat lore to appear in Contat's time was *Les Chats* (Rotterdam, 1728) by Francois Augustin Paradis de Moncrif. Although it was a mock treatise aimed at a sophisticated audience, it drew on a vast array of popular superstitions and proverbs, many of which appeared in the collections of folklorists a century and a half later.

28 C. S. L. Davies, *Peace, Print and Protestantism* (St. Albans, Hertz, 1977). The other references come from the sources cited in note 14. Among the many dictionaries of proverbs and slang, see André-Joseph Panckoucke, *Dictionnaire des proverbs françois et des façons de parler burlesques, et familiéres* (Paris, 1748) and Gaston Esnault, *Dictionnaire historique des argots français* (Paris, 1965).

29 Rolland, *Faune populaire*, p. 118. See note 14 for the other sources on which this account is based.

30 Emile Chautard, *La Vie étrange de l'argot* (Paris, 1931), pp. 367-68. The following expressions come from Panckoucke, *Dictionnaire des proverbs*

françois; Esnault, *Dictionnaire historique des argots français;* and *Dictionnaire de l'Académic francaise* (Paris, 1762), which contains a surprising amount of polite cat lore. The impolite lore was transmitted in large measure by children's games and rhymes, some of them dating from the sixteenth century: Claude Gaignebet, *Le Folklore obscène des enfants* (Paris, 1980), p. 260.

31 Sébillot, *Le Folk-lore de France*, III, 93-94.

32 Panckoucke, *Dictionnaire des proverbs françois*, p. 66.

Making Connections through Discussion and Writing

1. What is the primary source that Darnton uses to begin his inquiry into early eighteenth-century French social history?

   _____
   _____
   _____
   _____

2. What incident does he read about which causes him to realize he does not understand the society he is reading about?

   _____
   _____
   _____
   _____

3. Underline the sources Darnton cites as he continues to explore the meaning of the events Contat describes in his journal.

4. What leads Darnton to explore folklore, superstition, and village rituals?

   _____
   _____
   _____
   _____

5. Darnton graphically describes actions that he admits are repulsive. What is his purpose in doing this?

   _____
   _____
   _____
   _____
   _____
   _____

6. How does Darnton's historical account of event, recording, and interpretation illustrate the principles outlined by Luke Timothy Johnson?

   _____
   _____
   _____
   _____
   _____
   _____
   _____

Richard B. Morris

The Discovery of the Past and the Idea of Progress

Richard B. Morris (1904–1989) was an American historian, scholar, and author. An authority on early American legal and diplomatic history, he was Gouveneur Morris Professor of History at Columbia University from 1959–1973. His works include *Government and Labor in Early America* (1946) and *The Peacemakers* (1967). In the following essay, taken from his book *Time's Arrow (1985)*, Morris examines a basic Western assumption about historical progress.

Vocabulary . . . .

allegorically	imminent
chronology	insidious
cyclical	primordial
deterministic	promulgating
ecclesiastical	reprieve
entity	vortex

The people who lived during the Renaissance knew nothing of the idea of progress. Possibly this can be ascribed partly to their reverence for antiquity, and partly to the fact that some of the medieval ideas about time had not yet been discarded. The Renaissance was a period during which the rediscovery of the ancient classics and the myth of a golden age combined to create the belief that the achievements of the classical era were not likely to be equaled in modern times. Since, like their predecessors, the men[1] of the Renaissance believed that the time that remained was quite limited, they found it difficult to form a conception of social or intellectual progress. Although they sometimes interested themselves in the ancient idea of cyclical time, they generally felt little inclination to question the idea that the world and humanity were in their old age.

Thanks to the invention of the mechanical clock and to the work of poets like Petrarch and scientists like Galileo, time was becoming an abstract entity that could be saved, wasted, discussed, and used to regulate everyday life. However, no one had yet realized that time was something that might stretch endlessly into the past and into the future. One might say that the kind of time that expresses itself as hours and seconds had been discovered, but that time that goes on for eons had not.

Through the eighteenth century, the Biblical chronology, which implied that the world was less than six thousand years old, was generally accepted. Although it wasn't until 1650 that Archbishop James Ussher set the date of creation at 4004 B.C., the idea that the world was created somewhere around 4000 B.C. was already common in medieval times. During the Renaissance, then, the world was regarded as something that was not very old.

We can get a better idea of the Renaissance view of the past if we look at Biblical chronology in terms of generations rather than years. "4000 B.C." and "six thousand years" are concepts that are too abstract to be very meaningful. Most of us tend to think of six thousand years as simply "a very long time." In the psychological sense, there is not that much difference between six thousand years and six million; both are far longer than a human lifetime.

But consider this: If the world was less than six

thousand years old, and if the chronology given in the Old Testament was true, then Moses' mother, Jochebed, could easily have known Jacob. Jacob could have been acquainted with Noah's son Shem. And Shem probably would have known Methuselah. Methuselah was only 243 years old when Adam died. Since Adam is supposed to have been created only five days after time began, the entire period from the Creation to the Exodus was spanned by no more than five or six generations (admittedly, some of them were long ones; Methuselah is supposed to have lived to be 969 years old). And yet this period was, according to medieval and Renaissance thought, far longer than the time that remained. Is it any wonder that the medievals became preoccupied with eternity, or that the people of the Renaissance lacked any notion of progress?

When the Protestant Reformation got under way in the early sixteenth century, belief in Biblical chronology was strengthened, at least in those nations whose inhabitants accepted the new Protestant faiths. The Protestants rejected the authority of the Roman Catholic Church and emphasized a literal interpretation of the Bible in its place. Where Catholic scholars, since the time of St. Augustine in the early fifth century, had been willing to interpret Biblical passages allegorically, the Protestants insisted that the books of the Bible had been dictated by God, and that they were consequently an authoritative historical record. Martin Luther, for example, ridiculed the Copernican hypothesis that the earth revolved around the sun, and appealed to a literal interpretation of scripture to support his arguments. He pointed out that the Bible stated that Joshua had made the sun—not the earth—stand still. Luther also took 4000 B.C. as the date of Creation, and concluded that the world would shortly come to an end. 'The world will perish shortly," he said. "The last day is at the door, and I believe the world will not endure a hundred years."

When "new stars" (actually supernova explosions) were seen in the sky in 1572 and 1604, they were widely interpreted to be omens of imminent destruction. Previously, the constellations had been thought to be changeless. When the supernovae were observed, this was taken to mean that the corruption that was omnipresent on earth had spread to the heavens. And when astronomers observed sunspots through that new instrument, the telescope, this was taken to be evidence that the sun was decaying also.

To the Elizabethan poet John Donne, even the mountains were a symptom of decay. Accepting the then-common idea that the earth had originally been a perfect sphere, Donne spoke of mountains and valleys as "warts and pockholes in the face of th' Earth," and admonished, "Thinke so; but yet confesse, in this the world's proportion disfigured is."

Donne's contemporary, Sir Walter Raleigh, concurred. When Raleigh began writing his *History of the World* in 1604 while a prisoner in the Tower of London (he had been sentenced to death for high treason; a reprieve would later delay his execution until 1618), he accepted the Biblical chronology implicitly. Raleigh's own date for the Creation was 4032 B.C. Since, like most of his contemporaries, he believed that the world was destined to last for six thousand years, he concluded that less than four hundred years remained.

In the 1630s, the author and physician Sir Thomas Browne expressed similar sentiments, and explained why it was useless to concern oneself with such ideas as that of progress. "'Tis too late to be ambitious," Browne said. "The great Mutations of the World are acted, or Time may be too short for our designes."

The modern conception of the great, perhaps boundless, extent of time was introduced into Western thought in a rather roundabout way. Ideas about time began eventually to change, not because Biblical chronology was suddenly rejected, or because philosophers and scientists began to draw new conclusions about the nature of time, but because there was a growing understanding of the nature of physical law. A new conception of time grew up and began to spread in what was almost an insidious manner.

After Galileo's work became known, philosophers and scientists slowly began to realize that the behavior of physical objects could be described in mathematical terms. This led to the idea that there existed laws of nature that had been established by God to regulate His Creation. This concept, incidentally, was quite new; the idea of a "law of nature" would have been incomprehensible to most medieval thinkers. Its nearest equivalent in medieval times was that of natural law. But natural law had nothing to do with the behavior of physical objects; on the contrary, it was a moral law that governed human behavior.

The new idea that nature itself was subject to laws depended upon the implicit assumption that such laws did not change with time. Indeed, the suggestion that they did would have seemed almost blasphemous. If there were laws of nature, their divine origin implied that they must remain fixed for all time.

If the universe was governed by laws that did not change, then it was hard to believe that the world was decaying in the way that many Renaissance and Reformation thinkers believed. God's creation might eventually be destroyed. However, one had a right to expect that things would go on more or less in the same way for the foreseeable future. A lawful universe should not suddenly fall apart.

Although the argument is a rather complicated one, it proceeds by clear, logical steps. It is an argument that would almost certainly have been accepted by the leading thinkers of the seventeenth century, if it had ever been stated. But, strangely, it does not appear that it was ever made explicit. It was an ideal that was unconsciously assumed.

Unconscious assumptions are part of the thought of every age. For example, if the classical Greeks had not unconsciously assumed that the world could be understood by means of pure thought (as opposed to myth and religion), there never would have been any such thing as Greek philosophy. During the Middle Ages, the all-encompassing authority of the church and the validity of divine revelation were rarely questioned; a belief in their validity was one of the unconscious assumptions of the age. Since the time of Galileo, scientists have been making unconscious assumptions that are philosophical in nature, and that probably cannot be proved. They have assumed, first, that the universe is ultimately comprehensible, and second, that experimentation and the use of mathematical inference are the tools most likely to bring this comprehension about. These ideas seem so natural that most of us would think it silly to question them. However, there is really no way that we can be sure that they are true. For all we know, there may be things about the universe that we will never comprehend.

Modern philosophy is said to have begun with Descartes. So perhaps it is not surprising that he should have been the first to expound the new scientific outlook in detail. It was only after Descartes' writings became known that discussions of the "laws of nature" became common. It was Cartesian philosophy that was largely responsible for promulgating the idea that mankind lived in a universe whose workings were governed by law.

Paradoxically, practically all of Descartes' own scientific theories were wrong. Although he made significant contributions to mathematics, his ideas about physics and cosmology generally turned out to be erroneous. For example, he thought that the motion of the bodies in the solar system was akin to the motion of water in a whirlpool. The planets, he said, were carried around by a celestial vortex. Other vortices, he added, could be found around other stars.

In the end, this particular error stimulated the advance of science more than it impeded it. After Descartes, it was realized that there was a possibility that the universe might be very large, perhaps even infinite, in extent. If the stars were bodies like the sun, then planetary systems might be innumerable. Though the theory of vortices was to be disproved by Newton, Descartes advanced the Copernican hypothesis by displacing the earth even farther from the center of the universe. In Descartes' cosmology, neither the earth nor the sun was the center of God's creation.

Descartes was also the originator of the idea of cosmic evolution. Descartes realized that if the universe was governed by fixed laws, then these laws might also determine its evolution in time. He suggested that the universe was originally in a state of primordial chaos that was "as disordered as the poets could ever imagine." According to Descartes, as time passed, the operation of natural laws caused stars to be created. According to his theory, the formation of stars was inevitable. He seems to have reached the conclusion that the laws of nature operated in a deterministic way long before Laplace invented his famous argument.

According to Descartes' theory, the earth was originally a small star. After a time, clouds *similar* to sunspots were formed on its surface. Eventually, several layers of these clouds came into existence. As they piled up, the vortex surrounding the earth was diminished, and then destroyed. Thus the earth, together with the air that surrounded it, fell toward the sun until it was captured by the sun's vortex. More time passed, and "the mountains, seas, springs and rivers could form themselves naturally, and metals appear in the mines, and plants grow in the countryside." Presumably, a similar process could take place at many other places in the universe. If Descartes' theory was correct, there could be numerous inhabited worlds.

But as soon as Descartes presented his theory, he was careful to repudiate it. He stressed that he only meant to say that the earth *could* have evolved in this manner, adding that "we know perfectly well that they [the earth and the stars] never did arise in this way." Revelation tells us, Descartes admonished, that the world was created all at once by God.

No one really knows whether Descartes believed in his evolutionary theory or not. There are passages in his writings that make it clear that he had no desire to bring ecclesiastical censure down upon himself. He had heard of the manner in which the church had treated Galileo, and he had no desire to become a martyr to science himself. His repudiation of the theory could have been sincere; he might have been giving it only as an example of the manner in which the laws of nature could operate. On the other hand, he might really have believed it, and inserted disclaimers in order to protect himself against charges of heresy.

However, one thing is clear. Descartes did not share the opinion, expressed by many of his contemporaries, that the world would soon come to an end. On the contrary, he was one of the first advocates of the idea of progress. Apparently he felt that humanity could look forward to a future of indefinite length during which there would be invented "an infinity of devices by which we might enjoy, without any effort, the fruits of the earth and all its commodities." That which was known, he went on, "is almost nothing compared to what remains to be known." In Descartes' view, the future promised advances in medicine as well as in science and technology. Eventually, he said, mankind could free itself "of an infinity of illnesses, both of the body and mind, and perhaps even also the decline of age, if we knew enough about their causes and about all the remedies which nature has provided us." ∎

Notes

[1] My omission of Renaissance women is intentional; in this age, men were still the ones who dominated intellectual intercourse.

Making Connections through Discussion and Writing

1. Underline the passages in which Morris supports his claim that persons in the Renaissance thought "the world and humanity were in their old age."

2. What are the sources Morris draws from to support this claim?

   _____
   _____
   _____
   _____

3. Circle the paragraph in which Morris introduces his idea that notions of time began to expand after the Renaissance.

4. Why does the idea of "laws of nature" allow for a change in the concept of time?

   _____
   _____
   _____
   _____
   _____

5. What, according to Morris, is the difference between "laws of nature" and the earlier idea of "natural law"?

   _____
   _____
   _____
   _____
   _____
   _____

6. Which of Luke Timothy Johnson's three components of historical knowledge does Morris' article primarily represent?

   _____
   _____
   _____
   _____

7. How do Morris' sources differ from those examined by Robert Darnton?

   _____
   _____
   _____
   _____
   _____
   _____

8. How do you think the Biblical view of history as a linear progression (rather than the cyclical views of many earlier peoples) contributed to the idea of progress?

_____

_____

_____

_____

_____

9. List some specific developments (such as inoculations against communicable diseases or the discovery and utilization of electricity) since the Renaissance that you believe have added to the belief in progress.

_____

_____

_____

_____

_____

_____

_____

_____

_____

_____

_____

_____

_____

10. What makes the idea of progress problematic; that is, what difficulties must be dealt with when we attempt to affirm that there has been a positive movement through historical time?

_____

_____

_____

_____

_____

_____

_____

_____

_____

_____

_____

Kay Boyle
Winter Night

Kay Boyle (1902–1992), an American short-story writer, novelist, and poet, was born in St. Paul, Minnesota, resided in Europe for about twenty years before World War II, and moved to Germany after the war. She published her first collection of stories, *Wedding Day and Other Stories,* in 1930. She has since published over thirty books, including novels, children's books, nonfiction, and translations. Her poetry and short stories were compiled in two collections, *Collected Poems* (1962) and *Fifty Stories* (1980). She won the O. Henry Memorial Award for best short story in 1934 for "The White Horses of Vienna" and again in 1941 for her short story "Defeat." Boyle demonstrates an exceptional talent for examining the subtle details of relationships between Americans and Europeans in light of the individual's intense need for love, as seen in the following story, "Winter Night."

There is a time of apprehension which begins with the beginning of darkness, and to which only the speech of love can lend security. It is there, in abeyance, at the end of every day, not urgent enough to be given the name of fear but rather of concern for how the hours are to be reprieved from fear, and those who have forgotten how it was when they were children can remember nothing of this. It may begin around five o'clock on a winter afternoon when the light outside is dying in the windows. At that hour the New York apartment in which Felicia lived was filled with shadows, and the little girl would wait alone in the living room, looking out at the winter-stripped trees that stood black in the park against the isolated ovals of unclean snow. Now it was January, and the day had been a cold one; the water of the artificial lake was frozen fast, but because of the cold and the coming darkness, the skaters had ceased to move across its surface. The street that lay between the park and the apartment house was wide, and the two-way streams of cars and busses, some with their headlamps already shining, advanced and halted, halted and poured swiftly on to the tempo of the traffic signals' altering lights. The time of apprehension had set in, and Felicia, who was seven, stood at the window in the evening and waited before she asked the question. When the signals below would change from red to green again, or when the double-decker bus would turn the corner below, she

would ask it. The words of it were already there, tentative in her mouth, when the answer came from the far end of the hall.

"Your mother," said the voice among the sound of kitchen things, "she telephoned up before you came in from nursery school. She won't be back in time for supper. I was to tell you a sitter was coming in from the sitting parents' place."

Felicia turned back from the window into the obscurity of the living room, and she looked toward the open door, and into the hall beyond it where the light from the kitchen fell in a clear yellow angle across the wall and onto the strip of carpet. Her hands were cold, and she put them in her jacket pockets as she walked carefully across the living-room rug and stopped at the edge of light.

"Will she be home late?" she said.

For a moment there was the sound of water running in the kitchen, a long way away, and then the sound of the water ceased, and the high, Southern voice went on:

"She'll come home when she gets ready to come home. That's all I have to say. If she wants to spend two dollars and fifty cents and ten cents' carfare on top of that three or four nights out of the week for a sitting parent to come in here and sit, it's her own business. It certainly ain't nothing to do with you or me. She makes her money, just like the rest of us does. She works all day down there in the office, or whatever it is, just like the rest of us

---

Reprinted by permission of the Estate of Kay Boyle and the Watkins/Loomis Agency.

works, and she's entitled to spend her money like she wants to spend it. There's no law in the world against buying your own freedom. Your mother and me, we're just buying our own freedom, that's all we're doing. And we're not doing nobody no harm."

"Do you know who she's having supper with?" said Felicia from the edge of dark. There was one more step to take, and then she would be standing in the light that fell on the strip of carpet, but she did not take the step.

"Do I know who she's having supper with?" the voice cried out in what might have been derision, and there was the sound of dishes striking the metal ribs of the drainboard by the sink. "Maybe it's Mr. Van Johnson, or Mr. Frank Sinatra, or maybe it's just the Duke of Wincers[1] for the evening. All I know is you're having soft-boiled egg and spinach and applesauce for supper, and you're going to have it quick now because the time is getting away."

The voice from the kitchen had no name. It was as variable as the faces and figures of the women who came and sat in the evenings. Month by month the voice in the kitchen altered to another voice, and the sitting parents were no more than lonely aunts of an evening or two who sometimes returned and sometimes did not to this apartment in which they had sat before. Nobody stayed anywhere very long any more, Felicia's mother told her. It was part of the time in which you lived, and part of the life of the city, but when the fathers came back, all this would be miraculously changed. Perhaps you would live in a house again, a small one, with fir trees on either side of the short brick walk, and Father would drive up every night from the station just after darkness set in. When Felicia thought of this, she stepped quickly into the clear angle of light, and she left the dark of the living room behind her and ran softly down the hall.

The drop-leaf table stood in the kitchen between the refrigerator and the sink, and Felicia sat down at the place that was set. The voice at the sink was speaking still, and while Felicia ate it did not cease to speak until the bell of the front door rang abruptly. The girl walked around the table and went down the hall, wiping her dark palms in her apron, and, from the drop-leaf table, Felicia watched her step from the angle of light into darkness and open the door.

"You put in an early appearance," the girl said, and the woman who had rung the bell came into the hall. The door closed behind her, and the girl showed her into the living room, and lit the lamp

on the bookcase, and the shadows were suddenly bleached away. But when the girl turned, the woman turned from the living room too and followed her, humbly and in silence, to the threshold of the kitchen. "Sometimes they keep me standing around waiting after it's time for me to be getting on home, the sitting parents do," the girl said, and she picked up the last two dishes from the table and put them in the sink. The woman who stood in the doorway was a small woman, and when she undid the white silk scarf from around her head, Felicia saw that her hair was black. She wore it parted in the middle, and it had not been cut, but was drawn back loosely into a knot behind her head. She had very clean white gloves on, and her face was pale, and there was a look of sorrow in her soft black eyes. "Sometimes I have to stand out there in the hall with my hat and coat on, waiting for the sitting parents to turn up," the girl said, and, as she turned on the water in the sink, the contempt she had for them hung on the kitchen air. "But you're ahead of time," she said, and she held the dishes, first one and then the other, under the flow of steaming water.

The woman in the doorway wore a neat black coat, not a new-looking coat, and it had no fur on it, but it had a smooth velvet collar and velvet lapels. She did not move, or smile, and she gave no sign that she had heard the girl speaking above the sound of water at the sink. She simply stood looking at Felicia, who sat at the table with the milk in her glass not finished yet.

"Are you the child?" she said at last, and the voice was low, and the pronunciation of the words a little strange.

"Yes, this here's Felicia," the girl said, and the dark hands dried the dishes and put them away. "You drink up your milk quick now, Felicia, so's I can rinse your glass."

"I will wash the glass," said the woman. "I would like to wash the glass for her," and Felicia sat looking across the table at the face in the doorway that was filled with such unspoken grief. "I will wash the glass for her and clean off the table," the woman was saying quietly. "When the child is finished, she will show me where her night things are."

"The others, they wouldn't do anything like that," the girl said, and she hung the dishcloth over the rack. "They wouldn't put their hand to housework, the sitting parents. That's where they got the name for them," she said.

Whenever the front door closed behind the girl in the evening, it would usually be that the sitting parent who was there would take up a book of fairy stories and read aloud for a while to Felicia; or else would settle herself in the big chair in the living room and begin to tell the words of a story in drowsiness to her, while Felicia took off her clothes in the bed room, and folded them, and put her pajamas on, and brushed her teeth, and did her hair. But this time, that was not the way it happened. Instead, the woman sat down on the other chair at the kitchen table, and she began at once to speak, not of good fairies or bad, or of animals endowed with human speech, but to speak quietly, in spite of the eagerness behind her words, of a thing that seemed of singular importance to her.

"It is strange that I should have been sent here tonight," she said, her eyes moving slowly from feature to feature of Felicia's face, "for you look like a child that I knew once, and this is the anniversary of that child."

"Did she have hair like mine?" Felicia asked quickly, and she did not keep her eyes fixed on the unfinished glass of milk in the shyness any more.

"Yes, she did. She had hair like yours," said the woman, and her glance paused for a moment on the locks which fell straight and thick on the shoulders of Felicia's dress. It may have been that she thought to stretch out her hand and touch the ends of Felicia's hair, for her fingers stirred as they lay clasped together on the table, and then they relapsed into passivity again. "But it is not the hair alone, it is the delicacy of your face, too, and your eyes the same, filled with the same spring lilac color," the woman said, pronouncing the words carefully. "She had little coats of golden fur on her arms and legs," she said, "and when we were closed up there, the lot of us in the cold, I used to make her laugh when I told her that the fur that was so pretty, like a little fawn's skin on her arms, would always help to keep her warm."

"And did it keep her warm?" asked Felicia, and she gave a little jerk of laughter as she looked down at her own legs hanging under the table, with the bare calves thin and covered with a down of hair.

"It did not keep her warm enough," the woman said, and now, the mask of grief had come back upon her face. "So we used to take everything we could spare from ourselves, and we would sew them into cloaks and other kinds of garments for her and for the other children...."

"Was it a school?" said Felicia when the woman's voice had ceased to speak.

"No," said the woman softly, "it was not a school, but still there were a lot of children there. It was at camp—that was the name the place had; it was a camp. It was a place where they put people until they could decide what was to be done with them." She sat with her hands clasped, silent a moment, looking at Felicia. "That little dress you have on," she said, not saying the words to anybody, scarcely saying them aloud. "Oh, she would have liked that little dress, the little buttons shaped like little hearts, and the white collar—"

"I have four school dresses," Felicia said. "I'll show them to you. How many dresses did she have?"

"Well, there, you see, there in the camp," said the woman, "she did not have dresses except the little skirt and the pullover. That was all she had. She had brought just a handkerchief of her belongings with her, like everybody else—just enough for three days away from home was what they told us, so she did not have enough to last the winter. But she had her ballet slippers," the woman said, and her clasped fingers did not move. "She had brought them because she thought during her three days away from home she would have the time to practice her ballet."

"I've been to the ballet," Felicia said suddenly, and she said it so eagerly that she stuttered a little as the words came out of her mouth. She slipped quickly down from the chair and went around the table to where the woman sat. Then she took one of the woman's hands away from the other that held it fast, and she pulled her toward the door. "Come into the living room and I'll do a pirouette for you," she said, and then she stopped speaking, her eyes halted on the woman's face. "Did she—did the little girl—could she do a pirouette very well?" she said.

"Yes, she could. At first she could," said the woman, and Felicia felt uneasy now at the sound of sorrow in her words. "But after that she was hungry. She was hungry all winter," she said in a low voice. "We were all hungry, but the children were the hungriest. Even now," she said, and the voice went suddenly savage, "when I see milk like that, clean, fresh milk standing in a glass, I want to cry out loud, I want to beat my hands on the table, because it did not have to be..." She had drawn her fingers abruptly away from Felicia now, and Felicia stood before her, cast off, forlorn, alone again in the time of apprehension. "That was three years ago," the woman was saying, and one hand was lifted, as in weariness, to shade her face. "It was somewhere else, it was in another country," she said, and behind her hand her eyes were turned upon the substance of a world in which Felicia had played no part.

"Did—did the little girl cry when she was hungry?" Felicia asked, and the woman shook her head.

"Sometimes she cried," she said, "but not very much. She was very quiet. One night when she heard the other children crying, she said to me, 'You know, they are not crying because they want something to eat. They are crying because their mothers have gone away.'"

"Did the mothers have to go out to supper?" Felicia asked, and she watched the woman's face for the answer.

"No," said the woman. She stood up from her chair, and now that she put her hand on the little girl's shoulder, Felicia was taken into the sphere of love and intimacy again. "Shall we go into the other room, and you will do your pirouette for me?" the woman said, and they went from the kitchen and down the strip of carpet on which the clear light fell. In the front room, they paused hand in hand in the glow of the shaded lamp, and the woman looked about her, at the books, the low tables with the magazines and ash trays on them, the vase of roses on the piano, looking with dark, scarcely seeing eyes at these things that had no reality at all. It was only when she saw the little white clock on the mantelpiece that she gave any sign, and then she said quickly: "What time does your mother put you to bed?"

Felicia waited a moment, and in the interval of waiting the woman lifted one hand and, as if in reverence, touched Felicia's hair.

"What time did the little girl you knew in the other place go to bed?" Felicia asked.

"Ah, God, I do not know. I do not remember," the woman said.

"Was she your little girl?" said Felicia softly, stubbornly.

"No," said the woman. "She was not mine. At least, at first she was not mine. She had a mother, a real mother, but the mother had to go away."

"Did she come back late?" asked Felicia.

"No, ah, no, she could not come back, she never came back," the woman said, and now she turned, her arm around Felicia's shoulders, and she sat down in the low soft chair. "Why am I saying all this to you, why am I doing it?" she cried out in grief, and she held Felicia close against her. "I had thought to speak of the anniversary to you, and that was all, and now I am saying these other things to you. Three years ago today, exactly, the little girl became my little girl because her mother went away. That is all there is to it. There is nothing more."

Felicia waited another moment, held close against the woman and listening to the swift, strong heartbeats in the woman's breast.

"But the mother," she said then in the small, persistent voice, "did she take a taxi when she went?"

"This is the way it used to happen," said the woman, speaking in hopelessness and bitterness in the softly lightened room. "Every week they used to come into the place where we were and they would read a list of names out. Sometimes it would be the names of children they would read out, and then a little later they would have to go away. And sometimes it would be the grown people's names, the names of the mothers or big sisters, or other women's names. The men were not with us. The fathers were somewhere else, in another place."

"Yes," Felicia said. "I know."

"We had been there only a little while, maybe ten days or maybe not so long," the woman went on, holding Felicia against her still, "when they read the name of the little girl's mother out, and that afternoon they took her away."

"What did the little girl do?" Felicia said.

"She wanted to think up the best way of getting out so that she could go find her mother," said the woman, "but she could not think of anything good enough until the third or fourth day. And then she tied her ballet slippers up in the hankerchief again, and she went up to the guard standing at the door." The woman's voice was gentle, controlled now. "She asked the guard please to open the door so that she could go out. 'This is Thursday,' she said, 'and every Tuesday and Thursday I have my ballet lessons. If I miss a ballet lesson, they do not count the money off, so my mother would just be paying for nothing, and she cannot afford to pay for nothing. I missed my ballet lesson on Tuesday,' she said to the guard, 'and I must not miss it again today.'"

Felicia lifted her head from the woman's shoulder, and she shook her hair back and looked in question and wonder at the woman's face.

"And did the man let her go?" she said.

"No, he did not. He could not do that," said the woman. "He was a soldier and he had to do what he was told. So every evening after her mother went, I used to brush the little girl's hair for her," the woman went on saying. "And while I brushed it, I used to tell her the stories of the ballets. Sometimes I would begin with *Narcissus*,[2] the woman said, and she parted Felicia's locks with her fingers, "so if you will go and get your brush now, I will tell it while I brush your hair."

"Oh, yes," said Felicia, and she made two

whirls as she went quickly to the bedroom. On the way back, she stopped and held on to the piano with the fingers of one hand while she went up on her toes. "Did you see me? Did you see me standing on my toes?" she called the woman, and the woman sat smiling in love and contentment at her.

"Yes, wonderful, really wonderful," she said. "I am sure I have never seen anyone do it so well." Felicia came spinning toward her, whirling in pirouette after pirouette, and she flung herself down in the chair close to her, with her thin bones pressed against the woman's soft, wide hip. The woman took the silver-backed, monogrammed brush and the tortoise-shell comb in her hands, and now she began to brush Felicia's hair. "We did not have any soap at all and not very much water to wash in, so I never could fix her as nicely and prettily as I wanted to," she said, and the brush stroked regularly, carefully down, caressing the shape of Felicia's head.

"If there wasn't very much water, then how did she do her teeth?" Felicia said.

"She did not do her teeth," said the woman, and she drew the comb through Felicia's hair. "There were not any toothbrushes or tooth paste, or any thing like that."

Felicia waited a moment, constructing the unfamiliar scene of it in silence, and then she asked the tentative question.

"Do I have to do my teeth tonight?" she said.

"No," said the woman, and she was thinking of something else, "you do not have to do your teeth."

"If I am your little girl tonight, can I pretend there isn't enough water to wash?" said Felicia.

"Yes," said the woman, "you can pretend that if you like. You do not have to wash," she said, and the comb passed lightly through Felicia's hair.

"Will you tell me the story of the ballet?" said Felicia, and the rhythm of the brushing was like the soft, slow rocking of sleep.

"Yes," said the woman. "In the first one, the place is a forest glade with little pale birches growing in it, and they have green veils over their faces and green veils drifting from their fingers, because it is the springtime. There is the music of a flute," said the woman's voice softly, softly, "and creatures of the wood are dancing—"

"But the mother," Felicia said as suddenly as if she had been awaked from sleep. "What did the little girl's mother say when she didn't do her teeth and didn't wash at night?"

"The mother was not there, you remember," said the woman, and the brush moved steadily in her hand. "But she did send one little letter back.

Sometimes people who went away were able to do that. The mother wrote it in a train, standing up in a car that had no seats," she said, and she might have been telling the story of the ballet still, for her voice was gentle and the brush did not falter on Felicia's hair. "There were perhaps a great many other people standing up in the train with her, perhaps all trying to write their little letters on the bits of paper they had managed to hide on them, or that they had found in forgotten corners as they traveled. When they had written their letters, then they must try to slip them out through the boards of the car in which they journeyed, standing up," said the woman, "and these letters fell down on the tracks under the train, or they were blown into the fields or onto the country roads, and if it was a kind person who picked them up, he would seal them in envelopes and send them to where they were addressed to go. So a letter came back like this from the little girl's mother," the woman said, and the brush followed the comb, the comb the brush in steady pursuit through Felicia's hair. "It said good-by to the little girl, and it said please to take care of her. It said: 'Whoever reads this letter in the camp, please take good care of my little girl for me, and please have her tonsils looked at by a doctor if this is possible to do.'"

"And then," said Felicia softly, persistently, "what happened to the little girl?"

"I do not not know. I cannot say," the woman said. But now the brush and comb had ceased to move, and in the silence Felicia turned her thin, small body on the chair, and she and the woman suddenly put their arms around each other. "They must all be asleep now, all of them," the woman said, and in the silence that fell on them again, they held each other closer. "They must be quietly asleep somewhere, and not crying all night because they are hungry and because they are cold. For three years I have been saying 'They must all be asleep, and the cold and the hunger and the seasons or night or day or nothing matters to them—'"

It was after midnight when Felicia's mother put her key in the lock of the front door, and pushed it open, and stepped into the hallway. She walked quickly to the living room, and just across the threshold she slipped the three blue foxskins from her shoulders and dropped them, with her little velvet bag, upon the chair. The room was quiet, so quiet that she could hear the sound of breathing in it, and no one spoke to her in greeting as she crossed toward the bedroom door. And then, as startling as a slap across her delicately tinted face, she saw the woman lying sleeping on the divan, and Felicia, in her school dress still, asleep within the woman's arms. ■

Notes

[1] Van Johnson, Frank Sinatra, . . . Duke of Wincers—Johnson was an American actor popular in the 1490s and 1950s; Frank Sinatra has been a popular American singer for several decades; and the Duke of Wincers is probably the Duke of Windsor.

[2] *Narcissus*—a ballet based on the Greek mythological figure who fell in love with his own reflection.

Making Connections through Discussion and Writing

1. In the scene where the sitter enters the story, underline the details the author gives that show her to be different from other sitters Felicia has had.

2. a. Circle the images of light and dark in the story.

   b. Describe what meanings the author hints at by these images.

   _____
   _____
   _____
   _____
   _____
   _____
   _____
   _____
   _____

3. State the motive the sitter has to begin telling Felicia about the other child.

   _____
   _____
   _____
   _____

4. a. What does the sitter omit from the tale she tells Felicia?

   _____
   _____
   _____

   b. Why does she omit this?

   _____
   _____
   _____

5. By this story within the story, the character of Felicia learns something about a historical event. The reader too learns something from the story as a whole and about this event and its effect upon the sitter. How do the knowledge of Felicia and the knowledge of the reader differ?

   _____
   _____
   _____
   _____
   _____
   _____

Synthesis/Essay Suggestions: Historical Knowledge

1. Compose a synthesis essay in which you discuss the different ways fiction and non-fiction deal with history. You may use Luke Timothy Johnson's ideas as a basis for comparing the methods of Kay Boyle in the story "Winter Night" and those of Robert Darnton in "Workers Revolt. . . ." You may also incorporate other works from *Encounters* such as "In Search of Our Mothers' Gardens" by Alice Walker and "The Historical Roots of Our Ecological Crisis" by Lynn White, Jr. You may want to note the different sources these authors draw from, their different goals, and the different ways they interpret and present their "historical facts."

2. If Luke Timothy Johnson were to critique the stories "Winter Night" by Kay Boyle and "Young Goodman Brown" by Nathaniel Hawthorne as histories, how might he treat them in terms of his idea of the "components" of historical knowledge?

3. Considering Morris' ideas on how humans think about time and progress, examine Darnton's descriptions of life in eighteenth-century France. You may want to discuss how ordinary activities and attitudes of humans have changed, progressed, or deteriorated through the past three hundred years. What conclusions do you reach about human progress?

Chapter 8

Ecology

*p*ersonal attitudes held toward nature reflect cultural assumptions that people may be unaware they have. These assumptions are often embedded in and transferred by stories handed down from one generation to another. For example, the fear of wolves was probably valid in a time when wolves posed some real threat to humans or to their livestock. People living in the forests or shepherding their sheep or goats on grasslands knew the danger of predatory animals wounding or killing their animals. Stories, such as the primitive version of "Little Red Riding Hood" (in which the wolf eats the little girl) conveyed to many generations a kind of primal fear of the dark woods and the dangerous wolves. The word "wolf" even became a common metaphor for a predatory, seducing man. Thus, cultural assumptions painting the wolf as a bad creature became a small, but firmly fixed, part of our mental furniture—our "worldview." The public gave approval as bounties were placed on wolves and the species was eradicated from large areas of the North American wild lands. Recent ecologists and naturalists, however, have urged the return of wolves into wilderness environments to maintain the "balance of nature." Scientific observation has demonstrated that the wolf serves a necessary function in keeping caribou, antelope, and deer herds healthier by thinning out the weak, sick, or old animals. Their main diet, as the Canadian author of *Never Cry Wolf*, Farley Mowat, discovered, consists of small rodents such as mice and ground squirrels, not the large herding mammals they were thought to live on. To convey these facts to a public conditioned to believe in wolves as evil, Mowat told the story of his experiences with wolves in the Canadian wilderness. Through observation, he established facts about their real diet and hunting habits. By telling these facts in an entertaining story, Mowat changed many attitudes about wolves.

Only by new stories, apparently, can the attitudes fostered by the old stories be replaced by truer or more relevant information. Aldo Leopold takes a similar approach as he tries to move readers from their pre-existing attitudes and assumptions to get them to "think . . . like a mountain." Once more, imaginative writing, presenting a new perspective on an old idea or matter, is employed as a way of better knowing reality.

The relationship between humans and their natural environment has been a fundamental factor of human history. The earth and seas have provided food and shelter, and through most of human history the natural environment has been respected and cared for; it has been our home, and we were stewards of its abundance.

The technological advances of Western civilization allowed for more efficient methods of producing crops, fuels, building materials, and consumer goods. The Industrial Revolution in the nineteenth century promoted an expanded consumption of raw materials. Without cultural assumptions that held humans responsible for good stewardship, exploitation and waste became common. Clear-cutting old forests for lumber marred the landscapes of the American South; buffalo were exterminated to make the plains safe for the intercontinental railroad; strip mining polluted the land and the rivers; factories polluted the air.

Attitudes toward nature and natural resources shifted in the twentieth century. Exploitation and waste of forests, petroleum, coal, farmland, and animal species that had characterized the settling of colonial lands and the resource-needy Industrial Revolution caused many thoughtful people of the past century to re-examine cultural attitudes towards the human-environment relationship. New awareness of the interrelationship of living things, the web of life, and the fragility of the earth's eco-structure arose as people like Aldo Leopold and Rachel Carson led societal awareness beyond the romantic appreciation of nature expressed by writers like Henry Thoreau and John Muir and painters like Thomas Moran and Albert Bierstadt. Movements of conservation and preservation led to new environmental laws, the establishment of better policies of land and resource management, and the setting aside of large tracts of national wilderness areas.

In this section of the book, we focus on attitudes lacking concern about the health of the earth and its creatures, which have led some thinkers, like Lynn White, Jr., to probe ancient ideas for the roots of Western attitudes about human dominance over the natural creation. In criticizing mainstream Christian attitudes and behaviors, he urges the resurrection of alternative approaches to nature—alternatives such as the reverence demonstrated by St. Francis toward fellow creatures. Writers and thinkers like Wendell Berry and Steven Bouma-Prediger respond to White with their own insights into what seem to them a truer picture of Biblical environmental values.

Vincent Rossi, an Eastern Orthodox scholar, focuses closely upon the being of a tree to reveal the levels of insight this major Christian tradition brings to the ecological question. From another tradition, Leslie Marmon Silko reveals Native American attitudes toward nature; these can help us foster renewed reverence and humility in our use of the natural environment. Finally, the poets W. S. Merwin and Mark Williams present nightmarish visions of the results of human arrogance in destroying our fellow creatures.

St. Francis of Assisi
The Canticle of Brother Sun

St. Francis of Assisi (1181?–1226), whose original name was Giovanni Francesco Bernardone, was an Italian who founded the Franciscan Order. His father was a prosperous textile merchant, but Francis rejected all of his family's wealth when he was about twenty-six and dedicated himself to taking care of the sick, the poor, and the leprous. He lived a life of asceticism, mysticism, and intense prayer. Desiring to completely imitate the life of Jesus, he gathered a band of believers of like mind and began a monastic order in 1209. He is reported to have received the stigmata, the marks of Jesus' wounds, after fasting forty days on Mount Alverno. He was canonized as a saint in 1228. "The Canticle of Brother Sun" was written during a time of intense solitude and prayer when Francis was on Mount Alverno. St. Francis expresses his joyous love of nature and his belief that things in creation are his brothers and sisters.

Vocabulary ....

> infirmity
> tribulation

Most High, all-powerful, good Lord,
Yours are the praises, the glory, the honor, and all blessing.
To You alone, Most High, do they belong,
and no man is worthy to mention Your name.
Praised be You, my Lord, with all your creatures,
especially Sir Brother Sun,
Who is the day and through whom You give us light.
And he is beautiful and radiant with great splendor;
and bears a likeness of You, Most High One.
Praised be You, my Lord, through Sister Moon and the stars,
in heaven You formed them clear and precious and beautiful.
Praised be You, my Lord, through Brother Wind,
and through the air, cloudy and serene, and every kind of weather
through which You give sustenance to Your creatures.
Praised be You, my Lord, through Sister Water,
which is very useful and humble and precious and chaste.
Praised be You, my Lord, through Brother Fire,
through whom You light the night
and he is beautiful and playful and robust and strong.
Praised be You, my Lord, through our Sister Mother Earth,
who sustains and governs us,
and who produces varied fruits with colored flowers and herbs.
Praised be You, my Lord, through those who give pardon for Your love
and bear infirmity and tribulation.

Blessed are those who endure in peace
for by You, Most High, they shall be crowned.
Praised be You, my Lord, through our Sister Bodily Death,
from whom no living man can escape.
Woe to those who die in mortal sin.
Blessed are those whom death will find in Your most holy will,
for the second death shall do them no harm.
Praise and bless my Lord and give Him thanks
serve Him with great humility. ∎

Making Connections through Discussion and Writing

1. Describe the relationships St. Francis depicts between God and nature, humans and nature, and God and humans.

   God and nature

   _____
   _____
   _____
   _____

   Humans and nature

   _____
   _____
   _____
   _____

   God and humans

   _____
   _____
   _____
   _____

2. a. Underline St. Francis' use of personification, and circle examples of parallelism in this prayer.

   b. Explain how these devices are used to convey his main theme.

   _____
   _____
   _____
   _____
   _____
   _____
   _____
   _____

3. What connections does St. Francis make between objects of nature and God?

   _____
   _____
   _____
   _____
   _____
   _____
   _____
   _____
   _____
   _____

4. In the second section of the Canticle, St. Francis moves from creation as a vehicle to praise God to a discussion of human dependence on Jesus Christ for pardon and enduring peace.
    a. Why is this shift significant?

    _____

    _____

    _____

    _____

    _____

    _____

    b. How does it help us to understand St. Francis' perception about creation and our relationship to it?

    _____

    _____

    _____

    _____

    _____

    _____

5. a. St. Francis refers to "our Sister Bodily Death." How is this image an unusual way to view death?

    _____

    _____

    _____

    _____

    _____

    _____

    b. How does the image function in the context of the poem?

    _____

    _____

    _____

    _____

    _____

    _____

Lynn White, Jr.

The Historical Roots of Our Ecologic Crisis

Lynn White, Jr., (1907–1987) was an internationally known medieval scholar and taught at Princeton and Stanford universities between 1933-1943. For fifteen years he served as president of Mills College, and later he joined the faculty of the University of California at Los Angeles, where he founded the center for Medieval and Renaissance Studies in 1964.

Vocabulary ....

anthropocentric	myxomatosis
atavism	Occidental
axioms	palliative
beatniks	perspicacity
carcinoma	philistine
corpus	placate
crescendo	Pleistocene
Crusaders	rudimentary
deforestation	sluggards
derogation	teleology
ecclesiastic	transmigration
glades	vernacular

A conversation with Aldous Huxley[1] not infrequently puts one at the receiving end of an unforgettable monologue. About a year before his lamented death he was discoursing on a favorite topic: man's unnatural treatment of nature and its sad results. To illustrate his point he told how, during the previous summer, he had returned to a little valley in England where he had spent many happy months as a child. Once it had been composed of delightful grassy glades; now it was becoming overgrown with unsightly brush because the rabbits that formerly kept such growth under control had largely succumbed to a disease, myxomatosis, that was deliberately introduced by the local farmers to reduce the rabbits' destruction of crops. Being something of a Philistine, I could be silent no longer, even in the interests of great rhetoric. I interrupted to point out that the rabbit itself had been brought as a domestic animal to England in 1176, presumably to improve the protein diet of the peasantry.

All forms of life modify their contexts. The most spectacular and benign instance is doubtless the coral polyp. By serving its own ends, it has created a vast undersea world favorable to thousands of other kinds of animals and plants. Ever since man became a numerous species he has affected his environment notably. The hypothesis that his fire-drive method of hunting created the world's great grasslands and helped to exterminate the monster mammals of the Pleistocene from much of the globe is plausible, if not proved. For 6 millennia at least, the banks of the lower Nile have been a human artifact rather than the swampy African jungle which nature, apart from man, would have made it. The Aswan Dam,[2] flooding 5000 square miles, is only the latest stage in a long process. In many regions terracing or irrigation, overgrazing, the cutting of forests by Romans to build ships to fight Carthaginians or by Crusaders to solve the logistics problems of their expeditions, have profoundly changed some ecologies. Observation that the French landscape falls into two basic types, the open fields of the north and the *bocage*[3] of the south and west, inspired Marc Bloch to undertake his classic study of medieval agricultural methods. Quite unintentionally, changes in human ways often affect nonhuman nature. It has been noted, for example, that the advent of the automobile eliminated huge flocks of sparrows that once fed on the horse manure littering every street.

The history of ecologic change is still so rudimentary that we know little about what really happened, or what the results were. The extinction of the European aurochs[4] as late as 1627 would seem to have been a simple case of overenthusiastic hunting. On more intricate matters it often is impossible to find solid information. For a thousand years or more the Frisians[5] and Hollanders have been pushing back the North Sea, and the process is culminating in our own time in the reclamation of the Zuider Zee.[6] What, if any, species of animals, birds, fish, shore life, or plants have died out in the process? In their epic combat with Neptune have the Netherlanders overlooked ecological values in such a way that the quality of human life in the Netherlands has suffered? I cannot discover that the questions have ever been asked, much less answered.

People, then, have often been a dynamic element in their own environment, but in the present state of historical scholarship we usually do not know exactly when, where, or with what effects man-induced changes came. As we enter the last third of the 20th century, however, concern for the problem of ecological backlash is mounting feverishly. Natural science, conceived as the effort to understand the nature of things, had flourished in several eras and among several peoples. Similarly there had been an age-old accumulation of technological skills, sometimes growing rapidly, sometimes slowly. But it was not until about four generations ago that Western Europe and North America arranged a marriage between science and technology, a union of the theoretical and the empirical approaches to our natural environment. The emergence in widespread practice of the Baconian[7] creed that scientific knowledge means technological power over nature can scarcely be dated before about 1850, save in the chemical industries, where it is anticipated in the 18th century. Its acceptance as a normal pattern of action may mark the greatest

event in human history since the invention of agriculture, and perhaps in nonhuman terrestrial history as well.

Almost at once the new situation forced the crystallization of the novel concept of ecology; indeed, the word *ecology* first appeared in the English language in 1873. Today, less than a century later, the impact of our race upon the environment has so increased in force that it has changed in essence. When the first cannons were fired, in the early 14th century, they affected ecology by sending workers scrambling to the forests and mountains for more potash, sulfur, iron ore, and charcoal, with some resulting erosion and deforestation. Hydrogen bombs are of a different order: a war fought with them might alter the genetics of all life on this planet. By 1285 London had a smog problem arising from the burning of soft coal, but our present combustion of fossil fuels threatens to change the chemistry of the globe's atmosphere as a whole, with consequences which we are only beginning to guess. With the population explosion, the carcinoma of planless urbanism, the new geological deposits of sewage and garbage, surely no creature other than man has ever managed to foul its nest in such short order.

There are many calls to action, but specific proposals, however worthy as individual items, seem too partial, palliative, negative: ban the bomb, tear down the billboards, give the Hindus contraceptives and tell them to eat their sacred cows. The simplest solution to any suspect change is, of course, to stop it, or, better yet, to revert to a romanticized past: make those ugly gasoline stations look like Anne Hathaway's cottage[8] or (in the Far West) like ghost-town saloons. The "wilderness area" mentality invariably advocates deep-freezing an ecology, whether San Gorgonio or the High Sierra,[9] as it was before the first Kleenex was dropped. But neither atavism nor prettification will cope with the ecologic crisis of our time.

What shall we do? No one yet knows. Unless we think about fundamentals, our specific measures may produce new backlashes more serious than those they are designed to remedy.

As a beginning we should try to clarify our thinking by looking in some historical depth, at the presuppositions that underlie modern technology and science. Science was traditionally aristocratic, speculative, intellectual in intent; technology was lower-class, empirical, action-oriented. The quite sudden fusion of these two, towards the middle of the 19th century, is surely related to the slightly prior and contemporary democratic revolutions which, by reducing social barriers, tended to assert a functional unity of brain and hand. Our ecologic crisis is the product of an emerging, entirely novel, democratic culture. The issue is whether a democratized world can survive its own implications. Presumably we cannot unless we rethink our axioms.

The Western Traditions of Technology and Science

One thing is so certain that it seems stupid to verbalize it: both modern technology and modern science are distinctively *Occidental*. Our technology has absorbed elements from all over the world, notably from China; yet everywhere today, whether in Japan or in Nigeria, successful technology is Western. Our science is the heir to all the sciences of the past, especially perhaps to the work of the great Islamic scientists of the Middle Ages, who so often outdid the ancient Greeks in skill and perspicacity: al-Razi in medicine, for example; or ibn-al-Haytham in optics; or Omar Khayyám in mathematics. Indeed, not a few works of such geniuses seem to have vanished in the original Arabic and to survive only in medieval Latin translations that helped to lay the foundations for later Western developments. Today, around the globe, all significant science is Western in style and method, whatever the pigmentation or language of the scientists.

A second pair of facts is less well recognized because they result from quite recent historical scholarship. The leadership of the West, both in technology and in science, is far older than the so-called Scientific Revolution of the 17th century or the so-called Industrial Revolution of the 18th century. These terms are in fact outmoded and obscure the true nature of what they try to describe—significant stages in two long and separate developments. By A.D. 1000 at the latest—and perhaps, feebly, as much as 200 years earlier—the West began to apply water power to industrial processes other than milling grain. This was followed in the late 12th century by the harnessing of wind power. From simple beginnings, but with remarkable consistency of style, the West rapidly expanded its skills in the development of power machinery, labor-saving devices, and automation. Those who doubt should contemplate that most monumental achievement in the history of automation: the weight-driven mechanical clock, which appeared in two forms in the early 14th century. Not in craftsmanship but in basic technological capacity, the Latin West of the later Middle Ages far outstripped

its elaborate, sophisticated, and aesthetically magnificent sister cultures, Byzantium and Islam.[10] In 1444 a great Greek ecclesiastic, Bessarion, who had gone to Italy, wrote a letter to a prince in Greece. He was amazed by the superiority of Western ships, arms, textiles, glass. But above all he was astonished by the spectacle of waterwheels sawing timbers and pumping the bellows of blast furnaces. Clearly, he had seen nothing of the sort in the Near East.

By the end of the 15th century the technological superiority of Europe was such that its small, mutually hostile nations could spill out over all the rest of the world, conquering, looting, and colonizing. The symbol of this technological superiority is the fact that Portugal, one of the weakest states of the Occident, was able to become, and to remain for a century, mistress of the East Indies. And we must remember that the technology of Vasco da Gama and Albuquerque was built by pure empiricism, drawing remarkably little support or inspiration from science.

In the present-day vernacular understanding, modern science is supposed to have begun in 1543, when both Copernicus and Vesalius published their great works. It is no derogation of their accomplishments, however, to point out that such structures as the *Fabrica* and the *De revolutionibus* do not appear overnight. The distinctive Western tradition of science, in fact, began in the late 11th century with a massive movement of translation of Arabic and Greek scientific works into Latin. A few notable books—*Theophrastus*, for example—escaped the West's avid new appetite for science, but within less than 200 years effectively the entire corpus of Greek and Muslim science was available in Latin, and was being eagerly read and criticized in the new European universities. Out of criticism arose new observation, speculation, and increasing distrust of ancient authorities. By the late 13th century Europe had seized global scientific leadership from the faltering hands of Islam. It would be as absurd to deny the profound originality of Newton, Galileo, or Copernicus as to deny that of the 14th century scholastic scientists like Buridan or Oresme on whose work they built. Before the 11th century, science scarcely existed in the Latin West, even in Roman times. From the 11th century onward, the scientific sector of Occidental culture has increased in a steady crescendo.

Since both our technological and our scientific movements got their start, acquired their character, and achieved world dominance in the Middle Ages, it would seem that we cannot understand their nature or their present impact upon ecology without examining fundamental medieval assumptions and developments.

Medieval View of Man and Nature

Until recently, agriculture has been the chief occupation even in "advanced" societies; hence, any change in methods of tillage has much importance. Early plows, drawn by two oxen, did not normally turn the sod but merely scratched it. Thus, cross-plowing was needed and fields tended to be squarish. In the fairly light soils and semiarid climates of the Near East and Mediterranean, this worked well. But such a plow was inappropriate to the wet climate and often sticky soils of northern Europe. By the latter part of the 7th century after Christ, however, following obscure beginnings, certain northern peasants were using an entirely new kind of plow, equipped with a vertical knife to cut the line of the furrow, a horizontal share to slice under the sod, and a moldboard to turn it over. The friction of this plow with the soil was so great that it normally required not two but eight oxen. It attacked the land with such violence that cross-plowing was not needed, and fields tended to be shaped in long strips.

In the days of the scratch-plow, fields were distributed generally in units capable of supporting a single family. Subsistence farming was the presupposition. But no peasant owned eight oxen: to use the new and more efficient plow, peasants pooled their oxen to form large plowteams, originally receiving (it would appear) plowed strips in proportion to their contribution. Thus, distribution of land was based no longer on the needs of a family but, rather, on the capacity of a power machine to till the earth. Man's relation to the soil was profoundly changed. Formerly man had been part of nature; now he was the exploiter of nature. Nowhere else in the world did farmers develop any analogous agricultural implement. Is it coincidence that modern technology, with its ruthlessness toward nature, has so largely been produced by descendants of these peasants of northern Europe?

This same exploitive attitude appears slightly before A.D. 830 in Western illustrated calendars. In older calendars the months were shown as passive personifications. The new Frankish calendars, which set the style for the Middle Ages, are very different: they show men coercing the world around them—plowing, harvesting, chopping trees, butchering pigs. Man and nature are two things, and man is master.

These novelties seem to be in harmony with larger intellectual patterns. What people do about their ecology depends on what they think about themselves in relation to things around them. Human ecology is deeply conditioned by beliefs about our nature and destiny—that is, by religion. To Western eyes this is very evident in, say, India or Ceylon. It is equally true of ourselves and of our medieval ancestors.

The victory of Christianity over paganism was the greatest psychic revolution in the history of our culture. It has become fashionable today to say that, for better or worse, we live in "the post-Christian age." Certainly the forms of our thinking and language have largely ceased to be Christian, but to my eye the substance often remains amazingly akin to that of the past. Our daily habits of action, for example, are dominated by an implicit faith in perpetual progress which was unknown either to Greco-Roman antiquity or to the Orient. It is rooted in, and is indefensible apart from, Judeo-Christian theology. The fact that Communists share it merely helps to show what can be demonstrated on many other grounds; that Marxism, like Islam, is a Judeo-Christian heresy. We continue today to live, as we have lived for about 1700 years, very largely in a context of Christian axioms.

What did Christianity tell people about their relations with the environment?

While many of the world's mythologies provide stories of creation, Greco-Roman mythology was singularly incoherent in this respect. Like Aristotle, the intellectuals of the ancient West denied that the visible world had had a beginning. Indeed, the idea of a beginning was impossible in the framework of their cyclical notion of time. In sharp contrast, Christianity inherited from Judaism not only a concept of time as non-repetitive and linear but also a striking story of creation. By gradual stages a loving and all-powerful God had created light and darkness, the heavenly bodies, the earth and all its plants, animals, birds, and fishes. Finally, God had created Adam and, as an afterthought, Eve to keep man from being lonely. Man named all the animals, thus establishing his dominance over them. God planned all of this explicitly for man's benefit and rule: no item in the physical creation had any purpose save to serve man's purposes. And, although man's body is made of clay, he is not simply part of nature: he is made in God's image.

Especially in its Western form, Christianity is the most anthropocentric religion the world has seen. As early as the 2nd century both Tertullian and Saint Irenaeus of Lyons were insisting that when God shaped Adam he was foreshadowing the image of the incarnate Christ, the Second

Adam. Man shares, in great measure, God's transcendence of nature. Christianity, in absolute contrast to ancient paganism and Asia's religions (except, perhaps, Zoroastrianism),[11] not only established a dualism of man and nature but also insisted that it is God's will that man exploit nature for his proper ends.

At the level of the common people this worked out in an interesting way. In antiquity every tree, every spring, every stream, every hill had its own *genius loci*, its guardian spirit. These spirits were accessible to men, but were very unlike men; centaurs, fauns, and mermaids show their ambivalence. Before one cut a tree, mined a mountain, or dammed a brook, it was important to placate the spirit in charge of that particular situation, and to keep it placated. By destroying pagan animism,[12] Christianity made it possible to exploit nature in a mood of indifference to the feelings of natural objects.

It is often said that for animism the Church substituted the cult of saints. True; but the cult of saints is functionally quite different from animism. The saint is not *in* natural objects; he may have special shrines, but his citizenship is in heaven. Moreover, a saint is entirely a man; he can be approached in human terms. In addition to saints, Christianity of course also had angels and demons inherited from Judaism and perhaps, at one remove, from Zoroastrianism. But these were all as mobile as the saints themselves. The spirits *in* natural objects, which formerly had protected nature from man, evaporated. Man's effective monopoly on spirit in this world was confirmed, and the old inhibitions to the exploitation of nature crumbled.

When one speaks in such sweeping terms, a note of caution is in order. Christianity is a complex faith, and its consequences differ in differing contexts. What I have said may well apply to the medieval West, where in fact technology made spectacular advances. But the Greek East, a highly civilized realm of equal Christian devotion, seems to have produced no marked technological innovation after the late 7th century, when Greek fire was invented. The key to the contrast may perhaps be found in a difference in the tonality of piety and thought which students of comparative theology find between the Greek and the Latin Churches. The Greeks believed that sin was intellectual blindness, and that salvation was found in illumination, orthodoxy—that is, clear thinking. The Latins, on the other hand, felt that sin was moral evil and that salvation was to be found in right conduct. Eastern theology has been intellectualist. Western theology has been voluntarist. The Greek saint contemplates;

the Western saint acts. The implications of Christianity for the conquest of nature would emerge more easily in the Western atmosphere.

The Christian dogma of creation, which is found in the first clause of all the Creeds, has another meaning for our comprehension of today's ecologic crisis. By revelation, God had given man the Bible, the Book of Scripture. But since God had made nature, nature also must reveal the divine mentality. The religious study of nature for the better understanding of God was known as natural theology. In the early Church, and always in the Greek East, nature was conceived primarily as a symbolic system through which God speaks to men: the ant is a sermon to sluggards; rising flames are the symbol of the soul's aspiration. This view of nature was essentially artistic rather than scientific. While Byzantium preserved and copied great numbers of ancient Greek scientific texts, science as we conceive it could scarcely flourish in such an ambience.

However, in the Latin West by the early 13th century natural theology was following a very different bent. It was ceasing to be the decoding of the physical symbols of God's communication with man and was becoming the effort to understand God's mind by discovering how his creation operates. The rainbow was no longer simply a symbol of hope first sent to Noah after the deluge: Robert Grosseteste, Friar Roger Bacon, and Theodoric of Freiberg produced startlingly sophisticated work on the topics of the rainbow, but they did it as a venture in religious understanding. From the 13th century onward, up to and including Leibniz and Newton, every major scientist, in effect, explained his motivations in religious terms. Indeed, if Galileo had not been so expert an amateur theologian he would have got into far less trouble: the professionals resented his intrusion. And Newton seems to have regarded himself more as a theologian than as a scientist. It was not until the late 18th century that the hypothesis of God became unnecessary to many scientists.

It is often hard for the historian to judge, when men explain why they are doing what they want to do, whether they are offering real reasons or merely culturally acceptable reasons. The consistency with which scientists during the long formative centuries of Western science said that the task and the reward of the scientist was "to think God's thoughts after him" leads one to believe that this was their real motivation. If so, then modern Western science was cast in a matrix of Christian theology. The dynamism of religious devotion, shaped by the Judeo-Christian dogma of creation, gave it impetus.

An Alternative Christian View

We would seem to be headed toward conclusions unpalatable to many Christians. Since both *science* and *technology* are blessed words in our contemporary vocabulary, some may be happy at the notions, first, that, viewed historically, modern science is an extrapolation of natural theology and, second, that modern technology is at least partly to be explained as an Occidental, voluntarist realization of the Christian dogma of man's transcendence of, and rightful mastery over, nature. But, as we now recognize, somewhat over a century ago science and technology—hitherto quite separate activities—joined to give mankind powers which, to judge by many of the ecologic effects, are out of control. If so, Christianity bears a huge burden of guilt.

I personally doubt that disastrous ecologic backlash can be avoided simply by applying to our problems more science and more technology. Our science and technology have grown out of Christian attitudes toward man's relation to nature which are almost universally held not only by Christians and neo-Christians but also by those who fondly regard themselves, as post-Christians. Despite Copernicus, all the cosmos rotates around our little globe. Despite Darwin, we are *not*, in our hearts, part of the natural process. We are superior to nature, contemptuous of it, willing to use it for our slightest whim. The newly elected governor of California, like myself a churchman but less troubled than I, spoke for the Christian tradition when he said (as is alleged), "when you've seen one redwood tree, you've seen them all." To a Christian a tree can be no more than a physical fact. The whole concept of the sacred grove is alien to Christianity and to the ethos of the West. For nearly 2 millennia Christian missionaries have been chopping down sacred groves, which are idolatrous because they assume spirit in nature.

What we do about ecology depends on our ideas of the man-nature relationship. More science and more technology are not going to get us out of the present ecologic crisis until we find a new religion, or rethink our old one. The beatniks, who are the basic revolutionaries of our time, show a sound instinct in their affinity for Zen Buddhism, which conceives of the man-nature relationship as very nearly the mirror image of the Christian view. Zen, however, is as deeply conditioned by Asian history as Christianity is by the experience of the West, and I am dubious of its viability among us.

Possibly we should ponder the greatest radical in Christian history since Christ: Saint Francis of Assisi. The prime miracle of Saint Francis is the fact that he did not end at the stake, as many of his left-wing followers did. He was so clearly heretical that a general of the Franciscan Order, Saint Bonaventura, a great and perceptive Christian, tried to suppress the early accounts of Franciscanism. The key to an understanding of Francis is his belief in the virtue of humility—not merely for the individual but for man as a species. Francis tried to depose man from his monarchy over creation and set up a democracy of all God's creatures. With him the ant is no longer simply a homily for the lazy, flames a sign of the thrust of the soul toward union with God: now they are Brother Ant and Sister Fire, praising the Creator in their own ways as Brother Man does in his.

Later commentators have said that Francis preached to the birds as a rebuke to men who would not listen. The records do not read so: he urged the little birds to praise God, and in spiritual ecstasy they flapped their wings and chirped rejoicing. Legends of saints, especially the Irish saints, had long told of their dealings with animals but always, I believe, to show their human dominance over creatures. With Francis it is different. The land around Gubbio in the Apennines[13] was being ravaged by a fierce wolf. Saint Francis, says the legend, talked to the wolf and persuaded him of the error of his ways. The wolf repented, died in the odor of sanctity, and was buried in consecrated ground.

What Sir Steven Runciman calls "the Franciscan doctrine of the animal soul" was quickly stamped out. Quite possibly it was in part inspired, consciously or unconsciously, by the belief in reincarnation held by the Cathar heretics[14] who at that time teemed in Italy and southern France, and who presumably had got it originally from India. It is significant that at just the same moment, about 1200, traces of metempsychosis are found also in western Judaism, in the Provencal *Cabbala*. But Francis held neither to transmigration of souls nor to pantheism. His view of nature and of man rested on a unique sort of pan-psychism of all things animate and inanimate, designed for the glorification of their transcendent Creator, who, in the ultimate gesture of cosmic humility, assumed flesh, lay helpless in a manger, and hung dying on a scaffold.

I am not suggesting that many contemporary Americans who are concerned about our ecologic crisis will be either able or willing to counsel with wolves or exhort birds. However, the present increasing disruption of the global environment is the product of a dynamic technology and science which were originating in the Western medieval world against which Saint Francis was rebelling in so original a way. Their growth cannot be understood historically apart from distinctive attitudes toward nature which are deeply grounded in Christian dogma. The fact that most people do not think of these attitudes as Christian is irrelevant. No new set of basic values has been accepted in our society to displace those of Christianity. Hence we shall continue to have a worsening ecologic crisis until we reject the Christian axiom that nature has no reason for existence save to serve man.

The greatest spiritual revolutionary in Western history, Saint Francis, proposed what he thought was an alternative Christian view of nature and man's relation to it: he tried to substitute the idea of the equality of all creatures, including man, for the idea of man's limitless rule of creation. He failed. Both our present science and our present technology are so tinctured with orthodox Christian arrogance toward nature that no solution for our ecologic crisis can be expected from them alone. Since the roots of our trouble are so largely religious, the remedy must also be essentially religious, whether we call it that or not. We must rethink and refeel our nature and destiny. The profoundly religious, but heretical, sense of the primitive Franciscans for the spiritual autonomy of all parts of nature may point a direction. I propose Francis as a patron saint for ecologists. ■

Notes

1. Aldous Huxley—(1894–1963) English writer, author of *Brave New World*

2. The Aswan Dam—the Aswan High Dam built on the Nile River in 1962

3. bocage—(French) a grove, woods

4. aurochs—cattle-like animals

5. Frisians—people in the area along the coast of Germany and Denmark

6. Zuider Zee—a large bay that the Hollanders are draining in an effort to gain more land

7. Baconian—Francis Bacon (1561-1626) an English philosopher and essayist who believed that real knowledge is that which can be scientifically studied in nature

8. Anne Hathaway's cottage—the childhood home of Shakespeare's wife; it is a famous thatched-roof cottage.

9. San Gorgonio . . . High Sierra—mountains in California

10. Byzantium and Islam—Byzantium (Greek culture) and Islam (Arab culture)

11. Zoroastrianism—a religion in which good and evil are seen to struggle for supremacy

12. animism—a belief that natural objects possess souls

13. Apennines—a mountain range that runs the length of Italy

14. Cathar heretics—believed in the dualism of the spiritual and material worlds

Making Connections through Discussion and Writing

1. a. Tracing the main line of argument White uses in this essay, list causes that have led to the contemporary ecological crisis.

   _____
   _____
   _____
   _____
   _____
   _____

   b. Briefly describe White's methods and how they illustrate the approach of an intellectual historian (a historian of ideas).

   _____
   _____
   _____
   _____
   _____
   _____
   _____
   _____
   _____

2. a. Explain why White finds the kind of plow that began to be used in northern Europe in the seventh century to be so significant.

   _____
   _____
   _____
   _____

   b. He says, "Man's relation to the soil was profoundly changed." How did it change?

   _____
   _____
   _____
   _____

   c. What were the consequences of this change?

   _____
   _____
   _____
   _____
   _____

3. In the section White introduces with "what did Christianity tell people about their relations with the environment?," he lists particular ideas in the Jewish and Christian scriptures that influenced the Western attitude toward nature. Summarize these ideas.

    _____

    _____

    _____

    _____

    _____

    _____

    _____

    _____

    _____

    _____

    _____

4. a. What differences of attitude does White find between the Eastern Orthodox realm of Christianity and the Western realm of Catholicism and the later Protestantism?

        _____

        _____

        _____

        _____

        _____

        _____

    b. What does he attribute these differences to?

        _____

        _____

        _____

    c. What are their consequences?

        _____

        _____

        _____

        _____

        _____

5. a. What Christian example does White give as a model for better attitudes toward nature?

        _____

        _____

    b. Why does he choose this example?

        _____

        _____

6. White claims that St. Francis "tried to depose man from his monarchy over creation and set up a democracy of all God's creatures." Later in the essay, he says that St. Francis "tried to substitute the idea of the equality of all creatures." Read Francis' "Canticle of Brother Sun," and find other material on St. Francis.
   a. Do you agree with White that Francis believes in the "equality of all creatures"?

   _____

   _____

   b. Explain what you find Francis' belief to be.

   _____

   _____

   _____

   _____

   _____

7 a. Suggest Christian or Hebrew teachings that could keep man from exploiting nature by a wasteful or destructive "domination" over it.

   _____

   _____

   _____

   _____

   _____

   b. What constitutes a Biblical view toward nature?

   _____

   _____

   _____

   _____

   _____

   _____

   _____

   _____

   _____

Wendell Berry

Christianity and the Survival of Creation

Wendell Berry (b. 1934), American poet, novelist, and essayist, teaches at the University of Kentucky. He has written more than numerous books, such as the novella *Fidelity* and the novel *Old Jack*. His writings deal primarily with life in rural Kentucky and with environmental concerns. The following selection was originally delivered as a lecture at the Southern Baptist Theological Seminary in Louisville, Kentucky, and was published in Berry's book of essays titled *Sex, Economy, Freedom and Community* (1993).

Vocabulary ....

assignation	indictment
chateau	paraphernalia
dualism	shibboleths

I

I confess that I have not invariably been comfortable in front of a pulpit; I have never been comfortable behind one. To be behind a pulpit is always a forcible reminder to me that I am an essayist and, in many ways, a dissenter. An essayist is, literally, a writer who attempts to tell the truth. Preachers must resign themselves to being either right or wrong; an essayist, when proved wrong, may claim to have been "just practicing." An essayist is privileged to speak without institutional authorization. A dissenter, of course, must speak without privilege.

I want to begin with a problem: namely, that the culpability of Christianity in the destruction of the natural world and the uselessness of Christianity in any effort to correct that destruction are now established cliches of the conservation movement. This is a problem for two reasons.

First, the indictment of Christianity by the anti-Christian conservationists is, in many respects, just. For instance, the complicity of Christian priests, preachers, and missionaries in the cultural destruction and the economic exploitation of the primary peoples of the Western Hemisphere, as of traditional cultures around the world, is notorious. Throughout the five hundred years since Columbus's first landfall in the Bahamas, the evangelist has walked beside the conqueror and the merchant, too often blandly assuming that their

causes were the same. Christian organizations, to this day, remain largely indifferent to the rape and plunder of the world and of its traditional cultures. It is hardly too much to say that most Christian organizations are as happily indifferent to the ecological, cultural, and religious implications of industrial economics as are most industrial organizations. The certified Christian seems just as likely as anyone else to join the military-industrial conspiracy to murder Creation.

The conservationist indictment of Christianity is a problem, second, because, however just it may be, it does not come from an adequate understanding of the Bible and the cultural traditions that descend from the Bible. The anti-Christian conservationists characteristically deal with the Bible by waving it off. And this dismissal conceals, as such dismissals are apt to do, an ignorance that invalidates it. The Bible is an inspired book written by human hands; as such, it is certainly subject to criticism. But the anti-Christian environmentalists have not mastered the first rule of the criticism of books: you have to read them before you criticize them. Our predicament now, I believe, requires us to learn to read and understand the Bible in the light of the present fact of Creation. This would seem to be a requirement both for Christians and for everyone concerned, but it entails a long work of true criticism—that is, of careful and judicious study, not dismissal. It entails, furthermore, the making of very precise distinctions between biblical instruction and the behavior of those peoples supposed to have been biblically instructed.

I cannot pretend, obviously, to have made so meticulous a study; even if I were capable of it, I would not live long enough to do it. But I have attempted to read the Bible with these issues in mind, and I see some virtually catastrophic discrepancies between biblical instruction and Christian behavior. I don't mean disreputable Christian behavior, either. The discrepancies I see are between biblical instruction and allegedly respectable Christian behavior.

If because of these discrepancies Christianity were dismissible, there would, of course, be no problem. We could simply dismiss it, along with the twenty centuries of unsatisfactory history attached to it, and start setting things to rights. The problem emerges only when we ask, Where then would we turn for instruction? We might, let us suppose, turn to another religion—a recourse that is sometimes suggested by the anti-Christian conservationists. Buddhism, for example, is certainly a religion that could guide us toward a right respect for the natural world, our fellow humans, and our fellow creatures. I owe a considerable debt myself to Buddhism and Buddhists. But there are an enormous number of people—and I am one of them—whose native religion, for better or worse, is Christianity. We were born to it; we began to learn about it before we became conscious; it is, whatever we think of it, an intimate belonging of our being; it informs our consciousness, our language, and our dreams. We can turn away from it or against it, but that will only bind us tightly to a reduced version of it. A better possibility is that this, our native religion, should survive and renew itself so that it may become as largely and truly instructive as we need it to be. On such a survival and renewal of the Christian religion may depend the survival of the Creation that is its subject.

II

If we read the Bible, keeping in mind the desirability of those two survivals—of Christianity and the Creation—we are apt to discover several things about which modern Christian organizations have kept remarkably quiet or to which they have paid little attention.

(1) We will discover that we humans do not own the world or any part of it: "The earth is the Lord's, and the fulness thereof: the world and they that dwell therein."[1] There is in our human law, undeniably, the concept and right of "land ownership."

But this, I think, is merely an expedient to safeguard the mutual belonging of people and places without which there can be no lasting and conserving human communities. This right of human ownership is limited by mortality and by natural constraints on human attention and responsibility; it quickly becomes abusive when used to justify large accumulations of "real estate," and perhaps for that reason such large accumulations are forbidden in the twenty-fifth chapter of Leviticus. In biblical terms, the "landowner" is the guest and steward of God: "The land is mine; for ye are strangers and sojourners with me."[2]

(2) We will discover that God made not only the parts of Creation that we humans understand and approve but all of it: "All things were made by him; and without him was not anything made that was made."[3] And so we must credit God with the making of biting and stinging insects, poisonous serpents, weeds, poisonous weeds, dangerous beasts, and disease-causing micro-organisms. That we may disapprove of these things does not mean that God is in error or that He ceded some of the work of Creation to Satan; it means that we are deficient in wholeness, harmony, and understanding—that is, we are "fallen."

(3) We will discover that God found the world, as He made it, to be good, that He made it for His pleasure, and that He continues to love it and to find it worthy, despite its reduction and corruption by us. People who quote John 3:16 as an easy formula for getting to Heaven neglect to see the great difficulty implied in the statement that the advent of Christ was made possible by God's love for the world—not God's love for Heaven or for the world as it might be but for the world as it was and is. Belief in Christ is thus dependent on prior belief in the inherent goodness—the lovability—of the world.

(4) We will discover that the Creation is not in any sense independent of the Creator, the result of a primal creative act long over and done with, but is the continuous, constant participation of all creatures in the being of God. Elihu said to Job that if God "gather unto himself his spirit and his breath; all flesh shall perish together."[4] And Psalm 104 says, "Thou sendest forth thy spirit, they are created." Creation is thus God's presence in creatures. The Greek Orthodox theologian Philip Sherrard has written that "Creation is nothing less than the manifestation of God's hidden Being."[5] This means that we and all other creatures live by a sanctity that is inexpressibly intimate, for to every creature, the gift of life is a portion of the breath and spirit of

God. As the poet George Herbert put it:

Thou art in small things great, not small in any . . . For thou art infinite in one and all.[6]

We will discover that for these reasons our destruction of nature is not just bad stewardship, or stupid economics, or a betrayal of family responsibility; it is the most horrid blasphemy. It is flinging God's gifts into His face, as if they were of no worth beyond that assigned to them by our destruction of them. To Dante, "despising Nature and her goodness" was a violence against God.[7] We have no entitlement from the Bible to exterminate or permanently destroy or hold in contempt anything on the earth or in the heavens above it or in the waters beneath it. We have the right to use the gifts of nature but not to ruin or waste them. We have the right to use what we need but no more, which is why the Bible forbids usury and great accumulations of property. The usure, Dante said, "condemns Nature . . . for he puts his hope elsewhere."[8]

William Blake was biblically correct, then, when he said that "everything that lives is holy."[9] And Blake's great commentator Kathleen Raine was correct both biblically and historically when she said that "the sense of the holiness of life is the human norm."[10]

The Bible leaves no doubt at all about the sanctity of the act of world-making, or of the world that was made, or of creaturely or bodily life in this world. We are holy creatures living among other holy creatures in a world that is holy. Some people know this, and some do not. Nobody, of course, knows it all the time. But what keeps it from being far better known than it is? Why is it apparently unknown to millions of professed students of the Bible? How can modern Christianity have so solemnly folded its hands while so much of the work of God was and is being destroyed?

III

Obviously, "the sense of the holiness of life" is not compatible with an exploitive economy. You cannot know that life is holy if you are content to live from economic practices that daily destroy life and diminish its possibility. And many if not most Christian organizations now appear to be perfectly at peace with the military-industrial economy and its "scientific" destruction of life. Surely, if we are to remain free and if we are to remain true to our religious inheritance, we must maintain a separation between church and state. But if we are to maintain any sense or coherence or meaning in our lives, we cannot tolerate the present utter disconnection

between religion and economy. By "economy" I do not mean "economics," which is the study of money-making, but rather the ways of human housekeeping, the ways by which the human household is situated and maintained within the household of nature. To be uninterested in economy is to be uninterested in the practice of religion; it is to be uninterested in culture and in character. Probably the most urgent question now faced by people who would adhere to the Bible is this: What sort of economy would be responsible to the holiness of life? What, for Christians, would be the economy, the practices and the restraints, of "right livelihood"? I do not believe that organized Christianity now has any idea. I think its idea of a Christian economy is no more or less than the industrial economy—which is an economy firmly founded on the seven deadly sins and the breaking of all ten of the Ten Commandments. Obviously, if Christianity is going to survive as more than a respecter and comforter of profitable iniquities, then Christians, regardless of their organizations, are going to have to interest themselves in economy—which is to say, in nature and in work. They are going to have to give workable answers to those who say we cannot live without this economy that is destroying us and our world, who see the murder of Creation as the only way of life.

The holiness of life is obscured to modern Christians also by the idea that the only holy place is the built church. This idea may be more taken for granted than taught; nevertheless, Christians are encouraged from childhood to think of the church building as "God's house" and most of them could think of their houses or farms or shops or factories as holy places only with great effort and embarrassment. It is understandably difficult for modern Americans to think of their dwellings and workplaces as holy, because most of these are, in fact, places of desecration, deeply involved in the ruin of Creation.

The idea of the exclusive holiness of church buildings is, of course, wildly incompatible with the idea, which the churches also teach, that God is present in all places to hear prayers. It is incompatible with Scripture. The idea that a human artifact could contain or confine God was explicitly repudiated by Solomon in his prayer at the dedication of the Temple: "Behold, the heaven and the heaven of heavens cannot contain thee: how much less this house that I have builded?"[11] And these words of Solomon were remembered a thousand years later by Saint Paul, preaching at Athens:

God that made the world and all things therein,
seeing that he is lord of heaven and earth,
dwelleth not in temples made with hands . . .
For in him we live, and move, and have our
being; as certain also of your own poets have
said. [12]

Idolatry always reduces to the worship of something "made with hands," something confined within the terms of human work and human comprehension. Thus, Solomon and Saint Paul both insisted on the largeness and the at-largeness of God, setting Him free, so to speak, from *ideas* about Him. He is not to be fenced in, under human control, like some domestic creature; He is the wildest being in existence. The presence of His spirit in us is our wildness, our oneness with the wilderness of Creation. That is why subduing the things of nature to human purposes is so dangerous and why it so often results in evil, in separation and desecration. It is why the poets of our tradition so often have given nature the role not only of mother or grandmother but of the highest earthly teacher and judge, a figure of mystery and great power. Jesus' own specifications for his church have nothing at all to do with masonry and carpentry but only with people; his church is "where two or three are gathered together in my name."[13]

The Bible gives exhaustive (and sometimes exhausting) attention to the organization of religion: the building and rebuilding of the Temple; its furnishings; the orders, duties, and paraphernalia of the priesthood; the orders of rituals and ceremonies. But that does not disguise the fact that the most significant religious events recounted in the Bible do not occur in "temples made with hands." The most important religion in that book is unorganized and is sometimes profoundly disruptive of organization. From Abraham to Jesus, the most important people are not priests but shepherds, soldiers, property owners, workers, housewives, queens and kings, manservants and maidservants, fishermen, prisoners, whores, even bureaucrats. The great visionary encounters did not take place in temples but in sheep pastures, in the desert, in the wilderness, on mountains, on the shores of rivers and the sea, in the middle of the sea, in prisons. And however strenuously the divine voice prescribed rites and observances, it just as strenuously repudiated them when they were taken to *be* religion:

Your new moons and your appointed feasts
my soul hateth: they are a trouble unto me; I am
weary to bear them.

And when you spread forth your hands, I
will hide mine eyes from you: yea, when you
make many prayers, I will not hear: your hands
are full of blood.

Wash you, make you clean; put away the
evil of your doings from before mine eyes; cease
to do evil;

Learn to do well; seek judgment, relieve the
oppressed, judge the fatherless, plead for the
widow.[14]

Religion, according to this view, is less to be celebrated in rituals than practiced in the world.

I don't think it is enough appreciated how much an outdoor book the Bible is. It is a "hypaethral book," such as Thoreau talked about—a book open to the sky. It is best read and understood outdoors, and the farther outdoors the better. Or that has been my experience of it. Passages that within walls seem improbable or incredible, outdoors seem merely natural. This is because outdoors we are confronted everywhere with wonders; we see that the miraculous is not extraordinary but the common mode of existence. It is our daily bread. Whoever really has considered the lilies of the field or the birds of the air and pondered the improbability of their existence in this warm world within the cold and empty stellar distances will hardly balk at the turning of water into wine—which was, after all, a very small miracle. We forget the greater and still continuing miracle by which water (with soil and sunlight) is turned into grapes.

It is clearly impossible to assign holiness exclusively to the built church without denying holiness to the rest of Creation, which is then said to be "secular." The world, which God looked at and found entirely good, we find none too good to pollute entirely and destroy piecemeal. The church, then, becomes a kind of preserve of "holiness," from which certified lovers of God assault and plunder the "secular" earth.

Not only does this repudiate God's approval of His work; it refuses also to honor the Bible's explicit instruction to regard the works of the Creation as God's revelation of Himself. The assignation of holiness exclusively to the built church is therefore logically accompanied by the assignation of revelation exclusively to the Bible. But Psalm 19 begins, "The heavens declare the glory of God; and the firmament sheweth his handiwork." The word of God has been revealed in facts from the moment of the third verse of the first chapter of Genesis: "Let there be light: and there was light." And Saint Paul states the rule: "The invisible things of him from the creation of the world are clearly seen, being understood by the things that are made."[15] Yet from this free, generous, and sensible view of things, we come to the idolatry of the book: the idea that nothing is true that cannot be (and has not been already) written. The misuse of the Bible thus logically accompanies the abuse of nature: if you are going to destroy creatures without respect, you will want to reduce them to "materiality"; you will want to deny that there is spirit or truth in them, just as you will want to believe that the only holy creatures, the only creatures with souls, are humans—or even only Christian humans.

By denying spirit and truth to the nonhuman Creation, modern proponents of religion have legitimized a form of blasphemy without which the nature- and culture-destroying machinery of the industrial economy could not have been built—that is, they have legitimized bad work. Good human work honors God's work. Good work uses no thing without respect, both for what it is in itself and for its origin. It uses neither tool nor material that it does not respect and that it does not love. It honors nature as a great mystery and power, as an indispensable teacher, and as the inescapable judge of all work of human hands. It does not dissociate life and work, or pleasure and work, or love and work, or usefulness and beauty. To work without pleasure or affection, to make a product that is not both useful and beautiful, is to dishonor God, nature, the thing that is made, and whomever it is made for. This is blasphemy: to make shoddy work of the work of God. But such blasphemy is not possible when the entire Creation is understood as holy and when the works of God are understood as embodying and thus revealing His spirit.

In the Bible we find none of the industrialist's contempt or hatred for nature. We find, instead, a poetry of awe and reverence and profound cherishing, as in these verses from Moses' valedictory blessing of the twelve tribes:

> And of Joseph he said, Blessed of the Lord be his land, for the precious things of heaven, for the dew, and for the deep that croucheth beneath,
> And for the precious fruits brought forth by the sun, and for the precious things put forth by the moon,
> And for the chief things of the ancient mountains, and for the precious things of the lasting hills,
> And for the precious things of the earth and fullness thereof, and for the good will of him that dwelt in the bush.[16]

IV

I have been talking, of course, about a dualism that manifests itself in several ways: as a cleavage, a radical discontinuity, between Creator and creature, spirit and matter, religion and nature, religion and economy, worship and work, and so on. This dualism, I think, is the most destructive disease that afflicts us. In its best-known, its most dangerous, and perhaps its fundamental version, it is the dualism of body and soul. This is an issue as difficult as it is important, and so to deal with it we should start at the beginning.

The crucial test is probably Genesis 2:7, which gives the process by which Adam was created: "The Lord God formed man of the dust of the ground, and breathed into his nostrils the breath of life: and man became a living soul." My mind, like most people's, has been deeply influenced by dualism, and I can see how dualistic minds deal with this verse. They conclude that the formula for man-making is man = body + soul. But that conclusion cannot be derived, except by violence, from Genesis 2:7, which is not dualistic. The formula given in Genesis 2:7 is not man = body + soul; the formula there is soul = dust + breath. According to this verse, God did not make a body and put a soul into it, like a letter into an envelope. He formed man of dust; then, by breathing His breath into it, he made the dust live. The dust, formed as man and made to live, did not *embody* a soul; it *became* a soul. "Soul" here refers to the whole creature. Humanity is thus presented to us, in Adam, not as a creature of two discrete parts temporarily glued together but as a single mystery.

We can see how easy it is to fall into the dualism of body and soul when talking about the inescapable worldly dualities of good and evil or time and eternity. And we can see how easy it is, when Jesus asks, "For what is a man profited, if he shall gain the whole world, and lose his own soul?"[17] to assume that he is condemning the world and appreciating the disembodied soul. But if we give to "soul" here the sense that it has in Genesis 2:7, we see that he is doing no such thing. He is warning that in pursuit of so-called material possessions, we can lose our understanding of ourselves as "living souls"—that is, as creatures of God, members of the holy community of Creation. We can lose the possibility of the atonement of that membership. For we are free, if we choose, to make a duality of our one living soul by disowning the breath of God that is our fundamental bond with one another and with other creatures.

But we can make the same duality by disowning the dust. The breath of God is only one of the divine gifts that make us living souls; the other is the dust. Most of our modern troubles come from our misunderstanding and misvaluation of this dust. Forgetting that the dust, too, is a creature of the Creator, made by the sending forth of His spirit, we have presumed to decide that the dust is "low." We have presumed to say that we are made of two parts: a body and a soul, the body being "low" because made of dust, and the soul "high." By thus valuing these two supposed-to-be parts, we inevitably throw them into competition with each other, like two corporations. The "spiritual" view, of course, has been that the body, in Yeats's phrase, must be "bruised to pleasure soul." And the "secular" version of the same dualism has been that the body, along with the rest of the "material" world, must give way before the advance of the human mind. The dominant religious view, for a long time, has been that the body is a kind of scrip issued by the Great Company Store in the Sky, which can be cashed in to redeem the soul but is otherwise worthless. And the predictable result has been a human creature able to appreciate or tolerate only the "spiritual" (or mental) part of Creation and full of semiconscious hatred of the "physical" or "natural" part, which it is ready and willing to destroy for "salvation," for profit, for "victory," or for fun. This madness constitutes the norm of modern humanity and of modern Christianity.

But to despise the body or mistreat it for the sake of the "soul" is not just to burn one's house for the insurance, nor is it just self-hatred of the most deep and dangerous sort. It is yet another blasphemy. It is to make nothing—and worse than nothing—of the great Something in which we live and move and have our being.

When we hate and abuse the body and its earthly life and joy for Heaven's sake, what do we expect? That out of this life that we have presumed to despise and this world that we have presumed to destroy, we would somehow salvage a soul capable of eternal bliss? And what do we expect when with equal and opposite ingratitude, we try to make of the finite body an infinite reservoir of dispirited and meaningless pleasures?

Times may come, of course, when the life of the body must be denied or sacrificed, times when the whole world must literally be lost for the sake of one's life as a "living soul." But such sacrifice, by people who truly respect and revere the life of the earth and its Creator, does not denounce or degrade the body but rather exalts it and acknowledges its holiness. Such sacrifice is a refusal to allow the body to serve what is unworthy of it.

V

If we credit the Bible's description of the relationship between Creator and Creation, then we cannot deny the spiritual importance of our economic life. Then we must see how religious issues lead to issues of economy and how issues of economy lead to issues of art. By "art" I mean all the ways by which humans make the things they need. If we understand that no artist—no maker—can work except by reworking the works of Creation, then we see that by our work we reveal what we think of the works of God. How we take our lives from this world, how we work, what work we do, how well we use the materials we use, and what we do with them after we have used them—all these are questions of the highest and gravest religious significance. In answering them, we practice, or do not practice, our religion.

The significance—and ultimately the quality—of the work we do is determined by our understanding of the story in which we are taking part.

If we think of ourselves as merely biological creatures, whose story is determined by genetics or environment or history or economics or technology, then, however pleasant or painful the part we play, it cannot matter much. Its significance is that of mere self-concern. "It is a tale / Told by an idiot, full of sound and fury, / Signifying nothing," as Macbeth says when he has "supp'd full with horrors" and is "aweary of the sun."[18]

If we think of ourselves as lofty souls trapped temporarily in lowly bodies in a dispirited, desperate, unlovable world that we must despise for Heaven's sake, then what have we done for this question of significance? If we divide reality into two parts, spiritual and material, and hold (as the Bible does *not* hold) that only the spiritual is good or desirable, then our relation to the material Creation becomes arbitrary, having only the quantitative or mercenary value that we have, in fact and for this reason, assigned to it. Thus, we become the judges and inevitably the destroyers of a world we did not make and that we are bidden to understand as a divine gift. It is impossible to see how good work might be accomplished by people who think that our life in this world either signifies nothing or has only a negative significance.

If, on the other hand, we believe that we are living souls, God's dust and God's breath, acting our parts among other creatures all made of the same dust and breath as ourselves; and if we understand that we are free, within the obvious limits of mortal human life to do evil or good to ourselves and to the other creatures—then all our acts have a supreme significance. If it is true that we are living souls and morally free, then all of us are artists. All of us are makers, within mortal terms and limits, of our lives, of one another's lives, of things we need and use.

This, Ananda Coomaraswamy wrote, is "the normal view," which "assumes . . . not that the artist is a special kind of man, but that every man who is not a mere idler or parasite is necessarily some special kind of artist."[19] But since even mere idlers and parasites may be said to work inescapably, by proxy or influence, it might be better to say that everybody is an artist—either good or bad, responsible or irresponsible. Any life, by working or not working, by working well or poorly, inescapably changes other lives and so changes the world. This is why our division of the "fine arts" from "craftsmanship," and "craftsmanship" from "labor," is so arbitrary, meaningless, and destructive. As Walter Shewring rightly said, both "the plowman and the potter have a cosmic function."[20] And bad art in any trade dishonors and damages Creation.

If we think of ourselves as living souls, immortal creatures, living in the midst of a Creation that is mostly mysterious, and if we see that everything we make or do cannot help but have an everlasting significance for ourselves, for others, and for the world, then we see why some religious teachers have understood work as a form of prayer. We see why the old poets invoked the muse. And we know why George Herbert prayed, in his poem "Mattens":

> Teach me thy love to know;
> That this new light, which now I see,
> May both the work and workman show.[21]

Work connects us both to Creation and to eternity. This is the reason also for Mother Ann Lee's famous instruction: "Do all your work as though you had a thousand years to live on earth, and as you would if you knew you must die tomorrow."[22]

Explaining "the perfection, order, and illumination" of the artistry of Shaker furniture makers, Coomaraswamy wrote, "All tradition has seen in the Master Craftsman of the Universe the exemplar of the human artist or 'maker by art,' and we are told to be perfect, *even as* your Father in heaven is perfect.'" Searching out the lesson, for us, of the Shakers' humble, impersonal, perfect artistry, which refused the modern divorce of utility and beauty, he wrote, "Unfortunately, we do not desire to be such as the Shaker was; we do not propose to 'work as though we had a thousand years to live, and as though we were to die tomorrow.' Just as we

desire peace but not the things that make for peace, so we desire art but not the things that make for art . . . we have the art that we deserve. If the sight of it puts us to shame, it is with ourselves that the reformation must begin.[23]

Any genuine effort to "re-form" our arts, our ways of making, must take thought of "the things that make for art." We must see that no art begins in itself; it begins in other arts, in attitudes and ideas antecedent to any art, in nature, and in inspiration. If we look at the great artistic traditions, as it is necessary to do, we will see that they have never been divorced either from religion or from economy. The possibility of an entirely secular art and of works of art that are spiritless or ugly or useless is not a possibility that has been among us for very long. Traditionally, the arts have been ways of making that have placed a just value on their materials or subjects, on the uses and the users of the things made by art, and on the artists themselves. They have, that is, been ways of giving honor to the works of God. The great artistic traditions have had nothing to do with what we call "self-expression." They have not been destructive of privacy or exploitive of private life. Though they have certainly originated things and employed genius, they have no affinity with the modern cults of originality and genius. Coomaraswamy, a good guide as always, makes an indispensable distinction between genius in the modern sense and craftsmanship: "Genius inhabits a world of its own. The master craftsman lives in a world inhabited by other men; he has neighbors."[24] The arts, traditionally, belong to the neighborhood. They are the means by which the neighborhood lives, works, remembers, worships, and enjoys itself.

But most important of all, now, is to see that the artistic traditions understood every art primarily as a skill or craft and ultimately as a service to fellow creatures and to God. An artist's first duty, according to this view, is technical. It is assumed that one will have talents, materials, subjects—perhaps even genius or inspiration or vision. But these are traditionally understood not as personal properties with which one may do as one chooses but as gifts of God or nature that must be honored in use. One does not dare to use these things without the skill to use them well. As Dante said of his own art, "far worse than in vain does he leave the shore . . . who fishes for the truth and has not the art."[25] To use gifts less than well is to dishonor them and their Giver. There is no material or subject in Creation that in using, we are excused from using well; there is no work in which we are excused from being able and responsible artists.

VI

In denying the holiness of the body and of the so-called physical reality of the world—and in denying support to the good economy, the good work, by which alone the Creation can receive due honor—modern Christianity generally has cut itself off from both nature and culture. It has no serious or competent interest in biology or ecology. And it is equally uninterested in the arts by which humankind connects itself to nature. It manifests no awareness of the specifically Christian cultural lineages that connect us to our past. There is, for example, a splendid heritage of Christian poetry in English that most church members live and die without reading or hearing or hearing about. Most sermons are preached without any awareness at all that the making of sermons is an art that has at times been magnificent. Most modern churches look like they were built by robots without reference to the heritage of church architecture or respect for the place; they embody no awareness that work can be worship. Most religious music now attests to the general assumption that religion is no more than a vaguely pious (and vaguely romantic) emotion.

Modern Christianity, then, has become as specialized in its organizations as other modern organizations, wholly concentrated on the industrial shibboleths of "growth," counting its success in numbers, and on the very strange enterprise of "saving" the individual, isolated, and disembodied soul. Having witnessed and abetted the dismemberment of the households, both human and natural, by which we have, our being as creatures of God, as living souls, and having made light of the great feast and festival of Creation to which we were bidden as living souls, the modern church presumes to be able to save the soul as an eternal piece of private property. It presumes moreover to save the souls of people in other countries and religious traditions, who are often saner and more religious than we are. And always the emphasis is on the individual soul. Some Christian spokespeople give the impression that the highest Christian bliss would be to get to Heaven and find that you are the only one there—that you were right and all the others wrong. Whatever its twentieth-century dress, modern Christianity as I know it is still at bottom the religion of Miss Watson, intent on a dull and superstitious rigmarole by which supposedly we can avoid going to "the bad place" and instead go to "the good place." One can hardly help sympathizing with Huck Finn when he says, "I made up my mind I wouldn't try for it."[26]

Despite its protests to the contrary, modern Christianity has become willy-nilly the religion of the state and the economic status quo. Because it has been so exclusively dedicated to incanting anemic souls into Heaven, it has been made the tool of much earthly villainy. It has, for the most part, stood silently by while a predatory economy has ravaged the world, destroyed its natural beauty and health, divided and plundered its human communities and households. It has flown the flag and chanted the slogans of empire. It has assumed with the economists that "economic forces" automatically work for good and has assumed with the industrialists and militarists that technology determines history. It has assumed with almost everybody that "progress" is good, that it is good to be modern and up with the times. It has admired Caesar and comforted him in his depredations and defaults. But in its de facto alliance with Caesar, Christianity connives directly in the murder of Creation. For in these days, Caesar is no longer a mere destroyer of armies, cities, and nations. He is a contradicter of the fundamental miracle of life. A part of the normal practice of his power is his willingness to destroy the world. He prays he says, and churches everywhere compliantly pray with him. But he is praying to a God whose works he is prepared at any moment to destroy. What could be more wicked than that, or more mad?

The religion of the Bible, on the contrary, is a religion of the state and the status quo only in brief moments. In practice, it is a religion for the correction equally of people and of kings. And Christ's life, from the manger to the cross, was an affront to the established powers of his time, just as it is to the established powers of our time. Much is made in churches of the "good news" of the Gospels. Less is said of the Gospels' bad news, which is that Jesus would have been horrified by just about every "Christian" government the world has ever seen. He would be horrified by our government and its works, and it would be horrified by him. Surely no sane and thoughtful person can imagine any government of our time sitting comfortably at the feet of Jesus while he is saying, "Love your enemies, bless them that curse you, do good to them that hate you, and pray for them that despitefully use you and persecute you."[27]

In fact, we know that one of the businesses of governments, "Christian" or not, has been to reenact the crucifixion. It has happened again and again and again. In *A Time for Trumpets*, his history of the Battle of the Bulge, Charles B. MacDonald tells how the SS Colonel Joachim Peiper was forced to withdraw from a bombarded chateau near the town of La Gleize, leaving behind a number of severely wounded soldiers of both armies. "Also left behind," MacDonald wrote, "on a whitewashed wall of one of the rooms in the basement was a charcoal drawing of Christ, thorns on his head, tears on his cheeks—whether drawn by a German or an American nobody would ever know."[28] This is not an image that belongs to history but rather one that judges it. ■

Author's Notes

[1] Psalms 24:1. (All Biblical quotations are from the King James Version.)

[2] Leviticus 25:23

[3] John 1:3

[4] Job 34:14–15

[5] Philip Sherrard, *Human Image, World Image* (Ipswich, Suffolk, England: Golgonooza Press, 1992), 152.

[6] George Herbert, "Providence" lines 41 and 44, from *The Poems of George Herbert*, ed. by Helen Garner (London: Oxford University Press, 1961), 54.

[7] Dante Alighiere, *The Divine Comedy*, trans. by Charles S. Singleton, Bollingen Series 1 XXX, and *Inferno*, canto XI, lines 46-488 (Princeton, NJ: Princeton University Press, 1970).

[8] Dante Alighieri, *Inferno*, canto XI, lines 109-11.

[9] William Blake, *Complete Writings*, ed, by Geoffrey Keynes (London: Oxford University Press, 1966), 160.

[10] Kathleen Raine, *Golgonooza: City of Imagination* (Ipswich, Suffolk, England: Golgonooza Press, 1991), 28.

[11] I Kings 8:27.

[12] Acts 17:24 and 28.

[13] Matthew 18:20

[14] Isaiah 1:13-17

[15] Romans 1:20.

[16] Deuteronomy 33:13-16.

[17] Matthew 16:26.

[18] William Shakespeare, *Macbeth*, ed. by Kenneth Muir (Cambridge, MA: Harvard University Press, 1957), V.v. lines 13, 26-28, 49.

[19] Anada K. Coomaraswamy, *Christian and Oriental Philosophy of Art* (New York: Dover. 1957), 98.

[20] Walter Shewring, *Artist and Tradesman* (Marlborough, MA: Paulinus Press, 1984), 19.

[21] Herbert, *The Poems of George Herbert*, 54.

[22] June Sprigg, By Shaker Hands, Hanover, NH: University Press of New England, 1990), 33.

[23] Anada K. Coomaraswamy, *Selected Papers*, vol. I (Princeton NJ: Princeton University Press, 1997), 255, 259.

[24] Coomaraswamy, *Christian and Oriental Philosophy of Art*, 99.

[26] Mark Twain, *Adventures of Huckleberry Finn*, in *Mississippi Writings* (New York: Library of America, 1982), 626.

[27] Matthew 5:44.

[28] Charles B. MacDonald, *A Time for Trumpets* (New York: Bantam Books, 1984), 458.

Making Connections through Discussion and Writing

1. Reread the address by Berry, marking his major points by marginal notations.

2. a. What does Berry say is the difference between Christian behavior and Biblical teaching?

   _____
   _____
   _____
   _____
   _____
   _____
   _____

   b. Why does Berry make this distinction?

   _____
   _____
   _____
   _____
   _____

3. What sets the standard that Berry would want society to live up to in its attitudes toward nature?

   _____
   _____
   _____
   _____
   _____

4. What Biblical doctrines does Berry speak of that reveal God's attitude toward material reality?

   _____
   _____
   _____
   _____

5. What does Berry mean by his use of the word "economy"?

   _____
   _____
   _____

6. What is Berry's attitude toward the modern separation of reality into areas designated "sacred" and "secular"?

_____
_____
_____
_____

7. Citing particular points made by each author, briefly compare Berry's attitude toward work with that expressed by Dorothy L. Sayers in her essay "Why Work?"

_____
_____
_____
_____
_____
_____
_____
_____
_____
_____

8. a. What points does Berry make in part V of his address that provide insight into the subject of Christian aesthetics?

_____
_____
_____
_____
_____

   b. How does Berry relate the two subjects of ecology and aesthetics?

_____
_____
_____
_____

9. Explain how Berry relates assumptions about human nature (such as dualism) to attitudes toward material creation, work, and art.

_____
_____
_____
_____
_____
_____
_____
_____

Steven Bouma-Prediger

Is Christianity Responsible for the Ecological Crisis?

Steven Bouma-Prediger (b. 1957), former chair of the Philosophy Department at North Park College in Chicago, is now professor of religion at Hope College, in Holland, Michigan. His areas of research and publication are theology of nature, ecological ethics, and philosophy of religion. He is a member of the Evangelical Environmental Network and the Christian Environmental Council. His publications include *The Greening of Theology: The Ecological Models of Rosemary Radford Ruether, Joseph Sittler, and Jürgen Moltmann* (1995) and, with Virginia Vroblesky, *Assessing the Ark: A Christian Perspective on Nonhuman Creatures and Endangered Species Act* (1997). His latest publications include *Evocations of Grace: The Writings of Joseph Sittler on Ecology, Theology, and Ethics* (2000) and *For the Beauty of the Earth: A Christian View for Creation Care* (2002). In the following article, Professor Bouma-Prediger responds to the issues raised by Lynn White, Jr., in his influential article "The Historical Roots of Our Ecologic Crisis."

Vocabulary ....

apologetics	eschatology
apposite	eschaton
cogent	eschews
deleterious	exegeses
desacralizing	monotheism
egregious	*non sequitur*
ephemeral	problematic

Introduction

It is rare that a week passes without learning of some new ecological disaster. With each newspaper and television report we are shaken from our comfortable ignorance about the state of our early home and confronted with an ecological crisis that, like a crescendo, is growing to unimaginable and genuinely frightening proportions: Global warming, holes in the ozone layer, toxic wastes, oil spills, acid rain, drinking water contamination, overflowing landfills, topsoil erosion, species extinction, destruction of the rain forests, leakage of nuclear waste, lead poisoning, desertification, smog.

If our anecdotal observations need any confirmation, there are plenty of more highly trained earth-watchers speaking out about the current state of the planet. For example, biologist Calvin DeWitt

states that "a crisis of degradation is enveloping the earth"—a crisis genuinely unique in human history in its destructive capability. He lists "seven major degradations brought on by our assault on creation": (1) land conversion and habitat destruction, e.g., land lost due to deforestation; (2) species extinction; (3) degradation of the land, e.g., loss of topsoil to wind and water erosion; (4) resource conversion and production of wastes and hazards; (5) global toxification, e.g., oil spills; (6) the greenhouse effect and ozone depletion; (7) human and cultural degradation, e.g., the displacement of agriculture by agribusiness.[1] Such is the plight of the earth.

It is equally rare that a week passes without hearing of how Christianity, and usually religion in general, is to blame for our ecological crisis. For example:

Steven Bouma-Prediger, "Is Christianity Responsible for the Ecological Crisis?", *Christian Scholar's Review* XXV:2. Copyright © 1995 by *Christian Scholar's Review*; reprinted by permission.

To the extent that man fulfills the command to be fruitful and multiply, his assault on this planet will continue. Religions assume that whatever sacrifices may be necessary to accommodate more of humanity should be made by species other than us.

Having created God in man's own image, Western religion has adopted an anthropocentric mythology that separates God from Creation, soul from body, and man from Earth. It is this dualism that prevents us from relating not only to the natural world, but to ourselves.

The sky-god religions—Judaism, Christianity, and Islam—are the most corrosive forces on this planet. Monuments to irrationality under the guise of faith and spirituality, they focus people's hatred and distrust of one another as time runs out on the possibility that mutual respect and cooperation can save the Earth from suicide.

These responses, in a recent issue of *Sierra*—the official publication of the Sierra Club—were made to the question: has organized religion benefited or harmed the planet?[2] Views such as these are not unusual or uncommon today. They are, rather, all too prevalent, for many people blame Christianity for the present ecological crisis. Directly or indirectly, many argue, the Christian faith is responsible for ecological degradation since it in various ways legitimates and encourages the exploitation of the earth. Such is, to use the language of James Nash, the "ecological complaint against Christianity."[3]

In this project I intend to examine these claims. More exactly, in this paper I seek to ask and answer two main questions. First, what precisely is the ecological complaint against Christianity? And second, are these various criticisms concerning the contribution of Christianity to ecological degradation well-founded? My thesis is that the ecological complaint against Christianity correctly understood is not well-founded. Hence this endeavor can be viewed as a project in apologetics: an attempt to render the Christian faith credible, especially (though not exclusively) via the use of arguments. To be exact, since apologetics can take two different forms—negative apologetics, which involves the rebuttal of arguments against Christianity, and positive apologetics, or the presentation of constructive arguments for Christianity—this endeavor is a project in negative apologetics since I intend only to examine and rebut specific charges leveled against the Christian faith.

It is important, however, to note an important distinction implied in the thesis statement above. Despite the fact that, as I will argue in the bulk of this article, the ecological complaint against Christianity is seriously flawed, a satisfactory response to the complaint must include, as James Nash insists, "a forthright confession that at least much of the complaint is essentially true."[4] Nash's comments on this matter deserve a full hearing:

It will not do to draw a neat distinction between Christianity and Christendom, between the faith itself and perversions of it by its practitioners. That distinction may be formally or logically true, as I agree, but it is facile and unconvincing when applied to history. We cannot so easily distinguish between the faith and the faithful. The fact is that Christianity—*as interpreted and affirmed* by billions of its adherents over the centuries and in official doctrines and theological exegeses—has been ecologically tainted…. The bottom line is that Christianity itself cannot escape an indictment for ecological negligence and abuse.[5]

While I disagree with Nash's near categorical disavowal of any legitimate distinction between authentic Christian faith and misunderstandings or perversions of it by Christians themselves, his point must be taken seriously. As Nash properly acknowledges. "Christianity has done too little to discourage and too much to encourage the exploitation of nature"; thus "ongoing repentance is warranted."[6]

Thus it is not only non-Christians who must be convinced that Christianity is not *necessarily* ecologically bankrupt, but many *Christians* must *also* be persuaded that their faith has rich resources for creating a robust ecological theology and ethic of earthkeeping. And so the apologetic task applies just as much to *Christians* as to non-Christian critics. We Christians must read the Bible with new eyes—open to its surprising ecological insights, e.g., from texts like Genesis 9 and Psalm 104. We must read and re-read our own histories—open to their hidden treasures, e.g., learnings from Desert Fathers and Celtic saints. And we must openly and honestly acknowledge our ecological sins of omission and commission. As usual, Joseph Sittler articulately captures the heart of the matter:

When we turn the attention of the church to a definition of the Christian relationship with the natural world, we are not stepping away from grave and proper theological ideas; we are stepping right into the middle of them. There is a deeply rooted, genuinely Christian motivation for attention to God's creation, despite the fact that many church people consider ecology to be a secular concern. "What does environmental preservation have to do with Jesus Christ and his church?" they ask. They could not be more shallow or more wrong.[7]

Is the Ecological Complaint Cogent?

The ecological complaint against Christianity is, in general, the claim that the Christian faith is at fault for the current ecological crisis. As James Nash puts it: "The ecological complaint is the charge that the Christian faith is the culprit in the crisis. Christianity is the primary or at least a significant cause of ecological degradation."[8] Christianity, especially Christian theology, is ecologically bankrupt, and given its influence in Western culture, it is morally blameworthy with respect to the plight of the earth. The implication usually drawn from this claim is that people today must discard the Christian tradition and look elsewhere for a perspective which will provide an adequate response to the ecological challenges before us. There are a variety of different arguments given to support this claim. Let us attend to four of the most common.

The first argument is that monotheism in general and Christianity in particular is the primary if not sole cause of the despoilation of the earth. For example, influential historian Arnold Toynbee asserts that

> some of the major maladies of the present-day world—for instance recklessly extravagant consumption of nature's irreplaceable treasures, and the pollution of those of them that man has not already devoured—can be traced back in the last analysis to a religious cause, and that this cause is the rise of monotheism.[9]

Specifically, Toynbee argues that the Genesis 1:28 command to have dominion and subdue the earth has not only permitted but directed humankind to dominate and exploit creation.[10] Given this diagnosis, Toynbee claims that the remedy for what ails us "lies in reverting from the *Weltanschauung* [worldview] of monotheism to the *Weltanschauung* of pantheism."[11] In sum, this argument asserts that the Christian sacred scriptures, especially this most important text in Genesis chapter 1, sets humanity over against nature and thus encourages humans to conquer and exploit the natural world.

There are, however, numerous problems with this argument. Does Genesis 1-2 actually license the exploitation of creation? Does dominion mean domination? This is not the place for extensive biblical exegesis, but a few remarks are in order. First, both Genesis chapters 1 and 2 speak about both who humans are and what humans are to do. They speak both of being and doing. With respect to being, Genesis 1:26 clearly distinguishes between human creatures and non-human creatures by speaking only of the former as created *imago dei*—in the image (*selem*) and likeness (*demûth*) of God. Whatever this means, and the debate still rages, it shows that humans are distinct in some important sense—*unique* among all the creatures to come from God's hand. The story of the naming of the animals in Genesis 2:19-20, among other things, likewise points to human uniqueness.

But what is often ignored or intentionally overlooked is that humans are not only distinct in some sense but one with the other creatures—*embedded* in creation as it were. For example, the creation of humans does not occur on a day different from the creation of other animals. On the sixth day, as Genesis 1:24-31 tells it, all kinds of living creatures come forth: humans and the beasts of the earth have something in common. And as Genesis 2:7 indicates, earth-creature (*adām*) is made from the earth (*adāmāh*). Humans, too, are made of dust. In short, a close reading of these texts indicates that we humans are not only different from but significantly *similar* to our non-human neighbors. Other creatures, to take seriously the language of Joseph Sittler, are our sisters and brothers.[12]

With respect to doing, it must be acknowledged that the Hebrew verbs in Genesis 1:26-28 indicate that one dimension of the human calling is mastery. The earth-creature is called to subdue (*kābash*) and have dominion over (*rādāh*) other creatures. But again, this is only part of the picture. For example, Genesis 2:5 speaks of humans serving the earth (*adām* is to *ābad* the *adāmah*). And Genesis 2:15 also defines the human calling in terms of *service*. We are to serve (*ābad*) and protect (*shāmar*) the garden that is creation—literally be a slave to the earth for its own good. In short, to focus only on the dominion text and then to interpret it as necessarily entailing domination is faulty exegesis of the first order. Toynbee is quite selective in his reading of Genesis 1-2.

As indicated in the introduction, insofar as the history of Christian practice has contributed to ecological degradation, Christianity is, to use Nash's phrase, "ecologically tainted." More exactly, insofar as Christians have in fact misread the Bible, and the Genesis texts in particular, and on that basis engaged in ecologically destructive of exploitative actions, Toynbee is right and we Christians have much to repent of. However, even if Toynbee's reading of the Genesis text and its history of interpretation were correct, is it true that the ecological crisis can be traced back to a single cause? Nash, among others, rightly cautions against any such historical explanation: "The single cause theory for the emergence of our ecological crisis is pathetically simplistic. . . . In historical reality, many complex and interwoven causes were involved—and Christian thought was probably not the most prominent one."[13] The fine historical work of both Carolyn Merchant and Clarence Glacken also repudiates any simple-minded theory of single causation with respect to ecological degradation.[14] Present as well as past, ecological degradation has *many* causes. As Nash succinctly puts it: "the ecological complaint against Christianity appears to be a serious historical oversimplification."[15] In short, there are a variety of problems with this first argument.

Farmer and poet Wendell Berry articulates a second argument for why Christianity is at fault for the current ecological crisis. States Berry:

> The contempt for the world or the hatred of it, that is exemplified by the wish to exploit it for the sake of cash and by the willingness to despise it for the sake of "salvation," has reached a terrifying climax in our own time. The rift between soul and body, the Creator and the Creation, has admitted the entrance into the world of the machinery of the world's doom.[16]

This argument claims that the emphasis within the Christian tradition on dualisms of soul and body, spirit and matter, denigrates the earth and sanctions its misuse and exploitation. More exactly, the argument is that since there is a dualism between spirit and matter, soul and body, such that the former is of greater value than the latter, and since lack of value implies lack of ethical duty, Christianity fosters a careless attitude toward things material and thus is at fault for the plundering of the earth. In sum, this argument maintains that Christianity harbors a number of world-negating dualisms which have contributed to the current ecological crisis.

But this argument, too, invites a number of questions. For example, are these dualisms biblical? And do they represent the only perspective within

the tradition? Again, this is not the place to engage in an extensive discussion of this issue. A few comments are, however, apposite. First, it is not at all clear that either the Old or New Testament supports the kind of body/soul dualism assumed here.[17] A widely accepted reading of biblical anthropology affirms a functional holism in which the body is not devalued. While the body is separate from and inferior to the soul for Plato, this is not the case for scripture.[18] So also with respect to the supposed dualism between matter and spirit in which matter is devalued. A variety of biblical texts and many basic Christian doctrines derived from the Bible, e.g., creation, incarnation, eschatology, affirm that for God, matter matters. Since the initial premise is unacceptable, the argument is not sound.

In addition, while there clearly is within the Christian faith a *contemptus mundi* [contempt of the world] tradition based on dualisms of this sort, such a tradition is but one amidst many. As Nash reminds his readers, "Christianity is no monolith: it has had multiple strains with radically different emphases."[19] More precisely, Nash rightly states that this form of the ecological complaint "overlooks the complex, ambiguous, and diversified character of Christian history" and thus misses "the varied voices—albeit minorities—for ecological sensitivity in Christian history."[20] As Paul Santmire clearly shows, Christianity has within it creation-*affirming* as well as creation-negating traditions. And as Santmire persuasively argues, in contrast to the "spiritual motif" which adopts certain of these dualisms, the "ecological motif"—that vision of human existence which acknowledges human rootedness in the world of nature and desires to celebrate God's presence in and with the whole natural order—eschews these dualisms and yet is one of the dominant theological motifs in Christian history.[21] Thus the claim that Christianity necessarily perpetuates creation-denying dualisms and so is at fault for the ecological crisis, is problematic.

A third argument often cited by critics derives from perceived inadequacies in Christian eschatology. For example, it is argued that Christian eschatology negates any rationale for preserving the earth since the second coming of Jesus will usher in a *completely new* form of existence. In other words, since Christian eschatology posits an other-worldly mode of future existence, humans need not care for the present world. Biblical texts like 2 Peter 3:10 and Matthew 24:36-44 are often cited in support of this position. James Watt, the Reagan era Secretary of Interior and devout Christian, exemplified this view when, in response to a question about why his agency was acting contrary to its expressed mandate, reportedly said, "I don't know how many future generations we can count on before the Lord returns." In sum, this argument contends that since the world is ephemeral, unimportant, and will ultimately be destroyed, we need not live in an ecologically affirming way.

But is this eschatology accurate? Will the earth be burned up to nothing in the eschaton? Does Christian eschatology necessarily entail an ecologically bankrupt ethic? Once again, space and time preclude a thorough response, but certain things need to be said. First, the last clause of 2 Peter 3:10, "and the earth and the works that are upon it will be burned up" (RSV), is perhaps the most egregious mistranslation in the entire New Testament. A biblical text often cited to support a basic discontinuity between this world and the world to come, almost all versions translate the Greek in a similar creation-negating manner.[22] However, the Greek verb in question here is *heurethēsetai*, from *heureskein* or "to find" and from which we get the English expression "Eureka." In other words, the text states that after a refiner's fire of purification, the new earth will be *found*, not destroyed. Thus the text rightly rendered speaks of a basic *continuity* rather than discontinuity of this world with the next. Creation is not ephemeral and unimportant—some way-station until the eschaton—but rather our home, now and always.

Furthermore, if the James Watt eschatology is correct, then how do we understand Genesis 9:1-17? Here, at the end of that all too familiar story of Noah, the text speaks of a covenant which God made. However, this covenant, contrary to the usual language which speaks of the "Noahic covenant," is made with *all creation*. Six times in verses 8-17 the text tells us that God made a covenant not only with humans but also with our non-human neighbors—indeed, with the earth itself. God establishes his covenant with every living creature *(kol nephesh hayyāh)* that is with you, the birds, the cattle, and every beast of the earth with you, as many as came out of the ark (verses 9-10 and verse 12); the earth *(ha erets)* (verse 13); every living creature of all flesh *(kol nephesh hayyāh)* (verse 15 and verse 16); all flesh *(kol bāsacuteār)* that is upon the earth (verse 17). This everlasting covenant, God's first and original covenant—before the covenants with Abraham or Moses or David—is with *all* creation. A creation-negating eschatology cannot make sense of this crucial text.

Finally, even if Watt and others were right about the eventual destruction of the earth at the eschaton, why does it necessarily follow that we

should not care for creation now? It is simply a *non sequitur* to argue that because the earth will be destroyed in the future that therefore humans should allow it to be exploited in the present. To use an analogy, why is it permissible for me to plunder your house just because some time in the future it will be torn down? Like the previous two, this third argument has various problems. One of the central premises is unacceptable, and even if one grants this premise, the conclusion does not follow. The claim that Christian eschatology is essentially anti-ecological is mistaken.

Fourthly and finally, medieval historian Lynn White, Jr., is his famous and oft reprinted 1967 essay "The Historical Roots of Our Ecologic Crisis," claims that because of its role in the rise of modern science and technology, "Christianity bears a huge burden of guilt" for the present situation.[23] More exactly, White argues that by emphasizing both divine and human transcendence over nature (and thus by desacralizing nature), "Christianity made it possible to exploit nature in a mood of indifference to the feelings of natural objects."[24] In addition, White argues that the Christian doctrine of creation implies that "since God had made nature, nature also [in addition to the Bible] must reveal the divine mentality," thus encouraging empirical investigations of the natural world so that humans could "understand the mind of God by discovering how his creation operates."[25] In short, White claims that "modern Western science was cast in a matrix of Christian theology." More precisely, it was the "Judeo-Christian dogma of creation" which gave the impetus to Western science.[26]

White therefore concludes that since Christianity made possible the growth of modern science and technology, and since science and technology have given us unprecedented and uncontrolled power over nature—power the misuse of which Christianity has sanctioned—Christianity is responsible for the current plight of the earth. White's own summary of his argument is worth quoting in full:

> We would seem to be heading toward conclusions unpalatable to many Christians. Since both *science* and *technology* are blessed words in our contemporary vocabulary, some may be happy at the notions, first, that, viewed historically, modern science is an extrapolation of [Christian] natural theology and, second, that modern technology is at least partly to be explained as an Occidental, voluntarist realization of

the Christian dogma of man's transcendence of, and rightful mastery over, nature. But, as we now recognize, somewhat over a century ago science and technology—hitherto quite separate activities—joined to give mankind powers which, to judge by many of the ecologic effects, are out of control. If so, Christianity bears a huge burden of guilt.[27]

In sum, Christianity is indirectly if not directly responsible for the current ecological crisis.

Much ink has been spilt responding to White's thesis, and much could be said here in response. But, as with the previous arguments, a few remarks will suffice. Wesley Granberg-Michaelson summarizes well a number of the conclusions reached in "the past twenty years of discussion" since White's article was published.

> First, White's description of biblical teaching regarding the environment is selective and highly distorted. Second, his argument that Christianity paved the way for the scientific and technological revolutions is very questionable. And third, his assumption that environmental destruction has flowed solely from the mindset of Western culture, and not from others, is historically dubious.[28]

In contrast to White, Granberg-Michaelson presents a persuasive alternative explanation for the contemporary ecological crisis, finding much of the blame to rest with certain ecologically deleterious assumptions of the modern Western worldview, e.g., the model of the world as machine, the overemphasis on economic progress, and with the captivity of the Christian church to that worldview.[29]

From what has been argued heretofore, it should be obvious that White's description of biblical teaching is, as Granberg-Michaelson claims, distorted. Like Toynbee in the first argument above, White focuses on only certain texts while ignoring others. Thus his premise that biblical Christianity understands dominion only as domination is mistaken. Also, White's claim that Christian thought was a necessary condition for the rise of modern science in the West is disputed. While this thesis has its able defenders,[30] it also has its competent critics.[31] And so another of White's premises is at least questionable. And as Granberg-Michaelson points out, White's historical claim that ecological degradation is somehow linked uniquely with the modern Western worldview is dubious indeed. As Nash among many others rightly states, "ecological

crises are not peculiar to Christian-influenced cultures. Non-Christian cultures have also caused severe or irreparable harm to their ecosystems."[32] Ecological degradation is no respecter of religions. So in a number of significant respects White's argument is problematic.

But let us grant, for the sake of argument, that White is right about all of his claims. Let us assume that his premises are acceptable. Christianity was an essential contributor to the development of modern science and technology. Science and technology have given us great power over nature. The Christian tradition encourages mastery over nature, thereby promoting the "if we can, we must" logic of our technological society. Even if we accept his premises his argument is still problematic, for his conclusion that "Christianity bears a huge burden of guilt" for the ecological crisis does *not* follow because it relies on the questionable historical claim that science and technology are the principal causes of the crisis. While science and technology certainly have played a role in contributing to the current situation, many argue that other factors, especially economic factors, are equally if not more important?[33] There is, in other words, reason to doubt White's unargued assumption about the dominant causal role of science and technology. In summary, while extremely influential, the Lynn White thesis is not as plausible as many believe.

Conclusion

I have argued in this paper that the ecological complaint against Christianity is, in its various specific forms, seriously flawed. In providing the best summary to date, Nash argues that the complaint tends:

> to reduce the explanation of the complex ecological crisis to a single cause, to exaggerate the authority of Christianity in cultures, to minimize the fact that non-Christian cultures also have been environmental despoilers, to overlook the number of dissenting opinions in Christian history, and to underestimate the potential for ecological reform in Christianity.[34]

The ecological complaint fails to substantiate the assertion that Christianity properly understood is irremediably or intrinsically ecologically bankrupt, or that Christian thought and practice is the cause of the ecological crisis. And so the implication that Christianity itself must be rejected or abandoned is likewise unjustified.[35]

My goal here was a modest one: to rebut criticisms which assert the ecological bankruptcy of the Christian faith or claim that Christianity is necessarily anti-ecological. I have not argued for why Christians should, on inner-Christian grounds, be better caretakers of creation, though many compelling arguments exist, since the persuasiveness of such a constructive case for Christian earthkeeping depends in part on first dismantling the kinds of objections raised by the ecological complaint against Christianity. My main concern was merely to respond to certain objections. But in addition to rebutting criticisms, I have also acknowledged that since we Christians have not always been good keepers of creation, we need to begin (and perhaps end) with confession and repentance. While the Christian faith is not necessarily anti-ecological, we have too often acted as if it was. Many of our practices as Christians have in fact not served the earth but rather despoiled it.

Arguments, however, important as they are, are limited. Apologetics as traditionally conceived, valuable though it is, is of limited worth. For right doctrine and correct belief mean little unless they become incarnate in action. In an article prophetically linking ecology and evangelism, Joseph Sittler pointedly reminds us of the dangers of cogent arguments and orthodox theology divorced from living, breathing, shalom-giving action in our everyday life:

> If *in piety* the church says, "The earth is the Lord's and the fullness thereof" (Psalm 24:1), and *in fact* is no different in thought and action from the general community, who will be drawn by her word and worship to "Come and see" that her work or salvation has any meaning? Witness in saying is irony and bitterness if there be no witness in doing.[36] ■

Author's Notes

[1] Calvin DeWitt, "Assaulting the Gallery of God: Human Degradation of Creation," *Sojourners* (February-March 1990): 19-21.

[2] *Sierra* (May-June 1993): 112.

[3] James Nash so titles chapter 3 in his excellent book *Loving Nature: Ecological Integrity and Christian Responsibility* (Nashville: Abingdon, 1991).

[4] *Ibid.*, 72.

[5] *Ibid.* Or as the subtitle of H. Paul Santmire's fine historical survey of the Christian tradition indicates, Christian theology has in the past represented at best "an ambiguous ecological promise." See *The Travail of Nature* (Philadelphia: Fortress, 1985).

[6] Nash, *Loving Nature*, 72, 74.

[7] Joseph Sittler, *Gravity and Grace* (Minneapolis: Augsburg, 1986), 15.

[8] Nash, *Loving Nature*, 68.

[9] Arnold Toynbee, "The Religious Background of the Present Environmental Crisis," in *Ecology and Religion in History*, eds. David and Eileen Spring (New York: Harper and Row, 1974), 146.

[10] Ibid., 147. Many others make this same charge, e.g., Ian McHarg, "The Place of Nature in the City of Man," in *Western Man and Environmental Ethics*, ed. Ian Barbour (Reading: Addison-Wesley, 1973): 174-175.

[11] Toynbee, "The Religious Background," 148.

[12] See e.g., Joseph Sittler, "Ecological Commitment as Theological Responsibility," *Zygon* 5 (June 1970): 175.

[13] Nash, *Loving Nature*, 75

[14] See Carolyn Merchant, *the Death of Nature* (San Francisco: Harper and Row, 1980), and Clarence Glacken, *Traces on the Rhodian Shore* (Berkeley: University of California, 1967).

[15] Nash, Loving Nature, 77.

[16] Wendell Berry, "A Secular Pilgrimage," in *Western Man and Environmental Ethics*, 135. See also the writings of influential feminist Rosemary Radford Ruether, e.g., *Sexism and Gold-Talk* (Boston: Beacon, 1983) for articulation of this criticism.

[17] Backing for this claim can be found in H.W. Wolff, *Anthropology of the Old Testament* (Philadelphia: Fortress, 1981); G. E. Ladd, *Theology of the New Testament* (Grand Rapids: Eerdmans, 1974), chs. 29, 34; H. Ridderbos, *Paul: An Outline of His Theology* (Grand Rapids: Eerdmans, 1975), chs. 3, 6; G. C. Berkouwer, *Man: The Image of God* (Grand Rapids: Eerdmans, 1962), ch. 6. A very insightful and well-argued recent treatment of this issue is found in John Cooper, *Body, Soul, and Life Everlasting* (Grand Rapids: Eerdmans, 1989).

[18] See, e.g., Plato's *Phaedo* and *Phaedrus*.

19 Nash, *Loving Nature*, 79.

20 *Ibid*

21 Santmire, *The Travail of Nature*, ch. 2. See also Susan Power Bratton, *Christianity, Wilderness, and Wildlife* (Scranton: University of Scranton, 1993).

22 For example, "the earth also and the works therein shall be burned up" (KJV); "the earth and everything in it will vanish" (TEV); "the earth and everything in it will be laid bare" (NIV); "the earth and everything in it will be stripped bare" (NEB); "the earth and everything in it will be burned up to nothing" (Phillips); the French and Spanish equivalents of the TEV render the last verb "will cease to exist (*cessera d'exister*)" and "will be burned up (*sera quemada*)" respectively. The 1985 update of Luther's German Bible comes closer to the true reading when it translates the last clause "the earth and the works upon it will find their judgment (*werden ihr Urteil finden*)." The recently completed New RSV renders this text even more accurately when it translates the last clause "and the earth and everything that is done on it will be disclosed." Only the new Dutch translation (*Niewe Vertaling* 1975) faithfully captures the meaning of the best Greek text: "and the earth and the works upon it will be found (*en de aarde en de werken daarop zullen gevonden worden*)." For corroboration of this reading, see Richard Bauckharn, *Word Biblical Commentary 50: Jude and 2 Peter* (Waco: Word, 1983), 303-322

23 Lynn White, Jr., "The Historical Roots of Our Ecologic Crisis," in *Western Man and Environmental Ethics*, 27. Originally published in *Science* 155 (March 10, 1967): 1203-1207.

24 *Ibid.*, 25.

25 *Ibid.*, 26.

26 *Ibid.*, 27.

27 *Ibid.* Most references to White's thesis stop here—with a declaration that Christianity is at fault. However, in an often ignored section of the article entitled "An Alternative Christian View," White goes on to argue that "since the roots of our trouble are so largely religious, the remedy must also be essentially religious, whether we call it that or not." And thus given his diagnosis, White proceeds to offer a prescription: "I propose Francis (of Assisi) as a patron saint for ecologists" (p. 30). In other words, contrary to many accounts, White's own 'solution' is *not* to abandon Christianity but to draw upon other more creation-affirming aspects of that very tradition.

28 Wesley Granberg-Michaelson, *Ecology and Life* (Waco: Word, 1988), 33. For other critical responses to the Lynn White thesis, see, e.g., the essays by Louis Moncrief and Rene Dubos in *Western Man and Environmental Ethics*; Rene Dubos, "Franciscan Conservation versus Benedictine Stewardship," in Spring and Spring, *Ecology and Religion in History*; Nash, *Loving Nature*, ch. 3.

29 Granberg-Michaelson, *Ecology and Life*. 33-45.

30 See, e.g., Eugene Klaaren, *Religious Origins of Modern Science* (Grand Rapids: Eerdmans, 1977) and Roger Hooykaas, *Religion and the Rise of Modern Science* (Edinburgh: Scottish Academic, 1972).

31 See, e.g., David Lindberg and Ronald Numbers, *God and Nature* (Berkeley: University of California, 1986).

32 Nash, *Loving Nature*. 89.

33 For example, in *Capitalism and Progress* (Grand Rapids: Eerdmans, 1979) Bob Goudzwaard argues that modern capitalism (and socialism), with its ultimate belief in economic progress, has been a significant contributor to ecological degradation. Brian Walsh and Richard Middleton, in *The Transforming Vision* (Downers Grove: InterVarsity, 1984), also point to a misplaced faith in economic prosperity or economism as one of the leading factors in ecological despoilation. And Alan Miller makes a similar argument in ch. 5 of *Gaia Connections* (Savage, Maryland: Rowman and Littlefield, 1991).

34 Nash, p *Loving Nature*, 74.

35 Many thanks to my colleagues at North Park College for helpful comments on this paper, and thanks also to Caroline Simon and William Hasker for suggestions for improving both the clarity and the cogency of my argument.

36 Joseph Sittler, "Evangelism and the Care of the Earth," in *Preaching and the Witnessing Community*, ed. Herman Stuempfle (Philadelphia: Fortress, 1973), 104.

Making Connections through Discussion and Writing

1. a. Underline the passage where Bouma-Prediger states his thesis and states the two questions he intends to answer concerning the charges against Christianity.

    b. Summarize his thesis and questions below.

    _____
    _____
    _____
    _____
    _____
    _____
    _____

2. a. In the paragraph that follows his thesis, how does Bouma-Prediger limit or condition his defense of Christianity's role in the ecological crisis?

    _____
    _____
    _____
    _____
    _____
    _____

    b. Why is this admission important for his argument?

    _____
    _____
    _____
    _____

3. Bouma-Prediger's essay is a clearly organized argument. List the four points he refutes in the body of his text.

    _____
    _____
    _____
    _____
    _____
    _____
    _____
    _____
    _____
    _____

4. Explain why you do or do not think Bouma-Prediger represents Wendell Berry's view accurately.

_____

_____

_____

_____

_____

_____

5. Read Lynn White, Jr.'s essay, "The Historical Roots of Our Ecologic Crisis."

   a. Does Bouma-Prediger treat Lynn White, Jr.'s views accurately? Explain your answer.

   _____

   _____

   _____

   _____

   _____

   b. Does his footnote on the final section of White's essay clarify White's attitude appropriately? Explain your answer.

   _____

   _____

   _____

   _____

   _____

6. Restate Bouma-Prediger's conclusion and the final concessions and responses he makes to White's argument.

_____

_____

_____

_____

_____

_____

_____

_____

_____

_____

_____

_____

_____

_____

Vincent Rossi

Seeing the Forest for the Trees

Vincent Rossi (b. 1947), an Eastern Orthodox priest, theologian, teacher, lecturer, and environmental activist, teaches at Heald College in Santa Rosa, California. He founded *Epiphany Journal*, a respected quarterly focused on issues relating to spirituality, theology, and the environment. He served as executive director of the Religious Education and Environment Project (REEP) in London, England, from 1998–2000. The following article appeared in the journal *Religion and the Forest* as a condensed version of a much longer essay.

Vocabulary ....

apex	primordial
ethos	subsuming
liturgy	therapeutic
ontology	wantonly

According to Orthodox scholar Bishop Kallistos Ware, Fr. Amphilochios was an ecologist long before environmental concern became fashionable. "Do you know," the elder said, "God gave us one more commandment, which is not recorded in Scripture? It is the commandment, *'Love the trees.'* When you plant a tree, you plant hope, you plant peace, you plant love, and you will receive God's blessing."

It is recounted that when the elder heard the confessions of local farmers, he would regularly give as a penance the task of planting a tree, while he himself would go about the island watering young trees during times of drought. His Christian love for trees transformed Patmos, the island where St. John the Evangelist lived. Where photographs taken around the turn of the century reveal barren countryside, a thick and healthy forest now grows.

Many other examples could be found of people who combined a deep love of God and a love of trees. The story of John Chapman (1774–1845), better known as Johnny Appleseed, who wandered the American frontier, a Bible in one hand, a bag of seeds in the other, planting trees and herbs, who was considered a healer and something of a saint by Indian and settler alike, comes to mind. Are these just unusual examples of religious piety that one can admire but dismiss as irrelevant to one's spiritual life? After all, so the reasoning goes, trees are not people, but plants, put on earth for human use. Or is there truth to the teaching of Elder Amphilochios that there is an implicit "eleventh commandment" in the Bible that enjoins human beings to love the trees? Is it possible that there is a spiritual link between the way we treat God's creation and the state of our relationship to God?

Should Christians recognize that, just as the First Epistle of John teaches that anyone who says he loves God but hates his brother is a liar, it is equally if implicitly true to say that anyone who says he loves God, but willingly participates or acquiesces in the wanton destruction of forests, is also deceiving himself? Is there Scriptural evidence that God actually cares how we treat forests and the rest of His creation?

I believe the Elder from Patmos is right. There is a link between love of trees and love of God. In the first place, it is clear from Scripture that respecting, protecting and honoring nature as the creation of God is a fundamental duty of all Christians.

The principal text outlining human responsibility for earth stewardship, including forests, is Genesis 2:15, with its key verbs "to cultivate" and "to keep." Supporting this text are a number of others, including Rom. 8:19-20 and 2 Cor. 5:17-21 which indicate our God-given vocation to reconcile and restore creation to its God-ordained natural order. More specifically, within human responsibility for earth stewardship, the care of forests and trees possesses a special place in Biblical ecology. Let us turn now to the witness of Scripture.

Scripture is rich with references to trees and forests. The words "tree" and "trees," "forest" and "forests," occur hundreds of times in the Bible. These occurrences may be grouped into general categories and contexts. Among them are references to trees and forests as:

1. a species created by God and of intrinsic value: (Gen. 1:11-12, 2:9)

2. a source of food; a natural resource or source of wealth: (Gen. 1:29; 2 Kgs. 19:23; Neh. 2:8; Ezek. 39:10)

3. a natural part of the local or planetary ecosystem: (1 Sam. 22:5; 1 Kgs. 7:2; Mt. 21:19-21; Rev. 7:3)

4. a sign of and/or response to God's blessing or punishment: (Isa. 41:19-20; Rev. 7:1)

5. a simile or metaphor modeled on the tree's natural properties: (Ps. 1:3; Isa. 56:3; Mk. 13:28; Rev. 6:13). A great many tree references are of this category.

6. a sign of the natural world in harmony with itself: (Gen. 2:9; Ps. 104:16-17; Song 2:10-13)

7. a paradigm of the cosmic world tree; primordial living symbol of human knowledge and life: (Gen. 2:9, 17; 3:1-24; Rev. 2:7, 22:2)

8. symbol of the Cross of Christ: (Acts 5:30; Gal. 3:13; 1 Pt. 2:24)

This represents only a small sample of the hundreds of biblical references to forests and trees. Human beings excepted, no other living organism appears as often as trees in Scripture. On the basis of textual prominence alone, the tree is the most important non-human living organism in Scripture.

But is there a larger and deeper significance to trees and forests in the Bible? The importance of the images of trees and forests in Scripture cannot be attributed merely to numerical frequency alone. There must be a deeper meaning that delineates the revelation of the Holy Spirit as it relates to forests and trees, and that reveals the attitude that God expects human beings to take to the trees and forests He has created. There is.

This deeper meaning emerges out of the differences and the relationship between the *kinds* of references to forests and trees. I refer especially to the ways that Scripture uses the image of the tree.

The categories above give us a clue. Characteristically, Scripture uses the image of trees and forests in three basic ways, plus a subsuming fourth, which represent three kinds of the Scriptural tree, corresponding roughly to the Pauline trichotomy of body, soul and spirit, plus a transcending fourth, representing the presence of the Holy Spirit that is "everywhere present and fillest all things." We may call these three types of tree usages the Natural Tree, the Metaphoric Tree and the Symbolic Tree. Subsuming the functions of the previous kinds of tree while transcending them is the fourth kind of tree which we may call the Iconic Tree.

The Natural Tree

We meet the "natural tree" as part of the integrated order of the natural world. Throughout Scripture there is a warm, loving quality to the references to trees, almost as though they were "relatives" of the Biblical writer or familiar members of his community. And that, precisely, is what they were. The trees mentioned in the Bible—species such as hazel, chestnut, poplar, olive, palm, fig, bramble, cedar, pomegranate, hyssop, fir, juniper, bay, almond, apple, oak, acacia, myrtle, cypress, pine, willow, mustard, sycamore, almug, holly, galgal—were part of an ecological community called the Land of Israel, a community acutely aware of the interdependence of all the elements of life on earth, including human culture.

Forests and trees are also often mentioned in Scripture as a source of food, shelter, fuel, commerce and artistic expression. This approximates the way human societies from time immemorial have used trees.

What is especially significant is how Scripture deals with trees and forests as used by people. The Bible does not forbid the cutting and harvesting of trees for human use. The cedars of Lebanon were used in the construction of the Temple of Jerusalem (1 Kgs. 5:1-10). However, this is not the end of the story of the natural tree.

Following the injunction to "cultivate" and "keep," Scripture indicates a strong preference for Godly stewardship. This is strikingly shown in the injunction against cutting down the trees of an enemy in time of war (Deut. 21:19). This restraint is remarkable, given the context of warfare, when it is characteristic of human nature to abandon ordinary ethical rules to conquer the enemy. The Bible emphatically tells us that all is not "fair in love and war" when it comes to the natural world, and specifically when it comes to trees.

The verse following, which seems at first glance to mitigate the law against destroying trees in time of war, upon close reading actually confirms the law of restraint: *"Only the trees which are not trees for food you may destroy and cut down, to build siegeworks against the city that makes war with you . . ."* (Deut. 21:20). The *Torah* of God makes it clear that only the trees that are not "trees for food" may be cut down, for the *"tree of the field is man's food."*

God tells his people that under no circumstances may you endanger the food supply, not even war. More than this, the destruction of non fruit-bearing trees is also prohibited. Deuteronomy specifies that the cutting of non fruit-bearing trees is allowed only for building siegeworks. By the principle of restraint, remarkably enjoined even in time of war, and by the specification that trees must be spared, the Bible clearly implies and points to that "eleventh commandment" insisted upon by the holy Elder Amphilochios of Patmos: trees are to be protected, nurtured and, yes, loved, not only for their benefit as food, but for their role in the harmony of the environment, and for their own sake as a creation of God.

The Metaphoric Tree

By the "metaphoric tree" I mean the Scriptural use of the image of forests and trees in simile, metaphor, allegory, analogy or parable for teaching basic moral and spiritual principles. The metaphorical use of the tree-image is by far the largest category of references to trees and forests in the New Testament. Just as natural references to trees are on the physical-natural level, or the level of the body, so the metaphoric tree in Scripture relates to the level of the soul. To say soul is to say the moral-ethical and therapeutic-spiritual. This is the pre-eminent level of Scriptural teaching concerned with the way to salvation. The Book of Psalms offers many examples, none better than the first lines of Psalm 1:

1 Blessed is the man that walketh not in the counsel of the ungodly, nor standeth in the way of sinners . . .

3 And he shall be like a tree planted by the rivers of water, that bringeth forth his fruit in season. . . .

All the books attributed to Solomon contain tree references, some of which are acute observations of trees in nature, others are metaphoric. It is noteworthy that when the Bible wishes to demonstrate that Solomon is the wisest of all men, it speaks in terms of his knowledge of the natural world, in particular, of trees.

The metaphoric tree is prominent in the parables of Jesus. The parables of the fig tree (Mt. 24:32) and the mustard seed (Lk. 13:19) are two of the most outstanding.

The Symbolic Tree

What we are calling "the natural tree" represents the Scriptural awareness of the intrinsic value of trees and of the central role played by trees in ecological balance, as well as the use of trees for food, shelter, and commerce. The "metaphoric tree" represents the figurative use of trees for the teachings necessary for salvation to satisfy the needs of the soul. Beyond these two levels or types of tree, a third tree-image occurs in the Bible, which we are calling the "symbolic tree."

The Holy Spirit in Scripture employs the image of the tree to reveal truths about the cosmos, about humanity, about God's will in creation, and thus, about the deepest principles of the order of nature and life. This function of trees in Scripture we call "The Symbolic Tree."

The most important context in which the symbolic tree appears is the story of God creating the Edenic Paradise in the center of which He planted two trees, the Tree of Knowledge of Good and Evil and the Tree of Life (Genesis 2:8-17).

This passage is part of the "second creation story" of Genesis Two, which scholars agree is older than the creation story of Genesis One. We must not let the familiarity of this story blind us to its remarkable features, especially as they relate to our theme. Aside from man, trees are the first living thing mentioned. It is highly significant that of all the things that could have been mentioned, *only* trees are actually mentioned. This is a strong indication that *Scripture singles out the tree as representative of the biosphere as a whole.* Without directly pointing it out, Scripture is bearing witness to the pre-eminent value of trees in the organic world.

Two categories of trees are distinguished in Genesis 2: those "pleasant to the sight" and those "good for food." Both link trees to human physical and psychological well-being and represent the gift-nature of trees to humanity. Without introduction or explanation, the Sacred Narrative reveals the Tree of Life and the Tree of the Knowledge of Good and Evil in the midst of the Garden. Here we confront the primordial symbol of the sacred World Tree, which is a universal symbol in human consciousness.

In the Genesis Two creation story, our primary concern is the *image* of the tree. Why the *tree*? Why does the Holy Spirit use the tree to symbolize life? Why is human consciousness, across cultures and times, so accepting of the tree as the universal symbol of life?

To answer this question we must ask and attempt to answer another: What is a symbol? Commonly, this word is used as a synonym for "figure" or "sign" and is opposed to what is "real," such as when someone says that something is "only a symbol." But symbols can mean more than this. A symbol may be distinguished from a metaphor in that the latter is a figure of speech in which we speak of one thing in terms of another; whereas a symbol is not specifically linguistic and may represent physical objects and visual representations. One may speak metaphorically about a tree, but one cannot say, for example, that the tree is a metaphor of the cross, because a tree, as a physical object, is not a metaphor. One might properly say that the tree is a symbol of the cross. Because symbols are not figures of speech, but signifying objects, the representational definition of symbol—symbol as "only" a sign—does not exhaust the meaning or function of symbol.

A symbol is also capable of "vertical" significance by making visible a higher meaning. Further, a symbol, by the meaning of its form, its "transparency," may be the manifestation of a higher, invisible reality. Such was the view of the Fathers of the Church. The very physical presence of the symbol *represents* the higher reality it points to and reveals. Thus "symbol" and "reality" may not be opposites, but may coincide. As an example of this kind of "living" symbolism, Bishop Kallistos Ware cites Edward Carpenter's (1844–1929) vision of a tree:

"Has any one of us ever seen a Tree? I certainly do not think that I have—except most superficially . . . Once the present writer seemed to have a partial vision of a tree. It was a beech, standing isolated and leafless in early spring. Suddenly I was aware of its skyward-reaching arms and up-turned fingertips, as if some vivid life (or electricity) was streaming through them far into the spaces of heaven, and of its roots plunged in the earth and drawing the same energies from below. The day was quite still and there was no movement in the branches, but in that moment the tree was no longer a separate organism, but a vast being ramifying far into space, sharing and uniting the life of Earth and Sky, and full of most amazing activity."

Bishop Ware comments, "Here is a vision of joyful wonder, inspired by an underlying sense of mystery. The tree has become a symbol pointing beyond itself, a sacrament that embodies some deep secret at the heart of the universe."

Carpenter's experience, plus the bishop's comment, provide insight into the tree as symbol. Something in the nature of the tree makes it a symbol of life itself. The tree's upright form; its threefold structure of roots-trunk-branches; its intimate connection with the four elements—roots deep in the earth, branches high in the air, its power to transform sunlight and draw up water; its longevity and stability; its silent generosity, offering shade, shelter and sustenance to all other living things; its created capacity to "unite the life of Earth and Sky," all these qualities of the tree make it a powerful, central and universal symbol of life.

Yet this capacity in the tree to be a symbol only hints at the depths of that "deep secret at the heart of the universe" embodied by the symbolic tree and glimpsed by those blessed with even a "partial vision" similar to Edward Carpenter's. For the life we have been speaking of is created life. But the Tree of Life in Paradise confers eternal life. The tragic consequence of Adam's sin reveals the luminous reality of the Tree of Life just at the moment that he loses all contact with it.

> Then the LORD God said, "Behold, the man has become like one of us, knowing good and evil; now, lest he . . . take also of the tree of life, and eat, and live forever," therefore the LORD God sent him from the garden of Eden, to till the ground from which he was taken. He drove out the man; and . . . he placed the cherubim, and a flaming sword which turned every way to guard the way to the tree of life. (Gen. 3:22-24).

The loss of access to the Tree of Life meant death and expulsion from paradise. The "deep secret at the heart of the universe" still lies beyond the flaming sword of the cherubim. Nevertheless its presence may yet be intuited and felt, as did Edward Carpenter, in the transparent symbol of a living tree, truly *seen*.

If a symbol is, in its highest meaning, the reflection of a higher reality, then the sin of Adam can be seen as attachment to the symbol instead of the higher reality. The symbol had become an idol. Choosing the created symbol over the uncreated Life it symbolized, Adam lost not only the Tree of

Life, but the tree as the symbol of life. The fatal descent had begun, from the paradisal vision of trees "pleasant to the sight," as transparent symbols of life, to the infernal sight of "clear-cutting": the brutal stripping of entire mountainsides of their forests to feed the world's appetite for wood. Nevertheless, natural things have not lost their inner nature; they still praise God their Creator. The trees and all else in creation wait with earnest expectation for the manifestation of the sons of God (Rom. 8:19), that is, human beings redeemed by Christ and members of His body, so that they once again may see both the forest and the trees. Restoring this Christian unitive vision of creation as a cosmic sacrament points us to the Iconic Tree.

The Iconic Tree

The mystery of life is that even the life of fallen nature partakes somehow of the Life beyond life, even though without redemption access to the Tree of Life remains blocked by separation, sin and death. As a great saint of the early Church, Dionysios the Areopagite, wrote in his enormously influential work, *The Divine Names*, "Life" is one of the names of God:

> *The Divine Life beyond life is the Giver and Creator of life. All life and living movement comes from a Life which is above every life and beyond the source of life. From this Life souls have their indestructibility and every living being and plant has life.*

St. Maximos the Confessor (580-662), a profound student of Dionysios, sums up the whole tradition in a few words:

> *Death in the true sense is separation from God, and 'the sting of death is sin' (1 Cor. 15:56). Adam, who received the sting, became . . . an exile from the tree of life and from God; and this was necessarily followed by the body's death. Life, in the true sense, is He who said, "I am the Life" (Jn. 11:25).*

With his allusion to John 11:25 (*"Jesus said to her, I am the resurrection and the life. He who believes in me, though he die, yet shall he live"*), St. Maximos gives us the link to the Iconic Tree to which the symbol of the tree is pointing. For with the Incarnation, Crucifixion, Resurrection and Ascension of Christ, the glory of the cross of our Lord Jesus Christ (Gal. 6:14) has transformed the image of the tree from symbol to icon.

In order to understand how the symbol of the tree becomes an icon, we need to touch on the meaning of icons in the Orthodox Church. The icon is not merely religious "art." Iconography is sacred art with a primarily liturgical function, which is to manifest the unity of creation with heaven in the liturgy.

According to the Orthodox understanding of icons, icons make present that which they re-present. Therefore, the icon is the apex of symbolism in which the visible reveals the invisible in a *sacramental* manner. As we have seen, a symbol contrary to some opinion, is not necessarily opposed to "reality," and can signify much more than mere "representation." In fact, the essence of the symbol is to make known by manifesting a reality beyond itself. According to the Bible, the world was created by God so that He might be made known:

> *. . . because what may be known of God is manifest in them, for God has shown it to them. For since the creation of the world His invisible attributes are clearly seen, being understood by the things that are made, even His eternal power and Godhead (Rom. 1:19-20).*

As Orthodox theologian Fr. Alexander Schmemann writes: "the world is symbolical in virtue of its being created by God"; to be "symbolical" thus belongs to its ontology, the symbol being not only the way to perceive reality, but also a means of *participation*. It is this natural symbolism of the world that is reflected in the understanding of the early Church that the universe is itself a Book, the *Liber Mundi*, or "Book of Nature," through which the wisdom, power and glory of God might be known.

Philip Sherrard, one of the foremost theologians of this century, says that it is crucial that we learn to "read the book of nature, the *Liber Mundi*, in a way totally different from that in which we have been taught to read it. It demands that we read it in a way similar to that in which the great spiritual expositors tell us that we should read the Bible—we have to learn to look on the world as the exterior expression of a hidden, interior, spiritual world."

The Book of Job says the same thing more directly:

> *But ask the beasts, and they will teach you; and the birds of the air and they will tell you. Or speak to the earth and it will teach you; Who among all these does not know that the Lord has done this, in whose hand is the life of every living thing (Job 12:7-10)?*

To perceive the living symbolism of natural things—to read the Book of Nature—is to perceive the spiritual presence of which each natural form is the image—or icon. There is an inherent "sacramentality" to creation because the Divine presence in and through and beyond each created thing gives each its uniqueness, transparency and meaning. To read the Book of Nature is to move from creation to symbol to sacrament. That movement from symbol to sacrament is an "iconic" movement. For the tree, its iconic movement came as Christ Jesus was crucified at Golgotha. At that moment, the image of the tree, source of the wood that formed the instrument upon which our salvation was wrought, became forever a symbol of the cross.

There are five instances in the New Testament in which "tree" is used for the cross: three in Acts, one in Galatians, and one in First Peter. Remarkably, each of these is a divine moment filled by the Holy Spirit in which the Spirit-directed preaching of the Good News revealed the form, contours and scope of the Christian faith.

1. **The Witness to the Religious Authorities—the Power of the Gospel:** Acts 5:30 shows Peter, standing before the chief priests after his miraculous escape from prison by an angel of the Lord, fearlessly bearing witness to the Good News:
   The God of our fathers raised up Jesus, whom you slew and hanged on a tree.

2. **The Witness to the Gentiles—the Universal Scope of the Gospel:** Acts 10:39 shows St. Peter again, this time teaching the pagan centurion Cornelius, after his vision of the great sheet filled with all manner of creatures and being instructed of God that "what God hath cleansed, that call thou not common":
   And we are witnesses of all things which he did both in the land of the Jews, and in Jerusalem; whom they slew and hanged on a tree.

3. **The Witness to the Jewish People—the Gospel as the Fulfillment of Salvation History in Christ:** Acts 13:29 shows St. Paul in Antioch, preaching a magnificent sermon in which he shows that the entire history of salvation is fulfilled in Christ Jesus.
   And when they had fulfilled all that was written of him, they took him down from the tree, and laid him in a sepulchre.

4. **The Witness to the Early Church—the Gospel as the Transformation of the Covenant in Christ:** Galatians 3:13. Here Paul teaches the doctrine of faith in Christ, how we cannot be justified by the Law, but only by faith in God and Christ.
   Christ hath redeemed us from the curse of the law, being made a curse for us: for it is written, Cursed is every one that hangeth on a tree.

5. **The Witness to all Christians—the Gospel Command to Follow Christ on the Path of Suffering:** 1 Peter 2:24 evokes the suffering of Christ on the tree of the Cross as an example for all Christians:
   Who his own self bare our sins in his own body on the tree, that we, being dead to sins, should live unto righteousness: by whose stripes ye were healed.

In each of these primordial moments of the revelation of the Gospel, the image of the tree as the cross was invoked as the heart of the Gospel. This cannot be mere coincidence.

Liturgy and the Liturgical Ethos

We have seen that Holy Scripture bears witness to the importance of trees, not as objects of worship, but as one of the most complete manifestations in the created order of the wisdom, goodness and mercy of God.

We have seen that awareness of the interdependence of life is prominent in the Bible, and that the Bible knows trees to be of central importance to the balance and harmony of the living community on earth.

We have seen that Scripture utilizes the figurative value of the nature, growth and function of trees to teach moral lessons and spiritual wisdom.

Finally we have seen that the Christian revelation draws upon the symbolism of the tree and the natural sacramentality of creation to reveal that Christ Himself is the "deep secret at the heart of the universe." But what are we as Christians to do with this knowledge?

Scripture tells us that the proper response to the revelation of God's truth, goodness, beauty, wisdom, life and mercy is praise and thanksgiving. The Church calls us to the Eucharist: communion in the Kingdom in thanksgiving. Putting the two together means that the truly human task on earth, combining the healing of disorder, the manifestation of the Gospel and the perfecting of praise, is to develop a liturgical ethos, to liturgize the world. What does this mean? And how do trees relate to liturgy and the development of a liturgical ethos?

Liturgy, *leitourgia* in Greek, means the "work of the people" [*leit*-people, *ergon*-work]. Scripture tells us the work of the people of God is thanksgiving and praise. . . .

We have seen that from the beginning of Revelation and the history of our salvation God used trees to teach humanity.

We have seen the amazing emphasis upon trees in the Bible and in the teaching of the early Church. The liturgical ethos—the heart of a Christian response to creation—is centered around acts of praise and thanksgiving. As the earth, including all creatures, from microbes to the human microcosm, and the macrocosmic universe as well, are created by God with a symbolic ontology and a sacramental potentiality, they fulfill their existence also in praise. Indeed, the Christian mind and heart must truly reflect a liturgical ethos, which is to give voice to the song of praise for all creation. Of all plants the tree most fully symbolizes the blessings that God has bestowed upon us through creation. The presence of the tree in the natural environment and in Scripture is a sign of health, hope, goodness, fertility, abundance and order. The destruction of trees in Scripture is a sign of God's wrath and punishment for all transgressions of the order of nature and spirit.

Presently the forests of the world are being wantonly destroyed to an unprecedented degree by the hand of man. Clearly the entire witness of the Christian Revelation calls Christians to protect the trees. Christians should be at the forefront of any campaign to restore the forests of the world.

Growing trees are a sign of hope, peace and love, as the Elder from Patmos has said. Landscapes wantonly stripped of their forest cover, hillsides ravaged to feed the insatiable greed of the market, can such sins against nature be anything but signs of an inevitable day of judgment? Good deeds may not forestall this day. Nevertheless it is a universal Christian duty to protect the forests.

Love the trees. Love the trees. ■

Name: _____ Section: _____ Date: _____

Making Connections through Discussion and Writing

1. Briefly explain what Rossi means by the label "the natural tree."

_____
_____
_____
_____
_____

2. Briefly explain the differences he finds in "the metaphoric tree," "the symbolic tree," and "the iconic tree."

_____
_____
_____
_____
_____
_____
_____
_____
_____

3. What two responses to trees does Rossi advocate as "liturgy" ("work of the people")?

_____
_____
_____
_____
_____
_____
_____

4. In St. Francis' praise to God for His creation in "The Canticle of Brother Sun", what levels of Rossi's categories of meaning (natural, metaphoric, symbolic, iconic) do you think Francis achieves?

_____
_____
_____
_____
_____
_____
_____

5. Explain how Rossi's views are shaped by an analogical imagination (a way of thinking that sees reality in terms of relationships or analogies, e.g., seeing the life of a person in terms of the changing seasons of a year).

    _____

    _____

    _____

    _____

    _____

    _____

    _____

    _____

    _____

    _____

Aldo Leopold

Thinking Like a Mountain

Aldo Leopold (1887–1948), known as the "father of wildlife conservation in America," was educated at the Yale Forestry School, the first graduate forestry school in the United States. He worked in the U.S. Forest Service for over twenty years, then joined the faculty of the University of Wisconsin, holding the chair of Game Management. Leopold is best known for his classic collection of essays, *A Sand County Almanac*, and has been honored internationally as a pioneering environmental scientist. In the following essay, Leopold personifies a mountain to allow readers to rethink the issues of ecological balance in nature.

Vocabulary ....

anaemic
defoliated
desuetude
extirpate
ineducable

mêlée
molder
rimrock
tyro

A deep chesty bawl echoes from rimrock to rimrock, rolls down the mountain, and fades into the far blackness of the night. It is an outburst of wild defiant sorrow, and of contempt for all the adversities of the world.

Every living thing (and perhaps many a dead one as well) pays heed to that call. To the deer it is a reminder of the way of all flesh, to the pine a forecast of midnight scuffles and of blood upon the snow, to the coyote a promise of gleanings to come, to the cowman a threat of red ink at the bank, to the hunter a challenge of fang against bullet. Yet behind these obvious and immediate hopes and fears there lies a deeper meaning, known only to the mountain itself. Only the mountain has lived long enough to listen objectively to the howl of a wolf.

Those unable to decipher the hidden meaning know nevertheless that it is there, for it is felt in all wolf country, and distinguishes that country from all other land. It tingles in the spine of all who hear wolves by night, or who scan their tracks by day. Even without sight or sound of wolf, it is implicit in a hundred small events: the midnight whinny of a pack horse, the rattle of rolling rocks, the bound of a fleeing deer, the way shadows lie under the spruces. Only the ineducable tyro can fail to sense the presence or absence of wolves, or the fact that mountains have a secret opinion about them.

My own conviction on this score dates from the day I saw a wolf die. We were eating lunch on a high rimrock, at the foot of which a turbulent river elbowed its way. We saw what we thought was a doe fording the torrent, her breast awash in white water. When she climbed the bank toward us and shook out her tail, we realized our error: it was a wolf. A half-dozen others, evidently grown pups, sprang from the willows and all joined in a welcoming mêlée of wagging tails and playful maulings. What was literally a pile of wolves writhed and tumbled in the center of an open flat at the foot of our rimrock.

In those days we had never heard of passing up a chance to kill a wolf. In a second we were pumping lead into the pack, but with more excitement than accuracy: how to aim a steep downhill shot is always confusing. When our rifles were empty, the old wolf was down, and a pup was dragging a leg into impassable slide-rocks.

We reached the old wolf in time to watch a

fierce green fire dying in her eyes. I realized then, and have known ever since, that there was something new to me in those eyes—something known only to her and to the mountain. I was young then, and full of trigger-itch; I thought that because fewer wolves meant more deer, that no wolves would mean hunters' paradise. But after seeing the green fire die, I sensed that neither the wolf nor the mountain agreed with such a view.

Since then I have lived to see state after state extirpate its wolves. I have watched the face of many a newly wolfless mountain, and seen the south-facing slopes wrinkle with a maze of new deer trails. I have seen every edible bush and seedling browsed, first to anaemic desuetude, and then to death. I have seen every edible tree defoliated to the height of a saddlehorn. Such a mountain looks as if someone had given God a new pruning shears, and forbidden Him all other exercise. In the end the starved bones of the hoped-for deer herd, dead of its own too-much, bleach with the bones of the dead sage, or molder under the high-lined junipers.

I now suspect that just as a deer herd lives in mortal fear of its wolves, so does a mountain live in mortal fear of its deer. And perhaps with better cause, for while a buck pulled down by wolves can be replaced in two or three years, a range pulled down by too many deer may fail of replacement in as many decades.

So also with cows. The cowman who cleans his range of wolves does not realize that he is taking over the wolf's job of trimming the herd to fit the range. He has not learned to think like a mountain. Hence we have dustbowls, and rivers washing the future into the sea.

We all strive for safety, prosperity, comfort, long life, and dullness. The deer strives with his supple legs, the cowman with trap and poison, the statesman with pen, the most of us with machines, votes, and dollars, but it all comes to the same thing: peace in our time. A measure of success in this is all well enough, and perhaps is a requisite to objective thinking, but too much safety seems to yield only danger in the long run. Perhaps this is behind Thoreau's dictum: In wildness is the salvation of the world. Perhaps this is the hidden meaning in the howl of the wolf, long known among mountains, but seldom perceived among men. ∎

Making Connections through Discussion and Writing

1. Underline the sentences in paragraphs two, three, and five that indicate the narrator's sense that the mountain has a different perception of the cry of a wolf than do deer, coyotes, hunters, and cowboys.

2. What incident first led Leopold into "thinking like a mountain"?

   _____
   _____
   _____
   _____

3. Sum up the lesson that Leopold wants his readers to realize by "thinking like a mountain."

   _____
   _____
   _____
   _____
   _____
   _____
   _____
   _____

4. Explain the reasoning that leads Leopold to claim, rather abruptly, that humans have not learned "to think like a mountain. . . . Hence we have dustbowls, and rivers washing the future into the sea."

   _____
   _____
   _____
   _____
   _____
   _____
   _____
   _____
   _____
   _____
   _____
   _____
   _____

Leslie Marmon Silko

Landscape, History, and the Pueblo Imagination

Leslie Marmon Silko (b. 1948) was born in Albuquerque, New Mexico, of mixed heritage: Laguna Pueblo Indian, Mexican, and Caucasian. She grew up on the Laguna Pueblo reservation where she still lives, a place and culture that figure strongly in her works; she often writes about American Indian ritual and folklore. Some of her short stories have been compiled into *Storyteller* (1981), and her poems appear in *Laguna Woman: Poems* (1974). Her novel, *Ceremony*, was published in 1977. Silko's writing frequently involves relationships among people and between people and the land, a theme that appears in the following essay.

Vocabulary ....

arroyo	necromancers
imbued	petroglyphs
intrinsic	pictographs
mesa	solstice
middens	

From a High Arid Plateau in New Mexico

You see that after a thing is dead, it dries up. It might take weeks or years, but eventually if you touch the thing, it crumbles under your fingers. It goes back to dust. The soul of the thing has long since departed. With the plants and wild game the soul may have already been borne back into bones and blood or thick green stalk and leaves. Nothing is wasted. What cannot be eaten by people or in some way used must then be left where other living creatures may benefit. What domestic animals or wild scavengers can't eat will be fed to the plants. The plants feed on the dust of these few remains.

The ancient Pueblo people buried the dead in vacant rooms or partially collapsed rooms adjacent to the main living quarters. Sand and clay used to construct the roof make layers many inches deep once the roof has collapsed. The layers of sand and clay make for easy gravedigging. The vacant room fills with cast off objects and debris. When a vacant room has filled deep enough, a shallow but adequate grave can be scooped in a far corner. Archaeologists have remarked over formal burials complete with elaborate funerary objects excavated in trash middens of abandoned rooms. But the rocks and adobe mortar of collapsed walls were valued by the ancient people. Because each rock had been carefully selected for size and shape, then chiseled to an even face. Even the pink clay adobe melting with each rainstorm had to be prayed over, then dug and carried some distance. Corn cobs and husks, the rinds and stalks and animal bones were not regarded by the ancient people as filth or garbage. The remains were merely resting at a midpoint in their journey back to dust. Human remains are not so different. They should rest with the bones and rinds where they all may benefit living creatures—small rodents and insets—until their return is completed. The remains of things—animals and plants, the clay and the stones—were treated with respect. Because for the ancient people all these things had spirit and being.

The antelope merely consents to return home with the hunter. All phases of the hunt are conducted with love. The love the hunter and the people have for the Antelope People. And the love of the antelope who agree to give up their meat and blood so that human beings will not starve. Waste

---

of meat or even the thoughtless handling of bones cooked bare will offend the antelope spirits. Next year the hunters will vainly search the dry plains for antelope. Thus it is necessary to return carefully the bones and hair, and the stalks and leaves to the earth who first created them. The spirits remain close by. They do not leave us.

The dead become dust, and in this becoming they are once more joined with the Mother. The ancient Pueblo people called the earth the Mother Creator of all things in this world. Her sister, the Corn Mother, occasionally merges with her because all succulent green life rises out of the depths of the earth.

Rocks and clay are part of the Mother. They emerge in various forms, but at some time before, they were smaller particles or great boulders. At a later time they may again become what they once were. Dust.

A rock shares this fate with us and with animals and plants as well. A rock has being or spirit, although we may not understand it. The spirit may differ from the spirit we know in animals or plants or in ourselves. In the end we all originate from the depths of the earth. Perhaps this is how all beings share in the spirit of the Creator. We do not know.

From the Emergence Place

Pueblo potters, the creators of petroglyphs and oral narratives, never conceived of removing themselves from the earth and sky. So long as the human consciousness remains *within* the hills, canyons, cliffs, and the plants, clouds, and sky, the term *landscape*, as it has entered the English language, is misleading. "A portion of territory the eye can comprehend in a single view" does not correctly describe the relationship between the human being and his or her surroundings. This assumes the viewer is somehow *outside* or *separate from* the territory he or she surveys. Viewers are as much a part of the landscape as the boulders they stand on. There is no high mesa edge or mountain peak where one can stand and not immediately be part of all that surrounds. Human identity is linked with all the elements of Creation through the clan: you might belong to the Sun Clan or the Lizard Clan or the Corn Clan or the Clay Clan. Standing deep within the natural world, the ancient Pueblo understood the thing as it was—the squash blossom, grasshopper, or rabbit itself could never be created by the human hand. Ancient Pueblos took the modest view that the thing itself (the landscape) could not be improved upon. The ancients

did not presume to tamper with what had already been created. Thus *realism*, as we now recognize it in painting and sculpture, did not catch the imaginations of Pueblo people until recently.

The squash blossom itself is *one thing*: itself. So the ancient Pueblo potter abstracted what she saw to be the key elements of the squash blossom—the four symmetrical petals, the four symmetrical stamens in the center. These key elements, while suggesting the squash flower, also link it with the four cardinal directions. By representing only its intrinsic form, the squash flower is released from a limited meaning of restricted identity. Even in the most sophisticated abstract form, a squash flower or a cloud or a lightning bolt became intricately connected with a complex system of relationships which the ancient Pueblo people maintained with each other, and with the populous natural world they lived within. A bolt of lightning is itself, but at the same time it may mean much more. It may be a messenger of good fortune when summer rains are needed. It may deliver death, perhaps the result of manipulations by the Gunnadeyahs[1], destructive necromancers. Lightning may strike down an evildoer. Or lightning may strike a person of good will. If the person survives, lightning endows him or her with heightened power.

Pictographs and petroglyphs of constellations or elk or antelope, draw their magic in part from the process wherein the focus of all prayer and concentration is upon the thing itself, which, in its turn, guides the hunter's hand. Connection with the spirit dimensions requires a figure or form which is all-inclusive. A "lifelike" rendering of an elk *is* too restrictive. Only the elk *is* itself. A *realistic* rendering of an elk would be only one particular elk anyway. The purpose of the hunt rituals and magic is to make contact with *all* the spirits of the Elk.

The land, the sky, and all that is within them— the landscape—includes human beings. Interrelationships in the Pueblo landscape are complex and fragile. The unpredictability of the weather, the aridity and harshness of much of the terrain in the high plateau country explain in large part the relentless attention the ancient Pueblo people gave the sky and the earth around them. Survival depended upon harmony and cooperation not only among human beings, but among all things—the animate and the less animate, since rocks and mountains were known to move, to travel occasionally.

The ancient Pueblos believed the Earth and the Sky were sisters (or sister and brother in the post-Christian version). As long as good family relations are maintained, then the Sky will continue to bless her sister, the Earth, with rain, and the Earth's children will continue to survive. But the old stories recall incidents in which troublesome spirits or beings threaten the earth. In one story, a malicious ka'tsina,[2] called the Gambler, seizes the Shiwana, or Rainclouds, the Sun's beloved children. The Shiwana are snared in magical power late one afternoon on a high mountain top. The Gambler takes the Rainclouds to his mountain stronghold where he locks them in the north room of his house. What was his idea? The Shiwana were beyond value. They brought life to all things on earth. The Gambler wanted a big stake to wager in his games of chance. But such greed, even on the part of only one being, had the effect of threatening the survival of all life on earth. Sun Youth, aided by old Grandmother Spider, outsmarts the Gambler and the rigged game, and the Rainclouds are set free. The drought ends, and once more life thrives on earth.

Through the Stories We Hear Who We Are

All summer the people watch the west horizon, scanning the sky from south to north for rain clouds. Corn must have moisture at the time the tassels form. Otherwise pollination will be incomplete, and the ears will be stunted and shriveled. An inadequate harvest may bring disaster. Stories told at Hopi, Zuni, and at Acoma and Laguna describe drought and starvation as recently as 1900. Precipitation in west-central New Mexico averages fourteen inches annually. The western pueblos are located at altitudes over 5,600 feet above sea level, where winter temperatures at night fall below freezing. Yet evidence of their presence in the high desert plateau country goes back ten thousand years. The ancient Pueblo people not only survived in this environment, but many years they thrived. In A.D. 1100 the people at Chaco Canyon had built cities with apartment buildings of stone five stories high. Their sophistication as skywatchers was surpassed only by Mayan and Inca astronomers. Yet this vast complex of knowledge and belief, amassed for thousands of years, was never recorded in writing.

Instead, the ancient Pueblo people depended upon collective memory through successive generations to maintain and transmit an entire culture, a world view complete with proven strategies for survival. The oral narrative, or "story," became the medium in which the complex of Pueblo knowl-

edge and belief was maintained. Whatever the event or the subject, the ancient people perceived the world and themselves within that world as part of an ancient continuous story composed of innumerable bundles of other stories.

The ancient Pueblo vision of the world was inclusive. The impulse was to leave nothing out. Pueblo oral tradition necessarily embraced all levels of human experience. Otherwise, the collective knowledge and beliefs comprising ancient Pueblo culture would have been incomplete. Thus stories about the Creation and Emergence of human beings and animals into this World continue to be retold each year for four days and four nights during the winter solstice. The "humma-hah" stories related events from the time long ago when human beings were still able to communicate with animals and other living things. But, beyond these two preceding categories, the Pueblo oral tradition knew no boundaries. Accounts of the appearance of the first Europeans in Pueblo country or of the tragic encounters between Pueblo people and Apache raiders were no more and no less important than stories about the biggest mule deer ever taken or adulterous couples surprised in cornfields and chicken coops. Whatever happened, the ancient people instinctively sorted events and details into a loose narrative structure. Everything became story.

Traditionally everyone, from the youngest child to the oldest person, was expected to listen and to be able to recall or tell a portion, if only a small detail, from a narrative account or story. Thus the remembering and retelling were a communal process. Even if a key figure, an elder who knew much more than others, were to die unexpectedly, the system would remain intact. Through the efforts of a great many people, the community was able to piece together valuable accounts and crucial information that might otherwise have died with an individual.

Communal storytelling was a self-correcting process in which listeners were encouraged to speak up if they noted an important fact or detail omitted. The people were happy to listen to two or three different versions of the same event or the same humma-hah story. Even conflicting versions of an incident were welcomed for the entertainment they provided. Defenders of each version might joke and tease one another, but seldom were there any direct confrontations. Implicit in the Pueblo oral tradition was the awareness that loyalties, grudges, and kinship must always influence the narrator's choices as she emphasizes to listeners this is the way *she* has always heard the story told. The ancient Pueblo people sought a communal truth, not an absolute. For them this truth lived somewhere within the web of differing versions, disputes over minor points, outright contradictions tangling with old feuds and village rivalries.

A dinner-table conversation, recalling a deer hunt forty years ago when the largest mule deer ever was taken, inevitably stimulates similar memories in listeners. But hunting stories were not merely after-dinner entertainment. These accounts contained information of critical importance about behavior and migration patterns of mule deer. Hunting stories carefully described key landmarks and locations of fresh water. Thus a deer-hunt story might also serve as a "map." Lost travelers, and lost piñon-nut gatherers, have been saved by sighting a rock formation they recognize only because they once heard a hunting story describing this rock formation.

The importance of cliff formations and water holes does not end with hunting stories. As offspring of the Mother Earth, the ancient Pueblo people could not conceive of themselves within a specific landscape. Location, or "place" nearly always plays a central role in the Pueblo oral narratives. Indeed, stories are most frequently recalled as people are passing by a specific geographical feature or the exact place where a story takes place. The precise date of the incident often is less important than the place or location of the happening. "Long, long ago," "a long time ago," "not too long ago," and "recently" are usually how stories are classified in terms of time. But the places where the stories occur are precisely located, and prominent geographical details recalled, even if the landscape is well known to listeners. Often because the turning point in the narrative involved a peculiarity or special quality of a rock or tree or plant found only at that place. Thus, in the case of many of the Pueblo narratives, it is impossible to determine which came first: the incident or the geographical feature which begs to be brought alive in a story that features some unusual aspect of this location.

There is a giant sandstone boulder about a mile north of Old Laguna, on the road to Paguate. It is ten feet tall and twenty feet in circumference. When I was a child, and we would pass this boulder driving to Paguate village, someone usually made reference to the story about Kochininako, Yellow Woman, and the Estrucuyo, a monstrous giant who nearly ate her. The Twin Hero Brothers saved Kochininako, who had been out hunting rabbits to take home to feed her mother and sisters. The Hero Brothers had heard her cries just in time. The

Estrucuyo had cornered her in a cave too small to fit its monstrous head. Kochininako had already thrown to the Estrucuyo all her rabbits, as well as her moccasins and most of her clothing. Still the creature had not been satisfied. After killing the Estrucuyo with their bows and arrows, the Twin Hero Brothers slit open the Estrucuyo and cut out its heart. They threw the heart as far as they could. The monster's heart landed there, beside the old trail to Paguate village, where the sandstone boulder rests now.

It may be argued that the existence of the boulder precipitated the creation of a story to explain it. But sandstone boulders and sandstone formations of strange shapes abound in the Laguna Pueblo area. Yet most of them do not have stories. Often the crucial element in a narrative is the terrain—some specific detail of the setting.

A high dark mesa rises dramatically from a grassy plain fifteen miles southeast of Laguna, in an area known as Swanee. On the grassy plain one hundred and forty years ago, my great-grandmother's uncle and his brother-in-law were grazing their herd of sheep. Because visibility on the plain extends for over twenty miles, it wasn't until the two sheepherders came near the high dark mesa that the Apaches were able to stalk them. Using the mesa to obscure their approach, the raiders swept around from both ends of the mesa. My great-grandmother's relatives were killed, and the herd lost. The high dark mesa played a critical role: the mesa had compromised the safety which the openness of the plains had seemed to assure. Pueblo and Apache alike relied upon the terrain, the very earth herself, to give them protection and aid. Human activities or needs were maneuvered to fit the existing surroundings and conditions. I imagine the last afternoon of my distant ancestors as warm and sunny for late September. They might have been traveling slowly, bringing the sheep closer to Laguna in preparation for the approach of colder weather. The grass was tall and only beginning to change from green to a yellow which matched the late-afternoon sun shining off it. There might have been comfort in the warmth and the sight of the sheep fattening on good pasture which lulled my ancestors into their fatal inattention. They might have had a rifle whereas the Apaches had only bows and arrows. But there would have been four or five Apache raiders, and the surprise attack would have canceled any advantage the rifles gave them.

Survival in any landscape comes down to making the best use of all available resources. On that particular September afternoon, the raiders made better use of the Swanee terrain than my poor ancestors did. Thus the high dark mesa and the story of the two lost Laguna herders became inextricably linked. The memory of them and their story resides in part with the high black mesa. For as long as the mesa stands, people within the family and clan will be reminded of the story of that afternoon long ago. Thus the continuity and accuracy of the oral narratives are reinforced by the landscape—and the Pueblo interpretation of that landscape is *maintained.*

The Migration Story: An Interior Journey

The Laguna Pueblo migration stories refer to specific places—mesas, springs, or cottonwood trees—not only locations which can be visited still, but also locations which lie directly on the state highway route linking Paguate village with Laguna village. In traveling this road as a child with older Laguna people I first heard a few of the stories from that much larger body of stories linked with the Emergence and Migration. It may be coincidental that Laguna people continue to follow the same route which, according to the Migration story, the ancestors followed south from the Emergence Place. It may be that the route is merely the shortest and best route for car, horse, or foot traffic between Laguna and Paguate Villages. But if the stories about boulders, springs, and hills are actually remnants from a ritual that retraces the creation and emergence of the Laguna Pueblo people as a culture, as the people they became, then continued use of that route creates a unique relationship between the ritual-mythic world and the actual, everyday world. A journey from Paguate to Laguna down the long incline of Paguate Hill retraces the original journey from the Emergence Place, which is located slightly north of the Paguate village. Thus the landscape between Paguate and Laguna takes on a deeper significance: the landscape resonates the spiritual or mythic dimension of the Pueblo world even today.

Although each Pueblo culture designates a specific Emergence Place—usually a small natural spring edged with mossy sandstone and full of cattails and wild watercress—it is clear that they do not agree on any single location or natural spring as the one and only true Emergence Place. Each Pueblo group recounts its own stories about Creation, Emergence, and Migration, although they all believe that all human beings, with all the ani-

mals and plants, emerged at the same place and at the same time.

Natural springs are crucial sources of water for all life in the high desert plateau country. So the small spring near Paguate village is literally the source and continuance of life for the people in the area. The spring also functions on a spiritual level, recalling the original Emergence Place and linking the people and the spring water to all other people and to that moment when the Pueblo people became aware of themselves as they are even now. The Emergence was an emergence into a precise cultural identity. Thus the Pueblo stories about the Emergence and Migration are not to be taken as literally as the anthropologists might wish. Prominent geographical features and landmarks which are mentioned in the narratives exist for ritual purposes, not because the Laguna people actually journeyed south for hundreds of years from Chaco Canyon or Mesa Verde,[3] as the archaeologists say, or eight miles from the site of the natural springs at Paguate to the sandstone hilltop at Laguna.

The eight miles, marked with boulders, mesas, springs, and river crossings, are actually a ritual circuit or path which marks the interior journey the Laguna people made: a journey of awareness and imagination in which they emerged from being within the earth and from everything included in earth to the culture and people they became, differentiating themselves for the first time from all that had surrounded them, always aware that interior distances cannot be reckoned in physical miles or in calendar years.

The narratives linked with prominent features of the landscape between Paguate and Laguna delineate the complexities of the relationship which human beings must maintain with the surrounding natural world if they hope to survive in this place. Thus the journey was an interior process of the imagination, a growing awareness that being human is somehow different from all other life—animal, plant, and inanimate. Yet we are all from the same source: the awareness never deteriorated into Cartesian duality,[4] cutting off the human from the natural world.

The people found the opening into the Fifth World too small to allow them or any of the animals to escape. They had sent a fly out through the small hole to tell them if it was the world which the Mother Creator had promised. It was, but there was the problem of getting out. The antelope tried to butt the opening to enlarge it, but the antelope enlarged it only a little. It was necessary for the badger with her long claws to assist the antelope, and at last the opening was enlarged enough so that all the people and animals were able to emerge up into the Fifth World. The human beings could not have emerged without the aid of antelope and badger. The human beings depended upon the aid and charity of the animals. Only through interdependence could the human beings survive. Families belonged to clans, and it was by clan that the human being joined with the animal and plant world. Life on the high arid plateau became viable when the human beings were able to imagine themselves as sisters and brothers to the badger, antelope, clay, yucca, and sun. Not until they could find a viable relationship to the terrain, the landscape they found themselves in, could they *emerge.* Only at the moment the requisite balance between human and *other* was realized could the Pueblo people become a culture, a distinct group whose population and survival remained stable despite the vicissitudes of climate and terrain.

Landscape thus has similarities with dreams. Both have the power to seize terrifying feelings and deep instincts and translate them into images—visual, aural, tactile—into the concrete where human beings may more readily confront and channel the terrifying instincts or powerful emotions into rituals and narratives which reassure the individual while reaffirming cherished values of the group. The identity of the individual as a part of the group and the greater Whole is strengthened, and the terror of facing the world alone is extinguished.

Even now, the people at Laguna Pueblo spend the greater portion of social occasions recounting recent incidents or events which have occurred in the Laguna area. Nearly always, the discussion will precipitate the retelling of older stories about similar incidents or other stories connected with a specific place. The stories often contain disturbing or provocative material, but are nonetheless told in the presence of children and women. The effect of these inter-family or inter-clan exchanges is the reassurance for each person that she or he will never be separated or apart from the clan, no matter what might happen. Neither the worst blunders or disasters nor the greatest financial prosperity and joy will ever be permitted to isolate anyone from the rest of the group. In the ancient times, cohesiveness was all that stood between extinction and survival, and, while the individual certainly was recognized, it was always as an individual simultaneously bonded to family and clan by a complex bundle of custom and ritual. You are never

the first to suffer a grave loss or profound humiliation. You are never the first, and you understand that you will probably not be the last to commit or be victimized by a repugnant act. Your family and clan are able to go on at length about others now passed on, others older or more experienced than you who suffered similar losses.

The wide deep arroyo near the Kings Bar (located across the reservation borderline) has over the years claimed many vehicles. A few years ago, when a Viet Nam veteran's new red Volkswagen rolled backwards into the arroyo while he was inside buying a six-pack of beer, the story of his loss joined the lively and large collection of stories already connected with that big arroyo. I do not know whether the Viet Nam veteran was consoled when he was told the stories about the other cars claimed by the ravenous arroyo. All his savings of combat pay had gone for the red Volkswagen. But this man could not have felt any worse than the man who, some years before, had left his children and mother-in-law in his station wagon with the engine running. When he came out of the liquor store his station wagon was gone. He found it and its passengers upside down in the big arroyo. Broken bones, cuts and bruises, and a total wreck of the car. The big arroyo has a wide mouth. Its existence needs no explanation. People in the area regard the arroyo much as they might regard a living being, which has a certain character and personality. I seldom drive past that wide deep arroyo without feeling a familiarity with and even a strange affection for this arroyo. Because as treacherous as it may be, the arroyo maintains a strong connection between human beings and the earth. The arroyo demands from us the caution and attention that constitute respect. It is this sort of respect the old believers have in mind when they tell us we must respect and love the earth.

Hopi Pueblo elders have said that the austere and, to some eyes, barren plains and hills surrounding their mesa-top villages actually help to nurture the spirituality of the Hopi *way.* The Hopi elders say that Hopi people might have settled in locations far more lush where daily life would not have been so grueling. But there on the high silent sandstone mesas that overlook the sandy arid expanses stretching to all horizons, the Hopi elders say the Hopi people must "live by their prayers" if they are to survive. The Hopi way cherishes the intangible: the riches realized from interaction and interrelationships with all beings above all else. Great abundances of material things, even food, the Hopi elders believe, tend to lure human attention away from what is most valuable and important. The views of the Hopi elders are not much different from those elders in all the Pueblos.

The bare vastness of the Hopi landscape emphasizes the visual impact of every plant, every rock, every arroyo. Nothing is overlooked or taken for granted. Each ant, each lizard, each lark is imbued with great value simply because the creature is there, simply because the creature is alive in a place where any life at all is precious. Stand on the mesa edge at Walpai and look west over the bare distances toward the pale blue outlines of the San Francisco peaks where the ka'tsina spirits reside. So little lies between you and the sky. So little lies between you and the earth. One look and you know that simply to survive is a great triumph, that every possible resource is needed, every possi-

ble ally—even the most humble insect or reptile. You realize you will be speaking with all of them if you intend to last out the year. Thus it is that the Hopi elders are grateful to the landscape for aiding them in their quest as spiritual people. ■

Notes

[1] Gunnadeyahs—In Laguna culture, they are creatures with skills in black magic.

[2] Ka'tsina—spirit beings. Kachina masks are worn in Pueblo ceremonial dances.

[3] Chaco Canyon, Mesa Verde—two important Pueblo locations in the American Southwest

[4] Cartesian duality—the separation of the physical and spiritual worlds

Name: _____ Section: _____ Date: _____

Making Connections through Discussion and Writing

1. In this essay, Leslie Marmon Silko explains the interrelationships between the Pueblo way of life and its history through her discussions of several key factors in Pueblo culture: burial practices, art, stories, the Emergence Place, a sense of community, and migration. Describe each factor, explaining how it reflects Pueblo thinking and maintains Pueblo culture.

burial practices

_____
_____
_____
_____

art

_____
_____
_____
_____

stories

_____
_____
_____
_____

The Emergence Place

_____
_____
_____
_____

community

_____
_____
_____
_____

migration

_____
_____
_____
_____

2. Although recycling may seem to be a "new" practice in contemporary American culture, Silko describes ancient Pueblo recycling practice—although she never uses the term "recycling."

   a. What are some of these practices?

   _____

   _____

   _____

   _____

   _____

   b. How do they reflect the Pueblo view of the interrelationship between all created things and the earth?

   _____

   _____

   _____

   _____

   _____

3. What does Silko mean by the following statements?
   "The ancient Pueblo people sought a communal truth, not an absolute" (paragraph 16).

   _____

   _____

   _____

   _____

   _____

   "Thus the journey was an interior process of the imagination, a growing awareness that being human is somehow different from all other life—animal, plant, and inanimate" (paragraph 27).

   _____

   _____

   _____

   _____

   _____

4. a. Underline Silko's references to landscape.

   b. Write a statement that summarizes how the Pueblo Indians view landscape.

   _____

   _____

   _____

   _____

   _____

c. Explain how landscape is connected to Pueblo myth.

_____

_____

_____

_____

_____

_____

5. Explain why Silko says the English definition of "landscape . . . 'a portion of territory the eye can comprehend in a single view . . .' does not correctly describe the relationship between the human being and his or her surroundings."

_____

_____

_____

_____

_____

_____

_____

_____

_____

_____

_____

_____

_____

_____

Mark Williams

Nightmare #4 (Extinction)

Mark Williams (b. 1963) graduated from Oral Roberts University in 1986 with a B.A. in English Literature, winning the Outstanding English Student award. He then attended Yale Law School. He now is completing a poetic autobiography, while co-owning and running a graphic design business in Tuscon, Arizona.

RIVER

I am stepping through a field
I remember as being once green as green
paint but now the same lead
color as the sky dead as eyes
blind with cataracts
        and make my slow way
to the river I know is up ahead
my eyes fixed on my feet as not to puncture
my foot with broken glass to avoid
the large peel of tire rubber
patches of grease and a pile of bullet
shells left from some hunter's spree
and finally stand at the edge
of the water the color
of ashes and blood
        I see the animals floating by
in the slow moving swirls each one
badly disfigured each one the last
one of its kind they try to tell me
something through their oblong eyes
and by the pained tilt of their heads
        But I already know
what they are trying to say
Knew how this day would one day come
I try to say that I understand what we have done
and how I am sorry but the words
must sound like bullets to them now
for they have no way of rising from the dark
water that carries them to oblivion
they have no way of forgiving me. ■

Making Connections through Discussion and Writing

1. One of the techniques Williams uses in his poem is enjambment, the lack of punctuation at the ends of lines. With this, he often creates a tentative meaning at the end of one line that is modified by the beginning of the next line. An example is "for they have no way of rising from the dark," which lets us read "dark" as a noun—suggesting a general death—or oblivion. The next line, "water that carries them to oblivion," provides the noun "water," which causes us to reread the earlier "dark" as an adjective.

    a. Underline other similar line enjambments that cause you to shift your thinking slightly as you read the lines.

    b. What is gained by such a poetic technique?

    _____

    _____

    _____

    _____

    _____

2. How do the images of the second stanza of the poem create a sense of danger surrounding the narrator's journey?

    _____

    _____

    _____

    _____

    _____

3. a. Circle images of the river's color and speed.

    b. How do these images help reinforce the thematic significance of the poem?

    _____

    _____

    _____

    _____

    _____

4. Why is the detail of words sounding "like bullets" to the dead animals such a powerfully evocative image?

    _____

    _____

    _____

    _____

W. S. Merwin

Unchopping a Tree

W. S. Merwin (b. 1927) was born in New York City, the son of a Presbyterian minister. He was educated at Princeton and is known as a prolific poet and translator. He has translated works from Spanish, Portuguese, Latin, French, and Russian, using conventional poetic forms and free verse; his most famous translations are *The Poem of the Cid* (1959) and *The Song of Roland* (1963). His poetry is remote, with austere metaphors and hints of Eastern mysticism. Some of his works include *The Moving Target* (1963) and *Opening the Hands: Poems* (1983). *Houses and Travellers* (1977) is a collection of prose parables. He has received many awards for his poetry, including a Pulitzer Prize in 1971 for his collection of poems *A Carrier of Ladders*.

Vocabulary ....

arduous   panoply
bole   subcutaneous
inert

Start with the leaves, the small twigs, and the nests that have been shaken, ripped, or broken off by the fall; these must be gathered and attached once again to their respective places. It is not arduous work, unless major limbs have been smashed or mutilated. If the fall was carefully and correctly planned, the chances of anything of the kind happening will have been reduced. Again, much depends upon the size, age, shape, and species of the tree. Still, you will be lucky if you can get through this stage without having to use machinery. Even in the best of circumstances it is a labor that will make you wish often that you had won the favor of the universe of ants, the empire of mice, or at least a local tribe of squirrels, and could enlist their labors and their talents. But no, they leave you to it. They have learned, with time. This is men's work. It goes without saying that if the tree was hollow in whole or in part, and contained old nests of birds or mammal or insect, or hoards of nuts or such structures as wasps or bees build for their survival, the contents will have to be repaired where necessary, and reassembled, insofar as possible, in their original order, including the shells of nuts already opened. With spiders' webs you must simply do the best you can. We do not have the spider's weaving equipment, nor any substitute for the leaf's living bond with its point of attachment and nourishment. It is even harder to simulate the latter when the leaves have once become dry—as they are bound to do, for this is not the labor of a moment. Also it hardly needs saying that this is the time for repairing any neighboring trees or bushes or other growth that may have been damaged by the fall. The same rules apply. Where neighboring trees were of the same species it is difficult not to waste time conveying a detached leaf back to the wrong tree. Practice, practice. Put your hope in that.

Now the tackle must be put into place, or the scaffolding, depending on the surroundings and the dimensions of the tree. It is ticklish work. Almost always it involves, in itself, further damage to the area, which will have to be corrected later. But as you've heard it can't be helped. And care now is likely to save you considerable trouble later. Be careful to grind nothing into the ground.

At last the time comes for the erecting of the trunk. By now it will scarcely be necessary to remind you of the delicacy of this huge skeleton. Every motion of the tackle, every slight upward heave of the trunk, the branches, their elaborately re-assembled panoply of leaves (now dead) will draw from you an involuntary gasp. You will watch for a leaf or a twig to be snapped off yet again. You will listen for the nuts to shift in the hollow limb and you will hear whether they are indeed falling into place or are spilling in disorder—in which case, or in the event of anything else of the kind—operations will have to cease, of course, while you correct the matter. The raising itself is no small enterprise, from the moment when the chains tighten around the old bandages until the bole hangs vertical above the stump, splinter above splinter. Now the final straightening of the splinters themselves can take place (the preliminary work is best done while the wood is still green and soft, but at times when the splinters are not badly twisted most of the straightening is left until now, when the torn ends are face to face with each other). When the splinters are perfectly complementary the appropriate fixative is applied. Again we have no duplicate of the original substance. Ours is extremely strong, but it is rigid. It is limited to surfaces, and there is no play in it. However the core is not the part of the trunk that conducted life from the roots up into the branches and back again. It was relatively inert. The fixative for this part is not the same as the one for the outer layers and the bark, and if either of these is involved in the splintered section they must receive applications of the appropriate adhesives. Apart from being incorrect and probably ineffective, the core fixative would leave a scar on the bark.

When all is ready the splintered trunk is lowered onto the splinters of the stump. This, one might say, is only the skeleton of the resurrection. Now the chips must be gathered, and the sawdust, and returned to their former positions. The fixative for the wood layers will be applied to chips and sawdust consisting only of wood. Chips and sawdust consisting of several substances will receive applications of the correct adhesives. It is as well, where possible, to shelter the materials from the elements while working. Weathering makes it harder to identify the smaller fragments. Bark sawdust in particular the earth lays claim to very quickly. You must find your own ways of coping with this problem. There is a certain beauty, you will notice at moments, in the pattern of the chips as they are fitted back into place. You will wonder to what extent it should be described as natural, to what extent man-made. It will lead you on to speculations about the parentage of beauty itself, to which you will return.

The adhesive for the chips is translucent, and not so rigid as that for the splinters. That for the bark and its subcutaneous layers is transparent and runs into the fibers on either side, partially dissolving them into each other. It does not set the sap flowing again but it does pay a kind of tribute to the preoccupations of the ancient thoroughfares. You could not roll an egg over the joints but some of the mine-shafts would still be passable, no doubt for the first exploring insect who raises its head in the tight echoless passages. The day comes when it is all restored, even the moss (now dead) over the wound. You will sleep badly, thinking of the removal of the scaffolding that must begin the next morning. How you will hope for sun and a still day!

The removal of the scaffolding or tackle is not so dangerous, perhaps, to the surroundings, as its installation, but it presents problems. It should be taken from the spot piece by piece as it is detached, and stored at a distance. You have come to accept it there, around the tree. The sky begins to look naked as the chains and struts one by one vacate their positions. Finally the moment arrives when the last sustaining piece is removed and the tree stands again on its own. It is as though its weight for a moment stood on your heart. You listen for a thud of settlement, a warning creak deep in the intricate joinery. You cannot believe it will hold. How like something dreamed it is, standing there all by itself. How long will it stand there now? The first breeze that touches its dead leaves all seems to flow into your mouth. You are afraid the motion of the clouds will be enough to push it over. What more can you do? What more can you do?

But there is nothing more you can do.
Others are waiting.
Everything is going to have to be put back. ■

Making Connections through Discussion and Writing

1. A description of a step-by-step process is usually a form of composition used to instruct people on basic procedural matters. Cookbooks, automobile manuals, operating instructions for electronic devices, steps for assembling component parts—these are examples of the "process" rhetorical pattern. Readers can usually assume that such a process reveals a task that can be easily completed. Why would Merwin choose such a pattern to tell about a task that cannot be done?

_____
_____
_____
_____

2. a. Describe the order of the repair of the tree.

_____
_____
_____
_____

   b. How does this order differ from a natural order of growth?

_____
_____
_____
_____

3. a. Authors create an ironic tone through the disparity between what is being said and the manner in which it is said. Analyze the tone of this piece and the method Merwin uses to create irony.

   tone _____
_____
_____
_____

   method _____
_____
_____
_____

   b. What are the assumptions or views toward nature taken by the narrator?

_____
_____
_____
_____

c. Is the reader expected to take another view, or does the piece suggest that the author has a different point of view from that of the narrator?

_____

_____

_____

_____

d. Explain your answer.

_____

_____

_____

_____

_____

4. a. Explain the shift of tone of the ending lines of the piece.

_____

_____

_____

_____

b. What does this tone suggest about the consequences of irreparable damage to nature?

_____

_____

_____

_____

c. What does the whole piece suggest about the decisive consequences of human actions?

_____

_____

_____

_____

5. The popular singer/composer Joni Mitchell sings of those who would "pave Paradise and put in a parking lot." Working in a small group with other students, create a process description instructing a restoration of a natural condition that has been changed by man (such as a dam on a river).

_____

_____

_____

_____

_____

_____

_____

_____

W. S. Merwin

The Last One

In this poem, W. S. Merwin uses surrealistic images and echoes from the Biblical account of creation to suggest the horror of human's thoughtless destruction of nature, their killing "the last one" of a species, simply because they have the power to do so.

Well they'd made up their minds to be everywhere because why not.
Everywhere was theirs because they thought so.
They with two leaves they whom the birds despise.
In the middle of stones they made up their minds.
They started to cut.

Well they cut everything because why not.
Everything was theirs because they thought so.
It fell into its shadows and they took both away.
Some to have some for burning.

Well cutting everything they came to the water.
They came to the end of the day there was one left standing.
They would cut it tomorrow they went away.
The night gathered in the last branches.
The shadow of the night gathered in the shadow on the water.
The night and the shadow put on the same head.
And it said Now.

Well in the morning they cut the last one.
Like the others the last one fell into its shadow.
It fell into its shadow on the water.
They took it away its shadow stayed on the water.

Well they shrugged they started trying to get the shadow away.
They cut right to the ground the shadow stayed whole.
They laid boards on it the shadow came out on top.
They shone lights on it the shadow got blacker and clearer.
They exploded the water the shadow rocked.
They built a huge fire on the roots.
They sent up black smoke between the shadow and the sun.
The new shadow flowed without changing the old one.
They shrugged they went away to get stones.

They came back the shadow was growing.
They started setting up stones it was growing.
They looked the other way it went on growing.

They decided they would make a stone out of it.
They took stones to the water they poured them into the shadow.
They poured them in they poured them in the stones vanished.
The shadow was not filled it went on growing.
That was one day.

The next day was just the same it went on growing.
They did all the same things it was just the same.
They decided to take its water from under it.
They took away water they took it away the water went down.
The shadow stayed where it was before.
It went on growing it grew onto the land.
They started to scrape the shadow with machines.
When it touched the machines it stayed on them.
They started to beat the shadow with sticks.
Where it touched the sticks it stayed on them.
They started to beat the shadow with hands.
Where it touched the hands it stayed on them.
That was another day.

Well the next day started about the same it went on growing.
They pushed lights into the shadow.
Where the shadow got onto them they went out.
They began to stomp on the edge it got their feet.
And when it got their feet they fell down.
It got into eyes the eyes went blind.

The ones that fell down it grew over and they vanished.
The ones that went blind and walked into it vanished.
The ones that could see and stood still
It swallowed their shadows.
Then it swallowed them too and they vanished.
Well the others ran.

The ones that were left went away to live if it would let them.
They went as far as they could.
The lucky ones with their shadows. ■

Making Connections through Discussion and Writing

1. a. Underline the repeated words and parallel structures throughout this poem.

    b. What is the effect of the rhythm created by such techniques?

    _____
    _____
    _____
    _____

2. a. What is Merwin describing in lines 3 and 4 of the poem?

    _____
    _____
    _____
    _____

    b. How do these lines indicate the relationship between human beings and nature?

    _____
    _____
    _____
    _____
    _____

3. a. Merwin describes the shadow in a surrealistic way. What do you think the shadow symbolizes?

    _____
    _____
    _____
    _____

    b. What emotional effect does this description have on a reader?

    _____
    _____
    _____
    _____

    c. What is suggested thematically by the shadow's power?

    _____
    _____
    _____
    _____

4. a.   Describe how an ironic tone is established in the first two lines of the poem.

_____

_____

_____

_____

    b.   How does the reasoning suggested by "because why not" and "because they thought so" add to the irony?

_____

_____

_____

_____

    c.   What do these phrases suggest about the attitude of the tree cutters?

_____

_____

_____

_____

5. What does Merwin suggest about the ones who seem to get away, who "went away to live if it would let them"?

_____

_____

_____

_____

6. a.   Circle the lines that suggest or allude to the Genesis account of the days of creation.

    b.   What is Merwin's purpose in using these Biblical echoes?

_____

_____

_____

_____

7. a.   Describe and compare the tone of Williams' poem "Nightmare #4 (Extinction)" and the tone achieved by Merwin's poem "The Last One."

_____

_____

_____

_____

    b.   Which seems more ironic? Explain your answer.

_____

_____

_____

_____

    c.   How do these authors use tone to communicate their themes?

_____

_____

_____

Synthesis/Essay Suggestions: Ecology

1. Write an essay in which you synthesize the views of W. S. Merwin with those of Mark Williams and Vincent Rossi.

2. The poets and the essayists of this section suggest symbolic meanings or values of natural objects. Identify some of the natural objects that bear symbolic meaning. Discuss how the authors use these symbols to persuade their readers to an ecological ethic.

3. Write an essay in which you employ Sayers' ideas about consumption and the meaning of work (in her essay "Why Work?") to urge a renewed emphasis on Christian stewardship of the environment, drawing on the materials from the "Ecology" section, such as the Lynn White, Jr., essay, as you make your point.

4. Write a synthesis essay using "The Canticle of Brother Sun," "The Historical Roots of Our Ecologic Crisis," and "Unchopping a Tree." Discuss the similar or different ways they deal with the subject of humanity's relationship to nature, especially the environment.

5. Write an essay in which you synthesize the views toward nature and the human place in it as expressed by St. Francis, W. S. Merwin, and Lynn White, Jr. Describe the variety of literary genres the authors use to communicate their views. What effects are achieved by each approach? Suggest how the different approaches may be designed for different audiences or for different purposes.

6. Lynn White, Jr., suggests that modern Christians should learn from the Franciscan attitude toward nature, as explained in "The Historical Roots of Our Ecologic Crisis." Could Silko's philosophy of the relationship between humans and nature also contribute to a Christian view? Explain your answer.

7. Thomas Howard in "Myth: A Flight to Reality" suggests that the modern view of the relationship of nature and humans has been diminished because of a lack of mythic dimension. Silko describes a people for whom this mythic dimension shapes their perceptions of reality. Explain how each author argues for the importance of myth in pointing a society toward meaning.

8. In "The Historical Roots of Our Ecologic Crisis," Lynn White, Jr., speaking of general Christian attitudes toward nature, writes, "To a Christian a tree can be no more than a physical fact." How do you think Rossi would respond to this charge?

Part Three

Encounters: Mystery and Manners

"The fiction writer is concerned with the mystery that is lived . . . with ultimate
mystery as we find it embodied in the concrete world of sense experience."
(Flannery O'Connor, "The Teaching of Literature")

Writers use language to explore, question, and shape their notions of reality. Essayists may follow a logical analytical method as they test an idea or opinion (the name of the genre, "essay," originated from the French word for "testing" or "trial," *essai* or *assai*). Poets and fiction writers place characters in situations that often involve tensions requiring a working out of confusion or conflict to resolve issues and achieve a renewed sense of harmony or clarity. These writers are presenting images that say to readers "This is real life. This is how life looks and sounds and feels. This is what it is like to be in love. This is what jealousy feels like." They take the whole range of human emotions and explore them within the specific environments their word images build in readers' imaginations. Many writers, even some of the ones described as "realists," discover that, in their art, intensely imagined life reveals unexpected dimensions of meaning, and their art often evokes depths of feeling and insight not apparent from the surfaces of literal meaning. Ernest Hemingway was convinced that if he rendered his images of life "good enough" they would mean "many things." Robert Frost believed that a successful poem would surprise its maker and reader with unexpected insights, ending in a "clarification of life—not necessarily a great clarification . . . but in a momentary stay against confusion" ("The Figure a Poem Makes").

The work of a writer, then, witnesses to an order, meaning, and significance in human experience. The poet or fiction writer presents images of life—not abstractions, philosophies, doctrines, or theories, but images—that, when well made, convey to the attentive reader the sense of reality, with all its layered density of feeling and significance. When we read such mimetic writings with the thoughtfulness that we accord our own personal experiences, we are rewarded with enriched understandings, empathies, and knowledge gained from the vast universe of human artistic expression.

The experience of a transcendent presence within a moment of time is one that is conveyed most effectively through story telling and poetic writing. From the theophanies of the Old Testament and accounts of religious mystics throughout Christian history to the stories and poems of contemporary religious thinkers and writers, readers can participate in the feelings of awe, humility, and ecstasy that accompany such an experience of what we call the "holy." What cannot be explained directly may be suggested, hinted at, or evoked by the richly imagistic language of poetry and fiction.

One of America's finest contemporary fiction writers, Flannery O'Connor, often lectured on the craft of writing, taking care to explain how a writer's beliefs shape a worldview that is reflected in his or her fiction. O'Connor, a devout Christian, clearly articulates her belief that ordinary life is permeated with the mystery of divine grace. She presents her characters as being free to accept or reject this grace, and she makes clear that their choices have ultimate consequences. As a craftsman of her art, she resists moralizing or making abstract thematic statements, finding these approaches appropriate for expository prose, for editorials, essays, and sermons, but not for mimetic writings like poems, stories, or plays. Writers of these forms must reveal meaning through the images of concrete human situations. Ordinary occurrences and conflicts, the dialects and customs of a particular region, these are the manners that writers use to reveal "mystery"—the actions of grace. The writer, especially in modern fiction, poetry, and drama, speaks to an audience through characters and situations; writers rarely speak through their own voices. In a sense, they "hide" their personal attitudes, trusting their art to reveal a theme and a sense of reality.

O'Connor faulted many of the efforts to write religious literature because "it tends to minimize the importance and dignity of life here and now in favor of life in the next world or in favor of the miraculous manifestations of grace" ("The Church and the Fiction Writer"). To the incarnational imagination of O'Connor, ordinary life was dense with meaning; she did not need to explicitly state its significance in abstract language—she merely needed to portray human life as truthfully and concretely as she could. The meanings then, she trusted, would take care of themselves.

The authors selected for Part Three—from the nineteenth-century poets Wordsworth and Hopkins, to the contemporary Annie Dillard and Gjertrud Schnackenberg—attest to the presence of mystery in life, some quality that seems both immanent and transcendent, to which humans respond with a sense of awe. Many identify this quality with the presence of God. Some, like Whitman and Wordsworth in their poems represented here, focus on the human reactions of awe, humility, and joy that such a presence creates. These authors reveal their attempts to express the experience of the holy in works that depend on images drawn from daily life—chestnuts, caged birds, leaves falling from trees, fathers caring for their children, a man trying to validate his sense of wonder at life by tattooing his body, and widows managing their farms and hired hands. These are the common characters and events to which the writer points us to find meaning, and in their limited existences—their caged lives, their dirt fields, their crude dialects—incarnate grace abounds.

Chapter 9

Christian Aesthetics

S ince the time of Plato, aesthetics has dealt with the good, the true, and the beautiful. The Church has dealt comprehensively with the idea of the true (in doctrinal formulations) and with the good (in ethical teaching). It has been more reticent to engage in the arts—to explore the idea of the beautiful—fearing the encroachment of worldly ideas and pleasures. The church needs to provide a clear voice on aesthetics to contemporary culture. In our modern and post-modern society, the purpose of art often seems to be to shock. At one extreme, artists present vulgar depictions featuring Jesus Christ in offensive and sometimes blasphemous situations and the Virgin Mary shown in disrepute. In popular arts, such as film and rap music, there has been an effusion of profane language, of inappropriate sexual conduct, and a disregard for all that is sacred. Some of what passes for art today is nothing more than the glorification of that which is the evil, the false, and the ugly.

While much art continues to reveal the traditional values of the good, the true, and the beautiful, current culture engulfs us in such a mixture of effects and stimuli that the individual often feels there are no clear criteria for evaluation. When discussing a topic with such a broad range as art, we must be careful not to make too many generalizations. Certainly, art does and should display truth about life; it should not be hesitant to address the ugly. In fact, Christianity shows one of the ugliest acts in human history, the crucifixion of Jesus Christ, as an event of momentous significance, for the sacrifice of our Lord resulted in the redemption of humanity. Religious artists, from Giotto and Grünewald to Rouault and Chagall, have revealed beauty in this vision of the redemption of the "ugly" in their masterful portrayals of the crucifixion. Ultimately, art should lead the viewer to discover the transcendent and to see more clearly what his or her humanity means. What does it mean to know God? What is the essence of a human being? What motivates people to love and hate, to heal and hurt, to give and take? The power of art—whether a painting, a film, a sculpture, a novel, or a song—is the power to reflect, to reveal truth, and to transform.

This section begins with Plato, for in many ways he was the first to show the way towards understanding the ideal—that which humans feel lies beyond their empirical experience. Plato affirms the aspiration toward the ideal world where truth, goodness, and beauty reside. Plato's philosophy, however, in contrast to Christian thought, fails to validate the arts as vehicles of communicating these ideals. To Plato, the material world is simply a shadow of true or ideal reality, and the arts, representing a further diminishment of the ideal, are therefore shadows of shadows. As Christian thinkers, both Dorothy L. Sayers and Madeleine L'Engle are concerned with the shape of a Christian philosophy of the arts and the definition of true art. Demonstrating an aesthetic revealed by the relationship of the Trinity, Sayers shows how the eternal becomes the framework by which the earthly is to be formed. L'Engle is determined to show that the division between the sacred and secular is both arbitrary and unnecessary, asserting that "all true art is incarnational, and therefore 'religious.'"

Plato

Parable of the Cave

Plato (427?–348 B.C.?) was a Greek philosopher born in Athens of a noble family. At first he was interested in politics but became disillusioned upon seeing the injustice of the Athenian democracy, especially after the execution of his teacher, Socrates. Searching for answers to the mystery of the universe, Plato adopted philosophy as the vehicle for his quest. The primary medium Plato used to present his philosophical system was the dialogue, a literary form using conversation, myth, and dramatic setting. Known most for his philosophy, which states that the true essence of all things exists in the Ideal World and that the objects we observe are simply manifestations of that world, Plato influenced many of the early Christian theologians, particularly Augustine. The parable below illustrates clearly Plato's concept of the material world, its relationship to the Ideal World, and how this knowledge is revealed to the unenlightened.

Vocabulary ....

benefactors

spangled

felicitate

And now, I said, let me show in a figure how far our nature is enlightened or unenlightened:— Behold! human beings living in an underground den, which has a mouth open toward the light and reaching all along the den; here they have been from their childhood, and have their legs and necks chained so that they cannot move, and can only see before them, being prevented by the chains from turning round their heads. Above and behind them a fire is blazing at a distance, and between the fire and the prisoners there is a raised way; and you will see, if you look, a low wall built along the way, like the screen which marionette players have in front of them, over which they show the puppets.

I see.

And do you see, I said, men passing along the wall carrying all sorts of vessels, and statues and figures of animals made of wood and stone and various materials, which appear over the wall? Some of them are talking, others silent.

You have shown me a strange image, and they are strange prisoners.

Like ourselves, I replied; and they see only their own shadows, or the shadows of one another, which the fire throws on the opposite wall of the cave?

True, he said; how could they see anything but the shadows if they were never allowed to move their heads?

And of the objects which are being carried in like manner they would only see the shadows?

Yes, he said.

And if they were able to converse with one another, would they not suppose that they were naming what was actually before them?

Very true.

And suppose further that the prison had an echo which came from the other side, would they not be sure to fancy when one of the passers-by spoke that the voice which they heard came from the passing shadow?

No question, he replied.

To them, I said, the truth would be literally nothing but the shadows of the images.

That is certain.

And now look again, and see what will naturally follow if the prisoners are released and disabused of their error. At first, when any of them is

---

From *The Dialogues of Plato*, translated by Benjamin Jowett.

liberated and compelled suddenly to stand up and turn his neck round and walk and look toward the light, he will suffer sharp pains; the glare will distress him, and he will be unable to see the realities of which in his former state he had seen the shadows; and then conceive some one saying to him, that what he saw before was an illusion, but that now, when he is approaching nearer to being and his eye is turned toward more real existence, he has a clearer vision—what will be his reply? And you may further imagine that his instructor is pointing to the objects as they pass and requiring him to name them—will he not be perplexed? Will he not fancy that the shadows which he formerly saw are truer than the objects which are now shown to him?

Far truer.

And if he is compelled to look straight at the light, will he not have a pain in his eyes which will make him turn away to take refuge in the objects of vision which he can see, and which he will conceive to be in reality clearer than the things which are now being shown to him?

True, he said.

And suppose once more, that he is reluctantly dragged up a steep and rugged ascent, and held fast until he is forced into the presence of the sun himself, is he not likely to be pained and irritated? When he approaches the light his eyes will be dazzled, and he will not be able to see anything at all of what are now called realities.

Not all in a moment, he said.

He will require to grow accustomed to the sight of the upper world. And first he will see the shadows best, next the reflections of men and other objects in the water, and then the objects themselves; then he will gaze upon the light of the moon and the stars and the spangled heaven; and he will see the sky and the stars by night better than the sun or the light of the sun by day?

Certainly.

Last of all he will be able to see the sun, and not mere reflections of him in the water, but he will see him in his own proper place, and not in another; and he will contemplate him as he is.

Certainly.

He will then proceed to argue that this is he who gives the season and the years, and is the guardian of all that is in the visible world, and in a certain way the cause of all things which he and his fellows have been accustomed to behold?

Clearly, he said, he would first see the sun and then reason about him.

And when he remembered his old habitation and the wisdom of the den and his fellow-prisoners, do you not suppose that he would felicitate himself on the change, and pity them?

Certainly he would.

And if they were in the habit of conferring honors among themselves on those who were quickest to observe the passing shadows and to remark which of them went before, and which followed after, and which were together; and who were therefore best able to draw conclusions as to the future, do you think that he would care for such honors and glories, or envy the possessors of them? Would he not say with Homer,[1]

> Better to be the poor servant of a poor master,

and to endure anything, rather than think as they do and live after their manner?

Yes, he said, I think that he would rather suffer anything than entertain these false notions and live in this miserable manner.

Imagine once more, I said, such an one coming suddenly out of the sun to be replaced in his old situation; would he not be certain to have his eyes full of darkness?

To be sure, he said.

And if there were a contest, and he had to compete in measuring the shadows with the prisoners who had never moved out of the den, while his sight was still weak, and before his eyes had become steady (and the time which would be needed to acquire this new habit of sight might be very considerable), would he not be ridiculous? Men would say of him that he went and down he came without his eyes, and that it was better not even to think of ascending; and if any one tried to loose another and lead him up to the light, let them only catch the offender, and they would put him to death.

No question, he said.

This entire allegory, I said, you may now append, dear Glaucon, to the previous argument; the prison-house is the world of sight, the light of the fire is the sun, and you will not misapprehend me if you interpret the journey upwards to be the ascent of the soul into the intellectual world according to my poor belief, which, at your desire, I have expressed—whether rightly or wrongly God knows. But, whether true or false, my opinion is that in the world of knowledge the idea of good appears last of all, and is seen only with an effort; and, when seen, is also inferred to be the universal author of all things beautiful and right, parent of light and of the lord of light in this visible world, and the immediate source of reason and truth in the intellectual; and that this is the power upon which he who would act rationally either in public or private life must have his eye fixed.

I agree, he said, as far as I am able to understand you.

Moreover, I said, you must not wonder that those who attain to this beatific vision are unwilling to descend to human affairs; for their souls are ever hastening into the upper world where they desire to dwell; which desire of theirs is very natural, if our allegory be trusted.

Yes, very natural.

And is there anything surprising in one who passes from divine contemplations to the evil state of man, misbehaving himself in a ridiculous manner; if, while his eyes are blinking and before he has become accustomed to the surrounding darkness, he is compelled to fight in courts of law, or in other places, about the images or the shadows of images of justice, and its endeavoring to meet the conceptions of those who have never yet seen absolute justice?

Anything but surprising, he replied.

Any one who has common sense will remember that the bewilderments of the eyes are of two kinds, and arise from two causes, either from coming out of the light or from going into the light, which is true of the mind's eye, quite as much as of the bodily eye; and he who remembers this when he sees any one whose vision is perplexed and weak, will not be too ready to laugh; he will first ask whether that soul of man has come out of the brighter life, and is unable to see because unaccustomed to the dark, or having turned from darkness to the day is dazzled by excess of light. And he will count the one happy in his condition and state of being, and he will pity the other, or, if he have a mind to laugh at the soul which comes from below into the light, there will be more reason in this than in the laugh which greets him who returns from above out of the light into the den.

That, he said, is a very just distinction.

But then, if I am right, certain professors of education must be wrong when they say that they can put a knowledge into the soul which was not there before, like sight into blind eyes.

They undoubtedly say this, he replied.

Whereas, our argument shows that the power and capacity of learning exists in the soul already; and that just as the eye was unable to turn from darkness to light without the whole body, so too the instrument of knowledge can only by the movement of the whole soul be turned from the world of becoming into that of being, and learn by degrees to endure the sight of being, and of the brightest and best of being, or in other words, of the good.

Very true.

And must there not be some art which will effect conversion in the easiest and quickest manner; not implanting the faculty of sight, for that exists already, but has been turned in the wrong direction, and is looking away from the truth?

Yes, he said, such an art may be presumed.

And whereas the other so-called virtues of the soul seem to be akin to bodily qualities, for even when they are not originally innate they can be implanted later by habit and exercise, the virtue of wisdom more than anything else contains a divine element which always remains, and by this conversion is rendered useful and profitable; or, on the other hand, hurtful and useless. Did you never observe the narrow intelligence flashing from the keen eye of a clever rogue—how eager he is, how clearly his paltry soul sees the way to his end; he is the reverse of blind, but his keen eyesight is forced into the service of evil, and he is mischievous in proportion to his cleverness?

Very true, he said.

But what if there had been a circumcision of such natures in the days of their youth; and they had been severed from those sensual pleasures, such as eating and drinking, which, like leaden weights, were attached to them at their birth, and which drag them down and turn the vision of their souls upon the things that are below—if, I say, they had been released from these impediments and turned in the opposite direction, the very same faculty in them would have seen the truth as keenly as they see what their eyes are turned to now.

Very likely.

Yes, I said; and there is another thing which is likely, or rather a necessary inference from what has preceded, that neither the uneducated and uninformed of the truth, nor yet those who never make an end of their education, will be able ministers of State; not the former, because they have no single aim of duty which is the rule of all their actions, private as well as public; nor the latter, because they will not act at all except upon compulsion, fancying that they are already dwelling apart in the islands of the blest.

Very true, he replied.

Then, I said, the business of us who are the founders of the State will be to compel the best minds to attain that knowledge which we have already shown to be the greatest of all—they must continue to ascend until they arrive at the good; but when they have ascended and seen enough we must not allow them to do as they do now.

What do you mean?

I mean that they remain in the upper world: but this must not be allowed; they must be made to descend again among the prisoners in the den, and partake of their labors and honors, whether they are worth having or not.

But is not this unjust? he said; ought we to give them a worse life, when they might have a better?

You have again forgotten, my friend, I said, the intention of the legislator, who did not aim at making any one class in the State happy above the rest; the happiness was to be in the whole State, and he held the citizens together by persuasion and necessity, making them benefactors of the State, and therefore benefactors of one another; to this end he created them, not to please themselves, but to be his instruments in binding up the State.

True, he said, I had forgotten.

Observe, Glaucon, that there will be no injustice in compelling our philosophers to have a care and providence of others; we shall explain to them that in other States, men of their class are not obliged to share in the toils of politics: and this is reasonable, for they grow up at their own sweet will, and the government would rather not have them. Being self-taught, they cannot be expected to show any gratitude for a culture which they have never received. But we have brought you into the world to be rulers of the hive, kings of yourselves and of the other citizens, and have educated you far better and more perfectly than they have been educated, and you are better able to share in the double duty. Wherefore each of you, when his turn comes, must go down to the general underground abode, and get the habit of seeing in the dark. When you have acquired the habit, you will see ten thousand times better than the inhabitants of the den, and you will know what the several images are, and what they represent, because you have seen the beautiful and just and good in their truth. And thus our State which is also yours will be a reality, and not a dream only, and will be administered in a spirit unlike that of other States, in which men fight with one another about shadows only and are distracted in the struggle for power, which in their eyes is a great good. Whereas the truth is that the State in which the rulers are most reluctant to govern is always the best and most quietly governed, and the State in which they are most eager, the worst.

Quite true, he replied.

And will our pupils, when they hear this, refuse to take their turn at the toils of State, when they are allowed to spend the greater part of their time with one another in the heavenly light?

Impossible, he answered; for they are just men, and the commands which we impose upon them are just; there can be no doubt that every one of them will take office as a stern necessity, and not after the fashion of our present rulers of State.

Yes, my friend, I said; and there lies the point. You must contrive for your future rulers another and a better life than that of a ruler, and then you may have a well-ordered State; for only in the State which offers this, will they rule who are truly rich, not in silver and gold, but in virtue and wisdom, which are the true blessings of life. Whereas if they go to the administration of public affairs, poor and hungering after their own private advantage, thinking that hence they are to snatch the chief good, order there can never be; for they will be fighting about office, and the evil and domestic broils which thus arise will be the ruin of the rulers themselves and of the whole State.

Most true, he replied.

And the only life which looks down upon the life of political ambition is that of true philosophy. Do you know of any other?

Indeed, I do not, he said.

And those who govern ought not to be lovers of the task? For, if they are, there will be rival lovers, and they will fight.

No question.

Who then are those whom we shall compel to be guardians? Surely they will be the men who are wisest about affairs of State, and by whom the State is best administered, and who at the same time have other honors and another and a better life than that of politics?

They are the men, and I will choose them, he replied.

And now shall we consider in what way such guardians will be produced, and how they are to be brought from darkness to light—as some are said to have ascended from the world below to the gods?

By all means, he replied.

The process, I said, is not the turning over of an oyster-shell, but the turning round of a soul passing from a day which is little better than night to the true day of being, that is, the ascent from below which we affirm to be true philosophy?

Quite so. ■

Notes

[1] Homer—an ancient Greek writer believed to have written *The Odyssey* and *The Iliad*

Making Connections through Discussion and Writing

1. Summarize the "Parable of the Cave" in your own words.

    _____
    _____
    _____
    _____
    _____
    _____
    _____
    _____
    _____
    _____
    _____
    _____
    _____
    _____
    _____
    _____
    _____
    _____
    _____
    _____
    _____
    _____

2. In one column below, list some concrete items in the parable; in the second, their allegorical representation.

    _____   _____
    _____   _____
    _____   _____
    _____   _____
    _____   _____
    _____   _____
    _____   _____

3. a. Would the prisoner have been better off never going to the light? Explain.

    _____
    _____
    _____
    _____
    _____
    _____
    _____

b. When developing our personal philosophy, we may find that the challenge of changing our ideas often makes us want to retreat to our old ways of thinking. Give an example of a personal belief, the change of which has been painful or even isolating.

_____
_____
_____
_____
_____
_____
_____
_____
_____

4. Compare Plato's use of allegory to one of Jesus' parables in the New Testament. Why is the use of story a convincing method of persuasion?

_____
_____
_____
_____
_____

5. Compare what Plato says about the prisoner who returns to the cave to what Jesus says about the Old Testament prophets (see Matthew 5:12). Why are bearers of truth often rejected when their message contradicts the common belief of the day?

_____
_____
_____
_____
_____

6. Explain how the meaning of the "Parable of the Cave" relates to the idea of knowledge.

_____
_____
_____
_____
_____
_____

Dorothy L. Sayers
Towards a Christian Aesthetic[1]

In the following essay, Sayers emphasizes the importance of the Trinity as the foundation for true art. She sees the act of the artist mirrored in the relationship of the Godhead. Sayers explores this subject further in her fine book on Christian aesthetics, *The Mind of the Maker*, published in 1941.

Vocabulary . . . .

aesthetic	hedonistic
archetypal	incarnation
arpeggios	inculcate
austere	placidly
bawdy	spurious
braying	sublimated
clamor	Trinitarian
debauch	Unitarian
edifying	venially

I have been asked to speak about the arts in this country [England]—their roots in Christianity, their present condition, and the means by which (if we find that they are not flourishing as they should) their mutilated limbs and withering branches may be restored by re-grafting into the main trunk of Christian tradition.

This task is of quite peculiar difficulty, and I may not be able to carry it out in exactly the terms that have been proposed to me. And that for a rather strange reason. In such things as politics, finance, sociology, and so on, there really are a philosophy and a Christian tradition; we do know more or less what the Church has said and thought about them, how they are related to Christian dogma, and what they are supposed to *do* in a Christian country.

But oddly enough, we have no Christian aesthetic—no Christian philosophy of the arts. The Church as a body has never made up her mind about the arts, and it is hardly too much to say that she has never tried. She has, of course, from time to time puritanically denounced the arts as irreligious and mischievous, or tried to exploit the arts as a means to the teaching of religion and morals—but I shall hope to show you that both these attitudes are false and degrading, and are founded upon a completely mistaken idea of what art is supposed to be and do. And there have, of course, been plenty of writers on aesthetics who happened to be Christians, but they seldom made any consistent attempt to relate their aesthetic to the central Christian dogmas. Indeed, so far as European aesthetic is concerned, one feels that it would probably have developed along precisely the same lines had there never been an Incarnation to reveal the nature of God—that is to say, the nature of *all* truth. But that is fantastic. If we commit ourselves to saying that the Christian revelation discovers to us the nature of all truth, then it must discover to us the nature of the truth about art among other things. It is absurd to go placidly along explaining art in terms of a pagan aesthetic, and taking no notice whatever of the complete revolution of our ideas about the nature of things that occurred, or should have occurred, after the first Pentecost. I will go so far as to maintain that the extraordinary confusion of our minds about the nature and function of art is principally due to the fact that for nearly two thousand years we have been trying to reconcile a pagan, or at any rate a Unitarian, aesthetic with a Christian—that is, a Trinitarian and Incarnational—

From *Creed or Chaos* © 1949 by Dorothy L. Sayers. Reprinted by permission of the Estate of Dorothy Sayers and the Watkins/Loomis Agency.

theology. Even that makes us out too intelligent. We have not tried to reconcile them. We have merely allowed them to exist side by side in our minds; and where the conflict between them became too noisy to be overlooked, we have tried to silence the clamor by main force, either by brutally subjugating art to religion, or by shutting them up in separate prison cells and forbidding them to hold any communication with one other.

Now, before we go any further, I want to make it quite clear that what I am talking about now is aesthetic (the philosophy of art) and not about art itself as practiced by the artists. The great artists carry on with their work on the lines God has laid down for them, quite unaffected by the aesthetic worked out for them by philosophers. Sometimes, of course, artists themselves dabble in aesthetic, and what they have to say is very interesting, but often very misleading. If they really are great and true artists, they make their poem (or whatever it is) first, and then set about reconciling it with the fashionable aesthetic of their time; they do not produce their work to conform to their notions of aesthetic—or, if they do, they are so much the less artists, and the work suffers. Secondly, what artists chatter about to the world and to one another is not as a rule their art but the technique of their art. They will tell you, as critics, how it is they produce certain effects (the poet will talk about assonance, alliteration, and meter; the painter about perspective, balance and how he mixes his colors, etc.)—and from that we may get the misleading impression that the technique is the art, or that the aim of art is to produce some sort of effect. But this is not so. We cannot go for a march unless we have learned, through long practice, how to control the muscles of our legs; but it is not true to say that the muscular control *is* the march. And while it is a fact that certain tricks produce "effects"—like Tennyson's use of vowels and consonants to produce the effect of a sleepy murmuring in "The moan of doves in immemorial elms," or of metallic clashing in "The bare black cliff clanged round him"—it is not true that the poem is merely a set of physical, or even of emotional, effects. What a work of art really is and does we shall come to later. For the moment I want only to stress the difference between aesthetic and art and to make it clear that a great artist will produce great art, even though the aesthetic of his time may be hopelessly inadequate to explain it.

For the origins of European aesthetic we shall, of course, turn to Greece; and we are at once brought up against the two famous chapters in

which Plato discusses the arts and decides that certain kinds of art, and in particular certain kinds of poetry, ought to be banished from the perfect State. Not all poetry—people often talk as though Plato had said this, but he did not; certain kinds he wished to keep, and this makes his attitude all the more puzzling because, though he tells us quite clearly why he disapproves of the rejected kinds, he never explains what it is that makes the other kinds valuable. He never gets down to considering, constructively, what true art is or what it does. He tells us only about what are (in his opinion) the bad results of certain kinds of art—nor does he ever tackle the question whether the bad moral results of which he complains may not be due to a falseness *in* the art, i.e., to the work's being pseudo-art[2] or inartistic art. He seems to say that certain forms of art are inherently evil in themselves. His whole handling of the thing seems to us very strange, confused, and contradictory; yet his aesthetic has dominated all our critical thinking for many centuries and has influenced, in particular, the attitude of the Church more than the Church perhaps knows. So it is necessary that we should look at Plato's argument. Many of his conclusions are true—though often, I think, he reaches them from the wrong premises. Some of them are, I think, demonstrably false. But especially, his whole grasp of the subject is inadequate. That is not Plato's fault. He was one of the greatest thinkers of all time, but he was a pagan; and I am becoming convinced that no pagan philosopher could produce an adequate aesthetic, simply for lack of a right theology. In this respect, the least in the Kingdom of Heaven is greater than John the Baptist.

What does Plato say?

He begins by talking about stories and myths, and after dismissing as beneath consideration the stories and poems that are obviously badly written, he goes on to reject those that are untrue, or that attribute evil and disgusting behavior to the gods, or that tend to inculcate bad and vulgar passions or antisocial behavior in the audience. After this (which sounds very much like what moralists and clergymen are always saying nowadays) he leaves the subject-matter and goes on to certain *forms* of poetry and art—those forms that involve *mimesis*—the mimetic arts. Now *mimesis* can be translated as "imitation" or "representation"; and we can at once see that certain forms of art are more mimetic than others: drama, painting, and sculpture are, on the whole, mimetic—some natural object or action is represented or imitated (though we may find exceptions in modernist and surrealist paintings that seem to represent nothing in heaven or earth). Music, on the other hand, is not mimetic—nothing is imitated from the natural world (unless we count certain effects such as the noise of drums in a martial piece, or trills and arpeggios representing the song of birds or the falling of water, down to the squeaks, brayings, twitterings, and whistlings of cinema organs). In the Third Book of the *Republic,* Plato says he will allow the mimetic arts, provided that the imitation or representation is of something morally edifying, that sets a good example; but he would banish altogether the representation of unworthy objects, such as national heroes wallowing about in floods of tears, and people getting drunk, or using foul language. He thinks this kind of thing bad for the actors and also for the audience. Nor (which seems odd to us) are actors to imitate anything vulgar or base, such as artisans plying their trades, galley slaves or bos'ns;[3] nor must there be any trivial nonsense about stage effects and farmyard imitations. Nothing is to be acted or shown except what is worthy to be imitated, the noble actions of wise men—a gallery of good examples.

We may feel that Plato's theater would be rather on the austere side. But in the Tenth Book he hardens his heart still further. He decides to banish *all* mimetic art, all representation of every kind—and that for two reasons.

The first reason is that imitation is a kind of cheat. An artist who knows nothing about carpentering may yet paint a carpenter so that, if the picture is set up at a distance, children and stupid people may be deceived into thinking that it really is a carpenter. Moreover, in any case, the realities of things exist only in Heaven in an ideal and archetypal form; the visible world is only a pale reflection or bad imitation of the heavenly realities; and the work of art is only a cheating imitation of the visible world: therefore, representational art is merely an imitation of an imitation—a deceptive trick that tickles and entertains while turning men's minds away from the contemplation of the eternal realities.

At this point some of you will begin to fidget and say, "Hi! Stop! Surely there is a difference between mimicry intended to deceive and representation. I admit that there are such things as tin biscuit boxes got up to look like the works of Charles Dickens, which may deceive the unwary, and that very simple-minded people in theaters have been known to hiss the villain or leap on the stage to rescue the heroine—but as a rule we know perfectly well that the imitation is only imitation

and not meant to take anyone in. And surely there's a difference between farmyard imitations and John Gielgud playing Hamlet. And besides—even if you get an exact representation of something—say, a documentary film about a war, or an exact verbal reproduction of a scene at the Old Bailey[4]—that's not the same thing as *Coriolanus* or the trial scene in *The Merchant of Venice;* the work of art has something different, something more—poetry or a sort of a something . . ." and here you will begin to wave your hands about vaguely.

You are, of course, perfectly right. But let us for the moment just make a note of how Plato's conception of art is influenced by his theology—the visible world imitating, copying, reflecting a world of eternal changeless forms already existent elsewhere; and the artist, conceived of as a sort of craftsman or artisan engaged in *copying* or imitating something that exists already in the visible world.

Now let us take his [Plato's] second reason for banishing all representational art. He says that even where the action represented is in itself good and noble, the effect on the audience is bad, because it leads them to dissipate the emotions and energies that ought to be used for tackling the problems of life. The feelings of courage, resolution, pity, indignation, and so on are worked up in the spectators by the mimic passions on the stage (or in pictures or music) and then frittered away in a debauch of emotion over these unreal shadows, leaving the mind empty and slack, with no appetite except for fresh sensations of an equally artificial sort.

Now, that is a real indictment against a particular kind of art, which we ought to take seriously. In the jargon of modern psychology, Plato is saying that art of this kind leads to phantasy and daydreaming. Aristotle, coming about fifty years after Plato, defended this kind of art: he said that undesirable passions, such as pity and terror, were in this way *sublimated*—you worked them off in the theater, where they could do no harm. If, he means, you feel an inner urge to murder your wife, you go and see *Othello* or read a good, gory thriller, and satisfy your blood-lust that way, and if we had the last part of his *Poetics,* which dealt with comedy, we should probably find it suggested, in the same way, that an excess of sexual emotion can be worked off by going to a good, dirty farce or vulgar music hall, and blowing the whole thing away in a loud, bawdy laugh.

Now, people still argue as to whether Plato or Aristotle was right about this. But there are one or two things I want you to notice. The first is that what Plato is really concerned to banish from his perfect state is the kind of art that aims at mere entertainment—the art that dissipates energy instead of directing it into some useful channel. And though Aristotle defends "art for entertainment," it is still the same kind of art he is thinking about.

The second thing is that both Plato and Aristotle—but especially Plato—are concerned with the moral effect of art. Plato would allow representational art so long as he thought that it had the effect of canalizing the energies and directing them to virtuous action—he only banishes it, on further consideration, because he has come to the conclusion that *no* representational art of any kind—not even the loftiest tragedy—is successful in bracing the moral constitution. He does not tell us very clearly what poetry he will keep, or why, except that it is to be what we should call a lyrical kind, and, presumably, bracing and tonic in sentiment, and directly inculcating the love of the good, the beautiful and the true.

Thirdly: Plato lived at the beginning, and Aristotle in the middle, of the era that saw the collapse and corruption of the great Greek civilization. Plato sees the rot setting in and cries out like a prophet to his people to repent while there is yet time. He sees the theater audience is in fact looking to the theater for nothing but amusement and entertainment, that their energies are, in fact, frittering themselves away in spurious emotion—sob-stuff and sensation, and senseless laughter, phantasy and day-dreaming, and admiration for the merely smart and slick and clever and amusing. And there is an ominous likeness between his age and ours. We too have audiences and critics and newspapers assessing every play and book and novel in terms of its "entertainment value," and a whole generation of young men and women who dream over novels and wallow in day-dreaming at the cinema, and who seemed to be in a fair way of doping themselves into complete irresponsibility over the conduct of life until war came, as it did to Greece, to jerk them back to reality. Greek civilization was destroyed; ours is not yet destroyed. But it may be well to remember Plato's warning: "If you receive the pleasure-seasoned Muse, pleasure and pain will be kings in your city instead of law and agreed principles."

And there is something else in Plato that seems to strike a familiar note. We seem to know the voice that urges artists to produce works of art "with a high moral tone"—propaganda works, directed to

improving young people's minds and rousing them to a sense of their duties, "doing them good," in fact. And at the same time, we find—among artists and critics alike—a tendency to repudiate representational art, in favor of something more austere, primitive, and symbolic, as though the trouble lay *there*.

It is as though, in the decline of Greece, and in what is known as the "Decline of the West," both Plato and we agreed in finding something wrong with the arts—a kind of mutual infection, by which the slick, sentimental, hedonistic art corrupts its audience, and the pleasure-loving, emotional audience in turn corrupts the arts by demanding of them nothing but entertainment value. And the same sort of remedy is proposed in both cases—first, to get rid of "representationalism"—which, it is hoped, will take away the pleasure and entertainment and so cure the audience's itch for amusement; secondly, to concentrate on works that provide a direct stimulus to right thinking and right action.

What we have really got here is a sort of division of art into two kinds: Entertainment Art, which dissipates the energies of the audience and pours them down the drain; and another kind of art that canalizes energy into a sort of millstream to turn the wheel of action—and this we may perhaps call Spellbinding Art. But do these two functions comprise the whole of art? Or are they art at all? Are they perhaps only accidental effects of art, or false art—something masquerading under the name of art—or menial tasks to which we enslave art? Is the real nature and end of art something quite different from either? Is the real trouble something wrong with our aesthetic, so that we do not know what we ought to look for in art, or how to recognize it when we see it, or how to distinguish the real thing from the spurious imitation?

Suppose we turn from Plato to the actual poets he was writing about—to Aeschylus,[5] for instance, the great writer of tragedies. Drama, certainly, is a representational art, and therefore, according to Plato, pleasure art, entertainment art, emotional and relaxing art, sensational art. Let us read the *Agamemnon*.[6] Certainly it is the representation by actors of something—and of something pretty sensational: the murder of a husband by an adulterous wife. But it is scarcely sensational entertainment in the sense that a thriller novel on the same subject is sensational entertainment. A day-dreaming, pleasure-loving audience would hardly call it entertainment at all. It is certainly not relaxing. And I doubt whether it either dissipates our passions in Plato's sense or sublimates them in Aristotle's sense, any more than it canalizes them for any particular action, though it may trouble and stir us and plunge us into the mystery of things. We might extract some moral lessons from it; but if we ask ourselves whether the poet wrote that play in order to improve our minds, something inside us will, I think, say no. Aeschylus was trying to tell us something, but nothing quite so simple as that. He is saying something—something important something—enormous. And here we shall be suddenly struck with the inadequacy of the strictures against "representational art." "This" we shall say, "is not the copy or imitation of something bigger and more real than itself. It is bigger and more real than the real-life action that it represents. That a false wife should murder a husband—that might be a paragraph in the *News of the World* or a thriller to read in the train—but when it is shown to us like this, by a great poet, it is as though we went behind the triviality of the actual event to the cosmic significance behind it. And, what is more, this is not a representation of the actual event at all; if a BBC reporter had been present at the murder with a television set and microphone, what we heard and saw would have been nothing like this. This play is not anything that ever happened in this world—it is something happening in the mind of Aeschylus, and it had never happened before." *True Art*

Now here, I believe, we are getting to something—something that Plato's heathen philosophy was not adequate to explain—but which we can begin to explain by the light of Christian theology. Very likely the heathen poet could not have explained it either—if he had made the attempt, he too would have been entangled in the terms of his philosophy. But we are concerned, not with what he might have said, but with what he did. Being a true poet, he was true in his work—that is, his art was that point of truth in him that was true to the eternal truth, and only to be interpreted in terms of eternal truth.

The true *work* of art, then, is something new—it is not primarily the copy or representation of anything. It may involve representation, but that is not what makes it a work of art. It is not manufactured to specification, as an engineer works to a plan—though it may involve compliance with the accepted rules for dramatic presentation and may also contain verbal "effects" that can be mechanically accounted for. We know very well, when we compare it with so called works of art that *are* "turned out to pattern," that in this connection neither circumcision availeth anything nor uncircumcision, but a new *creature*. Something has been created.

This word—this idea of art as *creation*—is, I believe, the one important contribution that Christianity has made to aesthetics. Unfortunately, we are likely to use the words "creation" and "creativeness" very vaguely and loosely because we do not relate them properly to our theology. But it is significant that the Greeks had not this word in their aesthetic at all. They looked on a work of art as a kind of *techné*, a manufacture. Neither, for that matter, was the word in their theology—they did not look on history as the continual act of God fulfilling itself in creation.

How do we say that God creates, and how does this compare with the act of creation by an artist? To begin with, of course, we say that God created the universe "out of nothing"—He was bound by no conditions of any kind. Here there can be no comparison: the human artist is *in* the universe and bound by its conditions. He can create only within that framework and out of that material that the universe supplies. Admitting that, let us ask in what way God creates. Christian theology replies that God, who is a Trinity, creates by, or through, His Second Person, His Word or Son, who is continually begotten from the First Person, the Father, in an eternal creative activity. And certain theologians have added this very significant comment: the Father, they say, is only known to himself by beholding His image in His Son.

Does that sound very mysterious? We will come back to the human artist and see what it means in terms of *his* activity. But first, let us take note of a new word that has crept into the argument by way of Christian theology—the word *Image*. Suppose, having rejected the words "copy," "imitation," and "representation" as inadequate, we substitute the word "image" and say that what the artist is doing is to *image forth* something or the other, and connect that with St. Paul's phrase: "God . . . hath spoken to us by His Son, the brightness of this glory and *express image* of his person." Something which, by being an image, *expresses* that which it images. Is that getting us a little nearer to something? There is something that is, in the deepest sense of the words, *unimaginable*, known to Itself (and still more, to us) only by the image in which it expresses Itself through creation; and, says Christian theology very emphatically, the Son, who is the express image, is not the copy, or imitation, or representation of the Father, nor yet inferior or subsequent to the Father in any way—in the last resort, in depths of their mysterious being, the unimaginable and the image are *one and the same*.

Now for our poet. We said, when we were talking of the *Agamemnon,* that this work of art seemed to be "something happening in the mind of Aeschylus." We may now say, perhaps, more precisely, that the play is the *expression* of this interior happening. But what, exactly, was happening?

There is a school of criticism that is always trying to explain, or explain away, a man's works of art by trying to dig out the events of his life and his emotions *outside* the works themselves, and saying, "These are the real Aeschylus, the real Shakespeare, of which the poems are only faint imitations." But any poet will tell you that this is the wrong way to go to work. It is the old, pagan aesthetic that explains nothing—or that explains all sorts of things about the work *except* what makes it a work of art. The poet will say: "My poem is the expression of my experience." But if you then say, "What experience?" he will say, "I can't tell you anything about it, except what I have said in the poem—the poem is the experience." The Son and the Father are *one*; the poet himself did not know what his experience was until he created the poem which revealed his own experience to himself.

To save confusion, let us distinguish between an *event* and an *experience.* An event is something that happens to one, but one does not necessarily experience it. To take an extreme instance: suppose you are hit on the head and get a concussion and, as often happens, when you come to, you cannot remember the blow. The blow on the head certainly happened to you, but you did not *experience* it; all you experience is the after-effects. You only experience a thing when you can express it—however haltingly—to your own mind. You may remember the young man in T. S. Eliot's play, *The Family Reunion,* who says to his relations:

> You are all people
> To whom nothing has happened,
>   at most a continual impact
> Of external events. . . .

He means that they have got through life without ever really *experiencing* anything because they have never tried to express to themselves the real nature of what has happened to them.

A poet is a man who not only suffers "the impact of external events," but experiences them. He puts the experience into words in his own mind, and in so doing recognizes the experience for what it is. To the extent that we can do that, we are all poets. A "poet" so-called is simply a man like ourselves with an exceptional power of revealing his experience by expressing it, so that not only he, but we ourselves, recognize that experience as our own.

I want to stress the word *recognize.* A poet does not see something—say the full moon—and say: "This is a very beautiful sight—let me set about finding words for the appropriate expression of what people ought to feel about it." That is what the literary artisan does, and it means nothing. What happens is that then, or at some time after, he finds himself saying words in his head and says to himself: "Yes—that is right. *That* is the experience the full moon was to me. I recognize it in expressing it, and now I know what it was." And so, when it is a case of mental or spiritual experience—sin, grief, joy, sorrow, worship—the thing reveals itself to him in words and so becomes fully experienced for the first time. By thus recognizing it in its expression, he makes it his own—integrates it into himself. He no longer feels himself battered passively by the impact of external events; it is no longer something happening *to* him, but something happening *in* him; the reality of the event is communicated to him in activity and power. So that the act of the poet in creation is seen to be threefold—a trinity—experience, expression, and recognition: the unknowable reality in the experience; the image of that reality known in its expression; and power in the recognition; the whole making up the single and indivisible act of a creative mind.

Now, what the poet does for himself, he can also do for us. When he has imaged forth his experience he can incarnate it, so to speak, in a material body—words, music, painting—the thing we know as a work of art. And since he is a man like the rest of us, we shall expect that our experience will have something in common with his. In the image of *his* experience, we can *recognize* the image of some experience of our own— something that had happened to us, but which we had never understood, never formulated or expressed to ourselves, and therefore never known as a real experience. When we read the poem, or see the play or picture or hear the music, it is though a light were turned on inside us. We say: "Ah! I recognize that! That is something that I obscurely felt to be going on in and about me, but I didn't know what it was and couldn't express it. But now that the artist has made its image— imaged it forth—for me, I can possess and take hold of it and make it my own and turn it into a source of knowledge and strength." This is the *communication of the image in power,* by which the third person of the poet's trinity brings us, through the incarnate image, into direct knowledge of the in itself unknowable and unimaginable reality. "No man cometh to the Father save by Me," said the incarnate Image; and He added, "but the Spirit of Power will lead you into all truth."

This recognition of the truth that we get in the artist's work comes to us as a revelation of new truth. I want to be clear about that. I am not referring to the sort of patronizing recognition we give to a writer by nodding our heads and observing: "Yes, yes, very good, very true—that's just what I'm always saying." I mean the recognition of a truth that tells us something about ourselves that we had *not* been "always saying," something that puts a new knowledge of ourselves within our grasp. It is new, startling, and perhaps shattering— and yet it comes to us with a sense of familiarity. We did not know it before, but the moment the poet has shown it to us, we know that, somehow or other, we had always really known it.

Very well. But, frankly, is that the sort of thing the average British citizen gets, or expects to get, when he goes to the theater or reads a book? No, it is not. In the majority of cases, it is not in the least what he expects, or what he wants. What he looks for is not this creative and Christian kind of art at all. He does not expect or desire to be upset by sudden revelations about himself and the universe. Like the people of Plato's decadent Athens, he has forgotten or repudiated the religious origins of all art. He wants entertainment, or, if he is a little more serious-minded, he wants something with a moral, or to have some spell or incantation put on him to instigate him to virtuous action.

Now, entertainment and moral spell-binding have their uses, but they are not art in the proper sense. They may be the incidental effects of good art; but they may also be the very aim and essence of false art. And if we continue to demand of the arts only these two things, we shall starve and silence the true artist and encourage in his place the false artist, who may become a very sinister force indeed.

Let us take the amusement art: what does that give us? Generally speaking, what we demand and get from it is the enjoyment of the emotions that usually accompany experience without having had the experience. It does not reveal us to ourselves; it merely *projects* on to a mental screen a picture of ourselves as we already fancy ourselves to be— only bigger and brighter. The manufacturer of this kind of entertainment is not by any means interpreting and revealing his own experience to himself and us—he is either indulging his own daydreams, or—still more falsely and venially—he is saying: "What is it the audience think they would

like to have experienced? Let us show them that, so that they can wallow in emotion by pretending to have experienced it." This kind of pseudo-art is "wish fulfillment" or "escape" literature in the worst sense—it is an escape, not from the "impact of external events" into the citadel of experienced reality, but an escape from reality and experience into a world of merely external events—the progressive externalization of consciousness. For occasional relaxation this is all right; but it can be carried to the point where, not merely art, but the whole universe of phenomena becomes a screen on which we see the magnified projection of our unreal selves, as the object of equally unreal emotions. This brings about the complete corruption of the consciousness, which can no longer recognize reality in experience. When things come to this pass, we have a civilization that lives for amusement—a civilization without guts, without experience, and out of touch with reality.

Or take the spell-binding kind of art. This at first sight seems better because it spurs us to action; and it also has its uses. But it too is dangerous in excess because once again it does not reveal reality in experience, but only projects a lying picture of the self. As the amusement-art seeks to produce the *emotions* without the experience, so *this* pseudo-art seeks to produce the *behavior* without the experience. In the end it is directed to putting the behavior of the audience beneath the will of the spell-binder, and its true name is not "art," but "art magic." In its vulgarest form it becomes pure propaganda. It can (as we have reason to know) actually succeed in making its audience into the thing it desires to have them—it can really in the end corrupt the consciousness and destroy experience until the inner selves of its victims are wholly externalized and made the puppets and instruments of their own spurious passions. This is why it is dangerous for anybody—even for the Church—to urge artists to produce works of art for the express purpose of "doing good to people." Let her by all means encourage artists to express their own Christian experience and communicate it to others. That is the true artist saying: "Look! recognize your experience in my own." But "edifying art" may only too often be the pseudo-artist corruptly saying: "This is what you are supposed to believe and feel and do—and I propose to work you into a state of mind in which you will believe and feel and do as you are told." This pseudo-art does not really communicate power to us; it merely exerts power over us.

What is it, then, that these two pseudo-arts—

the entertaining and the spell-binding—have in common? And how are they related to true art? What they have in common is the falsification of consciousness; and they are to art as the *idol* is to the Image. The Jews were forbidden to make any image for worship because before the revelation of the threefold unity in which Image and Unimaginable are one, it was only too fatally easy to substitute the idol for the image. The Christian revelation set free all the images, by showing that the true image subsisted within the Godhead Itself—it was neither copy, nor imitation, nor representation, nor inferior, nor subsequent, but the brightness of the glory, and the express image of the Person—the very mirror in which reality knows itself and communicates itself in power.

But the danger still exists, and it always will recur whenever the Christian doctrine of the Image is forgotten. In our aesthetic, that doctrine has never been fully used or understood, and in consequence our whole attitude to the artistic expression of reality has become confused, idolatrous, and pagan. We see the arts degenerating into mere entertainment that corrupts and relaxes our civilization, and we try in alarm to correct this by demanding a more moralizing and bracing kind of art. But this is only setting up one idol in place of the other. Or we see that art is becoming idolatrous, and we suppose that we can put matters right by getting rid of the representational element in it. But what is wrong is not the representation itself, but the fact that what we are looking at, and what we are looking *for,* is not the Image *but* is an idol. Little children, keep yourselves from idols.

It has become a commonplace to say that the arts are in a bad way. We are in fact largely given over to the entertainers and the spellbinders; and because we do not understand that these two functions do not represent the true nature of art, the true artists are, as it were, excommunicate and have no audience. But there is here not, I think, so much a relapse from a Christian aesthetic as a failure ever to find and examine a real Christian aesthetic, based on dogma and not on ethics. This may not be a bad thing. We have at least a new line of country to explore, that has not been trampled on and built over and fought over by countless generations of quarrelsome critics. What we have to start from is the Trinitarian doctrine of creative mind, and the light that that doctrine throws on the true nature of images.

The great thing, I am sure, is not to be nervous about God—not to try and shut out the Lord Immanuel from *any* sphere of truth. Art is not He—we must not substitute art for God; yet this also is He for it is one of His Images and therefore reveals His nature. Here we see in a mirror darkly—we behold only the images; elsewhere we shall see face to face, in the place where Image and Reality are one. ■

Notes

1 Author's note—It will be immediately obvious how deeply this paper is indebted to R. G. Collingwood's *Principles of Art*, particularly as regards the disentangling of "Art Proper" (expression and imagination) from the pseudo-arts of "amusement and magic." The only contribution I have made of my own (exclusive of incidental errors) has been to suggest, however tentatively, a method of establishing the principles of "Art Proper" upon that Trinitarian doctrine of the nature of creative mind that does, I think, really underlie them. On this foundation it might perhaps be possible to develop a Christian aesthetic, which, finding its source and sanction in the theological center, would be at once more characteristically Christian and of more universal application than any aesthetic whose contact with Christianity is made only at the ethical circumference.—D.L.S.

2 pseudo-art—false art. Sayers believes some art falls below the standard she describes in the essay.

3 bos'ns—abbreviation for a Navy term "boatswain," which is a petty officer

4 Old Bailey—jail

5 Aeschylus—(525–456 B.C.) Greek dramatist

6 *Agamemnon*—a tragedy by Aeschylus

Making Connections through Discussion and Writing

1. Divide this essay into sections, identifying the main themes and topics of each section by labeling them in the margins.

2. a. Sayers presents a brief history of aesthetic philosophy. Summarize the specific ideas of Plato and Aristotle concerning the nature of art and its effects on society.

   Plato
   _____
   _____
   _____
   _____
   _____

   Aristotle
   _____
   _____
   _____
   _____
   _____

   b. According to Sayers, how are Plato's and Aristotle's definitions and defenses of art incomplete?
   _____
   _____
   _____
   _____

3. Plato's ideal republic excludes representational art; Sayers' aesthetic does not. How does Sayers defend representation art as legitimate?
   _____
   _____
   _____
   _____

4. a. According to Sayers, what is the most important contribution Christianity has made to aesthetics?
   _____ incarnation
   _____

   b. Why is it important?
   _____
   _____

5. a. What distinction does Sayers make between entertainment art and spellbinding art?   *look later in text*

    _____

    _____

    _____

    _____

    b. Give examples from modern culture—film, books, art, television, or music—to illustrate these two types of art.

    _____

    _____

    _____

    _____

    _____

    _____

    _____

    _____

    _____

    _____

    _____

6. a. Describe how Sayers uses the doctrine of the Trinity to define true art.

    _____

    _____

    _____

    _____

    b. List below the threefold correlation she sees between the creative act of the artist and the Trinity.

    _____

    _____

    _____

    _____

    _____

7. Explain how Sayers reevaluates the idea of the image in art by referring to Jesus Christ and the doctrine of the Incarnation.

    _____

    _____

    _____

    _____

    _____

    _____

8. a. According to Sayers, why is it dangerous to "produce works of art for the express purpose of doing good to people"?

_____

_____

_____

_____

_____

_____

   b. Compare Sayers' statement above to Flannery O'Connor's statement in "Novelist and Believer" where she writes that "[e]ver since there have been such things as novels, the world has been flooded with bad fiction for which the religious impulse has been responsible." Discuss your findings.

_____

_____

_____

_____

_____

_____

9. Sayers discusses the mutual infection that has invaded art: a corrupted art and a corrupted audience. Obviously the connection between a society's art and its morality is not coincidental. The High Middle Ages and the Renaissance were times of great faith and creative energy in art as reflected in Gothic cathedrals and in the paintings of Michelangelo.

   a. Select a particular artistic achievement from these earlier ages, and contrast it to a modern creative work.

_____   _____

_____   _____

_____   _____

_____   _____

_____   _____

_____   _____

_____   _____

   b. What are some similarities and differences that you notice?

_____

_____

_____

_____

_____

c. Why do you think these similarities and differences exist?

_____

_____

_____

10. Write an essay in which you define your idea of true art. Include in your definition some examples of the kind of art that illustrates your main point. If you disagree with Sayers, present her position clearly before refuting it.

Madeleine L'Engle
from Icons of the True

Madeleine L'Engle (1918-2007) was the world-renowned author of over 40 books including many children's books such as *A Wrinkle in Time* (1962), which won the Newberry Award, and *A Swiftly Tilting Planet* (1978), which received the American Book Award. She has also written *A Wind in the Door* (1973), *A Ring of Endless Light, A Circle of Quiet, Walking on Water*, and *And It Was Good.* She often writes in the library at the Cathedral Church of St. John the Divine in New York. L'Engle travels widely, speaking to audiences across North America and overseas. Excerpted from L'Engle's book *Walking on Water: Reflections on Faith and Art*, the following essay has the loose, flowing structure of a journal. L'Engle's opinions on art and faith are boldly expressed and supported by examples and intuitive insights rather than by closely argued analysis. As an imaginative artist with a deeply Christian outlook, L'Engle speaks from her own and others' experiences.

Vocabulary ....

android	munificent
Annunciation	pandered
anonymity	pellucid
cosmos	presumptuous
embroiled	pusillanimous
fugue	retribution
goy	smarmy
Hassidic	soppy
icon	unmitigated

It has often struck me with awe that some of the most deeply religious people I know have been, on the surface, atheists. Atheism is a peculiar state of mind; you cannot deny the existence of that which does not exist. I cannot say, "That chair is not there," if there is no chair there to say it about.

Many atheists deny God because they care so passionately about a caring and personal God and the world around them is inconsistent with a God of love, they feel, and so they say, "There is no God." But even when one denies God, to serve music, or painting, or words is a religious activity, whether or not the conscious mind is willing to accept that fact. Basically there can be no categories such as "religious" art and "secular" art, because all true art is incarnational, and therefore "religious."

The problem of pain, of war and the horror of war, of poverty and disease is always confronting us. But a God who allows no pain, no grief, also allows no choice. There is little unfairness in a colony of ants, but there is also little freedom. We human beings have been given the terrible gift of free will, and this ability to make choices, to help write our own story, is what makes us human, even when we make the wrong choices, abusing our freedom and the freedom of others. The weary and war-torn world around us bears witness to the wrongness of many of our choices. But lest I stumble into despair I remember, too, seeing the white, pinched-faced little children coming to the pediatric floor of a city hospital for open-heart surgery, and seeing them, two days later, with colour in their cheeks, while the nurses tried to slow down their wheel-chair races. I remember, too, that there is now a preventative for trachoma, still the chief cause of blindness in the world. And I remember that today few mothers die in childbirth, and our graveyards no longer contain the mute witness of five little stones in a row, five children of one family, dead in a week of scarlet fever or diptheria.

George MacDonald[1] gives me renewed strength during times of trouble—times when I have seen people tempted to deny God—when he says, "The Son of God suffered unto death, not that men might not suffer, but that their sufferings might be like his."

Jesus, too, had to make choices, and in the eyes of the world some of his choices were not only contrary to acceptable behaviour, but were foolish in the extreme. He bucked authority by healing on the Sabbath; when he turned his steps towards Jerusalem he was making a choice which led him to Calvary.

It is the ability to choose which makes us human.

This ability, this necessity to choose, is an important element in all story. Which direction will the young man take when he comes to the crossroads? Will the girl talk with the handsome stranger? Should the child open the forbidden door?

Oedipus[2] killed the man he met at the crossroads, and even though he did not know that the man was his father, that did not allow him to escape the retribution which followed his choice. He married a woman he did not know to be his mother, but his lack of knowledge did not make him "innocent." Though we may cry out, "But I didn't know!" our anguish does little to forestall the consequences of our actions. To the nonbeliever, the person who sees no cosmos in chaos, we are all the victims of the darkness which surrounds our choices; we have lost our way; we do not know what is right and what is wrong; we cannot tell our left hand from our right. There *is* no meaning.

But to serve any discipline of art, be it to chip a David[3] out of an unwieldly piece of marble, to take oils and put a clown on canvas, to write a drama about a young man who kills his father and marries his mother and suffers for these actions, to hear a melody and set the notes down for a string quartet, is to affirm meaning, despite all the ambiguities and tragedies and misunderstanding which surround us.

Aeschylus[4] writes, "In our sleep, pain that cannot forget falls drop by drop upon the heart and in our own despair, against our will, comes wisdom through the awful grace of God."

We see that wisdom and that awful grace in the silence of the Pièta,[5] in Gerard Manley Hopkins' poems; in Poulenc's organ concerto; but we do not find it in many places where we would naturally expect to find it. This confusion comes about because much so-called religious art is in fact bad art, and therefore bad religion. Those angels rendered by grown-ups who obviously didn't believe in angels and which confused the delegates at Ayia Napa[6] are only one example. Some of those soppy pictures of Jesus, looking like a tubercular, fair-haired, blue-eyed goy, are far more secular than a Picasso[7] mother and child. The Lord Jesus who rules my life is not a sentimental, self-pitying weakling. He was a Jew, a carpenter, and strong. He took into his own heart, for our sakes, that pain which brings "wisdom through the awful grace of God."

It is impossible for an artist to attempt a graphic reproduction of Jesus in any way that is meant to be literal. I sympathize with the Hassidic teaching that it is wrong to try in any way to make pictures of God or his prophets. The Muslims have this philosophy, too, hence the intricate, nonrepresentational designs on the mosques.

But in a way both miss the point which the Eastern Orthodox artists are taught when they study the painting of icons. The figure on the icon is not meant to represent literally what Peter or John or any of the apostles looked like, nor what Mary looked like, nor the child, Jesus. But, the orthodox painter feels, Jesus of Nazareth did not walk around Galilee faceless. The icon of Jesus may not look like the man Jesus two thousand years ago, but it represents some *quality* of Jesus, or his mother, or his followers, and so becomes an open window through which we can be given a new glimpse of the love of God. Icons are painted with firm discipline, much prayer, and anonymity. In this way the iconographer is enabled to get out of the way, to listen, to serve the work.

An icon is a symbol, rather than a sign. A sign may point the way to something, such as: *Athens—10 kilometers.* But the sign is not Athens, even when we reach the city limits and read *Athens.* A symbol, however, unlike a sign, contains within it some quality of what it represents. An icon of the Annunciation, for instance, does more than point to the angel and the girl; it contains, for us, some of Mary's acceptance and obedience, and so affects our own ability to accept, to obey.

Francis of Assisi[8] says that "In pictures of God

and the blessed Virgin painted on wood, God and the blessed Virgin are held in mind, yet the wood and the painting ascribe nothing to themselves, because they are just wood and paint; so the servant of God is a kind of painting, that is, a creature of God in which God is honoured for the sake of his benefits. But he ought to ascribe nothing to himself, just like the wood or the painting, but should render honour and glory to God alone."

I travel with a small icon, a picture pasted on wood, which was given to me with love, so that the picture, the wood, and the love have become for me a Trinity, an icon of God. Of themselves they are nothing; because they are also part of God's munificent love they are everything.

An iconographer is a devout and practising Christian, but all true art has an iconic quality. An Eastern Orthodox theologian, Timothy Kallistos Ware, writes (and where? in a magazine called *Sobornost,* probably about a decade ago edited by the Rev. Canon A. M. Allchin, of Canterbury Cathedral, England) that

> an abstract composition by Kandinsky[9] or Van Gogh's[10] landscape of the cornfield with birds . . . is a real instance of divine transfiguration, in which we see matter rendered spiritual and entering into the "glorious liberty of the children of God." This remains true, even when the artist does not personally believe in God. Provided he is an artist of integrity, he is a genuine servant of the glory which he does not recognize, and unknown to himself there is "something divine" about his work. We may rest confident that at the last judgment the angels will produce his works of art as testimony on his behalf.

(Angels again!)

We may not like that, but we call the work of such artists un-Christian or non-Christian at our own peril. Christ has always worked in ways which have seemed peculiar to many men, even his closest followers. Frequently the disciples failed to understand him. So we need not feel that we have to understand how he works through artists who do not consciously recognize him. Neither should our lack of understanding cause us to assume that he cannot be present in their work.

A sad fact which nevertheless needs to be faced is that a deeply committed Christian who wants to write stories or paint pictures or compose music to the glory of God simply may not have been given the talent, the gift, which a non-Christian, or even an atheist, may have in abundance. God is no respecter of persons, and this is something we are reluctant to face.

We would like God's ways to be like our ways, his judgments to be like our judgments. It is hard for us to understand that he lavishly gives enormous talents to people we would consider unworthy, that he chooses his artists with as calm a disregard of surface moral qualifications as he chooses his saints.

Often we forget that he has a special gift for each one of us, because we tend to weigh and measure such gifts with the coin of the world's market place. The widow's mite[11] was worth more than all the rich men's gold because it represented the focus of her life. Her poverty was rich because all she had belonged to the living Lord. Some unheard-of Elizabethan woman who led a life of selfless love may well be brought before the throne of God ahead of Shakespeare, for such a person may be a greater force for good than someone on whom God's blessings seem to have been dropped more generously. As Emmanuel, Cardinal Suhard says, "To be a witness does not consist in engaging in propaganda, nor even in stirring people up, but in being a living mystery. It means to live in such a way that one's life would not make sense if God did not exist."

The widow's mite and Bach's St. Matthew's Passion[12] are both "living mysteries," both witness to lives which affirm the loving presence of God.

Kandinsky and Van Gogh say more than they know in their paintings. So does a devout man who is not a Christian, but a Jew and a philosopher, Martin Buber. Listen: "You should utter words as though heaven were opened within them and as though you did not put the word into your mouth, but as though you had entered the word." Buber was certainly not consciously thinking of the second Person of the Trinity when he wrote that. Nevertheless his words become richer for me when I set them alongside these: "In the beginning was the Word, and the Word was with God, and the Word was God."

Plato, too, all that distance away in time and space from Bethlehem, seems often to be struggling towards an understanding of incarnation, of God's revelation of himself through particularity. Of course, because I am a struggling Christian, it's inevitable that I superimpose my awareness of all that happened in the life of Jesus upon what I'm reading, upon Buber, upon Plato, upon the Book of Daniel. But I'm not sure that's a bad thing. To be truly Christian means to see Christ everywhere, to know him as all in all.

I don't mean to water down my Christianity into a vague kind of universalism, with Buddha and Mohammed all being more or less equal to Jesus—not at all! But neither do I want to tell God (or my friends) where he can and cannot be seen! We human beings far too often tend to codify God, to feel that we know where he is and where he is not, and this arrogance leads to such things as the Spanish Inquisition,[13] the Salem witch burnings[14], and has the result of further fragmenting an already broken Christendom.

We live by revelation, as Christians, as artists, which means that we must be careful never to get set into rigid molds. The minute we begin to think we know all the answers, we forget the questions, and we become smug like the Pharisee who listed all his considerable virtues, and thanked God that he was not like other men.

Unamuno[15] might be describing the artist as well as the Christian as he writes, "Those who believe they believe in God, but without passion in the heart, without anguish of mind, without uncertainty, without doubt, and even at times without despair, believe only in the idea of God, and not in God himself."

When I was in college I knew that I wanted to be a writer. And to be a writer means, as everyone knows, to be published.

And I copied in my journal from Tchekov's[16] letters: "You must once and for all give up being worried about successes and failures. Don't let that concern you. It's your duty to go on working steadily day by day, quite quietly, to be prepared for mistakes, which are inevitable, and for failures."

I believed those words then, and I believe them now, though in the intervening years my faith in them has often been tested. After the success of my first novels I was *not* prepared for rejections, for the long years of failure. Again I turned to Tchekov. "The thought that I must, that I ought to, write, never leaves me for an instant." Alas, it *did* leave me, when I had attacks of false guilt because I was spending so much time at the typewriter and in no way pulling my own weight financially. But it never left me for long.

I've written about that decade of failure in *A Circle of Quiet*. I learned a lot of valuable lessons during that time, but there's no doubt that they were bitter. This past winter I wrote in my journal, "If I'd read these words of Rilke's[17] during the long years of rejection they might have helped, because I could have answered the question in the affirmative:

You are looking outward, and that above all you should not do now. Nobody can counsel and help you, nobody. There is only one single way. Go into yourself. Search for the reason that bids you to write; find out whether it is spreading out its roots in the deepest places of your heart, acknowledge to yourself whether you would have to die if it were denied you to write. This above all—ask yourself in the stillest hour of your night: *Must* I write? Delve into yourself for a deep answer. And if this should be affirmative, if you may meet this earnest question with a strong and simple "I must," then build your life according to this necessity; your life even into its most indifferent and slightest hour must be a sign of this urge and testimony to it.

That is from *Letters to a Young Poet*, and surely Rilke speaks to all of us who struggle with a vocation of words.

The writer does want to be published; the painter urgently hopes that someone will see the finished canvas (Van Gogh was denied the satisfaction of having his work bought and appreciated during his lifetime; no wonder the pain was more than he could bear); the composer needs his music to be heard. Art is communication, and if there is no communication it is as though the work had been still-born.

The reader, viewer, listener, usually grossly underestimates his importance. If a reader cannot create a book along with the writer, the book will never come to life. Creative involvement: that's the basic difference between reading a book and watching TV. In watching TV we are passive; sponges; we do nothing. In reading we must become creators. Once the child has learned to read alone, and can pick up a book without illustrations, he must become a creator, imagining the setting of the story, visualizing the characters, seeing facial expressions, hearing the inflection of voices. The author and the reader "know" each other; they meet on the bridge of words.

So there is no evading the fact that the artist yearns for "success," because that means that there has been a communication of the vision: that all the struggle has not been invalid.

Yet with each book I write I am weighted with a deep longing for anonymity, a feeling that books should not be signed, reviews should not be read. But I sign the books; I read the reviews.

Two writers I admire express the two sides of this paradox. They seem to disagree with each other completely, and yet I believe that each is right.

E. M. Forster[18] writes:

> . . . all literature tends towards a condition of anonymity, and that, so far as words are creative, a signature merely distracts from their true significance.
>
> I do not say that literature "ought" not to be signed . . . because literature is alive, and consequently "ought" is the wrong word. It wants not to be signed. That is my point. It is always tugging in that direction . . . saying, in effect, "I, not the author, really exist."
>
> The poet wrote the poem, no doubt. But he forgot himself while he wrote it, and we forget him while we read. . . . We forget, for ten minutes, his name and our own, and I contend that this temporary forgetfulness, this momentary and mutual anonymity, is sure evidence of good stuff.
>
> Modern education promotes the unmitigated study of literature, and concentrates our attention on the relation between a writer's life—his surface life—and his work. That is the reason it is such as curse.
>
> Literature wants not to be signed.

And yet I know whom I am quoting, for Forster signed his work.

W. H. Auden[19] writes:

> Our judgement of an established author is never simply an aesthetic judgment. In addition to any literary merit it may have, a new book by him has a historic interest for us as the act of a person in whom we have long been interested. He is not only a poet or a novelist; he is also a character in our biography.

We cannot seem to escape paradox; I do not think I want to.

Forster refers to *"his* surface life and *his* work;" Auden says, *"He* is not only a poet or a novelist; *he* is also a character in our biography." That *his* and that *he* refers as much to Jane Austin and George Sand as to Flaubert and Hemingway.[20] It is a generic *his* and *he*, and not exclusively masculine.

I am a female, of the species man. Genesis is very explicit that it takes both male and female to make the image of God, and that the generic word, man, includes both.

God created man in his own image, male and female.

That is Scripture, therefore I refuse to be timid about being part of *man*kind. We of the female sex are half of mankind, and it is pusillanimous to resort to he/she, him/her, or even worse, android words. I have a hunch that those who would do so have forgotten their rightful heritage.

I know that I am fortunate in having grown up in a household where no sexist roles were imposed upon me. I lived in an atmosphere which assumed equality with all its differences. When mankind was referred to it never occurred to me that I was not part of it, or that I was in some way being excluded. My great-great-grandmother, growing up on the St. John's river in times of violence and hardship, had seven homes burned down; nevertheless she spoke casually in seven languages. Her daughter-in-law ran a military hospital, having been brought up at the court of Spain where she was her ambassador father's hostess; her closest friend was the princess Eugenie, soon to be Empress, and two young women rode and competed with the princess's brothers in all sports; to prove their bravery, each drove a sharp knife into the flesh of the forearm without whimper. Others of my female forbears crossed the country in covered wagons, and knew how to handle a gun as well as any man.

Perhaps it is this background which has made me assume casually that of course I am not excluded when anyone refers to a novelist—or anyone else—as *he* or *him*. My closest woman friend is a physician, and so is my daughter-in-law. Not all women have been as fortunate as I have been. When my books were being rejected during the fifties it was not because of my sex, it was because the editors did not like what I was writing. It was my words which were being rejected, not my femaleness.

Because I am a story-teller I live by words. Perhaps music is a purer art form. It may be that when we communicate with life on another planet, it will be through music, not through language or words.

But I am a story-teller and that involves language, for me the English language, that wonderfully rich, complex, and oftimes confusing tongue. When language is limited, I am thereby diminished, too.

In time of war language always dwindles, vocabulary is lost; and we live in a century of war. When I took my elder daughter's tenth grade vocabulary cards up to the school from which she had graduated, less than a decade after she had left, the present tenth grade students knew almost none of them. It was far easier for my daughter to read Shakespeare in high school than it was for students coming along just a few years after her.

This diminution is world-wide. In Japan, after the Second World War, so many written characters were lost, that it is difficult, if not impossible, for the present day college student to read the works of the great classical masters. In Russia, even if Solzhenytzin[21] were allowed to be read freely, it would not be easy for the average student to read his novels, for again, after revolution and war, vocabulary fell away. In one of Solzhenytzin's books his hero spends hours at night reading the great Russian dictionary which came out in the late nineteenth century, and Solzhenytzin himself draws on this work, and in his writing he is redeeming language, using the words of Tolstoy[22] and Dostoyevsky,[23] using the words of the people of the street, bringing language back to life as he writes.

So it has always been. Dante,[24] writing in exile when dukedoms and principalities were embroiled in wars, was forging language as he wrote his great science-fiction fantasies.

We think because we have words, not the other way around. The more words we have, the better able we are to think conceptually. Yet another reason why *Wrinkle*[25] was so often rejected is that there are many words in it which would never be found on a controlled vocabulary list for the age-group of the ten-to-fourteen-year-old. *Tesseract*, for instance. It's a real word, and one essential for the story.

As a child, when I came across a word I didn't know, I didn't stop reading the story to look it up, I just went on reading. And after I had come across the word in several books, I knew what it meant; it had been added to my vocabulary. This still happens. When I started to read Teilhard de Chardin's *The Phenomenon of Man*, I was determined to understand it. I read intelligently, with a dictionary beside me, stopping to look up the scientific words which were not familiar to me. And I bogged down. So I put aside the dictionary and read as though I were reading a story, and quickly I got drawn into the book, fascinated by his loving theology, and understood it far better, at a deeper level, than if I had stuck with the dictionary.

Is this contradiction? I don't think so. We played with my daughter's vocabulary words during dinner. We kept a dictionary by the table, just for fun. But when we read, we read. We were capable of absorbing far more vocabulary when we read straight on than when we stopped to look up every word. Sometimes I will jot down words to be looked up later. But we learn words in many ways, and much of my vocabulary has been absorbed by my subconscious mind, which then kindly blips it up to my conscious mind when it is needed.

A friend of mine at a denominational college reported sadly one of his students came to complain to him about a visiting professor. This professor was having the students read some twentieth century fiction, and the student was upset both at the language of this fiction, and the amount of what she considered to be immoral sex.

My friend, knowing the visiting professor to be a person of both intelligence and integrity, urged the student to go and talk with him about these concerns.

"Oh, I couldn't do that," the student said. "He isn't a Christian."

"He" is a Roman Catholic.

If we fall into Satan's trap of assuming that other people are not Christians because they do not belong to our own particular brand of Christianity, no wonder we become incapable of understanding the works of art produced by so-called non-Christians, whether they be atheists, Jews, Buddhists, or anything else outside a frame of reference we have made into a closed rather than an open door.

If I cannot see evidence of incarnation in a painting of a bridge in the rain by Hokusai,[26] a book by Chaim Potok[27] or Isaac Bashevis Singer,[28] in music by Bloch[29] or Bernstein,[30] then I will miss its significance in an Annunciation by Franciabigio,[31] the final chorus of the St. Matthew Passion, the words of a sermon by John Donne.[32]

One of the most profoundly moving moments at Ayia Napa came for me when Jesse, a student from Zimbabwe, told me, "I am a good Seventh Day Adventist, but you have shown me God." Jesse will continue to be a good Seventh Day Adventist as he returns to Africa to his family; I will struggle with my own way of belief; neither of us felt the need or desire to change the other's Christian frame of reference. For that moment, at least, all our doors and windows were wide open; we were not carefully shutting out God's purifying light, in order to feel safe and secure; we were bathed in the same light that burned and yet did not consume the bush. We walked barefoot on holy ground.

I happen to love spinach, but my husband, Hugh, does not; he prefers beets, which I don't much care for—except the greens. Neither of us thinks less of the other because of this difference in taste. Both spinach and beets are vegetables; both are good for us. We do not have to enjoy precisely the same form of balanced meal.

We also approach God in rather different ways, but it is the same God we are seeking, just as Jesse and I, in our totally different disciplines, worship the same Lord.

Stories, no matter how simple, can be vehicles of truth; can be, in fact, icons. It's no coincidence that Jesus taught almost entirely by telling stories, simple stories dealing with the stuff of life familiar to the Jews of his day. Stories are able to help us to become more whole, to become Named. And Naming is one of the impulses behind all art; to give a name to the cosmos we see despite all the chaos.

God asked Adam to name all the animals, which was asking Adam to help in the creation of their wholeness. When we name each other, we are sharing in the joy and privilege of incarnation, and all great works of art are icons of Naming.

When we look at a painting, or hear a symphony, or read a book, and feel more Named, then, for us, that work is a work of Christian art. But to look at a work of art and then to make a judgment as to whether or not it is art, and whether or not it is Christian, is presumptuous. It is something we cannot know in any conclusive way. We can know only if it speaks within our own hearts, and leads us to living more deeply with Christ in God.

One of my professors, Dr. Caroline Gordon, a deeply Christian woman, told our class, "We do not judge great art. It judges us." And that very judgment may enable us to change our lives, and to renew our commitment to the Lord of Creation.

But how difficult it is for us not to judge; to make what, in current jargon, is called "a value judgment!" And here we blunder into paradox again. Jesus said, "Judge not, that you be not judged!" And yet daily we must make decisions which involve judgments:

We had peanut butter sandwiches yesterday because they are Tod's favourites. Today it's Sarah's turn and we'll have bologna with lots of mustard.

I will not let my child take this book of fairy tales out of the library because fairy tales are untrue.

I will share these wonderful fairy tales with my child because they are vehicles of hidden truths.

I will not talk with the Roman Catholic professor lest he make me less Christian than I think I am.

I will not talk to the Jewish scientist in the next apartment or Hitler and the Storm Troopers[33] might send me to a concentration camp.

I will not read this book because it might shake my belief in the answers I am so comfortable with.

Zeal for thine house hath eaten me up.

But Bertrand Russell[34] says, "Zeal is a bad mark for a cause. Nobody has any zeal about arithmetic. It is not the vaccinationists but the antivaccinationists who generate zeal. People are zealous for a cause when they are not quite positive that it is true."

It is hard for us to believe now that there were antivaccinationists, when vaccinations have succeeded in wiping small-pox from the planet. It is hard for us to believe that Dr. Semmelweis[35] was almost torn to pieces when he suggested that physicians should wash their hands before delivering babies, in order to help prevent the septicemia or puerperal fever which killed so many women after childbirth. It is hard for us to believe that Bach was considered heretical when he put the thumb under instead of over the fingers on the keyboard. It is hard for us to believe that Shakespeare was considered a trivial playwright because he was too popular. But great negative zeal was expended in all of these cases.

We all tend to make zealous judgments, and thereby close ourselves off from revelation. If we feel that we already know something in its totality, then we fail to keep our ears and eyes open to that which may expand or even change that which we so zealously think we know.

My non-Christian friends and acquaintances are zealous in what they "know" about Christianity, and which bears little or no relationship to anything I believe.

A friend of mine, Betty Beckwith, in her book, *If I Had the Wings of the Morning*, writes about taking her brain-damaged child to a Jewish doctor. He said, "You people think of us as the people who killed your Christ." Spontaneously she replied, "Oh, no. We think of you as the people who gave him to us."

In the literary world today, Christianity has pretty well replaced sex as the present pet taboo, not only because Christianity is so often distorted by Christians as well as non-Christians, but because it is too wild and free for the timid.

How many of us really want life, life more abundant, life which does not promise any fringe benefits or early retirement plans? Life which does not promise the absence of pain, or love which is not vulnerable and open to hurt? The number of people who attempt to withdraw from life through the abuse of alcohol, tranquilizers, barbiturates, is statistically shocking.

How many of us dare to open ourselves to that truth which would make us free? Free to talk to Roman Catholics or charismatics or Jews, as Jesus was free to talk to tax collectors or publicans or

Samaritans. Free to feast at the Lord's table with those whose understanding of the Body and Blood may be a little different from ours. Free to listen to angels. Free to run across the lake when we are called.

What is a true icon of God to one person may be blasphemy to another. And it is not possible for us flawed human beings to make absolute, zealous judgments as to what is and what is not religious art. I know what is religious art for me. You know what is religious art for you. And they are not necessarily the same. Not everybody feels pulled up to heavenly heights in listening to the pellucid, mathematically precise structure of a Bach fugue. The smarmy picture of Jesus which I find nauseating may be for someone else, a true icon.

Another problem about identifying what is and what is not religious art, is that religious art transcends its culture and reflects the eternal, and while we are alive we are caught within our culture. All artists reflect the time in which they live, but whether or not their work also has that universality which lives in any generation or culture is nothing we can know for many years. Also, art which is truly iconographic for one period may have little to say to another. My parents, who were in their thirties at the time of the First World War, loved Romantic[36] music, Chopin,[37] Wagner[38]—how they loved Wagner! But Wagner has little to say to me. The reasonable, peaceful world in which my parents grew up, the world which was far too civilized for war, was broken forever by the horror of World War I. My father went to fight in the war to end war, and for the rest of his life he had to live with the knowledge that not only had his war not ended war, it was the beginning of a century of near-total war.

My generation, and my children's, living in this embattled and insane period, find more nourishment in the structure of Bach and Mozart[39] than the lush romanticism of Wagner. Wagner is fine if the world around one is stable. But when the world is, indeed, in chaos, then an affirmation of cosmos becomes essential.

Usually, after the death of a well known artist, there comes a period of eclipse of his work. If the artist reflects only his own culture, then his works will die with that culture. But if his works reflect the eternal and universal, they will revive. It's difficult to believe that for several centuries after Shakespeare's death he was virtually unknown. William Green,[40] his contemporary, was considered a better playwright than the too popular Will, who pandered to public taste. But was it pandering? Art should communicate with as many people as pos-

sible, not just with a group of the esoteric elite. And who remembers Green today?

Bach, too, was eclipsed, and remembered as a good church organist rather than a composer, and for a long time that putting of the thumb under the fingers was held against him; no wonder the thumb had been very little used in keyboard music until Bach came along with this "radical" departure from custom.

Bach might have been forgotten forever had not Mendelssohn[41] discovered some monks wrapping parcels in music manuscript—and gave the St. Matthew Passion back to the world.

The St. Matthew Passion is an icon of the highest quality for me, an open door into the realm of the numinous. Bach, of course, was a man of deep and profound religious faith, a faith which shines through his most secular music. As a matter of fact, the melody of his moving chorale, *O sacred head now wounded,* was the melody of a popular street song of the day, but Bach's religious genius was so great that it is now recognized as one of the most superb pieces of religious music ever written.

There is nothing so secular that it cannot be sacred, and that is one of the deepest messages of the Incarnation. ■

Notes

[1] George MacDonald—(1824–1905) Scottish author known especially for his fairy tales

[2] Oedipus—a figure in Greek mythology

[3] David—Michaelangelo's famous marble statue of the psalmist

[4] Aeschylus—(525–456 B.C.) Greek dramatist

[5] Pièta—Michaelangelo's famous statue of Mary holding the lifeless body of Jesus

[6] Ayia Napa—a conference L'Engle attended

[7] Picasso—Pablo Picasso (1881–1973) famous Spanish artist

[8] Francis of Assisi—(1181?–1226) an Italian monk who founded the Order of Franciscans

[9] Kandinsky—Wassily Kandinsky (1866–1944) considered the father of abstract painting

[10] Van Gogh—Vincent Van Gogh (1853–1890) post-impressionist Dutch painter

[11] widow's mite—See Mark 12:41–44.

[12] St. Matthew Passion—a music composition by J. S. Bach

13 Spanish Inquisition—a tribunal that judged and condemned many people as heretics, primarily during the 1100s–1200s

14 Salem Witch burnings—In the 1690s hundreds of people were brought to trial in Salem, Massachusetts, accused of being witches. Twenty received the death penalty.

15 Unamuno—Miguel de Unamuno (1864–1936) Spanish philosopher and writer

16 Tchekov—Anton Tchekov (1860–1904) Russian writer

17 Rilke—Rainer Maria Rilke (1875–1926) German poet

18 E. M. Forster—Edward Morgan Forster (1879–1970) English novelist

19 W. H. Auden—Wystan Hugh Auden (1907–1973) English poet and dramatist

20 Jane Austen, George Sand, Flaubert, Hemingway—writers: Jane Austen (1775–1817) English novelist; George Sand (1804–1876) French writer; Gustav Flaubert (1821–1880) French novelist; Ernest Hemingway (1899–1961) American writer

21 Solzhenytzin—Alexander Solzhenitsyn (b. 1918) Russian author

22 Tolstoy—Count Leo Tolstoy (1824–1910) Russian novelist

23 Dostoyevsky—Fyodor Dostoyevsky (1821–1881) Russian novelist

24 Dante—Dante Alighieri (1265–1321) Italian poet

25 *Wrinkle*—Madeleine L'Engle's book *A Wrinkle in Time*

26 Hokusai—(1760–1849) Japanese painter and wood engraver who influenced the Impressionists

27 Chaim Potok—(b. 1929) Jewish-American novelist

28 Isaac Bashevis Singer—(b. 1904) Jewish-American writer

29 Bloch—Ernest Bloch (1880–1959) Swiss-born American composer

30 Bernstein—Leonard Bernstein (1918–1990) American composer, conductor, and musician

31 Franciabigio—Italian Renaissance painter who followed the style of Michelangelo

32 John Donne—(1571–1631) English metaphysical poet

33 Storm Troopers—a sub-group of Hitler's military forces

34 Bertrand Russell—(1872–1970) English philosopher and mathematician

35 Dr. Semmelweis—Ignaz Philipp Semmelweis (1818–1865) Hungarian doctor who first used antiseptic methods

36 Romantic music—nineteenth-century style of music that emphasizes emotion and personal feelings

37 Chopin—Frédéric Chopin (1810–1849) composer and pianist

38 Wagner—Richard Wagner (1813–1883) German composer, author, and conductor

39 Mozart—Wolfgang Amadeus Mozart (1756–1791) Austrian composer

40 William Green—playwright and contemporary of Shakespeare

41 Mendelssohn—Felix Mendelssohn (1809–1847) German pianist, and composer

Making Connections through Discussion and Writing

1. a. L'Engle makes some unusual assertions in her opening reflections. Paraphrase her first two paragraphs.

   _____
   _____
   _____
   _____
   _____
   _____

   _____
   _____
   _____
   _____
   _____
   _____

   b. Do you agree that art cannot be categorized as "sacred" or "secular" because "all true art is incarnational, and therefore 'religious'"? Explain your answer.

   _____
   _____
   _____
   _____

   c. In what sense, or at what level, might this be true?

   _____
   _____
   _____
   _____

2. a. Use marginal notations to divide the essay into sections.

   b. List L'Engle's main points below, summarizing them in your own words.

   _____
   _____
   _____
   _____
   _____
   _____
   _____
   _____
   _____

3. a. How does L'Engle distinguish between a "symbol" and a "sign"?

    _____

    _____

    _____

    _____

    b. Which does she believe to be an "icon"?

    _____

    _____

    c. Find an example of a traditional religious icon from the Eastern Orthodox tradition. (You may need to look in an art history book or an encyclopedia for this.) Compare it with a religious painting from the Renaissance or later. What are the different qualities or characteristics of each?

    religious icon   religious painting

    _____   _____

    _____   _____

    _____   _____

    _____   _____

    _____   _____

    _____   _____

    _____   _____

    d. Discuss how she sees these iconic qualities functioning in art.

    _____

    _____

    _____

    _____

4. a. L'Engle quotes Timothy Kallistos as saying, "[T]here is 'something divine' about the work of a non-believing artist." What does he mean by this?

    _____

    _____

    _____

    b. How do you respond to this idea? Provide sound support for your answer.

    _____

    _____

    _____

    _____

5. L'Engle quotes Dr. Caroline Gordon: "We do not judge great art. It judges us."
    a. What does she mean by this?

    _____

    _____

b.   What are some examples of art that has judged you?

_____

_____

c.   In what way did judgment happen?

_____

_____

d.   How did you respond to it?

_____

_____

6. a.   Underline L'Engle's allusions to specific thinkers, writers, or other kinds of artists.

b.   List examples of the works of some of these people.

_____

_____

_____

_____

c.   How does L'Engle react to the artist and his or her work?

_____

_____

_____

_____

_____

7. a.   What, for L'Engle, is so important about the ability to choose?

_____

_____

_____

b.   Think of ways human beings are limited in their free will and thereby hindered in their growth as persons. Suggest some specific ways that religious faith can either promote or discourage freedom.

_____

_____

_____

_____

_____

_____

8. Comment on the paradox L'Engle sees concerning an author's desire to be known and read and her sense of "longing for anonymity."

_____

_____

_____

_____

_____

_____

9. a. L'Engle concludes this essay with the statement, "There is nothing so secular that it cannot be sacred, and that is one of the deepest messages of the Incarnation." Explain what she means by this.

_____

_____

_____

_____

   b. How does she tie this into the Incarnation?

_____

_____

   c. Examine some artistic work from contemporary culture—a movie, a book, a popular song. How can you approach it in such a way as to reveal its sacred dimension by relating it to the doctrine of the Incarnation?

_____

_____

_____

_____

_____

_____

_____

10. Consider and write briefly on how the doctrine of God's creating the universe affirms human creativity.

_____

_____

_____

_____

_____

_____

_____

_____

_____

_____

_____

_____

_____

Richard Wilbur

A Baroque Wall-Fountain in the Villa Sciarra[1]

Richard Wilbur (b. 1921), an American poet whose carefully crafted poetry, which usually contains rhyme and regular meter, is known for its use of reason as a framework to discuss the meaning of life experiences. He has been influenced by the metaphysical poets, especially Andrew Marvell, and by Wallace Stevens. His books of poetry include *The Beautiful Changes* (1947); *Things of This World* (1956), a book that won a Pulitzer Prize; *The Poems of Richard Wilbur* (1963); *Walking to Sleep: New Poems and Translations* (1969); and *The Mind-Reader* (1976). He is also known for his elegant translations of French drama. Wilbur contrasts two Roman fountains in this meditative poem, using their differences to suggest two contrasting attitudes toward human life. The poem may be read as the speaker's interior argument, an argument that is resolved only through insights achieved in the process of the poem itself. It is a good example of Robert Frost's description of a poem as an act of discovery in his essay "The Figure a Poem Makes."

Vocabulary . . . .

addling	reproving
cavorting	reticulum
clambering	scrim
cockle	trefoil
insatiety	

Under the bronze crown
Too big for the head of the stone cherub whose feet
A serpent has begun to eat,
Sweet water brims a cockle and braids down

Past scattered mosses, breaks
On the tipped edge of a second shell, and fills
The massive third below. It spills
In threads then from the scalloped rim, and makes

A scrim or summery tent
For a faun-ménage[2] and their familiar goose.
Happy in all that ragged, loose
Collapse of water, its effortless descent

And flatteries of spray,
The stocky god upholds the shell with ease,
Watching, about his shaggy knees,
The goatish innocence of his babes at play;

His fauness all the while
Leans forward, slightly, into a clambering mesh
Of water-lights, her sparkling flesh
In a saecular[3] ecstasy, her blinded smile

Bent on the sand floor
Of the trefoil pool, where ripple-shadows come
And go in swift reticulum,
More addling to the eye than wine, and more

Interminable to thought
Than pleasure's calculus. Yet since this all
Is pleasure, flash, and waterfall,
Must it not be too simple? Are we not

change in thought

More intricately expressed
In the plain fountains that Maderna set
Before St. Peter's[4]—the main jet
Struggling aloft until it seems at rest

In the act of rising, until
The very wish of water is reversed,
That heaviness borne up to burst
In a clear, high, cavorting head, to fill

With blaze, and then in gauze
Delays, in a gnatlike shimmering, in a fine
Illumined version of itself, decline,
And patter on the stones its own applause?

If that is what men are
Or should be, if those water-saints display
The pattern of our aretè,[5]
What of these showered fauns in their bizarre,

Spangled, and plunging house?
They are at rest in fulness of desire
For what is given, they do not tire
Of the smart of the sun, the pleasant water-douse

And riddled pool below,
Reproving our disgust and our ennui[6]
With humble insatiety.
Francis,[7] perhaps, who lay in sister snow

Before the wealthy gate
Freezing and praising, might have seen in this
No trifle, but a shade of bliss[8]—
That land of tolerable flowers, that state

closest thing to heaven

As near and far as grass
Where eyes become the sunlight, and the hand
Is worthy of water: the dreamt land
Toward which all hungers leap, all pleasures pass. ■

infinite

Everyone deserves life

windows to the soul

toward the dreamt land

Notes

1. baroque—a period (late sixteenth century through the first of the eighteenth century) in European art and music. The style is ornate, grandiose, and freer than the symmetrical style of the Renaissance, which preceded the baroque period.

2. faun-ménage—a group of fauns

3. saecular—age-old, ancient

4. Maderna set / Before St. Peter's—Carlo Maderno, an artist, created the central facade on St. Peter's basilica in Rome.

5. aretè—(Greek) excellence, quality

6. ennui—(French) boredom

7. Francis—St. Francis of Assisi, whose love of God's creatures prompted him to refer to them in terms of brotherly relationship

8. According to the *Oxford English Dictionary* (the OED), "bliss" means "the place of bliss, paradise, heaven." This meaning was first noted in English in 971 A.D.

Making Connections through Discussion and Writing

1. Wilbur, like Hopkins in "The Caged Skylark," uses physical things to suggest more abstract qualities about humans and their ultimate destinies. Here the two fountains symbolize two ways of describing what humans seek as meaningful fulfillment of their lives. Paraphrase the poem by putting it in paragraph form (not poetry) in your own words. Be careful to stay with the literal level; that is, do not provide symbolic meaning or evaluation in your paraphrase.

    _____
    _____
    _____
    _____
    _____
    _____
    _____
    _____
    _____
    _____
    _____

2. List the physical details of the two fountains as they are described by the poet, then draw a sketch of them. Compare your sketch of the baroque fountain to the frontispiece photograph of this fountain.

    _____   _____
    _____   _____
    _____   _____
    _____   _____
    _____   _____
    _____   _____
    _____   _____
    _____   _____

3. a. Note the transitions in the poem by drawing a line where the poet's attention shifts from one fountain to another and where his description shifts to reflection.

    b. Why does he ask if the baroque fountain may not be "too simple"?

    _____
    _____
    _____
    _____

c. Why does he think the fountains in front of St. Peter's Cathedral might be better emblems of human life?

_____

_____

_____

d. What human qualities do these latter fountains suggest?

_____

_____

_____

4. a. Circle the line in the tenth stanza that suggests the plain fountain may represent not only human striving, but also a kind of spiritual pride.

b. How does this prepare for the movement back to a further meditation on the baroque fountain?

_____

_____

_____

_____

5. a. Natural appetites (for example, the need for food and drink) are soon satisfied. If one eats or drinks beyond the point of being content, a disgust or sickness may result. With this in mind, explain the poet's observation that the baroque fauns, who "are at rest in fullness of desire / For what is given," reprove "our disgust and our ennui / With humble insatiety."

_____

_____

_____

b. If they are continually filled with that which they continually long for, how do they represent a condition that humans cannot now share?

_____

_____

_____

c. In what way is their "insatiety" a reproof to us?

_____

_____

_____

_____

6. The mention of St. Francis of Assisi, the patron saint of Italy and one of the most revered figures of Christian history, provides an authoritative note of interpretation to bring the narrator's musings to a close. What does the narrator suggest that Francis might have seen in the baroque fountain?

_____

_____

_____

_____

_____

_____

7. Explain what you think the narrator is referring to when he speaks of "a shade of bliss," "That land," "that state," "the dreamt land" toward which "all hungers leap," "all pleasures pass."

_____

_____

_____

_____

8. Do you think the last line of the poem incorporates images that suggest a synthesis of the meanings Wilbur finds in both the baroque fountain and the plain fountains before St. Peter's? Explain your answer.

_____

_____

_____

_____

_____

_____

Synthesis/Essay Suggestions: Christian Aesthetics

1. Wendell Berry, in his address "Christianity and the Survival of Creation" (in Part Two of this book), and Flannery O'Connor, in "Novelist and Believer," expand on Madeleine L'Engle's idea of great art being beyond the personality of the artist—of art having a kind of "anonymity"—by their emphasis that the purpose of art is not merely "self-expression." Berry states, "The great artistic traditions have had nothing to do with what we call 'self-expression.'" O'Connor says, "The novelist doesn't write to express himself." Write an essay explaining what these authors believe the purpose of art is, giving examples of specific works that fulfill this purpose. Note how the art of one who believes its purpose is to express the self might differ from the art of one who seeks, in Flannery O'Connor's words, to render a vision he believes to be true "so that it can be transferred, as nearly whole as possible, to his reader."

2. According to some of the authors in this textbook, the act of the artist is very much connected with key doctrines of the Church: the Trinity, Incarnation, Creation, and Resurrection. Examining the excerpt from "On Fairy Stories" by J. R. R. Tolkien and the essays "Novelist and Believer" by Flannery O'Connor and "Towards a Christian Aesthetic" by Dorothy Sayers, explain how the pertinent doctrines illuminate their understanding of art and the artist. Especially note how the creative urge both emanates from and points back to God. Why are these ideas important? How does understanding these ideas help the artist and the observer alike appreciate the value of all true art? After analyzing these works and answering the above questions, compose an essay formulating your own aesthetic by which you can evaluate art.

3. Madeleine L'Engle asserts that any art that speaks truly of the human condition—that makes one feel affirmed or "named"—can be considered "Christian art." Flannery O'Connor, on the other hand, states that while human emotions are universal subjects of art, an artist's belief does affect his or her work, for the emotion portrayed must be placed within a moral context. The artist must decide whether the emotion is "adequate or inadequate, whether it is moral or immoral, whether it is good or evil." "And his theology," she says, " . . . will have a direct bearing on this." Distinguish the differences between these two views, explaining them and giving examples of literature that you think supports each view. Compose your own statement about the role of the artist's theological beliefs in shaping his or her art, synthesizing the views of O'Connor and L'Engle.

Chapter 10

Myth, Fairy Tale, and the Moral Imagination

The imagination is the gift that has been given to human beings in order to open the scrim that separates the seen and the unseen. Once the curtain is lifted, we realize that we have been participants in the play all along and that we have been too afraid or too ignorant to remove the masks that we were wearing and to see what we have never seen before. As the writers in this chapter illustrate, it is through the imagination that we discover new realms by realizing that our own world is filled with the wonder of words and the power of images. Imagination gives us wings so we may soar into the ordinary plane of our existence and find there beauty and majesty, which then impel us toward the far-off country, the land where elves and fairies and angels and gods dwell.

Unfortunately, for some reason (and we fear for all the wrong ones) Christians have often resisted or even condemned the imagination. They have rejected myth and do not realize, according to C. S. Lewis in "Myth Became Fact," "The heart of Christianity is a myth which is also a fact. The old myth of the Dying God without ceasing to be myth, comes down from the heaven of legend and imagination to the earth of history. . . . By becoming fact it does not cease to be myth: that is the miracle." Somehow, as Clyde S. Kilby in "Christian Imagination" reminds us, "Christians often turn out to have an unenviable corner on the unimaginative and the commonplace." Here lies the rub: by becoming less imaginative, we in some way lose a part of the depth of our Christianity. Lewis continues, "We must not, in false spirituality, withhold our imaginative welcome. If God chose to be mythopoeic—and is not the sky itself a myth—shall we refuse to be mythopathic?" In "Myth: A Flight to Reality," Thomas Howard notes that high myth is still celebrated in the Church even though she often fails to acknowledge it, "for we still sing Kyrie and Gloria and Sanctus, and break bread and pour wine, and call them the body and blood of God."

Sin has entered the imagination, and only as it is redeemed can humans truly see. Kilby notes,

> The fall of man can hardly be more forcefully felt than simply in noting what we all do with a fresh snowfall or the first buds of spring. On Monday, they fill us with delight and meaning, and on Tuesdays we ignore them. No amount of shouting to us that this is all wrong changes the fact for very long. . . . Only some esthetic power akin to God's own creativity has the capability for renewal, for giving us the power to see.

This "power akin to God's own creativity" has been described by J. R. R. Tolkien in "On Fairy Stories" as subcreation. He believes that human beings need to participate in "the land of fairy-story" as he did; he asks that his readers "receive my withered leaves, as a token that my hand at least once held a little of the gold." Through the inspiration of the Creator and the raw materials of the primary world, the subcreator is able to create a world that contains an "inner consistency of reality" and "may be a far-off gleam or echo of evangelium [good news] in the real world." He contends that "in Fantasy he [the Christian] may actually assist in the effoliation and multiple enrichment of creation." Tolkien's story "Leaf by Niggle" is his illustration of this statement, for Niggle, who is "a painter by nature," only seems to catch glimpses of the tree and the leaves that he desires to paint while he is in this realm, yet at the end of the tale when he has journeyed to the mountains, Niggle discovers that his gift has made the kingdom of Heaven richer for himself and for others.

Fairy tales are also important because they shape the imagination and depict virtue. Walter Wangerin, Jr., in "Flying the Night Wind," writes, "Fairy tales shaped me." He continues, "Children meet the problems of the world with their imagination, and the fairy tale honors and feeds and abets the imagination. As a child, I never analyzed the tale I read; I felt it; I sank inside of it; I lived its experience through to the happy conclusion." Fairy tales also inculcate moral values. Vigen Guroian in his essay "Awakening the Moral Imagination" asserts, "In these stories the virtues glimmer as if in a looking glass, and wickedness and deception are unmasked of their pretensions to goodness and truth. These stories make us face the unvarnished truth about ourselves while compelling us to consider what kind of people we want to be." Fairy tales should never be feared by a Christian; they should be embraced. G. K. Chesterton in "Dragooning the Dragon" tells us the reason: "The child learns without being taught that life contains some element of enmity. His own dreams would provide him with dragons; what the legend provides is St. George."

Clyde S. Kilby

The Christian Imagination

Born in Johnson City, Tennessee, son of a carpenter and educated at the University of Arkansas, University of Minnesota, and New York University where he received his Ph.D. in 1931, Clyde S. Kilby (1902–1986) taught at Wheaton College for more than forty years, serving as chair of the English Department from 1951–1966. He was a Presbyterian and is probably most famous for his work with the Oxford Christians. He became the curator of the Marion E. Wade Center, which contains one of the finest collections of the letters and works of George MacDonald, C. S. Lewis, J. R. R. Tolkien, Charles Williams, G. K. Chesterton, Dorothy Sayers, and Owen Barfield. He is best known as an expert on the writings of C. S. Lewis and J. R. R. Tolkien, and some of his works include *The Christian World of C. S. Lewis, Images of Salvation in the Fiction of C. S. Lewis*, and *Tolkien and the Silmarillion*. In the essay below, Kilby laments the lack of imagination among some segments of Christendom, particularly evangelicals, and yearns for this to change. He asserts, "Only some esthetic power akin to God's own creativity has the capability for renewal, for giving us the power to see."

The Bible: A Work of the Imagination

I want to base what I have to say on three facts which I think indisputable.

The first is that the Bible belongs to literature; that is, it is a piece of art. Does it make any difference that the Book we look upon as holy comes to us in literary form rather than in the form of abstract doctrine or systematic theology? Is the poetry of the Bible a fact plus an artistic decoration? If we summarize the Twenty-third Psalm to declare that God cares for his children as a good shepherd cares for his sheep, do the poetry and the prose summary amount to the same thing? If so, why the poetry in the first place? What change takes place when a piece of poetry is turned into a piece of doctrine or of practical exhortation?

How is the divine inspiration of the Bible related to the great oddity that the longest of the Psalms was written in the form of an acrostic? Was the acrostic form from God or only from the poet? The best authority I know of on the Bible as literature, Richard G. Moulton, points out the large variety of literary forms in the Scripture—epic cycles, orations, dramatic anthems, war anthems, festal hymns, litanies, acrostics, elegies, national anthems, odes, sonnets, epigrams, rhapsodies, vision cycles, encomiums, and so forth. Did God inspire the form or only the content of the Bible? Is its form only a man-made incidental? Should Christian teachers ever encourage students to read the Bible as literature?

Why the "indirection" of saying that a godly man is like a tree planted by the rivers of water, and the extreme exaggeration of saying that the floods and the trees of the fields clap their hands and sing? Are such expressions to be dismissed as mere adornments, embroidery, as feathers—perhaps very pretty ones—that are to be removed from the turkey before its caloric and real meaning can come into existence?

Why isn't the Bible plain, expository, concrete? Why those numerous and difficult paradoxes flung at the reader, such as Jeremiah 17:9—"The heart is deceitful above all things, and desperately wicked," and Romans 10:10—"With the heart man believeth unto righteousness"? Why the oddity of Paul's prayer in Ephesians 3:19, that Christians may know the love of Christ, which *passeth knowledge,* or of Hebrews 4:11, "*Labour* . . . to enter into . . . *rest,*" and the frequent wordplay even in our Lord's own language? All of which suggests the literary quality of the Bible.

The second indisputable fact is that, because one—and possibly the greatest—ingredient of literature is imagination, we must say that the Bible is an imaginative book. There is no literature without imagination—strong, honest, often daring imagination.

God, the Imaginer

The third indisputable fact is that the greatest artist of all, the greatest imaginer of all, is the one who appears at the opening of Genesis. Esthetics has to do with form, design, harmony, beauty. Perhaps the key word is "form." Now the earth, says Genesis, was without form. God shaped the creation into form—light and darkness, the heavens, the teeming waters, the multitudinous fauna and flora. He shaped birds and roses and morning glories and dandelions, the hippo and the alligator, the mammoth and the giraffe, and man in his own image. And we are told that he looked upon each thing he had shaped and saw that it was good. The whole he saw to be "*very* good." Even after the fall of man the Bible treats nature as beautiful, with God as its maker and wielder. Job, the Psalms and numerous other books celebrate—perhaps to a point a bit scary to some Christians—the intimate relationship of God and his creation. God did not, as so many of us, think that the esthetic was an incidental for leisure time.

And we can also add that God is an architect. The Scripture tells us in no uncertain detail that God put his spirit into the workmen who built Solomon's temple and that it required seventy thousand men to bear burdens and eighty thousand to hew timbers in the mountains, with thirty-three hundred supervisors, over a period of seven years. It is altogether proper, I think, to imagine God telling Solomon how to carve the magnificent lilies to go at the top of the great columns. More glorious still is the final fulfillment God promises in Ephesians 1 where he says (Phillips' translation): "He purposes in his sovereign will that all human history shall be consummated in Christ, that everything that exists in Heaven or earth shall find its perfection and fulfillment in him." No greater esthetic consummation is possible.

The Failure of Imagination in Evangelical Christianity

Now when we look from these three facts to contemporary evangelical Christianity we find a great oddity. The people who spend the most time with the Bible are in large numbers the "foes" of art and the sworn foes of imagination. And I grow in the feeling that these people have quite an astonishing indifference to the created world. Evangelicals hear the great "I am" of God but they are far less aware of the "I am" of his handiwork.

Furthermore, when evangelicals dare attempt any art form it is generally done badly.

As to the evangelical's skittishness toward imagination, I have looked into the Scriptures and I cannot find such a prejudice there. One prominent evangelical holds that the triad of truth-goodness-beauty is Greek in origin and the Hebrew concept is only that of the true and the holy. I doubt it. I doubt it primarily because of the glorious beauty I see every day in God's handiwork, but I also doubt it from looking at Scripture. The Revised Standard Version shows ninety uses of the words *beauteous, beautiful, beautify* and *beauty* (the King James Version uses seventy-six of these words), and overwhelmingly in a favorable sense. I see no esthetic difference between God's word and his creative work. Even if his world were purely a functional one, the bee and the flower around which it buzzes would be equally glorious, equally fantastic, equally miraculous.

How can it be that with a God who created birds and the blue of the sky, and who before the foundation of the world wrought out a salvation more romantic than Cinderella, with a Christ who encompasses the highest heaven and deepest hell, with the very hairs of our heads numbered, with God closer than hands and feet, Christians often turn out to have an unenviable corner on the unimaginative and the commonplace?

God shamelessly flings out the rainbow, but some Christians paint the bumpers of their autos black or shun attractive clothing, apparently on the ground that whatever is shiny is sinful. An evangelical sees a picture of a mission board and writes a warning against the worldliness that is creeping in because some of the members have handkerchiefs tucked in their coat pockets. Yet when the Lord talks of espousing Israel (Ezekiel 16:10ff.), he says, "I clothed you also with embroidered cloth . . . I swathed you in fine linen and covered you with silk. And I decked you with ornaments, and put bracelets on your arms, and a chain on your neck. And I put . . . earrings in your ears, and a beautiful crown upon your head. . . . You were decked with gold and silver; and your raiment was of fine linen, and silk, and embroidered cloth."

Evangelical Christians have had one of the purest of motives and one of the worst of outcomes. The motive is never to mislead by the smallest fraction of an iota in the precise nature of salvation, to live it and state it in its utter purity. But the unhappy outcome has too often been to elevate the cliché. The motive is that the gospel shall not be misunderstood, not sullied, not changed in jot or tittle. The outcome has often been merely the reactionary, static and hackneyed.

Take evangelical poetry as an example. Some

years ago I sent an inquiry to Christian editors. The all but unanimous response was that they published little or no poetry because what they received was simply trash. The same is more or less true of all our other creative efforts. I had given up the hope of ever seeing an evangelical novel that had any artistic merit when I came upon Olov Hartman's *The Holy Masquerade*.[1] When I began to praise it, someone asked me if the author really was an evangelical! I don't know.

But to come a little closer to home, it appears that the cliche has marked the evangelical's creative efforts because it first marked his thought and life. C. S. Lewis talks about the child who on Easter morning was heard whispering to himself, "Chocolate eggs and Jesus risen." In our desperate evangelical desire for a clear, logical depiction of Jesus risen we have tended to remove the chocolate eggs. P. T. Forsyth describes the glory and expectation that permeated early Christianity when, as he says: "Life received a horizon in place of a boundary. The Christian Faith introduced the witness of the true Infinite, not a mere mathematical infinity or extension, nor a dynamical infinity of energy, but the Infinite of spiritual thought, passion, purpose, and power—the thought and purpose of God, the passion of his holy redeeming love, and the power of the Holy Ghost."

For this expectant and viable Christianity we have somehow come to elevate the trite and the static as our rule. Our efforts to keep the Gospel pure and the way of salvation clear have led us almost exclusively to the expository, frontal, exegetical, functional and prosaic. We want the Word of God and everything pertaining to Christianity to be as simple as two times two, yet over against this stands the Bible itself as example, I believe, of another sort of thing.

There is a simplicity which diminishes and a simplicity which enlarges, and evangelicals have too often chosen the wrong one. The first is that of the cliché—simplicity with mind and heart removed. The other is that of art. The first falsifies by its exclusions, the second encompasses. The first silently denies the multiplicity and grandeur of creation, salvation and indeed all things. The second symbolizes and celebrates them. The first tries to take the danger out of Christianity and with the danger often removes the actuality. The second suggests the creative and sovereign God of the universe with whom there are no impossibilities. The contrast suggests that *not* to imagine is what is sinful. The symbol, the figure, the image, the parable—in short, the artistic method—so pungent in the Lord's teaching and acting, are often notewor-

thy for their absence in ours. Is this not a case of humanism far more reprehensible than the sort of humanism we often decry?

In an article discussing religious writing, Sydney Harris told of seeing in *The Saturday Evening Post* a cartoon of a boy sitting at the piano. The boy's father was wincing and saying to the mother, "He's trustworthy, loyal, helpful, and friendly . . . and untalented." Harris says the religious manuscripts he receives are the most painful ones he looks at and that ninety-nine out of one hundred religious books are useless. And what applies to our writing very often also marks our whole way of life. One very wrong thing we have done is to see the unsaved as objects, something destitute not only of salvation but of any worthy thoughts about God. An adequate imagination would have saved us from the mistake of turning men into things.

Even the pulpit, or so it seems to me, is often marked by a strange negativism. I have known at least one devoted pastor who stated that he would never use an illustration other than those in the Scriptures. Did Christ ever by the least hint suggest any such method? Did he ever suggest that he meant to exhaust the parabolic and the illustrative? Did Christ not instead confirm the Arabian adage that the best teacher is the one who can change men's ears to eyes? Much of the preaching I have heard, though it faithfully repeats the Christian message, bears little resemblance to that of Christ. Phillips' translation of Mark 11:19 says that Christ's teaching had "captured the imagination of the people." I seldom have such an experience from the sermons I hear. I get the impression that Christ's parables generally developed from a quick look at whatever object was at hand—bushel measures, a house with a shaky foundation, dowry coins worn by a woman, sheep, a common flower. It seems to me no less astonishing how little of this sort of thing rubs off on men in our evangelical seminaries.

Pastors seem beset with the conviction that statement is the only correct way. I am starkly admonished, for instance, to love, as though I did not know this fully as well as the preacher, as though I had not already beaten myself a thousand times with this cudgel. What I need instead is the opening of some little door through which I can enter, some little path through the tangle of my own selfishness, some glimpse of a person who practiced love last week. But what is the use of repeating to me, as though my soul were blind, what my conscience and the Holy Spirit habitually tell me?

Learning to Live Imaginatively

One critic said that Robert Frost was good as a poet because he thought of himself as a farmer and that, had he ever once called himself a poet, he would at that moment have become a literary shoemaker. The phrase "esthetic distance" means that the human attitude must prevail over the professional one. We need esthetic distance in our Christian way of life. St. Paul tells us to be instant in season and out of season, but he also tells us to be anxious in nothing. Our excuse for our esthetic failure has often been that we must be about the Lord's business, the assumption being that the Lord's business is never esthetic.

We must not take something infinitely large, glorious and precious and, even unintentionally, diminish it to what is small, fixed and patent. As evangelicals we wish never to misrepresent God and salvation. Yet some of us have developed an ear as big as a barn door in our practice of pitching the coin on the counter and listening not only to its Christian ring but expecting also the tinkle of our own favorite evangelical language. The cliché deadens whatever it touches, however good or great. It is the call to indifference, to the slavery of the commonplace, to nonthought and nonfeeling. Evangelicalism, I believe, is greatly in need of fresh and meaningful imagination.

A great principle of art and esthetics is that of the necessity of renewal. The freshness of being, says Alfred North Whitehead, evaporates under mere repetition; a static value, however good, suffers from claustrophobia. God has created a world with the paradoxical qualities of utter law and utter uniqueness. Orthodox Christians accent the first but almost ignore the second. The fall of man can hardly be more forcefully felt than simply in noting what we all do with a fresh snowfall or the first buds of spring. On Monday they fill us with delight and meaning, and on Tuesday we ignore them. No amount of shouting to us that this is all wrong changes the fact for very long. Detachment and the upside-down view are a constant necessity to circumvent the ruts, the tags, the clichés everywhere awaiting us. Only some esthetic power akin to God's own creativity has the capability for renewal, for giving us the power to see.

Art is a means of renewing our eyes and our hearts. I am not here talking simply about what goes on in the art or music department of a college; I am talking of a way, and I think a God-given way, for us to recognize his voice and his world. All institutions and practices tend to diminish their center and accent their periphery. The genuinely holy act of yesterday is only too easily hypostatized into the act minus the holiness, of today. One of Jonathan Blanchard's favorite phrases was *corruptio optima pessima*—The best thing, when not used in the right way, becomes the most loathsome.

Perhaps our hymns are an example. We mummify them into books and most of us sing them without the least notice of their meaning. John Newton and William Cowper formed an agreement to write a hymn each Sunday night covering their experiences of the previous week. They accepted, as we do not, the exhortation of the psalmist to sing to the Lord a new song.

With this meager mention of the principle of renewal let me go on to another and final principle that I believe we should consider. Perhaps the deepest thrust of the esthetic is toward the expression of being. "Life is a petty thing," says Ortega, "unless it is moved by the indomitable urge to extend its boundaries. Only in proportion as we are desirous of living more do we really live." Artists tell us that the creative process is more of an exploration and a profound learning than it is the production of a canvas or a piece of music. It is an act filled at once with joy and pain.

In the best essay I've ever read on the creative act, Stephen Spender says: "I dread writing poetry . . . a poem is a terrible journey . . . the writing of a poem brings one face to face with one's own personality with all its familiar and clumsy limitations. In every other phase of existence, one can exercise the orthodoxy of a conventional routine. . . . In Poetry, one is wrestling with a god." If our evangelical preaching efforts at creativeness had this quality of search to the point of knowing really who we are, I think a different situation might prevail.

That man and life are almost pure mysteries ought to permeate our constant thoughts. Mark Van Doren says that man is "a nervous animal, straining to comprehend what he contains, straining even to contain it."

I think one implication of this is that we ought to assume that students know more than we estimate they do. Nothing is more destructive in the classroom than telling students what they already know. The same is true for the sermon. Life is never static. It is dynamic.

Keeping orthodox is a high and necessary aim. But one of the best ways, I think, of destroying our orthodoxy is to make "keeping orthodox" an all-encompassing and tight-lipped aim. Orthodoxy is better retained when regarded as a by-product of a far higher aim, the love of God and the expectant search into his truth. ■

Author's Note

1 Olov Hartman, *The Holy Masquerade* (Grand Rapids: Eerdmans, 1964).

Making Connections through Discussion and Writing

1. What are the three "indisputable facts" upon which Kilby bases his argument concerning the imagination?

    _____
    _____
    _____

2. Why does Kilby believe that imagination has failed in evangelical Christianity?

    _____
    _____
    _____

3. a. What does Kilby mean by "a simplicity which diminishes and a simplicity which enlarges"?

    _____
    _____

    b. List the characteristics of each below.

    simplicity that diminishes   simplicity that enlarges

    _____   _____
    _____   _____
    _____   _____
    _____   _____
    _____   _____
    _____   _____
    _____   _____
    _____   _____
    _____   _____
    _____   _____

4. a. How does Kilby define "esthetic distance"?

    _____
    _____
    _____

    b. Explain what he means by this definition.

    _____
    _____
    _____

5. a. What excuse has been given by evangelicals for "esthetic failure"?

_____

_____

   b. What does Kilby mean when he asserts that a renewal needs to take place in esthetics?

_____

_____

_____

_____

6. a. After reading Kilby's essay, define the Christian imagination.

_____

_____

   b. Note below specific weaknesses and strengths that you have observed in the relationship of aesthetics and the Church.

strengths   weaknesses

_____   _____

_____   _____

_____   _____

_____   _____

_____   _____

_____   _____

_____   _____

Thomas Howard
Myth: A Flight to Reality

Thomas Howard (b. 1934) was an English professor at Gordon College and later taught at St. John Seminary (both located in Massachusetts). Brother of the famous missionary and writer Elisabeth Elliott, he was born into an evangelical family. While attending Wheaton College in the 1950s, he joined the Episcopal Church because of his newfound love for liturgical worship. His spiritual pilgrimage continued, and in 1985 he joined the Catholic Church after writing *Evangelical Is Not Enough*. He has authored many books and articles on topics ranging from the arts and the imagination to C. S. Lewis and Christian apologetics. He has written such books as *Christ the Tiger* (1967), *The Achievement of C. S. Lewis* (1980), *C. S. Lewis: Man of Letters* (1987), and *The Novels of Charles Williams* (1991). In the essay below, Howard demonstrates the crucial importance of myth in the life of the individual. In his introduction to this selection, he writes:

> *The crucial question is, What realities do the unlifelike conventions or details of myth express? They include deity, transcendence, glory, heroism, courage, goodness, beauty, and a dozen others. Are these things real? If so, myth is not a flight from reality but to reality. Paradoxically, modern realistic literature, which has exiled the gods and heroes from its world, represents the real flight from reality.*

Vocabulary . . . .

blithely	interdict
contemporaneity	jurisprudence
demur	peremptory
doctrinaire	shards
evanescent	unabashedly
immutable	

Let me begin with the premise that when we speak of "myth" we don't mean something that is untrue. The important thing about myth is not that it involves an event that never occurred on this planet, or out of it for that matter. The stories of Zeus and Odysseus[1] are not myths by virtue of the fact that they didn't happen. On the contrary, they are myths at least partly because they occurred in a realm that is beyond the reach of the geographers' and historians' tools.

The question whether or not they occurred somewhere around a place we know geographically as the Aegean or the Baltic,[2] or so many years before Pericles,[3] is irrelevant. The question about myth is not whether the tales it tells have happened in our history or prehistory. There is probably no one alive today who would insist that they have occurred in that way.

But on the other hand, the people (nearly everybody, in effect) who blithely assume that of course these things didn't happen may be whistling in the dark. How do *they* know? Unless you are a doctrinaire materialist and live in a tiny universe whose limits are determined by microscopes, telescopes, and measurements like 186,000 miles a second, you will always wonder what's going on just outside your lens frame. A Christian, especially, living as he does in a huge universe all

From *The Christian Imagination: Essays on Literature and the Arts* by Thomas Howard, 1981. Reprinted by permission of Baker Book House Company.

ringing with the footfalls of hurrying seraphim, cherubim, archangels, angels, men, and devils, will never be too peremptory concerning what creatures aren't in on the traffic. He can only demur and say, "Elves? I don't know much about them. I've never come across one (worse luck)."

The question about the myth is, rather, How true do they ring? Does such and such a tale or set of tales suppose a world that convinces us by its own integrity, that is, its fidelity, to its own laws? Is the fabric of that world whole and tough? Or is it tattered? Does it hold together by some binding energy that is really at work in it? Or must it be basted together by pins and threads borrowed from some other world?

Perhaps it's here that we come upon the rather elusive clues to what makes myth different from other kinds of tales. We can say that myth represents a world created by the imagination. For one thing, there is a sense in which real myth must be large. You can't have a myth with only one incident, or one or two characters in it. The individual episodes form part of a whole landscape. Myth, moreover, has to do with a whole world, not necessarily a world of any particular geography or chronology. You can have an imagined geography (utopia or Lilliput[4]) and not have what we call real myth. Or you can have our geography (Parnassus or Olympus) and yet have real myth.

What seems to be required is that there be a world, a whole world, that is remote from us and at the same time rooted in our world. We don't want our myths taking place in 1929, or even 1066, nor do we want them to occur in East Lansing or Gary, Indiana. If they did, they would have a distressing tendency to keep draining into the dry sand of history or contemporaneity. But on the other hand, remote and entire in themselves as they must be, we do want them to be in some sense rooted in our world, that is, in our understanding of experience. We don't want them to be crowded or spoiled by the immediate world, but we do want them to ring bells that our ears can hear.

The Meaning of Myth

The whole poetic or artistic or mythic phenomenon that we find when we look at the history of human imagination represents, I think, the search for perfection. Now you can give this perfection a hundred names—truth, beauty, goodness, wholeness, bliss, repose, order, form, the eternal, and so on—depending on what you want to stress at the moment. There's no word in human language that will name it adequately. Let's call it *perfection* here. We all have imaginings of it (some poets would urge that we have memories of it). Perfection hounds us remorselessly. It is what stands over against every experience we have of nostalgia, frustration, and desire. We find sooner or later all the data of our experience to be faulted—our bodies, our minds, our wills, our relationships, our landscapes, our states, our institutions, our programs.

Politics, medicine, ecology, and jurisprudence are our efforts to repair the damage. Most of what we do, starting with brushing our teeth in the morning, would be seen by the angels as a waste of time, since they don't know what it is to be almost wholly occupied with shoring things up. When we've been allowed to take time from our plowing and fighting and brushing our teeth, we have tried to say something about perfection and our experience of the discrepancy that we feel between ourselves and perfection. We want tranquility and we find tumult. We want permanence and we find decay. We want order and we find havoc. We want health and we find sickness. We want strength and we find weakness. We want beauty and we find horror.

But we neither can nor will settle for this state of affairs. We are driven by who knows what—it's the Holy Ghost—to complain about this discrepancy, to oppose it, and to transcend it. We write about our experience, and we sing about it, and we reenact it because we think that somehow if we can stand off from it and get a look at it, we can get a hold of it once more. We signal our awareness of perfection by making something approximating perfection out of our experience—something true, beautiful, good, and incorruptible. Myth is one version of this effort.

Distance and Identity in Myth

I do not think the words *art* and *myth* are synonymous, but perhaps myth stands at the pinnacle of the narrative art. In it you will find more or less perfectly manifested what is implicit in all art: distance from the immediate but identity of substance. Myth stands off from our experience, but it is *about* our experience.

Perhaps a distinction needs to be made here. We should speak of *high myth* when we are talking about those great tales that come out of the Mediterranean and the North, since the loose term *myth* can refer also to the controlling atmosphere or set of ideas or pool of presuppositions that govern an era. The twentieth century, for example, operates within a secularist myth. The Middle Ages operated inside a Christian one. And so forth.

You get in high myth a fairly pure example of what art is about: distance and identity. Perhaps this is why you used to have frames around paintings. Such and such a scene or person or event was "in there," and you, the viewer, had leisure to regard it and contemplate it. You were free from any entanglement. By the same token, when you read one of the older novels you can look *at* the experience being described precisely because you aren't called upon to sort it out. Of course, part of the genius of the whole thing is that you *do* get involved. But it is an involvement that is not cluttered by having to attend to a thousand trifling details. You are free to get a grip on things exactly because you are at a remove from them.

By the same token, if we move the world of myth away from the immediate, out of the twentieth century or the nineteenth or the eighteenth or the tenth, out of our calendar completely, we disengage it from the fuss of our world, and by thus setting it free from our time, we set ourselves free with respect to it. For time may be *the* tragic dimension of human experience. It is the agent and vehicle of change and decay and death. If we can get free from time, we can approach bliss. This is why poetry and the promise of paradise are so attractive to us. They all offer an escape from time. And the escape seems to be an escape *from* the unreal, from the transitory and evanescent, *to* the solid and immutable, that is, the real.

So we need distance, probably both chronological and geographical. We like the formula, "Once upon a time in a far off land." That's the best opening for a story—there's no question about it. For at that point we can settle in. There's no danger of any clutter and intrusion from the immediate world. If we sat down to read a story that began "At eleven o'clock on the morning of Friday, October 16, 1970, in the living room at 210 East Seminary in Wheaton, Illinois, an old crone began to stir her brew," we'd say, "Wait! Stop! It won't work. It's no good." The trouble is that we know that room. It's too defenseless against the postman and plumber and electrician, and we don't want *them* in our midst.

The Fate of Myth in the Modern World

Of course, it will be observed here that most of the writing that engages our attention now is realistic in this way. Isn't *this* art and therefore a form of myth? What about Updike and Saul Bellow and all the fiction that gets published now, to say nothing of cinema and theater? The whole avalanche of contemporary imagery tumbles out of our living rooms and kitchens, and bathrooms and bedrooms. What about all this? Can't things be local and contemporary?

It may be here that we come upon the trouble that the mythmakers and storytellers have nowadays, and indeed the trouble with the whole era. For they have to make their images out of what their world is made of. There has to be some identity of substance between what they make and what we know, so that we can recognize it. And it turns out that the stuff our world is made of won't shape up into high myth. Oh, you can make something out of it—cigarette ashes and tiny situations—but you can't get anything huge and wonderful and breathtaking and beautiful.

Why not? Because the world that gave birth to the high myths—to those huge worlds of story that are remote from us but terrifyingly close—that world has disappeared. It has disappeared under our interdict. For we have decided (sometime in the Renaissance it was and we finished the job in the eighteenth century) to recreate the world. It's a very small one now, limited as it is by microscopes and telescopes and computers, and asphalt parking lots at MacDonald's hamburger stands. And it's a horror. It is, above all, boring, for mystery has fled from it. We have announced to anyone who cares to listen—and somehow one imagines that the angels and elves aren't all that enthralled by the information—that we can explain everything. We know what our forefathers never guessed: that if you take things apart you can explain them and thus master them. And we're dead right. You certainly can master them. The only difficulty is that the thing you've got the mastery of is a pile of pieces all taken apart. We haven't found the spells (since we don't believe in spells) to put them back together again. We're in the position of all the king's men in "Humpty Dumpty."

By the eighteenth century the myth became sovereign that the analytic and rational capacity is absolutely adequate for unscrambling the mystery of the universe. Somewhere in the process the gods fled. The irony is that in the very effort of modern art to disentangle human experience from the transcendent, human experience turned to ashes. In painting and sculpture the focus is on less and less, until indeed there is less there than meets the eye. We are told that we must no longer ask what a work of art *means,* since all that matters is that it is.

The problem of the modern writer is obvious. He can't make bricks without straw. He can't make a rope out of sand. He can't create heroes and evoke courage and nobility and courtesy out of the materials that his world furnishes him. He may feel that what we have now is the truth of the matter.

On the other hand, the modern writer may be unhappy with the way things are. He may, like Francois Mauriac or Flannery O'Connor or Tolkien,[5] think that the time is out of joint, that what we have is most emphatically *not* the way things are, in which case he can try various things. He can try to find tiny pieces in the pile that is left of the world in the twentieth century—pieces which, if put together in a certain way or held up to a certain light, may bring back an old memory that once upon a time it wasn't broken like that. Or, like Flannery O'Connor, the storyteller can hail us, shout at us with frightening images to try to remind us that what we've made is not, in fact, very satisfactory. Or, like Tolkien, the mythmaker can step away from things and hold up for us some unabashedly ancient shapes, since he can find nothing at hand that will suit his purpose. When we have entered Tolkien's remote world we find that it is a true one, and therefore true of ours.

But apart from a few plucky spirits like this, what are the mythmakers giving us? You wonder whether the poets and artists are really fulfilling their ancient office, which is to see further than the rest of us, to see the mysteries and bear witness somehow to what they see in an imagery drawn from our world.

The Necessity of Myth

If we believe that the pile of broken pieces is a late and false creation, and that the world the old bards knew was, in fact, the world where our real life lies, then it must be confessed that, reactionary as it sounds, a return is indicated. At least some sort of return. Remember that not all returns are bad. A return to health after sickness, a return to shore after a voyage, a return to home after estrangement, to liberty after prison—these are salutary returns. Let's have no cant about reactionism.

The chances of a writer finding inside the modern world an imagery that will suggest the big, real, whole world are slim. The writer will have eventually to lift his sights away from the shards and catch once more the vision that was born in olden days when an imagery of heroes and elves and gods was alive. He'll have to search for it with all his heart, and he will, if he looks hard enough, find at least something. He'll find that, despite the cold and lethal myth that holds the whole world in a frosty sovereignty, there are pockets of warmth and life. The old vision, the vision that was affirmed in the high myths, is kept alive and nourished in the households of good and humble people everywhere. And (we wish it were true) in the church. At least it is still celebrated in the church, for we still sing *Kyrie* and *Gloria* and *Sanctus,* and break bread and pour wine, and call them the body and blood of God.

The human spirit at its best is impatient with the small and local and fragmented. It demands images of greatness and wholeness. The world of the imagination that I have called myth is a repository of such images—images of courage and glory and mystery and romance and deity and heroism. Excursions into that world are never a flight away from reality; they are, rather, a flight to reality.

Notes

1. Zeus, Odysseus—Greek mythological figures

2. Aegean, Baltic—seas; the area around Greece

3. Pericles—(500?–419 B.C.) a Greek statesman who advocated democracy

4. Lilliput—an imaginary land in Jonathan Swift's book *Gulliver's Travels*

5. Francois Mauriac, Flannery O'Connor, Tolkien—Mauriac (1885–1970) a French writer; O'Connor (1925–1964) an American writer; J. R. R. Tolkien (1892–1973) an English writer and professor

Making Connections through Discussion and Writing

1. a. Paraphrase Howard's description of myth.

    _____

    _____

    _____

    b. What does he say about myth and truth?

    _____

    _____

    _____

2. According to Howard, why is myth necessary for society?

    _____

    _____

    _____

3. a. What distinction does Howard make between art and myth in the third section of his essay?

    _____

    _____

    _____

    b. What does he mean by "high myth"?

    _____

    _____

4. How does Howard describe the function of distance and identity in myth?

    _____

    _____

    _____

    _____

5. Explain Howard's statement, "Time may be the tragic dimension of human experience."

    _____

    _____

    _____

    _____

6. a. According to Howard, when did humans desert their sense of mystery and wonder before the universe and begin thinking that the extent of reality is the measurable?

    _____

    _____

b.   How has this shift affected society?

_____

_____

7.   Why does Howard believe that twentieth-century readers and writers have a difficult time with the subject of myth?

_____

_____

_____

_____

8.   Why is myth necessary for modern society, according to Howard?

_____

_____

_____

_____

_____

_____

C. S. Lewis

Sometimes Fairy Stories May Say Best What's to Be Said

In the essay below, Lewis discusses his distinction between the "Author" and the "Man" and why he considers the form of the fairy tale so capable of expressing the story he wishes to tell. He especially emphasizes that the story emanates from imaginative images and characters; it does not, with most authors, begin with a predetermined theme or as an abstract moral, doctrinal, or didactic idea. The story, Lewis says, "bubbles up" from the author and dictates the form that it should take.

Vocabulary ....

edifying   patronizing

In the sixteenth century when everyone was saying that poets (by which they meant all imaginative writers) ought 'to please and instruct', Tasso[1] made a valuable distinction. He said that the poet, as poet, was concerned solely with pleasing. But then every poet was also a man and a citizen; in that capacity he ought to, and would wish to, make his work edifying as well as pleasing.

Now I do not want to stick very close to the renaissance ideas of 'pleasing' and 'instructing'. Before I could accept either term it might need so much redefining that what was left of it at the end would not be worth retaining. All I want to use is the distinction between the author as author and the author as man, citizen, or Christian. What this comes to for me is that there are usually two reasons for writing an imaginative work, which may be called Author's reason and the Man's. If only one of these is present, then, so far as I am concerned, the book will not be written. If the first is lacking, it can't; if the second if lacking, it shouldn't.

In the Author's mind there bubbles up every now and then the material for a story. For me it invariably begins with mental pictures. This ferment leads to nothing unless it is accompanied with the longing for a Form: verse or prose, short story, novel, play or what not. When these two things click you have the Author's impulse complete. It is now a thing inside him pawing to get out. He longs to see that bubbling stuff pouring into that Form as the housewife longs to see the new jam pouring into the clean jam jar. This nags him all day long and gets in the way of his work and his sleep and his meals. It's like being in love.

While the Author is in this state, the Man will of course have to criticize the proposed book from quite a different point of view. He will ask how the gratification of this impulse will fit in with all the other things he wants, and ought to do or be. Perhaps the whole thing is too frivolous and trivial (from the Man's point of view, not the Author's) to justify the time and pains it would involve. Perhaps it would be unedifying when it was done. Or else perhaps (at this point the Author cheers up) it looks like being 'good', not in a merely literary sense, but 'good' all around.

This may sound rather complicated but it is really very like what happens about other things. You are attracted by a girl; but is she the sort of girl you'd be wise, or right, to marry? You would like to have lobster for lunch; but does it agree with you and is it wicked to spend that amount of money on a meal? The Author's impulse is a desire (it is very like an itch), and of course, like every other desire, needs to be criticized by the whole Man.

Let me now apply this to my own fairy tales. Some people seem to think that I began by asking myself how I could say something about Christianity to children; then fixed on the fairy tale as an instrument; then collected information about child-psychology and decided what age group I'd write for; then drew up a list of basic Christian truths and hammered out 'allegories' to embody them. This is all pure moonshine. I couldn't write in that way at all. Everything began with images; a faun carrying an umbrella, a queen on a sledge, a magnificent lion. At first there wasn't even anything Christian about them; that element pushed itself in of its own accord. It was part of the bubbling.

Then came the Form. As these images sorted themselves into events (i.e., became a story) they seemed to demand no love interest and no close psychology. But the Form which includes these things is the fairy tale. And the moment I thought of that I fell in love with the Form itself; its brevity, its severe restraints on description, its flexible traditionalism; its inflexible hostility to all analysis, digression, inflections and 'gas'. I was now enamoured of it. Its very limitations of vocabulary became an attraction; as the hardness of the stone pleases the sculptor or the difficulty of the sonnet delights the sonneteer.

On that side (as Author) I wrote fairy tales because the Fairy Tale seemed the ideal Form for the stuff I had to say.

Then of course the Man in me began to have his turn. I thought I saw how stories of this kind could steal past a certain inhibition which had paralysed much of my own religion in childhood. Why did one find it so hard to feel as one was told one ought to feel about God or about the sufferings of Christ? I thought the chief reason was that one was told one ought to. An obligation to feel can freeze feelings. And reverence itself did harm. The whole subject was associated with lowered voices; almost as if it were something medical. But supposing that by casting all these things into an imaginary world, stripping them of their stained-glass and Sunday school associations, one could make them for the first time appear in their real potency? Could one not thus steal past those watchful dragons? I thought one could.

That was the Man's motive. But of course he could have done nothing if the Author had not been on the boil first.

You will notice that I have throughout spoken of Fairy Tales, not 'children's stories'. Professor J. R. R. Tolkien in *The Lord of the Rings*[2] has shown that the connection between fairy tales and children is not nearly so close as publishers and educationalists think. Many children don't like them and many adults do. The truth is, as he says, that they are now associated with children because they are out of fashion with adults; have in fact retired to the nursery as old furniture used to retire there, not because the children had begun to like it but because their elders had ceased to like it.

I was therefore writing 'for children' only in the sense that I excluded what I thought they would not like or understand; not in the sense of writing what I intended to be below adult attention. I may of course have been deceived, but the principle at least saves one from being patronizing. I never wrote down to anyone; and whether the opinion condemns or acquits my own work, it certainly is my opinion that a book worth reading only in childhood is not worth reading even then. The inhibitions which I hoped my stories would overcome in a child's mind may exist in a grown-up's mind too, and may perhaps be overcome by the same means.

The Fantastic or Mythical is a Mode available at all ages for some readers; for others, at none. At all ages, if it is well used by the author and meets the right reader, it has the same power: to generalize while remaining concrete, to present in palpable form not concepts or even experiences but whole classes of experience, and to throw off irrelevancies. But at its best it can do more, it can give us experiences we have never had and thus instead of 'commenting on life', can add to it. I am speaking, of course, about the thing itself, not my own attempts at it.

'Juveniles', indeed! Am I to patronize sleep because children sleep sound? Or honey because children like it? ■

Notes

1 Tasso—Torquato Tasso (1544–1595) an Italian poet

2 *The Lord of the Rings*—Tolkien's fantasy trilogy. Lewis goes on to paraphrase and quote from Tolkien's essay, "On Fairy Stories."

Making Connections through Discussion and Writing

1. a. According to Lewis, there are two roles within the self that an artist is responsible to. Explain these in one sentence each.

    _____
    _____
    _____

    _____
    _____
    _____

    b. What conflicts emerge between these roles?

    _____
    _____
    _____

    c. Why is it necessary for an artist to respect both roles?

    _____
    _____
    _____

2. a. Describe how some of Lewis' readers viewed the manner in which Lewis wrote fairy tales.

    _____
    _____
    _____
    _____

    b. How does Lewis present his methodology?

    _____
    _____
    _____
    _____

3. a. What values does Lewis find in myth and fantasy that lead him to choose the fairy tale form to tell his story?

    _____
    _____
    _____
    _____

b.   How does he view his audience?

_____

_____

_____

_____

4.   Lewis asks the following question when explaining about the challenges faced in writing of the "potency" of his faith: "Could one not thus steal past those watchful dragons? I thought one could." What does this question mean in context?

_____

_____

_____

_____

_____

_____

5.   How does Lewis respond to the idea that fairy tales are only for children?

_____

_____

_____

_____

_____

_____

G. K. Chesterton

Dragooning the Dragon

In the following piece, G. K. Chesterton defends in a humorous and straightforward manner the telling of fairy tales to children. He contends that these tales are more captivating for children than the everyday "truths" adults believe.

Vocabulary ....

dragooning

We all know the people who think it wicked to tell children fairy tales which they are not required to believe, though of course not wicked to teach them false doctrines or false news which they are required to believe. They hold that the child must be guarded from the danger of supposing that all frogs turn into princesses or that any pumpkin will at any minute turn into a coach and six[1] and that he must rather reserve his faith for the sober truth told in the newspapers, which will tell him that all Socialists are Satanists or that the next Act of Parliament will mean work and wealth for all. We ourselves have generally found that children were quite sufficiently intelligent to question the first and that grown-up people were quite sufficiently stupid to swallow the second. It almost looks as if there were something wrong about education; or perhaps something wrong about growing up. But the latest news in the educational world is that a more moderate reform is under consideration; and the reformers admit that there is a distinction to be made. One or two fairy tales about pretty things like flowers or butterflies, it is loftily admitted, may do no harm. But fairy tales about dragons and giants, because they are ugly things, may have a dreadful effect upon the delicate instinct for beauty. Schoolmasters discussed the question recently in the light of the most recent psychology of esthetics. For our part, we have seldom seen a schoolmaster who was half so decorative as a dragon. And though a giant may appear gross or grotesque, he is not necessarily less so when (as in the case of one or two professors) he is reduced to the dimensions of a dwarf. The human race must be a very horrible sight to the human child, if he is really so sensitive an esthetic as all

that. But it must be admitted that the objection was not exclusively esthetic, but also partly ethical. On moral grounds also it was urged that the child may read stories about beanstalks, but not stories about giants; the learned educationists having apparently forgotten that they both occur in the same story. Children, it appears, are not to read about giants and witches because it will encourage cruelty; as the child "will certainly sympathise with the torturers." This would seem to be an extreme dogma of Original Sin by the Calvinists[2] rather than the Catholic definition of it. Why a little boy reading about another little boy pursued by a dragon should suppose himself to be a dragon, which he is not, instead of a boy, which he is, we have no idea; we suppose it is the dragon complex. Anyhow, psychologists suffer from what may be called the contradiction complex; and we need not say that they contradict themselves flatly even on that one small point. For they also say that the tale of the dragon will produce morbid terror and panic; so that it would almost seem as if the little boy were a little boy after all. But he is a rather curious little boy, who exultantly enjoys eating himself at the same moment that he is mad and miserable with fear of being eaten by himself; his complex is evidently very complex indeed. Meanwhile, it might perhaps be pointed out that a child generally goes very eagerly to his father or his friend for the experience of fairy tales; whereas he can remain in complete isolation and ignorance, and still have the experience of fear. The child learns without being taught that life contains some element of enmity. His own dreams would provide him with dragons; what the legend provides is St. George.[3] ∎

IRONY

From *Everlasting Man* by G. K. Chesterton, published 1925.

Notes

[1] a coach and six—a coach with six horses; an allusion to the Cinderella story

[2] Calvinists—followers of the teachings of John Calvin (1509–1564), a leader of the Reformation

[3] St. George—a Christian martyr of the 3rd or 4th century. The patron saint of England, St. George has been especially venerated as a protecting saint by orthodox Christians in Russia. The stories about his slaying a dragon are from a late medieval legend.

J. R. R. Tolkien

from On Fairy Stories

J. R. R. Tolkien (1892–1973), a philologist and Medieval professor, was born in Bloemfontein, South Africa, and was educated at Oxford University. He is most noted for his fantasy novels, which include *The Hobbit* (1937) and the trilogy *The Lord of the Rings*, containing *The Fellowship of the Ring* (1954), *The Two Towers* (1955), and *The Return of the King* (1956), works that were actually begun when Tolkien was a student of philology at Oxford. He created the Elvish language and then developed a mythology around this new tongue. He was a member of the famous Inklings group that included C. S. Lewis, Charles Williams, and Owen Barfield. In the following short excerpt from his long essay "On Fairy Stories," Tolkien discusses the role of the author as subcreator and describes how the Christian Story authenticates and enlivens the fairy tale.

Vocabulary . . . .

abrogated

Probably every writer making a secondary world, a fantasy, every sub-creator, wishes in some measure to be a real maker, or hopes that he is drawing on reality: hopes that the peculiar quality of this secondary world (if not all the details) are derived from Reality, or are flowing into it. If he achieves a quality that can fairly be described by the dictionary definition: 'inner consistency of reality', it is difficult to conceive how this can be, if the work does not in some way partake of reality. The peculiar quality of the 'joy' in successful Fantasy can thus be explained as a sudden glimpse of the underlying reality or truth. It is not only a 'consolation' for the sorrow of this world, but a satisfaction, and an answer to that question 'Is it true?' The answer to this question that I gave at first was (quite rightly): 'If you have built your little world well, yes: it is true in that world.' That is enough for the artist (or the artist part of the artist). But in the 'eucatastrophe'[1] we see in a brief vision that the answer may be greater—it may be a far-off gleam or echo of *evangelium*[2] in the real world. The use of this word gives a hint of my epilogue. It is a serious and dangerous matter. I am a Christian, and so at least should not be suspected of wilful irreverence. Knowing my own ignorance and dullness, it is perhaps presumptuous of me to touch upon such a

theme; but if by grace what I say has in any respect any validity, it is, of course, only one facet of a truth incalculably rich: finite only because the capacity of Man for whom this was done is finite.

I would venture to say that approaching the Christian Story from this direction, it has long been my feeling (a joyous feeling) that God redeemed the corrupt making-creatures, men, in a way fitting to this aspect, as to others, of their strange nature. The Gospels contain a fairy-story, or a story of a larger kind which embraces all the essence of fairy-stories. They contain many marvels—peculiarly artistic,[3] beautiful, and moving: 'mythical' in their perfect, self-contained significance; and at the same time powerfully symbolic and allegorical; and among the marvels is the greatest and most complete conceivable eucatastrophe. The Birth of Christ is the eucatastrophe of Man's history. The Resurrection is the eucatastrophe of the story of the Incarnation. This story begins and ends in joy. It has pre-eminently the 'inner consistency of reality'. There is no tale ever told that men would rather find was true, and none which so many sceptical men have accepted as true on its own merits. For the Art of it has the supremely convincing tone of Primary Art, that is, of Creation. To reject it leads either to sadness or to wrath.

It is not difficult to imagine the peculiar excitement and joy that one would feel, if any specially beautiful fairy-story were found to be 'primarily' true, its narrative to be history, without thereby necessarily losing the mythical or allegorical significance that it had possessed. It is not difficult, for one is not called upon to try and conceive anything of a quality unknown. The joy would have exactly the same quality, if not the same degree, as the joy which the 'turn' in a fairy-story gives: such joy has the very taste of primary truth. (Otherwise its name would not be joy.) It looks forward (or backward: the direction in this regard is unimportant) to the Great Eucatastrophe. The Christian joy, the *Gloria,* is of the same kind; but it is pre-eminently (infinitely, if our capacity were not finite) high and joyous. Because this story is supreme; and it is true. Art has been verified. God is the Lord, of angels, and of men—and of elves. Legend and History have met and fused.

But in God's kingdom the presence of the greatest does not depress the small. Redeemed Man is still man. Story, fantasy, still go on, and should go on. The Evangelium has not abrogated legends; it has hallowed them, especially the 'happy ending'. The Christian has still to work, with mind as well as body, to suffer, hope, and die; but he may now perceive that all his bents and faculties have a purpose, which can be redeemed. So great is the bounty with which he has been treated that he may now, perhaps, fairly dare to guess that in Fantasy he may actually assist in the effoliation[4] and multiple enrichment of creation. All tales may come true; and yet, at the last, redeemed, they may be as like and as unlike the forms that we give them as Man, finally redeemed, will be like and unlike the fallen that we know. ■

Notes

[1] eucatastrophe—the happy ending

[2] evangelium—the story of the Gospel of Jesus Christ

[3] Author's note—The Gospels are not artistic in themselves; the Art is here in the story itself, not in the telling. For the Author of the story was not the evangelists. "Even the world itself could not contain the books that should be written," if that had been fully written down.

[4] effoliation—The word is related to exfoliation (to unfold as a leaf) and also to foliation (to form into a leaf).

Making Connections through Discussion and Writing

1. According to Tolkien, what should be the relationship of reality and fantasy for the subcreator?

   _____
   _____
   _____
   _____

2. What does Tolkien mean by the "inner consistency of reality" in a fairy story?

   _____
   _____
   _____
   _____

3. a. According to Tolkien, what is the Christian Story?

   _____
   _____
   _____

   b. How does it lend credence to fairy tales? In other words, how has the Gospel validated fairy tales?

   _____
   _____
   _____
   _____

4. Discuss Tolkien's use of the word "eucatastrophe," explaining its significance for both the Christian Story and fantasy.

   _____
   _____
   _____
   _____
   _____
   _____
   _____

5. a. What is the joy Tolkien describes?

   _____
   _____

b.   How does it relate to fairy story?

_____

_____

_____

6.   Tolkien writes, "God is the Lord, of angels, and of men—and of elves. Legend and history have met and fused." C. S. Lewis says, "Christianity is a myth that is also a fact."

a.   What do you think these authors mean by these statements?

_____

_____

_____

_____

b.   What is your response to these ideas?

_____

_____

_____

_____

J. R. R. Tolkien

Leaf by Niggle

At the end of his essay "On Fairy Stories," Tolkien contends that "in Fantasy he [the Christian] may actually assist in the effoliation and multiple enrichment of creation." The fairy story below, "Leaf By Niggle," is his illustration of this very statement, for Niggle "was the sort of painter who can paint leaves better than trees." Niggle participates in the process of effoliation—of forming a leaf in his painting—thus, assisting in the "enrichment of creation." When Parish, Niggle's neighbor, finally enters Niggle's Country, he is astonished at what is there, for he sees Niggle's Picture fully formed. He remarks, "But it did not look like this then, not *real*." To which the shepherd, who is the guide into the country, replies, "No, it was only a glimpse then, . . . but you might have caught the glimpse, if you had ever thought it worthwhile to try"; hence, the idea Tolkien is asserting: myth points to reality. Then Niggle's Parish becomes established—a place where those first introduced to Heaven go. As a result, both Parish and Niggle are filled with joy: "They both laughed. Laughed—the Mountains rang with it!" Somehow, because the artist Niggle has participated in the act of subcreation, the kingdom of heaven has become richer and the joy resonant in that place has filled the lives of its inhabitants lives.

There was once a little man called Niggle, who had a long journey to make. He did not want to go, indeed the whole idea was distasteful to him; but he could not get out of it. He knew he would have to start some time, but he did not hurry with his preparations.

Niggle was a painter. Not a very successful one, partly because he had many other things to do. Most of these things he thought were a nuisance; but he did them fairly well, when he could not get out of them: which (in his opinion) was far too often. The laws in his country were rather strict. There were other hindrances, too. For one thing, he was sometimes just idle, and did nothing at all. For another, he was kindhearted, in a way. You know the sort of kind heart: it made him uncomfortable more often than it made him do anything; and even when he did anything, it did not prevent him from grumbling, losing his temper, and swearing (mostly to himself). All the same, it did land him in a good many odd jobs for his neighbour, Mr. Parish, a man with a lame leg. Occasionally he even helped other people from further off, if they came and asked him to. Also, now and again, he remembered his journey, and began to pack a few things in an ineffectual way: at such times he did not paint very much.

He had a number of pictures on hand; most of them were too large and ambitious for his skill. He was the sort of painter who can paint leaves better than trees. He used to spend a long time on a single leaf, trying to catch its shape, and its sheen, and the glistening of dewdrops on its edges. Yet he wanted to paint a whole tree, with all of its leaves in the same style, and all of them different.

There was one picture in particular which bothered him. It had begun with a leaf caught in the wind, and it became a tree; and the tree grew, sending out innumerable branches, and thrusting out the most fantastic roots. Strange birds came and settled on the twigs and had to be attended to. Then all round the Tree, and behind it, through the gaps in the leaves and boughs, a country began to open out; and there were glimpses of a forest marching over the land, and of mountains tipped with snow. Niggle lost interest in his other pictures; or else he took them and tacked them on to the edges of his great picture. Soon the canvas became so large that he had to get a ladder; and he ran up and down it, putting in a touch here, and rubbing out a patch there. When people came to call, he seemed polite enough, though he fiddled a little with the pencils on his desk. He listened to what they said, but underneath he was thinking all the time about his big canvas, in the tall shed that had been built for it out in his garden (on a plot where once he had grown potatoes).

He could not get rid of his kind heart. "I wish I was more strong-minded!" he sometimes said to himself, meaning that he wished other people's troubles did not make him feel uncomfortable. But for a long time he was not seriously perturbed. "At any rate, I shall get this one picture done, my real picture, before I have to go on that wretched journey," he used to say. Yet he was beginning to see that he could not put off his start indefinitely. The picture would have to stop just growing and get finished.

One day, Niggle stood a little way off from his picture and considered it with unusual attention and detachment. He could not make up his mind what he thought about it, and wished he had some friend who would tell him what to think. Actually it seemed to him wholly unsatisfactory, and yet very lovely, the only really beautiful picture in the world. What he would have liked at that moment would have been to see himself walk in, and slap him on the back, and say (with obvious sincerity): "Absolutely magnificent! I see exactly what you are getting at. Do get on with it, and don't bother about anything else! We will arrange for a public pension, so that you need not."

However, there was no public pension. And one thing he could see: it would need some concentration, some *work*, hard uninterrupted work, to finish the picture, even at its present size. He rolled up his sleeves, and began to concentrate. He tried for several days not to bother about other things. But there came a tremendous crop of interruptions. Things went wrong in his house; he had to go and serve on a jury in the town; a distant friend fell ill; Mr. Parish was laid up with lumbago; and visitors kept on coming. It was springtime, and they wanted a free tea in the country: Niggle lived in a pleasant little house, miles away from the town. He cursed them in his heart, but he could not deny that he had invited them himself, away back in the winter, when he had not thought it an "interruption" to visit the shops and have tea with acquaintances in the town. He tried to harden his heart; but it was not a success. There were many things that he had not the face to say *no* to, whether he thought them duties or not; and there were some things he was compelled to do, whatever he thought. Some of his visitors hinted that his garden was rather neglect-

ed, and that he might get a visit from an Inspector. Very few of them knew about his picture, of course; but if they had known, it would not have made much difference. I doubt if they would have thought that it mattered much. I dare say it was not really a very good picture, though it may have had some good passages. The Tree, at any rate, was curious. Quite unique in its way. So was Niggle; though he was also a very ordinary and rather silly little man.

At length Niggle's time became really precious. His acquaintances in the distant town began to remember that the little man had got to make a troublesome journey, and some began to calculate how long at the latest he could put off starting. They wondered who would take his house, and if the garden would be better kept.

The autumn came, very wet and windy. The little painter was in his shed. He was up on the ladder, trying to catch the gleam of the westering sun on the peak of a snow-mountain, which he had glimpsed just to the left of the leafy tip of one of the Tree's branches. He knew that he would have to be leaving soon: perhaps early next year. He could only just get the picture finished, and only so so, at that: there were sonic corners where he would not have time now to do more than hint at what he wanted.

There was a knock on the door. "Come in!" he said sharply, and climbed down the ladder. He stood on the floor twiddling his brush. It was his neighbour, Parish: his only real neighbour, all other folk lived a long way off. Still, he did not like the man very much: partly because he was so often in trouble and in need of help; and also because he did not care about painting, but was very critical about gardening. When Parish looked at Niggle's garden (which was often) he saw mostly weeds; and when he looked at Niggle's pictures (which was seldom) he saw only green and grey patches and black lines, which seemed to him nonsensical. He did not mind mentioning the weeds (a neighbourly duty), but he refrained from giving any opinion of the pictures. He thought this was very kind, and he did not realize that, even if it was kind, it was not kind enough. Help with the weeds (and perhaps praise for the pictures) would have been better.

"Well, Parish, what is it?" said Niggle.

"I oughtn't to interrupt you, I know," said Parish (without a glance at the picture). "You are very busy, I'm sure."

Niggle had meant to say something like that himself, but he had missed his chance. All he said was: "Yes."

"But I have no one else to turn to," said Parish.

"Quite so," said Niggle with a sigh: one of those sighs that are a private comment, but which are not made quite inaudible. "What can I do for you?"

"My wife has been ill for some days, and I am getting worried," said Parish. "And the wind has blown half the tiles off my roof, and water is pouring into the bedroom. I think I ought to get the doctor. And the builders, too, only they take so long to come. I was wondering if you had any wood and canvas you could spare, just to patch me up and see me through for a day or two." Now he did look at the picture.

"Dear, dear!" said Niggle. "You *are* unlucky. I hope it is no more than a cold that your wife has got. I'll come round presently, and help you move the patient downstairs."

"Thank you very much," said Parish, rather coolly. "But it is not a cold, it is a fever. I should not have bothered you for a cold. And my wife is in bed downstairs already. I can't get up and down with trays, not with my leg. But I see you are busy. Sorry to have troubled you. I had rather hoped you might have been able to spare the time to go for the doctor, seeing how I'm placed; and the builder too, if you really have no canvas you can spare."

"Of course," said Niggle; though other words were in his heart, which at the moment was merely soft without feeling at all kind. "I could go. I'll go, if you are really worried."

"I am worried, very worried. I wish I was not lame," said Parish.

So Niggle went. You see, it was awkward. Parish was his neighbour, and everyone else a long way off. Niggle had a bicycle, and Parish had not, and could not ride one. Parish had a lame leg, a genuine lame leg which gave him a good deal of pain: that had to be remembered, as well as his sour expression and whining voice. Of course, Niggle had a picture and barely time to finish it. But it seemed that this was a thing that Parish had to reckon with and not Niggle. Parish, however, did not reckon with pictures; and Niggle could not alter that. "Curse it!" he said to himself, as he got out his bicycle.

It was wet and windy, and daylight was waning. "No more work for me today!" thought Niggle, and all the time that he was riding, he was either swearing to himself, or imagining the strokes of his brush on the mountain, and on the spray of leaves beside it, that he had first imagined in the spring. His fingers twitched on the handlebars. Now he was out of the shed, he saw exactly the way in which to treat that shining spray which framed the distant vision of the mountain. But he had a sinking feeling in his heart, a sort of fear that he would never now get a chance to try it out.

Niggle found the doctor, and he left a note at the builder's. The office was shut, and the builder had gone home to his fireside. Niggle got soaked to the skin, and caught a chill himself. The doctor did not set out as promptly as Niggle had done. He arrived next day, which was quite convenient for him, as by that time there were two patients to deal with, in neighbouring houses. Niggle was in bed, with a high temperature, and marvellous patterns of leaves and involved branches forming in his head and on the ceiling. It did not comfort him to learn that Mrs. Parish had only had a cold, and was getting up. He turned his face to the wall and buried himself in leaves.

He remained in bed some time. The wind went on blowing. It took away a good many more of Parish's tiles, and some of Niggle's as well: his own roof began to leak. The builder did not come. Niggle did not care; not for a day or two. Then he crawled out to look for some food (Niggle had no wife). Parish did not come round: the rain had got into his leg and made it ache; and his wife was busy mopping up water, and wondering if "that Mr. Niggle" had forgotten to call at the builder's. Had she seen any chance of borrowing anything useful, she would have sent Parish round, leg or no leg; but she did not, so Niggle was left to himself.

At the end of a week or so Niggle tottered out to his shed again. He tried to climb the ladder, but it made his head giddy. He sat and looked at the picture, but there were no patterns of leaves or visions of mountains in his mind that day. He could have painted a far-off view of a sandy desert, but he had not the energy.

Next day he felt a good deal better. He climbed the ladder, and began to paint. He had just begun to get into it again, when there came a knock on the door.

"Damn!" said Niggle. But he might just as well have said "Come in!" politely, for the door opened all the same. This time a very tall man came in, a total stranger.

"This is a private studio," said Niggle. "I am busy. Go away!"

"I am an Inspector of Houses," said the man, holding up his appointment-card, so that Niggle on his ladder could see it.

"Oh!" he said.

"Your neighbour's house is not satisfactory at all," said the Inspector.

"I know," said Niggle. "I took a note to the builders a long time ago, but they have never come. Then I have been ill."

"I see," said the Inspector. "But you are not ill now."

"But I'm not a builder. Parish ought to make a complaint to the Town Council, and get help from the Emergency Service."

"They are busy with worse damage than any up here," said the Inspector. "There has been a flood in the valley, and many families are homeless. You should have helped your neighbour to make temporary repairs and prevent the damage from getting more costly to mend than necessary. That is the law. There is plenty of material here: canvas, wood, waterproof paint."

"Where?" asked Niggle indignantly.

"There!" said the Inspector, pointing to the picture.

"My picture!" exclaimed Niggle.

"I dare say it is," said the Inspector. "But houses come first. That is the law."

"But I can't . . ." Niggle said no more, for at that moment another man came in. Very much like the Inspector he was, almost his double: tall, dressed all in black.

"Come along!" he said. "I am the Driver."

Niggle stumbled down from the ladder. His fever seemed to have come on again, and his head was swimming; he felt cold all over.

"Driver? Driver?" he chattered. "Driver of what?"

"You, and your carriage," said the man. "The carriage was ordered long ago. It has come at last. It's waiting. You start today on your journey, you know."

"There now!" said the Inspector. "You'll have to go; but it's a bad way to start on your journey, leaving your jobs undone. Still, we can at least make some use of this canvas now."

"Oh, dear!" said poor Niggle, beginning to weep. "And it's not, not even finished!"

"Not finished?" said the Driver. "Well, it's finished with, as far as you're concerned, at any rate. Come along!"

Niggle went, quite quietly. The Driver gave him no time to pack, saying that he ought to have done that before, and they would miss the train; so all Niggle could do was to grab a little bag in the hall. He found that it contained only a paint-box and a small book of his own sketches: neither food nor clothes. They caught the train all right. Niggle was feeling very tired and sleepy; he was hardly aware of what was going on when they bundled him into his compartment. He did not care much: he had forgotten where he was supposed to be going, or what he was going for. The train ran almost at once into a dark tunnel.

Niggle woke up in a very large, dim railway station. A Porter went along the platform shouting, but he was not shouting the name of the place; he was shouting *Niggle!*

Niggle got out in a hurry, and found that he had left his little bag behind. He turned back, but the train had gone away.

"Ah, there you are!" said the Porter. "This way! What! No luggage? You will have to go to the Workhouse."

Niggle felt very ill, and fainted on the platform. They put him in an ambulance and took him to the Workhouse Infirmary.

He did not like the treatment at all. The medicine they gave him was bitter. The officials and attendants were unfriendly, silent, and strict; and he never saw anyone else, except a very severe doctor, who visited him occasionally. It was more like being in a prison than in a hospital. He had to work hard, at stated hours: at digging, carpentry, and painting bare boards all one plain colour. He was never allowed outside, and the windows all looked inwards. They kept him in the dark for hours at a stretch, "to do some thinking," they said. He lost count of time. He did not even begin to feel better, not if that could be judged by whether he felt any pleasure in doing anything. He did not, not even in getting into bed.

At first, during the first century or so (I am merely giving his impressions), he used to worry aimlessly about the past. One thing he kept on repeating to himself, as he lay in the dark: "I wish I had called on Parish the first morning after the high winds began. I meant to. The first loose tiles would have been easy to fix. Then Mrs. Parish might never have caught cold. Then I should not have caught cold either. Then I should have had a week longer." But in time he forgot what it was that he had wanted a week longer for. If he worried at all after that, it was about his jobs in the hospital. He planned them out, thinking how quickly he could stop that board creaking, or rehang that door, or mend that table-leg. Probably he really became rather useful, though no one ever told him so. But that, of course, cannot have been the reason why they kept the poor little man so long. They may have been waiting for him to get better, and judging "better" by some odd medical standard of their own.

At any rate, poor Niggle got no pleasure out of life, not what he had been used to call pleasure. He was certainly not amused. But it could not be denied that he began to have a feeling of—well, satisfaction: bread rather than jam. He could take up a task the moment one bell rang, and lay it aside promptly the moment the next one went, all tidy and ready to be continued at the right time. He got through quite a lot in a day, now; he finished small things off neatly. He had no "time of his own" (except alone in his bed-cell), and yet he was becoming master of his time; he began to know just what he could do with it. There was no sense of rush. He was quieter inside now, and at resting-time he could really rest.

Then suddenly they changed all his hours; they hardly let him go to bed at all; they took him off carpentry altogether and kept him at plain digging, day after day. He took it fairly well. It was a long while before he even began to grope in the back of his mind for the curses that he had practically forgotten. He went on digging, till his back seemed broken, his hands were raw, and he felt that he could not manage another spadeful. Nobody thanked him. But the doctor came and looked at him.

"Knock off!" he said. "Complete rest—in the dark."

Niggle was lying in the dark, resting completely; so that, as he had not been either feeling or thinking at all, he might have been lying there for hours or for years, as far as he could tell. But now he heard Voices: not voices that he had ever heard before. There seemed to be a Medical Board, or perhaps a Court of Inquiry, going on close at hand, in an adjoining room with the door open, possibly, though he could not see any light.

"Now the Niggle case," said a Voice, a severe voice, more severe than the doctor's.

"What was the matter with him?" said a Second Voice, a voice that you might have called gentle, though it was not soft—it was a voice of authority, and sounded at once hopeful and sad. "What was the matter with Niggle? His heart was in the right place."

"Yes, but it did not function properly," said the First Voice. "And his head was not screwed on tight enough: he hardly ever thought at all. Look at the time he wasted, not even amusing himself! He never got ready for his journey. He was moderately well-off, and yet he arrived here almost destitute, and had to be put in the paupers' wing. A bad case, I am afraid. I think he should stay some time yet."

"It would not do him any harm, perhaps," said the Second Voice. "But, of course, he is only a little man. He was never meant to be anything very much; and he was never very strong. Let us look at the Records. Yes. There are some favourable points, you know."

"Perhaps," said the First Voice; "but very few that will really bear examination."

"Well," said the Second Voice, "there are these. He was a painter by nature. In a minor way, of course; still, a Leaf by Niggle has a charm of its own. He took a great deal of pains with leaves, just for their own sake. But he never thought that that made him important. There is no note in the Records of his pretending, even to himself, that it excused his neglect of things ordered by the law."

"Then he should not have neglected so many," said the First Voice.

"All the same, he did answer a good many Calls."

"A small percentage, mostly of the easier sort, and he called those Interruptions. The Records are full of the word, together with a lot of complaints and silly imprecations."

"True; but they looked like interruptions to him, of course, poor little man. And there is this: he never expected any Return, as so many of his sort call it. There is the Parish case, the one that came in later. He was Niggle's neighbour, never did a stroke for him, and seldom showed any gratitude at all. But there is no note in the Records that Niggle expected Parish's gratitude; he does not seem to have thought about it."

"Yes, that is a point," said the First Voice; "but rather small. I think you will find Niggle often merely forgot. Things he had to do for Parish he put out of his mind as a nuisance he had done with."

"Still, there is this last report," said the Second Voice, "that wet bicycle-ride. I rather lay stress on that. It seems plain that this was a genuine sacrifice: Niggle guessed that he was throwing away his last chance with his picture, and he guessed, too, that Parish was worrying unnecessarily."

"I think you put it too strongly," said the First Voice. "But you have the last word. It is your task, of course, to put the best interpretation on the facts. Sometimes they will bear it. What do you propose?"

"I think it is a case for a little gentle treatment now," said the Second Voice.

Niggle thought that he had never heard anything so generous as that Voice. It made Gentle Treatment sound like a load of rich gifts, and the summons to a King's feast. Then suddenly Niggle felt ashamed. To hear that he was considered a case for Gentle Treatment overwhelmed him, and made him blush in the dark. It was like being publicly praised, when you and all the audience knew that the praise was not deserved. Niggle hid his blushes in the rough blanket.

There was a silence. Then the First Voice spoke

to Niggle, quite close. "You have been listening," it said.

"Yes," said Niggle.

"'Well, what have you to say?"

"Could you tell me about Parish?" said Niggle. "I should like to see him again. I hope he is not very ill? Can you cure his leg? It used to give him a wretched time. And please don't worry about him and me. He was a very good neighbour, and let me have excellent potatoes very cheap, which saved me a lot of time."

"Did he?" said the First Voice. "I am glad to hear it."

There was another silence. Niggle heard the Voices receding. "Well, I agree," he heard the First Voice say in the distance. "Let him go on to the next stage. Tomorrow, if you like."

Niggle woke up to find that his blinds were drawn, and his little cell was full of sunshine. He got up, and found that some comfortable clothes had been put out for him, not hospital uniform. After breakfast the doctor treated his sore hands, putting some salve on them that healed them at once. He gave Niggle some good advice, and a bottle of tonic (in case he needed it). In the middle of the morning they gave Niggle a biscuit and a glass of wine; and then they gave him a ticket.

"You can go to the railway station now," said the doctor. "The Porter will look after you. Good-bye."

Niggle slipped out of the main door, and blinked a little. The sun was very bright. Also he had expected to walk out into a large town, to match the size of the station; but he did not. He was on the top of a hill, green, bare, swept by a keen invigorating wind. Nobody else was about. Away down under the hill he could see the roof of the station shining.

He walked downhill to the station briskly, but without hurry. The Porter spotted him at once.

"This way!" he said, and led Niggle to a bay, in which there was a very pleasant little local train standing: one coach, and a small engine, both very bright, clean, and newly painted. It looked as if this was their first run. Even the track that lay in front of the engine looked new: the rails shone, the chairs were painted green, and the sleepers gave off a delicious smell of fresh tar in the warm sunshine. The coach was empty.

"Where does this train go, Porter?" asked Niggle.

"I don't think they have fixed its name yet," said the Porter. "But you'll find it all right." He shut the door.

The train moved off at once. Niggle lay back in his seat. The little engine puffed along in a deep cutting with high green banks, roofed with blue sky. It did not seem very long before the engine gave a whistle, the brakes were put on, and the train stopped. There was no station, and no signboard, only a flight of steps up the green embankment. At the top of the steps there was a wicket-gate in a trim hedge. By the gate stood his bicycle; at least, it looked like his, and there was a yellow label tied to the bars with NIGGLE written on it in large black letters.

Niggle pushed open the gate, jumped on the bicycle, and went bowling downhill in the spring sunshine. Before long he found that the path on which he had started had disappeared, and the bicycle was rolling along over a marvellous turf. It was green and close; and yet he could see every blade distinctly. He seemed to remember having seen or dreamed of that sweep of grass somewhere or other. The curves of the land were familiar somehow. Yes: the ground was becoming level, as it should, and now, of course, it was beginning to rise again. A great green shadow came between him and the sun. Niggle looked up, and fell off his bicycle.

Before him stood the Tree, his Tree, finished. If you could say that of a Tree that was alive, its leaves opening, its branches growing and bending in the wind that Niggle had so often felt or guessed, and had so often failed to catch. He gazed at the Tree, and slowly he lifted his arms and opened them wide.

"It's a gift!" he said. He was referring to his art, and also to the result; but he was using the word quite literally.

He went on looking at the Tree. All the leaves he had ever laboured at were there, as he had imagined them rather than as he had made them; and there were others that had only budded in his mind, and many that might have budded, if only he had had time. Nothing was written on them, they were just exquisite leaves, yet they were dated as clear as a calendar. Some of the most beautiful—and the most characteristic, the most perfect examples of the Niggle style—were seen to have been produced in collaboration with Mr. Parish: there was no other way of putting it.

The birds were building in the Tree. Astonishing birds: how they sang! They were mating, hatching, growing wings, and flying away singing into the Forest, even while he looked at them. For now he saw that the Forest was there too, opening out on either side, and marching away into the distance. The Mountains were glimmering far away.

After a time Niggle turned towards the Forest. Not because he was tired of the Tree, but he seemed to have got it all clear in his mind now, and was aware of it, and of its growth, even when he was not looking at it. As he walked away, he discovered an odd thing: the Forest, of course, was a distant Forest, yet he could approach it, even enter it, without its losing that particular charm. He had never before been able to walk into the distance without turning it into mere surroundings. It really added a considerable attraction to walking in the country, because, as you walked, new distances opened out; so that you now had doubled, treble, and quadruple distances, doubly, trebly, and quadruply enchanting. You could go on and on, and have a whole country in a garden, or in a picture (if you preferred to call it that). You could go on and on, but not perhaps for ever. There were the Mountains in the background. They did get nearer, very slowly. They did not seem to belong to the picture, or only as a link to something else, a glimpse through the trees of something different, a further stage: another picture.

Niggle walked about, but he was not merely pottering. He was looking round carefully. The Tree was finished, though not finished with—"Just the other way about to what it used to be," he thought—but in the Forest there were a number of inconclusive regions, that still needed work and thought. Nothing needed altering any longer, nothing was wrong, as far as it had gone, but it needed continuing up to a definite point. Niggle saw the point precisely, in each case.

He sat down under a very beautiful distant tree—a variation of the Great Tree, but quite individual, or it would be with a little more attention—and he considered where to begin work, and where to end it, and how much time was required. He could not quite work out his scheme.

"Of course!" he said. "What I need is Parish. There are lots of things about earth, plants, and trees that he knows and I don't. This place cannot be left just as my private park. I need help and advice: I ought to have got it sooner."

He got up and walked to the place where he had decided to begin work. He took off his coat. Then, down in a little sheltered hollow hidden from a further view, he saw a man looking round rather bewildered. He was leaning on a spade, but plainly did not know what to do. Niggle hailed him. "Parish!" he called.

Parish shouldered his spade and came up to him. He still limped a little. They did not speak, just nodded as they used to do, passing in the lane; but now they walked about together, arm in arm. Without talking, Niggle and Parish agreed exactly where to make the small house and garden, which seemed to be required.

As they worked together, it became plain that Niggle was now the better of the two at ordering his time and getting things done. Oddly enough, it was Niggle who became most absorbed in building and gardening, while Parish often wandered about looking at trees, and especially at the Tree.

One day Niggle was busy planting a quickset hedge, and Parish was lying on the grass near by, looking attentively at a beautiful and shapely little yellow flower growing in the green turf. Niggle had put a lot of them among the roots of his Tree long ago. Suddenly Parish looked up: his face was glistening in the sun, and he was smiling.

"This is grand!" he said. "I oughtn't to be here, really. Thank you for putting in a word for me."

"Nonsense," said Niggle. "I don't remember what I said, but anyway it was not nearly enough."

"Oh yes, it was," said Parish. "It got me out a lot sooner. That Second Voice, you know: he had me sent here; he said you had asked to see me. I owe it to you."

"No. You owe it to the Second Voice," said Niggle. "We both do."

They went on living and working together: I do not know how long. It is no use denying that at first they occasionally disagreed, especially when they got tired. For at first they did sometimes get tired. They found that they had both been provided with tonics. Each bottle had the same label: *A few drops to be taken in water from the Spring, before resting.*

They found the Spring in the heart of the Forest; only once long ago had Niggle imagined it, but he had never drawn it. Now he perceived that it was the source of the lake that glimmered, far away and the nourishment of all that grew in the country. The few drops made the water astringent, rather bitter, but invigorating; and it cleared the head. After drinking they rested alone; and then they got up again and things went on merrily. At such times Niggle would think of wonderful new flowers and plants, and Parish always knew exactly how to set them and where they would do best. Long before the tonics were finished they had ceased to need them. Parish lost his limp.

As their work drew to an end they allowed themselves more and more time for walking about, looking at the trees, and the flowers, and the lights and shapes, and the lie of the land. Sometimes they sang together; but Niggle found that he was now beginning to turn his eyes, more and more often, towards the Mountains.

The time came when the house in the hollow, the garden, the grass, the forest, the lake, and all the country was nearly complete, in its own proper fashion. The Great Tree was in full blossom.

"We shall finish this evening," said Parish one day. "After that we will go for a really long walk."

They set out next day, and they walked until they came right through the distances to the Edge. It was not visible, of course: there was no line, or fence, or wall; but they knew that they had come to the margin of that country. They saw a man, he looked like a shepherd; he was walking towards them, down the grass-slopes that led up into the Mountains.

"Do you want a guide?" he asked. "Do you want to go on?"

For a moment a shadow fell between Niggle and Parish, for Niggle knew that he did now want to go on, and (in a sense) ought to go on; but Parish did not want to go on, and was not yet ready to go.

"I must wait for my wife," said Parish to Niggle. "She'd be lonely. I rather gathered that they would send her after me, some time or other, when she was ready, and when I had got things ready for her. The house is finished now, as well as we could make it; but I should like to show it to her. She'll be able to make it better, I expect: more homely. I hope she'll like this country, too." He turned to the shepherd. "Are you a guide?" he asked. "Could you tell me the name of this country?"

"Don't you know?" said the man. "It is Niggle's Country. It is Niggle's Picture, or most of it: a little of it is now Parish's Garden."

"Niggle's Picture!" said Parish in astonishment. "Did *you* think of all this, Niggle? I never knew you were so clever. Why didn't you tell me?"

"He tried to tell you long ago," said the man; "but you would not look. He had only got canvas and paint in those days, and you wanted to mend your roof with them. This is what you and your wife used to call Niggle's Nonsense, or That Daubing."

"But it did not look like this then, not *real*," said Parish.

"No, it was only a glimpse then," said the man; "but you might have caught the glimpse, if you had ever thought it worth while to try."

"I did not give you much chance," said Niggle. "I never tried to explain. I used to call you Old Earth-grubber. But what does it matter? We have lived and worked together now. Things might have been different, but they could not have been better. All the same, I am afraid I shall have to be going on. We shall meet again, I expect: there must be many more things we can do together. Good-bye!" He shook Parish's hand warmly: a good, firm, honest hand it seemed. He turned and looked back for a moment. The blossom on the Great Tree was shining like flame. All the birds were flying in the air and singing. Then he smiled, and nodded to Parish, and went off with the shepherd.

He was going to learn about sheep, and the high pasturages, and look at a wider sky, and walk ever further and further towards the Mountains, always uphill. Beyond that I cannot guess what became of him. Even little Niggle in his old home could glimpse the Mountains far away, and they got into the borders of his picture; but what they are really like, and what lies beyond them, only those can say who have climbed them.

"I think he was a silly little man," said Councillor Tompkins. "Worthless, in fact; no use to Society at all."

"Oh, I don't know," said Atkins, who was nobody of importance, just a schoolmaster. "I am not so sure: it depends on what you mean by *use.*"

"No practical or economic use," said Tompkins. "I dare say he could have been made into a serviceable cog of some sort, if you schoolmasters knew your business. But you don't, and so we get useless people of his sort. If I ran this country I should put him and his like to some job that they're fit for, washing dishes in a communal kitchen or something, and I should see that they did it properly. Or I would put them away. I should have put *him* away long ago."

"Put him away? You mean you'd have made him start on the journey before his time?"

"Yes, if you must use that meaningless old expression. Push him through the tunnel into the great Rubbish Heap: that's what I mean."

"Then you don't think painting is worth anything, not worth preserving, or improving, or even making use of?"

"Of course, painting has uses," said Tompkins. "But you couldn't make use of his painting. There is plenty of scope for bold young men not afraid of new ideas and new methods. None for this old-fashioned stuff. Private day-dreaming. He could not have designed a telling poster to save his life. Always fiddling with leaves and flowers. I asked him why, once. He said he thought they were pretty! Can you believe it? He said *pretty!* "What, digestive and genital organs of plants?" I said to him; and he had nothing to answer. Silly footler."

"Footler," sighed Atkins. "Yes, poor little man, he never finished anything. Ah well, his canvases have been put to 'better uses,' since he went. But I am not sure, Tompkins. You remember that large one, the one they used to patch the damaged house next door to his, after the gales and floods? I found a corner of it torn off, lying in a field. It was damaged, but legible: a mountain-peak and a spray of leaves. I can't get it out of my mind."

"Out of your what?" said Tompkins.

"Who are you two talking about?" said Perkins, intervening in the cause of peace: Atkins had flushed rather red.

"The name's not worth repeating," said Tompkins. "I don't know why we are talking about him at all. He did not live in town."

"No," said Atkins; "but you had your eye on his house, all the same. That is why you used to go and call, and sneer at him while drinking his tea. Well, you've got his house now, as well as the one in town, so you need not grudge him his name. We were talking about Niggle, if you want to know, Perkins."

"Oh, poor little Niggle" said Perkins. "Never knew he painted."

That was probably the last time Niggle's name ever came up in conversation. However, Atkins preserved the odd corner. Most of it crumbled; but one beautiful leaf remained intact. Atkins had it framed. Later he left it to the Town Museum, and for a long while "Leaf: by Niggle" hung there in a recess, and was noticed by a few eyes. But eventually the Museum was burnt down, and the leaf, and Niggle, were entirely forgotten in his old country.

"It is proving very useful indeed," said the Second Voice. "As a holiday, and a refreshment. It is splendid for convalescence; and not only for that, for many it is the best introduction to the Mountains. It works wonders in some cases. I am sending more and more there. They seldom have to come back."

"No, that is so," said the First Voice. "I think we shall have to give the region a name. What do you propose?"

"The Porter settled that some time ago," said the Second Voice. *"Train for Niggle's Parish in the bay:* he has shouted that for a long while now. Niggle's Parish. I sent a message to both of them to tell them."

"What did they say?"

"They both laughed. Laughed—the Mountains rang with it!" ■

Making Connections through Discussion and Writing

1. a. What is Niggle's occupation?

   _____

   b. What are some struggles he faces?

   _____
   _____
   _____
   _____

2. a. Who is Mr. Parish?

   _____
   _____

   b. What is the significance of his name?

   _____
   _____

   c. What is his purpose in the story?

   _____
   _____
   _____

   d. How does who he is and what he does at the beginning of the story, especially concerning his relationship with Niggle, relate to the formation of Niggle's Parish at the end of the tale?

   _____
   _____
   _____
   _____

3. After reading "On Fairy Stories" in which J. R. R. Tolkien explains the role of a subcreator, discuss how Niggle fits this definition and fulfills his purpose. Particularly, how is his occupation significant in his role as subcreator?

   _____
   _____
   _____
   _____
   _____

4. a. List below the concrete images and their symbolic meanings. Especially note the Inspector or Driver, the Carriage, the Workhouse, and the Mountains. Include in your list below any other symbolic details you observe.

images   symbolic meanings
_____   _____
_____   _____
_____   _____
_____   _____
_____   _____
_____   _____
_____   _____

  b. Explain Tolkien's use of symbols in the story.
_____
_____
_____
_____

5. When Niggle arrives at his destination after his time at the Workhouse, he sees his tree completely finished. What does this say about Niggle (who was "a painter by nature"), about his art, and about his new world?
_____
_____
_____
_____

6. At the end of the story, Niggle and Parish are filled with joy—the Heavens are filled with their laughter. How does this joy relate to the work of the subcreator and the message of the Gospel as Tolkien discusses in "On Fairy Stories"?
_____
_____
_____
_____

7. Assume the role of a subcreator, and write a fairy story along the same lines as "Leaf by Niggle."

Vigen Guroian

Awakening the Moral Imagination: Teaching Virtues through Fairy Tales

Vigen Guroian (b. 1948) received his Ph.D. in Theology from Drew University in 1978 and is currently Professor of Theology and Ethics at Loyola College in Baltimore, Maryland. Along with his responsibilities as husband and father, Guroian sits on numerous editorial boards including *The Journal of Religious Ethics, Pro Ecclesia*, and *Christian Bio-Ethics*. He has published over one hundred articles in books and journals on a range of subjects including liturgy and ethics, marriage and family, children's literature, ecology, genocide, and medical ethics. Two of his recent books, *Inheriting Paradise: Meditations on Gardening* (1999) and *Tending the Heart of Virtue: How Classic Stories Awaken a Child's Moral Imagination* (1998), have received national press and media attention. The following article has been included as a chapter in *Tending the Heart of Virtue;* here Guroian expresses the power of the fairy tale to teach virtue and inculcate moral conduct.

When Mendal was already the far-famed and much-hated rabbi of Kotzak, he once returned to the little town in which he was born. There he visited the teacher who taught him his alphabet when he was a child and read five books of Moses with him. But he did not go to see the teacher who had given him further instruction, and at a chance meeting the man asked his former pupil whether he had any cause to be ashamed of his teacher. Mendal replied: 'You taught me things that can be refuted, for according to one interpretation they can mean this, according to another, that. But my first teacher taught me true teachings which cannot be refuted, and they have remained with me as such. That is why I owe him special reverence.'

—from *Tales of the Hasidim*, Martin Buber

The notion that fairy tales and fantasy stories stimulate and instruct the moral imagination of the young is, of course, not new. The Victorians certainly held to that notion when they brought the fairy tale into the nursery. In our day, we have seen a resurgence of interest in the fairy tale. The renowned psychiatrist Bruno Bettleheim gave this an important impetus twenty years ago with his publication of *The Uses of Enchantment: The Meaning and Importance of Fairy Tales* (1975). "It hardly requires emphasis at this moment in our history" Bettelheim wrote, that children need "a moral education . . . [that teaches] not through abstract ethical concepts but through that which seems tangibly right and therefore meaningful. . . . The child finds this kind of meaning through fairy tales."[1]

Just in the past several years William J. Bennett has edited three highly successful anthologies that include ample samplings of classic fairy tales and modern children's stories.[2] With *The Book of Virtues* (1994) and *The Moral Compass and A Children's Book of Virtues* (1955), Bennett seems to have tapped a tremendous thirst among parents and teachers for literary resources that they might use in nurturing the moral imagination of children. They need, and are asking for direction in how to influence the moral character of the young.

For this reason it is surprising to me how little has been written on the moral meaning in fairy tales. Literary criticism on fairy tales and modern children's literature is a relatively new enterprise that has not yet accumulated a substantial or impressive corpus of interpretation, and the studies done by psychologists and educators mostly address the special concerns of these disciplines. One would have thought that ethicists might do better. Yet religious and philosophical ethicists have not reflected a great deal on children as moral learners nor written much on children's literature. Perhaps this is because, like so many others, they have subscribed to the falsehood that children are at a pre-moral stage and that socialization rather than moral formation is more appropriate to their kind. But intuitively and from our experience as parents and teachers we ought to know that it is not that simple.

The American writer Flannery O'Connor spoke a simple but profound truth when she said that "a story is a way to say something that can't be said any other way. . . . You tell a story because a statement would be inadequate."[3] The great fairy tales and fantasy stories capture the meaning of morality through vivid depictions of struggles between good and evil where characters must make difficult choices between right and wrong, or heroes and villains contest the very fate of imaginary worlds. The great stories avoid didacticism and supply the imagination with important symbolic information about the shape of our world and appropriate responses to its inhabitants. The contemporary moral philosopher Alasdair MacIntyre sums this up eloquently:

> It is through hearing stories about wicked stepmothers, lost children, good but misguided kings, wolves that suckle twin boys, youngest sons who receive no inheritance but must make their own way in the world and eldest sons who waste their inheritance . . . , that children learn or mislearn what a child and what a parent is, what the cast of characters may be in the drama into which they have been born and what the ways of the world are. Deprive children of stories and you leave them unscripted, anxious stutterers in their actions as in their words.[4]

Musing on the wisdom and ethics of the fairy tale, G.K. Chesterton observes that the genre sparks a special way of seeing that is indispensable to morality. Chesterton writes: "I am concerned with a certain way of looking at life, which was created in me by the fairy tales, but has since been meekly ratified by mere facts."[5] I am calling this way of looking at life the moral imagination. For Chesterton is suggesting what the moral imagination is when he remarks: "We can say why we take liberty from a man who takes liberties. But we cannot say why an egg can turn into a chicken any more than we can

say why a bear could turn into a fairy prince. As *ideas*, the egg and the chicken are further from each other than the bear and the prince; for no egg itself suggests a chicken, whereas some princes do suggest bears."[6] Likewise, we can say that values are set by the free market or by the state and assess what we are up against and how we should trade our wares or parley our talents; but we cannot know, except within the context of the entire story, why what seemed to be courage in one character turned out to be stupid bravado, while what looked like disloyalty in another character turned out to be creative fidelity to a greater good.

Moral living is about being responsive and responsible toward other people. And virtues are those traits of character that enable persons to use their freedom in morally responsible ways. The mere ability, however, to use moral principles to justify one's actions does not make a virtuous person. The great Jewish philosopher Martin Buber tells the story of how he fell into "the fatal mistake of *giving instruction* in ethics" by presenting ethics as formal rules and principles. Buber discovered that very little of this kind of education gets "transformed into character-building substance." In his little gem of moral and educational philosophy, an essay appropriately entitled "The Education of Character," Buber recalls: "I try to explain to my pupils that envy is despicable, and at once I feel the secret resistance of those who are poorer than their comrades. I try to explain that it is wicked to bully the weak, and at once I see a suppressed smile on the lips of the strong. I try to explain that lying destroys life, and something frightful happens: the worst habitual liar of the class produces a brilliant essay on the destructive power of lying."[7]

Mere instruction in morality is not sufficient to nurture the virtues. It might even backfire, especially when the presentation is heavily exhortative and the pupil's will is coerced. Instead, a compelling vision of the goodness of goodness itself needs to be presented in a way that is attractive and stirs the imagination. A good moral education addresses both the cognitive and affective dimensions of human nature. Stories are an irreplaceable medium of this kind of moral education. This is the education of character.

The Greek word for character literally means an *impression*. Moral character is an impression stamped upon the self. Character is defined by its orientation, consistency, and constancy. Today we often equate freedom with morality and goodness. But this is naïve because freedom is transcendent and the precondition of choice itself. Depending upon his character, an individual will be drawn toward either goodness or wickedness. Moral and immoral behavior is freedom enacted either for good or for ill.

The great fairy tales and children's fantasy stories attractively depict character and virtue. In these stories the virtues glimmer as if in a looking glass, and wickedness and deception are unmasked of their pretensions to goodness and truth. These stories make us face the unvarnished truth about ourselves while compelling us to consider what kind of people we want to be.

"Beauty and the Beast" is one of the most beloved of all the fairy tales just because it contrasts goodness with badness in a way that is appealing to the imagination. It is also a story that depicts with special force the mystery of virtue itself. Virtue is the "magic" of the moral life for it often appears in the most unexpected persons and places and with surprising results. At the beginning of the story, we are told that a very rich merchant had three "daughters [all of whom] were extremely handsome, especially the youngest: [so she was] called 'The little Beauty.'" But nothing more is said about Beauty's physical attributes. Instead, the story draws our attention to her virtuous character. Beauty's moral goodness—her "inner beauty"—is contrasted with her sisters' pride, vanity, and selfishness—their "inner ugliness." Although Beauty's sisters were physically attractive they "had a great deal of pride, because they were rich . . . [they] put on ridiculous airs . . . and laughed at their sister [Beauty], because she spent . . . her time in reading good books." By contrast, Beauty was "charming, sweet tempered . . . spoke . . . kindly to poor people," and truly loved her father.[8]

Because she is virtuous, Beauty is able to "see" the virtues in Beast that lie hidden beneath his monstrous appearance. At her first supper in the monster's castle, Beauty says to Beast: "That is true [I find you ugly] . . . for I cannot lie, but I believe you are very good-natured." And when Beast tries her the more with his repeated self-deprecatory remarks, Beauty responds emphatically: "Among mankind . . . there are many that deserve that name [Beast] more than you, and I prefer you, just as you are, to those, who, under a human form, hide a treacherous, corrupt, and ungrateful heart."[9] The sharp contrast between Beauty's goodness and her sisters' badness, which is masked by their physical attractiveness, parallels the irony that the Beast who is repulsive physically is good and virtuous.

"Beauty and the Beast" teaches the simple but important lesson that appearances can be deceptive, that what is seen is not always what it appears to be.

Similarly, this great fairy tale also bids us to imagine what the outcome might have been had Beauty's sisters been put in her position. No doubt they would not have recognized or appreciated the goodness beneath Beast's monstrous appearance. Nor does it seem at all likely that they would have made Beauty's courageous and fortuitous choice. The story portrays the paradoxical truth that unless virtue is in a person she will not be able to find, appreciate, or embrace virtue in another.

"Beauty and the Beast" embraces one last important moral truth: a person's decisions in life will define what kind of person she becomes. In this sense also our destinies are not fated: we decide our own destinies. At the end of the story, the "beautiful lady" who has visited Beauty in her dreams appears at Beast's castle and brings with her Beauty's entire family. The fairy then says to Beauty: "Beauty . . . come and see the reward of your judicious choice; you have preferred virtue before either wit or beauty, and deserve to have a person in whom these qualifications are united: you are going to be a great queen."[10] Beauty's sisters, however, are unhappy in their marriages because they chose their spouses solely upon the basis of good looks and wit. Through greed, jealousy, and pride their hearts have become like stone. So they are turned into statues, but retain their consciousness that they might behold their sister's happiness until they admit their own faults.

Like all the great fairy tales, "Beauty and the Beast" invites us to draw analogies between its imaginary world and the world in which we live. It supplies the imagination with information that the self also uses to distinguish what is true from what is not. But how, we might ask, is the imagination itself awakened, and how is it made moral? These are important questions for the moral educator, and they are not so easily answered.

Buber's frank discussion of the mistakes he made when he first taught ethics helps us to see how difficult awakening and nurturing the moral imagination is. Buber's mistakes are not uncommon. They are often committed today, especially when the role of reason in human conduct is overestimated and the roles of the will and the imagination are underestimated. This hazard is increased by a utilitarian and instrumentalist ethos that has seeped to the moral tap roots of our culture.

Despite the overwhelming evidence that we are failing to transmit morality effectively to our children, we persist in teaching ethics as if it comes from a "how to" manual for successful living. Moral educators routinely introduce moral principles and even the virtues themselves to students as if they are practical instruments for achieving success. When we tell our children that standards of social utility and material success are the measurements of the value of moral principles and virtues, then it is not likely that our pedagogy is going to transform the minds or convert the hearts of young people. As Buber observed in his own classroom, all that we will accomplish is to confirm the despair of the weak, darken the envy of the poor, justify the greed of the rich, and encourage the aggression of the strong.

Much of what passes for moral education fails to nurture the moral imagination. Yet, only a pedagogy that awakens and enlivens the moral imagination will persuade the child or the student that courage is the ultimate test of good character, that honesty is essential for trust and harmony among persons, and that humility and a magnanimous spirit are goods greater than the prizes won by selfishness, pride, or the unscrupulous exercise of position and power.

The moral imagination is not a *thing*, not so much a faculty even, as the very process by which the self makes metaphors out of images given by experience and then employs these metaphors to find and suppose moral correspondences in experience. The moral imagination is active, for well or ill, strongly or weakly, every moment of our lives, in our sleep as well as when we are awake. But it needs nurture and proper exercise. Otherwise it will atrophy like a muscle that is not used. The richness or the poverty of the moral imagination depends upon the richness or the poverty of experience. When human beings are young and dependent upon parents and others who assume custodial care for them, they are especially open to formation through experiences provided by these persons. When we argue or discuss what kind of education or recreation our children should have we are acknowledging these realities.

Unfortunately, more often than not, this society is failing to provide children with the kinds of experience that nurture and build the moral imagination. One measure of the impoverishment of the moral imagination in the rising generation is their inability to recognize, make, or to use metaphors. My college students do not lack an awareness of morality, although they might be confused or perplexed about its basis or personal ownership. But when they read a novel they are perplexed because they are unable to find the inner connections of character, action, and narrative provided by the author's own figurative imagination. Sadly, the only kind of story many of my undergraduate students seem to be able to follow are news reports and sitcom scripts.

Several years ago, I administered a surprise quiz in a course on theology and literature in which I asked the students to list and explain five metaphors that they had found in John Updike's early novel *Rabbit, Run*. The majority of the class was unable to name five metaphors. Some students did not even identify the metaphor in the book's title, which I had purposively discussed in the preceding class meeting. It was not that these young people lacked a practical definition of a metaphor. They had been provided with such a definition over and over again in English courses. They lacked, however, a personal knowledge of metaphor that only an active imagination engenders. I suspect that in the past these students had gotten the idea that all they needed to do was look for the so-called "facts" in a book. Facts are things whose meaning belongs to their use and whose use requires relatively little interpretation. We are living in a culture in which metaphor is discarded for the so-called "facts." We train minds to catch these "facts" much as one breaks in a baseball glove. Meanwhile, the imagination is neglected and is left unguarded and untrained.

Fairy tales and fantasy stories transport the reader into *other worlds* that are fresh with wonder, surprise, and danger. They challenge the reader to make sense out of those *other worlds*, to navigate his way through them, and to imagine himself in the place of the heroes and heroines who populate those worlds. The safety and assurance of these imaginative adventures is that risks can be taken without having to endure all of the consequences of failure; the joy is in discovering how these risky adventures might eventuate in satisfactory and happy outcomes. Yet the concept of self is also transformed. The images and metaphors in these stories stay with the reader even after he has returned to the "real" world.

After a child has read Hans Christian Andersen's *The Snow Queen* or C.S. Lewis's *The Lion, the Witch, and the Wardrobe*, her moral imagination is bound to have been stimulated and sharpened. These stories offer powerful images of good and evil and show her how to love through the examples of the characters she has come to love and admire. This will spur her imagination to translate these experiences and images into the constitutive elements of self identity and into metaphors she will use to interpret her own world. She grows increasingly capable of moving about in that world with moral intent.

When the moral imagination is wakeful, the virtues come to life, filled with personal and existential, as well as social, significance. The virtues needn't be the dry and lifeless data of moral theories or the ethical version of hygienic rules in health science classes; they can take on a life that attracts and awakens the desire to own them for oneself. We need desperately to adopt forms of moral pedagogy that are faithful to the ancient and true vocation of the teacher—to make persons into mature and whole human beings, able to stand face to face with the truth about themselves and others, and desiring to correct their faults and to emulate goodness and truth wherever it is found. We need to take greater advantage of the power in stories to humanize the young, whether these be Buber's beloved tales of the Hasidim or the stories we commonly refer to as fairy tales.

"Values" is the chief buzz-word of the contemporary educational scene. The word carries with it the full burden of our concerns over the decline of morality. Teaching values, whether family values, democratic values, or religious values, is touted as the remedy for our moral confusion. Of course, this consensus about the need for stronger moral values immediately cracks and advocates retreat when the inevitable question is raised as to which values should be taught. I do not think that the current debate over values lends much promise of clarifying what we believe in or what morality we should be teaching our children. Values certainly are not the answer to moral relativism. Quite to the contrary, values talk is entirely amenable to moral relativism.

In her book, *The Demoralization of Society: From Victorian Virtues to Modern Values,* Gertrude Himmelfarb exposes what some students of Western morals have known all along, that values is a rather new term in our moral vocabulary. Its history reaches back not much farther than the late-nineteenth century. The German philosopher Friedrich Nietzsche seems to have been the inventor of our modern use of the term as a category of morality. Nietzsche was opposed to what we call "effeminate" Christianity and advocated the "Ubermensch" or superior human being with the courage to defy conventional religious morality and invent his own values. In his famous essay entitled *Beyond Good and Evil,* Nietzsche used values in this new way, not as a verb meaning to value or esteem something, nor as a singular noun, meaning the measure of a thing (the economic value of money, labor, or property), but in the plural, connoting the moral beliefs and attitudes of a society or of the individual.[9] In his turn of the phrase "transvaluation of values," Nietzsche summed up his thesis about the "death of God" and the birth of his new "noble type of man." Nietzsche described this new kind of human being as "a determiner of [his own] values" who judges right from wrong upon the basis of what is good or injurious to himself. Thus the values of conventional morality were false values bound to be replaced by the self made values of the truly autonomous and free individual.

Nietzsche's innovative use of values did not gain immediate approval or acceptance. Even as late as the 1928 edition, the *Oxford English Dictionary* did not list values in the plural form referring to moral qualities. More recently, the 1992 edition of the *Oxford Modern English Dictionary* defines values not only in the modern sense of moral qualities but assigns them a subjectivistic character. The dictionary's editors give this definition: Values refers to *"one's* standards, *one's judgement* of what is valuable or important in life" (the emphases are mine). Another way of putting it is that values belong to those things we call individual lifestyles, and in common discourse a lifestyle is something we choose and even exchange for another according to our personal preferences and tastes, much in the same way that we might replace one wardrobe with another. Himmelfarb is justified when she says: "'Values' [has] brought with it the assumptions that all moral ideas are subjective and relative, that they are mere customs and conventions, that they have a purely instrumental and utilitarian purpose, and that they are peculiar to specific individuals and societies."[11]

In our consumerist society moral values may even take on the characteristics of material commodities. We easily assume that personal freedom is about *choosing* values for oneself in an unregulated and ever expanding marketplace of moralities and lifestyles. *Choosing* values turns out not to be much different from shopping for groceries at the supermarket or selecting building supplies at the home improvement store. As a society, we are learning how to regard morality and values as matters of taste and personal satisfaction. For some people married heterosexual monogamy is a value and for others it is a romantic relationship with one or several lovers, male or female or both. Some people say abortion is wrong and they do not approve of it; but these same people also say that for others abortion may be all right. This is possible only if values are the creation of the self and are not universally binding moral norms. If one scratches just beneath the surface of the moral outlook of many Americans one bumps into the rather naively but also often vehemently held assumption that the individual is the architect of his or her own morality built out of value "blocks" that the individual independently picks and stacks. We suddenly run into the ghost of Friedrich Nietzsche.

There are real and very important differences between what we now call values and the virtues as they had traditionally been understood. Let me put it this way. A value is like a smoke ring. Its shape is initially determined by the smoker; but once it is released there is no telling what shape it will take. One thing is certain, however. Once a smoke ring has left the smoker's lips it has already begun to evaporate into thin air. Volition and volatility are the character of smoke rings and values both. By contrast, a virtue might be compared to a stone whose nature is permanence. We might throw a stone into a pond where it will lie at the bottom with other stones. But if, at some later date, we should want to retrieve that stone from the bottom of the pond, we can be sure that the shape of the stone has not changed and that we will be able to distinguish it from the rest of the stones.

The virtues define the character of a person, his enduring relationship to the world, and what will be his end. Whereas, values, according to their common usage, are the instruments or components of moral living that the self chooses for itself and that the self may disregard without necessarily jeopardizing its identity. Accordingly, values are subordinate and relative to the self's own autonomy, which is understood as the self's highest value and essential quality. But when we say in the older speech of character that Jack is virtuous and that he is a courageous person, we are saying that the virtue of courage belongs to the very essence of who and what Jack is. Being courageous is not subject to a willing for it to be so or a willing for it not to be so. Virtues and vices define the will itself and also properly describe the willing person. The color orange is both a quality of an orange and an inescapable description of it. If we find an object, however, that looks like an orange but is brown, it must either be an orange that has gone bad or it is not an orange at all. Similarly, it makes no moral

sense to say that a courageous man has decided to be a coward. We cannot say on the basis of some subsequent behavior that we have observed in Jack that he must have decided to become a coward. If Jack's late actions were indeed cowardly and not courageous then we are obliged, rather, to revise our original description of Jack.

Thus, I am contending that what seems so self-evident to many of our contemporaries about the centrality of values to moral living might not be true, nor be consistent with human nature, nor take into account adequately the larger share of human reality over which we each personally have little or no choice or control. Rather, the best of sources in the Western tradition have argued that morality is much more than, indeed qualitatively different from, the sum of the values that an essentially autonomous self chooses for itself. Classical, Jewish, and Christian sources such as Plato, Aristotle, and Cicero, or Augustine, John Chrysostom, Maimonides, Thomas Aquinas, and John Calvin insist that morality is neither plural nor subjective. Instead, they maintain that human morality is substantial, universal, and relational in character, founded and rooted in a permanent Good, or in a higher moral law, or in the being of God. From this standpoint, values and decisions whose claims of legitimacy extend no further than individual volition are as effervescent as the foam that floats on top the waves. They cannot be reliable guides to moral living.

The great teachers of our historic culture insist that morality is deeper and more substantial than effervescent foam. It stands to reason, they insist, that where there are waves and foam there is a deeper body of water. These sources describe a sea of substantial morality that lies beneath the ephemeral and ever-changing surface expressions of emotion, taste, and satisfaction in ordinary human intercourse. They describe character as the gravity that keeps us afloat and virtues as the sails that propel us and the instruments that help us to maintain our course even when the ship is being rocked by stormy waters and high seas.

Sailors need to know when to use ballast or throw down the anchor, lest the ship sink and they drown. In like manner, the virtues enable us to respond correctly to those moments of life that are the moral equivalents to such conditions at sea. However, an ability to discern these moments and respond appropriately entails more than formal techniques of decision-making; just as successful sailing requires that one knows more than just the techniques of good navigation. As the latter requires a knowledge of and familiarity with the sea that cannot be taught in books but can only be learned from sea-faring itself, so the moral life requires that we also *be* virtuous. The virtues are not just the moral equivalent of techniques of good sailing; rather they are the way as well as the end of goodness and happiness. If we assume, however, as so many of the textbooks would have us believe, that problems and quandaries are the whole subject matter of ethics and that the decisions we make are the purpose of morality, then we are likely to interpret even the virtues in the same superficial, utilitarian way that we already think of values. But if we pay heed to the ancient sources we will recognize that the virtues are related to a much thicker and deeper moral reality. We will see the virtues as the qualities of character that we need in order to steer our way through the complicated and mysterious sea of morality into which we all have been placed. For such journeying a pocket full of values is neither sufficient ballast nor substitute for sails, compass, or sextant.

Years ago in a series of essays entitled, simply enough, "Education, or the Mistake About the Child,"[12] G.K. Chesterton entered into a debate that was no less important then than it is today. That debate is about what counts for moral education. In conclusion, I want to review what Chesterton had to say, thus bringing this conversation around full circle to the claim I made at the start, that stories, especially fairy tales, are invaluable resources for the moral education of children.

Modern educators have not been well disposed toward traditional fairy tales and their like. They write them off as too violent or not contemporary enough and so forth and so on. They favor "practical" and "realistic" stories—stories about the lives children live today that easily lend themselves to distillation into useful themes, principles, and values. What some educators can't find they create. Off of the pens of values textbook writers, stories spill whose sole purpose is to clarify so-called moral problems or "draw-out" reasons for making intelligent moral decisions. These stories are of the disposable kind, made to be discarded like empty cartons once the important "stuff" that has been packed in them has been extracted. Teaching reasoning skills, not the virtues, is considered the means to a moral education; values-clarification, not character, is regarded as the goal.

These educators think that moral education is like teaching children reading or arithmetic. But that is not even quite accurate, because in the case of moral education children are supposed to be permitted to discover and clarify for themselves their own values and personal moral stance in the world. Yet we do not permit children to invent their own math: we teach them the multiplication tables; nor do we encourage children to make up their own personal alphabets: we teach them how to read. What might one suppose would be the outcome of an education that did permit children to invent their own alphabets and math? No doubt the result would be confusion or chaos. Ought we to be surprised at the outcome of our recent efforts to help children clarify their own values, in point of fact invent their own personal moralities?

In his own inimitable way, G.K. Chesterton exposed the flaw and deception in this modern approach to moral education. And he identified the dogmatizing in its anti-dogmatic rhetoric. In our day this modern approach is justified by prior commitments to certain psychological theories that elevate personal autonomy and self-realization above what is dismissively called external authority. The teacher must not introduce values into the classroom but work, instead, to "draw out" from children their own moral beliefs and through a process of clarification help them to better formulate their own values. But here is how Chesterton characterized this historic debate:

> The important point is . . . that you cannot . . . get rid of authority in education. . . . The educator drawing out is just as arbitrary and coercive as the instructor pouring in: for he draws out what he chooses. He decides what in the child shall be developed and what shall not be developed. He does not (I suppose) draw out the neglected faculty of forgery. He does not (so far, at least) lead out, with timid steps, a shy talent for torture. The only result of this pompous and precise distinction between the educator and the instructor is that the instructor pokes where he likes and the educator pulls where he likes.[13]

In answer to the skeptics, Chesterton stated what he thought to be obvious. Whether we admit it or not, education is bound to indoctrinate and bound to coerce. Rabbi Mendal especially thanked and praised his first teacher because he faithfully inculcated in his young student the necessary rudiments of culture and passed on the essentials of a religious and moral way of life. The *Oxford English Dictionary* defines indoctrination as to imbue with learning or bring into a knowledge of something, such as a dogma. Chesterton argued that an authentic moral education is not possible unless something like this occurs. He spoke of the responsibility to affirm "the truth of our human tradition and hand it on with a voice of authority. That is the one eternal education; to be sure enough that something is true that you dare to tell it to a child."[14]

The real corruptions of moral education are an imperious moralizing, on the one hand, and the indulgence of spurious argument and undisciplined opinion, on the other. Nevertheless, a valid and effective moral education is bound to be coercive at times and even do a kind of violence, whether or not opinion is "drawn out" from the student or dogma is "put into" him.

> Exactly the same intellectual violence is done to the creature who is poked and pulled. Now we must all accept the responsibility of this intellectual violence. Education is violent; because it is creative. It is creative because it is human. It is reckless as playing on the fiddle; as dogmatic as drawing a picture; as brutal as building a house. In short it is what all human action is; it is an interference with life and growth.[15]

But Chesterton was not an advocate of the blunt and heavy instrument; nor am I. This is one reason why fairy tales appealed to him so much. Fairy tales might not qualify as scientific hypotheses or theories, but they do resonate with the deepest qualities of humanness, of freedom, and of the moral imagination. At the same time, they deny the materialism and psychological determinism that lurk behind much of the modern talk of human liberation, and they discredit the hubris of reason and rationality that displaces faith and confidence in truth. Again, they show us a way of envisioning the world—a world in which everything that is need not have been and the *real* moral law connotes freedom and not necessity. The fairy-tale philosopher, wrote Chesterton, is "glad that the leaf is green precisely because it could have been scarlet. . . . He is pleased that snow is white on the strictly reasonable ground that it might have been black. Every colour has in it a bold quality as of choice; the red of garden roses is not only decisive but dramatic, like spilt blood. He feels that something has been *done*,"[16] that there is something *willful* in all of it as if someone decided that things ought to be this way instead of another way and that these things are repeated either in order to improve them or simply because they are a source of delight in their repetition. The fairy-tale

philosopher respects the deeper mystery of freedom in its transcendent source.

Second, fairy tales show us that there is a difference between what is logically possible and what is morally felicitous, between what is rationally do-able and what is morally permissible. In fairy tales the character of real law belongs to neither natural necessity nor rational determinism. Rather, real law is a comprehensible sign of a primal, unfathomable freedom and of a numinous reality and will. Real law, the realest law, can be obeyed or broken, and in either case for the very same reason—because the creature is both subject of and participant in this primal freedom. Fairy tale heroes are called to be both free and responsible, thus virtuous and respectful of the moral law.

Fairy tale and modern fantasy stories project fantastic other worlds; but they also pay close attention to real moral "laws" of character and virtue. These laws ought not to be high-handedly shoved down the throats of children (or of anyone else). More accurately, they are norms of behavior that obtain in patterns of relation between agent, act, other, and world. Rational cognition is capable of grasping these norms. They become habit, however, only when they are lived, or, as in the case of fairy tales, experiences vicariously and imaginatively through the artful delineation of character and plot in story. Thus, while fairy tales are not a substitute for life experience, they have the great capacity to shape our moral constitution without the shortcomings of either rigidly dogmatic schooling or values-clarification education.

By portraying wonderful and frightening worlds in which ugly beasts are transformed into princes and evil persons are turned to stones and good persons back to flesh, fairy tales remind us of moral truths whose ultimate claims to normativity and permanence we would not think of questioning. Love freely given is better than obedience that is coerced. Courage that rescues the innocent is noble; whereas, cowardice that betrays others for self-gain or self-preservation is worthy only of disdain. Fairy tales say plainly that virtue and vice are opposites and not just a matter of degree. They show us that the virtues fit into character and complete our world in the same way that goodness naturally fills all things.

I realize that the views I have expressed defy what the advocates of late-modernity or post-modernity insist upon, that there is no such thing as a common human condition or a perennial literature that lends expression to the experience of that condition. I do not expect to persuade those who are entrenched in these positions to change their minds. I can only appeal to that certain "stuff" of human existence that the human imagination takes hold of and makes moral sense of in fairy tales. I mean such things as: the joy in the birth of a first child and the crippling sorrow of illness and deformity, childhood fears of getting lost matched by childhood desires to escape parental authority, the love that binds siblings together and the rivalry that tears them apart, the naming we do that gives identity and the naming we also do that confuses identity, the curses of dread male-factors and the blessings of welcome benefactors, the agony of unrequited love and the joy of love that is reciprocated.

I could go on. But the skeptics and critics will not be satisfied. The skeptics say there is nothing of commonality in such things, just individual lives and the particular conditions in which these lives flourish or fail. I am not convinced. Nothing of what these people say is proven, and as I grow older and become more traveled and my memory fills with so many different lives and human faces, the wisdom of fairy tales, the wisdom of a common human condition underlying and running through all of the diversity and difference, seems far more reasonable than moral and cultural relativism. One last thing in which I agree with Chesterton. Fairy tales lead us toward a belief in something that, if it were not also so veiled in a mystery, common sense alone would affirm: if there is a story there must surely also be a story-teller. ∎

Author's Notes

1 Bruno Bettleheim, *The Uses of Enchantment* (New York: Alfred A. Knopf, Inc., 1975). p. 5.

2 William J. Bennett, ed., *The Book of Virtues* (New York: Simon and Schuster, 1993).

3 Flannery O'Connor, *Mystery and Manners* (New York: Farrar, Straus and Giroux, 1990), p. 96.

4 Alasdair MacIntyre, *After Virtue: A Study in Moral Theory,* 2nd ed. (Notre Dame, IN: University of Notre Dame Press, 1984), p. 216.

5 Gilbert K. Chesterton, *Orthodoxy* (Garden City, NY: Doubleday and Co., 1959), p. 50.

6 *Ibid.,* p. 52.

7 Martin Buber, *Between Man and Man* (New York: Macmillan Pub. Co., Inc., 1978), p. 105.

8 Ionia and Peter Opie, eds., *The Classic Fairy Tales* (New York: Oxford University Press, 1980), pp. 182–183. This is the English translation of Madame de Beaumont's version of the fairy tale published originally in French in 1756, subsequently translated into English in 1761.

9 *Ibid.,* p. 190.

10 *Ibid.,* p. 195.

11 Gertrude Himmelfarb, *The Demoralization of Society: From Victorian Virtues to Modern Values* (New York: Alfred A. Knopf, 1995), p. 10.

12 These are collected in Gilbert K. Chesterton, *What's Wrong with the World* (New York: Dodd, Mead and Co., 1910).

13 *Ibid.,* p. 253.

14 *Ibid.,* p. 254.

15 *Ibid.,* p. 253.

16 Chesterton, *Orthodoxy,* p. 59.

Making Connections through Discussion and Writing

1. How does Guroian describe the moral imagination?

_____

_____

_____

_____

_____

2. a. Explain Guroian's statement: "The mere ability, however, to use moral principles to justify one's actions does not make a virtuous person."

_____

_____

_____

_____

_____

   b. Why is "mere instruction in morality . . . not sufficient to nurture the virtues"?

_____

_____

_____

_____

3. How does Guroian describe moral character?

_____

_____

_____

_____

4. What do fairy tales do to shape the moral imagination?

_____

_____

_____

_____

5. a. List below some fairy tales Guroian describes.

_____

_____

_____

   b. What particular virtues are emphasized by these tales?

_____

_____

_____

6. According to Guroian, how are virtues related to the development of the moral imagination?

_____

_____

_____

7. a. What distinction does Guroian make between values and virtues?

_____

_____

_____

   b. What can virtues accomplish that values cannot?

_____

_____

_____

8. a. How does G. K. Chesterton deal with modern educators?

_____

_____

_____

   b. What does he see as moral education?

_____

_____

9. a. What are fairy tales able to accomplish in children that modern educational theory cannot?

_____

_____

   b. List specific purposes that the fairy tale accomplishes.

_____

_____

10. a. Think of some fairy tales that were meaningful to you. List them, and describe how they affected you.

   Fairy tale   Effect

   _____   _____

   _____   _____

   _____   _____

   _____   _____

   _____   _____

   b. How was your moral imagination developed?

_____

_____

Walter Wangerin, Jr.
Flying the Night Wind

Walter Wangerin, Jr., (b. 1944) was born in Portland, Oregon, his father an educator, his mother a businesswoman. He has degrees from Concordia Theological Seminary, Miami University, and Christ Seminary. Presently a full-time writer, Wangerin has worked as a migrant peapicker, lifeguard, ghetto youth worker, producer and announcer at a radio station, an English professor, and even a Lutheran pastor. At one time, while writing the book *Crying for a Vision,* he even lived among the Lakota Indians in order to portray their legends more accurately. Wangerin has written more than twenty devotional, fiction, and non-fiction books for both children and adults. Probably his most famous work is *The Book of the Dun Cow* (1978), a book of fantasy patterned after the beast fables, that explores the perennial battle of good and evil. It won numerous awards including Best Children's Book of the Year by both *School Library Journal* and *New York Times* (1978) and the National Religious Book Award (1980). Its sequel, *The Book of Sorrows,* followed in 1985. Other works include *Ragman and Other Cries of Faith* (1984) and *Miz Lil and the Chronicles of Grace* (1988). He is currently writer-in-residence at Valparaiso University; writes articles for *The Lutheran* magazine, a monthly publication of the Evangelical Lutheran Church in America; and is the featured speaker for the *Lutheran Vespers* radio program. In the essay below, Walter Wangerin demonstrates how fairy tales, particularly those of Hans Christian Andersen, shaped his imagination.

Personal Essay

When I was a child, I spake as a child, I understood as a child. When I became a man I put away childish things, but the man I became was shaped in childhood, and that shape remains forever.

Fairy tales shaped me. I have since "put them away." That is, the adult is a mostly rational creature, aware that fairy tales are not "real" but are a fantasy, an entertaining escape from the problems of the world.

But as a child all full of wonder, I approached the fairy tale as something real indeed. Children meet the problems of the world with their imagination, and the fairy tale honors and feeds and abets the imagination. As a child, I never analyzed the tale I read; I felt it; I sank inside of it; I *lived* its experience through to the happy conclusion.

The tales of Hans Christian Andersen *were* my world for a while. They named and shaped the universe in which I dwelt, and something of that shape has remained forever: not the fantasy, but the faith that created the fantasy continues even now to explain existence.

When my father bought a thick, pictureless book containing all the tales of Hans Christian Andersen and began to read them to his children, he did me a kindness more profound than mere entertainment. Those things that were horrible and senseless in my external world were, in Andersen's world, horrible still; but his stories gave them a sense (often a spiritual sense) that I could grasp, by which the horror might be mastered, if not by me then by someone, by goodness, by God. Andersen was my whispering, laughing, wise companion when I most needed companionship.

"Ready?" Dad asks. I nod. I curl tight beneath the covers. "Once upon a time," Dad reads, "there lived in a village two men who had the same name; they were both called Claus. . . ."

Little Claus and Big Claus: This is the first of all the tales my father chooses to read to us. It's an astonishing beginning. There is violence here: horse killings, grandmother killings, old men sent to heaven, and a great, rich fool apparently drowned. But the violence accords with nightmares of my own.

And the violence is funny! I listen and laugh, and my father laughs, too. What is happening? Violence is being reduced to something manageable; and because I am the one laughing at it, scorning it, recognizing the blustering silliness of it, then I am larger than it, capable of triumphing over it. This story does not deny the monster in me or the cruelties of the general society. Rather, it empowers me.

I identify with Little Claus. In contrast to the big and brutal Big Claus, I am poor and weak (though cleverer by half), hobbled by kindness while he is strong in amorality. In the beginning I have one horse and he has four. All week long he plows with all five, but on Sundays the team is mine. And because I am not sinless, either, vanity makes me cry out: "Giddy-up, all my horses!"

This infuriates Big Claus. "Four of those horses are mine," he yells. "If you say that again, I'll knock your horse in the head, and then you will have none."

But I am not sinless. (This is a troubling fact; both in my life and in this story—which makes the story true.) In spite of his threat, the passing of churchgoers stirs my vanity again, and I cry: "Giddy-up, all my horses!"

So Big Claus comes and knocks my only horse dead.

I *like* Little Claus. I want to be—I am—him. I dislike Big Claus. I sever myself from—and I am not—him, even though he represents a real iniquity in me. But within the story, by laughter and luck and cleverness (but call luck "grace"), I amputate this evil which I don't want to be.

And here is how I do it. I tan the hide of my murdered horse. I take it to market to sell it. On the way I have the "luck" to witness a farmer's wife involved in an impropriety with a deacon while her husband is absent: she's feeding the deacon a fine dinner in her kitchen. Just before the farmer returns, she hides the dinner in the oven and the deacon in an empty chest. I see all this, and then the good farmer invites me inside for food.

"I'm sorry, dear, we have no food," says the farmer's wife.

But I, who am cleverer by half than deacons and wives and Big Claus, too, step on the hide of my murdered horse. I make it squeak and interpret the squeaks as a prophecy that there is dinner ready-made in the oven. There is, and the farmer is amazed by my wonderful horsehide. Moreover, I step on it again, and it squeaks again, declaring that there's a devil-deacon in that chest. There is! So the farmer buys my horse's hide for a whole bushel of money and sends the deacon-in-a-chest away with me. I'm so clever that I cannot quit this cleverness: when I come to a river, I pretend out loud that I'm going to toss the chest in it. The deacon roars and pleads and bargains, until I sell him his freedom for another bushel of money. I am rich.

And what do I do to the Brutal Big Claus? Why, I use his stupidity and his greed against him.

"Where did you get all that money from?" cries Big Claus.

"Oh, that was for my horsehide. I sold it last night."

Immediately Big Claus hurries home and takes an ax and knocks all four of his horses in their heads. He skins them and runs to market to humiliate himself. Who would buy horsehides for bushels of money?

And so my story goes: I trick Big Claus into knocking his poor grandmother in the head. Ah, me, but the man is dumb! And his nature is violent altogether! Finally, I trick Big Claus into jumping into the river himself, and so I am rid of dumbness, greed, and brutality all at once.

Dad closes the book. He turns out the light and leaves. But I am flying the night wind, living still in a good, good story—"good" in that evil is overcome and suffers its due, in that the Old Adam need not forever be my master. But I discover the truth in experience, laughing till the tears run down my cheeks, not in remote and intellectual lessons that my poor brain can scarcely translate into "real life."

Hans Andersen has persuaded me of optimism, a tough and abiding optimism, not the pollyanna sugar that merely sweetens the facts of evil and suffering, danger and death.

I cannot run. I am short, hampered by big buttocks, hunched with a miserable miscoordination, generally inferior in the contests of children—unable to run. But in the track meets of the fifth grade, they make me run the 100-yard dash. It causes me a vomitous anxiety. I have nightmares of running under water. My dreams are not untrue, for when the starting gun goes off, I stumble and am the last to leave the line; slowly, slowly I suffer my way to the end of the race, and when I arrive, people have departed to run in other races. I am humiliated. Ellery Yurchuck cries out, "He walks like a girl!" I do. I burn with shame, I cannot do what other children do so thoughtlessly. I cannot run.

But Dad reads of a duckling more ugly than others, and I listen with unspeakable sympathy for that duck. "I know, I know," I murmur.

The ugliness alone—not wickedness, not cruelty, not any error on our part—brings shame upon us, the ugly duckling and I. Other ducklings are cute, in the image of our mother. But we were hatched from a larger, vagrant egg—an odd beginning, producing an odd shape. Therefore, we are pecked and pushed and scorned. Our wonderful mother defends us; but we only feel pity for her that she should so unjustly suffer for our own troubles. Merely that she loves us is cause for pain. Oh, it is so complicated to be ugly!

For our own sakes she says, "I wish you were far away"—from pain and teasing, she means. But we take her literally. We run away to other barnyards, never to see her again.

On our own we discover "the way of the world." It includes the death of the few who befriend us: Hunters kill two kindly wild ganders. It includes a sneering judgment against all the things we cannot do: Can't lay eggs like chickens, can't arch our backs like cats. *Do, do, do,* cries society; but we can *do* nothing it likes and therefore are the uglier.

It is utterly natural that in the end we wish to die. Sorrow drives us to such extremities, even though we are but a child and a duckling.

In the dead of a dreary winter we notice three swans moving in absolute elegance, nobility, and beauty. Surely, they, too, will despise our ugliness, and their spite will be as intense as their distant beauty. Surely, then, they will kill us. In fact, we desire to die by beauty rather than by any other means. It seems right. We think to ourselves, "It is better to be killed by them than to be bitten by the other ducks."

But here appears the outrageous grace that we never anticipated: all along, while we were ugly indeed, another mercy was working within us, uncaused by us but given to us purely as a gift. What was this mercy? What sort of gift is given now to us? Why, it is we ourselves, transfigured!

"'Kill me,' whispered the poor creature, and bent his head humbly while he waited for his death." So goes the story, and thus do we surrender ourselves. "Humbly. . . ," writes Andersen. "Humbly," my father reads, and I more than hear it; I feel such humility in my heart. I am the one who cannot run. But what does such humility reveal to me?

In Andersen's words: "But what was that he saw in the water? It was his own reflection; and he was no longer an awkward, clumsy, gray bird, so ungainly and so ugly. He was a swan! It does not matter that one is born in the henyard as long as one has lain in a swan's egg." And Andersen goes

on to name the goodness that has existed in all our sorrow, the duckling's and mine. Andersen names the grace upon grace that we have received, and the graciousness that we shall show hereafter: "He was thankful that he had known so much want, and gone through so much suffering, for it made him appreciate his present happiness and loveliness of everything about him all the more. . . . Everyone agreed that the new swan was the most beautiful of them all. The older swans bowed toward him."

But does pride or vengeance then rear up in him or in me? No, and that is much the point: for the suffering transfigures us even to the soul. Humility showed us our new selves; humility remains in our hearts to keep these selves both beautiful and *virtuous:* "He felt so shy that he hid his head beneath his wing. He was too happy, but not proud, for a kind heart can never be proud."

So then, there is hope—not only that there may emerge from my ugly self a beauty, but also that the suffering that my ugliness has caused is ultimately valuable, making my beautiful self also a good and sympathetic self. In the end I shall love the world the more; and even the people who once did me dishonor, I shall honor.

Can any child receive a better impress on his person, a subtler, more spiritual shape than this, that he be taught grace and to be gracious? And what is more fortified than the self-esteem that comes as a gift from God?

Night after night my father reads the stories from a thick book with pastel-colored pages, pink and blue and yellow. Night after night I live the adventures that order my turbulent days and shape my waking self, my instincts, my faith, my adulthood to come. Optimism grows in me, and hope in the midst of suffering, and this third thing too, perhaps the most difficult thing of all: forgiveness for my own most self-centered and wretched sins. Not the doctrine of forgiveness. Not the concept. Forgiveness *in fact*, as a mold to my experience ever hereafter. Andersen's world is a dramatic enactment of theologies that the child simply cannot grasp in the abstract.

The north wind whistles at the eaves, an almost malevolent warning. "This story," my father murmurs, the pipe gone dead beside him, "is called *The Red Shoes.*"

A fatherless girl named Karen appears before me. She is not aware of me, but I am of her. I join her. We are one. And we are both very vain. We think that we are more than pretty: gorgeous. We want everyone to notice how splendid we are; therefore, even at inappropriate times, we slip our little feet into a pair of patent-leather shoes so red, so red, O Lord, that we shine!

This is how vain we are, and this is how the story begins: at the funeral of our mother we follow the coffin in red shoes. And we are noticed. A kindly old woman notices us. We think it's because of our red shoes and our gorgeousness. But it is her love that sees us; she is moved by the sight of a newly orphaned child. So by grace we are granted a second mother, for the woman takes us in and raises us as her own.

Her eyes grow dim. Ours stay sharp for red adornments. When the time of our confirmation arrives, and when we must buy shoes for the holy occasion, the old woman thinks we've bought black, but it is red we carry home, and it is red we wear to church. Everyone notices our bright red feet. We are so proud! Our mind is scarcely on the words of our "covenant with God to be a good Christian." We are thinking of red shoes.

Then it happens that the old woman, our second mother, grows sick, as our first mother had. Once we were ignorant of the world, of the laws of God, and of our own wicked tendencies. But now we have been taught and scolded and warned. This time we ought to know better. Nevertheless, we do again exactly what we have done before.

On the very night when the doctors say that the old woman is dying, we contemplate the red shoes, the alluring red shoes, the bright red shoes so perfect for our gorgeousness. There is a dance tonight. Looking leads to touching, and touching leads to donning; and as soon as the shoes are on our feet, we have to go. We leave the dying woman behind and steal away to dance.

And we do dance. We laugh and whirl the whole night through; for once we have begun, we cannot stop. It is the shoes that are dancing now. The red shoes! Dancing and dancing wherever they wish, taking us with them, down the stairs and out the door. And while they are dancing, the old woman dies.

I know this only too well.

For I have dealt with my mother as though she were nothing to me. My mother the dim-eyed old woman, my mother the stepmother, who unjustly (so it seemed to me) punished me for many things, could easily be dismissed. I have run out to play when I knew she didn't want me to go. I have stayed gone too long, causing her anguish at my absence. And when she confronted me with my fault, I have whistled. I have reduced her, once or twice, to tears at my cold impertinence. She has gone into her bedroom and shut the door and grieved in a deep frustration. Then I was burned by guilt to hear her hurt. She was ill in her bedroom, dying. She said so: *Dying.* "I am sick to death of your disobedience," she said. O Mama! Never again! But always my demons have been too powerful for me, and I have done it again in spite of every resolution.

I am Karen, surrendering to sin until my sin has taken me over completely—and even when I want to stop, I cannot. Even when my heart desires goodness, it has it not. Dancing and dancing, our shoes have taken us into the street.

We dance toward the church. Maybe there is help for us in church. But at the door an angel appears, dressed in white, holding a shining sword.

"You shall dance," he declares, "dance in your red shoes until you become pale and thin. When you pass a house where proud and vain children live, there you shall knock on the door so that they will see you and fear your fate. Dance, you shall dance. Dance!"

"Mercy!" scream Karen and I together. But we cannot hear what the angel answers, because the red shoes carry us away and away, always dancing.

One morning in a lonely place we dance past a solitary cottage. The man who comes out when we cry is the Executioner. "I am the one," he says, "who cuts off the heads of evil men."

"No," we plead, "for then I should not be able to repent. But cut off our feet instead."

We confess our sins (isn't this enough?), and the Executioner cuts off our feet, and the red shoes go dancing away into the forest. For us the kindly Executioner carves wooden feet. He teaches us the psalm that penitent people sing. We kiss his hand and go.

Now have we suffered enough?

We go again to the church. Is this what it takes? That we are severed of our sin? Will ritual and formality receive us now? No, no, this isn't enough. For when we come to the door, the red shoes arrive ahead of us and dance and dance to block our way. In horror we flee. O God! The sins keep coming back! What can we *do* to be free?

So now we despair. Nothing we do can save us. Not true sorrow, which we have done. Not true goodness, which we have done. Do this, do that— we've done it all, and still the shoes, they mock us.

Therefore, let us live in misery till we die. We deserve no better.

We go to the minister's house and ask for work. In pity he takes us in, gives us his roof and food. We work very hard, though hopelessly, for we know this changes nothing—our feet are still wooden. In the evening the minister reads to his children from the Bible and we listen; but we make no great account of the listening, because we are wiser now and know this changes nothing.

On Sunday, the minister's whole family goes to church. We are invited, too, but our eyes fill with tears. They go without us.

In a tiny room we sit down to read a psalm book. The wind blows hither the music of the church organ. We hear it, and we weep. We lift our face and whisper simply: "O God, help me."

All at once the sunlight seems doubly bright in the room, and the angel of God is standing before us: in the tiny room of the minister's house, in the attic bedroom where my father is reading. This is the very same angel who held a sword at the church's door—but now he holds a rose branch thick with flowers. He raises the branch and touches the ceiling above Karen and above my bed. The ceiling suddenly sails aloft, and where he touched it a golden star appears. He brushes the walls of my attic, and they widen. Lo, here is the church organ! The congregation is sitting and holding their psalm books and singing. The church has come to us, to Karen and me! When the psalm is done, someone sees us and smiles and whispers, "It is good that you came, Karen."

And this is what Karen replies: so these are the words in my mouth, too, brilliant with significance: "This is his mercy."

Mercy! It never was what we might do that could save us. It never was our work, our penitence, our goodness that would forgive us and bring us back to God. We can do nothing! It always was the pure love and mercy of God—*God's* doing, given us freely as a gift.

Mercy. Mercy is the healing that had waited for us all along. Love. Pure, holy love, unpurchased, undeserved.

When my father reads the final sentences of this story, I am crying. I am tingling. For I am not learning, but rather am *experiencing* the highest truth of our faith. Not in doctrine, but in fact it is releasing me from the sins against my mother, even as it is imprinting me for adulthood, to show in what I speak, to shine through what I write forever. In the deeps of my bones I know and believe in forgiveness, for I have lived it. ■

Making Connections through Discussion and Writing

1. According to Wangerin, what are some of the benefits of reading fairy tales?

   _____

   _____

   _____

   _____

2. List below the three fairy tales Wangerin discusses, and write beside each one the virtue or virtues he believes it typifies.

   fairy tales   virtues

   _____   _____

   _____   _____

   _____   _____

   _____   _____

   _____   _____

   _____   _____

   _____   _____

3. In what ways did fairy tales shape Walter Wangerin's world?

   _____

   _____

   _____

   _____

4. a. Using Vigen Guroian's essay, "Awakening the Moral Imagination: Teaching Virtues through Fairy Tales," explain how the virtues Wangerin discusses are inculcated into the reader.

   _____

   _____

   _____

   _____

   _____

   b. Why are fairy tales able to accomplish this?

   _____

   _____

   _____

   _____

   _____

5. Describe Wangerin's method of effectively drawing the reader into his discussion of fairy tales.

_____

_____

_____

_____

_____

6. a. Think of a fairy tale or story that you particularly remember from your childhood. What kind of effect did it have on you?

_____

_____

_____

_____

_____

_____

    b. What was its lasting impression?

_____

_____

_____

_____

_____

Frederick Buechner

The Annunciation

Frederick Buechner (b. 1926) was educated at Princeton University and Union Theological Seminary. An ordained Presbyterian minister, Buechner is best known for his earlier novels, his autobiographical accounts, and his books of meditations. While most of his novels are set in contemporary America, two, *Godric* (1981) and *Brendan* (1987), are based on the lives of these early English and Irish saints. In this sermon, Buechner asserts the value and power of storytelling.

In the sixth month the angel Gabriel was sent from God to a city of Galilee named Nazareth, to a virgin betrothed to a man whose name was Joseph, of the house of David, and the virgin's name was Mary. And he came to her and said, "Hail, O favored one, the Lord is with you!" But she was greatly troubled at the saying, and considered in her mind what sort of greeting this might be. And the angel said to her, "Do not be afraid, Mary, for you have found favor with God. And behold you will conceive in your womb and bear a son, and you shall call his name Jesus.

He will be great, and will be called the Son of the Most High;

and the Lord God will give to him the throne of his father; David,

and he will reign over the house of Jacob for ever;

and of his kingdom there will be no end."

And Mary said to the angel, "How can this be, since I have no husband?" And the angel said to her,

"The Holy Spirit will come upon you,

and the power of the Most High will overshadow you;

therefore the child to be born will be called holy, the Son of God."

Luke 1:26-35 RSV

"In the sixth month the angel Gabriel was sent from God to a city of Galilee named Nazareth, to a virgin betrothed to a man whose name was Joseph, of the house of David; and the virgin's name was Mary," and that is the beginning of a story—a time, a place, a set of characters, and the implied promise, which is common to all stories, that something is coming, something interesting or significant or exciting is about to happen. And I

would like to start out by reminding my reader that in essence this is what Christianity is. If we whittle away long enough, it is a story that we come to at last. And if we take even the fanciest and most metaphysical kind of theologian or preacher and keep on questioning him far enough—Why is this so? All right, but why is that so? Yes, but how do we know *that* it's so?—even he is forced finally to take off his spectacles and push his books off to one side and say, "Once upon a time there was . . . ," and then everybody leans forward a little and starts to listen. Stories have enormous power for us, and I think that it is worth speculating why they have such power. Let me suggest two reasons.

One is that they make us want to know what is coming next, and not just out of idle curiosity either because if it is a good story, we *really* want to know, almost fiercely so, and we will wade through a lot of pages or sit through a lot of endless commercials to find out. There was a young woman named Mary, and an angel came to her from God, and what did he say? And what did she say? And then how did it all turn out in the end? But the curious thing is that if it is a good story, we want to know how it all turns out in the end even if we have heard it many times before and know the outcome perfectly well already. Yet why? What is there to find out if we already know?

And that brings me to the second reason why I think stories have such power for us. They force us to consider the question, "Are stories true?" Not just, "Is *this* story true?"—was there really an angel? Did he really say, "Do not be afraid"?—but are any stories true? Is the claim that all stories make a true claim? Every storyteller, whether he is

Shakespeare telling about Hamlet or Luke telling about Mary, looks out at the world much as you and I look out at it and sees things happening—people being born, growing up, working, loving, getting old, and finally dying—only then, by the very process of taking certain of these events and turning them into a story, giving them form and direction, does he make a sort of claim about events in general, about the nature of life itself. And the storyteller's claim, I believe, is that life has meaning—that the things that happen to people happen not just by accident like leaves being blown off a tree by the wind but that there is order and purpose deep down behind them or inside them and that they are leading us not just anywhere but somewhere. The power of stories is that they are telling us that life adds up somehow, that life itself is like a story. And this grips us and fascinates us because of the feeling it gives us that if there is meaning in any life—in Hamlet's, in Mary's, in Christ's—then there is meaning also in our lives. And if this is true, it is of enormous significance in itself, and it makes us listen to the storyteller with great intensity because in this way all his stories are about us and because it is always possible that he may give us some clue as to what the meaning of our lives is.

The story that Christianity tells, of course, claims to give more than just a clue, in fact to give no less than the very meaning of life itself and not just of some lives but of all our lives. And it goes a good deal further than that in claiming to give the meaning of God's life among men, this extraordinary tale it tells of the love between God and man, love conquered and love conquering, of long-lost love and love that sometimes looks like hate. And so, although in one sense the story Christianity tells is one that can be so simply told that we can get the whole thing really on a very small Christmas card or into the two crossed pieces of wood that form its symbol, in another sense it is so vast and complex that the whole Bible can only hint at it. Where does the story of God and man begin, for instance? Biblically speaking, you would have to say that it begins with Genesis and the picture we get of the Spirit of God brooding over the dark waters of chaos before the great "Let there be light!" of Creation sounded. But that amounts to saying that it has no beginning in time at all. Or where do we say that it ends? With the Crucifixion perhaps, where man brings the story to an end by killing God, or with nuclear war perhaps, where man brings it to an end by killing himself. But the answer to this is, "Behold, I create new heavens and a new earth!" and "He that believeth in me, though he were dead, yet shall he live," so the Christian story is beyond time altogether.

Yet it is also in time, the story of the love between God and man. There is a time when it begins, and therefore there is a time before it begins, when it is coming but not yet here, and this is the time Mary was in when Gabriel came to her. It is Advent: the time just before the adventure begins, when everybody is leaning forward to hear what will happen even though they already know what will happen and what will not happen, when they listen hard for meaning, their meaning, and begin to hear, only faintly at first, the beating of unseen wings.

The angel said to her, "'Hail, O favored one, the Lord is with you!' But she was greatly troubled at the saying, and considered in her mind what sort of greeting this might be." And well she might have been troubled if she had any idea of what lay ahead for her and her baby, and to one degree or another we must believe that she did. In the great medieval paintings of the scene, the Annunciation, the air is painted in gold leaf, and the figures of Mary and Gabriel stand there as still as death. There is no movement. None. Even the robe of the angel, still billowed out by the winds of Heaven, is frozen, and so is the wind itself. Time itself seems to have stopped. It is a moment beyond time. And of course there is truth in these ancient paintings because when our vision of the world suddenly deepens and brightens—when we suddenly see an angel where before we saw only empty space, when in a flash of light we have the uncanny sense that our lives are not just happening to us but are trying to tell us something of unspeakable importance—then for a moment we are stunned. We are stopped dead in our tracks, and the whole world holds its breath, and even the air becomes as rich and impenetrable as gold. But that is only part of the truth, because when angels draw near, as they do, the earth begins to shake beneath our feet as it began to shake beneath Mary's feet, which was why she was greatly troubled. Instead of everything standing still and sure, suddenly nothing is standing still, and everything is unsure. Something new and shattering is breaking through into something old. Something is trying to be born. And if the new thing is going to be born, then the old thing is going to have to give way, and there is agony in the process as well as joy, just as there is agony in the womb as it labors and contracts to bring forth the new life.

But this is the language of poetry, and I use it because it is the language in which the

Annunciation is described and the only language in which it can be described. But there are other languages to describe other things. How, for instance, do you describe this world of ours in revolution, a world beneath whose oceans at this moment an American atomic submarine is cruising armed with missiles whose explosive power exceeds that of all the bombs set off in the two world wars? What is trying to happen? Something is trying to happen, we can be sure of that, and the earth is shaking beneath our feet at its approach.

Men have seen something; the Communists have seen it no less clearly than we and in some ways perhaps more clearly. And what men have seen is something that has never existed anywhere in history and exists nowhere today except in their vision of it: a world where men live together as brothers. "No more shall there be in it an infant that lives but a few days, or an old man who does not fill out his days. They shall not labor in vain, or bear children for calamity. The wolf and the lamb shall feed together, the lion shall eat straw like the ox; and dust shall be the serpent's food. They shall not hurt or destroy in all my holy mountain, says the Lord."

These are Isaiah's words for it, the words of poetry again. But it is the same world that Communism is talking about in the words of Marxian economic theory, the same world that the Western Alliance is talking about in the words of Christian Democracy, a world that never was on land or sea but a world that is pressing in upon us through our vision of it. So what do the nations do? Two things at once, I think, and things that contradict each other and are always at war. On the one hand, they are trying to materialize the vision, to bring it about. The tools they use are the weapons they have forged in their factories and the political and economic ideas they have forged in their heads. The price that they are all but willing to pay for it is death because there are times when even death seems not too high a price to pay for life, new life. And yet at the same time, and with the same tools, they are trying to prevent its being brought about, to bring about instead not the world of their vision but a man-made version of it, a more reasonable and less demanding facsimile where the serpent gets a little more than dust to eat, and the lion is allowed an occasional taste of blood. We try to fend off this world we yearn for where men live together as brothers because there is something in each of us that wants to live not for his brother but for himself. We fend it off because we know in our terrible wisdom that the price we must pay for it *is*

death, the death of self and all the values of self, the death that must take place before the life can come.

In an odd way it is so comforting to talk about history, even the tragic history of our own times, because it is so much *out there* somewhere, outside these walls, beyond the town limits, across the river. And all the wars and the threat of war are out there too, and with them the strange thing which is not an angel because we believe there are no angels but which is something of great terror and great beauty gathering to a brightness. The world waits. History waits and labors. Something draws near, and we love its being far away there rather than here, among ourselves. Except, of course, that it is here among us too and within us as we wait for the story to begin, the story whose end we already know and yearn to know again and wish we did not know: the story whose meaning may be our meaning, as we wait for the child to be born.

For this is what Gabriel comes to announce, and Mary stands there as still as life in her blue mantle with her hands folded on her lap, and the terrible salutation is caught like a bird's wing in the golden net of the air—*Ave Maria gratia plena. Dominus tecum.* And then she hears him say, "Behold, you will conceive in your womb and bear a son, and you shall call his name. . . ." But she knows his name before Gabriel says it, just as we also know his name, because the child who is going to be born is our child as he is her child. He is that which all the world's history and all of our own inner histories have been laboring to bring forth. And it will be no ordinary birth but a virgin birth because the birth of righteousness and love in this stern world is always a virgin birth. It is never men nor the nations of men nor all the power and wisdom of men that bring it forth but always God, and that is why the angel says, "The child to be born will be called the Son of God."

Here at the end let me tell a story which seems to me to be a kind of parable of the lives of all of us. It is a peculiarly twentieth-century story, and it is almost too awful to tell: about a boy of twelve or thirteen who, in a fit of crazy anger and depression, got hold of a gun somewhere and fired it at his father, who died not right away but soon afterward. When the authorities asked the boy why he had done it, he said that it was because he could not stand his father, because his father demanded too much of him, because he was always after him, because he hated his father. And then later on, after he had been placed in a house of detention somewhere, a guard was walking down the corridor late one night when he heard sounds from the boy's room, and he stopped to listen. The words that he heard the boy sobbing out in the dark were, "I want my father, I want my father."

Our father. We have killed him, and we will kill him again, and our world will kill him. And yet he is there. It is he who listens at the door. It is he who is coming. It is our father who is about to be born. Through Jesus Christ our Lord. ∎

Making Connections through Discussion and Writing

1. a.   Underline the two reasons Buechner gives for the power of stories.

    b.   Briefly restate these reasons in your own words.

    _____
    _____
    _____
    _____

    _____
    _____
    _____
    _____

2. What does Buechner mean by saying that the Christian story is so small it can be told on a Christmas card or by "two crossed pieces of wood," yet so vast it "is beyond time altogether"?

    _____
    _____
    _____
    _____
    _____

3. What does Buechner see as the significance of Advent?

    _____
    _____
    _____
    _____

4. What does Buechner find suggested by the great medieval paintings of the Annunciation—by the gold leaf air and the stillness of the figures?

    _____
    _____
    _____

5. How does Buechner's discussion about the vision of our "tragic history"—the vision of both communism and democracy—relate to his primary subject, the power of the Christian story?

    _____
    _____
    _____
    _____

6. What assumptions lie behind Buechner's assertion that "He is that which all the world's history and all of our own inner histories have been laboring to bring forth" and that it is "never men nor the nations of men nor all the power and wisdom of men that bring it forth but always God"?

    _____

    _____

    _____

    _____

    _____

7. How does the story that Buechner ends his sermon with relate to the theme of the Annunciation?

    _____

    _____

    _____

    _____

    _____

Synthesis/Essay Suggestions: Myth, Fairy Tale, and the Moral Imagination

1. Write a one-sentence summary stating the main points about myth and fairy tales made in Tolkien's "On Fairy-Stories," Chesterton's "Dragooning the Dragon," Lewis' "Sometimes Fairy Stories May Say Best What's to Be Said," and Howard's "Myth: A Flight to Reality." Synthesize their ideas in an original essay in which you define and defend the use of fairy tales or myth and explain the role Christianity plays in the telling of these.

2. Choose a modern mythic figure (e.g., Superman, Batman, Indiana Jones, Luke Skywalker), and write about this figure applying some of the principles the authors in the chapter espouse.

3. Using Tolkien's definition of subcreator in "On Fairy Stories," explain how Lewis, Chesterton, Tolkien, and Howard describe this process. Pay close attention to their definition of myth and their beliefs concerning the creation of other worlds. Feel free to read some additional works by these authors, focusing on essays or fairy stories. Then write an essay examining subcreation, its methodology and purpose, as well as its effectiveness in conveying the message of the author.

4. Chesterton writes briefly and wittily about the value of fairy tales in his essay "Dragooning the Dragon." Scholars and authors since Chesterton, such as Bruno Bettelheim in his book *The Uses of Enchantment*, have continued to study fairy tales, finding values similar to those suggested by Chesterton. The essay by Vigen Guroian develops several ideas about these values. Identify and analyze the methods by which Guroian develops Chesterton's observations and asserts the importance of classic fairy tales.

Chapter 11

Epiphanies: The Transcendent Presence

Sometimes in the most ordinary moment—in the observation of nature, the viewing of a painting, the reading of a book, or a conversation with a friend—we discover something extraordinary. We see something we have not seen before, and our lives are fuller because of the event. Literature, art, and music have recorded such moments, and religious mystics have constructed their lives around them. These moments reveal something beyond ourselves, thus enriching our vision of this world.

For example, Moses experienced theophanies (visions of God) at various times in his life. He was confronted with the mysterious presence of God—when he encountered God in the burning bush, when he received the Law at Mt. Sinai, when he prayed that God would forgive the rebellious Israelites for worshipping the golden calf. In the latter experience recorded in the Book of Exodus, Moses "sees" the face of God: "So the Lord spoke to Moses, face to face, as a man speaks to his friend" (Ex. 33:11, NKJV). Here we can conclude that Moses saw God's face apart from His full glory because later in the passage, following this sacred moment, Moses beseeches God, "Please, show me your glory." To which God replies, "You cannot see My face; for no man shall see Me, and live," the implication being that no human can see the complete glory of God. Moses had glimpsed God's face, but not His fullness. So in response to Moses' plea to see His glory, God shows Moses His back, not his face; in fact, he covers Moses' eyes as He passes by.

Humans are able to see God only because He first sees them. Nicholas of Cusa in his book *The Vision of God* writes of God's seeing us. He emphasizes God as omnivoyant (the all-seeing One). As Clyde Miller has indicated, the title of this book allows for a twofold meaning: "God's all-seeing gaze upon, or vision of, human creatures, and for our human vision or mystical sighting of God." Evelyn Underhill also observes, "The Absolute Glance falls equally, simultaneously, and unflickeringly on all. Within this Perfect Vision the small life of man is lived; it conditions his limited spiritual experience. Only because God first looks at him, can man desire to look at God." Using an icon of God, Nicholas of Cusa meditates on Him, exclaiming, "O Lord my God, the longer I look upon Thy face the more keenly dost Thou seem to turn the glance of Thine eyes upon me! . . . But I perceive, not with my fleshly eyes, which look on this icon of Thee, but with the eyes of my mind and understanding, the invisible truth of Thy Face, which therein is signified, under a shadow and limitation." He concludes, "Even so is Thy face turned toward all faces that look upon Thee. Thy glance, Lord, is Thy face."

In various ways, the authors in this chapter of the book see or at least desire to see the face of God—to find Him in relationship to others as in "Supernatural Love" by Gjertrud Schnackenberg, in nature as with the poems of Gerard Manley Hopkins, or even in the darkness of the night as described by Rainer Rilke in his poem "Do Not Be Troubled, God." Sometimes the experience is frightening, as in Annie Dillard's "A Field of Silence," when she discovers that "holiness is a force . . . but I didn't want to see it, God or no God. . . . I turned away, willful, and the whole show vanished." Dillard finds that when human beings draw nearer to God, they realize how far from Him they actually are. Sometimes the vision is unexpected, as when the host in "A Christmas Story" allows his gaze to fall "on an old man who happened to be sitting at the table in his line of vision, looking about and thinking of nothing at all." At other times, it is so obvious that we do not see it, as Thomas Merton illustrates in "The General Dance" when he views the presence of God in children at play, in the migration of birds, and in the splash of a frog in a pond. The mystic Julian of Norwich is able to perceive God's hand even in something small—as small as a hazelnut—for "God made it," "God loveth it," and "God keepeth it." These selections demonstrate the various writers' experiences of the transcendent presence in their moments of epiphany.

Julian of Norwich
from The Revelations of Divine Love

Julian of Norwich (b. 1342; died after 1416), probably born in Norwich, England, is a celebrated medieval mystic whose *The Revelations of Divine Love* is believed by many to be one of the greatest works produced during this time—a writing that relates religious visionary experiences with intensity and insight. When she was thirty years old and seriously ill, she experienced a series of sixteen revelations or "showings" of Christ's suffering and of the Blessed Virgin. She was healed of her sickness on May 13, 1373. Julian wrote two accounts of her visions; the second, which is the longer version, was written 20 or 30 years after the first one. She lived the latter part of her life as an anchoress or recluse at St. Julian's Church, Norwich. Although she labeled herself as "unlettered," the evidence points to the contrary, for she was a caring, intuitive, and educated individual. Many came to her for her counsel, including Margery Kempe, another medieval mystic known for her ecstatic visions. Julian's book *The Revelations of Divine Love* deals with the profoundest mysteries of God, including predestination, foreknowledge, and theodicy. In the excerpt below, Julian of Norwich shows that all things are sustained by God, even something small—as small as a hazelnut—for "God made it," "God loveth it," and "God keepeth it."

The Fifth Chapter

How God is to us everything that is good, tenderly wrapping us round; and everything that is made is nothing in regard to Almighty God; and how man hath no rest until he counteth himself and all things as nothing, for the love of God.

In the same time that I saw this sight of his head bleeding, our good Lord shewed a ghostly[1] sight of his homely[2] loving. I saw that he is to us everything that is good and strengthening for our help. He is our clothing that, for love, wrappeth us up and windeth us about; embraceth us, all becloseth us and hangeth about us, for tender love; so that he can never leave us. And so, in this sight, I saw that he is to us everything that is good, as I understand it.

Also in this he shewed a little thing, the size of a hazelnut, which seemed to lie in the palm of my hand; and it was as round as any ball. I looked upon it with the eye of my understanding, and thought, "What may this be?" I was answered in a general way, thus: "It is all that is made." I wondered how long it could last; for it seemed as though it might suddenly fade away to nothing, it was so small. And I was answered in my understanding: "It lasts, and ever shall last; for God loveth it. And even so hath everything being—by the love of God."

In this little thing I saw three properties. The first is that God made it: the second, that God loveth it: the third, that God keepeth it. And what beheld I in this? Truly, the Maker, the Lover and the Keeper. And until I am substantially oned[3] to him, I can never have full rest nor true bliss; that is to say, until I am so fastened to him that there is no created thing at all between my God and me. And this little thing that is made—it seemed as though it would fade away to nothing, it was so small. We need to have knowledge of this—that we should reckon as naught[4] everything that is made, to love and have God who is unmade. For this is the reason why we are not at all in ease of heart and of soul: that we seek here rest in this thing that is so little and where no rest is in: we know not our God that is almighty, all-wise and all-good. For he is very rest. It is his will to be known and it is his pleasure that we rest us in him. All that is beneath him sufficeth[5] not to us. And this is the reason why no soul can be in rest until it is naughted[6] of everything that

Excerpts from *The Revelations of Divine Love*, by Julian of Norwich, translated by James Walsh. Copyright © 1978 by The Missionary Society of St. Paul the Apostle in the State of New York. Used with permission of Paulist Press. www.paulistpress.com

is made. When the soul is willingly naughted, for love, so as to have him who is All, then is she able to receive ghostly[1] rest.

And also our good Lord shewed that it is the greatest pleasure to him that a simple soul come to him nakedly, plainly and homely.[2] This is the kind yearning of the soul, through the touching of the Holy Ghost, as I am given to understand by this shewing:

> God, of thy goodness, give me thyself; for thou art enough to me, and I can nothing ask that is less that would be full worship of thee. And if I ask anything that is less, ever me wanteth; for in thee only have I all.

These words, through the goodness of God, are full love-some to the soul, and full near touch the will of our Lord. For his goodness full filleth all his creatures and all his blessed works, without end. For he is the endlessness, and he made us only for himself; and he restored us by his blessed passion[7] and ever keepeth us in his blessed love. And all this of his goodness. ■

Notes

[1] ghostly—spiritual

[2] homely—familiar, simple

[3] substantially oned—essentially united

[4] reckon as naught—consider as nothing

[5] sufficeth—satisfy

[6] naughted—detached

[7] passion—the sufferings of Christ between the Last Supper and His Crucifixion

Name: _____ Section: _____ Date: _____

Making Connections through Discussion and Writing

1. a. Underline the images Julian of Norwich uses <u>to describe the love of God and His relationship with the believer</u>.

   b. Explain the metaphor she seeks to establish.

   _____
   _____
   _____
   _____

2. a. God shows Julian "a little thing." To what does Julian compare it to express its size and shape?
   <u>HAZLENUT</u>
   _____

   b. What does God say about the "little thing"?
   _____
   _____

   c. What are the three properties of "this little thing"?
   _____
   _____
   _____

   d. How do these properties reflect God?
   _____
   _____
   _____
   _____

3. a. According to Julian, how does the individual find "full rest" or "true bliss"?
   _____
   _____
   _____

   b. How should one approach God?
   _____
   _____

4. a. How does Julian describe the goodness of God?
   _____
   _____
   _____

b.   Why is this goodness important to the believer?

_____

_____

_____

5.   As established earlier, Julian is concerned with the relationship of God and the believer. List below the characteristics of this relationship as she describes them. In other words, in one column list God's response to us, in the other our response to God.

God's response to us   Our response to God

_____   _____

_____   _____

_____   _____

_____   _____

_____   _____

_____   _____

_____   _____

_____   _____

Annie Dillard

A Field of Silence

Annie Dillard (b. 1945) was born in Pittsburgh, Pennsylvania. She wrote about her life in the Roanoke Valley, publishing her observations in *Pilgrim at Tinker Creek*, which received a Pulitzer Prize in 1975. Her works include *Holy the Firm* (1978), *Teaching a Stone to Talk* (1982), *Living by Fiction* (1982), *Encounters with Chinese Writers* (1984), *An American Childhood* (1987), *The Writing Life* (1989), and *For the Time Being* (1999). Dillard is often considered a modern mystic because her writings reflect supernatural, revelatory experiences that occur in conjunction with nature. Exhibiting her interest in science, poetry, the mystics, and theology, "A Field of Silence," written in 1978, is an example of one such experience.

Vocabulary . . . .

arrhythmically	loped
cicadas	Platonic
din	ruckus
enjambments	stridulations
impeccable	surrealistic

There is a place called "the farm" where I lived once, in a time that was very lonely. Fortunately I was unconscious of my loneliness then, and felt it only deeply, bewildered, in the half-bright way that a puppy feels pain.

I loved the place, and still do. It was an ordinary farm, a calf-raising, haymaking farm, and very beautiful. Its flat, messy pastures ran along one side of the central portion of a quarter-mile road in the central part of an island, an island in Puget Sound,[1] so that from the high end of the road you could look west toward the Pacific, to the Sound and its hundred islands, and from the other end—and from the farm—you could see east to the water between you and the mainland, and beyond it the mainland's mountains slicked smooth with snow.

I liked the clutter about the place, the way everything blossomed or seeded or rusted; I liked the hundred half-finished projects, the smells and the way the animals always broke loose. It is calming to herd animals. Often a regular rodeo breaks out— two people and a clever cow can kill a morn-ing—but still, it is calming. You laugh for a while, exhausted, and silence is restored; the beasts are back in their pastures, the fences not fixed but disguised as if they were fixed, ensuring the animals' temporary resignation; and a great calm descends, a lack of urgency, a sense of having to invent something to do until the next time you must run and chase cattle.

The farm seemed eternal in the crude way the earth does—extending, that is, a very long time. The farm was as old as earth, always there, as old as the island, the Platonic form of "farm," of human society itself and at large, a piece of land eaten and replenished a billion summers, a piece of land worked on, lived on, grown over, plowed under, and stitched again and again, with fingers or with leaves, in and out and into human life's thin weave. I lived there once.

I lived there once and I have seen, from behind the barn, the long roadside pastures heaped with silence. Behind the rooster, suddenly, I saw the silence heaped on the fields like trays. That day the green hayfields supported silence evenly sown; the fields bent just so under the even pressure of silence, bearing it, even, palming it aloft: cleared fields, part of a land, a planet, they did not buckle beneath the heel of silence, nor split up scattered to bits, but instead lay secret, disguised as time and matter as though that were nothing, ordinary—disguised as fields like those which bear the silence only because they are spread, and the silence spreads over them, great in size.

I do not want, I think, ever to see such a sight again. That there is loneliness here I had granted, in the abstract—but not, I thought, inside the light of God's presence, inside his sanction, and signed by his name.

I lived alone in the farmhouse and rented; the owners, Angus and Lynn, in their twenties, lived in another building just over the yard. I had been reading and restless for two or three days. It was morning. I had just read at breakfast an Updike story,[2] "Packed Dirt, Churchgoing, A Dying Cat, A Traded Car," which moved me. I heard our own farmyard rooster and two or three roosters across the street screeching. I quit the house, hoping at heart to see Lynn or Angus, but immediately to watch our rooster as he crowed.

It was Saturday morning late in the summer, in early September, clear-aired and still. I climbed the barnyard fence between the poultry and the pastures; I watched the red rooster, and the rooster, reptilian, kept one alert and alien eye on me. He pulled his extravagant neck to its maximum length, hauled himself high on his legs, stretched his beak as if he were gagging, screamed, and blinked. It was a ruckus. The din came from everywhere, and only the most rigorous application of reason could persuade me that it proceeded in its entirety from this lone and maniac bird.

After a pause, the roosters across the street would start, answering the proclamation, or cranking out another round, arrhythmically, interrupting. In the same way there is no pattern nor sense to the massed stridulations of cicadas; their skipped beats, enjambments, and failed alterations jangle your spirits, as though each of those thousand insects, each with identical feelings, were stubbornly deaf to the others, and loudly alone.

I shifted along the fence to see if Lynn or Angus was coming or going. To the rooster I said nothing, but only stared. And he stared at me: we were both careful to keep the wooden fence slat from our line of sight, so that this profiled eye and my two eyes could meet. From time to time I looked beyond the pastures to learn if anyone might be seen on the road.

When I was turned away in this manner, the silence gathered and struck me. It bashed me broadside from nowhere, as if I'd been hit by a plank. It dropped from the heavens above me like yard goods; ten acres of fallen, invisible sky choked the fields. The pastures on either side of the road turned green in a surrealistic fashion, monstrous, impeccable, as if they were holding their breath. The roosters stopped. All the things of the world— the fields and the fencing, the road, a parked orange truck— were stricken and self-conscious. A world pressed down on their surfaces, a world battered just within their surfaces, and that real world, so near to emerging, had got stuck.

There was only silence. It was the silence of matter caught in the act and embarrassed. There were no cells moving, and yet there were cells. I could see the shape of the land, how it lay holding silence. Its poise and its stillness were unendurable, like the ring of the silence you hear in your skull when you're little and notice you're living, the ring which resumes later in life when you're sick.

There were flies buzzing over the dirt by the henhouse, moving in circles and buzzing, black dreams in chips off the one long dream, the dream of the regular world. But the silent fields were the real world, eternity's outpost in time, whose look I remembered but never like this, this God-blasted, paralyzed day. I felt myself tall and vertical, in a blue shirt, self-conscious, and wishing to die. I heard the flies again; I looked at the rooster who was frozen looking at me.

Then at last I heard whistling, human whistling far on the air, and I was not able to bear it. I looked around, heartbroken; only at the big yellow Charolais[3] farm far up the road was there motion— a woman, I think, dressed in pink, and pushing a wheelbarrow easily over the grass. It must have been she who was whistling and heaping on top of the silence those hollow notes of song. But the slow sound of the music—the beautiful sound of the music ringing the air like a stone bell—was isolate and detached. The notes spread into the general air and became the weightier part of silence, silence's last straw. The distant woman and her wheelbarrow were flat and detached, like mechanized and pink-painted properties for a stage. I stood in pieces, afraid I was unable to move. Something had unhinged the world. The houses and roadsides and pastures were buckling under the silence. Then a Labrador, black, loped up the distant driveway, fluid and cartoonlike, toward the pink woman. I had to try to turn away. Holiness is a force, and like the others can be resisted. It was given, but I didn't want to see it, God or no God. It was as if God had said, "I am here, but not as you have known me. This is the look of silence, and of loneliness unendurable: it too has always been mine, and now will be yours." I was not ready for a life of sorrow, sorrow deriving from knowledge I could just as well stop at the gate.

I turned away, willful, and the whole show vanished. The realness of things disassembled. The whistling became ordinary, familiar; the air above the fields released its pressure and the fields lay hooded as before. I myself could act. Looking to the rooster I whistled to him myself, softly, and some hens appeared at the chicken house window, greeted the day, and fluttered down.

Several months later, walking past the farm on the way to a volleyball game, I remarked to a friend, by way of information, "There are angels in those fields." Angels! That silence so grave and so stricken, that choked and unbearable green! I have rarely been so surprised at something I've said. Angels! What are angels? I had never thought of angels, in any way at all.

From that time I began to think of angels. I considered that sights such as I had seen of the silence must have been shared by the people who said they saw angels. I began to review the thing I had seen that morning. My impression now of those fields is of thousands of spirits—spirits trapped, perhaps, by my refusal to call them more fully, or by the paralysis of my own spirit at that time—thousands of spirits, angels in fact, almost discernible to the eye, and whirling. If pressed I would say they were three or four feet from the ground. Only their motion was clear (clockwise, if you insist); that, and their beauty unspeakable.

There are angels in those fields, and I presume, in all fields, and everywhere else. I would go to the lions for this conviction, to witness this fact. What all this means about perception, or language, or angels, or my own sanity, I have no idea. ■

Notes

[1] Puget Sound—Seattle, Washington, is situated on Puget Sound, an inlet of water.

[2] Updike story—John Updike (b. 1932) is an American author. The story referred to is the final story of his early collection titled *Pigeon Feathers*. In the story Updike discusses how insight into faith comes in unexpected ways.

[3] Charolais—a type of cattle

Making Connections through Discussion and Writing

1. a. Dillard equates a piece of land with silence. What is her purpose for doing this?

    _____

    _____

    b. What insight concerning silence does this comparison give the reader?

    _____

    _____

    _____

2. What does Dillard mean by the "Platonic form of 'farm'"?

    _____

    _____

    _____

    _____

3. a. What does Dillard mean when she writes, "But the silent fields were the real world, eternity's outpost in time"?

    _____

    _____

    _____

    b. How does this "real world" relate to the "Platonic form of 'farm'"?

    _____

    _____

    _____

    c. Why is it important to know that the fields were the "real world"?

    _____

    _____

    _____

    d. What epiphany does she experience?

    _____

    _____

    _____

    _____

    e. How does this relate to the later revelation she has about her epiphany?

    _____

    _____

    _____

    _____

4. a. Dillard uses several examples of repetition. Underline all of the examples that you can find.

    b. Why does she use repetition?

    _____

    _____

    _____

    c. In what way does repetition further her purpose?

    _____

    _____

    _____

5. What role does the rooster play in Dillard's movement from the surroundings of the farm to her vision-
    ary experience?

    _____

    _____

    _____

    _____

6. Discuss the kind of language that Dillard uses, including what is unusual about it and how it compares
    to normal narrative language.

    _____

    _____

    _____

    _____

    _____

    _____

7. a. Underline Dillard's thesis.

    b. Where in the essay does it appear?

    _____

    _____

    c. Look again at the essay to examine how Dillard organizes it and then describe her organization.

    _____

    _____

    _____

    d. Explain why the organization is important to her overall thesis.

    _____

    _____

    _____

    _____

8. Why do you think Dillard does not understand her vision until much later?

_____
_____
_____

9. a. Explain what Dillard is saying in her last paragraph.

_____
_____
_____
_____
_____

   b. Does Dillard have an objectively verifiable vision of the "silent" world, or does she simply imagine this? Explain.

_____
_____
_____
_____

   c. Does her vision give credibility to the story, or does it detract from it? Explain.

_____
_____
_____
_____

   d. How can one verify the accuracy of any revelation?

_____
_____
_____
_____
_____

Annie Dillard

A Christmas Story

In the following selection, which was published in *Harper's Magazine* in 1976, Dillard relates a story of a feast in which the gaze of the host upon an old man brings him clarity of vision, thus enabling him to fully appreciate the beauty and richness of life.

Vocabulary ....

damask

pallid

whorled

Once there was a great feast held in a banquet hall of such enormous proportions that you could not believe men built such a thing. Two thousand chandeliers hung from the ceiling; lumber cut from all the world's forests made the vast and parti-colored floor. Great loose areas of the hall were given to various activities: there were dances and many kinds of gaming; a corner was devoted to the sick and injured, and another to the weaving of cloth. Children chanted rhymes wherever they gathered, and young men sought pretty girls in greenhouses or behind the damask hanging of booths and stalls.

The feast lasted all night long. Guests sat at a table as long as a river that stretched down the middle of the hall. No one cloth could cover such a table, nor could one centerpiece suffice. So the table was decorated in hundreds of different themes, with different combinations of colors and kinds of tableware, with various carved figures and various drinks, and with lively musicians in costume playing to each set of guests a special music.

There was only a single course served to the guests, but that was a soup made of so many ingredients it seemed to contain all other dishes. The soup was served continuously, all night long, and there were so many guests that all the places at the table were always taken, and the benches always full, when the servants ladled the soup into the endlessly decorated array of metal, glass, wood and pottery bowls.

Now, the host of this feast was a young man of tremendous wealth and power who stood behind a curtain on a balcony above the great hall, and watched the guests as they ate and drank at the long table. He thought: "All night long people have been eating as much soup as they wanted, and then coming back to the table for more. It is good that they enjoy themselves. But not one person has seen or really understood the excellence of that soup."

So the host parted the curtain a crack more and let his gaze fall. It fell directly on an old man who happened to be sitting at the table in his line of vision, looking about and thinking of nothing at all. At once the old man felt an overwhelming sense of power, an impact as if his spirit had been struck broadside and wakened to a flood of light. He bowed his head and saw, through charged eyes, his bowl of soup that had come alive and was filled to endless depths with wonderful things.

There were green fields in his soup bowl, with carrots growing, one by one, in slender rows. As he watched, transfixed, men and women in bright vests and scarves came and pulled the carrots, one by one, out of the soil, and carried them in baskets to shaded kitchens, where they scrubbed them with yellow brushes under running water. He saw whitefaced cattle lowing and wading in rivers, with dust on the whorled and curly white hair between their ears. He saw tomatoes in kitchen gardens set out as seedlings by women in plaid shirts and by strong-handed men; and he watched the tomatoes as, before his eyes, the light from the sun blew each one up like a balloon. Cells on the root hairs of beans swelled and divided, and squashes grew spotted and striped in the fall. Wine aged in caves,

---

and the barrel-maker went home to his wife through sunlight and shade.

He saw the ocean, and he seemed to be in the ocean himself, swimming over orange crabs that looked like coral, or off the deep Atlantic banks where whitefish school. Or again he saw the tops of poplars, and the whole sky brushed with clouds in pallid streaks, under which wild ducks flew with outstretched necks, and called, one by one, and flew on.

All these things the old man saw in his soup.

Scenes grew in depth and sunlit detail under his eyes, and were replaced by ever more scenes, until, with the flight of wild ducks, the worlds resolved into one blue sky, now streaked, now clear, and, at last, into soup again, dark soup, fragrant in its bowl. The host had let the curtain fall shut.

The man blinked and moved his head from side to side. "I see now," he said to himself, "that this is truly an excellent soup, praise God." And he ate his bowlful, and joined the dancers in a daze, a kind of very energetic daze. ∎

Making Connections through Discussion and Writing

1. What does Dillard mean when she describes "the world in a bowl of soup"?

    _____
    _____
    _____
    _____
    _____
    _____

2. a. Underline the imagery Dillard uses to indicate the abundance of the feast.

    b. What does this abundance suggest about God's creation and man's relationship to God?

    _____
    _____
    _____
    _____

3. a. Who does the host represent?

    _____
    _____

    b. How does he function in the story?

    _____
    _____
    _____

4. a. What is the theme of the story?

    _____
    _____

    b. What is the significance of the title, "A Christmas Story"?

    _____
    _____
    _____

    c. How does the title relate to the theme of the story?

    _____
    _____
    _____

5. a. In this story, Dillard is interested in the idea of seeing and being seen. What are some examples?

    _____
    _____
    _____
    _____

    b. Why is this important to the narrative?

    _____
    _____
    _____

    c. How can it be related to the omnivoyance of God?

    _____
    _____
    _____

6. a. What dance is the old man participating in?

    _____
    _____

    b. What does his experience teach him about God?

    _____
    _____
    _____

7. Compare this story to Thomas Merton's essay "The General Dance." How does Dillard's story "provide a glimpse of the cosmic dance" that Merton discusses?

    _____
    _____
    _____
    _____
    _____
    _____
    _____
    _____
    _____
    _____
    _____

Thomas Merton
from The General Dance

Thomas Merton (1915–1968) was ordained a Catholic priest in 1949. After his conversion, he became a Trappist monk and continued to influence the world around him through writing more than fifty books as well as dozens of essays. He is known for his ability to critically and satirically evaluate contemporary culture. His most famous book, *The Seven Storey Mountain*, (1948)—considered a classic of modern spiritual literature—is the autobiography of his early life. While visiting the Dalai Lama—the leader of Tibetan monks—in Bangkok, Thailand, in 1968, his life was abruptly ended when he was accidentally electrocuted. The selection below is from *New Seeds of Contemplation* (1961) and invites all of humanity to forsake themselves and the world and join in the cosmic dance of God. His later books include *Seeds of Destruction* (1964) and *Mystics and Zen Masters* (1967).

. . . What is serious to men is often very trivial in the sight of God. What in God might appear to us as "play" is perhaps what He Himself takes most seriously. At any rate the Lord plays and diverts Himself in the garden of His creation, and if we could let go of our own obsession with what we think is the meaning of it all, we might be able to hear His call and follow Him in His mysterious, cosmic dance. We do not have to go very far to catch echoes of that game, and of that dancing. When we are alone on a starlit night; when by chance we see the migrating birds in autumn descending on a grove of junipers to rest and eat; when we see children in a moment when they are really children; when we know love in our own hearts; or when, like the Japanese poet Bashō we hear an old frog land in a quiet pond with a solitary splash—at such times the awakening, the turning inside out of all values, the "newness," the emptiness and the purity of vision that make themselves evident, provide a glimpse of the cosmic dance.

For the world and time are the dance of the Lord in emptiness. The silence of the spheres is the music of a wedding feast. The more we persist in misunderstanding the phenomena of life, the more we analyze them out into strange finalities and complex purposes of our own, the more we involve ourselves in sadness, absurdity and despair. But it does not matter much, because no despair of ours can alter the reality of things, or stain the joy of the cosmic dance which is always there. Indeed, we are in the midst of it, and it is in the midst of us, for it beats in our very blood, whether we want it to or not.

Yet the fact remains that we are invited to forget ourselves on purpose, cast our awful solemnity to the winds and join in the general dance. ∎

Making Connections through Discussion and Writing

1. a. Explain Merton's statement, "What is serious to men is often very trivial in the sight of God."
    _____
    _____
    _____

    b. If God is concerned about everything, how can anything be trivial?
    _____
    _____
    _____

2. What does Merton mean by "the cosmic dance"?
    _____
    _____
    _____
    _____

3. According to Merton, how can we catch a glimpse of the cosmic dance?
    _____
    _____
    _____
    _____
    _____
    _____

4. The Scriptures proclaim, "The heavens declare the glory of God" (Psalm 19:1). From the Middle Ages through the seventeenth century, many people took this literally and believed that the planets sang in harmony the praises of God. What new twist does Merton put on this idea when he writes, "The silence of the spheres is the music of a wedding feast"?
    _____
    _____
    _____
    _____
    _____

5. a. Explain what Merton means when he says that the cosmic dance is a part of us whether we acknowledge it or not.
    _____
    _____
    _____

b. How would this idea be understood from the vantage point of a mystic (such as Julian of Norwich)?

_____

_____

_____

c. What relevance does it have for our lives today?

_____

_____

_____

6. Compare this essay to Dillard's "A Christmas Story." How do Merton's comments about the cosmic dance help us understand the old man's reaction to his bowl of soup and the discovery of his place in the scheme of God's universe?

_____

_____

_____

_____

_____

_____

7. a. Identify the controlling metaphor (the metaphor that determines the structure of the writing) in Merton's "The General Dance" and Dillard's "A Christmas Story."

_____

_____

_____

_____

b. How does metaphor help us understand a part of God that is beyond human comprehension?

_____

_____

_____

_____

William Wordsworth
I Wandered Lonely as a Cloud

William Wordsworth (1770–1850), born in Westmoreland and educated at Cambridge, was one of England's best known poets. Along with his friend Samuel Taylor Coleridge, he published *Lyrical Ballads* in 1798, the "Preface" of which was in many ways responsible for the beginning of the English Romantic movement. He was influenced by Jean Jacques Rousseau's philosophical ideas, and his poems reflect his interest in nature as a healing balm for the ills of society. "Lines Composed a Few Miles Above Tintern Abbey," "The World is Too Much with Us," as well as "I Wandered Lonely as a Cloud," are among his best known poems. Wordsworth states in his "Preface" to *Lyrical Ballads*, "I have said that poetry is the spontaneous overflow of powerful feelings; it takes its origin from emotion recollected in tranquillity: the emotion is contemplated till, by a species of reaction, the tranquillity gradually disappears, and an emotion, kindred to that which was before the subject of contemplation, is gradually produced, and does itself actually exist in the mind." This creative process, Wordsworth continues, moves the poet to a "state of enjoyment, an experience of emotions that he should convey to the Reader—and those passions, if his Reader's mind be sound and vigourous, should always be accompanied with an overbalance of pleasure." These ideas take some of their best shape in the poem "I Wandered Lonely as a Cloud" where Wordsworth describes a meaningful moment when he observes the beauty of daffodils. The event had most likely occurred in 1802, about two years before the composition of the poem, when he was on a walk with his sister Dorothy (which she records in her diary); the poem contains many of her recollections as well as his own. Dorothy Wordsworth writes:

> When we were in the woods beyond Gowbarrow Park we saw a few daffodils close to the water-side. We fancied that the lake had floated the seeds ashore, and the little colony had so sprung up. But as we went along there were more and yet more; and at last, under the boughs of the trees, we saw that there was a long belt of them along the shore, about the breadth of a country turnpike road. I never saw daffodils so beautiful. They grew among the mossy stones about and about them; some rested their heads upon these stones as on a pillow for weariness; and the rest tossed and reeled and danced, and seemed as if they verily laughed with the wind, that flew upon them over the Lake; they looked so gay, ever glancing, ever changing. This wind blew directly over the Lake to them. There was here and there a little knot, and a few stragglers a few yards higher up, but they were so few as not to disturb the simplicity, unity, and life of that one busy highway.

Vocabulary ....

jocund   pensive

I wandered lonely as a cloud
That floats on high o'er vales and hills,
When all at once I saw a crowd,
A host, of golden daffodils;
Beside the lake, beneath the trees,
Fluttering and dancing in the breeze.

Continuous as the stars that shine
And twinkle on the milky way,
They stretched in never-ending line
Along the margin of a bay:
Ten thousand saw I at a glance,
Tossing their heads in sprightly dance.

The waves beside them danced; but they
Outdid the sparkling waves in glee;
A poet could not but be gay,
In such a jocund company;
I gazed—and gazed—but little thought
What wealth the show to me had brought:

For oft, when on my couch I lie
In vacant or in pensive mood,
They flash upon that inward eye
Which is the bliss of solitude;
And then my heart with pleasure fills,
And dances with the daffodils. ■

Notes

Author's Note: "Written at Town-end, Grasmere. The Daffodils grew and still grow on the margin of Ullswater, and probably may be seen to this day as beautiful in the month of March, nodding their golden heads beside the dancing and foaming waves."

Wordsworth also notes that lines 21 and 22, which he considered the "best lines" of the poem, were written by his wife, Mary.

Making Connections through Discussion and Writing

1. a. Describe the occasion that inspired the poem.

_____

_____

   b. Why does the speaker emphasize that he journeyed alone?

_____

_____

_____

2. a. Underline the similes in the poem.

   b. How do they cause Wordsworth's experience to become more meaningful for the reader?

_____

_____

_____

_____

3. a. Circle the words that portray the daffodils' movement in the poem.

   b. How does that movement serve as a contrast to Wordsworth's wandering?

_____

_____

_____

   c. What do these words suggest about Nature?

_____

_____

_____

_____

4. Compare the experience that Wordsworth describes in the poem with the one noted by Dorothy Wordsworth in her diary. List similarities and differences below.

similarities   differences

_____   _____

_____   _____

_____   _____

_____   _____

_____   _____

_____   _____

_____   _____

5. In the last stanza, the poet reflects on his walk in the woods with his sister. How has the poet taken the literal event, experienced the "emotion recollected in tranquillity," and then shaped his poem from the relived moment rather than its original occurrence?

    _____

    _____

    _____

    _____

    _____

    _____

    _____

Robert Frost

Desert Places

In the following poem, Frost depicts the internal loneliness experienced by the speaker as being greater than that expressed by nature and the universe.

Vocabulary ....

benighted   lairs

Snow falling and night falling fast, oh, fast
In a field I looked into going past,
And the ground almost covered smooth in snow,
But a few weeds and stubble showing last.

The woods around it have it—it is theirs.
All animals are smothered in their lairs.
I am too absent-spirited to count;
The loneliness includes me unawares.

And lonely as it is that loneliness
Will be more lonely ere it will be less—
A blanker whiteness of benighted snow
With no expressions, nothing to express.

They cannot scare me with their empty spaces
Between stars—on stars where no human race is.
I have it in me so much nearer home
To scare myself with my own desert places. ■

From *Complete Poems of Robert Frost*, Holt, Rinehart and Winston, Inc., 1916.

Making Connections through Discussion and Writing

1. Revealing despair more overtly than some other poems by Frost, "Desert Places" evokes specific images to create a melancholy tone. Underline three images that communicate this feeling.

2. In his loneliness, the speaker feels alienated from nature. How does he express this as he looks at the field?

   _____

   _____

   _____

   _____

3. Frost parallels two seemingly dissimilar images, desert and space, in the poem. List characteristics of each.

   desert   space

   _____   _____

   _____   _____

   _____   _____

   _____   _____

   _____   _____

   _____   _____

4. a. What does the speaker mean by the lines, "I have it in me so much nearer home / To scare myself with my own desert places"?

   _____

   _____

   _____

   _____

   b. What is he afraid of?

   _____

   _____

5. The subject of this poem is personal loneliness and a sense of meaninglessness in the universe. Frost says in his essay "The Figure a Poem Makes" that a poem brings "a momentary stay against confusion." How does this poem, with its rather bleak ending, bring any kind of defense against hopelessness or a sense of meaninglessness?

   _____

   _____

   _____

   _____

Walt Whitman

When I Heard the Learn'd Astronomer

Walter Whitman (1819–1892), who chose to be called "Walt" after he started his writing career, was born to a Quaker family in West Hills located near Huntington, Long Island. He taught briefly in the Long Island area and worked as a journalist for various newspapers including the *Brooklyn Eagle.* In 1855 he self-published the first of nine editions of *Leaves of Grass*, a book of poetry that includes the first version of his major poem, "Song of Myself," called by some a "personal epic"—a poem that reflects the theme of individualism yet sums up the more universal experiences of life in nineteenth-century America. In fact, he sent a copy to Ralph Waldo Emerson, who responded to Whitman in a letter, "I greet you at the beginning of a great career." His subjects range broadly on a variety of topics, all distinctly American, including the Civil War and the assassination of Abraham Lincoln as well as railroads and steamers, cities and plains, carpenters and farmers. Whitman once remarked, "The United States themselves are essentially the greatest poem." In the poem below, the speaker contemplates the difference between experiencing the stars through the medium of a lecture and his personal perception of their presence in the night sky.

When I heard the learn'd astronomer,
When the proofs, the figures, were ranged in columns before
    me,
When I was shown the charts and diagrams, to add, divide,
    and measure them,
When I sitting heard the astronomer where he lectured with
    much applause in the lecture-room,
How soon unaccountable I became tired and sick,
Till rising and gliding out I wander'd off by myself,
In the mystical moist night-air, and from time to time,
Look'd up in perfect silence at the stars. ∎

Making Connections through Discussion and Writing

1. a. Underline all the words that signify a scientific discussion of astronomy.

    b. Why does the speaker leave the lecture?

    _____

    _____

    _____

    _____

    _____

2. a. The speaker of this poem is seeking to learn about the heavens. What does he learn in the "perfect silence" that he misses in the "much applause"?

    _____

    _____

    _____

    _____

    b. How does his aloneness enable him to see what he is unable to experience in the crowd?

    _____

    _____

    _____

    _____

3. a. What is the theme of this poem?

    _____

    b. What does it say about one's experience with nature?

    _____

    _____

    _____

    _____

4. a. Circle examples of alliteration in the poem.

    b. How does this poetic technique help convey the theme?

    _____

    _____

    _____

    _____

5. The poet senses that there is more to the universe than mathematical formulations and manifold charts and diagrams. What is it about "the mystical moist night air" that enables him to see and causes him to become speechless in the presence of nature?

_____

_____

_____

_____

Gerard Manley Hopkins
The Caged Skylark

Gerard Manley Hopkins (1844–1889) was born at Stratford, England, and educated at Oxford. He was originally Anglican but converted to Roman Catholicism and was ordained a Jesuit priest in 1877. Having burned his earlier poems in 1868 when first deciding to enter the priesthood, Hopkins, upon the suggestion of Rector Father Jones, later composed one of his most famous works, "The Wreck of the Deutschland," a poem dealing with the tragedy of a shipwreck at sea where five nuns drowned. Hopkins lived the last five years of his life in Dublin, Ireland, as Professor of Greek and Latin Literature in the Catholic University College. Succumbing to the stress of marking numerous examinations, experiencing frustration with the Irish for their hatred of England, and feeling that his work would not be valued, Hopkins grew weaker in body and spirit. He died of typhoid when he was only 44 years old. Some of Hopkins' most famous poems include those that extol God's presence in nature such as "The Windhover," "God's Grandeur," and "Pied Beauty." During periods of severe depression, he composed such sonnets as "Carrion Comfort," "To seem the stranger," "I wake and feel," "No worst, there is none," "Patience, hard thing," and "My own heart." These are known as his "terrible" sonnets because of their dark tone. With his experiments in rhythm and his revival of alliteration, which had characterized Old English poetry, Hopkins is considered by many as a forerunner of twentieth-century poetry. In the following poem, Hopkins reflects on the earthly life of humans and the Christian belief of the resurrection of the body. The analogy he draws from nature enables his persona and his readers to better understand one of the great mysteries of the faith.

Vocabulary . . . .

| scanted | wring |
| uncumbered | |

As a dare-gale skylark scanted in a dull cage
   Man's mounting spirit in his bone-house, mean house, dwells—
   That bird beyond the remembering his free fells;[1]
This in drudgery, day-laboring-out life's age.

Though aloft on turf[2] or perch or poor low stage,
   Both sing sometimes the sweetest, sweetest spells,
   Yet both droop deadly sometimes in their cells
Or wring their barriers in bursts of fear or rage.

Not that the sweet-fowl, song-fowl, needs no rest—
Why, hear him, hear him babble and drop down to his nest,
   But his own nest, wild nest, no prison.

Man's spirit will be flesh-bound, when found at best,
But uncumbered: meadow-down is not distressed
For a rainbow footing it nor he for his bones risen. ∎

Notes

[1] fell—a British term for a barren hill

[2] turf—It was a custom to put a piece of clover turf inside a bird's cage.

Name: _____ Section: _____ Date: _____

Making Connections through Discussion and Writing

1. a. Circle the compound words that Hopkins creates.

   b. List them below, and define them.

   word   definition

   _____   _____
   _____   _____
   _____   _____
   _____   _____
   _____   _____
   _____   _____
   _____   _____
   _____   _____

2. a. Describe the caged skylark.

   _____
   _____
   _____

   b. List all the comparisons Hopkins makes between humans and skylarks in the first three stanzas.

   _____
   _____
   _____
   _____
   _____

3. a. What new comparison does he make in the fourth stanza?

   _____
   _____

   b. Complete the analogy that Hopkins draws: the skylark in a cage is like man in his earthly body; the skylark in his own nest is like_____.

   c. Explain its meaning.

   _____
   _____
   _____
   _____

509

4. a. How does "flesh-bound" relate to "his bones risen"?

    _____

    _____

    _____

    b. How does the image of the bird in "his nest . . . his own nest, wild nest, no prison" relate to human destiny?

    _____

    _____

    _____

    _____

    _____

    c. How does the New Testament teaching on the resurrection of the body clarify what Hopkins means here?

    _____

    _____

    _____

    _____

5. a. Explain the following image from the poem: "meadow-down is not distressed / For a rainbow footing it nor he for his bones risen."

    _____

    _____

    _____

    _____

    b. How does this image bring insight into the reality of the resurrection?

    _____

    _____

    _____

6. Paraphrase the poem, being careful to clarify the unusual phrases Hopkins uses.

    _____

    _____

    _____

    _____

    _____

    _____

    _____

    _____

    _____

    _____

    _____

7. a. Analyze Hopkins' unusual meter by placing accents above the stressed syllables in this poem.

    b. Mark the rhyming words (as in the first stanza, a b b a).

8. This poem is an example of which verse form?

    _____

9. a. What is the theme of this poem?

    _____

    b. What does the affirmation made here add to a definition of human nature and destiny?

    _____

    _____

    _____

    _____

Gerard Manley Hopkins
Spring

In the following two poems, "Spring" and "Spring and Fall," Gerard Manley Hopkins is concerned with the seasons of nature and their connection with the seasons of life, particularly spring and autumn, the first filling the soul with joy, the second with foreboding.

Nothing is so beautiful as Spring—
    When weeds, in wheels, shoot long and lovely and lush;
    Thrush's eggs look little low heavens, and thrush
Through the echoing timber does so rinse and wring
The ear, it strikes like lightnings to hear him sing;
    The glassy peartree leaves and blooms, they brush
    The descending blue; that blue is all in a rush
With richness; the racing lambs too have fair their fling.

What is all this juice and all this joy?
    A strain of the earth's sweet being in the beginning
In Eden garden.—Have, get, before it cloy,
    Before it cloud, Christ, lord, and sour with sinning,
Innocent mind and Mayday in girl and boy,
    Most, O maid's child, thy choice and worthy the winning. ■

Making Connections through Discussion and Writing

1. a. Hopkins presents a list of things that remind him of spring. Underline them.

   b. Paraphrase his descriptions of these items.

   _____
   _____
   _____
   _____
   _____
   _____
   _____
   _____
   _____

2. a. The spring Hopkins describes is alive with movement and richness. List the images that depict the vibrancy of nature.

   _____
   _____
   _____
   _____
   _____
   _____

   b. Explain how they present the speaker's view of spring.

   _____
   _____
   _____
   _____
   _____

3. a. What does the speaker mean by "The descending blue; that blue is all in a rush / With richness"?

   _____
   _____
   _____
   _____

   b. Explain the connection of "blue" with his various descriptions of nature.

   _____
   _____
   _____
   _____

4. a.   How are the descriptions of nature in the first stanza echoes of Eden?

_____

_____

_____

_____

   b.   How is spring a fitting symbol for the Eden that is now lost?

_____

_____

_____

_____

5. a.   Circle the alliterative words Hopkins uses.

   b.   Why is this poetic technique effective for Hopkins' theme?

_____

_____

_____

_____

6. a.   Who is the "maid's child" Hopkins mentions?

_____

_____

   b.   How is this child connected to the innocence of spring and the Garden of Eden?

_____

_____

_____

_____

Gerard Manley Hopkins
Spring and Fall

to a young child

Márgarét, áre you grieving
Over Goldengrove unleaving?
Leáves líke the things of man, you
With your fresh thoughts care for, can you?
Ah! ás the heart grows older
It will come to such sights colder
By and by, nor spare a sigh
Though worlds of wanwood[1] leafmeal[2] lie;
And yet you will weep and know why.
Now no matter, child, the name:
Sórrow's spríngs áre the same.
Nor mouth had, no nor mind, expressed
What heart heard of, ghost[3] guessed:
It's the blight man was born for,
It is Margaret you mourn for. ∎

Notes

[1] wanwood—autumn woods

[2] leafmeal—leaves turning into mulch

[3] ghost—spirit

Making Connections through Discussion and Writing

1. a. To whom is the poem addressed?

     _____

    b. Why do you think Hopkins would choose this person?

     _____

     _____

2. a. Describe the speaker?

     _____

    b. What is his tone in the poem?

     _____

     _____

3. a. What is Margaret grieving over?

     _____

     _____

    b. According to the end of the poem, what should she be grieving over?

     _____

     _____

    c. Why does the poem take this twist?

     _____

     _____

4. a. Circle four unusual words in the poem.

    b. List them below, and define them.

    word   definition

    _____   _____

    _____   _____

    _____   _____

    _____   _____

    c. What is the theme in this poem?

     _____

     _____

d.   How do these words amplify the theme?

_____

_____

_____

_____

_____

5.   Paraphrase lines 3-4 and 12-13. Make sure the final sentences are written in clear, concise, and coherent English.

_____

_____

_____

_____

_____

_____

_____

_____

_____

_____

6.   a.   Pay special attention to the title of the poem. What is the relationship of spring and fall?

_____

_____

_____

_____

b.   Discuss how the title "Spring and Fall" is reflected in the poem.

_____

_____

_____

_____

c.   How does the word "blight" relate to spring and fall?

_____

_____

_____

7.   Compare and contrast the two poems by Hopkins: "Spring" and "Spring and Fall." Specifically note the tone of each poem, the approach toward the subject matter, and their individual resolution.

tone _____

_____

_____

_____

approach _____
_____
_____
_____
_____

subject _____
_____
_____
_____
_____

resolution _____
_____
_____
_____
_____

Rainer Maria Rilke
Do Not Be Troubled, God

Rainer Maria Rilke (1875–1926) was a German poet born in Prague. He attended military school, a trade school, and the University of Prague, but was dissatisfied with them all. He married Clara Westhoff, a German artist, in 1901. His early works reflect his desire for religious vision; his later works particularly demonstrate his ability to communicate spiritual insights and truths through his masterful use of imagery and lyrical diction. Many consider him the most influential German poet of the twentieth century. His books include *Letters to a Young Poet* (1903), *Duino Elegies* (1922), and *Sonnets to Orpheus* (1922). The two poems included here show his informal tone as he speaks to God. Like the seventeenth-century poet George Herbert, Rilke speaks in defense of human weakness and need, defending these before a God who is his intimate friend, not a harsh and distant judge.

Vocabulary . . . .

      beggary   charlatan

Do not be troubled, God, though they say "mine"
of all things that permit it patiently.
They are like wind that lightly strokes the boughs
and says: MY tree.

They hardly see
how all things glow that their hands seize upon,
so that they cannot touch
even the utmost fringe and not be singed.

They will say "mine" as one will sometimes call
the prince his friend in speech with villagers,
this prince being very great—and far away.
They call strange walls "mine," knowing not at all
who is the master of the house indeed.
They still say "mine," and claim possession, though
each thing, as they approach, withdraws and closes;
a silly charlatan perhaps thus poses
as owner of the lightning and the sun.
And so they say: my life, my wife, my child,
my dog, well knowing all that they have styled
their own: life, wife, child, dog, remain
shapes foreign and unknown,
that blindly groping they must stumble on.
This truth, be sure, only the great discern,
who long for eyes. The others WILL not learn
that in the beggary of their wandering

they cannot claim a bond with any thing,
but, driven from possessions they have prized,
not by their own belongings recognized,
they can OWN wives no more than they own flowers,
whose life is alien and apart from ours.

God, do not lose your equilibrium.
Even he who loves you and discerns your face
in darkness, when he trembles like a light
you breathe upon,—he cannot own you quite.
And if at night one holds you closely pressed,
locked in his prayer so you cannot stray,
        you are the guest
        who comes, but not to stay.

God, who can hold you? To yourself alone
belonging, by no owner's hand disturbed,
you are like unripened wine that unperturbed
grows ever sweeter and is all its own. ■

Making Connections through Discussion and Writing

1. The beginning of this poem is a bit startling for the reader because the speaker tells God not to be troubled. What do you think the speaker means here?

   _____
   _____
   _____
   _____
   _____

2. a. The speaker presents various examples of "owning." Underline the examples he gives to indicate the human penchant toward owning possessions and people.

   b. According to the speaker, how must an experience with God differ from this kind of possessiveness?

   _____
   _____
   _____
   _____
   _____

3. a. The poem presents the view that man foolishly thinks he can possess something or someone, but he "cannot claim a bond with anything." Does this poem reveal the emptiness of humanity or the fullness of God?

   _____
   _____

   b. How can our emptiness prepare us to know God?

   _____
   _____
   _____
   _____
   _____

4. a. Underline the simile describing God that comes in the last two lines of the poem.

   b. What is the speaker asserting about the nature of God in this simile?

   _____
   _____
   _____
   _____
   _____
   _____

Rainer Maria Rilke
You, Neighbor God

You, neighbor God, if sometimes in the night
I rouse you with loud knocking, I do so
only because I seldom hear you breathe
and know: you are alone.
And should you need a drink, no one is there
to reach it to you, groping in the dark.
Always I hearken. Give but a small sign.
I am quite near.

Between us there is but a narrow wall,
and by sheer chance; for it would take
merely a call from your lips or from mine
to break it down,
and that without a sound.
The wall is builded of your images.

They stand before you hiding you like names,
And when the light within me blazes high
that in my inmost soul I know you by,
the radiance is squandered on their frames.

And then my senses, which too soon grow lame,
exiled from you, must go their homeless ways. ■

Making Connections through Discussion and Writing

1. a. In this poem, Rilke recognizes a wall that exists between the speaker and God. What constitutes this wall?

_____

_____

_____

   b. How does it work to block the speaker from fully experiencing the presence of God through his inner experience of "light"?

_____

_____

_____

_____

_____

2. a. What is the speaker's attitude toward his paradoxical experience of knowing God and yet still being separated from God?

_____

_____

_____

_____

   b. How does the poem move toward a "resolution" of this problem?

_____

_____

_____

_____

3. Compare this poem to the parable of the neighbor who needs a favor in the night (Luke 11:5-8). What differences and similarities exist between the speaker of the poem and the friend who comes at midnight in the parable?

   similarities   differences

   _____   _____

   _____   _____

   _____   _____

   _____   _____

   _____   _____

   _____   _____

   _____   _____

   _____   _____

4. a. Rilke sees language itself (of saying and not saying, speaking and not speaking) as blocking our immediate and full comprehension of God. Using examples from both poems, explain the function of language to draw us near to or move us away from God.

    b. Compare these ideas to the purpose of the poet. How does Rilke attempt to reveal God through this use of language?

5. a. The two poems by Rilke attribute to God more human emotions than are often associated with the divine. Given the limitations of language, do you think God may be more effectively described by human emotions, as Rilke does, or by more abstract formulations, such as Paul Tillich's phrase "the ground of being"?

    b. What are the advantages and disadvantages of each way of speaking about God?

    c. Which of these may better serve as a "window" into the nature of God? Why?

Gjertrud Schnackenberg
Supernatural Love

Gjertrud Schnakenberg (b. 1953), a contemporary American poet, was born in Tacoma, Washington. She earned a B.A. from Mount Holyoke College, graduating *summa cum laude,* and in 1985 received an honorary doctorate from that same institution. She lived two years at the American Academy in Rome and has won numerous awards, including the Rome Prize of the American Academy and Institute of Arts and Letters, *The Paris Review* Conners Prize, and the Brandeis University Creative Arts Citation. Her poetry has been anthologized in *The Norton Anthology of Modern Poetry.* Her first two collections of poems were *Portraits and Elegies* (1982) and *The Lamplit Answer* (1985). Her newest book is titled *Gilded Lapse of Time* (1994). The poem below, from *The Lamplit Answer,* illustrates the intuitive insight a child possesses concerning the kingdom of Heaven—a perception that an adult seeks to obtain through more rational processes.

Vocabulary ....

        fathomed

My father at the dictionary-stand
Touches the page to fully understand
The lamplit answer, tilting in his hand

His slowly scanning magnifying lens.
A blurry, glistening circle he suspends
Above the word "Carnation." Then he bends

So near his eyes are magnified and blurred,
One finger on the miniature word,
As if he touched a single key and heard

A distant, plucked, infinitesimal string,
"The obligations due to everything
That's smaller than the universe." I bring

My sewing needle close enough that I
Can watch my father through the needle's eye,
As through a lens ground for a butterfly

Who peers down flower hallways toward a room
Shadowed and fathomed as this study's gloom
Where, as a scholar bends above a tomb

To read what's buried there, he bends to pore
Over the Latin blossom, I am four,
I spill my pins and needles on the floor

Trying to stitch "Beloved" X by X.[1]
My dangerous, bright needle's point connects
Myself illiterate to this perfect text

I cannot read. My father puzzles why
It is my habit to identify
Carnations as "Christ's flowers," knowing I

Can give no explanation but "Because."
Word-roots blossom in speechless messages
The way the thread behind my sampler[2] does

Where following each X I awkward move
My needle through the word whose root is love.
He reads, "A pink variety of Clove.

Carnatio, the Latin, meaning flesh."
As if the bud's essential oils brush
Christ's fragrance through the room, the iron-fresh

Odor carnations have floats up to me,
A drifted, secret, bitter ecstasy,
the stems squeak in my scissors, *Child, it's me,*

He turns the page to "Clove" and reads aloud:
"The clove, a spice, dried from a flower-bud."
Then twice, as if he hasn't understood,

He reads, "From French, for *clou,* meaning a nail."
He gazes, motionless. "Meaning a nail."
The incarnation blossoms, flesh and nail,

I twist my threads like stems into a knot
And smooth "Beloved," but my needle caught
Within the threads, *Thy blood so dearly bought,*

The needle strikes my finger to the bone.
I lift my hand, it is myself I've sewn,
The flesh laid bare, the threads of blood my own,

I lift my hand in startled agony
And call upon his name. "Daddy daddy"—
My father's hand touches the injury

As lightly as he touched the page before,
Where incarnation bloomed from roots that bore
The flowers I called Christ's when I was four. ∎

Notes

[1] X by X—The letters in "beloved" that the little girl is stitching are made up of tiny crosses or X-shaped stitches, a technique known as "cross stitch."

[2] sampler—a display or sample of different types of needlework designs and stitches. Often a sampler includes the alphabet or a saying to demonstrate skill at making letters. Completed samplers are usually hung in picture frames.

Making Connections through Discussion and Writing

1. a. Who is the speaker of the poem?

   _____

   b. What does the insight of the speaker motivate the father to do?

   _____

   _____

2. a. What are the activities that the two characters in the poem are engaged in?

   _____

   _____

   _____

   b. How are these activities related?

   _____

   _____

3. Why is it significant that the child does not yet know how to read?

   _____

   _____

4. a. What does the father discover about the root word sources of "carnation" and "clove"?

   _____

   _____

   _____

   b. How does his discovery relate to the child's intuition?

   _____

   _____

   _____

5. a. Who is the speaker of the words *"Child, it's me"* in stanza 13?

   _____

   b. How does this statement relate to the one in stanza 16, *"Thy blood so dearly bought"*?

   _____

   _____

   _____

6. What is significant about the child's accident with the needle and the father's response?

7. How does the title of the poem prepare the reader for its religious theme?

8. a.   Describe the relationship between the father and daughter.

   b.   What does the father give his daughter?

   c.   What does she give to him?

9. a.   Underline the Biblical allusions in the poem.

   b.   Describe how these work to elucidate the poem's meaning.

10. Explain how the insights about the universality of the Christian story that Frederick Buechner points out in "The Annunciation" elucidate the meanings suggested by the images (blood, nails, carnations, and "Daddy") that Gertrud Schnakenberg presents in her poem "Supernatural Love."

Li-Young Lee
The Gift

Li-Young Lee (b. 1957) was born in Jakarta, Indonesia, of Chinese parents. In 1959 Lee's father became a political prisoner for one year. The family fled Indonesia when the father was released, living in Hong Kong, Macau, and Japan before finally coming to America in 1964. Lee studied at several universities, including the University of Pittsburgh, the University of Arizona, and the State University of New York. He has since taught at various universities such as Northwestern University and the University of Iowa. Winner of many awards for his writing, Lee has published two volumes of poetry, *Rose* (1986) and *The City in Which I Love You* (1990). He published a prose autobiographical account, *The Winged Seed*, in 1995. The following poem is from his first book of poetry, *Rose*. Like Gjertrud Schnackenberg's poem, "Supernatural Love," this poem celebrates a father's action that establishes a lasting "gift" in the soul of the child.

To pull the metal splinter from my palm
my father recited a story in a low voice.
I watched his lovely face and not the blade.
Before the story ended, he'd removed
the iron sliver I thought I'd die from.

I can't remember the tale,
but hear his voice still, a well
of dark water, a prayer.
And I recall his hands,
two measures of tenderness
he laid against my face,
the flames of discipline
he raised above my head.

Had you entered that afternoon
you would have thought you saw a man
planting something in a boy's palm,
a silver tear, a tiny flame.
Had you followed that boy
you would have arrived here,
where I bend over my wife's right hand.

Look how I shave her thumbnail down
so carefully she feels no pain.
Watch as I lift the splinter out.
I was seven when my father
took my hand like this,

and I did not hold that shard
between my fingers and think,
Metal that will bury me,
christen it Little Assassin,
Ore Going Deep for My Heart.
And I did not lift up my wound and cry,
Death visited here!
I did what a child does
when he's given something to keep.
I kissed my father. ■

Making Connections through Discussion and Writing

1. a. Underline the four metaphors in the poem that the speaker in Li-Young Lee's poem introduces in the second stanza.

   b. Explain what is suggested by the images they present.

   _____
   _____
   _____
   _____

2. How does the poem's speaker, in the third stanza, directly involve the reader in this initial incident and then move the reader through time to a second incident?

   _____
   _____
   _____
   _____
   _____
   _____
   _____

3. What meanings do the lines "planting something in a boy's palm, / a silver tear, a tiny flame" suggest?

   _____
   _____
   _____
   _____
   _____
   _____
   _____

   b. How does the participle "planting" help link together the two incidents separated by time?

   _____
   _____
   _____
   _____

4. Explain how the father's action, in which "tenderness" and "discipline" are given, prepares for the son's care of his own wife.

   _____
   _____
   _____
   _____

5. a. What does the speaker not consider about the "shard" that his father had extracted?

_____

_____

_____

_____

   b. Why does he go into such detail about this?

_____

_____

_____

6. a. Explain the significance of his real reaction: "I kissed my father."

_____

_____

_____

_____

   b. How does this line bring the action of the poem to resolution, yielding a satisfying conclusion?

_____

_____

_____

_____

_____

_____

_____

_____

Mark Williams

Blind

The following poem records a moment of personal discovery for the speaker.

I woke that cold morning
and went to the killing tree
asked how a son
should kill the father
who took away
his eyes what should
the blind fingers look for
how should the unloved
arms react what path
should the feet take but the tree
was saying that hate is not
like this that it does not fall away
or change colors but is the old
disease that eats
through the limbs
and from underneath
rather the tree said
to lean my face
against the wind
and listen
and I would hear
my father's voice
calling my name
from eight directions
repeating my name
from the ache
of his own unloved body
then I would understand
how lonely he had been
how he had waited
all these years for me
to find him and tell him
he could live. ■

Making Connections through Discussion and Writing

1. a. Underline the adjectives in the first two lines of this poem that help set the tone suggested by the setting.

   b. Why do you think the speaker goes to the "killing tree" to speak of his hatred?

   _____

   _____

   _____

   c. What associations does the image "killing tree" evoke?

   _____

   _____

   _____

2. a. Bracket the questions the speaker puts to the tree.

   b. What do these questions reveal about the relationship he has had with his father?

   _____

   _____

   _____

   _____

3. a. The tree reveals something of the nature of hate to the speaker. What do you think it means by saying hate "does not fall away / or change colors"?

   _____

   _____

   _____

   _____

   b. What is suggested by the tree's description of what hate does do?

   _____

   _____

   _____

   _____

4. Think of the poem as an act, a process that brings a discovery to the speaker. What does the tree promise the speaker will learn from following its instruction to "lean [his] face / against the wind / and listen"?

   _____

   _____

   _____

   _____

5. What is the significance and emotional power of the father's calling the speaker's name, especially calling it "from the ache / of his own unloved body"?

_____

_____

_____

_____

6. a. Explain the paradox posed by the poem—that the "killing tree" speaks of life.

_____

_____

_____

_____

   b. How has the poem served as an epiphany?

_____

_____

_____

_____

   c. What images would you use to explore, in a poem you could write, your relationship with a parent?

_____

_____

_____

_____

Synthesis/Essay Suggestions: Epiphanies

1. Three poems in this section deal with parent-child relationships: "Supernatural Love" (Schnackenberg), "The Gift" (Lee), and "Blind" (Williams). What do the concerns of these poems suggest about the lasting influence of the early interactions between children and their parents? What do the fathers in the poems of Gjertrud Schnackenberg and Li-Young Lee provide that seems to be lacking in the father spoken of in Mark Williams' poem? Choose *one* of the following options for a synthesis exercise:

    a. Compose a brief essay in which you answer the questions above and go on to focus on your own early life. Identify an incident in which one of your parents treated you in such a way as to give you a "gift" that helped structure your personality or your way of dealing with life.

    b. Find and read the modern American poems "My Papa's Waltz" by Theodore Roethke and "Those Winter Sundays" by Robert Hayden; consider how the speakers of these poems remember their fathers. Compose a brief essay in which you compare their views with those of the three speakers in the Schnackenberg, Lee, and Williams poems.

    c. Write a poem in which you focus on an incident from your childhood that resulted in a lasting influence on your life.

2. Frederick Buechner ends his sermon "The Annunciation" with a story about a boy who kills his father, then grieves for him, saying, "I want my father, I want my father." Buechner suggests that this cry is somehow our own. In an essay, compare this insight, and the resolution Buechner states, to those expressed by the speaker in Mark Williams' poem, "Blind."

3. In this section several poems deal with the relationship of nature and human beings, including "I Wandered Lonely as a Cloud," "When I Heard the Learn'd Astronomer," "Desert Places," "Spring," and "Spring and Fall." Choose at least three of the poems, and in an essay discuss in detail the power of nature to provide insight into the meaning of life, the universe, and even the presence of God. Take into account the themes of the poems selected, and show how the poet moves from the ordinary to the extraordinary—from the immanent to the transcendent—from the natural to the supernatural.

4. Metaphor that derives from analogical thinking has been considered to be the heart of poetry. Most poems arrive at a sense of meaning or new insight through the linking of phenomena that the poet sees related in some way. Examine the controlling metaphor used in Gjertrud Schnackenberg's "Supernatural Love," Gerard Manley Hopkins' "Spring and Fall," and Li-Young Lee's "The Gift." In an essay, discuss how the metaphor is used to convey the theme of the poem, paying special attention to the novel way the poet looks at the world.

Chapter 12

The Sacred Ordinary: The Incarnational Imagination

In orthodox Christian belief, material reality is known as good, declared so by two fundamental doctrines: Creation and Incarnation. Creation suggests that all creatures carry the image of their divine maker, even as a human artist's work bears signs of its maker in its style and approach to its subject. God's accompanying affirmation that His making is "good" (the term used in Genesis chapter 1) removes the possibility that material reality can be, in itself, evil. The Incarnation of God in the human Jesus combines divinity and material reality—human reality—in a way that forever radically changes the nature of human life and destiny. Through the Incarnation, humans have become caught up into the life of God. The promise of Christ's resurrection is, according to St. Paul, that "we shall be like Him." This doctrine secures the worth of all material reality, for it has been divinized by the participation of God in it. The curtain that separated the Holy Place from the Holy of Holies, at the heart of the Jewish temple, split at the death of Christ (Matt. 27:51), signifying that no longer was the sacred confined to a particular place on earth; the categories of "holy" and "secular" were no longer valid in the view of faith, for God's Spirit was poured out upon the whole earth, as proclaimed by the Jewish prophet Joel and announced by St. Peter on the day of Pentecost following the ascension of Jesus.

The worldview that attends these doctrines, and the imagination shaped by them, finds in everyday reality (ordinary actions of human beings, normal occurrences of the natural world) the indwelling holiness of existence. Artists and thinkers with the vision to perceive such holiness in the ordinary remind us of, or awaken us to, their vision that this holiness surrounds us: we inhabit the kingdom of Heaven even now. Variously expressed, the kingdom is "among us," "within us"; it is like a "treasure hidden in a field" or a "pearl of great price" that we chance to find. Consider an example from the visual arts: Jan Vermeer's painting of a young woman pouring milk from a pitcher into a bowl, lit by warm sunlight streaming in from an open window, is a vision of earthly goodness, of the inherent holiness of common things—milk, pottery, wood, sunlight, and the woman herself. In the art of music, a single cello playing one of Bach's concertos reveals holiness in the order of reality. Beyond these achievements of high art, however, Christian thought affirms the holiness of even a menial job done well and with integrity—Bruna Sandoval's faithful cleaning of the church in Wilbur's poem "A Plain Song for Comadre," for example. Any work or human act that is not distorted by sin may be done "as to the Lord" and may reveal its intrinsic holiness—a research paper crafted well, a basketball game played skillfully, a person treated with respect and justice.

In this chapter of *Encounters*, Thomas Howard, a contemporary Christian teacher and author, instructs on the importance of Incarnation in the shaping and meaning of Christian art, and Flannery O'Connor vividly captures the action of grace erupting into the most ordinary moments and invading the common characters in her powerful stories—"Parker's Back," in which a tattooed man becomes a "Christ-bearer" like St. Christopher, and "The Displaced Person," in which the poor, "displaced" persons of the world become Christ-bearers to the proud and self-sufficient. Finally, C. S. Lewis sums up the significance of the Incarnation for human life and destiny in his remarkable sermon "The Weight of Glory."

Michelangelo

Mine Eyes That Are Enamored of Things Fair

Michelangelo (1473–1564) was one of the leading artists of the Italian Renaissance. He is primarily known as a sculptor, the creator of such famous works as *Moses, David*, and the *Pieta*, but he was also a master painter whose work on the Sistine Chapel ceiling traces Biblical history from creation to final judgment. He was the major designer of St. Peter's Cathedral in the Vatican. His writings are not well known, but the following poem expresses his belief in using earthly beauty to move an individual toward contemplation of heavenly beauty.

Mine eyes that are enamored of things fair
And this my soul that for salvation cries
      May nevermore heavenward rise
Unless the sight of beauty lifts them there.
      Down from the loftiest star
      A splendor falls on earth,
      And draws desire afar,
      To that which gave it birth.
So love and heavenly fire and counsel wise
The noble heart finds most in starlike eyes. ■

Making Connections through Discussion and Writing

1. What does the speaker mean when he says that his eyes "are enamored of things fair"?

   _____
   _____
   _____
   _____

2. Describe what the speaker means by the need of his soul?

   _____
   _____
   _____

3. What enables him to rise "heavenward"?

   _____
   _____
   _____

4. According to lines 5 and 6, where does beauty originate?

   _____
   _____
   _____
   _____

5. What do lines 7 and 8 suggest about the effect of beauty on the soul?

   _____
   _____
   _____
   _____
   _____

6. How do the last two lines affirm the speaker's belief concerning the function of earthly beauty?

   _____
   _____
   _____
   _____
   _____

7. The speaker finds beauty in the earthly image of "starlike eyes," but speaks of splendor coming from "the loftiest star." Beauty, it is suggested, is both around us and beyond us—both immanent and transcendent. How might you explain this dual nature of beauty in terms of both Platonic and Christian thought?

_____

_____

_____

_____

_____

_____

_____

_____

_____

_____

_____

_____

_____

_____

Thomas Howard
Mimesis and Incarnation

In the essay below, Thomas Howard explores the way the modern visual arts have developed in line with intellectual movements of the nineteenth and twentieth centuries. Drawing on the doctrine of the Incarnation to affirm both the concrete world known to our senses and the transcendent world of significance, he defends mimesis (the process of image-making) as the fundamental basis of uniting matter and meaning in art.

Vocabulary . . . .

abortive	hexahedrons
anachronistic	hiatus
anagogical	hierarchic
animistic	iconoclastic
annunciation	iconography
arcane	impetus
atavistic	inanity
automatism	inquisitorial
axiomatic	ire
bacchic	luminescence
banality	matrix
bibelots	metamorphosis
carnality	mimetic
cleavage	myopiconus
cognoscenti	otiose
colossus	pedestrian
concretion	perdition
connate	pietá
corollary	posit
desideratum	positivistic
disavowal	proximate
discredited	referent
dissolution	rhomboids
epoch	servile
equilibrium	solipsism
ethereal	trammels
evinces	transcendence
forswore	vacuity
gnostic	

Thomas Howard, "Mimesis and Incarnation," from *Imagination and the Spirit*, ed. Charles Huttar, © 1971 Wm. B. Eerdmans Publishing Co., Grand Rapids, Michigan. Reprinted by permission; all rights reserved.

There has, perhaps, never been an epoch in which the hiatus between serious artistic activity and common taste has been wider. What appears in the galleries and in the journals of poetry is addressed frequently to the cognoscenti, and leaves the public murmuring confusedly. Historically, this was not the case. Much of what we now call "great art" appeared in response to a direct commission from a patron or church, or, in the case of epic poetry, was addressed to a listening audience of mostly uneducated people. The assumption was that everyone would understand what was being offered. There were not two worlds—the one of the artists and the few, and the other of the masses. Even into the eighteenth and nineteenth centuries, the novels and poetry that are now read only in graduate studies were written for anyone who cared to buy a book.

The cleavage between artist and public is so total now, however, that it is doubtful whether the name of a single serious painter or poet is familiar in at all the same sense as are the names of popular entertainers. This, of course, raises the question of blame: has the public rejected the artist, or the artist the public?

This is a question that cannot be answered one way or the other, since both answers are right. Something can be said, however, about the present state of affairs. It is worth asking whence it arose and what sort of criticism is possible in the light of historic notions concerning the office of the artist and the nature of his world.

The public is understandably bewildered when it encounters soup tins, ropes, burlap, crumpled auto parts, plaster hamburgers, flags, and comics in the art museums, and is told by the critics that it ought to be impressed and moved. The popular response is, often enough, disgust, fear, embarrassment, or blankness.

The rationale offered by its practitioners for much of current art may itself follow various lines of thought. There is the dogmatic nonhumanism of Ad Reinhardt, for example, who insisted on the entire independence of the artistic endeavor, and disallowed most of the canons of nonrepresentational as well as representational art. The "op" artists employ their stripes, checkerboards, swirls of color, and dots with a rigor and exactitude second to none in the history of art, seeking not so much for images to be looked *at* as for forms that will arouse perceptual responses. The idea is to engage the viewer in an act that will, it is hoped, increase his awareness of his visual capacities, and hence contribute to that great end of all high art, the heightening of consciousness.

Other artists, angrily or happily aware of the metamorphosis of American life into a vast travelogue of cola billboards, parking meters, ribbons of macadam, and gleaming formica-and-steel drive-ins, urge that, since this is the stuff of our existence, this is to be the stuff of the mimetic arts. Insofar as the Greek vision involved the glory of the human form, that is what one sees in the iconography of the epoch; insofar as the medieval involved annunciations and pietas, that is what is figured; insofar as ours involves hamburgers, that is what we shall have. The artist is the seer who gives its own existence back to his age, transfigured for contemplation. Traditionally, the images in which he gives that existence back to the world are those that speak of the eternal, whether that be a religious eternity as in the Christian vision, or a nonpersonalistic eternity of pure form as in post-Enlightenment vision. Given the modern world, say these artists, we will give you your bibelots, which speak of nothing.

The "primary structuralists," whose work takes the shape of immense rhomboids, cubes, and hexahedrons, are seeking a nonillusive form. Since, in their view, the world is neither meaningful *nor* absurd ("It simply is," says Alain Robbe-Grillet[1]), the effort is to create solid, immediate objects that are nothing but what they are. They are "presences," it is urged, without meaning or referent.

It may help us see what is occurring in contemporary painting and sculpture if we inquire into the notions from which the mimetic activity of the last one hundred years derives.

Historically, it was felt that there is an onus of sublime affirmation laid upon high art. That is, that the office of the poet and artist is to "see life steadily and see it whole," in all of its beauty, ambiguity, and horror, and to find an imagery that not only figures that life truly, but takes the stuff of that life and transfigures it into forms that speak of ultimacy.

It is, perhaps, in the notion of sublimity that the discontinuity occurs between the art of earlier epochs and that which has arisen in the last century. Art traditionally proceeded on the assumption that there is an equation between Beauty and Truth, and had for its aim the figuring of Beauty in images faithful to human experience. In the nineteenth century this aim was forsworn in the name of Reality. There had been, in the wake of postmedieval methods of describing the world, a gradual dissolution of confidence in myths and other ideas that were not verifiable according to the terms of the new methodology.[2] Sibyls, prophets, angels, priests—everyone who tried to bring tidings from outside to the human situation—had been discredited. The field for investigation and for imagination was to be the one at hand. Since we see no titans, fauns, heroes, devils, or archangels at play there, we must assume, until they appear in our lenses, that there are none. Thus a positivistic view, and thus the *Zeitgeist*[3] that ensued.

Since we are to scrutinize our world dispassionately, we will posit Reality in our own terms as our starting point, and leave the erstwhile notion of Beauty to fend for itself. If it emerges from our experience, *tant mieux;*[4] if not, *tant pis.*[5] We will not conjure it from a realm about which nobody knows anything. The point was that the sublime is a notion referring to nothing that we can verify in our terms, and hence is inappropriate as a referent for modern imagery.

The man who announced the emancipation of painting from anachronistic notions of beauty and sublimity was Gustave Courbet. Reality is to be the province of the artist from here on, he declared. At about the same time, Whistler announced his attempt to "divest the picture from any outside sort of interest," in answer to Ruskin's charge that he had "flung a pot of paint in the public's face."

Proceeding from Courbet, Edouard Manet focussed attention on the medium itself. In his view, the province of the artist is paint and canvas, not what they "stand for." His "Fifer" aroused dismay when it appeared, for it was clear that the artist had made no attempt to subject his paint to the demands of three-dimensional illusion: on the contrary, here was a brightly colored doll, in effect pasted flat onto the canvas. The focus was on the thing itself, not on the idea of a real little boy with a fife. Manet and those who followed him tried to get a scientifically exact record of the patterns of light that the retina registers, not the image we construct in our imagination in response to the phenomenon. They felt that artistic activity must become less and less servile to our figuration of the external world, and more and more independent. The work of Renoir, Cézanne, Monet, Pissarro, Seurat, and Degas evinces this effort.

In the twentieth century, painting went in three directions from this beginning: toward Expressionism, toward Abstractionism, and toward Fantasy. Each exhibits its own special effort to discover significance in the world without reference to a discredited transcendence. Expressionism concerned itself with the emotional world, Abstractionism with questions of formal structure, and Fantasy with imagination, especially irregular imaginations and dreams.

The fathers of Expressionism were probably the "fauvists" (wild beasts), who aroused critical ire by appearing to do violence to human perception. Matisse, with his dancing curlicues, wanted to pursue the formal demands of design and color further than had been done up to that point. Rouault saw vividly the corruption of the world and figured this in his "ugly" portraits, hinting nonetheless at a residue of nobility in the human face. Kokoschka, Kirchner, and Beckmann assailed the public eye with images of vacuity and damnation.

Picasso, Braque, Leger, and Mondrian became occupied with formal questions, abstracting from the apparent world suggestions of geometric structure. Picasso scandalized everybody with his "Les Demoiselles d'Avignon," which represents the methodical and violent break-up of classical notions of beauty. This sort of thing (known as Cubism) attempts to find an alternative to the external world by discovering a "building material" of angular chunks of voids and spaces (one cannot help but recall some of Cézanne's work here). Braque worked with scraps of this and that (wood, fabric, newsprint, tickets), calling attention to texture itself rather than to anything scenic perceived through the "window" of traditional painting.

Up to this point there was still a reference to the external world. Whether in terms of texture or form or image, the matrix from which the imagery arose was still perceptibly of that world, although it was sometimes in the form of disavowal. But Wassily Kandinsky made the disavowal final. He abandoned representation entirely, and sought to present emotion directly on the canvas. He sought to invest pure form and color with a spiritual meaning quite apart from the familiar world of appearance, so that not only is it impossible to discover any imagery in his composition: it is a mistaken effort. There is none. Likewise, Piet Mondrian set about to apprehend "pure reality" in wholly nonrepresentational modes. He saw this reality to consist in an equilibrium achieved in terms of a balance of forms, and his blocks of primary color divided by heavy ruled lines are among the most familiar and pleasing objects of twentieth-century painting.

The third major stream in the painting of this century is that of Fantasy. The doctrine involved is that imagination is a more significant source for mimetic imagery than is the external world. It posits the psychoanalytic idea of a commonalty of subconscious images in all of us, although in its handling of these images it frequently becomes entirely private, so that the viewer may bring his own interpretation to the painting. In the dream visions of De Chirico, in the fairy-tale childhood memories of Chagall, and the "language of signs" of Klee, this sort of thing is visible. It is visible in the Dadaism of Duchamp and others, who declared that, as of the Great War, *all* value systems had become otiose and who preached nonsense as the desideratum, and in the Surrealism of Dali and Miro, who sought to explore "pure psychic automatism," that is, thought free from the trammels of reason, morals, or aesthetics.

A drastic departure from even these iconoclastic activities occurred in the work of Jackson Pollock, who announced the centrality of the *act* of painting. He forswore the attempt to figure anything at all on the canvas (dreams, pure form, signs, nonsense), substituting for these traditional activities an interest in the dynamics of the paint itself. It is not insulting to him to say that he poured and dribbled and threw the paint: that is precisely what he did. He moved, perhaps, as far as it is possible to move from the view of the painter's office as having anything to do with human existence.

We have already noted some of the post-Pollock activity, and it is possible to see in some of it a return to the world of appearances, albeit a return that insists that things are what they are, period.

The mimetic activity of the last century derives, then, directly from doctrines that attended the intellectual activity of the era. The doctrines entail, again, a final confidence in an analytic and descriptive methodology as the sole approach to the world. There is a circular movement involved, in that the early decision to exclude from inquiry all realms not scrutable by the methodology is followed by the dogma that there *are* no such realms, since the method does not perceive them. Corollary to this is the view that it is not possible to discover any principle of *significance* in appearances, in that there is nothing else to be signalled.

There is an alternative view possible, of course. It is the view, once universal, that the data of our world are significant. The human consciousness has, from the beginning, figured its intimation of this in its mimetic activity. The method involved was synthetic and anagogical rather than analytic and descriptive. The notion was that one thing signals another, that there is a continuum of significance from the lowest worm to the highest seraph, that there is a form, an order, a harmony, a dance in which all participate. It tended to feel, in contrast to our own epoch which urges that nothing means anything, that everything means everything. It believed in the image as a mode—perhaps *the* mode—of articulating what it suspected. It is visi-

ble in the imagery of all times and all places. And it uttered itself variously in the doctrines of Aristotle, Caxton, Sidney, Shelley, Wordsworth, Arnold, and Emerson—that the poet has upon him the high task of perceiving the myriad hierarchic interchanges among all things, and of figuring that perception in noble images.

This notion has, often enough, attended the religious view of the world. In the Egyptian, Assyrian, Greek, and animistic worlds, it was inseparable from religious vision: the imagery *was* religious. The conjunction of aesthetic and religious vision is, of course, most familiar to us in the West in medieval and Renaissance—that is, in Christian—imagery.

The Christian vision affirms the significance of the mimetic act. It does so because it sees here the human echo of activity connate with the origins of things, and because its own understanding of the world is one that involves the notion of the Incarnate Word.

It sees the original creative energy as describable by the term "Word." It understands this energy as tending toward utterance, that is, toward the articulation of significance, and indeed toward being, from nonsignificance and nonbeing (cf. human language, which, far more than serving merely as the mode by which we exchange ideas, in effect calls our world into being for us by *naming* it). It is an articulation tending always toward concretion and identity, and not, as might be supposed, toward abstraction and anonymity. The energy utters itself in terms that we apprehend as soil and rock and fire and flesh. It uttered its form most nobly in man, and eventually in The Man—Immanuel. Which is to say that this Word, the Ground of all form and significance, the Referent for all phenomena and imagery, is such that its self-articulation tends finally toward Incarnation.

And the Incarnate, called Logos, embraced the limitations of this world and proclaimed authenticity and freedom and glory to us not, as many prophets have done, via escape into the ether, but via participation in the actualities of human existence. The vision of glory declared here is one, not of dissolution and a denial of carnality, but on the contrary, of a restoration of concretion and specificity and flesh in the unity and harmony for which it was made. The Christian agrees with Plato up to a point, but, unlike Plato, he suspects that the Ideal, far from being an abstraction, is harder and "knobblier" (C. S. Lewis) than anything we knock our shins on here. He sees this world, not as illusion, but as figure—that is, as the species under which we now apprehend Actuality. And, because he understands the Incarnate to be the finally authentic utterance of Actuality, he must affirm the validity of the world which that Incarnate affirmed.

The Incarnational view, then, would entail at least the following notions: it would affirm the immediate (because it believes in the Incarnation); it would affirm the transcendent (because it believes in the Logos); it would see the commonplace as the vehicle of ultimacy (n.b.[6] the common manhood of the Incarnate, and also his pedestrian *modus vivendi*[7]); and it would insist on the public character of significance (again, because it believes in the Word).

A person who takes this view would have, then, various questions to ask concerning aesthetic theories and the imagery deriving from those theories. He would find himself, for a start, at a point midway between the two eternal human inclinations—the one that seeks Reality in an escape from this existence, and the other that disavows the transcendent in its effort to apprehend the actuality of this world. Historically, the former view is the one that has issued most often in sublime images: indeed, there is an element of this escapism in most religious imagery. But in its final form, the tendency is gnostic, and leads to a vision that becomes more and more ethereal and less and less congenial to any imagery at all, and hence leaves the province of art altogether, since mimetic activity must presuppose a robust affirmation of the concrete if it is to have any matrix from which its images are to rise. (Hence the poor artistic yield of religions and cults that seek Actuality in purely spiritual terms: their categories reduce the possibility of imagery; the Reformation faith might ask itself some hard questions here.)

The view that, on the other hand, seeks Actuality in the stuff at hand has much to be said for it. Besides giving an impetus to scientific inquiry, it has given us the great vision of the Impressionists. However, at the point at which this view excludes the transcendent altogether, and seeks Actuality *solely* in the world investigated by the sciences—at that point its grasp upon even *that* world begins to slip. For it becomes increasingly difficult to posit the notion of significance, and hence to draw images of power and sublimity from this matrix. Ironically, the quest for Actuality in these terms leads eventually either to a retreat from the recognizable into abstract and arcane forms (since the thing-as-it-appears-to-us is nonsignificant) or to a myopic crawl into an inner universe of fantasy which yields images of greater and greater grotesquery and inanity. Often enough, the early stages of this quest yield compelling and powerful images. The work of Duchamp, Mondrian, and Braque has surely opened our eyes to provinces of form and texture that we would have missed. And who can gainsay the power of the visions of horror in the work of Kirchner, Beckmann, and Grosz? Perhaps it took an antitranscendentalist view to make this imagery possible. But, however compelling or intriguing or unsettling or shocking or amusing or engaging or diverting the imagery may be, it is difficult to find in it that troubling thing we call, vaguely, greatness, which seems to rise from the simultaneous awareness of limitation and sublimity, and sees them both figured in the human situation. The mighty vision of a Michelangelo took the *donnée*[8] (the human form) and transfigured (not twisted) it into forms that spoke of the eternal. Perhaps we need the twisting as an image of perdition; but perdition is of proximate interest only. Sublimity alone is final.

Again, the Incarnational view, with its celebration of the commonplace, would have to inquire into the worth of the bizarre and arcane as appropriate vehicles of authenticity. For it would suspect, unlike the more intoxicating view that freedom and fulfillment lie in the bacchic and the occult, that this freedom and fulfillment lie in the obvious, and that participation in the given rhythms of existence (dawn and twilight, spring and fall, birth, marriage, work, eating and drinking) is the beginning of glory. Vermeer is the colossus towering above those who, on the one hand, seek increasingly peculiar images, and those who, on the other, insist flatly on the nothingness but inevitability of what is at hand (hamburgers and rubber tires). In contrast to the former, Vermeer found luminescence and sublimity in a *room corner*; against the latter, he found *luminescence and sublimity* in a room corner.

Finally, the Incarnational view would suspect that the truly significant is public in its nature, and that the private is of limited interest only. Because of the universal utterance of the Word, and because of the response to this in the great "Benedicite, omnia opera Domini," this view would look with suspicion on mimetic activity involving any esoteric doctrine or the tendency toward solipsism. Hence, while it is surely entirely permissible (and perhaps helpful to himself) for an artist to see his task to be the figuring of private visions and emotions directly on the canvas, the result is of minimal significance. High art is an eminently public thing, for, like the Word, it calls form from havoc and utters it in universal terms.

The criticism that this view would urge, then, against our own epoch, is one that will raise again the questions that are not asked. It will urge no atavistic return to the manageable ages of supposed ignorance. Nor will it be nostalgic for some twelfth-century equilibrium of sensibility.

But it will ask whether the dogmas deriving from postmedieval methodology are quite axiomatic after all. It will ask whether the exclusion of the ghoulies and ghosties and long-legged beasties (and Apollo and the Virgin of Chartres and Immanuel) from categories of inquiry is not abortive. It will doubt whether the human imagination will ever be satisfied with the edict that declares that man comes of age to the extent that he disavows the notions celebrated in the imagery of other ages—candor, valor, *caritas*,[9] beauty, glory. It will test with inquisitorial rigor the sensibility of an age whose imagery can speak truthfully only of banality and perdition and the immediate. And it will urge that only that mimesis rises beyond cleverness and topicality whose imagery figures the sublimity and fear in a handful of dust.[10] ■

Notes

1 Author's Note: As quoted in "The Shape of Art for Some Time to Come: Primary Structures," *Life*, LXIII, iv (July 28, 1967), 44A.

2 Author's Note: See, in this connection, Walter J. Ong, S. J., *Ramus, Method, and the Decay of Dialogue* (Cambridge, Mass, 1958), and Owen Barfield, *Saving the Appearances* (London, 1957).

3 *Zeitgeist*—(German) spirit of the times, worldview

4 *tant mieux*—(French) so much the better

5 *tant pis*—(French) too bad

6 n.b.: *nota bene*—(Latin) note well, take note

7 *modus vivendi*—(Latin) way of life

8 *donnée*—(French) a given, that which is present

9 *caritas*—(Latin) selfless love

10 fear in a handful of dust—This phrase is from T. S. Eliot's poem "The Wasteland," part 1, line 30.

Making Connections through Discussion and Writing

1. a. Howard introduces his essay with a description of the "cleavage" between the popular arts and the fine arts and that of the public and the artist. In one sentence, summarize Howard's point in the first two paragraphs of his essay.

_____

_____

_____

_____

_____

   b. List below examples that you are aware of that reveal this separation in the arts. Draw from your knowledge of such arts as music, fiction, films, etc.

_____

_____

_____

_____

_____

_____

2. Howard finds modern art taking three directions. Briefly describe these directions.

_____

_____

_____

_____

_____

_____

3. a. What does Howard mean by the phrase "discredited transcendence"?

_____

_____

_____

_____

   b. How does he view the three directions taken by modern art as reactions to this "discredited transcendence"?

_____

_____

_____

_____

4. a. Howard states several principles or "notions" that Incarnational art affirms. List these principles below.

_____

_____

_____

_____

_____

_____

b. Explain how these principles arise from Christian doctrines.

_____

_____

_____

_____

_____

c. Explain how Thomas finds these principles calling into question the methods and effects of much modern art.

_____

_____

_____

_____

_____

_____

5. a. Howard does not condemn modern art completely. What does he suggest such art can do?

_____

_____

_____

b. What does he believe it cannot achieve?

_____

_____

_____

6. Check the fine arts section of your academic library or on the Internet to find an example of a painting of the crucifixion by the Renaissance German painter Grünewald (one such painting is *The Isenheim Altarpiece* in the Unterlinden Museum in Colmar, France) and a print of Salvador Dali's painting of the crucifixion *(Corpus Hypercubus)*.

a. How do these works differ?

_____

_____

b. What do these works suggest about the artists' views of the Christian doctrine of the Incarnation?

_____

_____

_____

7. Find examples of paintings by Jan Vermeer and by Salvador Dali—particularly Dali's religious paintings.
    a. Which do you think Howard would classify as "mimetic," which as "gnostic"?

_____

_____

_____

    b. Explain your answer.

_____

_____

_____

_____

8. Evaluate some examples of modern religious art and music using criteria drawn from Howard's ideas.

_____

_____

_____

_____

_____

_____

_____

_____

_____

_____

_____

_____

_____

_____

_____

_____

Flannery O'Connor
Novelist and Believer

Flannery O'Connor (1925–1964), born in Savannah, Georgia, spent most of her life in the small town of Milledgeville, where she graduated from the Georgia State College for Women in 1945. She studied at the famed Writers' Workshop of the University of Iowa, receiving her M.F.A. degree in 1947. Diagnosed with the disease lupus while still a young woman, she was in pain and had to walk with crutches during most of her writing career. Considered a major American author, she is known for her unusual imagination, uncompromising religious vision, and superb literary style. Her fiction treats contemporary Southern life in terms of comedy and tragedy and reflects her strong Roman Catholic faith. She published two novels, *Wise Blood* (1952) and *The Violent Bear It Away* (1960). Her short stories, originally in two volumes—*A Good Man Is Hard to Find* (1955) and *Everything That Rises Must Converge* (1965)—were collected in *The Complete Stories* (1971). *The Habit of Being* (1979) contains her letters, and *Mystery and Manners* (1969), from which the essay below is taken, contains her speeches and essays. Here O'Connor asserts that literature reveals the beliefs of its author. To O'Connor, an author's theology is inherent in every stage of the text and reflects a worldview that either includes or excludes God.

Vocabulary . . . .

anagogically	ecumenism
atrophies	impinge
benighted	penitential
dogmatically	sacramentally

Being a novelist and not a philosopher or theologian, I shall have to enter this discussion at a much lower level and proceed along a much narrower course than that held up to us here as desirable. It has been suggested that for the purposes of this symposium,[1] we conceive religion broadly as an expression of man's ultimate concern rather than identify it with institutional Judaism or Christianity or with "going to church."

I see the utility of this. It's an attempt to enlarge your ideas of what religion is and of how the religious need may be expressed in the art of our time; but there is always the danger that in trying to enlarge the ideas of students, we will evaporate them instead, and I think nothing in this world lends itself to quick vaporization so much as the religious concern.

As a novelist, the major part of my task is to make everything, even an ultimate concern, as solid, as concrete, as specific as possible. The novelist begins his work where human knowledge begins—with the senses; he works through the limitations of matter, and unless he is writing fantasy, he has to stay within the concrete possibilities of his culture. He is bound by his particular past and by those institutions and traditions that this past has left to his society. The Judaeo-Christian tradition has formed us in the west; we are bound to it by ties which may often be invisible, but which are there nevertheless. It has formed the shape of our secularism; it has formed even the shape of modern atheism. For my part, I shall have to remain well within the Judaeo-Christian tradition. I shall have to speak, without apology, of the Church, even when the Church is absent; of Christ, even when Christ is not recognized.

If one spoke as a scientist, I believe it would be possible to disregard large parts of the personality

---

and speak simply as a scientist, but when one speaks as a novelist, he must speak as he writes—with the whole personality. Many contend that the job of the novelist is to show us how man feels, and they say that this is an operation in which his own commitments intrude not at all. The novelist, we are told, is looking for a symbol to express feeling, and whether he be Jew or Christian or Buddhist or whatever makes no difference to the aptness of the symbol. Pain is pain, joy is joy, love is love, and these human emotions are stronger than any mere religious belief; they are what they are and the novelist shows them as they are. This is all well and good so far as it goes, but it just does not go as far as the novel goes. Great fiction involves the whole range of human judgment; it is not simply an imitation of feeling. The good novelist not only finds a symbol for feeling, he finds a symbol and a way of lodging it which tells the intelligent reader whether this feeling is adequate or inadequate, whether it is moral or immoral, whether it is good or evil. And his theology, even in its most remote reaches, will have a direct bearing on this.

It makes a great difference to the look of a novel whether its author believes that the world came late into being and continues to come by a creative act of God, or whether he believes that the world and ourselves are the product of a cosmic accident. It makes a great difference to his novel whether he believes that we are created in God's image, or whether he believes we create God in our own. It makes a great difference whether he believes that our wills are free, or bound like those of the other animals.

St. Augustine[2] wrote that the things of the world pour forth from God in a double way: intellectually into the minds of the angels and physically into the world of things. To the person who believes this—as the western world did up until a few centuries ago—this physical, sensible world is good because it proceeds from a divine source. The artist usually knows this by instinct; his senses, which are used to penetrating the concrete, tell him so. When Conrad[3] said that his aim as an artist was to render the highest possible justice to the visible universe, he was speaking with the novelist's surest instinct. The artist penetrates the concrete world in order to find at its depths the image of its source, the image of ultimate reality. This in no way hinders his perception of evil but rather sharpens it, for only when the natural world is seen as good does evil become intelligible as a destructive force and a necessary result of our freedom.

For the last few centuries we have lived in a world which has been increasingly convinced that the reaches of reality end very close to the surface, that there is no ultimate divine source, that the things of the world do not pour forth from God in a double way, or at all. For nearly two centuries the popular spirit of each succeeding generation has tended more and more to the view that the mysteries of life will eventually fall before the mind of man. Many modern novelists have been more concerned with the processes of consciousness than with the objective world outside the mind. In twentieth-century fiction it increasingly happens that a meaningless, absurd world impinges upon the sacred consciousness of author or character; author and character seldom now go out to explore and penetrate a world in which the sacred is reflected.

Nevertheless, the novelist always has to create a world and a believable one. The virtues of art, like the virtues of faith, are such that they reach beyond the limitations of the intellect, beyond any mere theory that a writer may entertain. If the novelist is doing what as an artist he is bound to do, he will inevitably suggest that image of ultimate reality as it can be glimpsed in some aspect of the human situation. In this sense, art reveals, and the theologian has learned that he can't ignore it. In many universities, you will find departments of theology vigorously courting departments of English. The theologian is interested specifically in the modern novel because there he sees reflected the man of our time, the unbeliever, who is nevertheless grappling in a desperate and usually honest way with intense problems of the spirit.

We live in an unbelieving age but one which is markedly and lopsidedly spiritual. There is one type of modern man who recognizes spirit in himself but who fails to recognize a being outside himself whom he can adore as Creator and Lord; consequently he has become his own ultimate concern. He says with Swinburne,[4] "Glory to man in the highest, for he is the master of things," or with Steinbeck,[5] "In the end was the word and the word was with men." For him, man has his own natural spirit of courage and dignity and pride and must consider it a point of honor to be satisfied with this.

There is another type of modern man who recognizes a divine being not himself, but who does not believe that this being can be known analogically or defined dogmatically or received sacramentally. Spirit and matter are separated for him. Man wanders about, caught in a maze of guilt he can't identify, trying to reach a God he can't approach, a God powerless to approach him.

And there is another type of modern man who can neither believe nor contain himself in unbelief and who searches desperately, feeling about in all experience for the lost God.

At its best our age is an age of searchers and discoverers, and at its worst, an age that has domesticated despair and learned to live with it happily. The fiction which celebrates this last state will be the least likely to transcend its limitations, for when the religious need is banished successfully, it usually atrophies, even in the novelist. The sense of mystery vanishes. A kind of reverse evolution takes place, and the whole range of feeling is dulled.

The searchers are another matter. Pascal[6] wrote in his notebook, "If I had not known you, I would not have found you." These unbelieving searchers have their effect even upon those of us who do believe. We begin to examine our own religious notions, to sound them for genuineness, to purify them in the heat of our unbelieving neighbor's anguish. What Christian novelist could compare his concern to Camus[7]? We have to look in much of the fiction of our time for a kind of sub-religion which expresses its ultimate concern in images that have not yet broken through to show any recognition of a God who has revealed himself. As great as much of this fiction is, as much as it reveals a wholehearted effort to find the only true ultimate concern, as much as in many cases it represents religious values of a high order, I do not believe that it can adequately represent in fiction the central religious experience. That, after all, concerns a relationship with a supreme being recognized through faith. It is the experience of an encounter, of a kind of knowledge which affects the believer's every action. It is Pascal's experience after his conversion and not before.

What I say here would be much more in line with the spirit of our times if I could speak to you about the experience of such novelists as Hemingway[8] and Kafka[9] and Gide[10] and Camus, but all my own experience has been that of the writer who believes, again in Pascal's words, in the "God of Abraham, Isaac, and Jacob and not of the philosophers and scholars." This is an unlimited God and one who has revealed himself specifically. It is one who became man and rose from the dead. It is one who confounds the senses and the sensibilities, one known early on as a stumbling block. There is no way to gloss over this specification or to make it more acceptable to modern thought. This God is the object of ultimate concern and he has a name.

The problem of the novelist who wishes to write about a man's encounter with this God is how he shall make the experience—which is both natural and supernatural—understandable, and credible, to his reader. In any age this would be a problem but in our own, it is a well-nigh insurmountable one. Today's audience is one in which religious feeling has become, if not atrophied, at least vaporous and sentimental. When Emerson[11] decided, in 1832, that he could no longer celebrate the Lord's Supper unless the bread and wine were removed, an important step in the vaporization of religion in America was taken, and the spirit of that step has continued apace. When the physical fact is separated from the spiritual reality, the dissolution of belief is eventually inevitable.

The novelist doesn't write to express himself, he doesn't write simply to render a vision he believes true, rather he renders his vision so that it can be transferred, as nearly whole as possible, to his reader. You can safely ignore the reader's taste, but you can't ignore his nature, you can't ignore his limited patience. Your problem is going to be difficult in direct proportion as your beliefs depart from his.

When I write a novel in which the central action is a baptism, I am very well aware that for a majority of my readers, baptism is a meaningless rite, and so in my novel I have to see that this baptism carries enough awe and mystery to jar the reader into some kind of emotional recognition of its significance. To this end I have to bend the whole novel—its language, its structure, its action. I have to make the reader feel, in his bones if nowhere else, that something is going on here that counts. Distortion in this case is an instrument; exaggeration has a purpose, and the whole structure of the story or novel has been made what it is because of belief. This is not the kind of distortion that destroys; it is the kind that reveals, or should reveal.

Students often have the idea that the process at work here is one which hinders honesty. They think that inevitably the writer, instead of seeing what is, will see only what he believes. It is perfectly possible, of course, that this will happen. Ever since there have been such things as novels, the world has been flooded with bad fiction for which the religious impulse has been responsible. The sorry religious novel comes about when the writer supposes that because of his belief, he is somehow dispensed from the obligation to penetrate concrete reality. He will think that the eyes of the Church or of the Bible or of his particular theology have already done the seeing for him, and that his business is to rearrange this essential vision into satisfying patterns, getting himself as little dirty in the process as possible. His feeling about this may have been made more definite by one of those Manichean-type[12] theologies which sees the natural world as unworthy of penetration. But the real novelist, the one with an instinct for what he is about, knows that he cannot approach the infinite directly, that he must penetrate the natural human world as it is. The more sacramental his theology, the more encouragement he will get from it to do just that.

The supernatural is an embarrassment today even to many of the churches. The naturalistic bias has so well saturated our society that the reader doesn't realize that he has to shift his sights to read fiction which treats of an encounter with God. Let me leave the novelist and talk for a moment about his reader.

This reader has first to get rid of a purely sociological point of view. In the thirties we passed through a period in American letters when social criticism and social realism were considered by many to be the most important aspects of fiction. We still suffer with a hangover from that period. I launched a character, Hazel Motes, whose presiding passion was to rid himself of a conviction that Jesus had redeemed him. Southern degeneracy never entered my head, but Hazel said "I seen" and "I taken" and he was from East Tennessee, and so the general reader's explanation for him was that he must represent some social problem peculiar to that part of the benighted South.

Ten years, however, have made some difference in our attitude toward fiction. The sociological tendency has abated in that particular form and survived in another just as bad. This is the notion that the fiction writer is after the typical. I don't know how many letters I have received telling me that the South is not at all the way I depict it, some tell me that Protestantism in the South is not at all the way I portray it, that a Southern Protestant would never be concerned, as Hazel Motes is, with penitential practices. Of course, as a novelist I've never wanted to characterize the typical South or typical Protestantism. The South and the religion found there are extremely fluid and offer enough variety to give the novelist the widest range of possibilities imaginable, for the novelist is bound by the reasonable possibilities, not the probabilities, of his culture.

There is an even worse bias than these two, and that is the clinical bias, the prejudice that sees everything strange as a case study in the abnormal.

Freud[13] brought to light many truths, but his psychology is not an adequate instrument for understanding the religious encounter or the fiction that describes it. Any psychological or cultural or economic determination may be useful up to a point; indeed, such facts can't be ignored, but the novelist will be interested in them only as he is able to go through them to give us a sense of something beyond them. The more we learn about ourselves, the deeper into the unknown we push the frontiers of fiction.

I have observed that most of the best religious fiction of our time is most shocking precisely to those readers who claim to have an intense interest in finding more "spiritual purpose"—as they like to put it—in modern novels than they can at present detect in them. Today's reader, if he believes in grace at all, sees it as something which can be separated from nature and served to him raw as Instant Uplift. This reader's favorite word is compassion. I don't wish to defame the word. There is a better sense in which it can be used but seldom is—the sense of being in travail with and for creation in its subjection to vanity. This is a sense which implies a recognition of sin; this is a suffering-with, but one which blunts no edges and makes no excuses. When infused into novels, it is often forbidding. Our age doesn't go for it.

I have said a great deal about the religious sense that the modern audience lacks, and by way of objection to this, you may point out to me that there is a real return of intellectuals in our time to an interest in and a respect for religion. I believe that this is true. What this interest in religion will result in for the future remains to be seen. It may, together with the new spirit of ecumenism that we see everywhere around us, herald a new religious age, or it may simply be that religion will suffer the ultimate degradation and become, for a little time, fashionable. Whatever it means for the future, I don't believe that our present society is one whose basic beliefs are religious, except in the South. In any case, you can't have effective allegory in times when people are swept this way and that by momentary convictions, because everyone will read it differently. You can't indicate moral values when morality changes with what is being done, because there is no accepted basis of judgment. And you cannot show the operation of grace when grace is cut off from nature or when the very possibility of grace is denied, because no one will have the least idea of what you are about.

The serious writer has always taken the flaw in human nature for his starting point, usually the flaw in an otherwise admirable character. Drama usually bases itself on the bedrock of original sin, whether the writer thinks in theological terms or not. Then, too, any character in a serious novel is supposed to carry a burden of meaning larger than himself. The novelist doesn't write about people in a vacuum; he writes about people in a world where something is obviously lacking, where there is the general mystery of incompleteness and the particular tragedy of our own times to be demonstrated, and the novelist tries to give you, within the form of the book, a total experience of human nature at any time. For this reason the greatest dramas naturally involve the salvation or loss of the soul. Where there is no belief in the soul, there is very little drama. The Christian novelist is distinguished from his pagan colleagues by recognizing sin as sin. According to his heritage he sees it not as sickness or an accident of environment, but as a responsible choice of offense against God which involves his eternal future. Either one is serious about salvation or one is not. And it is well to realize that the maximum amount of seriousness admits the maximum amount of comedy. Only if we are secure in our beliefs can we see the comical side of the universe. One reason a great deal of our contemporary fiction is humorless is because so many of these writers are relativists and have to be continually justifying the actions of their characters on a sliding scale of values.

Our salvation is a drama played out with the devil, a devil who is not simply generalized evil, but an evil intelligence determined on its own supremacy. I think that if writers with a religious view of the world excel these days in the depiction of evil, it is because they have to make its nature unmistakable to their particular audience.

The novelist and the believer, when they are not the same man, yet have many traits in common—a distrust of the abstract, a respect for boundaries, a desire to penetrate the surface of reality and to find in each thing the spirit which makes it itself and holds the world together. But I don't believe that we shall have great religious fiction until we have again that happy combination of believing artist and believing society. Until that time, the novelist will have to do the best he can in travail with the world he has. He may find in the end that instead of reflecting the image at the heart of things, he has only reflected our broken condition and, through it, the face of the devil we are possessed by. This is a modest achievement, but perhaps a necessary one. ■

Notes

1 this symposium—a conference at Sweetbriar College, Virginia, in March of 1963

2 St. Augustine—(354–430) an Early Church father who wrote about Christian doctrine

3 Conrad—Joseph Conrad (1857–1924) English novelist

4 Swinburne—Charles Swinburne (1837–1909) English author

5 Steinbeck—John Steinbeck (1902–1968) American author

6 Pascal—Blaise Pascal (1623–1662) French philosopher, scientist, mathematician, and writer

7 Camus—Albert Camus (1913–1960) French philosopher, writer

8 Hemingway—Ernest Hemingway (1899–1961) American writer

9 Kafka—Franz Kafka (1883–1924) Austrian novelist

10 Gide—Andre Gide (1869–1951) French writer

11 Emerson—Ralph Waldo Emerson (1803–1882) American philosopher and writer

12 Manichean-type—belief in dualism. The spirit is seen as good and the body as evil.

13 Freud—Sigmund Freud (1856–1939) Austrian psychiatrist

Making Connections through Discussion and Writing

1. a. Underline Flannery O'Connor's statements that define her view of the purpose of a literary artist.

    b. Summarize her statements in your own words.

    _____

    _____

    _____

    _____

    _____

    _____

    _____

2. O'Connor claims that novelists' theology inescapably shapes their fiction, particularly as they portray good and evil. What dilemma does she think a Christian writer faces as he or she presents a fictional world to a society that lacks a strong and unified faith?

    _____

    _____

    _____

    _____

    _____

3. a. O'Connor identifies three ways modern people tend to deal with religious questions and the existence of God. List these here.

    _____

    _____

    _____

    _____

    _____

    b. How does she find these three attitudes expressed in various examples of modern literature?

    _____

    _____

    _____

    _____

    _____

    _____

4. a. How does O'Connor explain her complaint that "[e]ver since there have been such things as novels, the world has been flooded with bad fiction for which the religious impulse has been responsible"?

_____

_____

_____

_____

_____

b. What kind of fiction do you think she is referring to?

_____

_____

_____

_____

_____

c. Give some examples from your own reading experience.

_____

_____

_____

_____

_____

_____

Flannery O'Connor
Parker's Back

"Parker's Back" first appeared in *Esquire* in 1965. This was O'Connor's last story, much of it written during the final phases of her illness and published after her death. In it the author draws from Old Testament stories—Moses and the burning bush, Jonah's flight from God—to dramatize the search for meaning taken by an inarticulate man haunted by longings he cannot name or understand. He tries to satisfy these longings by covering his body with images, culminating with an icon-like portrait of Christ tattooed on his back. In tracing Parker's search for meaning, O'Connor wittily recapitulates (through the lives of contemporary rural characters) an ancient Christian debate over religious images, leaving the reader to decide whether Parker is a "Christopher" (a "Christ bearer") or an idolater.

Plot started from beginning

Parker's wife was sitting on the front porch floor, snapping beans. Parker was sitting on the step, some distance away, watching her sullenly. She was plain, plain. The skin on her face was thin and drawn as tight as the skin on an onion and her eyes were gray and sharp like the points of two icepicks. Parker understood why he had married her—he couldn't have got her any other way—but he couldn't understand why he stayed with her now. She was pregnant and pregnant women were not his favorite kind. Nevertheless, he stayed as if she had him conjured. He was puzzled and ashamed of himself.

The house they rented sat alone save for a single tall pecan tree on a high embankment overlooking a highway. At intervals a car would shoot past below and his wife's eyes would swerve suspiciously after the sound of it and then come back to rest on the newspaper full of beans in her lap. One of the things she did not approve of was automobiles. In addition to her other bad qualities, she was forever sniffing up sin. She did not smoke or dip, drink whiskey, use bad language or paint her face, and God knew some paint would have improved it, Parker thought. Her being against color, it was the more remarkable she had married him. Sometimes he supposed that she had married him because she meant to save him. At other times he had a suspicion that she actually liked everything she said she didn't. He could account for her one way or another; it was himself he could not understand.

She turned her head in his direction and said, "It's no reason you can't work for a man. It don't have to be a woman."

"Aw shut your mouth for a change," Parker muttered.

If he had been certain she was jealous of the woman he worked for he would have been pleased but more likely she was concerned with the sin that would result if he and the woman took a liking to each other. He had told her that the woman was a hefty young blonde; in fact she was nearly seventy years old and too dried up to have an interest in anything except getting as much work out of him as she could. Not that an old woman didn't sometimes get an interest in a young man, particularly if he was as attractive as Parker felt he was, but this old woman looked at him the same way she looked at her old tractor—as if she had to put up with it because it was all she had. The tractor had broken down the second day Parker was on it and she had set him at once to cutting bushes, saying out of the side of her mouth to the nigger, "Everything he touches, he breaks." She also asked him to wear his shirt when he worked; Parker had removed it even though the day was not sultry; he put it back on reluctantly.

This ugly woman Parker married was his first wife. He had had other women but he had planned never to get himself tied up legally. He had first seen her one morning when his truck broke down on the highway. He had managed to pull it off the road into a neatly swept yard on which sat a peeling two-room house. He got out and opened the hood of the truck and began to study the motor. Parker had an extra sense that told him when there was a woman nearby watching him. After he had leaned over the motor a few minutes, his neck began to prickle. He cast his eye over the empty yard and porch of the house. A woman he could not see was either nearby beyond a clump of honeysuckle or in the house, watching him out the window.

Suddenly Parker began to jump up and down and fling his hand about as if he had mashed it in the machinery. He doubled over and held his hand close to his chest. "God dammit!" he hollered, "Jesus Christ in hell! Jesus God Almighty damm! God dammit to hell!" he went on, flinging out the same few oaths over and over as loud as he could.

Without warning a terrible bristly claw slammed the side of his face and he fell backwards on the hood of the truck. "You don't talk no filth here!" a voice close to him shrilled.

Parker's vision was so blurred that for an instant he thought he had been attacked by some creature from above, a giant hawk-eyed angel wielding a hoary weapon. As his sight cleared, he saw before him a tall raw-boned girl with a broom.

"I hurt my hand," he said. "I HURT my hand." He was so incensed that he forgot that he hadn't hurt his hand. "My hand may be broke," he growled although his voice was still unsteady.

"Lemme see it," the girl demanded.

Parker stuck out his hand and she came closer and looked at it. There was no mark on the palm and she took the hand and turned it over. Her own hand was dry and hot and rough and Parker felt himself jolted back to life by her touch. He looked more closely at her. I don't want nothing to do with this one, he thought.

The girl's sharp eyes peered at the back of the stubby reddish hand she held. There emblazoned in red and blue was a tattooed eagle perched on a cannon. Parker's sleeve was rolled to the elbow. Above the eagle a serpent was coiled about a shield and in the spaces between the eagle and the serpent there were hearts, some with arrows through them. Above the serpent there was a spread hand of cards. Every space on the skin of Parker's arm, from wrist to elbow, was covered in some loud design. The girl gazed at this with an almost stupefied smile of shock, as if she had accidentally grasped a poisonous snake; she dropped the hand.

"I got most of my other ones in foreign parts," Parker said. "These here I mostly got in the United States. I got my first one when I was only fifteen year old."

"Don't tell me," the girl said, "I don't like it. I ain't got any use for it."

"You ought to see the ones you can't see," Parker said and winked. Two circles of red appeared like apples on the girl's cheeks and softened her appearance. Parker was intrigued. He did not for a minute think that she didn't like the tattoos. He had never yet met a woman who was not attracted to them.

Parker was fourteen when he saw a man in a fair, tattooed from head to foot. Except for his loins which were girded with a panther hide, the man's skin was patterned in what seemed from Parker's distance—he was near the back of the tent, standing on a bench—a single intricate design of brilliant color. The man, who was small and sturdy, moved about on the platform, flexing his muscles so that the arabesque of men and beasts and flowers on his skin appeared to have a subtle motion of its own. Parker was filled with emotion, lifted up as some people are when the flag passes. He was a boy whose mouth habitually hung open. He was heavy and earnest, as ordinary as a loaf of bread. When the show was over, he had remained standing on the bench, staring where the tattooed man had been, until the tent was almost empty.

Parker had never before felt the least motion of wonder in himself. Until he saw the man at the fair, it did not enter his head that there was anything out of the ordinary about the fact that he existed. Even then it did not enter his head, but a peculiar unease settled in him. It was as if a blind boy had been turned so gently in a different direction that he did not know his destination had been changed.

He had his first tattoo some time after—the eagle perched on the cannon. It was done by a local artist. It hurt very little, just enough to make it appear to Parker to be worth doing. This was peculiar too for before he had thought that only what did not hurt was worth doing. The next year he quit school because he was sixteen and could. He went to the trade school for a while, then he quit the trade school and worked for six months in a garage. The only reason he worked at all was to pay for more tattoos. His mother worked in a laundry and could support him, but she would not pay for any tattoo except her name on a heart, which he had put on, grumbling. However, her name was Betty Jean and nobody had to know it was his mother. He found out that the tattoos were attractive to the kind of girls he liked but who had never liked him before. He began to drink beer and get in fights. His mother wept over what was becoming of him. One night she dragged him off to a revival with her, not telling him where they were going. When he saw the big lighted church, he jerked out of her grasp and ran. The next day he lied about his age and joined the navy.

Parker was large for the tight sailor's pants but the silly white cap, sitting low on his forehead, made his face by contrast look thoughtful and almost intense. After a month or two in the navy, his mouth ceased to hang open. His features hardened into the features of a man. He stayed in the navy five years and seemed a natural part of the gray mechanical ship, except for his eyes, which were the same pale slate-color as the ocean and reflected the immense spaces around him as if they were a microcosm of the mysterious sea. In port Parker wandered about comparing the run-down places he was in to Birmingham, Alabama. Everywhere he went he picked up more tattoos.

He had stopped having lifeless ones like anchors and crossed rifles. He had a tiger and a panther on each shoulder, a cobra coiled about a torch on his chest, hawks on his thighs, Elizabeth II and Philip over where his stomach and liver were respectively. He did not care much what the subject was so long as it was colorful; on his abdomen he had a few obscenities but only because that seemed the proper place for them. Parker would be satisfied with each tattoo about a month, then something about it that had attracted him would wear off. Whenever a decent-sized mirror was available, he would get in front of it and study his overall look. The effect was not of one intricate arabesque of colors but of something haphazard and botched. A huge dissatisfaction would come over him and he would go off and find another tattooist and have another space filled up. The front of Parker was almost completely covered but there were no tattoos on his back. He had no desire for one anywhere he could not readily see it himself. As the space on the front of him for tattoos decreased, his dissatisfaction grew and became general.

After one of his furloughs, he didn't go back to the navy but remained away without official leave, drunk, in a rooming house in a city he did not know. His dissatisfaction, from being chronic and latent, had suddenly become acute and raged in him. It was as if the panther and the lion and the serpents and the eagles and the hawks had penetrated his skin and lived inside him in a raging warfare. The navy caught up with him, put him in the brig for nine months and then gave him a dishonorable discharge.

After that Parker decided that country air was the only kind fit to breathe. He rented the shack on the embankment and bought the old truck and took various jobs which he kept as long as it suited him. At the time he met his future wife, he was buying apples by the bushel and selling them for the same price by the pound to isolated homesteaders on back country roads.

"All that there," the woman said, pointing to his arm, "is no better than what a fool Indian would do. It's a heap of vanity." She seemed to have found the word she wanted. "Vanity of vanities," she said.

Well what the hell do I care what she thinks of it? Parker asked himself, but he was plainly bewildered. "I reckon you like one of these better than another anyway," he said, dallying until he thought of something that would impress her. He thrust the arm back at her. "Which you like best?"

"None of them," she said, "but the chicken is not as bad as the rest."

"What chicken?" Parker almost yelled.

She pointed to the eagle.

"That's an eagle," Parker said. "What fool would waste their time having a chicken put on themself?"

"What fool would have any of it?" the girl said and turned away. She went slowly back to the house and left him there to get going. Parker remained for almost five minutes, looking agape at the dark door she had entered.

The next day he returned with a bushel of apples. He was not one to be outdone by anything that looked like her. He liked women with meat on them, so you didn't feel their muscles, much less their old bones. When he arrived, she was sitting on the top step and the yard was full of children, all as thin and poor as herself; Parker remembered it was Saturday. He hated to be making up to a woman when there were children around, but it was fortunate he had brought the bushel of apples off the truck. As the children approached him to see what he carried, he gave each child an apple and told it to get lost; in that way he cleared out the whole crowd.

The girl did nothing to acknowledge his presence. He might have been a stray pig or goat that had wandered into the yard and she too tired to take up the broom and send it off. He set the bushel of apples down next to her on the step. He sat down on a lower step.

"Hep yourself," he said, nodding at the basket; then he lapsed into silence.

She took an apple quickly as if the basket might disappear if she didn't make haste. Hungry people made Parker nervous. He had always had plenty to eat himself. He grew very uncomfortable. He reasoned he had nothing to say so why should he say it? He could not think now why he had come or why he didn't go before he wasted another bushel of apples on the crowd of children. He supposed they were her brothers and sisters.

She chewed the apple slowly but with a kind of relish of concentration, bent slightly but looking out ahead. The view from the porch stretched off across a long incline studded with iron weed and across the highway to a vast vista of hills and one small mountain. Long views depressed Parker. You look out into space like that and you begin to feel as if someone were after you, the navy or the government or religion.

"Who them children belong to, you?" he said at length.

"I ain't married yet," she said. "They belong to momma." She said it as if it were only a matter of time before she would be married.

Who in God's name would marry her? Parker thought.

A large barefooted woman with a wide gap-toothed face appeared in the door behind Parker. She had apparently been there for several minutes.

"Good evening," Parker said.

The woman crossed the porch and picked up what was left of the bushel of apples. "We thank you," she said and returned with it into the house.

"That your old woman?" Parker muttered.

The girl nodded. Parker knew a lot of sharp things he could have said like "You got my sympathy," but he was gloomily silent. He just sat there, looking at the view. He thought he must be coming down with something.

"If I pick up some peaches tomorrow I'll bring you some," he said.

"I'll be much obliged to you," the girl said.

Parker had no intention of taking any basket of peaches back there but the next day he found himself doing it. He and the girl had almost nothing to say to each other. One thing he did say was, "I ain't got any tattoo on my back."

"What you got on it?" the girl said.

"My shirt," Parker said. "Haw."

"Haw, haw," the girl said politely.

Parker thought he was losing his mind. He could not believe for a minute that he was attracted to a woman like this. She showed not the least interest in anything but what he brought until he appeared the third time with two cantaloupes. "What's your name?" she asked.

"O. E. Parker," he said.

"What does the O. E. stand for?"

"You can just call me O. E.," Parker said. "Or Parker. Don't nobody call me by my name."

"What's it stand for?" she persisted.

"Never mind," Parker said. "What's yours?"

"I'll tell you when you tell me what them letters are the short of," she said. There was just a hint of flirtatiousness in her tone and it went rapidly to Parker's head. He had never revealed the name to any man or woman, only to the files of the navy and the government, and it was on his baptismal record which he got at the age of a month; his mother was a Methodist. When the name leaked out of the navy files, Parker narrowly missed killing the man who used it.

"You'll go blab it around," he said.

"I'll swear I'll never tell nobody," she said. "On God's holy word I swear it."

Parker sat for a few minutes in silence. Then he reached for the girl's neck, drew her ear close to his mouth and revealed the name in low voice.

"Obadiah," she whispered. Her face slowly brightened as if the name came as a sign to her. "Obadiah," she said.

The name still stank in Parker's estimation.

"Obadiah Elihue," she said in a reverent voice.

"If you call me that aloud, I'll bust your head open," Parker said. "What's yours?"

"Sarah Ruth Cates," she said.

"Glad to meet you, Sarah Ruth," Parker said.

Sarah Ruth's father was a Straight Gospel preacher but he was away, spreading it in Florida. Her mother did not seem to mind his attention to the girl so long as he brought a basket of something with him when he came. As for Sarah Ruth herself, it was plain to Parker after he had visited three times that she was crazy about him. She liked him even though she insisted that pictures on the skin were vanity of vanities and even after hearing him curse, and even after she had asked him if he was saved and he had replied that he didn't see it was anything in particular to save him from. After that, inspired, Parker had said, "I'd be saved enough if you was to kiss me."

She scowled. "That ain't being saved," she said.

Not long after that she agreed to take a ride in his truck. Parker parked it on a deserted road and suggested to her that they lie down together in the back of it.

"Not until after we're married," she said—just like that.

"Oh that ain't necessary," Parker said and as he reached for her, she thrust him away with such force that the door of the truck came off and he found himself flat on his back on the ground. He made up his mind then and there to have nothing further to do with her.

They were married in the County Ordinary's office because Sarah Ruth thought churches were idolatrous. Parker had no opinion about that one way or the other. The Ordinary's office was lined with cardboard file boxes and record books with dusty yellow slips of paper hanging on out of them. The Ordinary was an old woman with red hair who had held office for forty years and looked as dusty as her books. She married them from behind the iron-grill of a stand-up desk and when she finished, she said with a flourish, "Three dollars and fifty cents and till death do you part!" and yanked some forms out of a machine.

Marriage did not change Sarah Ruth a jot and it made Parker gloomier than ever. Every morning he decided he had had enough and would not return that night; every night he returned. Whenever Parker couldn't stand the way he felt, he would have another tattoo, but the only surface left on him now was his back. To see a tattoo on his own back he would have to get two mirrors and stand between them in just the correct position and this seemed to Parker a good way to make an idiot of himself. Sarah Ruth who, if she had had better sense, could have enjoyed a tattoo on his back, would not even look at the ones he had elsewhere. When he attempted to point out especial details of them, she would shut her eyes tight and turn her back as well. Except in total darkness, she preferred Parker dressed and with his sleeves rolled down.

"At the judgement seat of God, Jesus is going to say to you, 'What you been doing all your life besides have pictures drawn all over you?'" she said.

"You don't fool me none," Parker said, "you're just afraid that hefty girl I work for'll like me so much she'll say, 'Come on, Mr. Parker, let's you and me . . .'"

"You're tempting sin," she said, "and at the judgement seat of God you'll have to answer for that too. You ought to go back to selling the fruits of the earth."

Parker did nothing much when he was at home but listen to what the judgement seat of God would be like for him if he didn't change his ways. When he could, he broke in with tales of the hefty girl he worked for. "'Mr. Parker,'" he said she said, 'I hired you for your brains.'" (She had added, "So why don't you use them?")

"And you should have seen her face the first time she saw me without my shirt," he said. "'Mr. Parker,' she said, 'you're a walking panner-ram-

mer!'" This had, in fact, been her remark but it had been delivered out of one side of her mouth.

Dissatisfaction began to grow so great in Parker that there was no containing it outside of a tattoo. It had to be his back. There was no help for it. A dim half-formed inspiration began to work in his mind. He visualized having a tattoo put there that Sarah Ruth would not be able to resist—a religious subject. He thought of an open book with HOLY BIBLE tattooed under it and an actual verse printed on the page. This seemed just the thing for a while; then he began to hear her say, "Ain't I already got a real Bible? What you think I want to read the same verse over and over for when I can read it all?" He needed something better even than the Bible! He thought about it so much that he began to lose sleep. He was already losing flesh—Sarah Ruth just threw food in the pot and let it boil. Not knowing for certain why he continued to stay with a woman who was both ugly and pregnant and no cook made him generally nervous and irritable, and he developed a little tic in the side of his face.

Once or twice he found himself turning around abruptly as if someone were trailing him. He had had a granddaddy who had ended in the state mental hospital, although not until he was seventy-five, but as urgent as it might be for him to get a tattoo, it was just as urgent that he get exactly the right one to bring Sarah Ruth to heel. As he continued to worry over it, his eyes took on a hollow preoccupied expression. The old woman he worked for told him that if he couldn't keep his mind on what he was doing, she knew where she could find a fourteen-year-old colored boy who could. Parker was too preoccupied even to be offended. At any time previous, he would have left her then and there, saying drily, "Well, you go ahead on and get him then."

Two or three mornings later he was baling hay with the old woman's sorry baler and her broken down tractor in a large field, cleared save for one enormous old tree standing in the middle of it. The old woman was the kind who would not cut down a large old tree because it was a large old tree. She had pointed it out to Parker as if he didn't have eyes and told him to be careful not to hit it as the machine picked up hay near it. Parker began at the outside of the field and made circles inward toward it. He had to get off the tractor every now and then and untangle the baling cord or kick a rock out of the way. The old woman had told him to carry the rocks to the edge of the field, which he did when she was there watching. When he thought he could make it, he ran over them. As he circled the field his mind was on a suitable design for his back. The sun, the size of a golf ball, began to switch regularly from in front to behind him, but he appeared to see it both places as if he had eyes in the back of his head. All at once he saw the tree reaching out to grasp him. A ferocious thud propelled him into the air, and he heard himself yelling in an unbelievably loud voice, "GOD ABOVE!"

He landed on his back while the tractor crashed upside down into the tree and burst into flame. The first thing Parker saw were his shoes, quickly being eaten by the fire; one was caught under the tractor, the other was some distance away, burning by itself. He was not in them. He could feel the hot breath of the burning tree on his face. He scrambled backwards, still sitting, his eyes cavernous, and if he had known how to cross himself he would have done it.

His truck was on a dirt road at the edge of the field. He moved toward it, still sitting, still backwards but faster and faster; halfway to it he got up and began a kind of forward-bent run from which he collapsed on his knees twice. His legs felt like two old rusted rain gutters. He reached the truck finally and took off in it, zigzagging up the road. He drove past his house on the embankment and straight for the city, fifty miles distant.

Parker did not allow himself to think on the way to the city. He only knew that there had been a great change in his life, a leap forward into a worse unknown, and that there was nothing he could do about it. It was for all intents accomplished.

The artist had two large cluttered rooms over a chiropodist's office on a back street. Parker, still barefooted, burst silently in on him at a little after three in the afternoon. The artist, who was about Parker's own age—twenty-eight—but thin and bald, was behind a small drawing table, tracing a design in green ink. He looked up with an annoyed glance and did not seem to recognize Parker in the hollow-eyed creature before him.

"Let me see the book you got with all the pictures of God in it," Parker said breathlessly. "The religious one."

The artist continued to look at him with his intellectual, superior stare. "I don't put tattoos on drunks," he said.

"You know me!" Parker cried indignantly. "I'm O. E. Parker! You done work for me before and I always paid!"

The artist looked at him another moment as if he were not altogether sure. "You've fallen off some," he said. "You must have been in jail."

"Married," Parker said.

"Oh," said the artist. With the aid of mirrors the artist had tattooed on the top of his head a miniature owl, perfect in every detail. It was about the size of a half-dollar and served him as a show piece. There were cheaper artists in town but Parker had never wanted anything but the best. The artist went over to a cabinet at the back of the room and began to look over some art books. "Who are you interested in?" he said, "saints, angels, Christs or what?"

"God," Parker said.

"Father, Son or Spirit?"

"Just God," Parker said impatiently. "Christ. I don't care. Just so it's God."

The artist returned with a book. He moved some papers off another table and put the book down on it and told Parker to sit down and see what he liked. "The up-t-date ones are in the back," he said.

Parker sat down with the book and wet his thumb. He began to go through it, beginning at the back where the up-to-date pictures were. Some of them he recognized—The Good Shepherd, Forbid Them Not, The Smiling Jesus, Jesus the Physician's Friend, but he kept turning rapidly backwards and the pictures became less and less reassuring. One showed a gaunt green dead face streaked with blood. One was yellow with sagging purple eyes. Parker's heart began to beat faster and faster until it appeared to be roaring inside him like a great generator. He flipped the pages quickly, feeling that when he reached the one ordained, a sign would come. He continued to flip through until he had almost reached the front of the book. On one of the pages a pair of eyes glanced at him swiftly. Parker sped on, then stopped. His heart too appeared to cut off; there was absolute silence. It said as plainly as if silence were a language itself, GO BACK.

Parker returned to the picture—the haloed head of a flat stern Byzantine Christ with all-demanding eyes. He sat there trembling; his heart began slowly to beat again as if it were being brought to life by a subtle power.

"You found what you want?" the artist asked.

Parker's throat was too dry to speak. He got up and thrust the book at the artist, opened at the picture.

"That'll cost you plenty," the artist said. "You don't want all those little blocks though, just the outline and some better features."

"Just like it is," Parker said, "just like it is or nothing."

"It's your funeral," the artist said, "but I don't do that kind of work for nothing."

"How much?" Parker asked.

"It'll take maybe two days work."

"How much?" Parker said.

"On time or cash?" the artist asked. Parker's other jobs had been on time, but he had paid.

"Ten down and ten for every day it takes," the artist said.

Parker drew ten dollar bills out of his wallet; he had three left in. "You come back in the morning," the artist said, putting the money in his own pocket. "First I'll have to trace that out of the book."

"No no!" Parker said. "Trace it now or gimme my money back," and his eyes blared as if he were ready for a fight.

The artist agreed. Any one stupid enough to want a Christ on his back, he reasoned, would be just as likely as not to change his mind the next minute, but once the work was begun he could hardly do so.

While he worked on the tracing, he told Parker to go wash his back at the sink with the special soap he used there. Parker did it and returned to pace back and forth across the room, nervously flexing his shoulders. He wanted to go look at the picture again but at the same time he did not want to. The artist got up finally and had Parker lie down on the table. He swabbed his back with ethyl chloride and then began to outline the head on it with his iodine pencil. Another hour passed before he took up his electric instrument. Parker felt no particular pain. In Japan he had had a tattoo of the Buddha done on his upper arm with ivory needles; in Burma, a little brown root of a man had made a peacock on each of his knees using thin pointed sticks, two feet long; amateurs had worked on him with pins and soot. Parker was usually so relaxed and easy under the hand of the artist that he often went to sleep, but this time he remained awake, every muscle taut.

At midnight the artist said he was ready to quit. He propped one mirror, four feet square, on a table by the wall and took a smaller mirror off the lavatory wall and put it in Parker's hands. Parker stood with his back to the one on the table and moved the other until he saw a flashing burst of color reflected from his back. It was almost completely covered with little red and blue and ivory and saffron squares; from them he made out the lineaments of the face—a mouth, the beginning of heavy brows, a straight nose, but the face was empty; the eyes had not yet been put in. The impression for the moment was almost as if the artist had tricked him and done the Physician's Friend.

"It don't have eyes," Parker cried out.

"That'll come," the artist said, "in due time. We have another day to go on it yet."

Parker spent the night on a cot at the Haven of Light Christian Mission. He found these the best places to stay in the city because they were free and included a meal of sorts. He got the last available cot and because he was still barefooted, he accepted a pair of secondhand shoes which, in his confusion, he put on to go to bed; he was still shocked from all that had happened to him. All night he lay awake in the long dormitory of cots with lumpy figures on them. The only light was from a phosphorescent cross glowing at the end of the room. The tree reached out to grasp him again, then burst into flame; the shoe burned quietly by itself; the eyes in the book said to him distinctly GO BACK and at the same time did not utter a sound. He wished that he were not in this city, not in this Haven of Light Mission, not in a bed by himself. He longed miserably for Sarah Ruth. Her sharp tongue and icepick eyes were the only comfort he could bring to mind. He decided he was losing it. Her eyes appeared soft and dilatory compared with the eyes in the book, for even though he could not summon up the exact look of those eyes, he could still feel their penetration. He felt as though, under their gaze, he was as transparent as the wing of a fly.

The tattooist had told him not to come until ten in the morning, but when he arrived at that hour, Parker was sitting in the dark hallway on the floor, waiting for him. He had decided upon getting up that, once the tattoo was on him, he would not look at it, that all his sensations of the day and night before were those of a crazy man and that he would return to doing things according to his own sound judgement.

The artist began where he left off. "One thing I want to know," he said presently as he worked over Parker's back, "why do you want this on you? Have you gone and got religion? Are you saved?" he asked in a mocking voice.

Parker's throat felt salty and dry. "Naw," he said, "I ain't got no use for none of that. A man can't save his self from whatever it is he don't deserve none of my sympathy." These words seemed to leave his mouth like wraiths and to evaporate at once as if he had never uttered them.

"Then why . . ."

"I married this woman that's saved," Parker said. "I never should have done it. I ought to leave her. She's done gone and got pregnant."

"That's too bad," the artist said. "Then it's her making you have this tattoo."

"Naw," Parker said, "she don't know nothing about it. It's a surprise for her."

"You think she'll like it and lay off you a while?"

"She can't hep herself," Parker said. "She can't say she don't like the looks of God." He decided he had told the artist enough of his business. Artists were all right in their place but he didn't like them poking their noses into the affairs of regular people. "I didn't get no sleep last night," he said. "I think I'll get some now."

That closed the mouth of the artist but it did not bring him any sleep. He lay there, imagining how Sarah Ruth would be struck speechless by the face on his back and every now and then this would be interrupted by a vision of the tree of fire and his empty shoe burning beneath it.

The artist worked steadily until nearly four o'clock, not stopping to have lunch, hardly pausing with the electric instrument except to wipe the dripping dye off Parker's back as he went along. Finally he finished. "You can get up and look at it now," he said.

Parker sat up but he remained on the edge of the table.

The artist was pleased with his work and wanted Parker to look at it at once. Instead Parker continued to sit on the edge of the table, bent forward slightly but with a vacant look. "What ails you?" the artist said. "Go look at it."

"Ain't nothing ail me," Parker said in a sudden belligerent voice. "That tattoo ain't going nowhere. It'll be there when I get there." He reached for his shirt and began gingerly to put it on.

The artist took him roughly by the arm and propelled him between the two mirrors. "Now *look*," he said, angry at having his work ignored.

Parker looked, turned white and moved away. The eyes in the reflected face continued to look at him—still, straight, all-demanding, enclosed in silence.

"It was your idea, remember," the artist said. "I would have advised something else."

Parker said nothing. He put on his shirt and went out the door while the artist shouted, "I'll expect all of my money!"

Parker headed toward a package shop on the corner. He bought a pint of whiskey and took it into a nearby alley and drank it all in five minutes. Then he moved on to a pool hall nearby which he frequented when he came to the city. It was a well-lighted barn-like place with a bar up one side and

gambling machines on the other and pool tables in the back. As soon as Parker entered, a large man in a red and black checkered shirt hailed him by slapping him on the back and yelling, "Yeyyyyyy boy! O. E. Parker!"

Parker was not yet ready to be struck on the back. "Lay off," he said, "I got a fresh tattoo there."

"What you got this time?" the man asked and then yelled to a few at the machines. "O.E.'s got him another tattoo."

"Nothing special this time," Parker said and slunk over to a machine that was not being used.

"Come on," the big man said, "let's have a look at O.E.'s tattoo," and while Parker squirmed in their hands, they pulled up his shirt. Parker felt all the hands drop away instantly and his shirt fell again like a veil over the face. There was a silence in the pool room which seemed to Parker to grow from the circle around him until it extended to the foundations under the building and upward through the beams in the roof.

Finally some one said, "Christ!" Then they all broke into noise at once. Parker turned around, an uncertain grin on his face.

"Leave it to O.E.!" the man in the checkered shirt said. "That boy's a real card!"

"Maybe he's gone and got religion," someone yelled.

"Not on your life," Parker said.

"O.E.'s got religion and is witnessing for Jesus, ain't you, O.E.?" a little man with a piece of cigar in his mouth said wryly. "An original way to do it if I ever saw one."

"Leave it to Parker to think of a new one!" the fat man said.

"Yyeeeeeeyyyyyyyy boy!" someone yelled and they all began to whistle and curse in compliment until Parker said, "Aaa shut up."

"What'd you do it for?" somebody asked.

"For laughs," Parker said. "What's it to you?"

"Why ain't you laughing then?" somebody yelled. Parker lunged into the midst of them and like a whirlwind on a summer's day there began a fight that raged amid overturned tables and swinging fists until two of them grabbed him and ran to the door with him and threw him out. Then a calm descended on the pool hall as nerve shattering as if the long barn-like room were the ship from which Jonah had been cast into the sea.

Parker sat for a long time on the ground in the alley behind the pool hall, examining his soul. He saw it as a spider web of facts and lies that was not at all important to him but which appeared to be necessary in spite of his opinion. The eyes that were now forever on his back were eyes to be obeyed. He was as certain of it as he had ever been of anything. Throughout his life, grumbling and sometimes cursing, often afraid, once in rapture, Parker had obeyed whatever instinct of this kind had come to him—in rapture when his spirit had lifted at the sight of the tattooed man at the fair, afraid when he had joined the navy, grumbling when he had married Sarah Ruth.

The thought of her brought him slowly to his feet. She would know what he had to do. She would clear up the rest of it, and she would at least be pleased. It seemed to him that, all along, that was what he wanted, to please her. His truck was still parked in front of the building where the artist had his place, but it was not far away. He got in it and drove out of the city and into the country night. His head was almost clear of liquor and he observed that his dissatisfaction was gone, but he felt not quite like himself. It was as if he were himself but a stranger to himself, driving into a new country though everything he saw was familiar to him, even at night.

He arrived finally at the house on the embankment, pulled the truck under the pecan tree and got out. He made as much noise as possible to assert that he was still in charge here, that his leaving her for a night without word meant nothing except it was the way he did things. He slammed the car door, stamped up the two steps and across the porch and rattled the door knob. It did not respond to his touch. "Sarah Ruth!" he yelled, "let me in."

There was no lock on the door and she had evidently placed the back of a chair against the knob. He began to beat on the door and rattle the knob at the same time.

He heard the bed springs screak and bent down and put his head to the keyhole, but it was stopped up with paper. "Let me in!" he hollered, bamming on the door again. "What you got me locked out for?"

A sharp voice close to the door said, "Who's there?"

"Me," Parker said, "O.E."

He waited a moment.

"Me," he said impatiently, "O.E."

Still no sound from inside.

He tried once more. "O.E.," he said, bamming the door two or three more times. "O. E. Parker. You know me."

There was a silence. Then the voice said slowly, "I don't know no O.E."

"Quit fooling," Parker pleaded. "You ain't got

any business doing me this way. It's me, old O.E., I'm back. You ain't afraid of me."

"Who's there?" the same unfeeling voice said.

Parker turned his head as if he expected someone behind him to give him the answer. The sky had lightened slightly and there were two or three streaks of yellow floating above the horizon. Then as he stood there, a tree of light burst over the skyline.

Parker fell back against the door as if he had been pinned there by a lance.

"Who's there?" the voice from inside said and there was a quality about it now that seemed final. The knob rattled and the voice said peremptorily, "Who's there, I ast you?"

Parker bent down and put his mouth near the stuffed keyhole. "Obadiah," he whispered and all at once he felt the light pouring through him, turning his spider web soul into a perfect arabesque of colors, a garden of trees and birds and beasts.

"Obadiah Elihue!" he whispered.

The door opened and he stumbled in. Sarah Ruth loomed there, hands on her hips. She began at once, "That was no hefty blonde woman you was working for and you'll have to pay her every penny on her tractor you busted up. She don't keep insurance on it. She came here and her and me had us a long talk and I . . ."

Trembling, Parker set about lighting the kerosene lamp.

"What's the matter with you, wasting that kerosene this near daylight?" she demanded. "I ain't got to look at you."

A yellow glow enveloped them. Parker put the match down and began to unbutton his shirt.

"And you ain't going to have none of me this near morning," she said.

"Shut your mouth," he said quietly. "Look at this and then I don't want to hear no more out of you." He removed the shirt and turned his back to her.

"Another picture," Sarah Ruth growled. "I might have known you was off after putting some more trash on yourself."

Parker's knees went hollow under him. He wheeled around and cried, "Look at it! Don't just say that! *Look* at it!"

"I done looked," she said.

"Don't you know who it is?" he cried in anguish.

"No, who is it?" Sarah Ruth said. "It ain't anybody I know."

"It's him," Parker said.

"Him who?"

"God!" Parker cried.

"God? God don't look like that!"

"What do you know how he looks?" Parker moaned. "You ain't seen him."

"He don't *look*," Sarah Ruth said. "He's a spirit. No man shall see his face."

"Aw listen," Parker groaned, "this is just a picture of him."

"Idolatry!" Sarah Ruth screamed. "Idolatry! Enflaming yourself with idols under every green tree! I can put up with lies and vanity but I don't want no idolator in this house!" and she grabbed up the broom and began to thrash him across the shoulders with it.

Parker was too stunned to resist. He sat there and let her beat him until she had nearly knocked him senseless and large welts had formed on the face of the tattooed Christ. Then he staggered up and made for the door.

She stamped the broom two or three times on the floor and went to the window and shook it out to get the taint of him off it. Still gripping it, she looked toward the pecan tree and her eyes hardened still more. There he was—who called himself Obadiah Elihue—leaning against the tree, crying like a baby. ■

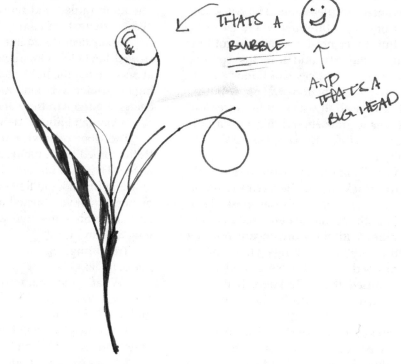

Making Connections through Discussion and Writing

1. (a.) Underline passages in which Parker reveals his desire for tattoos.

    b. Explain what his vision of the tattooed man awakened in Parker.

    _____
    _____
    _____
    _____
    _____

2. (a.) Put brackets around any allusions to Biblical stories or characters.

    b. How do these allusions reveal a spiritual dimension to Parker's actions?

    _____
    _____
    _____
    _____
    _____

3. Why does Parker select the stern Byzantine Christ as the image to wear on his back?

    _____
    _____
    _____
    _____

4. When Parker saw the tattooed man at the fair, he envisioned "a single intricate design"—"an arabesque of men and beasts and flowers"—that aroused his sense of wonder, yet his own attempts to emulate this vision resulted in an effect that was "not of one intricate arabesque of colors but of something haphazard and botched." At the end of the story, when Parker utters his name, "Obadiah," the narrator says that "he felt the light pouring through him, turning his spider web soul into a perfect arabesque of colors, a garden of trees and birds and beasts." Comment on the spiritual progress suggested by these descriptions, and be sure to explain the significance of Parker stating his full name to Sarah Ruth.

    _____
    _____
    _____
    _____
    _____
    _____
    _____
    _____
    _____
    _____

5. Sarah Ruth can articulate her idea of God much better than Parker can. How is her view influenced (or not influenced) by the Christian doctrine of the Incarnation?

    _____

    _____

    _____

    _____

    _____

    _____

    _____

    _____

    _____

6. (a.) Explain how Parker can be viewed as a "Christ-bearer."

    _____

    _____

    _____

    _____

    (b.) Why does Sarah Ruth, whose words seem to mark her as the "Christian" in the story, reject him and his tattoo?

    _____

    _____

    _____

7. Consider the last scenes of "Parker's Back," in which Parker is beaten by Sarah Ruth, then goes out and leans against a tree, crying like a baby. What symbolic motifs are present in the closing scenes that might point both to Parker's spiritual rebirth and to Christ's death?

    _____

    _____

    _____

    _____

8. What are some possible meanings of the title of the story?

    _____

    _____

    _____

    _____

9. a. How are you, as a reader, engaged by the issues of O'Connor's stories?

    _____

    _____

    _____

b. Do you identify with Parker or with Sarah Ruth? Why?

_____

_____

_____

_____

_____

_____

Flannery O'Connor
The Displaced Person

Flannery O'Connor published this extended short story, or novella, in the *Sewanee Review* in October 1954. The setting is a Southern farm shortly after World War II, when some refugees from the Nazi concentration camps were being resettled in the United States. The story illustrates—through the characters' various perceptions of the peacock, the displaced person, and Christ—O'Connor's belief that reality has manifold dimensions and multiple levels of meaning when viewed from a Christian perspective.

The peacock was following Mrs. Shortley up the road to the hill where she meant to stand. Moving one behind the other, they looked like a complete procession. Her arms were folded and as she mounted the prominence, she might have been the giant wife of the countryside, come out at some sign of danger to see what the trouble was. She stood on two tremendous legs, with the grand self-confidence of a mountain, and rose, up narrowing bulges of granite, to two icy blue points of light that pierced forward, surveying everything. She ignored the white afternoon sun which was creeping behind a ragged wall of cloud as if it pretended to be an intruder and cast her gaze down the red clay road that turned off from the highway.

The peacock stopped just behind her, his tail—glittering green-gold and blue in the sunlight—lifted just enough so that it would not touch the ground. It flowed out on either side like a floating train and his head on the long blue reed-like neck was drawn back as if his attention were fixed in the distance on something no one else could see.

Mrs. Shortley was watching a black car turn through the gate from the highway. Over by the toolshed, about fifteen feet away, the two Negros, Astor and Sulk, had stopped work to watch. They were hidden by a mulberry tree but Mrs. Shortley knew they were there.

Mrs. McIntyre was coming down the steps of her house to meet the car. She had on her largest smile but Mrs. Shortley, even from her distance, could detect a nervous slide in it. These people who were coming were only hired help, like the Shortleys themselves or the Negroes. Yet here was the owner of the place out to welcome them. Here she was, wearing her best clothes and a string of beads, and now bounding forward with her mouth stretched.

The car stopped at the walk just as she did and the priest was the first to get out. He was a long-legged black-suited old man with a white hat on and a collar that he wore backwards, which, Mrs. Shortley knew, was what priests did who wanted to be known as priests. It was this priest who had arranged for these people to come here. He opened the back door of the car and out jumped two children, a boy and a girl, and then, stepping more slowly, a woman in brown, shaped like a peanut. Then the front door opened and out stepped the man, the Displaced Person. He was short and a little sway-backed and wore gold-rimmed spectacles.

Mrs. Shortley's vision narrowed on him and then widened to include the woman and the two children in a group picture. The first thing that struck her as very peculiar was that they looked like other people. Every time she had seen them in her imagination, the image she had got was of the three bears, walking single file, with wooden shoes on like Dutchmen and sailor hats and bright coats with a lot of buttons. But the woman had on a dress she might have worn herself and the children were dressed like anybody from around. The man had on khaki pants and a blue shirt. Suddenly, as Mrs. McIntyre held out her hand to him, he bobbed down from the waist and kissed it.

Mrs. Shortley jerked her own hand up toward her mouth and then after a second brought it down and rubbed it vigorously on her seat. If Mr.

Shortley had tried to kiss her hand, Mrs. McIntyre would have knocked him into the middle of next week, but then Mr. Shortley wouldn't have kissed her hand anyway. He didn't have time to mess around.

She looked closer, squinting. The boy was in the center of the group, talking. He was supposed to speak the most English because he had learned some in Poland and so he was to listen to his father's Polish and say it in English and then listen to Mrs. McIntyre's English and say that in Polish. The priest had told Mrs. McIntyre his name was Rudolph and he was twelve and the girl's name was Sledgewig and she was nine. Sledgewig sounded to Mrs. Shortley like something you would name a bug, or vice versa, as if you named a boy Bollweevil. All of them's last name was something that only they themselves and the priest could pronounce. All she could make out of it was Gobblehook. She and Mrs. McIntyre had been calling them the Gobblehooks all week while they got ready for them.

There had been a great deal to do to get ready for them because they didn't have anything of their own, not a stick of furniture or a sheet or a dish, and everything had had to be scraped together out of things that Mrs. McIntyre couldn't use any more herself. They had collected a piece of odd furniture here and a piece there and they had taken some flowered chicken feed sacks and made curtains for the windows, two red and one green, because they had not had enough of the red sacks to go around. Mrs. McIntyre said she was not made of money and she could not afford to buy curtains. "They can't talk," Mrs. Shortley said. "You reckon they'll know what colors even is?" and Mrs. McIntyre had said that after what those people had been through, they should be grateful for anything they could get. She said to think how lucky they were to escape from over there and come to a place like this.

Mrs. Shortley recalled a newsreel she had seen once of a small room piled high with bodies of dead naked people all in a heap, their arms and legs tangled together, a head thrust in here, a head there, a foot, a knee, a part that should have been covered up sticking out, a hand raised clutching nothing. Before you could realize that it was real and take it into your head, the picture changed and a hollow-sounding voice was saying, "Time marches on!" This was the kind of thing that was happening every day in Europe where they had not advanced as in this country, and watching from her vantage point, Mrs. Shortley had the sudden intuition that the Gobblehooks, like rats with typhoid fleas, could

have carried all those murderous ways over the water with them directly to this place. If they had come from where that kind of thing was done to them, who was to say they were not the kind that would also do it to others? The width and breadth of this question nearly shook her. Her stomach trembled as if there had been a slight quake in the heart of the mountain and automatically she moved down from her elevation and went forward to be introduced to them, as if she meant to find out at once what they were capable of.

She approached, stomach foremost, head back, arms folded, boots flopping gently against her large legs. About fifteen feet from the gesticulating group, she stopped and made her presence felt by training her gaze on the back of Mrs. McIntyre's neck. Mrs. McIntyre was a small woman of sixty with a round wrinkled face and red bangs that came almost down to two high orange-colored penciled eyebrows. She had a little doll's mouth and eyes that were a soft blue when she opened them wide but more like steel or granite when she narrowed them to inspect a milk can. She had buried one husband and divorced two and Mrs. Shortley respected her as a person nobody had put anything over on yet—except, ha, ha, perhaps the Shortleys. She held out her arm in Mrs. Shortley's direction and said to the Rudolph boy, "And this is Mrs. Shortley. Mr. Shortley is my dairyman. Where's Mr. Shortley?" she asked as his wife began to approach again, her arms still folded. "I want him to meet the Guizacs."

Now it was Guizac. She wasn't calling them Gobblehook to their face. "Chancey's at the barn," Mrs. Shortley said. "He don't have time to rest himself in the bushes like them niggers over there."

Her look first grazed the tops of the displaced people's heads and then revolved downwards slowly, the way a buzzard glides and drops in the air until it alights on the carcass. She stood far enough away so that the man would not be able to kiss her hand. He looked directly at her with little green eyes and gave her a broad grin that was toothless on one side. Mrs. Shortley, without smiling, turned her attention to the little girl who stood by the mother, swinging her shoulders from side to side. She had long braided hair in two looped pigtails and there was no denying she was a pretty child even if she did have a bug's name. She was better looking than either Annie Maude or Sarah Mae, Mrs. Shortley's two girls going on fifteen and seventeen but Annie Maude had never got her growth and Sarah Mae had a cast in her eye. She compared the foreign boy to her son, H.C., and

H.C. came out far ahead. H.C. was twenty years old with her build and eyeglasses. He was going to Bible school now and when he finished he was going to start him a church. He had a strong sweet voice for hymns and could sell anything. Mrs. Shortley looked at the priest and was reminded that these people did not have an advanced religion. There was no telling what all they believed since none of the foolishness had been reformed out of it. Again she saw the room piled high with bodies.

The priest spoke in a foreign way himself, English but as if he had a throatful of hay. He had a big nose and a bald rectangular face and head. While she was observing him, his large mouth dropped open and with a stare behind her, he said, "Arrrrrr!" and pointed.

Mrs. Shortley spun around. The peacock was standing a few feet behind her, with his head slightly cocked.

"What a beauti-ful birdrrrd!" the priest murmured.

"Another mouth to feed," Mrs. McIntyre said, glancing in the peafowl's direction.

"And when does he raise his splendid tail?" asked the priest.

"Just when it suits him," she said. "There used to be twenty or thirty of those things on the place but I've let them die off. I don't like to hear them scream in the middle of the night."

"So beauti-ful," the priest said. "A tail full of suns," and he crept forward on tiptoe and looked down on the bird's back where the polished gold and green design began. The peacock stood still as if he had just come down from some sun-drenched height to be a vision for them all. The priest's homely red face hung over him, glowing with pleasure.

Mrs. Shortley's mouth had drawn acidly to one side, "Nothing but a peachicken," she muttered.

Mrs. McIntyre raised her orange eyebrows and exchanged a look with her to indicate that the old man was in his second childhood. "Well, we must show the Guizacs their new home," she said impatiently and she herded them into the car again. The peacock stepped off toward the mulberry tree where the two Negroes were hiding and the priest turned his absorbed face away and got in the car and drove the displaced people down to the shack they were to occupy.

Mrs. Shortley waited until the car was out of sight and then she made her way circuitously to the mulberry tree and stood about ten feet behind the two Negroes, one an old man holding a bucket half full of calf feed and the other a yellowish boy with a short woodchuck-like head pushed into a rounded felt hat. "Well," she said slowly, "yawl have looked long enough. What you think about them?"

The old man, Astor, raised himself. "We been watching," he said as if this would be news to her. "Who they now?"

"They come from over the water," Mrs. Shortley said with a wave of her arm. "They're what is called Displaced Persons."

"Displaced Persons," he said. "Well now. I declare. What do that mean?"

"It means they ain't where they were born at and there's nowhere for them to go—like if you was run out of here and wouldn't nobody have you."

"It seem like they here, though," the old man said in a reflective voice. "If they here, they somewhere."

"Sho is, " the other agreed. "They here."

The illogic of Negro-thinking always irked Mrs. Shortley. "They ain't where they belong to be at," she said. "They belong to be back over yonder where everything is still like they been used to. Over here it's more advanced than where they come from. But yawl better look out now," she said and nodded her head. "There's about ten million billion more just like them and I know what Mrs. McIntyre said."

"Say what?" the young one asked.

"Places are not easy to get nowadays, for white or black, but I reckon I heard what she stated to me," she said in a sing-song voice.

"You liable to hear most anything," the old man remarked, leaning forward as if he were about to walk off but holding himself suspended.

"I heard her say, 'This is going to put the Fear of the Lord into those shiftless niggers!'" Mrs. Shortley said in a ringing voice.

The old man started off. "She say something like that every now and then," he said. "Ha. Ha. Yes indeed."

"You better get on in the barn and help Mr. Shortley," she said to the other one. "What you reckon she pays you for?"

"He the one sont me out." The Negro muttered. "He the one gimme something else to do."

"Well you better get to doing it then," she said and stood there until he moved off. Then she stood a while longer, reflecting, her unseeing eyes directly in front of the peacock's tail. He had jumped into the tree and his tail hung in front of her, full of fierce planets with eyes that were each ringed in green and set against a sun that was gold in one second's light and salmon-colored in the next. She might have been looking at a map of the universe but she didn't notice it any more than she did the spots of sky that cracked the dull green of the tree. She was having an inner vision instead. She was seeing the ten million billion of them pushing their way into new places over here and herself, a giant angel with wings as wide as a house, telling the Negroes that they would have to find another place. She turned herself in the direction of the barn, musing on this, her expression lofty and satisfied.

She approached the barn from an oblique angle that allowed her a look in the door before she could be seen herself. Mr. Chancey Shortley was adjusting the last milking machine on a large black and white spotted cow near the entrance, squatting at her heels. There was about a half-inch of cigarette adhering to the center of his lower lip. Mrs. Shortley observed it minutely for half a second. "If she seen or heard of you smoking in this barn, she would blow a fuse," she said.

Mr. Shortley raised a sharply rutted face containing a washout under each cheek and two long crevices eaten down both sides of his blistered mouth. "You gonter be the one to tell her?" he asked.

"She's got a nose of her own," Mrs. Shortley said.

Mr. Shortley, without appearing to give the feat any consideration, lifted the cigarette stub with the sharp end of his tongue, drew it into his mouth, closed his lips tightly, rose, stepped out, gave his wife a good round appreciative stare, and spit the smoldering butt into the grass.

"Aw Chancey," she said, "haw haw," and she dug a little hole for it with her toe and covered it up. This trick of Mr. Shortley's was actually his way of making love to her. When he had done his courting, he had not brought a guitar to strum or anything pretty for her to keep, but had sat on her porch steps, not saying a word, imitating a paralyzed man propped up to enjoy a cigarette. When the cigarette got the proper size, he would turn his eyes to her and open his mouth and draw in the butt and then sit there as if he had swallowed it, looking at her with the most loving look anybody could imagine. It nearly drove her wild and every time he did it, she wanted to pull his hat down over his eyes and hug him to death.

"Well," she said, going into the barn after him. "the Gobblehooks have come and she wants you to meet them, says, 'Where's Mr. Shortley?' and I says, 'He don't have time . . .'"

"Tote up them weights," Mr. Shortley said, squatting to the cow again.

"You reckon he can drive a tractor when he don't know English?" she asked. "I don't think

she's going to get her money's worth out of them. That boy can talk but he looks delicate. The one can work can't talk and the one can talk can't work. She ain't any better off than if she had more niggers."

"I rather have a nigger if it was me," Mr. Shortley said.

"She says it's ten million more like them, Displaced Persons, she says that there priest can get her all she wants."

"She better quit messin with that there priest," Mr. Shortly said.

"He don't look smart," Mrs. Shortley said. "—kind of foolish."

"I ain't going to have the Pope of Rome tell me how to run no dairy." Mr. Shortley said.

"They ain't Eye-talians, they're Poles." She said. "From Poland where all them bodies were stacked up at. You remember all them bodies?"

"I give them three weeks here," Mr. Shortley said.

Three weeks later Mrs. McIntyre and Mrs. Shortley drove to the cane bottom to see Mr. Guizac start to operate the silage cutter, a new machine that Mrs. McIntyre had just bought because she said, for the first time, she had somebody who could operate it. Mr. Guizac could drive a tractor, use the rotary hay-baler, the silage cutter, the combine, the letz mill, or any other machine she had on the place. He was an expert mechanic, a carpenter, and a mason. He was thrifty and energetic. Mrs. McIntyre said she figured he would save her twenty dollars a month on repair bills alone. She said getting him was the best day's work she had ever done in her life. He could work milking machines and he was scrupulously clean. He did not smoke.

She parked her car on the edge of the cane field and they got out. Sulk, the young Negro, was attaching the wagon to the cutter and Mr. Guizac was attaching the cutter to the tractor. He finished first and pushed the colored boy out of the way and attached the wagon to the cutter himself, gesticulating with a bright angry face when he wanted the hammer or the screwdriver. Nothing was done quick enough to suit him. The Negroes made him nervous.

The week before, he had come upon Sulk at the dinner hour, sneaking with a croker sack into the pen where the young turkeys were. He had watched him take a frying-size turkey from the lot and thrust it in the sack and put the sack under his coat. Then he had followed him around the barn, jumped on him, dragged him to Mrs. McIntyre's back door and had acted out the entire scene for her, while the Negro muttered and grumbled and said God might strike him dead if he had been stealing any turkey, he had only been taking it to put some black shoe polish on its head because it had the sorehead. God might strike him dead if that was not the truth before Jesus. Mrs. McIntyre told him to go put the turkey back and then she was a long time explaining to the Pole that all Negroes would steal. She finally had to call Rudolph and tell him in English and have him tell his father in Polish, and Mr. Guizac had gone off with a startled disappointed face.

Mrs. Shortley stood by hoping there would be trouble with the silage machine but there was none. All of Mr. Guizac's motions were quick and accurate. He jumped on the tractor like a monkey and maneuvered the big orange cutter into the cane; in a second the silage was spurting in a green jet out of the pipe into the wagon. He went jolting down the row until he disappeared from sight and the noise became remote.

Mrs. McIntyre sighed with pleasure. "At last," she said, "I've got somebody I can depend on. For years I've been fooling with sorry people. Sorry people. Poor white trash and niggers," she muttered. "They've drained me dry. Before you all came I had Ringfields and Collins and Jarrells and Perkins and Pinkins and Herrins and God knows what all else and not a one of them left without taking something off this place that didn't belong to them. Not a one!"

Mrs. Shortley could listen to this with composure because she knew that if Mrs. McIntyre had considered her trash, they couldn't have talked about trashy people together. Neither of them approved of trash. Mrs. McIntyre continued with the monologue that Mrs. Shortley had heard oftentimes before. "I've been running this place for thirty years," she said, looking with a deep frown out over the field, "and always just barely making it. People think you're made of money. I have taxes to pay. I have the insurance to keep up. I have the repair bills. I have the feed bills." It all gathered up and she stood with her chest lifted and her small hands gripped around her elbows. "Ever since the Judge died," she said, "I've barely been making ends meet and they all take something when they leave. The niggers don't leave—they stay and steal. A nigger thinks anybody is rich he can steal from and that white trash thinks anybody is rich who can afford to hire people as sorry as they are. And all I've got is the dirt under my feet!"

You hire and fire, Mrs. Shortley thought, but she didn't always say what she thought. She stood by and let Mrs. McIntyre say it all out to the end but this time it didn't end as usual. "But at last I'm saved!" Mrs. McIntyre said. "One fellow's misery is the other fellow's gain. That man there," and she pointed where the Displaced Person had disappeared, "—he has to work! He wants to work!" She turned to Mrs. Shortley with her bright wrinkled face. "That man is my salvation!" she said.

Mrs. Shortley looked straight ahead as if her vision penetrated the cane and the hill and pierced through to the other side. "I would suspicion salvation got from the devil," she said in a slow detached way.

"Now what do you mean by that?" Mrs. McIntyre asked, looking at her sharply.

Mrs. Shortley wagged her head but would not say anything else. The fact was she had nothing else to say for this intuition had only at that instant come to her. She had never given much thought to the devil for she felt that religion was essentially for those people who didn't have the brains to avoid evil without it. For people like herself, for people of gumption, it was a social occasion providing the opportunity to sing; but if she had ever given it much thought, she would have considered the devil the head of it and God the hanger-on. With the coming of these displaced people, she was obliged to give new thought to a good many things.

"I know what Sledgewig told Annie Maude," she said, and when Mrs. McIntyre carefully did not ask her what but reached down and broke off a sprig of sassafras to chew, she continued in a way to indicate she was not telling all, "That they wouldn't be able to live long, the four of them, on seventy dollars a month."

"He's worth raising," Mrs. McIntyre said. "He saves me money."

This was as much as to say that Chancey had never saved her money. Chancey got up at four in the morning to milk her cows, in winter wind and summer heat, and he had been doing it for the last two years. They had been with her the longest she had ever had anybody. The gratitude they got was these hints that she hadn't been saved any money.

"Is Mr. Shortley feeling better today?" Mrs. McIntyre asked.

Mrs. Shortley thought it was about time she was asking that question. Mr. Shortley had been in bed two days with an attack. Mr. Guizac had taken his place in the dairy in addition to doing his own work. "No he ain't," she said. "That doctor said he was suffering from over-exhaustion."

"If Mr. Shortley is over-exhausted," Mrs. McIntyre said, "then he must have a second job on the side," and she looked at Mrs. Shortley with almost closed eyes as if she were examining the bottom of a milk can.

Mrs. Shortley did not say a word but her dark suspicion grew like a black thunder cloud. The fact was that Mr. Shortley did have a second job on the side and that, in a free country, this was none of Mrs. McIntyre's business. Mr. Shortley made whiskey. He had a small still back in the farthest reaches of the place, on Mrs. McIntyre's land to be sure, but on land that she only owned and did not cultivate, on idle land that was not doing anybody any good. Mr. Shortley was not afraid of work. He got up at four in the morning and milked her cows and in the middle of the day when he was supposed to be resting, he was off attending to his still. Not every man would work like that. The Negroes knew about his still but he knew about theirs so there had never been any disagreeableness between them. But with foreigners on the place, with people who were all eyes and no understanding, who had come from a place continually fighting, where the religion had not been reformed—with this kind of people, you had to be on the lookout every minute. She thought there ought to be a law against them. There was no reason they couldn't stay over there and take the place of some of the people who had been killed in their wars and butcherings.

"What's furthermore," she said suddenly, "Sledgewig said as soon as her papa saved the money, he was going to buy him a used car. Once they get them a used car, they'll leave you."

"I can't pay him enough money for him to save money," Mrs. McIntyre said. "I'm not worrying about that. Of course," she said then, "if Mr. Shortley got incapacitated, I would have to use Mr. Guizac in the dairy all the time and I would have to pay him more. He doesn't smoke," she said, and it was the fifth time within the week that she had pointed this out.

"It is no man," Mrs. Shortley said emphatically, "that works as hard as Chancey, or is as easy with a cow, or is more of a Christian," and she folded her arms and her gaze pierced the distance. The noise of the tractor and cutter increased and Mr. Guizac appeared coming around the other side of the cane row. "Which can not be said about everybody," she muttered. She wondered whether, if the Pole found Chancey's still, he would know what it was. The trouble with these people was, you couldn't tell what they knew. Every time Mr. Guizac smiles, Europe stretched out in Mrs. Shortley's imagination, mysterious and evil, the devil's experiment station.

The tractor, the cutter, the wagon passed, rattling and rumbling and grinding before them.

"Think how long that would have taken with men and mules to do it." Mrs. McIntyre shouted. "We'll get this whole bottom cut within two days at this rate."

"Maybe," Mrs. Shortley muttered, "if don't no terrible accident occur." She thought how the tractor had made mules worthless. Nowadays you couldn't give away a mule. The next thing to go, she reminded herself, will be niggers.

In the afternoon she explained what was going to happen to them, to Astor and Sulk who were in the cow loft, filling the manure spreader. She sat down next to the block of salt under a small shed, her stomach in her lap, her arms on top of it. "All you colored people better look out," she said. "You know how much you can get for a mule."

"Nothing, no indeed," the old man said, "not one thing."

"Before it was a tractor," she said, "it could be a mule. And before it was a Displaced Person, it could be a nigger. The time is going to come," she prophesied, "when it won't be no more occasion to speak of a nigger."

The old man laughed politely. "Yes indeed," he said. "Ha ha."

The young one didn't say anything. He only looked sullen but when she had gone in the house, he said, "Big Belly act like she know everything."

"Never mind," the old man said, "your place too low for anybody to dispute with you for it."

She didn't tell her fears about the still to Mr. Shortley until he was back on the job in the dairy. Then one night after they were in bed, she said, "That man prowls."

Mr. Shortley folded his hands on his bony chest and pretended he was a corpse.

"Prowls," she continued and gave him a sharp kick in the side with her knee. "Who's to say what they know and don't know? Who's to say if he found it he wouldn't go right to her and tell? Hope you know they don't make liquor in Europe? They drive tractors. They got them all kinds of machinery. Answer me."

"Don't worry me now," Mr. Shortley said, "I'm a dead man."

"It's them little eyes of his that's foreign," she muttered. "And that way he's got of shrugging." She drew her shoulders up and shrugged several times. "How come he's got anything to shrug about?" she asked.

"If everybody was as dead as I am, nobody would have no trouble," Mr. Shortley said.

"That priest," she muttered and was silent for a minute. Then she said, "In Europe they probably got some different way to make liquor but I reckon they know all the ways. They're full of crooked ways. They never have advanced or reformed. They got the same religion as a thousand years ago. It could only be the devil responsible for that. Always fighting amongst each other. Disputing. And then get us into it. Ain't they got us into it twice already and we ain't got no more sense to go over there and settle it for them and then they come on back over here and snoop around and find your still and go straight to her. And liable to kiss her hand any minute. Do you hear me?"

"No," Mr. Shortley said.

"And I'll tell you another thing," she said. "I wouldn't be a tall surprised if he don't know everything you say, whether it be in English or not."

"I don't speak no other language," Mr. Shortly murmured.

"I suspect," she said, " that before long there won't be no more niggers on this place. And I tell you what, I'd rather have niggers than them Poles. And what's furthermore, I aim to take up for the niggers when the time comes. When Gobblehook first come here, you recollect how he shook their hands, like he didn't know the difference, like he might have been as black as them, but when it come to finding out Sulk was taking turkeys, he gone on and told her. I known he was taking turkeys, I could have told her myself."

Mr. Shortley was breathing softly as if he were asleep.

"A nigger don't know when he has a friend," she said. "And I'll tell you another thing, I get a heap out of Sledgewig. Sledgewig said that in Poland they lived in a brick house and one night a man come and told them to get out of it before daylight. Do you believe they ever lived in a brick house?"

"Airs," she said. "That's just airs. A wooden house is good enough for me. Chancey," she said, "turn thisaway. I hate to see niggers mistreated and run out. I have a heap of pity for niggers and poor folks. Ain't I always had?" she asked. "I say ain't I always been a friend to niggers and poor folks?"

"When the time comes," she said, "I'll stand up for the niggers and that's that. I ain't going to see that priest drive out all the niggers."

Mrs. McIntyre bought a new drag harrow and a tractor with a power lift because she said, for the first time, she had someone who could handle machinery. She and Mrs. Shortley had driven to the back field to inspect what he had harrowed the day before. "That's been done beautifully!" Mrs. McIntyre said, looking out over the red undulating ground.

Mrs. McIntyre had changed since the Displaced Person had been working for her and Mrs. Shortley had observed the change very closely: she had begun to act like somebody who was getting rich secretly and she didn't confide in Mrs. Shortley the way she used to. Mrs. Shortley suspected that the priest was at the bottom of the change. They were very slick. First he would get her into his church and then he would get his hand in her pocketbook. Well, Mrs. Shortley thought, the more fool she! Mrs. Shortley had a secret herself. She knew something the Displaced Person was doing that would floor Mrs. McIntyre. "I still say he ain't going to work forever for seventy dollars a month," she murmured. She intended to keep her secret to herself and Mr. Shortley.

"Well," Mrs. McIntyre said, "I may have to get rid of some of this other help so I can pay him more."

Mrs. Shortley nodded to indicate she had known this for some time. "I'm not saying those niggers ain't had it coming," she said. "But they do the best they know how. You can always tell a nigger what to do and stand by until he does it."

"That's what the Judge said," Mrs. McIntyre said and looked at her with approval. The Judge was her first husband, the one who had left her the place. Mrs. Shortley had heard that she had married him when she was thirty and he was seventy-five, thinking she would be rich as soon as he died, but then the old man was a scoundrel and when his estate was settled, they found he didn't have a nickel. All he left her were the fifty acres and the house. But she always spoke of him in a reverent way and quoted his sayings, such as, "One fellow's misery is the other fellow's gain," and "The devil you know is better than the devil you don't."

"However," Mrs. Shortley remarked, "the devil you know is better than the devil you don't," and she had to turn away so that Mrs. McIntyre would not see her smile. She had found out what the Displaced Person was up to through the old man, Astor, and she had not told anybody but Mr. Shortley. Mr. Shortley had risen straight up in bed like Lazarus from the tomb.

"Shut your mouth!" he had said.

"Yes," she had said.

"Naw!" Mr. Shortley had said.

"Yes," she had said.

Mr. Shortley had fallen back flat.

"The Pole don't know any better," Mrs. Shortley had said. "I reckon that priest is putting him up to it is all. I blame the priest."

The priest came frequently to see the Guizacs and he would always stop in and visit Mrs. McIntyre too and they would walk around the place and she would point out her improvements and listen to his rattling talk. It suddenly came to Mrs. Shortley that he was trying to persuade her to bring another Polish family onto the place. With two of them here, there would be almost nothing spoken but Polish! The Negroes would be gone and there would be the two families against Mr. Shortley and herself! She began to imagine a war of words, to see the Polish words and the English words coming at each other, stalking forward, not sentences, just words, gabble, gabble, gabble, flung out high and shrill and stalking forward and then grappling with each other. She saw the Polish words, dirty and all-knowing and unreformed, flinging mud on the clean English words until everything was equally dirty. She saw them all piled up in a room, all the dead dirty words, theirs and hers too, piled up like the naked bodies in the newsreel. God save me, she cried silently, from the stinking power of Satan! And she started from that day to read the Bible with a new attention. She poured over the Apocalypse and began to quote from the Prophets and before long she had come to a deeper understanding of her existence. She saw plainly that the meaning of the world was a mystery that had been planned and she was not surprised to suspect that she had a special part in the plan because she was strong. She saw that the Lord God Almighty had created the strong people to do what had to be done and she felt that she would be ready when she was called. Right now she felt that her business was to watch the priest.

His visits irked her more and more. On the last one, he went about picking up feathers off the ground. He found two peacock feathers and four or five turkey feathers and an old brown hen feather and took them off with him like a bouquet. This foolish-acting did not deceive Mrs. Shortly any. Here he was: leading foreigners over in hordes to places that were not theirs, to cause disputes, to uproot niggers, to plant the Whore of Babylon in the midst of the righteous! Whenever he came on the place, she hid herself behind something and watched until he left.

It was on a Sunday afternoon that she had her vision. She had gone to drive in the cows for Mr. Shortley who had a pain in his knee and she was walking slowly through the pasture, her arms folded, her eyes on the distant low-lying clouds that looked like rows and rows of white fish washed up on a great blue beach. She paused after an incline to heave a sigh of exhaustion for she had an immense weight to carry around and she was not as young as she used to be. At times she could feel her heart, like a child's fist, clenching and unclenching inside her chest, and when the feeling came, it stopped her thought altogether and she would go about like a large hull of herself, moving for no reason; but she gained this incline without a tremor and stood at the top of it, pleased with herself. Suddenly while she watched, the sky folded back in two pieces like the curtain to a stage and a gigantic figure stood facing her. It was the color of the sun in the early afternoon, white-gold. It was of no definite shape but there were fiery wheels with fierce dark eyes in them, spinning rapidly all around it. She was not able to tell if the figure was going forward or backward because its magnificence was so great. She shut her eyes in order to look at it and it turned blood-red and the wheels turned white. A voice, very resonant, said the one word, "Prophesy!"

She stood there, tottering slightly but still upright, her eyes shut tight and her fists clenched and her straw sun hat low on her forehead. "The children of wicked nations will be butchered," she said in a loud voice. "Legs where arms should be, foot to face, ear in the palm of hand. Who will remain whole? Who will remain whole? Who?"

Presently she opened her eyes. The sky was full of white fish carried lazily on their sides by some invisible current and pieces of the sun, submerged some distance beyond them, appeared from time to time as if they were being washed in the opposite direction. Woodenly she planted one foot in front of the other until she had crossed the pasture and reached the lot. She walked through the barn like one in a daze and did not speak to Mr. Shortley. She continued up the road until she saw the priest's car parked in front of Mrs. McIntyre's house. "Here again," she muttered. "Come to destroy."

Mrs. McIntyre and the priest were walking in the yard. In order not to meet them face to face, she turned to the left and entered the feed house, a single-room shack piled on one side with flowered sacks of scratch feed. There were spilled oyster shells in one corner and a few old dirty calendars on the wall, advertising calf feed and various patent medicine remedies. One showed a bearded gentleman in a frock coat, holding up a bottle, and beneath his feet was the inscription, "I have been made regular by this marvelous discovery." Mrs. Shortley had always felt close to this man as if he were some distinguished person she was acquainted with but now her mind was on nothing but the dangerous presence of the priest. She stationed herself at a crack between two boards where she could look out and see him and Mrs. McIntyre strolling toward the turkey brooder, which was placed just outside the feed house.

"Arrrrr!" he said as they approached the brooder. "Look at the little biddies!" and he stooped and squinted through the wire.

Mrs. Shortley's mouth twisted.

"Do you think the Guizacs will want to leave me?" Mrs. McIntyre asked. "Do you think they'll go to Chicago or some place like that?"

"And why should they do that now?" asked the priest, wiggling his finger at a turkey, his big nose close to the wire.

"Money," Mrs. McIntyre said.

"Arrrr, give them some morrre then," he said indifferently. "They have to get along."

"So do I," Mrs. McIntyre muttered. "It means I'm going to have to get rid of some of the others."

"And arrre the Shortleys satisfactory?" he inquired, paying more attention to the turkeys than to her.

"Five times in the last month I've found Mr. Shortley smoking in the barn," Mrs. McIntyre said. "Five times."

"And arrre the Negroes any better?"

"They lie and steal and have to be watched all the time," she said.

"Tsk, tsk," he said. "Which will you discharge?"

"I've decided to give Mr. Shortley his month's notice tomorrow," Mrs. McIntyre said.

The priest scarcely seemed to hear her he was so busy wiggling his finger inside the wire. Mrs. Shortley sat down on an open sack of laying mash with a dead thump that sent feed dust clouding up around her. She found herself looking straight ahead at the opposite wall where the gentleman on the calendar was holding up his marvelous discovery but she didn't see him. She looked ahead as if she saw nothing whatsoever. Then she rose and ran to her house. Her face was an almost volcanic red.

She opened all the drawers and dragged out boxes and old battered suitcases from under the bed. She began to unload the drawers into the boxes, all the time without pause, without taking off the sunhat she had on her head. She set the two girls to doing the same. When Mr. Shortley came in, she did not even look at him but merely pointed one arm at him while she packed with the other. "Bring the car around to the back door," she said. "You ain't waiting to be fired!"

Mr. Shortley had never in his life doubted her

omniscience. He perceived the entire situation in half a second and, with only a sour scowl, retreated out the door and went to drive the automobile around to the back.

They tied the two iron beds to the top of the car and the two rocking chairs inside the beds and rolled the two mattresses up between the rocking chairs. On top of this they tied a crate of chickens. They loaded the inside of the car with the old suitcases and boxes, leaving a small space for Annie Maude and Sarah Mae. It took them the rest of the afternoon and half the night to do this but Mrs. Shortley was determined that they would leave before four o'clock in the morning, that Mr. Shortley should not adjust another milking machine on this place. All the time she had been working, her face was changing rapidly from red to white and back again.

Just before dawn, as it began to drizzle rain, they were ready to leave. They all got in the car and sat there cramped up between boxes and bundles and rolls of bedding. The square black automobile moved off with more than its customary grinding noises as if it were protesting the load. In the back, the two long bony yellow-haired girls were sitting on a pile of boxes and there was a beagle hound puppy and a cat with two kittens somewhere under the blankets. The car moved slowly, like some overfreighted leaking ark, away from their shack and past the white house where Mrs. McIntyre was sleeping soundly—hardly guessing that her cows would not be milked by Mr. Shortley that morning—and past the Pole's shack on top of the hill and on down the road to the gate where the two Negroes were walking, one behind the other, on their way to help with the milking. They looked straight at the car and its occupants but even as the dim yellow headlights lit up their faces, they politely did not seem to see anything, or anyhow, to attach significance to what was there. The loaded car might have been passing mist in the early morning half-light. They continued up the road at the same even pace without looking back.

A dark yellow sun was beginning to rise in a sky that was the same slick dark gray as the highway. The fields stretched away, stiff and weedy, on either side. "Where we goin?" Mr. Shortley asked for the first time.

Mrs. Shortley sat with one foot on a packing box so that her knee was pushed into her stomach. Mr. Shortley's elbow was almost under her nose and Sarah Mae's bare left foot was sticking over the front seat, touching her ear.

"Where we goin?" Mr. Shortley repeated and

when she didn't answer again, he turned and looked at her.

Fierce heat seemed to be swelling slowly and fully into her face as if it were welling up now for a final assault. She was sitting in an erect way in spite of the fact that one leg was twisted under her and one knee was almost into her neck, but there was a peculiar lack of light in her icy blue eyes. All the vision in them might have been turned around, looking inside her. She suddenly grabbed Mr. Shortley's elbow and Sarah Mae's foot at the same time and began to tug and pull on them as if she were trying to fit the two extra limbs onto herself.

Mr. Shortley began to curse and quickly stopped the car and Sarah Mae yelled to quit but Mrs. Shortley apparently intended to rearrange the whole car at once. She thrashed forward and backward, clutching at everything she could get her hands on and hugging it to herself. Mr. Shortley's head, Sarah Mae's leg, the cat, a wad of white bedding, her own big moon-like knee; then all at once her fierce expression faded into a look of astonishment and her grip on what she had loosened. One of her eyes drew near to the other and seemed to collapse quietly and she was still.

The two girls, who didn't know what had happened to her, began to say, "Where we goin, Ma? Where we goin?" They thought she was playing a joke and that their father, staring straight ahead at her, was imitating a dead man. They didn't know that she had had a great experience or ever been displaced in the world from all that belonged to her. They were frightened by the gray slick road before them and they kept repeating in higher and higher voices, "Where we goin, Ma? Where we goin?" while their mother, her huge body rolled back still against the seat and her eyes like blue-painted glass, seemed to contemplate for the first time the tremendous frontiers of her true country.

II

"Well," Mrs. McIntyre said to the old Negro, "we can get along without them. We've seen them come and seen them go—black and white." She was standing in the calf barn while he cleaned it and she held a rake in her hand and now and then pulled a corn cob from a corner or pointed to a soggy spot that he had missed. When she discovered the Shortleys were gone, she was delighted as it meant she wouldn't have to fire them. The people she hired always left her—because they were that kind of people. Of all the families she had had, the Shortleys were the best if she didn't count the Displaced Person. They had been not quite trash;

Mrs. Shortley was a good woman, and she would miss her but as the Judge used to say, you couldn't have your pie and eat it too, and she was satisfied with the D.P. "We've seen them come and seen them go," she repeated with satisfaction.

"And me and you," the old man said, stooping to drag his hoe under a feed rack, "is still here."

She caught exactly what he meant her to catch in his tone. Bars of sunlight fell from the cracked ceiling across his back and cut him in three distinct parts. She watched his long hands clenched around the hoe and his crooked old profile pushed close to them. You might have been here *before* I was, she said to herself, but it's mighty likely I'll be here when you're gone. "I've spent half my life fooling with worthless people," she said in a severe voice, "but now I'm through."

"Black and white," he said, "is the same."

"I am through," she repeated and gave her dark smock that she had thrown over her shoulders like a cape a quick snatch at the neck. She had a broad-brimmed black straw hat that had cost her twenty dollars twenty years ago and that she used now for a sunhat. "Money is the root of all evil," she said. "The Judge said so every day. He said he deplored money. He said the reason you niggers were so uppity was because there was so much money in circulation."

The old Negro had known the Judge. "Judge say he long for the day when he be too poor to pay a nigger to work," he said. "Say when that day come, the world be back on its feet."

She leaned forward, her hands on her hips and her neck stretched and said, "Well that day has almost come around here and I'm telling each and every one of you: you better look sharp. I don't have to put up with foolishness any more. I have somebody now who has to work!"

The old man knew when to answer and when not. At length he said, "We seen them come and we seen them go."

"However, the Shortleys were not the worst by far," she said. "I well remember those Garrits."

"They was before them Collinses." He said.

"No, before the Ringfields."

"Sweet Lord, them Ringfields!" he murmured.

"None of that kind *want* to work," she said.

"We seen them come and we seen them go," he said as if this were a refrain. "But we ain't never had one before," he said, bending himself up until he faced her, "like what we got now." He was cinnamon-colored with eyes that were so blurred with age that they seemed to be hung behind cobwebs.

She gave him an intense stare and held it until,

lowering his hands on the hoe, he bent down again and dragged a pile of shavings alongside the wheelbarrow. She said stiffly, "He can wash out that barn in the time it took Mr. Shortley to make up his mind he had to do it."

"He from Pole," the old man muttered.

"From Poland."

"In Pole it ain't like it is here," he said. "They got different ways of doing," and he began to mumble unintelligibly.

"What are you saying?" she said. "If you have anything to say about him, say it and say it aloud."

He was silent, bending his knees precariously and edging the rake along the underside of the trough.

"If you know anything he's done that he shouldn't, I expect you to report it to me," she said.

"It warn't like it was what he should ought or oughtn't," he muttered. "It was like what nobody else don't do."

"You don't have anything against him," she said shortly, "and he's here to stay."

"We ain't never had one like him before is all," he murmured and gave his polite laugh.

"Times are changing," she said. "Do you know what's happening to this world? It's swelling up. It's getting so full of people that only the smart thrifty energetic ones are going to survive," and she tapped the words, smart, thrifty, and energetic out on the palm of her hand. Through the far end of the stall she could see down the road to where the Displaced Person was standing in the open barn door with the green hose in his hand. There was a certain stiffness about his figure that seemed to make it necessary for her to approach him slowly, even in her thoughts. She had decided this was because she couldn't hold an easy conversation with him. Whenever she said anything to him, she found herself shouting and nodding extravagantly and she would be conscious that one of the Negroes was leaning behind the nearest shed, watching.

"No indeed!" she said, sitting down on one of the feed racks and folding her arms, "I've made up my mind that I've had enough trashy people on this place to last me a lifetime and I'm not going to spend my last years fooling with Shortleys and Ringfields and Collins when the world is full of people who *have* to work."

"Howcome they so many extra?" he asked.

"People are selfish," she said. "They have too many children. There's no sense in it any more."

He had picked up the wheelbarrow handles and was backing out the door and he paused, half

in the sunlight and half out, and stood there chewing his gums as if he had forgotten which direction he wanted to move in.

"What you colored people don't realize," she said, "is that I'm the one around here who holds all the strings together. If you don't work, I don't make any money and I can't pay you. You're all dependent on me but you each and every one act like the shoe is on the other foot."

It was not possible to tell from his face if he heard her. Finally he backed out with the wheelbarrow. "Judge say the devil he know is better than the devil he don't," he said in a clear mutter and trundled off.

She got up and followed him, a deep vertical pit appearing suddenly in the center of her forehead, just under the red bangs. "The Judge has long since ceased to pay the bills around here," she called in a piercing voice.

He was the only one of her Negroes who had known the Judge and he thought this gave him title. He had had a low opinion of Mr. Crooms and Mr. McIntyre, her other husbands, and in his veiled polite way, he had congratulated her after each of her divorces. When he thought it necessary, he would work under a window where he knew she was sitting and talk to himself, a careful roundabout discussion, question and answer and then refrain. Once she had got up silently and slammed the window down so hard that he had fallen backwards off his feet. Or occasionally he spoke with the peacock. The cock would follow him around the place, his steady eye on the ear of corn that stuck up from the old man's back pocket or he would sit near him and pick himself. Once from the open kitchen door, she had heard him say to the bird, "I remember when it was twenty of you walking about this place and now it's only you and two hens. Crooms it was twelve. McIntyre it was five. You and two hens now."

And that time she had stepped out of the door onto the porch and said, "MISTER Crooms and MISTER McIntyre! And I don't want to hear you call either of them anything else again. And you can understand this: when that peachicken dies there won't be any replacements."

She kept the peacock only out of a superstitious fear of annoying the Judge in his grave. He had liked to see them walking around the place for he said they made him feel rich. Of her three husbands, the Judge was the one most present to her although he was the only one she had buried. He was in the family graveyard, a little space fenced in the middle of the back cornfield, which his mother and father and grandfather and three great aunts and two infant cousins. Mr. Crooms, her second, was forty miles away in the state asylum and Mr. McIntyre, her last, was intoxicated, she supposed, in some hotel room in Florida. But the Judge, sunk in the cornfield with his family, was always at home.

She had married him when he was an old man and because of his money but there had been another reason that she would not admit then, even to herself: she had liked him. He was a dirty snuff-dipping Court House figure, famous all over the country for being rich, who wore hightop shoes, a string tie, a gray suit with a black stripe in it and a yellowed panama hat, winter and summer. His teeth and hair were tobacco-colored and his face a clay pink pitted and tracked with mysterious pre-historic-looking marks as if he had been unearthed among fossils. There had been a peculiar odor about him of sweaty fondled bills but he never carried money on him or had a nickel to show. She was his secretary for a few months and the old man with his sharp eye had seen at once that here was a woman who admired him for himself. The three years that he lived after they married were the happiest and most prosperous of Mrs. McIntyre's life, but when he died his estate proved to be bankrupt. He left her a mortgaged house and fifty acres that he had managed to cut the timer off before he died. It was as if, as the final triumph of a successful life, he had been able to take everything with him.

But she had survived. She had survived a succession of tenant farmers and dairymen that the old man himself would have found hard to outdo, and she had been able to meet the constant drain of a tribe of moody unpredictable Negroes, and she had even managed to hold her own against the incidental bloodsuckers, the cattle dealers and lumber men and the buyers and sellers of anything who drove up in pieced-together trucks and honked in the yard.

She stood slightly reared back with her arms folded under her smock and a satisfied expression on her face as she watched the Displaced Person turn off the hose and disappear inside the barn. She was sorry that the poor man had been chased out of Poland and run across Europe and had had to take up in a tenant shack in a strange country, but she had not been responsible for any of this. She had had a hard time herself. She knew what it was to struggle. People ought to have to struggle. Mr. Guizac had probably had everything given to him all the way across Europe and over here. He had probably not had to struggle enough. She had

given him a job. She didn't know if he was grateful or not. She didn't know anything about him except that he did the work. The truth was that he was not very real to her yet. He was a kind of miracle that she had seen happen and that she talked about but that she still didn't believe.

She watched as he came out of the barn and motioned to Sulk, who was coming around the back of the lot. He gesticulated and then took something out of his pocket and the two of them stood looking at it. She started down the lane toward them. The Negro's figure was slack and tall and he was craning his round head forward in his usual idiotic way. He was a little better than half-witted but when they were like that they were always good workers. The Judge had said always hire you a half-witted nigger because they don't have sense enough to stop working. The Pole was gesticulating rapidly. He left something with the colored boy and then walked off and before she rounded the turn in the lane, she heard the tractor crank up. He was on his way to the field. The Negro was still hanging there, gaping at whatever he had in his hand.

She entered the lot and walked through the barn, looking with approval at the wet spotless concrete floor. It was only nine-thirty and Mr. Shortley had never got anything washed until eleven. As she came out at the other end, she saw the Negro moving very slowly in a diagonal path across the road in front of her, his eyes still on what Mr. Guizac had given him. He didn't see her and he paused and dipped his knees and leaned over his hand, his tongue describing little circles. He had a photograph. He lifted one finger and traced it lightly over the surface of the picture. Then he looked up and saw her and seemed to freeze, his mouth in a half-grin, his finger lifted.

"Why haven't you gone to the field?" she asked.

He raised one foot and opened his mouth wider while the hand with the photograph edged toward his back pocket.

"What's that?" she said.

"It ain't nothing," he muttered and handed it to her automatically.

It was a photograph of a girl of about twelve in a white dress. She had blonde hair with a wreath in it and she looked forward out of light eyes that were bland and composed. "Who is this child?" Mrs. McIntyre asked.

"She his cousin," the boy said in a high voice.

"Well what are you doing with it?" she asked.

"She going to mah me," he said in an even higher voice.

"Marry you!" she shrieked.

"I pays half to get her over here," he said. "I pays him three dollar a week. She bigger now. She his cousin. She don't care who she mah she so glad to get away from there." The high voice seemed to shoot up like a nervous jet of sound and then fall flat as he watched her face. Her eyes were the color of blue granite when the glare falls on it, but she was not looking at him. She was looking down the road where the distant sound of the tractor could be heard.

"I don't reckon she goin to come nohow," the boy murmured.

"I'll see that you get every cent of your money back," she said in a toneless voice and turned and walked off, holding the photograph bent in two. There was nothing about her small stiff figure to indicate that she was shaken.

As soon as she got in the house, she lay down on her bed and shut her eyes and pressed her hand over her heart as if she were trying to keep it in place. Her mouth opened and she made two or three dry little sounds. Then after a minute she sat up and said aloud, "They're all the same. It's always been like this." And she fell back flat again. "Twenty years of being beaten and done in and they even robbed his grave!" and remembering that, she began to cry quietly, wiping her eyes every now and then with the hem of her smock.

What she had thought of was the angel over the Judge's grave. This had been a naked granite cherub that the old man had seen in the city one day in a tombstone store window. He had been taken with it at once, partly because its face reminded him of his wife and partly because he wanted a genuine work of art over his grave. He had come home with it sitting on the green plush train seat beside him. Mrs. McIntyre had never noticed the resemblance to herself. She had always thought it hideous but when the Herrins stole it off the old man's grave, she was shocked and outraged. Mrs. Herrin had thought it very pretty and had walked to the graveyard frequently to see it, and when the Herrins left the angel left with them, all but its toes, for the ax old man Herrin had used to break it off had struck slightly too high. Mrs. McIntyre had never been able to afford to have it replaced.

When she had cried all she could, she got up and went into the back hall, a closet-like space that was dark and quiet as a chapel and sat down on the edge of the Judge's black mechanical chair with her elbow on his desk. This was a giant roll-top piece of furniture pocked with pigeon holes full of dusty papers. Old bankbooks and ledgers were stacked in the half-open drawers and there was a small safe, empty but locked, set like a tabernacle in the center of it. She had left this part of the house unchanged since the old man's time. It was a kind of memorial to him, sacred because he had conducted his business here. With the slightest tilt one way or the other, the chair gave a rusty skeletal groan that sounded something like him when he had complained of his poverty. It had been his first principle to talk as if he were the poorest man in the world and she followed it, not only because he had but because it was true. When she sat with her intense constricted face turned toward the empty safe, she knew there was nobody poorer in the world than she was.

She sat motionless at the desk for ten or fifteen minutes and then as if she had gained some strength, she got up and got in her car and drove to the cornfield.

The road ran through a shadowy pine thicket and ended on top of a hill that rolled fan-wise down and up again in a broad expanse of tassled green. Mr. Guizac was cutting from the outside of the field in a circular path to the center where the graveyard was all but hidden by the corn, and she could see him on the high far side of the slope, mounted on the tractor with the cutter and wagon behind him. From time to time, he had to get off the tractor and climb in the wagon to spread the silage because the Negro had not arrived. She watched impatiently, standing in front of her black coupe with her arms folded under her smock, while he progressed slowly around the rim of the field, gradually getting close enough for her to wave to him to get down. He stopped the machine and jumped off and came running forward, wiping his red jaw with a piece of grease rag.

"I want to talk to you," she said and beckoned him to the edge of the thicket where it was shady. He took off the cap and followed her, smiling, but his smile faded when she turned and faced him. Her eyebrows, thin and fierce as a spider's leg, had drawn together ominously and the deep vertical pit had plunged down from under the red bangs into the bridge of her nose. She removed the bent picture from her pocket and handed it to him silently. Then she stepped back and said, "Mr. Guizac! You would bring this poor innocent child over here and try to marry her to a half-witted thieving black stinking nigger! What kind of a monster are you!"

He took the photograph with a slowly returning smile. "My cousin," he said. "She twelve here. First Communion. Six-ten now."

Monster! she said to herself and looked at him as

if she were seeing him for the first time. His forehead and skull were white where they had been protected by his cap but the rest of his face was red and bristled with yellow short hairs. His eyes were like two bright nails behind the gold-rimmed spectacles that had been mended over the nose with haywire. His whole face looked as if it might have been patched together out of several others. "Mr. Guizac," she said, beginning slowly and then speaking faster until she ended breathless in the middle of a word, "that nigger cannot have a white wife from Europe. You can't talk to a nigger that way. You'll excite him and besides it can't be done. Maybe it can be done in Poland but it can't be done here and you'll have to stop. It's all foolishness. That nigger don't have a grain of sense and you'll excite . . ."

"She in camp three year," he said.

"Your cousin," she said in a positive voice, "cannot come over here and marry one of my Negroes."

"She six-ten year," he said. "From Poland. Mamma die, pappa die. She wait in camp. Three camp." He pulled a wallet from his pocket and fingered through it and took out another picture of the same girl, a few years older, dressed in something dark and shapeless. She was standing against a wall with a short woman who apparently had no teeth. "She mamma," he said, pointing to the woman. "She die in two camp."

"Mr. Guizac," Mrs. McIntyre said, pushing the picture back at him, "I will not have my niggers upset. I cannot run this place without my niggers. I can run it without you but not without them and if you mention this girl to Sulk again, you won't have a job with me. Do you understand?"

His face showed no comprehension. He seemed to be piecing all these words together in his mind to make a thought.

Mrs. McIntyre remembered Mrs. Shortley's words: "He understands everything, he only pretends he don't so as to do exactly as he pleases," and her face regained the look of shocked wrath she had begun with. "I cannot understand how a man who calls himself a Christian," she said, "could bring a poor innocent girl over here and marry her to something like that. I cannot understand it. I cannot!" And she shook her head and looked into the distance with a pained blue gaze.

After a second he shrugged and let his arms drop as if he were tired. "She no care black," he said. "She in camp three year."

Mrs. McIntyre felt a peculiar weakness behind her knees. "Mr. Guizac," she said, "I don't want to have to speak to you about this again. If I do, you'll have to find another place yourself. Do you understand?"

The patched face did not say. She had the impression that he didn't see her there. "This is my place," she said. "I say who will come here and who won't."

"Ya," he said and put back on his cap.

"I am not responsible for the world's misery," she said as an afterthought.

"Ya," he said.

"You have a good job. You should be grateful to be here," she added, "but I'm not sure you are."

"Ya," he said and gave his little shrug and turned back to the tractor.

She watched him get on and maneuver the machine into the corn again. When he had passed her and rounded the turn, she climbed to the top of the slope and stood with her arms folded and looked grimly over the field. "They're all the same," she muttered, "whether they come from Poland or Tennessee. I've handled Herrins and Ringfields and Shortleys and I can handle a Guizac," and she narrowed her gaze until it closed entirely around the diminishing figure on the tractor as if she were watching him through a gunsight. All her life she had been fighting the world's overflow and now she had it in the form of a Pole. "You're just like all the rest of them," she said, "— only smart and thrifty and energetic but so am I. And this is my place," and she stood there, a small black-hatted, black-smocked figure with an aging cherubic face, and folded her arms as if she were equal to anything. But her heart was beating as if some interior violence had already been done to her. She opened her eyes to include the whole field so that the figure on the tractor was no larger than a grasshopper in her widened view.

She stood there for some time. There was a slight breeze and the corn trembled in great waves on both sides of the slope. The big cutter, with its monotonous roar, continued to shoot it pulverized into the wagon in a steady spurt of fodder. By nightfall, the Displaced Person would have worked his way around and around until there would be nothing on either side of the two hills but the stubble, and down in the center, risen like a little island, the graveyard where the Judge lay grinning under his desecrated monument.

III

The priest with his long bland face supported on one finger, had been talking for ten minutes about Purgatory while Mrs. McIntyre squinted furiously at him from an opposite chair. They were drinking ginger ale on her front porch and she kept rattling the ice in her glass, rattling her beads, rattling her bracelet like an impatient pony jingling its harness. There is no moral obligation to keep him, she was saying under her breath, there is absolutely no moral obligation. Suddenly she lurched up and her voice fell across his brogue like a drill into a mechanical saw. "Listen," she said, "I'm not theological. I'm practical! I want to talk to you about something practical!"

"Arrrrrrr," he groaned, grating to a halt.

She had put at least a finger of whiskey in her own ginger ale so that she would be able to endure his full-length visit and she sat down awkwardly, finding the chair closer to her than she had expected. "Mr. Guizac is not satisfactory," she said.

The old man raised his eyebrows in mock wonder.

"He's extra," she said. "He doesn't fit in. I have to have somebody who fits in."

The priest carefully turned his hat on his knees. He had a little trick of waiting a second silently and then swinging the conversation back into his own paths. He was about eighty. She had never known a priest until she had gone to see this one on the business of getting her the Displaced Person. After he had got her the Pole, he had used the business introduction to try to convert her—just as she had supposed he would.

"Give him time," the old man said. "He'll learn to fit in. Where is that beautiful birrrrd of yours?" he asked and then said, "Arrrrr, I see him!" and stood up and looked out over the lawn where the peacock and the two hens were stepping at a strained attention, their long necks ruffled, the cock's violent blue and the hens' silver-green, glinting in the late afternoon sun.

"Mr. Guizac," Mrs. McIntyre continued, bearing down with a flat steady voice, "is very efficient. I'll admit that. But he doesn't understand how to get on with my niggers and they don't like him. I can't have my niggers run off. And I don't like his attitude. He's not the least grateful for being here."

The priest had his hand on the screen door and he opened it, ready to make his escape. "Arrrr, I must be off," he murmured.

"I tell you if I had a white man who understood the Negroes, I'd have to let Mr. Guizac go," she said and stood up again.

He turned then and looked her in the face. "He has nowhere to go," he said. Then he said, "Dear lady, I know you well enough to know you wouldn't turn him out for a trifle!" and without waiting for an answer, he raised his hand and gave her his blessing in a rumbling voice.

She smiled angrily and said, "I didn't create this situation, of course."

The priest let his eyes wander toward the birds.

They had reached the middle of the lawn. The cock stopped suddenly and curving his neck backwards, he raised his tail and spread it with a shimmering timbrous noise. Tiers of small pregnant suns floated in a green-gold haze over his head. The priest stood transfixed, his jaw slack. Mrs. McIntyre wondered where she had ever seen such an idiotic old man. "Christ will come like that!" he said in a loud gay voice and wiped his hand over his mouth and stood there, gaping.

Mrs. McIntyre's face assumed a set puritanical expression and she reddened. Christ in the conversation embarrassed her the way sex had her mother. "It is not my responsibility that Mr. Guizac has nowhere to go," she said. "I don't find myself responsible for all the extra people in the world."

The old man didn't seem to hear her. His attention was fixed on the cock who was taking minute steps backwards, his head against the spread tail. "The Transfiguration," he murmured.

She had no idea what he was talking about. "Mr. Guizac didn't have to come here in the first place," she said, giving him a hard look.

The cock lowered his tail and began to pick grass.

"He didn't have to come in the first place," she repeated, emphasizing each word.

The old man smiled. "He came to redeem us," he said and blandly reached for her hand and shook it and said he must go.

If Mr. Shortley had not returned a few weeks later, she would have gone out looking for a new man to hire. She had not wanted him back but when she saw the familiar black automobile drive up the road and stop by the side of the house, she had the feeling that she was the one returning, after a long miserable trip, to her own place. She realized all at once that it was Mrs. Shortley she had been missing. She had had no one to talk to since Mrs. Shortley left, and she ran to the door, expecting to see her heaving herself up the steps.

Mr. Shortly stood there alone. He had on a black felt hat and a shirt with red and blue palm trees designed in it but the hollows in his long bitten blistered face were deeper than they had been a month ago.

"Well!" she said. "Where is Mrs. Shortley?"

Mr. Shortley didn't say anything. The change in his face seemed to have come from the inside; he looked like a man who had gone for a long time without water. "She was God's own angel," he said in a loud voice. "She was the sweetest woman in the world."

"Where is she?" Mrs. McIntyre murmured.

"Daid," he said. "She had herself a stroke on the day she left out of here." There was a corpse-like composure about his face. "I figure that Pole killed her," he said. "She seen through him from the first. She known he come from the devil. She told me so."

It took Mrs. McIntyre three days to get over Mrs. Shortley's death. She told herself that anyone would have thought they were kin. She rehired Mr. Shortley to do farm work though actually she didn't want him without his wife. She told him she was going to give thirty days' notice to the Displaced Person at the end of the month and that then he could have his job back in the dairy. Mr. Shortley preferred the dairy job but he was willing to wait. He said it would give him some satisfaction to see the Pole leave the place, and Mrs. McIntyre said it would give her a great deal of satisfaction. She confessed that she should have been content with the help she had in the first place and not have been reaching into other parts of the world for it. Mr. Shortley said he never had cared for foreigners since he had been in the first world's war and seen what they were like. He said he had seen all kinds then but that none of them were like us. He said he recalled the face of one man who had thrown a hand-grenade at him and that the man had little round eye-glasses exactly like Mr. Guizac's.

"But Mr. Guizac is a Pole, he's not a German," Mrs. McIntyre said.

"It ain't a great deal of difference in them two kinds," Mr. Shortley had explained.

The Negroes were pleased to see Mr. Shortley back. The Displaced Person had expected them to work as hard as he worked himself, whereas Mr. Shortley recognized their limitations. He had never been a very good worker himself with Mrs. Shortley to keep him in line, but without her, he was even more forgetful and slow. The Pole worked as fiercely as ever and seemed to have no inkling that he was about to be fired. Mrs. McIntyre saw jobs done in a short time that she had thought would never get done at all. Still she was resolved to get rid of him. The sight of his small stiff figure moving quickly here and there had come to be the most irritating sight on the place for her, and she felt she had been tricked by the old priest. He had said there was no legal obligation for her to keep the Displaced Person if he was not satisfactory, but then he had brought up the moral one.

She meant to tell him that *her* moral obligation was to her own people, to Mr. Shortley, who had fought in the world war for his country and not to Mr. Guizac who had merely arrived here to take advantage of whatever he could. She felt she must have this out with the priest before she fired the Displaced Person, When the first of the month came and the priest hadn't called, she put off giving the Pole notice for a little longer.

Mr. Shortley told himself that he should have known all along that no woman was going to do what she said she was when she said she was. He didn't know how long he could afford to put up with her shilly-shallying. He thought himself that she was going soft and was afraid to turn the Pole out for fear he would have a hard time getting another place. He could tell her the truth about this: that if she let him go, in three years he would own his own house and have a television aerial sitting on top of it. As a matter of policy, Mr. Shortley began to come to her back door every evening to put certain facts before her. "A white man sometimes don't get the consideration a nigger gets," he said, "but that don't matter because he's still white, but sometimes," and here he would pause and look off in the distance, "a man that's fought and bled and died in the service of his native land don't get the consideration of one of them like them he was fighting. I ast you: is that right?" When he asked her such questions he could watch her face and tell he was making an impression. She didn't look too well these days. He noticed lines around her eyes that hadn't been there when he and Mrs. Shortley had been the only white help on the place. Whenever he thought of Mrs. Shortley, he felt his heart go down like an old bucket into a dry well.

The old priest kept away as if he had been frightened by his last visit but finally, seeing that the Displaced Person had not been fired, he ventured to call again to take up giving Mrs. McIntyre instructions where he remembered leaving them off. She had not asked to be instructed but he instructed anyway, forcing a little definition of one of the sacraments or of some dogma into each conversation he had, no matter with whom. He sat on her porch, taking no notice of her partly mocking, partly outraged expression as she sat shaking her foot, waiting for an opportunity to drive a wedge into his talk. "For," he was saying, as if he spoke of something that had happened yesterday in town, "when God sent his Only Begotten Son, Jesus Christ, Our Lord"—he slightly bowed his head—"as a Redeemer to mankind, He . . ."

"Father Flynn!" she said in a voice that made him jump. "I want to talk to you about something serious!"

The skin under the old man's right eye flinched.

"As far as I'm concerned," she said and glared

at him fiercely, "Christ was just another D.P."

He raised his hands slightly and let them drop on his knees. "Arrrrrr," he murmured as if he were considering this.

"I'm going to let that man go," she said. "I don't have any obligation to him. My obligation is to the people who've done something for their country, not to the ones who've just come over to take advantage of what they can get." And she began to talk rapidly, remembering all her arguments. The priest's attention seemed to retire to some private oratory to wait until she got through. Once or twice his gaze roved out onto the lawn as if he were hunting some means of escape but she didn't stop. She told him she had been hanging onto this place for thirty years, always just barely making it against people who came from nowhere and were going nowhere, who didn't want anything but an automobile. She said she had found out they were the same whether they came from Poland or Tennessee. When the Guizacs got ready, she said, they would not hesitate to leave her. She told him how the people who looked rich were the poorest of all because they had the most to keep up. She asked him how he thought she paid her feed bills. She told him she would like to have her house done over but she couldn't afford it. She couldn't even afford to have the monument restored over her husband's grave. She asked him if he would like to guess what her insurance amounted to for the year. Finally she asked him if he thought she was made of money and the old man suddenly let out a great ugly bellow as if this were a comical question.

When the visit was over, she felt let down, though she had clearly triumphed over him. She made up her mind now that on the first of the month, she would give the Displace Person his thirty days' notice and she told Mr. Shortley so.

Mr. Shortley didn't say anything. His wife had been the only woman he was ever acquainted with who was never scared off from doing what she said. She said the Pole had been sent by the devil and the priest. Mr. Shortley had no doubt that the priest had got some peculiar control over Mrs. McIntyre and that before long she would start attending his Masses. She looked as if something was wearing her down from the inside. She was thinner and more fidgety, and not as sharp as she used to be. She would look at a milk can now and not see how dirty it was and he had seen her lips move when she was not talking. The Pole never did anything the wrong way but all the same he was very irritating to her. Mr. Shortley himself did things as he pleased—not always her way—but she

didn't seem to notice. She had noticed though that the Pole and all his family were getting fat; she pointed out to Mr. Shortley that the hollows had come out of his cheeks and that they saved every cent they made. "Yes'm, and one of these days he'll be able to buy and sell you out," Mr. Shortley had ventured to say, and he could tell that the statement had shaken her.

"I'm just waiting for the first," she had said.

Mr. Shortley waited too and the first came and went and she didn't fire him. He could have told anybody how it would be. He was not a violent man but he hated to see a woman done in by a foreigner. He felt that that was one thing a man couldn't stand by and see happen.

There was no reason Mrs. McIntyre should not fire Mr. Guizac at once but she put it off from day to day. She was worried about her bills and about her health. She didn't sleep at night or when she did she dreamed about the Displaced Person. She had never discharged anyone before; they had all left her. One night she dreamed that Mr. Guizac and his family were moving into her house and that she was moving in with Mr. Shortley. This was too much for her and she woke up and didn't sleep again for several nights; and one night she dreamed that the priest came to call and droned on and on saying, "Dear lady, I know your tender heart won't suffer you to turn the porrrrr man out. Think of the thousands of them, think of the ovens and the boxcars and the camps and the sick children and Christ Our Lord."

"He's extra and he's upset the balance around here," she said, "and I'm a logical practical woman and there are no ovens here and no camps and no Christ Our Lord and when he leaves, he'll make more money. He'll work at the mill and buy a car and don't talk to me—all they want is a car."

"The ovens and the boxcars and the sick children," droned the priest, "and our dear Lord."

"Just one too many," she said.

The next morning, she made up her mind while she was eating her breakfast that she would give him his notice at once, and she stood up and walked out of the kitchen and down the road with her table napkin still in her hand. Mr. Guizac was spraying the barn, standing in his swaybacked way with one hand on his hip. He turned off the hose and gave her an impatient kind of attention as if she were interfering with his work. She had not thought of what she would say to him, she had merely come. She stood in the barn door, looking severely at the wet spotless floor and the dripping stanchions. "Ya goot?" he said.

"Mr. Guizac," she said, "I can barely meet my

obligations now." Then she said in a louder, stronger voice, emphasizing each word, "I have bills to pay."

"I too," Mr. Guizac said. "Much, bills, little money," and he shrugged.

At the other end of the barn, she saw a long beak-nosed shadow glide like a snake halfway up the sunlit open door and stop; and somewhere behind her, she was aware of a silence where the sound of the Negroes shoveling had come a minute before. "This is my place," she said angrily. "All of you are extra. Each and every one of you are extra!"

"Ya," Mr. Guizac said and turned on the hose again.

She wiped her mouth with the napkin she had in her hand and walked off, as if she accomplished what she came for.

Mr. Shortley's shadow withdrew from the door and he leaned against the side of the barn and lit half a cigarette that he took out of his pocket. There was nothing for him to do now but wait on the hand of God to strike, but he knew one thing; he was not going to wait with his mouth shut.

Starting that morning, he began to complain and to state his side of the case to every person he saw, black or white. He complained in the grocery store and at the courthouse and on the street corner and directly to Mrs. McIntyre herself, for there was nothing underhanded about him. If the Pole could have understood what he had to say, he would have said it to him too. "All men was created free and equal," he said to Mrs. McIntyre, "and I risked my life and limb to prove it. Gone over there and fought and bled and died and come back on over here and find out who's got my job—just exactly who I been fighting. It was a hand-grenade come that near to killing me and I seen who throwed it—little man with eye-glasses just like his. Might have bought them at the same store. Small world," and he gave a bitter little laugh. Since he didn't have Mrs. Shortley to do the talking any more, he had started doing it himself and had found that he had a gift for it. He had the power of making other people see his logic. He talked a good deal to the Negroes.

"Whyn't you go back to Africa?" he asked Sulk one morning as they were cleaning out the silo. "That's your country, ain't it?"

"I ain't going there," the boy said. "They might eat me up."

"Well, if you behave yourself it isn't any reason you can't stay here," Mr. Shortley said kindly. "Because you didn't run away from nowhere. Your granddaddy was bought. He didn't have a thing to do with coming. It's the people that run away from where they come from that I ain't got any use for."

"I never felt no need to travel," the Negro said.

"Well," Mr. Shortley said, "if I was going to travel again, it would be to either China or Africa. You go to either of them two places and you can tell right away what the difference is between you and them. You go to these other places and the only way you can tell is if they say something. And then you can't always tell because about half of them know the English language. That's where we make our mistake," he said. "—letting all them people onto English. There'd be a heap less trouble if everybody only knew his own language. My wife said knowing two languages was like having eyes in the back of your head. You couldn't put nothing over on her."

"You sho couldn't," the boy muttered, and then he added, "She was fine. She was sho fine. I never known a finer white woman than her."

Mr. Shortley turned in the opposite direction and worked silently for a while. After a few minutes he leaned up and tapped the colored boy on the shoulder with the handle of his shovel. For a second he only looked at him while a great deal of meaning gathered in his wet eyes. Then he said softly, " Revenge is mine, saith the Lord."

Mrs. McIntyre found that everybody in town knew Mr. Shortley's version of her business and that everyone was critical of her conduct. She began to understand that she had a moral obligation to fire the Pole and that she was shirking it because she found it hard to do. She could not stand the increasing guilt any longer and on a cold Saturday morning, she started off after breakfast to fire him. She walked down to the machine shed where she heard him cranking up the tractor.

There was a heavy frost on the ground that made the fields look like the rough backs of sheep; the sun was almost silver and the woods stuck up like dry bristles on the sky line. The countryside seemed to be receding from the little circle of noise around the shed. Mr. Guizac was squatting on the ground beside the small tractor, putting in a part. Mrs. McIntyre hoped to get the fields turned over while he still had thirty days to work for her. The colored boy was standing by with some tools in his hand and Mr. Shortley was under the shed about to get up on the large tractor and back it out. She meant to wait until he and the Negro got out of the way before she began her unpleasant duty.

She stood watching Mr. Guizac, stamping her feet on the hard ground, for the cold was climbing like a paralysis up her feet and legs. She had on a heavy black coat and a red head-kerchief with her black hat pulled down on top of it to keep the glare out of her eyes. Under the black brim her face had an abstracted look and once or twice her lips moved silently. Mr. Guizac shouted over the noise of the tractor for the Negro to hand him a screwdriver and when he got it, he turned over on his back on the icy ground and reached under the machine. She could not see his face, only his feet and legs and trunk sticking impudently out from the side of the tractor. He had on rubber boots that were cracked and splashed with mud. He raised one knee and then lowered it and turned himself slightly. Of all the things she resented about him, she resented most that he hadn't left on his own accord.

Mr. Shortley had got on the large tractor and was backing it out from under the shed. He seemed to be warmed by it as if its heat and strength sent impulses up through him that he obeyed instantly. He had headed it toward the small tractor but he braked it on a slight incline and jumped off and turned back toward the shed. Mrs. McIntyre was looking fixedly at Mr. Guizac's legs lying flat on the ground now. She heard the brake on the large tractor slip and, looking up, she saw it move forward, calculating its own path. Later she remembered that she had seen the Negro jump silently out of the way as if a spring in the earth had released him and that she had seen Mr. Shortley turn his head with incredible slowness and stare silently over his shoulder and that she had started to shout to the Displaced Person but that she had not. She had felt her eyes and Mr. Shortley's eyes and the Negro's eyes come together in one look that froze them in collusion forever, and she had heard the little noise the Pole made as the tractor wheel broke his backbone. The two men ran forward to help and she fainted.

She remembered, when she came to, running somewhere, perhaps into the house and out again but she could not remember what for or if she had fainted again when she got there. When she finally came back to where the tractors were, the ambulance had arrived. Mr. Guizac's body was covered with the bent bodies of his wife and two children and by a black one which hung over him, murmuring words she didn't understand. At first she thought this must be the doctor but then with a feeling of annoyance she recognized the priest, who had come with the ambulance and was slipping something into the crushed man's mouth. After a minute he stood up and she looked first at his bloody pants legs and then at his face which was not averted from her but was as withdrawn and expressionless as the rest of the countryside. She only stared at him for she was too shocked by her experience to be quite herself. Her mind was not taking hold of all that was happening. She felt she was in some foreign country where the people bent over the body were natives, and she watched like a stranger while the dead man was carried away in the ambulance.

That evening, Mr. Shortley left without notice to look for a new position and the Negro, Sulk, was taken with a sudden desire to see more of the world and set off for the southern part of the state. The old man Astor could not work without company. Mrs. McIntyre hardly noticed that she had no help left for she came down with a nervous affliction and had to go to the hospital. When she came back, she saw that the place would be too much for her to run now and she turned her cows over to a professional auctioneer (who sold them at a loss) and retired to live on what she had, while she tried to save her declining health. A numbness developed in one of her legs and her hands and head began to jiggle and eventually she had to stay in bed all the time with only a colored woman to wait on her. Her eyesight grew steadily worse and she lost her voice altogether. Not many people remembered to come out to the country to see her except the old priest. He came regularly once a week with a bag of breadcrumbs and, after he had fed these to the peacock, he would come in and sit by the side of her bed and explain the doctrines of the Church. ■

Making Connections through Discussion and Writing

1. a. O'Connor often focused on the spiritual pride of her characters. In this story she presents at least two characters that manifest this kind of pride. Who are they?

    _____

    _____

    b. Underline passages or images that reveal their pride.

2. a. The priest, Mrs. McIntyre, and Mrs. Shortley comment on the peacock. Explain what their comments reveal about themselves and their moral perceptions.

    the priest

    _____

    _____

    _____

    Mrs. McIntyre

    _____

    _____

    _____

    Mrs. Shortley

    _____

    _____

    _____

    b. Describe how O'Connor uses the priest's comments to suggest that reality can be perceived as having levels of meaning.

    _____

    _____

    _____

    _____

3. a. Identify which characters' attitudes the narrator is reflecting in the following statements:

    "But with foreigners on the place, with people who were all eyes and no understanding, who had come from a place continually fighting, where the religion had not been reformed—with this kind of people, you had to be on the lookout every minute."

    _____

"His forehead and skull were white where they had been protected by his cap but the rest of his face was red and bristled with short yellow hairs. His eyes were like two bright nails behind his gold-rimmed spectacles that had been mended over the nose with haywire. His whole face looked as if it might have been patched together out of several others."

b. Explain how O'Connor uses her narrative voice in these passages, and describe the effect this narrator has on the reader's perception of the story.

_____

_____

_____

_____

_____

4. List at least four characters, either directly in the story or alluded to, who are "displaced." Describe the various ways they can be viewed as being displaced.

_____

_____

_____

_____

_____

_____

_____

_____

_____

_____

_____

_____

5. How do the Black farm workers' attitudes contrast with those of Mrs. Shortley and Mrs. McIntyre?

_____

_____

_____

_____

_____

a. How can they also be seen as "displaced" by the end of the story?

_____

_____

_____

6. a. Mrs. McIntyre says of Mr. Guizac, "That man is my salvation." Explain why this statement is perceived by the reader as being ironic.

   _____
   _____
   _____
   _____

   b. What do you think O'Connor is suggesting by this comment?

   _____
   _____
   _____
   _____

7. a. List Mrs. Shortley's visions.

   _____
   _____
   _____

   b. Discuss her interpretation of her visions and prophecy.

   _____
   _____
   _____
   _____
   _____

   c. Write a paragraph in which you describe Mrs. Shortley's prophecy. Discuss how her own life and death may be seen as fulfilling her prophecy.

   _____
   _____
   _____
   _____
   _____
   _____
   _____
   _____
   _____
   _____

8. a. Put brackets around the dialogue between the priest and Mrs. McIntyre that shows how their separate perceptions preclude their understanding each other.

   b. How does this dialogue produce an ironic effect for the reader?

   _____
   _____
   _____
   _____

c.   How does it suggest the symbolic function of the displaced person?

_____

_____

_____

_____

_____

_____

9.   a.   Identify the two Christ figures in the story.

_____

_____

_____

_____

_____

_____

b.   How do Mrs. McIntyre's actions toward them reveal her spiritual pride and blindness?

_____

_____

_____

_____

_____

_____

_____

Vigen Guroian
The Iconographic Fiction of Flannery O'Connor

In the essay below, Vigen Guroian presents a clear exposition of Flannery O'Connor's artistic intention as a Christian fiction writer. He explains how her vision and artistry are grounded in the Christian doctrine of the Incarnation and how her stories serve as icons to reveal the force of divine grace to her readers. Particular attention is given to the stories "The Enduring Chill" and "Parker's Back." Guroian's discussion is a model of a critical approach that probes the literal level of a story to gain insight into its symbolic and spiritual meanings.

Vocabulary . . . .

denouement	*kenosis*
Docetism	mandarins
double entendre	Manicheanism
Ecumenical	mastisis
ennui	plethora
furtive	proleptically
gnostic	wraiths
hubris	

"What the word says, the image shows silently; what we have heard, we have seen." That is how the Seventh Great Ecumenical Council held at Constantinople in 787 summarized its defense of the use of icons in Christian worship. What the council confessed to have heard from scripture and to believe is that God became man in Jesus Christ. According to the Gospel of John "the Word became flesh and dwelt among us, and we have seen his glory, the glory as of the only begotten of the Father, full of grace and truth" (John 1:13-14). Through an act of unfathomable *kenosis*, humility and love, the infinite had become finite, the uncircumscribable was circumscribed in a human being, and the invisible was made visible. In so far as the divine Word, the Only Begotten Son of the Father, had become flesh and took the body of a man, he and the saints could be painted on wood or represented in mosaic or mural art. The Old Testament prohibition against images had been lifted by God himself.

Flannery O'Connor did not use paint to make icons; however, she was an "iconographer" with words. For she embraced the Incarnation with utter seriousness in her life and in her fiction. To her close friend whom we know in the correspondence only as "A," she writes in September of 1955, "God became not only a man, but Man. This is the mystery of Redemption."[1] Some years later, in another letter to "A," O'Connor explains how this belief in the Incarnation ran up against the secularity of her audience as she was challenged to lend fresh expression to the Christian vision of life.

> The setting in which most modern fiction takes place is exactly a setting in which nothing is so little felt to be true as the reality of a faith in Christ. I know what you mean here but you haven't said what you mean. Fiction may deal with faith implicitly but explicitly it deals only with faith-in-a-person, or persons. What must be

From *The Intercollegiate Review*, Fall/Spring 2001, volume 36, no. 1-2 by Vigen Guroian. Copyright © 2001 by The Intercollegiate Review. Reprinted by permission.

unquestionable is what is implicitly implied as the author's attitude, and to do this the writer has to succeed in making the divinity of Christ seem consistent with the structure of all reality. This has to be got across implicitly in spite of a world that doesn't feel it, in spite of characters that don't live it.[2]

The ancient defenders of icons said essentially the same about paintings and the Incarnation. The icon made the divinity of Christ seem consistent with the structure of all reality, and most especially human existence. Icons of Christ and the saints testified to the real potential of human life, exceeding even the highest expectations of pagan humanism. God became man and made it possible for man to become God—not, of course, by nature God, but most assuredly by grace that transfigures life. The Incarnation made it possible for all believers in Jesus Christ "to be partakers of the divine nature" (2 Peter 1:4). Christian humanism introduced the ideas of Creation, Incarnation, and the sanctification of life while at the same time rejecting the strong prejudice of Hellenic culture that spirit is opposed to matter and that, therefore, God, who is spirit, would never enter the material world. In light of the Incarnation and bodily Resurrection and Ascension of Jesus Christ, human salvation could no longer be thought of as an escape of the captive soul from the prison of the body. The early church condemned as heresies Docetism and Manicheanism, two gnostic movements within Christianity, precisely because they embraced this dualism of matter and spirit. In her day, Flannery O'Connor combatted what she viewed as modern reincarnations of these ancient gnostic heresies. She detected the gnosticism in currents of contemporary spirituality that thrived even within the Christian churches. In her essay "The Nature and Aim of Fiction," O'Connor names the enemy:

> The Manicheans separated spirit and matter. To them all material things were evil. They sought pure spirit and tried to approach the infinite directly without any mediation of matter. This is also pretty much the modern spirit, and for the sensibility infected with it, fiction is hard if not impossible to write because fiction is so very much an incarnational art.[3]

This passage needs some explanation. After all, aren't moderns materialists? And yet O'Connor seems to maintain that contemporary people value material things less than spiritual reality. How is she able to say this in the face of society's massive appetite for material goods and obsession with the body and sex? O'Connor does not dispute this description of modern tastes and behavior. But she does point to a two-fold irony in it. First, this much-discussed and depicted sex is radically devalued sex—not that it is reduced to mere animal sex. Human sexuality is thoroughly permeated by spirit and always transcends mere instinct. Rather, modern sex is either trivialized by sentimentality or distorted into obscenity and pornography. Sentimentalized sex leaps over sin to "a mock state of innocence." Obscenity (and pornography) is also "essentially sentimental, for it leaves out the connection of sex with its hard purpose, and so far disconnects it from the meaning in life as to make it simply an experience for its own sake."[4] Sentimentalized and romanticized sex ultimately devalues the body, as it views the body as merely an instrument of the self, not constitutive of it. This frequently leads to alienation, *ennui*, and boredom. As for materialism and consumerism, the objects with which contemporary people clutter their lives do not satisfy their need for a meaningful life. The mandarins of marketing and advertising know this. So they constantly fuel this dissatisfaction and inflame the acquisitive spirit with incessant promises that the next purchase will quench the craving.

Thus, when modern people turn to religion, they often look for release from this syndrome, in flight from the body and materialism to peace of mind by the quickest means available. A plethora of mysticisms, transcendental religions, and new age spiritualities compete for the attention of the people. O'Connor writes: "Today's reader, if he believes in grace at all, sees it as something which can be separated from nature and served to him raw as instant Uplift."[5] As Frederick Asals has observed so wisely in his study of O'Connor's craft: "The central thrust in all of Flannery O'Connor's later fiction is to explode this . . . escapism or pseudotranscendence by insisting again and again that existence can only be *in* the body, *in* matter, whatever the horrors that may entail."[6] Even this astute assessment falls short of naming all that is at stake for O'Connor in her defense of incarnate being. Nature does not end in orgasm, a full stomach, or owning a late model luxury vehicle. Nature is both a window into and a path to the supernatural. O'Connor understands the special challenges that a secular age poses for a writer of fiction with orthodox Christian convictions and a sacramental vision of life. Even the "average Catholic reader" is smitten with the gnostic spirit, she observes. "By separating nature and grace as much as possible, he has reduced his conception of the supernatural to pious cliché"[7] and nature is emptied of grace. In a discussion of O'Connor's fiction, Peter S. Hawkins concludes that "what is distinctive about the modern era is that the conflict between nature and grace has been resolved by the elimination of the notion of grace altogether."[8] This may be an exaggeration. O'Connor did not believe that the modern person dismisses grace entirely. However, she does conclude that when modern people entertain grace as a possibility in their lives, they are inclined to think of it as a divine utility, not as a sacramental presence. Grace is an extra, alien ingredient added to nature by God, conjured up by priests and prayers, like gas pumped into an empty fuel tank—useful but not present under ordinary circumstances. What is more, this instrumentalist view of grace makes it "almost impossible to write about supernatural Grace," says O'Connor. Supernatural grace is not magic; it is not subject to human manipulation, or restricted to human needs. In an effort to impress this upon her readers, O'Connor says that in her fiction she approaches grace "almost negatively."[9] In practical terms this means that the majority of her protagonists strenuously resist the action of God upon them. The lesson they learn, often through suffering, is that grace is God's own free doing and can come upon anyone even in the face of his or her disbelief.

Although Thomas Aquinas and Catherine of Sienna may have helped shape her religious imagination, O'Connor felt acutely how different her location in life was from theirs. She recognized that the vast majority of people for whom she was writing lacked a vision of a unified world that comes from the hand of God, is fallen but redeemed by the Creator-Word, and is indwelt by the Holy Spirit. She assayed that only a small minority of her readers, and even fewer of her reviewers, shared her incarnational faith: even many Catholics did not take the Incarnation with deep seriousness as a rule for their lives or truly believe in the resurrection of the body. Nevertheless, O'Connor made it her task to show her readers that the world is surrounded by mystery and that the physical creation is itself an icon and a window into that mystery. In her essay "Novelist and Believer" she explains that the Christian novelist will reject the influence "of those Manichean-type theologies which . . . [see] the natural world as unworthy of penetration," because he knows that the infinite cannot be approached directly in his art. Rather, "he must penetrate the

natural human world as it is," without an ideological formula or hardened preconceptions of what lies behind it. "The more sacramental [the writer's] theology, the more encouragement he will get from it to do just that." With these prerequisites of belief the Christian writer of fiction seeks "to penetrate the concrete world"[10] with a confidence that he may catch a glimpse of, "the image of the source, the image of ultimate reality."[11]

Thus in Flannery O'Connor's stories, a pigpen momentarily becomes the place from whence Jacob's ladder reaches into the heavens and bears the saints upward; a line of tree tops may be experienced as the protecting wall of an Edenic garden sanctuary; and a water stain on a bedroom ceiling takes flight as a bird of pentecostal grace to cure one rebellious youth of his spiritual blindness. Much like the icon painter, O'Connor turns to inverted perspective and distorted form in order to impress upon her reader that the ordinary may be revelatory, that the natural bears the image of the supernatural. And like the icon painter, O'Connor's art is figural and typological. The images she paints with words and the mysteries that are revealed to her protagonists join the biblical world and its events with theirs, just as the iconographer paints his gospel scenes in such a manner that the Old Testament prefigurements of the New Testament events are gathered up in icons of Christ's birth and baptism or his transfiguration. In other words, for O'Connor fiction truly is an incarnational art.

Yet for these efforts, Flannery O'Connor was badly misunderstood. Her trouble was, as she well understood, that those who received her fiction lacked the biblical moorings and moral imagination to comprehend the true nature of her iconographic art. Modern interpreters of iconography have described the icon as primitive in one breath and idealistic in the next, not for once grasping its realism grounded in the Incarnation and revelation of transfigured life. When O'Connor first came on the scene, critics described her fiction as grotesque, and attributed to her the same metaphysical and moral dualism that she stood against. What possible respect could this writer have for the body when she routinely portrayed disfigured characters and, worse yet, put them through, what seemed to these critics, trials of gratuitous violence? They concluded that O'Connor was committed to the irreconcilableness of matter and spirit.

Hawkins sets the record straight, however, when he correctly observes that "the warfare she [O'Connor] wages is not, in fact, spirit against flesh, but rather, spirit *in* flesh. Her goal is not only to make it impossible to deny the sacred as present in the midst of the secular; it is to make it impossible to rest easy with any notion of secularity at all."[12] In her stories O'Connor describes a human drama in which flesh, in St. Paul's sense of *sarx* or sinful human nature, resists the action of grace by which God seeks to heal sin and destroy death. To her friend Cecil Dawkins, she states: "All human nature vigorously resists grace because grace changes us and the change is painful."[13] This, she insists, is as true for her readers as for the characters in her stories.

The psychosomatic unity of human personality and the Word's incarnation of this nature are the grounds of God's efforts to redeem the fallen creature that he has made in his own image. These are also the Christian truths that generate the drama of O'Connor's stories. Often her protagonists deny the divine image within them and resist God's redemptive purpose in their lives. In other words, they inveterately resist grace, until grace moves them to embrace the mystery of their existence within a revelation of divine meaning. In "The Enduring Chill," Asbury Fox is a young man filled with hubris and immersed in self-delusion about his talents as a writer. He rejects the Christian religion because he thinks it stands in the way of his artistic imagination and fulfillment as a writer. He says to a priest in the story, "God is an idea created by man" and "The artist prays by creating."[14] Asbury leaves his home on a country farm to live in New York City (the secular city) to make his mark on the literary world. But things do not go well for Asbury. He is not productive and he becomes ill.

His sickness weakens him so that he has no recourse but to return home to what he imagines will be his speedy demise. His sister Mary George, a principal of an elementary school and someone equally smitten with pride in her own intellect, sarcastically diagnoses Asbury's condition: "Asbury can't write so he gets sick,"[15] she quips. But Asbury's sickness is not just in his head. It is also genuinely physical. Later in the story, we learn that before leaving for the city, Asbury drank unpasteurized milk at the family farm in an unsuccessful attempt to make friends with two of the Negro workers. From this he contracts undulant fever, called "bangs" in cows, that causes painfully alternating chills and fevers in humans, though it is not fatal.

Asbury is one of O'Connor's modern gnostics, alienated from home and his own body, sick with the sin of pride, especially in his case intellectual hubris, and attracted to New Age sorts of mysticism that project man as his own savior and perfecter. Since childhood, Asbury has resisted that grace which is neither of his own conjuring nor in service to his selfish ways. A water stain on the ceiling above his bed is the sign of this grace that he resists. For as long as Asbury can remember, it has been there, taking the form of a fierce bird with icicles in its claws making ready to descend upon him. At the close of the story, Asbury lies in bed dreadfully sick but also aware that he is not going to die. "The old life in him [was] exhausted. He awaited the coming of a new." The fierce bird "appear[ed] all at once in motion," the Holy Ghost descended upon him, O'Connor announces, "emblazoned in ice instead of fire."[16]

"The Enduring Chill" is as complex a story as Flannery O'Connor penned, and we cannot touch upon all facets of its meaning. Several details in the story, however, point to its principal themes. Early in the story, O'Connor establishes that Asbury has a "peculiar" relationship to the bovine species. It is not just that he drinks their milk and gets sick. More important is the fact that although he is not a cow, he *can* get sick with a disease that *is* a cow disease. O'Connor reminds us that human beings share an animal nature with other creatures. During a car ride back to the farm, Asbury notices that "a small walleyed Guernsey . . . [is] watching him steadily as if she sense[s] some bond between them." With sardonic humor, O'Connor comments: "On the point of death, he found himself existing in a state of illumination that was totally out of keeping with the kind of talk he had to listen to from his mother. This was largely about cows with names like Daisy and Bessie Button and their intimate functions—their mastisis and their screw-worms and their abortions."[17]

Asbury's endeavors to practice an intellectual angelism are defeated. He wants to die, or more accurately, he wants to shed his body. But it is not his body, nor the bodies of the cows on the farm, that blocks his "illumination." A spiritual disease frustrates his creativity and prevents his happiness. "I think it is usually some form of self-inflation that destroys the free use of a gift," says O'Connor in one of her essays.[18] Ironically, the bird that descends upon him *is* a product of Asbury's own furtive imagination, suggesting that this young man's most creative period of life might lie ahead of him. He will live, and maybe even inherit the kingdom of God, in a physically diseased body but with humility, because "the last film of illusion . . . [has been] torn as if by a whirlwind from his eyes."[19]

Like the humanism of a Thomas More or a John Henry Newman, Flannery O'Connor's Christian humanism is grounded in an unwavering incarnational faith and sacramental vision. But faced with the modern temper, she chose a strategy that she gambled would shake the spiritual cataracts from her secular readers' eyes and open their vision to the operations of grace in the everyday world. In her essay "Novelist and Believer," she explains:

> When I write a novel in which the central action is a baptism, I am very well aware that for a majority of my readers, baptism is a meaningless rite, and so in my novel I have to see that this baptism carries enough awe and mystery to jar the reader into some kind of emotional recognition of its significance. To this end I have to bend the whole novel—its language, its structure, its action. I have to make the reader feel, in his bones if nowhere else, that something is going on here that counts. Distortion in this case is an instrument; exaggeration has a purpose, and the whole story or novel has been made what it is because of belief. This is not the kind of distortion that destroys; it is the kind that reveals, or should reveal.[20]

O'Connor does not limit herself, however, to the traditional sacraments to make her case. It is fitting that the last story she finished stands up as her most profound affirmation of the sanctity of our bodies as imprinted with the image of God and having a place of permanence in the redemptive purpose of God. For she completed "Parker's Back" in her hospital bed in defiance of her doctor's instructions not to press her own failing body any further. "Parker's Back" crowns the achievement of O'Connor's Christian humanism. In this story, she resoundingly rejects gnosticism and iconoclasm and shows that the Incarnation is the true source of lasting beauty, goodness, and truth. Without the slightest didacticism she builds the case that beauty and goodness are not ends in themselves but point to the Creator of those things in which they may be seen, enjoyed, and the truth known. Through a back country character, whom she describes "as ordinary as a loaf of bread"[21]—an only slightly disguised allusion to the bread of the Eucharist—she shows that divine truth is never an abstraction, but is always manifested concretely in the human being who praises God in his glory. Obadiah Elihue Parker is the opposite of Asbury Fox in almost every respect, except that like

Asbury he is driven by a desire for perfection. Asbury is an intellectual who thinks that he can create beauty and truth out of his own head, whereas Parker—for that is the name he goes by, since he is ashamed of his first and middle names—wants to wear beauty on his body. When O'Connor introduces us to him at the start of the story, Parker is twenty-eight years of age and has married a young woman named Sarah Ruth who is the daughter of a fundamentalist preacher. "They were married in the County Ordinary's office because Sarah Ruth thought churches were idolatrous."[22] But we have to be taken back to when Parker was fourteen years of age to fully understand what moves him throughout the story. In that year, at the fair, Parker set his eyes on a tattooed man whose entire body, from head to foot, was covered with images. O'Connor writes: "Until he saw the man at the fair, it did not enter his head that there was anything out of the ordinary about the fact that he existed." Parker does not exactly think these thoughts about mystery and life, for O'Connor makes it clear that he is a character moved more by instinct and emotion than by intellect. "It was as if a blind boy had been turned so gently in a different direction that he did not know his destination had been changed."[23]

Nevertheless, the course of Parker's life had been changed. For the first time, he entertained a vision of beauty. His search for God had begun. "The man, who was small and sturdy, moved on the platform, flexing his muscles so that the arabesque of men and beasts and flowers on his skin appeared to have a subtle motion of its own." From that moment on, Parker wanted the same for himself. He wanted to wear everything that there is on his body in bright color and beautiful design. He began to appropriate tattoos. But strangely, no tattoo kept him satisfied for very long; and "as the space on the front of him for tattoos decreased, his dissatisfaction grew and became general." No combination seemed to achieve the desired result. The overall effect was not the harmony of color and form and movement, the beauty Parker saw on the tattooed man, but "something haphazard and botched." Changing metaphor and perspective on human desire and the longing for happiness, O'Connor adds, "Hungry people made Parker nervous."[24]

When we meet Parker at the beginning of the story, his entire body is covered with tattoos, except for his back. "He had no desire for one anywhere he could not readily see it himself." Parker has no idea that he is being moved by and toward a profound theological truth. But through comic irony, O'Connor invites the reader to explore the serious notion that man is a microcosm of creation, that in the human being, whom God has created in his very own image, the whole universe reverberates. God intends that man be the custodian and priest of this creation, giving it order and blessing it to good use, even lending it his voice to glorify God. Once again, Parker does not think these things, but he does feel them, or more precisely, he "senses" them. It is revealed in his eyes, which O'Connor describes as "the same pale slate-color as the ocean and reflect[ing] the immense spaces around him as if they were a microcosm of the mysterious sea."[25]

To please his wife, for nothing seems to please her, especially not his tattoos, Parker is determined to have a tattoo done on his back that she will approve of. He is also moved by a "dissatisfaction [that] began to grow so great in Parker that there was no containing it outside of a tattoo. It had to be his back. There was no help for it." One day Parker crashes a tractor into a tree and sets it on fire. Immediately, he takes flight in his truck straight to the city fifty miles away where he visits the local tattoo artist. Parker is convinced that nothing short of a tattoo of God himself will please Sarah Ruth. He pages through a book of pictures of God and is caught by the "all-demanding eyes" of a Byzantine Christ, "as if he were being brought to life by a subtle power."[26] Parker is about to have himself inscribed by the image of him whom St. Paul calls the "express image" of God the Father and the archetypal image of our humanity. His earlier "skirmish" with the burning tree—an allusion to Moses' revelation on Sinai—signifies and foreshadows Parker's personal appropriation of the Incarnate God, inscribed on his own flesh.

In her description of Parker's crash into the tree that sends him on this mission to get tattooed one final time, O'Connor employs the ancient Christian double entendre of the sun and the Son of God. I have added the emphases to the text to highlight not only this use of the double entendre but also the other biblical allusions that she carefully plants within the scene.

> As he circled the field *his mind was on a suitable design for his back*. The *sun*, the size of a golfball, began to switch regularly from in front of him to behind him, but he appeared to see it both places *as if he had eyes in the back of his head*. All at once he saw the *tree* reaching out to grasp him: a ferocious thud propelled him into the air, and heard himself yelling in an unbelievably loud voice, 'GOD ABOVE!'

He landed on his *back* while the tractor crashed upside down into the *tree* and burst into *flame*. The first thing Parker saw were his *shoes* quickly eaten by fire. . . . He could feel the hot breath of the *burning tree* on his face. He scrambled backwards, still sitting, *his eyes cavernous* and if he had known how to *cross* himself he would have done it.[27]

Soon Parker will have "eyes in the back of his head," or more precisely on his back. His "cavernous" eyes mirror proleptically the eyes of the Byzantine icon of Christ. And the image of the burning tree anticipates the end of the story when Parker encounters another fiery tree that is his "cross."

We need to review briefly the action before this denouement. When he leaves the farm for the city, Parker has embarked on a transformative journey of discovery and revelation. When the tattoo artist taunts Parker, "Have you gone and got religion? Are you saved?" Parker objects, but his protestations seem "to leave his mouth like wraiths and to evaporate at once as if he never uttered them." On the way home, Parker stops at the local pool parlor where he is ridiculed when he shows off his tattoo. "O.E's got religion and is witnessing for Jesus." The locals throw him out of the building "as if the long barn like room were the ship from which Jonah had been cast into the sea." Like Jonah, Parker's resistance to his calling is to no avail. He is reminded once again that in some mysterious way he has become a follower of the One whose image he has had put on his back. "The eyes that were now forever on his back were eyes to be obeyed. He was as certain of it as he had ever been of anything." It is as if, like Jonah, Parker is driven to a foreign country where he truly comes to himself and completes his service to God. "It was as if he were himself but a stranger to himself, driving into a new country though everything he saw was familiar to him, even at night. "[28]

When Parker arrives at home just before dawn, the door is locked. He calls to Sarah Ruth. "A sharp voice close to the door said, 'Who's there?'" Parker answers, "O.E." "I don't know no O.E.," the voice answers. At that moment the sun comes up. "The sky had lighted slightly and there were two or three streaks of yellow floating above the horizon. Then as he stood there, a tree of light burst over the skyline." It is the lone pecan tree in the yard and Parker suddenly has an ecstatic religious experience: "He felt the light pouring through him, turning his spider web soul into a perfect arabesque of colors, a garden of trees, birds and beasts." This ecstatic moment is quickly extinguished, however, when Sarah Ruth expels him from their home. For when Parker uncovers his back and shows it to her, the results are not as he imagined. At first Sarah Ruth is confused. She does not recognize the face on his back. " It ain't no body I know,"[29] she says. Her words are packed with irony.

"It's him," Parker said.

"Him who?"

"God!" Parker cried.

"God? God don't look like that!"

"What do you know how he looks?" Parker moaned. "You ain't seen him."

"He don't *look*," Sarah Ruth said. "He's spirit. No man shall see his face. . . ."

> "Idolatry," Sarah Ruth screamed. "Idolatry. . . . I don't want no idolater in this house!" and she grabbed up the broom and began to thrash him across the shoulders with it . . . and large welts . . . formed on the face of the tattooed Christ. Then he staggered up and made for the door . . . still gripping [the broom] she looked toward the pecan tree and her eyes hardened still more. There he was—who called himself Obadiah Elihue—leaning against the tree, crying like a baby.[30]

The story ends this way. O'Connor gives it no full closure. The fate of this scourged and "crucified" figure is left unknown. But it seems clear that Parker has come to some deep subliminal understanding of the meaning of his name and the destiny it holds for him. Obadiah means "servant of God," which Parker has become, in spite of his aversion to God and religion. And Elihue means "God is he," with whom Parker has identified in the most intimate manner by carrying his image in his own flesh. What is more, Elihue is a variant of Elihu, who in the book of Job turns from explaining suffering as the result of human sin to interpreting it as part of the divine mystery of God's creation. Let us recall that Sarah Ruth as one writer said "sees his tattoos as 'vanity' and a sign of sinfulness, whereas to Parker they represent ineffable mystery." What is more, Parker signifies someone "whose home is a park, a walled garden like those in icons of the Expulsion from Paradise and of the New Jerusalem. Parker courted Sarah with apples and other fruit, an allusion to Eden."[31] When he arrives home at dawn, Parker imagines that he indeed has gotten to Eden. After being forced to repeat his full name Obadiah Elihue, he feels "the light pouring through him, turning his spider web soul into a perfect arabesque of colors, a garden of trees, and birds and beasts."

In *Voice of the Peacock*, Kathleen Feeley comments: "It seems strangely fitting that the story of a man led in mysterious ways to incarnate the Redeemer on his own body should be the final story of an author led by equally mysterious ways to make Redemption a reality in her fiction."[32] Feeley turns our attention back to the powerful incarnational vision that drove Flannery O'Connor's fiction and stood at the heart of her Christian humanism.

O'Connor's iconographic fiction was drawn out by the challenges to Christian orthodoxy that she felt compelled to answer. And "Parker's Back" in particular helps us to understand where and on what grounds she parts company with the fundamentalist religion of the South—a religion that on various occasions O'Connor said she otherwise stood beside as a Roman Catholic in opposition to the secular mind. Ironically, modern fundamentalism doesn't take the Incarnation seriously enough. It limits the limitless God to the written word and denies his presence in the physical creation. Sarah Ruth completely fails to detect God's presence in the drama that unfolds around her. She is unable to see the image of God in her husband and does not comprehend his participation in the suffering of Christ and redemptive victory on the cross. Could this be because she is a Christian gnostic? O'Connor leaves Sarah Ruth no better off in relation to God and humanity than the secular people she abhors. On another occasion, Flannery O'Connor penned these words about her art which crystallize in her characteristically homely way her remarkable incarnational and humanistic vision of life. "Fiction," she said, "is about everything human and we are made out of dust, and if you scorn getting yourself dusty, then you shouldn't try to write fiction. It's not a grand enough job for you."[33] Now that is a lesson not limited to writing but applicable to the whole of living. ∎

Author's Notes

1 Flannery O'Connor, *The Habit of Being*, ed. Sally Fitzgerald (New York: Farrar, Straus and Giroux, 1979), p. 102.

2 O'Connor, *Habit of Being*, p. 290.

3   Flannery O'Connor, *Mystery and Manners* (New York: Farrar, Straus and Giroux, 1969), p. 68.

4   O'Connor, *Mystery and Manners*, p. 148.

5   O'Connor, *Mystery and Manners*, p. 165.

6   Frederick Asals, *Flannery O'Connor: The Imagination of Extremity* (Athens, Georgia: The University of Georgia Press, 1982), p. 66.

7   O'Connor, *Mystery and Manners*, p. 147.

8   Peter S. Hawkins, *The Language of Grace* (Cowly Publications, 1983), p. 24.

9   O'Connor, *Habit of Being*, p. 144.

10   O'Connor, *Mystery and Manners*, p. 163.

11   O'Connor, *Mystery and Manners*, p. 157.

12   Hawkins, *Language of Grace*, p. 24.

13   O'Connor, *Habits of Being*, p. 307.

14   Flannery O'Connor, *The Complete Stories* (New York: Farrar, Straus and Giroux, 1992), p. 376.

15   O'Connor, *Complete Stories*, p. 373.

16   O'Connor, *Complete Stories*, p. 382.

17   O'Connor, *Complete Stories*, pp. 362, 367.

18   O'Connor, *Mystery and Manners*, p. 82.

19   O'Connor, *Complete Stories*, p. 382.

20   O'Connor, *Mystery and Manners*, p. 162.

21   O'Connor, *Complete Stories*, p. 513.

22   O'Connor, *Complete Stories*, p. 518.

23   O'Connor, *Complete Stories*, p. 513.

24   O'Connor, *Complete Stories*, p. 515.

25   O'Connor, *Complete Stories*, p. 514.

26   O'Connor, *Complete Stories*, pp. 519, 522.

27   O'Connor, *Complete Stories*, p. 520.

28   O'Connor, *Complete Stories*, pp. 524, 527.

29   O'Connor, *Complete Stories*, pp. 528, 529.

30   O'Connor, *Complete Stories*, pp. 529-530.

31   Credit is due here to a splendid little paper submitted in a course I taught in the summer of 2000 on the icon as theology. The paper, entitled "Ironic Icon," is by Annette M. Chappell and the quoted material is taken directly from that paper.

32   Kathleen Feeley, *Voice of the Peacock* (New York: Fordham University Press, 1982), pp. 15-51.

33   O'Connor, *Mystery and Manners*, p. 68.

C. S. Lewis
The Weight of Glory

C. S. Lewis preached the following sermon, "The Weight of Glory," at the Oxford University Church of St. Mary on June 8, 1941, to one of the largest audiences gathered there in modern times. Here Lewis, like Glen Tinder in the essay "Can We Be Good Without God?," affirms that humans are creatures of destiny, created and by the grace of the Incarnation, redeemed for divine Glory. Lewis believes this faith should affect our relationship with every human being because "there are no *ordinary* people."

If you asked twenty good men today what they thought the highest of the virtues, nineteen of them would reply, Unselfishness. But if you had asked almost any of the great Christians of old, he would have replied, Love. You see what has happened? A negative term has been substituted for a positive, and this is of more than philological importance. The negative idea of Unselfishness carries with it the suggestion not primarily of securing good things for others, but of going without them ourselves, as if our abstinence and not their happiness was the important point. I do not think this is the Christian virtue of Love. The New Testament has lots to say about self-denial, but not about self-denial as an end in itself. We are told to deny ourselves and to take up our crosses in order that we may follow Christ; and to nearly every description of what we shall ultimately find if we do so contains an appeal to desire. If there lurks in most modern minds the notion that to desire our own good and earnestly to hope for the enjoyment of it is a bad thing, I submit that this notion has crept in from Kant and the Stoics[1] and is no part of the Christian faith. Indeed, if we consider the unblushing promises of reward and the staggering nature of the rewards promised in the Gospels, it would seem that Our Lord finds our desires not too strong, but too weak. We are halfhearted creatures, fooling about with drink and sex and ambition when infinite joy is offered us, like an ignorant child who wants to go on making mud pies in a slum because he cannot imagine what is meant by the offer of a holiday at the sea. We are far too easily pleased.

We must not be troubled by unbelievers when they say that this promise of reward makes the Christian life a mercenary affair. There are different kinds of rewards. There is the reward which has no natural connection with the things you do to earn it and is quite foreign to the desires that ought to accompany those things. Money is not the natural reward of love; that is why we call a man mercenary if he marries a woman for the sake of her money. But marriage is the proper reward for a real lover, and he is not mercenary for desiring it. A general who fights well in order to get a peerage is mercenary; a general who fights for victory is not, victory being the proper reward of battle as marriage is the proper reward of love. The proper rewards are not simply tacked on to the activity for which they are given, but are the activity itself in consummation. There is also a third case, which is more complicated. An enjoyment of Greek poetry is certainly a proper, and not a mercenary, reward for learning Greek; but only those who have reached the stage of enjoying Greek poetry can tell from their own experience that this is so. The schoolboy beginning Greek grammar cannot look forward to his adult enjoyment of Sophocles[2] as a lover looks forward to marriage or a general to victory. He has to begin by working for marks, or to escape punishment, or to please his parents, or, at best, in the hope of a future good which he cannot at present imagine or desire. His position, therefore, bears a certain resemblance to that of the mercenary; the reward he is going to get will, in actual fact, be a natural or proper reward, but he will not know that till he has got it. Of course, he gets it gradually; enjoyment creeps in upon the mere drudgery, and nobody could point to a day or an hour when the one ceased and the other began. But it is just insofar as he approaches the reward that he becomes able to desire it for its own sake; indeed, the power of so desiring it is itself a preliminary reward.

The Christian, in relation to heaven, is in much the same position as this schoolboy. Those who have attained everlasting life in the vision of God doubtless know very well that it is no mere bribe, but the very consummation of their earthly discipleship; but we who have not yet attained it cannot know this in the same way, and cannot even begin to know it at all except by continuing to obey and finding the first reward of our obedience in our increasing power to desire the ultimate reward. Just in proportion as the desire grows, our fear lest it should be a mercenary desire will die away and finally be recognized as an absurdity. But probably this will not, for most of us, happen in a day; poetry replaces grammar, gospel replaces law, longing transforms obedience, as gradually as the tide lifts a grounded ship.

But there is one other important similarity between the schoolboy and ourselves. If he is an imaginative boy, he will, quite probably, be revelling in the English poets and romancers suitable to his age some time before he begins to suspect that Greek grammar is going to lead him to more and more enjoyments of this same sort. He may even be neglecting his Greek to read Shelley and Swinburne[3] in secret. In other words, the desire which Greek is really going to gratify already exists in him and is attached to objects which seem to him quite unconnected with Xenophon[4] and the verbs in μι. Now, if we are made for heaven, the desire for our proper place will be already in us, but not yet attached to the true object, and will even appear as the rival of that object. And this, I think, is just what we find. No doubt there is one point in which my analogy of the schoolboy breaks down. The English poetry which he reads when he ought to be doing Greek exercises may be just as good as the Greek poetry to which the exercises are leading him, so that in fixing on Milton[5] instead of journeying on to Aeschylus[6] his desire is not embracing a false object. But our case is very different. If a transtemporal, transfinite good is our real destiny, then any other good on which our desire fixes must be in some degree fallacious, must bear at best only a symbolical relation to what will truly satisfy.

In speaking of this desire for our own far-off country, which we find in ourselves even now, I feel a certain shyness. I am almost committing an indecency. I am trying to rip open the inconsolable secret in each one of you—the secret which hurts so much that you take your revenge on it by calling it names like Nostalgia and Romanticism and Adolescence; the secret also which pierces with such sweetness that when, in very intimate conversation, the mention of it becomes imminent, we grow awkward and affect to laugh at ourselves; the secret we cannot hide and cannot tell, though we desire to do both. We cannot tell it because it is a desire for something that has never actually appeared in our experience. We cannot hide it because our experience is constantly suggesting it, and we betray ourselves like lovers at the mention of a name. Our commonest expedient is to call it beauty and behave as if that had settled the matter. Wordsworth's expedient was to identify it with certain moments in his own past. But all this is a cheat. If Wordsworth[7] had gone back to those moments in the past, he would not have found the thing itself, but only the reminder of it; what he remembered would turn out to be itself a remembering. The books or the music in which we thought the beauty was located will betray us if we trust to them; it was not in them, it only came through them, and what came *through* them was longing. These things—the beauty, the memory of our own past— are good images of what we really desire; but if they are mistaken for the thing itself, they turn into dumb idols, breaking the hearts of their worshippers. For they are not the thing itself; they are only the scent of a flower we have not found, the echo of a tune we have not heard, news from a country we have never yet visited. Do you think I am trying to weave a spell? Perhaps I am; but remember your fairy tales. Spells are used for breaking enchantments as well as for inducing them. And you and I have need of the strongest spell that can be found to wake us from the evil enchantment of worldliness which has been laid upon us for nearly a hundred years. Almost our whole education has been directed to silencing this shy, persistent, inner voice; almost all our modern philosophies have been devised to convince us that the good of man is to be found on this earth. And yet it is a remarkable thing that such philosophies of Progress or Creative Evolution themselves bear reluctant witness to the truth that our real goal is elsewhere. When they want to convince you that earth is your home, notice how they set about it. They begin by trying to persuade you that earth can be made into heaven, thus giving a sop to your sense of exile in earth as it is. Next, they tell you that this fortunate event is still a good way off in the future, thus giving a sop to your knowledge that the fatherland is not here and now. Finally, lest your longing for the

some influence saying, "After
—— comes out, your life will
be so much better!"

transtemporal should awake and spoil the whole affair, they use any rhetoric that comes to hand to keep out of your mind the recollection that even if all the happiness they promised could come to man on earth, yet still each generation would lose it by death, including the last generation of all, and the whole story would be nothing, not even a story, for ever and ever. Hence all the nonsense that Mr. Shaw[8] puts into the final speech of Lilith, and Bergson's remark that the *élan vital* is capable of surmounting all obstacles, perhaps even death—as if we could believe that any social or biological development on this planet will delay the senility of the sun or reverse the second law of thermodynamics.

Do what they will, then, we remain conscious of a desire which no natural happiness will satisfy. Is it there any reason to suppose that reality offers any satisfaction to it? "Nor does the being hungry prove that we have bread." But I think it may be urged that this misses the point. A man's physical hunger does not prove that man will get any bread; he may die of starvation on a raft in the Atlantic. But surely a man's hunger does prove that he comes of a race which repairs its body by eating and inhabits a world where eatable substances exist. In the same way, though I do not believe (I wish I did) that my desire for Paradise proves that I shall enjoy it, I think it a pretty good indication that such a thing exists and that some men will. A man may love a woman and not win her; but it would be very odd if the phenomenon called "falling in love" occurred in a sexless world.

Here, then, is the desire, still wandering and uncertain of its object and still largely unable to see that object in the direction where it really lies. Our sacred books give us some account of the object. It is, of course, a symbolical account. Heaven is, by definition, outside our experience, but all intelligible descriptions must be of things within our experience. The scriptural picture of heaven is therefore just as symbolical as the picture which our desire, unaided, invents for itself; heaven is not really full of jewelry any more than it is really the beauty of Nature, or a fine piece of music. The difference is that the scriptural imagery has authority. It comes to us from writers who were closer to God than we, and it has stood the test of Christian experience down the centuries. The natural appeal of this authoritative imagery is to me, at first, very small. At first sight it chills, rather than awakes, my desire. And that is just what I ought to expect. If Christianity could tell me no more of the far-off land than my own temperament led me to surmise already, then Christianity would be no higher than myself. If it has more to give me, I expect it to be less immediately attractive than "my own stuff." Sophocles at first seems dull and cold to the boy who has only reached Shelley. If our religion is something objective, then we must never avert our eyes from those elements in it which seem puzzling or repellent; for it will be precisely the puzzling or the repellent which conceals what we do not yet know and need to know.

The promises of Scripture may very roughly be reduced to five heads. It is promised (1) that we shall be with Christ; (2) that we shall be like Him; (3) with an enormous wealth of imagery, that we shall have "glory"; (4) that we shall, in some sense, be fed or feasted or entertained; and (5) that we shall have some sort of official position in the universe—ruling cities, judging angels, being pillars of God's temple. The first question I ask about these promises is "Why any one of them except the first?" Can anything be added to the conception of being with Christ? For it must be true, as an old writer says, that he who has God and everything else has no more than he who has God only. I think the answer turns again on the nature of symbols. For though it may escape our notice at first glance, yet it is true that any conception of being with Christ which most of us can now form will be not very much less symbolical than the other promises; for it will smuggle in ideas of proximity in space and loving conversation as we now understand conversation, and it will probably concentrate on the humanity of Christ to the exclusion of His deity. And, in fact, we find that those Christians who attend solely to this first promise always do fill it up with very earthly imagery indeed—in fact, with hymeneal or erotic imagery. I am not for a moment condemning such imagery. I heartily wish I could enter into it more deeply than I do, and pray that I yet shall. But my point is that this also is only a symbol, like the reality in some respects, but unlike it in others, and therefore needs correction from the different symbols in the other promises. The variation of the promises does not mean that anything other than God will be our ultimate bliss; but because God is more than a Person, and lest we should imagine the joy of His presence too exclusively in terms of our present poor experience of personal love, with all its narrowness and strain and monotony, a dozen changing images, correcting and relieving each other, are supplied.

I turn next to the idea of glory. There is no getting away from the fact that this idea is very prominent in the New Testament and in early Christian writings. Salvation is constantly associated with palms, crowns, white robes, thrones, and splendour like the sun and stars. All this makes no immediate appeal to me at all, and in that respect I fancy I am a typical modern. Glory suggests two ideas to me, of which one seems wicked and the other ridiculous. Either glory means to me fame, or it means luminosity. As for the first, since to be famous means to be better known than other people, the desire for fame appears to me as a competitive passion and therefore of hell rather than heaven. As for the second, who wishes to become a kind of living electric light bulb?

When I began to look into this matter I was shocked to find such different Christians as Milton, Johnson, and Thomas Aquinas taking heavenly glory quite frankly in the sense of fame or good report. But not fame conferred by our fellow creatures— fame with God, approval or (I might say) "appreciation" by God. And then, when I had thought it over, I saw that this view was scriptural; nothing can eliminate from the parable the divine *accolade*, "Well done, thou good and faithful servant." With that, a good deal of what I had been thinking all my life fell down like a house of cards. I suddenly remembered that no one can enter heaven except as a child; and nothing is so obvious in a child—not in a conceited child, but in a good child—as its great and undisguised pleasure in being praised. Not only in a child, either, but even in a dog or a horse. Apparently what I had mistaken for humility had, all these years, prevented me from understanding what is in fact the humblest, the most childlike, the most creaturely of pleasures—nay, the specific pleasure of the inferior: the pleasure of a beast before men, a child before its father, a pupil before his teacher, a creature before its Creator. I am not forgetting how horribly this most innocent desire is parodied in our human ambitions, or how very quickly, in my own experience, the lawful pleasure of praise from those whom it was my duty to please turns into the deadly poison of self-admiration. But I thought I could detect a moment—a very, very short moment— before this happened, during which the satisfaction of having pleased those whom I rightly loved and rightly feared was pure. And that is enough to raise our thoughts to what may happen when the redeemed soul, beyond all hope and nearly beyond belief, learns at last that she has pleased Him whom she was created to please. There will be no room for vanity then. She will be free from the miserable illusion that it is her doing. With no taint of what we should now call self-approval she will most inno-

cently rejoice in the thing that God has made her to be, and the moment which heals her old inferiority complex forever will also drown her pride deeper than Prospero's book.[9] Perfect humility dispenses with modesty. If God is satisfied with the work, the work may be satisfied with itself; "it is not for her to bandy compliments with her Sovereign." I can imagine someone saying that he dislikes my idea of heaven as a place where we are patted on the back. But proud misunderstanding is behind that dislike. In the end that Face which is the delight or the terror of the universe must be turned upon each of us either with one expression or with the other, either conferring glory inexpressible or inflicting shame that can never be cured or disguised. I read in a periodical the other day that the fundamental thing is how we think of God. By God Himself, it is not! How God thinks of us is not only more important, but infinitely more important. Indeed, how we think of Him is of no importance except insofar as it is related to how He thinks of us. It is written that we shall "stand before" Him, shall appear, shall be inspected. The promise of glory is the promise, almost incredible and only possible by the work of Christ, that some of us, that any of us who really chooses, shall actually survive that examination, shall find approval, shall please God. To please God . . . to be a real ingredient in the divine happiness . . . to be loved by God, not merely pitied, but delighted in as an artist delights in his work or a father in a son—it seems impossible, a weight or burden of glory which our thoughts can hardly sustain. But so it is.

And now notice what is happening. If I had rejected the authoritative and scriptural image of glory and stuck obstinately to the vague desire which was, at the outset, my only pointer to heaven, I could have seen no connection at all between that desire and the Christian promise. But now, having followed up what seemed puzzling and repellent in the sacred books, I find, to my great surprise, looking back, that the connection is perfectly clear. Glory, as Christianity teaches me to hope for it, turns out to satisfy my original desire and indeed to reveal an element in that desire which I had not noticed. By ceasing for a moment to consider my own wants I have begun to learn better what I really wanted. When I attempted, a few minutes ago, to describe our spiritual longings, I was omitting one of their most curious characteristics. We usually notice it just as the moment of vision dies away, as the music ends, or as the landscape loses the celestial light. What we feel then has been well described by Keats[10] as "the journey homeward to habitual self." You know what I mean. For a few minutes we have had the illusion of belonging to that world. Now we wake to find that it is no such thing. We have been mere spectators. Beauty has smiled, but not to welcome us; her face was turned in our direction, but not to see us. We have not been accepted, welcomed, or taken into the dance. We may go when we please, we may stay if we can: "Nobody marks us." A scientist may reply that since most of the things we call beautiful are inanimate, it is not very surprising that they take no notice of us. That, of course, is true. It is not the physical objects that I am speaking of, but that indescribable something of which they become for a moment the messengers. And part of the bitterness which mixes with the sweetness of that message is due to the fact that it so seldom seems to be a message intended for us, but rather something we have overheard. By bitterness I mean pain, not resentment. We should hardly dare to ask that any notice be taken of ourselves. But we pine. The sense that in this universe we are treated as strangers, the longing to be acknowledged, to meet with some response, to bridge some chasm that yawns between us and reality, is part of our inconsolable secret. And surely, from this point of view, the promise of glory, in the sense described, becomes highly relevant to our deep desire. For glory means good report with God, acceptance by God, response, acknowledgement, and welcome into the heart of things. The door on which we have been knocking all our lives will open at last.

Perhaps it seems rather crude to describe glory as the fact of being "noticed" by God. But this is almost the language of the New Testament. St. Paul promises to those who love God not, as we should expect, that they will know Him, but that they will be known by Him (I Cor. 8:3). It is a strange promise. Does not God know all things at all times? But it is dreadfully re-echoed in another passage of the New Testament. There we are warned that it may happen to anyone of us to appear at last before the face of God and hear only the appalling words, "I never knew you. Depart from Me." In some sense, as dark to the intellect as it is unendurable to the feelings, we can be both banished from the presence of Him who is present everywhere and erased from the knowledge of Him who knows all. We can be left utterly and absolutely *outside*—repelled, exiled, estranged, finally and unspeakably ignored. On the other hand, we can be called in, welcomed, received, acknowledged. We walk every day on the razor edge between these two incredible possibilities. Apparently, then, our life-long nostalgia, our longing to be reunited with something in the universe from which we now feel cut off, to be on the inside of some door which we have always seen from the outside, is no mere neurotic fancy, but the truest index of our real situation. And to be at last summoned inside would be both glory and honour beyond all our merits and also the healing of that old ache.

And this brings me to the other sense of glory—glory as brightness, splendour, luminosity. We are to shine as the sun, we are to be given the Morning Star. I think I begin to see what it means. In one way, of course, God has given us the Morning Star already: you can go and enjoy the gift on many fine mornings if you get up early enough. What more, you may ask, do we want? Ah, but we want so much more—something the books on aesthetics take little notice of. But the poets and the mythologies know all about it. We do not want merely to *see* beauty, though, God knows, even that is bounty enough. We want something else which can hardly be put into words—to be united with the beauty we see, to pass into it, to receive it into ourselves, to bathe in it, to become part of it. That is why we have peopled air and earth and water with gods and goddesses and nymphs and elves— that, though we cannot, yet these projections can enjoy in themselves that beauty, grace, and power of which Nature is the image. That is why the poets tell us such lovely falsehoods. They talk as if the west wind could really sweep into a human soul; but it can't. They tell us that "beauty born of murmuring sound" will pass into a human face; but it won't. Or not yet. For if we take the imagery of Scripture seriously, if we believe that God will one day *give* us the Morning Star and cause us to *put on* the splendour of the sun, then we may surmise that both the ancient myths and the modern poetry, so false as history, may be very near the truth as prophecy. At present we are on the outside of the world, the wrong side of the door. We discern the freshness and purity of morning, but they do not make us fresh and pure. We cannot mingle with the splendours we see. But all the leaves of the New Testament are rustling with the rumour that it will not always be so. Some day, God willing, we shall get *in*. When human souls have become as perfect in voluntary obedience as the inanimate creation is in its lifeless obedience, then they will put on its glory, or rather that greater glory of which Nature is only the first sketch. For you must not think that I am putting forward any heathen fancy of being absorbed into Nature. Nature is mortal; we shall outlive her. When all the suns and nebulae have passed away, each one of you will still be alive. Nature is only the image, the symbol; but it is the symbol Scripture invites me to use. We are summoned to pass in through Nature, beyond her, into that splendour which she fitfully reflects.

And in there, in beyond Nature, we shall eat of the tree of life. At present, if we are reborn in Christ, the spirit in us lives directly on God; but the mind and, still more, the body receives life from Him at a thousand removes—through our ancestors, through our food, through the elements. The faint, far-off results of those energies which God's creative rapture implanted in matter when He made the worlds are what we now call physical pleasures; and even thus filtered, they are too much for our present management. What would it be to taste at the fountainhead that stream of which even these lower reaches prove so intoxicating? Yet that, I believe, is what lies before us. The whole man is to drink joy from the fountain of joy. As St. Augustine[11] said, the rapture of the saved soul will "flow over" into the glorified body. In the light of our present specialised and depraved appetites, we cannot imagine this *torrens voluptatis*,[12] and I warn everyone most seriously not to try. But it must be mentioned, to drive out thoughts even more misleading—thoughts that what is saved is a mere ghost, or that the risen body lives in numb insensibility. The body was made for the Lord, and these dismal fancies are wide of the mark.

Meanwhile the cross comes before the crown and tomorrow is a Monday morning. A cleft has opened in the pitiless walls of the world, and we are invited to follow our great Captain inside. The following Him is, of course, the essential point. That being so, it may be asked what practical use there is in the speculations which I have been indulging. I can think of at least one such use. It may be possible for each to think too much of his own potential glory hereafter; it is hardly possible for him to think too often or too deeply about that of his neighbour. The load, or weight, or burden of my neighbour's glory should be laid on my back, a load so heavy that only humility can carry it, and the backs of the proud will be broken. It is a serious thing to live in a society of possible gods and goddesses, to remember that the dullest and most uninteresting person you can talk to may one day be a creature which, if you saw it now, you would be strongly tempted to worship, or else a horror and a corruption such as you now meet, if at all, only in a nightmare. All day long we are, in some degree, helping each other to one or other of these destinations. It is in the light of these overwhelming possi-

bilities, it is with the awe and the circumspection proper to them, that we should conduct all our dealings with one another, all friendships, all loves, all play, all politics. There are no *ordinary* people. You have never talked to a mere mortal. Nations, cultures, arts, civilisations—these are mortal, and their life is to ours as the life of a gnat. But it is immortals whom we joke with, work with, marry, snub, and exploit—immortal horrors or everlasting splendours. This does not mean that we are to be perpetually solemn. We must play. But our merriment must be of that kind (and it is, in fact, the merriest kind) which exists between people who have, from the outset, taken each other seriously—no flippancy, no superiority, no presumption. And our charity must be a real and costly love, with deep feeling for the sins in spite of which we love the sinner—no mere tolerance, or indulgence which parodies love as flippancy parodies merriment. Next to the Blessed Sacrament itself, your neighbour is the holiest object presented to your senses. If he is your Christian neighbour, he is holy in almost the same way, for in him also Christ *vere latitat*[13]—the glorifier and the glorified, Glory Himself, is truly hidden. ■

Notes

1   Kant and the Stoics—Immanuel Kant (1724–1804) a German philosopher; he focused on reason and rationalism. The Stoics—followers of a Greek philosophy, founded in 308 B.C., that advocated rationalism and freedom from passions.

2   Sophocles—(496–406 B.C.) a Greek tragic dramatist, writer of *Oedipus*

3   Shelley and Swinburne—Percy Bysshe Shelley (1792–1822) and Algernon Charles Swinburne (1837–1909), two English poets

4   Xenophon—ancient Greek historian (c. 430–454)

5   Milton—John Milton (1608–1674) English poet and prose writer

6   Aeschylus—(525–456 B.C.) a Greek dramatist

7   Wordsworth—William Wordsworth (1770-1850) an English poet of the Romantic Period

8   George Bernard Shaw—(1856–1950) an Irish dramatist

9   Prospero is a character in Shakepeare's *The Tempest*, and through his book and staff he can conjure up tricks. At the end of the play,

Prospero announces that he is going to drown his book, thus renouncing his magical abilities

[10] Keats—John Keats (1795–1821) an English poet

[11] St. Augustine—(354–430) an early Christian theologian

[12] *Torreris voluptatis*—(Latin) following pleasures.

[13] *Vere latitat*—(Latin) he is truly hidden.

Making Connections through Discussion and Writing

1. Using a separate sheet of paper, outline this sermon, identifying the points that Lewis uses to support his argument.

2. What does Lewis mean when he says, "[I]f we consider the unblushing promises of reward . . . promised in the Gospels, it would seem that Our Lord finds our desires not too strong, but too weak"?

   _____
   _____
   _____
   _____
   _____

3. a. Lewis describes two aspects of glory. What are they?

   _____
   _____

   b. Explain the difference between the two.

   _____
   _____
   _____
   _____

4. As Lewis describes the fulfillment of glory, he gives a view of heaven that differs from many popular presentations today.
   a. Underline his references to heaven, and, in the space below, provide some examples of contemporary images of heaven.

   b. Explain the differences between Lewis' views and popular notions about heaven.

   _____
   _____
   _____
   _____
   _____
   _____
   _____

5. a. Explain why Lewis considers all human beings as having worth.

   _____
   _____
   _____
   _____

b. How has reading this sermon influenced your evaluation of your life and destiny and your attitude toward your neighbor?

_____

_____

_____

_____

_____

Synthesis/Essay Suggestions: The Sacred Ordinary

1. In an essay, discuss Michelangelo's idea of beauty, its origin and function, in light of Thomas Howard's treatment of the way incarnational art has both an immediate, imagistic presence and a transcendent significance or resonance of meaning. Include how the doctrine of the Incarnation adds to an understanding of Michelangelo's poem.

2. O'Connor states in her essay "Novelist and Believer" that the purpose of a novelist is to "render . . . his vision [of what he believes to be true] so that it can be transferred, as nearly whole as possible, to his reader." In her stories, she often accomplishes this "transfer of vision" by encouraging her readers to identify with her characters—in their spiritual temptations, their pride, their self-righteousness, and in their spiritual crises and insights. In an example essay, examine the narrative technique O'Connor employs in her stories as a method of developing this identification, and analyze her use of narrative voice, describing how it aids the transfer of the "vision" of her stories to her reader. Include examples from her stories to illustrate how her methods encourage allowing the reader to participate vicariously in the pride, fall, judgment, and redemption of the characters.

3. Dorothy L. Sayers, in "Toward a Christian Aesthetic," objects to "edifying art," finding it to be, all too often, a form of manipulating "pseudo-art" that is intended to exert power over its readers. In a brief essay, compare her idea on this subject with Flannery O'Connor's objection to the bad fiction arising from "religious impulse" and with C. S. Lewis' description of his own experience of writing (in paragraph six of his essay "Sometimes Fairy Stories May Say Best What's To Be Said"). Again considering Lewis' descriptions of his own writing process, discuss how literature can be written that is truly edifying.

4. Flannery O'Connor writes, "The novelist doesn't write to express himself, he doesn't write simply to render a vision he believes true, rather he renders his vision so that it can be transferred, as nearly whole as possible, to his reader." In an essay, discuss how you think Dorothy L. Sayers, who states that "the act of the poet in creation is seen to be threefold—a trinity—experience, expression, and recognition," would evaluate O'Connor's description of an artist's purpose. Explain how these descriptions have modified your own view of the purpose of art.

5. Using the essays in Part Three, particularly those of Sayers, L'Engle, O'Connor, Lewis, and Guroian, write an essay that discusses the characteristics of art these authors value. Explain how they affirm the way such art reveals reality, giving insight into human experience and pointing toward a transcendent meaning. Briefly explain the components of an aesthetic that these readings have helped you formulate.

6. C. S. Lewis' sermon "The Weight of Glory" describes the future glory of human destiny: "We are to shine as the sun, we are to be given the Morning Star." Glenn Tinder reinforces this view in his essay "Can We Be Good Without God?" (found in Part Two), where he writes that "the glory of a human being is placed in the future." Tinder thus links this glory with human destiny. Summarize both authors' idea of glory. Then explain the importance of this concept in relationship to humans' place in the universe. Note how this concept explains Lewis' assertion, "Next to the Blessed Sacrament itself, your neighbour is the holiest object presented to your senses."

7. In his sermon "The Weight of Glory," Lewis provides a description of what he thinks the joy of heaven will be like—the glory in which the "whole man is to drink joy from the fountain of joy." Use Lewis' ideas to better understand Richard Wilbur's description of the "shade of bliss" in his poem "The Baroque Wall-Fountain of the Villa Sciarra" (from Part Two of this book). Write your own description of heaven, using Lewis' sermon and Wilbur's poem as sources for your ideas.

Index